# THE ROMAN
# CITIZENSHIP

# THE ROMAN CITIZENSHIP

BY

A. N. SHERWIN-WHITE

SECOND EDITION

49901

OXFORD
AT THE CLARENDON PRESS

*Oxford University Press, Walton Street, Oxford* OX2 6DP

OXFORD  LONDON  GLASGOW
NEW YORK  TORONTO  MELBOURNE  WELLINGTON
KUALA LUMPUR  SINGAPORE  HONG KONG  TOKYO
DELHI  BOMBAY  CALCUTTA  MADRAS  KARACHI
NAIROBI  DAR ES SALAAM  CAPE TOWN

*First published 1939*
*New edition 1973*
*First published in paperback 1980*

**British Library Cataloguing in Publication Data**

Sherwin-White, Adrian Nicholas
  The Roman citizenship. – 2nd ed.
  1. Citizenship – Rome
  I. Title
  323.6'0937        JC85.C5          79–41370
  ISBN 0–19–814847–x

*Printed in Great Britain*
*at the University Press, Oxford*
*by Eric Buckley*
*Printer to the University*

# PREFACE

WHEN the first edition of this book, published in 1939, was exhausted, my learned friends, and especially Professor E. Badian, urged me to prepare a reprint with or without the addition of some account of recent developments of the subject, on the grounds of the general usefulness (so they said) of *Roman Citizenship* as an introduction to what has now become a vast subject. I decided that I would spoil the relative directness of the original version, in which discussion of the evidence generally predominates over scholarly controversy (apart from the excessive refutation of the unfortunate Dr. Rudolph), if I incorporated extensive criticism of modern theories into the script. So the original text has been reprinted with the correction of certain errors and misstatements, and a number of new chapters and appendices have been added which try to evaluate the principal contributions of recent scholarship, and also to extend the scope of the first edition. For the Republican period there is more evaluation than extension, although a new chapter explores in some detail the political objectives of the Italici in the Social War. The new Part Three discusses at length matters omitted or handled more summarily in the first edition: the technicalities of enfranchisement of provincial communes and grants of Latin status in the imperial period, the history of the enfranchisement of individuals by viritane grants, the evolution of dual citizenship, the manumission of slaves, the registration of citizenship, and the origins of *ius Italicum*. A fresh evaluation is attempted of the *Constitutio Antoniniana* in the light of recent work and fresh evidence. But on certain topics I have deliberately refrained from enlargement. Thus the recruitment of provincial senators is vastly better documented today than in 1939, but the additional detail has added little to the understanding of principles. Part Four, concerning the attitude of provincials towards Rome, does not directly touch on Roman citizenship, and is left in its original form, as an introduction to the evidence for a large theme with a developing literature that can no longer be contained in a brief compass. In the various additional sections I have tried to indicate what is valuable in recent historical writing, but I have not sought to record every aberration of scholarly opinion, and I have not tried to provide one of those total bibliographies in the modern fashion, which usurp the function of the bibliographical reviews, exaggerate the erudition of the author, and add to the expenses rather than the profit of the reader.

Of personal obligations I must record with gratitude the criticisms of Professor P. A. Brunt on my discussion of *ius Italicum*, and his insistence that something should be said about manumission, and the advice of Mr. M. W. Frederiksen on some matters of municipal legislation. I much regret that the final publication of the text of the remarkable *Tabula Banasitana* did not take place in time for me to be able to take full account of it.

I must also thank the Clarendon Press for their help in planning the somewhat unorthodox arrangement of this book, for their readiness to allow me adequate space, and for the patient assistance of their editors and proof readers at all times.

A. N. SHERWIN-WHITE

*March* 1973

# CONTENTS

PART III

## TECHNICAL PROBLEMS OF ROMAN STATUS

PART IV

## THE ATTITUDE OF THE PROVINCIALS
## TO THE EMPIRE

# PART I

# ROMAN CITIZENSHIP DURING THE REPUBLIC

# I

# ROME AND EARLY LATIUM

## INTRODUCTION

IT is impossible to study early Roman history as a whole without first forming a working hypothesis about the sources. Such a hypothesis is especially necessary in a general study, because by it would be determined many questions of chronology and many details concerning personalities. But here, where one is concerned with the development of constitutional practice, the best evidence for earlier practice, in times for which the evidence is in dispute, is the later practice itself, which has developed out of the earlier. What matters for the understanding of Rome's gradual mastery of political technique is not so much the exact dates and authors of various innovations as the relative order of events. Thus questions about the evidence which are relevant to points of detail may mostly be ignored. But on the major issue—the reliability of the general outline—it must be said that there seems to be no reason to doubt the justice of the view held by Beloch and De Sanctis, so far as concerns the basis of the whole structure, which is the accuracy of the *Fasti*. So long as this core is believed to be sound, critical reconstruction is possible, especially where the central tradition is buttressed by the common survival of constitutional practices to a later age.

Closely connected with this latter fact is a peculiar characteristic of Roman historical writing—its crystallization or fixation of tradition. Livy admittedly derives his information from earlier writers, dependent in turn upon other literary sources, which also may not owe much to the official archives of the Roman state. Yet Livy often describes events in phraseology which seems to have changed little from the first recording—oral or written—of the matter in question. A characteristic example of this is the formula *Romani facti, Romani fieri*, which is often used of communities which have been given the *civitas sine iure suffragi*.[1]

Even where there is nothing archaic in the form of words, facts themselves are often handed on without addition or alteration,

[1] See below, 41.

sometimes embedded in a general narrative, sometimes listed as so many items of a catalogue. Perhaps the most valuable chapter of Livy's first decade is that which contains, in the guise of a speech of Camillus, a catalogue of the reorganization of the Roman confederation which followed the last Latin war. Here the genuine character of the crystallized tradition is beyond doubt. Admittedly the gap between these events and the beginnings of Roman historical writing is not so alarmingly large. But there are passages describing very remote periods of history which inspire a similar confidence. Dionysius draws from Cato an account of the extension of Sabine influence towards Latium, well documented with place-names, Testruna, Reate, Cotyliae, Cures.[1] Despite the interval of three or four centuries which must be set between the events and the recording of them, the account has the ring of truth. Where independent evidence is lacking, our confidence must depend upon our belief in the strength of folk memory. This it is still possible to decry, but some at least of those who have investigated its reliability have not allowed for the necessary distinction between a primitive but civilized people and barbarous savages. At the same time our confidence may be confirmed by the probability that the *Annales Maximi*—the earliest documentary records of the early Republic —contained, amid much that is worthless, a kernel of solid tradition, not necessarily first recorded only in the third century.[2]

However, we are not reduced to simple faith in folk memory and the credibility of the *Annales Maximi* for the guarantee of the tradition. The inquiry concerns not so much persons and policies as the development of certain constitutional forms which were the very framework of the political life of Latium. The school of Niebuhr ultimately arrived at the belief that archaic Rome perished with all its records in a grand conflagration when the Gauls sacked the city.[3] The evidence for this view can be reduced to a single statement of Plutarch, based on the testimony of 'a certain Claudius'.[4] Since he goes on to add that the earlier history was then forged in the interests of the great families, it is clear that this is only another form of the problem of the *Fasti*, and that 'Claudius' was not insisting that all such documents

---

[1] Dion. Hal. 2. 49. 2–3.                    [2] De Sanctis, *Storia dei Romani*, i. 18 f.

[3] e.g. E. Pais, *Storia Critica di Roma*, i. 67 f.

[4] *Vita Numae* 1, ?Quadrigarius, in an Ἔλεγχος χρόνων; but the Ancients are not necessarily most reliable when most critical or 'scientific'.

as the *foedus Gabinum* had been destroyed. But even if we had not evidence for the preservation of at least some documents of Rome before the Gallic invasion, the task of this inquiry would not be impossible. The essential nature of the relationship between Rome and the Latins remains the same whether we accept the outline of the traditional account, or whether we confine the story of the Latin League to the half-century preceding 338 B.C. In the last resort, the solution of the great problems connected with the dating of the first Carthaginian and the Cassian treaties does not alter our conception of the background of political ideas and forms of association which influenced the growth of *civitas Romana* and *ius Latii*. The traditional chronology simply extends the period during which certain notions were being formed and consolidated. For the sceptical it is necessary to crowd the canvas, but both the detail and the general view remain the same.

## THE GEOGRAPHIC BACKGROUND

The difference between the Greek *polis* and the Latin *civitas* corresponds to the difference between the mountains of Greece and the hills of Latium.[1] The Latin city-states were not isolated from their neighbours by impassable mountains. The Latins could find safe refuge in their hill-tops, but the lands from which they drew their livelihood were separated by no mountain barriers from those of their neighbours. Latium is a plain, and that plain forms a natural unity; it is not broken but encircled by its hills. This geographical factor must guide discussion of the political history of the various communities which formed the population of the Latin plain. If their life attained to any degree of social complexity, they were bound to find some means of living on terms of peace with their neighbours. It was not possible for a state to develop internally and remain isolated in the fashion of the Greek cities, which felt the inconvenience of isolation only when social order was far advanced. In Latium inter-communal relations may be expected to predate the rise of the city-states, nor would it be surprising to find both that the division of the geographic or tribal unit into a number of smaller elements was never as complete as in Hellas, and that the Latins always retained more than a sentimental feeling of unity. Much that had to

[1] Cf. in general E. Kornemann, 'Polis und Urbs', *Klio*, 1905, 72 ff.

be artificially recreated in Hellas, by statesmen and philosophers, may never have disappeared from the consciousness of ordinary men in Latium.

Another consequence of the geographic character of Latium was that a great territorial state, such as Rome became in the sixth century, did not carry its own security. By increase of lands Rome became more vulnerable, and the necessity for an understanding with her neighbours became greater. Rome learned in infancy a lesson which other great Mediterranean powers gained only late in life; for a truly continental environment is rare in the borderlands of the Mediterranean. The Seven Hills offered little protection to the dwellers in the fields and villages of the extensive Roman territory. This is no less true of the other communities of Latium; their condition is to be judged in terms of 'continental' politics, where the frontier is often only an arbitrary line. The Greeks lived in mountain-walled valleys or on islands, the Phoenicians on peninsulas, but the Romans *in Latio*—on a plain.

Again, if ever Latium were seriously threatened by foreign invasion, the various communities would not be able to defend themselves effectively in isolation; some form of union for territorial defence would become necessary. A glance at a map thus shows that every practical argument was at hand for the political federation, or unification, of an area which geographically forms an undisputed unity. Such unification was in the interests of both great and small; over the watersheds of Anio, Turano, and Himella, there was an easy road from the central Apennines, if ever the men of the hills came to covet the lands of the plain, and likewise the Volscian hills offered easy descents into Latium. Only on the west has Latium a natural boundary of any strength in the swift waters of the Tiber. Yet a river can unite as well as separate; for the extension of Latium beyond the Tiber, by which the lower Tiber basin finally became a single political unit, was secured comparatively early. In the history of Rome her hills may be neglected, but not her river. It is difficult to assess the precise importance of Rome's position in assisting her rise to ecumenical empire, but that Rome first grew great in Latium because she controlled a crossing of the Tiber cannot be seriously doubted. So far as there was a northward and southward trade-route through Italy in early times, that route crossed the Tiber at Rome among other places; and although the *via campana* ran along the right bank of the Tiber, the east and westward salt route, the *via salaria* down the left bank of the Tiber, was controlled by Rome. The importance of these facts for the history of Roman federal institutions is that they emphasize that continental environment in which all Latin communities found themselves set. This means that Rome by her position was the immediate neighbour of the states and civilization of Etruria, that is, of a distinct and foreign people from whom she could not hold aloof; thus the inhabitants of the site of Rome would be more likely to develop some form of international system than those of Aricia or Bovillae.

It is worth noting that the very position of Rome casts doubt upon Mommsen's theory of 'natural enmity',[1] i.e. that Rome regarded herself as in a state of enmity with other communities until formal *amicitia* or alliance had been established. This view, within the later Republican period, had been combated in detail by others;[2] it suffices to recall that not only is there no trace of it in the seventh and sixth centuries, but that such a theory would have been most inconvenient for a community, however primitive, set at one of the great crossings of the Tiber. Since all Rome's international relations until the second half of the sixth century seem to have been worked out in dealings with men, either Latin or 'Sabine', with whom she shared common festivals and solemnities, it is hard to see where such an idea could have had its origin. The geographic unity of Latium must always have worked against such a principle.


## THE SOCIAL BACKGROUND OF THE SEVENTH-SIXTH CENTURIES

The natural geographic unity of Latium seems early to have dominated the racial diversity of its inhabitants. According to the archaeological evidence, the Alban hills mark the boundary of the cremating folk, and at Rome, at Ardea, and in the Alban hills themselves beside the cremators are found the remains of a wave of an inhuming population.[3] With this the literary evidence

---

[1] *St. R.* iii. 590 f.

[2] A. Heuss, 'Die völkerrechtlichen Grundlagen der römischen Aussenpolitik', *Klio*, Beiheft 31.

[3] Cf. *CAH* vii. 340; J. Whatmough, *The Foundations of Roman Italy*, ch. xi; also A. Blakeway, 'Demaratus', *JRS* 25 (1935), 129 ff.

so far agrees as to hold that the Roman people was not racially one. Contact with Hellas in the later Republic produced a crop of myths, attributing the origins of the Latin peoples to figures of the Greek legends. But if we set these aside, the literary tradition is at one in recognizing, first, a predominant race, the descendants of the folk of Alba and Lavinium, and next an infiltration of other elements. At Ardea the Ausones, the *Pelasgi* of Italy, are mentioned,[1] while at Rome there is a double intrusion of 'Sabines'. The fusion of these elements is represented in the stories of Titus Tatius and, later, of Attus Clausus, as an easy process. The series of common religious festivals in Latium,[2] and the existence at Rome of duplicated institutions such as the Salii Palatini and Salii Collini, go to support the accuracy of the traditional account. This quasi-national sense of unity despite racial diversity is of high importance, because it rendered familiar, in a crude form, that idea of incorporation without extinction of local peculiarities which is the key to the Roman unification of Italy and finally of the civilized world, the Orbis Terrarum.

The population which lived on the fertile soil of Latium, when these lands were rendered available by the cessation of volcanic activity, seems to have been extremely numerous. A dispute still rages over the meaning of what appear to be the remnants of a system of communal drainage, belonging to the earliest period, and suggesting the most intensive exploitation of the soil by a comparatively dense population. Even without this confirmatory evidence Pliny's list of 53 *populi* of early Latium, which had disappeared in later days, is proof enough that the population was large, as Livy also surmised, though for a different reason.[3]

Early Latium thus represented a miniature continent. The inhabitants were originally organized in small village communities, each a tiny *populus*, grouped together in religious leagues, each of which had its cult-centre. This left a mark on the story of Latium, which shows through, palimpsest-like, in the later period, when the federations of villages had been replaced by a group of considerable city-states. The famous march of Coriolanus, for example, is described[4] in terms of the village

[1] Cf. E. Pais, *Ancient Italy* (Chicago, 1908), 10.          [2] Below, 11.

[3] Cf. De la Blanchère, *Mélanges d'arch. et d'hist.*, 1882; T. Frank, *Economic History of Rome*, 11; G. De Sanctis, *Riv. Fil.* 1933, 290; P. Fraccaro, *Athenaeum*, 1928, 367–75; Plin. *NH* 3. 68–9; Livy 6. 12. 2–5.

[4] Livy 2. 39. 2–4. Dion. Hal. 8. 17–20.

system, but a precise dating of the emergence of fully conscious political units and political leagues is rendered hard by the irregularity of the processes of consolidation, and by anachronisms of terminology in the sources.

The outline of the tradition in Dionysius is that Alba Longa had exercised a political suzerainty over the Latin states of which she was the founder, and that with the destruction of Alba this hegemony passed to Rome. But it has been shown that Dionysius was largely influenced by his dependence on a Caesarian source of which the object was to glorify the family of Caesar, by tradition originally derived from Alba.[1] The version of Livy is more moderate: he seems to distinguish between the hegemony of all Latium, established by the last Tarquin, and the leadership of a narrower set of folk called 'Prisci Latini', the 'early Latins', a term which, like the 'casci Latini' of Ennius, here means the earliest neighbours of Rome whose memory survived in later days.[2] From Livy, supplemented by the sounder core of Dionysius, a catalogue can be found of the Prisci and their limits defined. The place-names involved in the conquests of the early kings, as described by either writer, are always the same. They form a selection from the vanished villages whose memory is also preserved in Pliny's list, and are given as a group, after the surrender of Collatia to the first Tarquin, thus—'Corniculum Ficulea vetus Cameria Crustumerium Ameriola Medullia Nomentum haec de Priscis Latinis aut qui ad Latinos defecerant capta oppida'.[3] With the addition of another group—Antemnae, Politorium, Caenina—they have appeared earlier in the stories of Tullus Hostilius, and even before him.[4] It is from these little places that the Roman kings are brought, Tullus from Medullia, and Servius from Corniculum.[5] These villages of the Prisci emerge again as independent communities even after the expulsion of the kings.[6] On the other hand, none of the Latin city-states of the fifth century figure among them, with the exception of Nomentum. Tusculum, Aricia and Ardea do not appear in Livy's narrative until the time of Superbus, while Lavinium is mentioned in a special category by itself.[7] Dionysius, in a passage

[1] M. Pohlenz, *Hermes* 1924, 181 ff.  [2] Ennius, *Annales* 1. 22 (20 b).
[3] Livy 1. 38. 4. Cf. Dion. Hal. 3. 49–50.
[4] Dion. Hal. 2. 33. 1; 36; 50. 4; 3. 1. 2; 34. 5; 37. 4.
[5] Dion. Hal. 3. 1. 2; 4. 1. 2.
[6] Dion. Hal. 5. 21. 2; 49. 3. Livy 2. 19.  [7] Livy 1. 14. 1; 49. 9; 50. 3; 57. 1.

referring to Tullus Hostilius that is undoubtedly anachronistic, names Cora and Suessa, two places at a comparatively great distance from Rome, but he makes amends by substituting Corilla for Livy's Aricia in the narrative about Superbus.[1]

The Prisci Latini on closer examination turn out to be, if the usual identifications are correct, the folk who occupied the narrow area, between the Anio and the Tiber, that separated Rome from the Sabine country.[2] The nearest of their villages, Antemnae and Caenina, were close to the Anio some fifteen kilometres from Rome. The description of even the larger units with which Rome came into touch towards the close of the sixth century likewise suggests that the notion of the city-state was little developed among the smaller peoples: Suessa was known as the city of the Pometini, and Ardea is summed up by Livy in the phrase: *Ardeam Rutuli habebant gens.*[3]

This evidence implies that the sphere of Roman influence was narrowly delimited within central Latium in the seventh and the earlier part of the sixth century, and that Rome could only make headway against the smaller Latin communities in her immediate neighbourhood, which had not yet passed beyond the stage of village organization. Rome had still to make contact with the larger and remoter units of Latium; for it is not possible to believe that Tibur and Praeneste did not exist at this period as comparatively large states, although it is certain that the villages only passed gradually under the sway of the greater powers. At the very end of the period Gabii, as an independent community, was too strong for Rome to swallow up and merge completely in herself.[4] These data provide the setting for the religious leagues and cult-centres, and render impossible the claim to a political hegemony of all Latium as complete as that which Dionysius attributes to the pre-Etruscan kings.

In Livy the first attempt at any wide hegemony is connected with Servius' establishment of a federal cult of Diana on the Aventine, while the claim to the heritage of Alba is made only by the second Tarquin.[5] The variant tradition in Dionysius, who assigns this claim to Tullus Hostilius, the conqueror of Alba,

---

[1] Dion. Hal. 3. 34. 3; 4. 45. 4; 50. 2. Cf. below, 11 n. 3.
[2] Cf. Beloch, *RG* 166 ff., and Map 1.
[3] Livy 1. 57. 1. 'The tribe of the Rutuli held Ardea.'
[4] Below, 19.                              [5] Below, 13 f.

must be rejected as anticipation of later events.[1] Dionysius describes how Hostilius was opposed by the Thirty Peoples at the council of Lucus Ferentinae under the leadership of two *praetores Latini* from Cora and Lavinium. This is the Latin League of later days, but when the fighting comes the communities named are those of the Prisci Latini once again—Medullia, Politorium, Tellene, etc.[2] The silence of Livy suggests that Dionysius has attached to one piece of genuine information, itself belonging to a later period,[3] a fictitious account, and fused together two strata of Latin history. Livy is entirely consistent and sober; he makes a bare mention of 'Latins with whom a treaty was made in the reign of Tullus', and these Latins are simply the narrow circle of the Prisci.[4] The particular anachronism which is the basis of Dionysius' account is the substitution of the league of the thirty states, which later met at the Lucus Ferentinae in the territory of Aricia, for the league of the Latins, which was composed of a larger number of smaller communities and met at the shrine of Juppiter Latiaris on the Alban mount. Rome's claim to dominate the former could not be based on her control of the latter.

## THE RELIGIOUS LEAGUES

Both in the literary tradition and in the epigraphic remains the religious leagues of Latium have left considerable traces. Their characteristic is that they are groups of varying numbers of communities, united by the bond of race in a common cult, each with its special shrine. The best-known is the league of Juppiter Latiaris with its centre on Monte Cavo.[5] The administration of this passed, according to tradition, from Alba Longa to Rome, by a process familiar in later history. This fact has worked havoc in the writing of Roman history, because it has been given a narrowly political meaning; but the custom of declaring a holy truce at the time of the Latin Festival shows that the control of the Latiar gave Rome no political hegemony in Latium.[6] Whether this league included

---

[1] Dion. Hal. 3. 34.    [2] Dion. Hal. 3. 34. 5; 38.
[3] Dion. Hal. 3. 34. 3. Cf. below, 14 The names of the two *praetores Latini* sound genuine—Ancus Publicius of Cora, Spusius Vecelius of Lavinium.
[4] Livy 1. 32. 3; 33.    [5] M. Gelzer, *RE* 'Latium', col. 947.
[6] As follows from Varro, *LL* 6. 25 and Varro *apud* Gell. *Noctes Atticae*, 1. 25. 1. Cf. Dion. Hal. 4. 49. 2.

all the *populi Latini* is uncertain, though probable. Pliny's list of numerous vanished partakers—*populi carnem in monte Albano soliti accipere*—suggests that the league was extensive.[1] The tradition that the last Tarquin enlarged it to include 47 *populi* some of whom were Volscian or Hernican, presumes that all the Latin communities were members.[2] Such enlargement, if it ever took place, must not be given a political significance, since the common source of Livy and Dionysius represents Superbus as gaining his ends through the control not of the Latiar but of the assembly of the Thirty Peoples at Lucus Ferentinae. The increase suggests, instead, a spontaneous impulse of the *populi Latini* towards unification around cult-centres.

Not all the religious guilds of Latium are so conspicuous in the tradition. There was a Lucus Dianae on Mount Corne 'sacratus a Latio' that has a federal sound.[3] At Ardea and Lavinium there existed shrines common to all Latins, according to Strabo.[4] The Lucus Feroniae shared by Latins and Sabines was perhaps a local affair near Rome, since it is connected with the warfare of Romans and Sabines.[5] These cults have received some illumination from Carcopino's study of the *sodales Arulenses* and the shrine of Volcanus at Ostia, in which he sees another of these small communal groups.[6] Perhaps the smallest of all is the cult of the Penates at Lavinium, shared between the *populus Laurens* and the *populus Romanus*.[7]

Far wider in scope and importance is the league of Diana at Aricia. The best evidence for the composition of this league is the well-known fragment of Cato :[8] 'Lucum Dianium in nemore Aricino Egerius Baebius dedicavit dic(t)ator Latinus. hi populi communiter Tusculanus Aricinus Lanuvinus Laurens Coranus Tiburtis Pometinus Ardeatis Rutulus.' This document belongs to a date earlier than that usually assigned to it. The presence in the list of the *populus Pometinus* shows that it is prior to the destruction of that community recorded by Livy.[9] The

---

[1] *NH* 3. 68 f. 'Folks who usually took the meat on the Alban mount.'
[2] Dion. Hal. 4. 49. 2.          [3] Plin. *NH* 16. 242.
[4] Strabo 5. 3. 5 (232 C).          [5] Dion. Hal. 3. 32. 1.
[6] J. Carcopino, *Virgile et les origines d'Ostie*, 82 ff., 157 ff.
[7] Varro, *LL* 5. 144. Livy 5. 52. 8. *ILS* 5004.
[8] Cato, *Orig.* 2. 58. 'Egerius Baebius the Latin dictator dedicated the grove of Diana in the wood of Aricia. The following folks acted conjointly.'
[9] Livy 2. 17.

reconstruction of the second book of Cato's *Origines*, from which it comes, supports an even earlier date. For the fragments collected by Peter show that Cato was dealing in this book with the earliest history and even with the mythical period of the great Latin, Hernican and Volscian cities, and by no means with the later centuries.[1] If the quotation is complete it illustrates an early stage in the unification of Latium, when a large, but not inclusive, selection of the more important Latin communities had drawn together in common worship around the shrine of Diana situated at the source of the Aqua Ferentina in the territory of Aricia.[2] The inclusion of distant Tibur and Cora is notable.

Whether or not this league, at this particular moment of its development, represented a political group is less certain. H. Rudolph points out that the best manuscript reading of the text is *dicator Latinus*, and argues that this is a purely religious functionary.[3] Whether there is any original distinction between *dicator* and *dictator* is not clear. In a far later period the *dicator* who administered a grove of Juppiter in the territory of Spoletium possessed quasi-magisterial functions,[4] and Rome had dictators with purely religious functions—*dictator clavi fingendi causa* and *dictator Latinarum feriarum causa*. More important is the apparent connection between the shrine of Aricia and the Concilium Latinorum which met at the Lucus Ferentinae. This identification seems to be secured by the fact that, when Superbus called a meeting of the Council of Ferentina, the leading part was taken by Herdonius of Aricia.[5] This consideration should dispose of the view that the league of Aricia was a separate organization from the Council of Ferentina, set up as a counter-body when Superbus gained control of the latter. Such a view, in any case, does not agree with the chronological indications of Cato.

The functions of this Council are adumbrated by a fragment of Cincius, which states that the Latins, including Rome, met at the Grove yearly for the administration of their common affairs.[6]

---

[1] e.g. frs. 61, 64, 67—the *via Salaria*.      [2] Beloch, *RG* 183.

[3] H. Rudolph, *Stadt und Staat im römischen Italien*, 12.

[4] *ILS* 4911, 'eius piacli moltaique dicatorei exactio estod.' Cf. below, 70 f. The two terms are perhaps by-forms of the same root *dic*, *dictator* having no connection with *dicto*, which does not mean 'command' in pre-Augustan Latin. Cf. *Thesaurus Linguae Latinae*, s.v. 'dicto', 1012 f.      [5] Livy 1. 50–1.

[6] Festus, s.v. 'praetor'. 'Alba diruta usque ad P. Decium Murem cos. populos Latinos ad caput Ferentinae quod est sub monte Albano consulere solitos et imperium communi consilio administrare.'

But while his terminal date is correct, his starting-point for this system is mythical. Nor is any assistance to be gained from a passage where Dionysius asserts that in the time of Tullus Hostilius the Council not only existed but possessed two praetors as federal officers; for the passage is an anachronistic anticipation of the system of the fourth century.[1] The first clear indication that this assembly possessed any political importance is offered by the tradition that Servius Tullius sought to acquire the political hegemony of Latium by the establishment of a rival cult of Diana on the Aventine.[2] This event also provides the earliest date to which we can assign, with any degree of confidence, an attempt on the part of Rome to enlarge her sphere in Latium, by means other than the conquest of new lands at the expense of the Prisci.

It is thus possible to maintain that by the middle of the sixth century the cult-centres, though still primarily religious, were capable of acquiring political importance. At what date the league of Aricia first assumed such importance remains uncertain. All that can be said is that in the period which preceded the Etruscan domination of Rome Latium was composed of a number of crossing and interrelated groups, some small and local, others tending to become complex and politically self-conscious. The big city-states were undoubtedly emerging, but the period of the sedentary tribe was perhaps not very remote. It is improbable that at this period there existed any single political group which embraced all the *populi* of Latium; the two forces which should engender this—the unifying factor of a single dominant state and the threat of foreign invasion—were still lacking.

It was extremely important for the history of the Latin people that they retained down to a late period in their development as city-states the practice of these intercommunal festivities and councils, and that the memory of the pre-urban, tribal organization of Latium was thus kept alive. For in this period must be placed the formation of that community of rights among Latini which was so fruitful an institution in later days. This question needs fuller consideration.[3] Here it is enough to say that it is easier to find the origin of certain conceptions, such as *ius commercii*, *ius conubii*, and *postliminium*, in a condition of society where

---

[1] Dion. Hal. 3. 34. 3. Above, 10. Cf. Livy 8. 3. 9, and below, 25.
[2] Livy 1. 45. Dion. Hal. 4. 25; 26. Varro, *LL* 5. 43.          [3] Below, 32 ff.

the concept of the state, with its attendant concept of the fixed domicile, is not strongly developed, above all in a society where the claim to legal recognition—if we may talk of law at all instead of custom—is based upon something like a geographic sense of national unity. Dionysius has much to say of the 'isopolity' that the Latins shared with one another.[1] To deny that he found anything in his sources to justify the use of such a phrase seems hard, for, though the language may be that of his own day, yet the phrase covers exactly the relationship in which a number of politically un-selfconscious communities, established in a single geographic area with well-defined limits, would stand to one another. It is precisely this late survival of the non-exclusive attitude which made possible the incorporation of Gabii and Tusculum within the Roman state, and led, when extended beyond the boundaries of Latium, to the creation of the *municipium*.

## THE EMERGENCE OF POLITICAL UNION

Upon the loosely organized federal system of early Latium there supervened a unifying influence, which is connected by tradition with the Etruscan domination of Rome. The outline of the familiar story represents so consistent an account that it cannot be rejected out of hand. With Servius and Superbus is associated the creation of some form of Roman domination in Latium.[2] When the Etruscan kings disappear the peoples of Latium, the Latin Name, seem to enjoy a greater degree of federal unity than in the earlier period, and Rome in particular emerges as the head of a considerable league of Latin states.

Livy and Dionysius assert that Superbus secured some form of domination in Latium by gaining control of the Council of Lucus Ferentinae. Their narrative is not very rich in convincing detail and contains mythical elements, such as the tale of Herdonius; but the cumulative effect, when the general story of the expansion of the Etruscan power in Campania is taken into account, is considerable.[3] It remains to decide what precisely were the limits of the Etruscan hegemony in Latium. Unless we believe that in the *sixth* century the Etruscans went by sea to

[1] Below, 32 n. 1.
[2] Cf. above, 10, where the Dionysian version of the hegemony of Tullus is rejected.　　　　　　　　　　[3] Livy 1. 50–1. Dion. Hal. 3. 45–8.

Campania, the story of their domination must be accepted. In the seventh century they left their mark in the great tombs of Praeneste, and in the sixth they were certainly powerful in Campania, but it does not follow that they dominated the whole block of territory between the Tiber and the Voltumnus. Rome and Praeneste are the essential points of control along the high road from Etruria to Campania, and at Rome too the remnants of archaic Graeco-Etruscan art testify to a strong Etruscan influence even if they do not by themselves prove Etruscan occupation.[1]

The alternative view, that the Etruscan domination in Campania was secured only by sea, and that Praeneste was the terminal point of their influence inland, is, however, possible, for there is a notable absence from the Liris valley, which connects Latium and Campania, of any archaeological material of an Etruscan or Graeco-Etruscan character.[2] This suggests that the Etruscans did not pass that way, and the suggestion is borne out by the literary evidence, which indicates that they were mainly interested in the control of the Tiber crossing and of the coastal plain with its harbours. For the core of the Etruscan hegemony in Latium consisted of Rome, Lavinium, Ardea, Antium, Circei, Suessa Pometia, and Tarracina. This view needs some amplification. It depends upon the acceptance of the testimony of Livy, and of the independent, confirmatory evidence offered by Polybius' account of the first treaty between Rome and Carthage. Many have doubted whether the date given by Polybius to this document is correct, for he assigns it to the first year of the Republican era. Various plausible, though speculative, reasons can be found why Rome and Carthage should have entered into an agreement at that time, of which the best is that the treaty simply reaffirmed the relations existing between the Carthaginians and the Tarquins. Alternatively it is possible that Carthage, to whose commercial advantage the treaty works, was eager to take advantage of the situation in Latium to check a commercial rival, or that the landed aristocracy who expelled the Etruscan merchant-dynasty were trying to play off the Carthaginians against the Etruscans.[3]

[1] Cf., e.g., E. D. van Buren, *Terracotta Revetments in Latium and Etruria*, plates 2, 3. 3, 4. 10, 2. 12, 3. 21, 1, 3. 32, 2.

[2] Cf. A. Blakeway, 'Demaratus', *JRS*, 1935, 129 ff. Gabrici, 'Cuma', *Mon. Ant.* 22. 343 ff. T. Frank, *Economic History of Rome*, 20 f.

[3] Polyb. 3. 22.

The battle for the authenticity of the Polybian date may not yet be over, although archaeological investigation has provided what was lacking before, the material presupposition of an ordered city life in Latium at the close of the sixth century.[1] But whatever the exact year of the treaty, it must at least belong to a period before the passing of Antium into Volscian hands and the separation of Tarracina from the rest of Latium—events that were accomplished by the first quarter of the fifth century—because these two states are called Latin peoples in the text.[2] Two categories of Latin states are mentioned: those of or near the coast are described as directly subject to Rome, and in addition Rome guarantees the peace of the rest of the Latin peoples 'such as are not subject'. The term used by Polybius for 'subject'—ὑπήκοος—is the normal Greek translation of the Latin socius, in the sense of 'dependent ally'.[3] So according to this treaty certain Latin peoples were directly bound to Rome as dependent allies, while towards the rest of Latium Rome stands in the position of an equal partner. This suggests that the cities named as allies, Ardea, Antium, Circei, Tarracina and probably Lavinium, represent the maximum extent of the Etrusco-Roman empire in Latium.[4] The conclusion is borne out by Livy who records considerable activity of Superbus in the coastal strip, at Ardea, Cercei and also Suessa Pometia, whereas inland his only achievements are the incorporation of Gabii, almost at the gate of Rome, and the dispatch of a colony, of which no details are given, to Signia.[5] This latter incident, if it can be accepted, is the only indication of Etruscan activity in the Liris valley. The contrast between the two spheres of interest supports the notion suggested by the Polybian treaty, that Rome did not claim as the result of Superbus' intrigues at Lucus Ferentinae to be the mistress of all Latium, and hence that the majority of the cities of that league are included in the category 'such as are not subject'. It would also seem that already at the close of the sixth century Rome's relations with the Latin peoples were taking two main forms: these are, first, specific agreements with particular communities—the subject allies in Polybius, and the Gabine treaty in the

[1] Cf. Gelzer, *RE* art. cit., col. 951.     [2] Polyb. 3. 22. 11.

[3] Cf. Stephanus, s.v.

[4] There is only a slight textual doubt about the inclusion of the Laurentes in Polybius' list.

[5] Livy 1. 56. 3; 57. 1; 60. 1. For Superbus and Gabii, cf. below, 19 f.

Livian tradition—and, second, general treaties involving the
Latins as a whole—the admission of Rome to a place, possibly
a leading place, in the League of Ferentina. But the two types
of relationship were not mutually exclusive, as Ardea, Suessa,
and Lavinium of the 'subject allies' belonged also to the general
league. Thus it would seem that the arrangements of the Etruscan period were a shadowy anticipation of the system of the
fourth century.[1]

The peoples named by the Polybian treaty are, when compared
to the group of Prisci Latini, large communities. This is what
distinguishes the later political confederations from the earlier
religious leagues. Until the process of synoecism had made considerable progress, there could be no large and important political
leagues. But the emergence of such units in Latium must not be
set too late. In the fifth century the *populi Latini* could readily
combine against foreign aggression. The appearance of the idea
of political union, which belongs to the latter part of the sixth
century, cannot be contemporary with the formation of the units
which alone made it possible. Still, it is true that, down to the
fifth century, the historians contain considerable references to the
smaller units of Latium; and during this last period it is clear that
Latium has not yet been reduced to the fourteen or fifteen states
of the fourth century. There was a time, whenever it may have
been, when Latium consisted of Thirty Peoples, the Triginta
Populi,[2] which figure represents a considerable change from the
period to which Pliny's lists and the system of the Prisci Latini
belong. In the fourth century they no longer exist, and even in
the fifth there is difficulty in reconstructing a satisfactory list.[3]
The fact that Dionysius inserts his list of the Thirty at the end of
the sixth century is not entirely to be regarded with suspicion.[4]
His list may be dubious in details, but its general character fits
well the tradition that this is the intermediate period—let us say
from the second half of the sixth century onwards—when Latium
still contained, besides the larger city-states, some dozen smaller
communities that maintained a separate existence.[5]

Doubtless these latter were gradually being swept into the
maw of their larger neighbours, and doubtless the name of

---

[1] Below, 26 ff.          [2] Livy 2. 18. 3. Dion. Hal. 3. 31. 4.
[3] Cf. De Sanctis, *Storia dei Romani*, ii. 101.          [4] Dion. Hal. 5. 61.
[5] Cf. below, 21 ff.

Triginta Populi was retained long after the reality had disappeared and the minor members were no longer independent. The growth of the power of Rome advances by a double process : the establishment of military control over Latium is accompanied by the extension of the Roman territory and of the citizen body. The tradition is more reliable for the second of these processes than for the first, partly because its preservation is less accidental. It has left its mark in those most obstinate of records, place-names and extra-urban cults, while the creation of political leagues has only occasionally been remembered by the lucky survival of actual documents.

The detailed account of the relations between Rome and Gabii in the time of Superbus illustrates the process of direct absorption. Gabii was a small community situated to the west of the group of Prisci Latini with which Rome had hitherto been mainly occupied. Livy and Dionysius, after mentioning certain attempts of Superbus to secure the submission of Gabii by violence, agree in the noteworthy statement that it eventually entered the Roman state unforced.[1] According to Dionysius this entry was mediated by a treaty, which gave to the Gabini the enjoyment of their own city and lands, together with 'isopolity'.[2] The character of this treaty has been much discussed. Dionysius' assertion that the terms which he describes were recorded on a leather shield that was kept in the temple of Semo Sancus and preserved to his own day can hardly be neglected. There is confirmatory evidence, in the special use of the *cinctus Gabinus*, the Gabine robe, and in the peculiar condition of Gabine land, to show that Gabii at an early date possessed an extraordinary position in relation to the Roman state; for *ager Gabinus* was juridically distinct from both *ager Romanus* and *ager peregrinus*, and the *cinctus Gabinus* was worn by Roman officials as a sacred vestment for certain solemnities.[3] There can, then, be little doubt that the Gabine treaty of Dionysius is a genuine fact. Nor is Gabii an isolated instance of such a policy. In another passage Dionysius states that Crustumerium was incorporated on similar terms by the first Tarquin.[4] This assertion may gain some slight support from the special distinction

---

[1] Livy 1. 54. 10. Dion. Hal. 4. 57. 3.    [2] Dion. Hal. 4. 58. 4.
[3] Varro, *LL* 5, 33. Cf. Beloch, *RG* 156. Livy 8. 9. 9; 10. 7. 3. Cato in Servius on *Aeneid* 5. 755. Festus, s.v. 'procincta classis'.
[4] Dion. Hal. 3. 49. 6.

drawn later between *ager Crustuminus* and other Roman territory
for the purposes of religion.[1] Either these statements are a reflection backwards to a remote epoch of a system inaugurated
later, or else they record a real change in the political method
of Rome. The parallel between these two instances and the incorporation of Tusculum in the fourth century is too exact to
be accidental. Tusculum also was a tiny community compared
to Rome; but even when surrounded on all sides by Roman
territory it was still too conscious of its own identity to be completely swallowed up in the Roman state.[2]

The incorporation of Gabii and of Crustumerium marks the
opening of a new era in the history of Rome. The days of simple
destruction and aggrandizement at the expense of the *populi
Latini* were over. The reason for this is that the villages, or groups
of them, have grown up into politically self-conscious townships.
The existence of the *foedus Gabinum* shows that tribal feeling was
no longer the preponderating influence in the life of the Latins,
and that the claims of local loyalty were growing strong; the
designation 'Gabinus' has become more than a description or an
address. The new form of incorporation suggests that at this time
the Triginta Populi were a reality and that synoecism in Latium
did not proceed at a regular pace. Some of the smaller cities
were able themselves to grow to moderate size before they
found their further extension blocked by the frontiers of some
greater neighbour. Political consolidation was to go further yet,
until the Thirty were reduced to about a dozen states;[3] but the
period was pre-eminently the time when the special character of
the Latin Name was fixed, for the *populi* appear to have been conscious both of their common origin and interests as Latins, and
also of their distinctive individuality as city-states. In a word, this
is the period of the Cassian treaty, and always the best reason for
accepting the fifth-century date of this document will remain the
fact that this arrangement of the data best explains the development of 'Latin rights', and the later Latin Name. Set the Cassian
treaty in the fourth century, and time enough is not allowed for
the slow growth of so permanent a political concept.

[1] Cf. Mommsen, *St. R.* iii. 824 n. 2. Livy 41. 13. 1–3. Pliny, *NH* 3. 52. But *ager
Veiens* was also similarly distinguished, Festus 189 M.

[2] Cf. Beloch, *RG* 211, 215. Livy 6. 26. 8; 33. 6; cf. below, 30, 60 n. 1.

[3] Below, 31 n. 6.

POLITICAL PRODUCTS OF THE WARS OF THE LATIN
LEAGUE

It is not until the fifth century that the Volscian and Aequian
tribes play an important part in the records of Latin history.
During the sixth century there is a series of notices of minor
movements of the Sabines which seem to indicate an infiltration
rather than an invasion.[1] The area affected was mainly the
country beyond the Anio. A long quotation from Cato shows that
the full force of the Sabine movement exhausted itself before
passing the north-eastern fringe of Latium.[2] But in the fifth
century a fresh danger appeared with the advance of the Volsci
into the hills to the south-east of Latium, their seizure of certain
strongholds such as Velitrae, and their influx into the coastal
plain as far as Antium.[3] This threat was a contributory motive in
the formation of the alliances between Rome and the other Latin
peoples known as the Cassian treaty, even as a little later the
advance of the Aequi was a compelling cause in the extension of
the Latin federation to the Hernici.[4]

These traditions are consistent and credible despite the attacks
which have been made upon them. The difficulties that have been
raised over the two treaties ascribed to Spurius Cassius are largely
due to the habit of regarding them as the Roman historians wish us
to regard them—as the assertion of Roman suzerainty over recalcitrant allies, rather than as the acceptance of the hegemony of the
greatest state in Latin by the others, at a time when their own
existence was seriously threatened. That on the collapse of the
strong Etruscan dynasty the hegemony won by the kings—
whatever it was—should collapse, was natural. That this hegemony was recovered at a stroke on the field of Regillus has
always been questioned, especially since the treaty that is said to
record the recovery, when examined, reveals no such state of
affairs.

The accounts of Livy and Dionysius show that the conclusion
of the Cassian treaty was immediately preceded by aggression on
the part of the Volsci and Aurunci, who succeeded in annexing

[1] Dion. Hal. 3. 28. 32, 40, 55, 56. Livy 1. 36 f. Cf. 2. 16.
[2] Dion. Hal. 2. 49. 2.
[3] First in Dion. Hal. 6. 25; 32. Livy 2. 22. Aurunci earlier in Livy 2. 16. 8 (Dion.
Hal. 6. 32). Later Aurunci are equated with Volsci, cf. Livy 2. 22. 2.
[4] First in Dion. Hal. 8. 62. 3; 63. 2; 68. 1. Cf. Livy 2. 30. 8; 40. 12; 41. 1.

the territory of the two Latin communities of Pometia and Cora.[1]
With the exception of the famous march of the Volsci under
Coriolanus to the Fossae Cloeliae, neither these nor later raids
seriously threatened Roman territory, for Rome was sheltered by
a ring of Latin states on whom the first attack always fell.
Nomentum, Pedum, Tibur, Praeneste, Tusculum above all,
Aricia, Lanuvium, Ardea—these formed a wall of comparative
security around Rome. Her interest in the fifth century lay in
seeing that the wall was strong, not in increasing her territory at
Latin expense. That tendency was resumed only when the
invasions had spent their force. The interest of the Latins equally
lay in gaining Roman aid, to save themselves from the raiders.
On these presuppositions the Cassian treaty can be accepted as
part of the genuine tradition, set at its traditional date, despite
the dubious character of other stories that have attached themselves to the name of its alleged mediator.[2]

Whether the document which Dionysius quotes as the Cassian
treaty contains the original text is another question.[3] It was not
impossible for Dionysius or one of his sources to have had access
to the original, for Cicero asserts that it existed down to his time,
inscribed on a bronze column which was to be found behind the
Rostra.[4] On the other hand, the text given by Dionysius is certainly incomplete, for Festus preserves a fragment of the treaty
which, while not contradicting, does not precisely correspond to
Dionysius' version.[5] Again, the terms of the treaty have been
modernized and atticized by Dionysius, especially in formal
details. But still, the effective content of the document fits the
situation recorded by the tradition. The treaty establishes peace
between the Latin cities and Rome, but not between the Latins
themselves, and it provides for a defensive alliance on equal terms
in case of attack from without Latium, and for the division of
spoils of war. There is a clear reference, in the article 'let
them not bring in wars'—or better, 'enemies'—'against each
other from outside', to a recent incident in which Romans had

---

[1] Livy 2. 16. 8; 22. 1–5. The treaty follows in 33. 4. Cf. Dion. Hal. 6. 91–4 and
95; and above, 21 n. 4.
[2] Gelzer, *RE* art. cit., col. 954. Beloch, *RG* 195, on Rosenberg's view in *Hermes* 54.
[3] Dion. Hal. 6. 95. Livy 2. 33. 9.
[4] Cic. *Pro Balbo* 53. He implies that it existed no longer. *Nuper* might refer to its
disappearance after 89 B.C., when it became obsolete. Cf. Livy 2. 33. 9.
[5] Festus, s.v. 'nancitor'.

co-operated with Etruscans against Aricia.[1] For the future such treachery is forbidden. These terms do not fit so well in the early fourth century, when Latium was on the offensive and recovering lost lands, and when also it is hard to make up the complement of the Thirty Peoples by whom this covenant was made.[2]

The objections brought against this document are that the relations between Rome and Latium do not, in the following period, always appear to be regulated by such a treaty on equal terms, such a *foedus aequum*, as Dionysius records; that Rome possessed other treaties with individual Latin states that might seem to preclude the existence of a general treaty; that Rome did not observe this treaty, and that in particular she neglected the clause which provided for the equal distribution of booty.

It is not to be denied that Livy in writing his history has succeeded in disguising the equal alliance as a Roman suzerainty, nor that under the cover of this treaty the Romans established a *de facto* supremacy, from which the Latins in the fourth century made continuous attempts to break away. But under the surface clear traces of the *foedus aequum* can be detected down to the time of the last Latin revolt. The other Latin cities are mentioned as fighting wars on their own account, *sine Romano aut duce aut auxilio*, though in Livy's story this is regarded as exceptional.[3] They fight in separate contingents,[4] conduct and settle affairs for themselves.[5] Especially important are two incidents from the fourth century, when the Latins lead a raid into Paelignian territory,[6] and later support the Sidicini against the Samnites.[7] Livy by the use of ambiguous phrases, tries to suggest that at the time of the latter incident, which preceded the final war of Latin independence, the Latins were already completely estranged from Rome, and the treaty in abeyance; but his own narrative makes it clear that the rupture of the *foedus* and the declaration of war did not come till later, for Latins and Romans were still at peace in the year following the incident.[8] The Roman reply to Samnite complaints shows the true position: 'there is nothing in the Latin treaty to prevent them fighting with whom they like'.[9]

[1] Livy 2. 14. 5–9.                                    [2] Below, 31 f.
[3] Livy 2. 53. 5; 3. 6. 5–6; 4. 45. 4.                [4] Livy 3. 22. 5.
[5] Livy 3. 23. 5, 'omnes sub iugum a Tusculanis missi.' Cf. Livy 4. 10. 5.
[6] Livy 7. 38. 1.                                     [7] Livy 8. 2. 5–8.
[8] Livy 8. 3. 8; 5. 1; 6. 8. Cf. Livy 7. 32. 9.
[9] Livy 8. 2. 13. Cf. Livy 8. 4. 2, 'sub umbra foederis aequi'.

Beside these facts may be set certain indications that the division of spoils was also maintained; yet here again Livy tries to colour the interpretation of events in a way more favourable to the dignity of Rome, by representing the division either as due to the graciousness of Rome, or else as the mere recovery of stolen property.[1] In addition the important institution of the Latin colony is not to be forgotten. Throughout the fifth and fourth centuries the Romans and Latins were establishing joint colonies. It is true that Rome, always interested in the conservation of man-power, secured control over the foundation of these colonies, and that a large number of the lots must have fallen to Roman citizens; but unless a large proportion were also handed over to Latins, the very nature of the colonies cannot be understood. In the earlier period the non-Roman element must have been the stronger, because several of these colonies had no hesitation in joining the Latin rather than the Roman side in the civil wars of the fourth century. Norba, Setia, and Circei do not stand alone.[2] The foundation of these colonies may be taken to represent the work-ing of the clause of the Cassian treaty which provided for the division of booty, since lands gained in warfare, or won back, were divided between Rome and her allies thereby, though not neces-sarily in equal proportions.

The passages in Livy which suggest that whatever treaty governed the relations of Rome and Latium down to 338 B.C. was not a *foedus aequum* are those where Rome is described as de-manding, or receiving, or complaining at the absence of, the Latin contingents for the wars, or where the Latins are refusing to supply the troops. All these passages imply that there was some sort of a treaty, and cannot be used to deny the existence of any. They speak of *milites ex instituto* or *ex foedere vetusto accepti*, or simply of *milites iussi* or *imperati*,[3] the levying officer sometimes being the consul, sometimes the dictator.[4] But there is no word of the term *milites ex formula togatorum*, known to the third and second centuries. The key to the interpretation of these facts is

---

[1] Livy 4. 29. 4, 'praedae pars sua cognoscentibus Latinis atque Hernicis reddita'. 4. 51. 8, 'Hernicis ipsum (oppidum) agerque dono datus.' 5. 19. 5. 'Latini Hernici-que . . . ad id bellum venere'. 20. 4, qui particeps esse praedae vellet. Veios iret 19. 8, 'ingenti praeda cuius pars maxima ad quaestorem redacta est, haud ita multum militi datum'.

[2] Livy 8. 3. 9. Cf. events at Velitrae, Livy 6. 17. 7; 8. 14. 5. Cf. below, 36.

[3] Livy 6. 10. 6; 7. 12. 7; 25. 5.       [4] Livy 3. 4. 11; 4. 26. 12

provided by the answer which, according to Livy, the rebellious Council at Lucus Ferentinae gave to the Roman demand for troops in 350 B.C.—*absisterent imperare iis quorum auxilio egerent.*[1] Thus the administrative act by which Rome gathered the allied troops together at this time was not based on the same principle as the later procedure *ex formula togatorum*, when Rome imposed the duty on the Latins by right of conquest. The terminology itself shows that the troops were sent *ex foedere* to the aid of the assailed state; frequently enough, for instance, the Romans go to help the Tusculani, when the Aequi were encamped 'in Algido'. It became an *institutum* for the Latin cities to send their soldiery each year to the city of their great ally. Now *institutum* is not a technical term of constitutional right, but a designation for a practice which could be, and on Livy's admission was, broken.[2]

The consistent account of the working of the *foedus aequum* which lies under the surface of Livy's narrative agrees admirably with the précis of early Latin history which is contained in a fragment of Cincius quoted by Festus.[3] Cincius, summing up the history of Latium in its own right, with Rome, for once, not holding the centre of the stage, speaks of Roman *imperatores* sent to command the federal forces 'by order of the Latin Name', and conversely of troops *a communi Latio missus* coming to Rome to meet their praetor. Since Roman consuls in the fifth century were probably called *praetores*, and since the federal officers of Latium[4] were also known as *praetores*, it was easy for the federal nature of some of Rome's early wars to escape notice. But Livy has not always obscured the truth; for in a curious passage in which he describes T. Quinctius as acting *pro consule* when in command of a joint force of Hernici and Latins, he must mean that Quinctius was exercising a federal command.[5] Livy is following a good source, for the same paragraph contains another archaism on which he expressly comments.[6] But the pro-magistracy itself is an impossible anachronism at such a date.

What had originally been a federal act may have passed under Roman control, in so far as Rome took over the conduct of the

---

[1] Livy 7. 25. 5, 'Let them stop giving orders to those whose help they need.'

[2] Livy 7. 12. 7, 'quod multis intermiserant annis.'

[3] s.v. 'praetor' cited above, 13 n. 6.                    [4] Cf. Livy 8. 3. 9.

[5] Livy 3. 4. 10–11, '. . . ipsum consulem Romae manere . . . pro consule T. Quinctium . . . cum sociali exercitu mitti'.

[6] 'subitarios milites—ita tum repentina auxilia appellabant'.

federal wars. One particular factor, in addition to the central position and predominant strength of Rome, probably favoured the transfer—the alliance with the Hernici. The introduction of a non-Latin people meant that the conduct of communal affairs could no longer be entirely directed by the council at Lucus Ferentinae, which was essentially a Latin tribal gathering, whose function was to appoint the *praetores Latini*. Two considerations support this view. First, although the war which introduced the Hernican alliance had been a federal affair,[1] the Hernici apparently formed a connection not with the *populi Latini* but with Rome.[2] Second, in later days the Hernici were independent of the Latins in their relation to Rome. They supplied separate contingents for the wars,[3] they had a separate council of their own *in circo quem maritimum vocant*, and their acts of rebellion against Roman authority proceeded independently of the movements in Latium.[4]

The conclusion of the treaty with the Hernici was a momentous event in two ways. It marks Rome's first adventure beyond the narrow limits of Latium, and it fixes the moment when Rome became more definitely the military focus of Latium that united a double federation of Latini and Hernici. Since there was no machinery for the selection of a joint commander, the leadership of the triple alliance inevitably fell to Rome, through whom alone the other two partners came into official contact.[5] So began that *institutum* of yearly sending troops to Rome, which developed into an iron rule and perverted the spirit of the *foedus aequum*.

Other arguments against the existence of the Cassian treaty are based on the relations known to have existed between Rome and various individual states. It is thought that separate *foedera* should have been excluded by the existence of a general *foedus*. But in the form known to us the Cassian treaty is nothing more than a defensive alliance extended by the addition of a single trading clause, though it is true that an entry in Festus suggests that Dionysius' version is not complete.[6] That Rome should have sought to amplify a *de facto* supremacy by securing closer ties between certain states and herself does not run counter to any

---

[1] Dion. Hal. 8. 65. 1 places it in the territory of Praeneste.

[2] Dion. Hal. 8. 69. 4. Livy 2. 41. 1.          [3] Livy 6. 10. 6–7.

[4] Livy 9. 42. 11. In 7. 6. 7 war is declared on the Hernici separately. In 6. 10–12 Hernici play only an inferior part; in the last revolt no part at all.

[5] Cf. Livy 2. 40. 13 for an analogy.          [6] s.v. 'nancitor'.

known condition of the Cassian treaty; nor do the Latins appear to have held that collective pacts and majority votes bound the dissentient to abstain from independent action, any more than the Greeks held that the existence of the Delian league, for example, prevented Athens from forming particular compacts with individual members of it. The conduct of the Hernican peoples in 321 provides a clear instance of separatist tendencies within a confederation.[1]

There was certainly a special treaty between Ardea and Rome in the fifth century. This is the basic fact behind the curious story of the land dispute between Aricia and Ardea that Rome was said to have settled, when invited to arbitrate, by awarding the disputed area to herself.[2] This story reflects the atmosphere of the second century and is anachronistic in its details, but the existence of the treaty is guaranteed independently of the anecdote.[3] The document was known to Licinius Macer, of the Second Annalistic, who found in it the names of the consuls for 444 B.C., for which hitherto no consuls had been known: it is thus probable that the anecdote, which Cicero also tells about Nola and Neapolis, was attributed to this period to explain the otherwise isolated fact of the formation or renewal of a treaty between Rome and Ardea in 444.[4]

Another certain instance of a special compact outside the framework of the Cassian treaty is the treaty of Lavinium. But it is specially improper to bring in this *foedus* against the *Cassianum*, because Rome's relation to Lavinium, her second 'metropolis', was most particular.[5] The addition to this list of a *foedus Aricinum*, however, cannot be established by Cicero's reference to the *municipium* of Aricia in his day as *iure foederatum*.[6] Some confirmation might perhaps be found in the fact that, in Livy's narrative, the Romans rushed to rescue Aricia from the grip of the Aurunci in the period after the battle of Lake Regillus and before the conclusion of the Cassian treaty.[7] Rome was certainly

[1] Livy 9. 42. 11. 'concilium populorum omnium habentibus Anagninis . . . praeter Aletrinatem Ferentinatemque et Verulanum omnes Hernici nominis populo Romano bellum indixerunt.'

[2] Livy 3. 71–2. Dion. Hal. 11. 52.

[3] Cf. Beloch, *RG* 147. Tribunician interference in foreign policy!

[4] Livy 4. 7. 10. Dion. Hal. 11. 62. 4. Cf. Cic. *Off*. 1. 33. Macer distinguishes the text of the treaty from his much-suspected *libri lintei*.

[5] Dion. Hal. 3. 11. 2. Livy 5. 52. 8. Cf. *ILS* 5004.

[6] Cic. *Phil*. 3. 15, 'in law, federated'. Cf. below, 61.          [7] Livy 2. 26. 6.

especially interested in Aricia, not only in the regal, but also in the early republican period.[1]

If the suggestion of a *foedus Aricinum* can be accepted, the most that the three instances of special treaties, Ardea, Lavinium, and Aricia, would suggest is that the Roman Republic was simply resuming the policy of the last of the Kings, who seem to have sought to combine a limited series of local alliances with a general confederation with the rest of Latium.[2] Rome naturally desired a more explicit understanding with those powers with which she was in immediate contact than with the remoter states of Latium. It is characteristic that the two peoples of whom most is heard in the fourth century, Tibur and Praeneste, are conspicuous by their absence from the records of the fifth. This means simply that the Cassian treaty satisfied the needs of these powers, and that neither party desired ampler arrangements. The two solitary references to Praeneste in the fifth century bear out this view. Dionysius refers to a federal war against the Aequi in the territory of Praeneste that preceded the formation of the Hernican alliance, and Livy records that Praeneste took no part in the Latin war that followed the expulsion of the Kings.[3] As long as Tibur and Praeneste looked after their sector of the Aequian front, the Cassian treaty sufficed. But when in the fourth century Rome's interests began to extend beyond Latium, she sought to implement the Cassian treaty in relation to precisely these two powers.[4] The meaning of these special treaties becomes clear when they are considered all together: they mark the gradual extension of Roman supremacy in Latium in a special way—the conversion of 'such as are not subject' into 'such as are subject'. While the traditional date of the Cassian treaty raises difficulties that are more apparent than real, the attribution of it to a date in the fourth century involves a serious contradiction; for Rome, in the fourth century, at first gradually and later completely abandoned the notion of a general league in favour of individual pacts. The latter were used, not merely to supplement, but to supplant the Cassian treaty. The reason for this can be gathered from the general history, not merely of Rome, but of Latium, during the century and a half that passed between the

---

[1] Cf. Livy 2. 14. 5–9.       [2] Cf. above, 18.
[3] Livy 2. 19. 2. Dion. Hal. 8. 65. 1.
[4] De Sanctis, *Storia dei Romani*, ii. 153 ff., 275 f.

formation of the Cassian treaty and the final break-up of the confederation in 334 B.C.

Despite the comparatively detailed account of Livy and Dionysius, in truth very little is known of what was happening in Latium during this century and a half, except where Roman interests are directly concerned. The traditional account of the breakdown of the Cassian system is that the undue preponderance of the Romans, who won back, under the shelter of the treaty, much of the power lost in the sixth century, stirred the Latins on two occasions, first between 385 and 358 B.C., when the Gallic invasion offered an opportunity, and again in 340 B.C., to break away from the threatening dominion of Rome. This view gains confirmation when we consider the growth of the Roman territory in this period.[1] The Aequian wars, though fought mainly in defence of Tusculum, had resulted in the territorial enrichment of Rome, especially by the acquisition of the *ager Labicanus* and the conquest of small territories like that of Corbio. Finally the incorporation of Tusculum meant that Latium was split in two by a great wedge of Roman land, running from the Tiber to the Algidus pass.[2] The Latin cities of the east were cut off from those of the west. At the time of the final outbreak the narrative of Livy shows that the *praetores Latini* from Circei and Setia could reach effectively only the western states.[3] While Rome was able to deal separately with the eastern cities, the Latins were compelled to seek a rendezvous outside Latium.[4] In the last campaign this course was not open to them, and the two groups fought separately, Tibur and Praeneste around Pedum, the rest near the Astura.[5]

Not only was Rome strengthening herself at the expense of a divided and weakened Latium, but the acquisition of the new Latium across the Tiber, the *ager Veiens*, had provided fresh fields for the increase of Roman manpower, so that the existence of ten legions in 338 B.C. appears almost credible.[6] The increased strength of Rome now ceased to be employed for the special

[1] Below, 31.
[2] Cf. Livy 7. 11. 3, 'foedae populationes in Labicano Tusculanoque et Albano agro'.
[3] Livy 8. 3. 9, 'praetores . . . per quos praeter Signiam Velitrasque et ipsas colonias Romanas Volsci etiam exciti ad arma erant'.
[4] Livy 8. 6. 8; 8. 19.                                    [5] Livy 8. 13. 4–5.
[6] Cf. Livy 7. 25. 8, 'etiam agresti iuventute decem legiones scriptae'. *Contra*, Polyb. 6. 19.

benefit of Latium. When the Volscian and Aequian peoples had been pushed back to their proper limits, the work of the defensive alliance was finished, and there was no further cause for communal wars. But Rome was not prepared to leave her new strength unemployed. The fourth century saw the extension of Roman power, first in southern Etruria and later in Campania. But this had nothing to do with the interests of the Latins, and each phase was met by a corresponding refusal to co-operate,[1] first in the long period of unrest from 385 to 358, then more briefly in the wars of 340–338 B.C. This connection of events shows clearly how the Romans, entering on a career of expansion outside Latium, found the collective treaty an unsuitable instrument for the exploitation of the military resources of Latium, and how the Latini and Hernici, aware that the balance of power had been upset, and that they were being territorially encircled, were forced to rise in defence of their liberties.

On the first occasion, Rome, in re-establishing order, dealt with most of the allies *en bloc* and restored the 'old treaty', as Livy calls it. Livy's narrative is borne out by the independent evidence of Polybius, who says that after the Gallic invasion the Romans again saw to their interests in Latium—language that lends little support to those who would attribute the origin of the Cassian treaty to this very period.[2] But with the two greatest states, Tibur and Praeneste, which had performed the act of formal surrender individually to her, Rome settled separately.[3] A little earlier a special settlement had also been made with Tusculum, which roused the indignation of the Latin federation. At least the annalistic tradition stigmatizes the Tusculani with the phrase, *deserto communi concilio Latinorum*.[4] Further evidence of the growing importance of individual pacts is given by the text of the second Carthaginian treaty. This document, which may belong to the year 348, recognizes, in addition to the two classes of subject allies and ordinary Latins known to the first treaty, a third class of superior *foederati* allied to Rome by special agreements.[5]

---

[1] Livy 6. 9–10. 6, on Etruscan wars, continues 'eodem anno ab Latinis Hernicisque res repetitae.' Livy 7. 38. 4–42, the garrison in Campania. Livy 7. 42. 8, 'Latinorum infidum iamdiu foedus'.        [2] Livy 7. 12. 7. Pol. 2. 18. 5.

[3] Livy 6. 29. 7. Cf. Diod. 16. 45. 8, for Praeneste. Livy 7. 19. 1 and Chronicle of Oxyrhynchus, Ol. 106, 1, for Tibur.

[4] Livy 6. 33. 6, 'deserting the joint council of Latium.'

[5] Polyb. 3. 24. 5–6. Diod. 16. 69. 1. Livy 7. 27. 2; 38. 2; cf. 9. 43. 26. Beloch,

It was not, however, till the settlement of 338 B.C. that this method of individual treatment was employed universally.[1]

The internal history of Latium supplies another clue to the breakdown of the Cassian system. The fragment of Cincius, supported by casual references in Livy, shows how much has been lost of the history of Latium in this period.[2] We probably possess less than half the stories of the border warfare. The recorded Roman interest on the Aequian front, for example, was mainly limited to attacks made on Tusculum from the post *in Algido*. Tibur and Praeneste, except for one mysterious reference to the latter, are barely mentioned in the fifth-century records.[3] Yet in the fourth century they emerge as powers capable of sustaining a war with Rome by themselves, each with a little league of incorporated cities. 'Eight towns were under the sway of Praeneste', writes Livy,[4] while Empulum and Sassulla, with 'other towns', stand in a similar relation to Tibur.[5] This seems to represent a development of the period. Like Rome, these two states emerge from the period of the invasions with an increase of lands and power. But this increase, like that of Rome, must have been at the expense of the remaining Triginta Populi which contracted the *foedus Cassianum*. In 338 no more than thirteen independent *populi* were left.[6] This continuous absorption of the smaller members of the federation by the greater, coupled with the replacement of others by newly created *coloniae Latinae*, meant that certain areas of Latium were withdrawn from the scope of the Cassian treaty; for the manpower of the *populi* that had lost their independence could only be exploited by Rome through a closer understanding with the greater powers that had absorbed them. The small *populus* had in effect ceased to be the normal unit in Latium; hence the political system could no longer be based upon it. The political atmosphere having changed and the separatism which was already prevalent in the fifth century having further

---

*RG* 308. But the third class might be allies from beyond Latium. Their citizens seem to be seafaring peoples, possibly the Caerites or even the Campani (cf. Livy 7. 29–30).

[1] Below, 96 ff.                                                   [2] Above, 13 n. 6, and 23 ff.
[3] Livy 2. 19. 2. Cf. Dion. Hal. 8. 65. 1; above, 26 n. 1, and 28 f.
[4] Livy 6. 29. 6.                                          [5] Livy 7. 18. 2; 19. 1. *Oppida* is used.
[6] Ardea,* Aricia, Circei,* Cora, Lanuvium, Lavinium, Nomentum, Norba,* Pedum, Praeneste, Setia,* Signia,* Tibur. Of these the five '*' are *coloniae*, like Nepet and Sutrium. Cf. Beloch, *RG* Index for further documentation.

intensified, it was inevitable that the collective pact should be replaced by individual treatment.

The fact that after a hundred years the *foedus Cassianum* was proving unworkable, and perhaps old-fashioned, need not cast any doubts upon its historicity and its effectiveness in the fifth century. It would be more truly surprising if the highly individual treatment to which Rome in the end submitted the Latins were the inspiration of the moment. The elaborate system of 338 did not spring ready-made from the head of some Camillus. The various instances of particularism in the earlier period should rather be regarded as a groping towards the final idea.

## SOCIAL AND LEGAL ASPECTS OF EARLY LATIUM

The substitution of separate pacts for the communal alliance corresponds to an alteration in the status of the individual *homo Latinus*. When Latium consisted of a great number of tiny communities, a man was simply a *Latinus*, a 'dweller in the plain', belonging to a certain village; for the term *Latini* is comparable in origin to 'the Peloponnesians' rather than to 'the Dorians'. Since those days the concept of local citizenship has hardened and taken on a truly political colour. In the settlement of 338 *conubium* and *commercium* are named as distinct *iura* for the first time, in the place of that vague isopolity, of which Dionysius speaks as still subsisting between all Latins in the early fifth century.[1] Their adventures in the following period, when they were continually forced to fall back on their strong places and town-centres, and to create new ones where such were lacking, doubtless had the effect of defining local citizenship at the expense of the earlier sentiment of geographic unity. Certain customs which a man had originally shared through his status as a Latin began to be regarded as privileges dependent upon residence within the territory of a given state, or as the corollary of duties performed for that state. These privileges could be shared with, or withheld from, a neighbour; but the older sentiment still had such strength left that in the fourth century Rome could extend her commonwealth by the incorporation of communities of fellow Latins—that is to say, Rome restored the former isopolity in a particular

---

[1] Dion. Hal. 6. 63. 4; 7. 53. 5; 8. 35. 2; 76, 2, etc.

area. This appears clearly when the contrast between two almost contemporary events is considered—the destruction of Etruscan Veii and the grant of Roman rights to Latin Tusculum.[1]

The relative strength of centripetal and centrifugal forces is nicely revealed by the dispositions of 338. Apart from Lavinium, which was specially privileged, and the *coloniae Latinae*, the two states that succeeded in maintaining their independence were just those which had developed the greatest independent power, and a corresponding sense of autonomy—Tibur and Praeneste; the smaller places more closely connected with the federal centre at Lucus Ferentinae, from which in the preceding half-century Tibur and Praeneste had been cut off, were easily incorporated in the Roman state.

The question arises, how many of the *iura* later associated with Latin rights had their origin in the social conditions prior to the dissolution of the Latin league, and how many were later adjustments of privilege that arose from the subsequent circumstances of the Latin Name? The answer to this question depends largely upon the importance which we assign to the persistence of the sense of pre-urban unity. It has been denied, for each in its turn, that the early Latins possessed any of these *iura*. But the idea that the numerous villages of the Prisci Latini were each cut off totally from its neighbour, as far as social relationship is concerned, although the neighbour was but a mile or two away, is not convincing. In the era of the fully developed city-state some degree of isolation may well be expected; yet the text of Livy, which is the basis of all discussion, states, in reference to the settlement of 338 B.C., 'ceteris Latinis populis conubia commerciaque et concilia inter se ademerunt.'[2] Hence all these had previously existed in Latium. In the face of this, the presence of a trading clause in the *foedus Cassianum* cannot be used to support the view that the Latini did not enjoy mutual *commercium*. Rather does this clause presuppose *commercium*, that is to say, not the bare power of buying and selling, which can be done subject to treaty regulations of the type suggested by the first Carthaginian treaty, but the right of a *Tiburtinus*, for example, to make contracts, etc. with a Roman enforceable in Roman courts according to Roman law and vice versa. With *commercium*, *conubium* goes hand in hand—the right to contract a marriage with a foreigner

[1] Cf. above, 19 f, and below, 59 n. 3.  [2] 8. 14. 10.

which will be upheld in a Roman court of law, with full validity of testamentary power and paternity rights.[1]

The existence of *commercium* and *conubium* is no small exception to the exclusiveness of local politics in fourth-century Latium. The power of acquiring the citizenship of another state by change of domicile—*ius mutandae civitatis* or *ius migrationis*—is debated ground. That in the second century the Latin colonies shared it with Rome and one another, is not disputed.[2] The modern view is that this was a concession to Roman citizens who exchanged their Roman citizen rights for Latin status on joining a Latin colony,[3] and that the purpose of the concession was to enable the Latin to end his days at Rome after doing his duty to the state. But this does not explain why the right applied not only to *Romani* but to colonists drawn from other Latin colonies, and also held good between other Latin communities; for there is no proof that the right was limited to Latins who had originally been Romani, nor even that the *ius* was limited to Latin colonies, and not equally open to, e.g. Praenestini, or even to Hernici. No distinction is drawn at any time during the Republic between two such grades of Latins.[4]

Moreover, the *ius civitatis mutandae* is closely connected with the *ius exilii* and *postliminium*. These practices reflect the same early stage of social organization which allowed a man to change his domicile at will, and which, in an extreme form, precluded any distinct sense of territorial citizenship. There is no doubt that *exilium* is primitive in origin. Late in the third century special legislation was necessary to extend the *ius exilii* to a non-Latin state;[5] in the earlier period there are numerous examples which show that the *exul* acquired the citizenship of the community to which he went. Collatinus' retirement to Lavinium is traditional,[6] likewise Camillus' to Ardea, where he is represented as calling the Ardeates *veteres amici, novi etiam cives mei*.[7] The liveliness and continuity of the notion are shown by the fact that Tibur and Praeneste retained the right, after the break-up of the Latin

---

[1] Below, 108 f.          [2] Below, 110 f.

[3] e.g. P. Fraccaro, 'L'organizzazione Politica dell'Italia Romana', *Atti del Congresso Internazionale di Diritto Romano*, (1) 1934, 207.

[4] Below, 37 n. 1, 104 f., 110 f.

[5] Livy 26. 3. 12, 'Cn. Fulvius exulatum Tarquinios abiit; id ei iustum exilium esse scivit plebs.'          [6] Livy 2. 2. 10–11. Cf. 3. 29. 7.

[7] Livy 5. 43–4, 'My old friends and new fellow citizens'.

League, till the Social War.[1] The subject is illuminated by the incident, in 311 B.C., of the Roman *tibicines* who went on strike and retired to Tibur. They, in fact, exercised the *ius exilii*; that is why the Senate could not touch them.[2] Down to the age of Cicero *exilium* remained a voluntary act,[3] and was only incidentally associated with the removal of political offenders from the state.

*Postliminium* is the corollary of *exilium*. It is the right of the voluntary exile and of the prisoner of war, i.e. the man who has become an exile contrary to his own or his city's will, to recover his original *civitas*. 'Etiam postliminio potest civitatis fieri mutatio', writes Cicero, and quotes an example: 'ad populum latum est ut is Publicius si domum revenisset et inde Romam redisset ne minus civis esset'.[4] The return of Camillus is probably an example of this practice;[5] but its early origin is also evident from its connection with *exilium* and the primitive custom of *rerum repetitio* or *reciperatio*,[6] and also from the formation and meaning of the word itself.

The number of *iura* that are late accretions can thus be reduced to a modest figure. Most obvious is the *ius suffragi ferendi*: one tribe was set aside at Rome in the *concilium plebis* in which Latins could cast their votes. Dionysius has taken this custom to be primitive,[7] but elsewhere it has left no trace until Livy's mention of it during the second Punic War.[8] As a primitive institution, beside the *ius mutandae civitatis* it seems superfluous;[9] but later, when Roman citizens were being drafted off in large numbers to Latin colonies, in distant parts of Italy, the custom, suggesting vaguely the yet unformed concept of a dual citizenship, becomes highly interesting.

Another institution that loses its meaning if transferred to the fourth century is the access to Roman citizenship *per magistratum*, by holding office in a Latin state. A. Zumpt, in his defence of the contrary view, while misusing the evidence of Livy and Asconius,

[1] Polyb. 6. 14. 8.

[2] Livy 9. 30. 5–10, 'eius rei religio tenuit senatum'.

[3] Cic. *Balb.* 28–9.

[4] Ibid. 'It was proposed before the people that if the man Publicius went back to his home and then returned to Rome he should nevertheless remain a Roman citizen.' Festus, s.v. 'Postliminium'. 'Change of citizenship can be effected also by *postliminium*.'

[5] Livy 5. 46. 10–11.

[6] Cf. Festus, loc. cit.

[7] Dion. Hal. 8. 72. 4.

[8] Livy 25. 3. 16.

[9] But cf. below, 112 f.

rightly pointed out that before the emancipation of the *plebs* at Rome, only the governing class of the Latin states would rank as equals of the Roman *patricii*, i.e. could claim to stand for election to the curule magistracies in addition to the ordinary privileges.[1] But this does not mean that they became Roman citizens while remaining in their native community. At such a time the idea of a *civis Romanus* domiciled *in agro peregrino*, neither performing *munera* nor holding *honores*, is absurd. The analysis of *civitas sine suffragio*, an idea conceived in the fourth century, will show this.[2]

The last manifestation of the tribal spirit of the Latins is to be found in the creation of the *coloniae Latinae*. The federal character of these colonies has often been denied.[3] The method of foundation is said to be the same, in Livy's notices, as that employed later for the citizen colonies, the *coloniae civium Romanorum*. Latins, it is asserted, were only admitted by the special favour of Rome. But this is to be misled by the tendentious, exclusively Roman, outlook of Livy. Colonies were founded by other powers than Rome, though we hear very little of them.[4] The Latins, Romans, and others had a joint interest in occupying the strong positions of Latium; why then should they not found joint colonies? 'Norbam in montes novam coloniam quae arx in Pomptino esset miserunt (Romani).'[5] That is in 491 B.C. But since the *ager Pomptinus* was not at that date Roman territory, the colony must have been a federal affair. Livy, it is true, calls these early Latin colonies *coloniae Romanae*,[6] but he also gives that title to the thirty Latin colonies of the third century without thereby confusing them with the citizen colonies.[7] Moreover, he once describes Pometia and Cora as 'duae coloniae Latinae'.[8] If these foundations were composed entirely of Roman citizens, it is difficult to understand why they were so often disloyal to their metropolis.[9] Again, the Ferentinates in 187 B.C. assumed that they had the right to join in Roman colonial foundations.[10] There are

---

[1] A. Zumpt, 'De Propagatione civitatis Romanae', *Studia Romana*, 365. Asc. *in Pis.* 3. Livy 23. 22. 5. Cf. Pliny, *NH* 7. 136, 'L. Fulvius Tusculanorum . . . consul eodemque honore cum transisset exornatus.'      [2] Below, 39 ff.
[3] e.g. Gelzer, art. cit. col. 958 ff.      [4] e.g. Livy 7. 27. 2.
[5] Livy 2. 34. 6. 'The Romans sent a new colony to Norba in the hills, to be a stronghold in the Pomptine territory.'
[6] Livy 7. 42. 8; 8. 3. 9.      [7] Livy 27. 9. 7.
[8] Livy 2. 16. 8.      [9] Cf. above, 24 n. 2.
[10] Livy 34. 42. 5, 'Novum ius . . . a Ferentinatibus temptatum ut Latini qui in coloniam Romanam nomina dedissent cives Romani essent.'

even some traces of federal action in the procedure at Antium, though this instance may be contaminated by the knowledge of later events.[1] Federal or not, the existence of these colonies bears out the conclusions based upon the evidence of the other customs. For their presupposition is that, when a Roman leaves his native state for another, he ceases to be a Roman citizen and reverts to the condition of a *homo Latinus*.

The combined effect of these various institutions is to show how firm was the foundation beneath the sentiment of Latin unity. The latter was thus enabled to persist, despite the separatist tendencies of the particular states. When in later years diverse instruments were required for the conquest and control of Italy, this valuable force was not forgotten. A new Latin Name replaced the old. Later again, *ius Latii* supplied an essential intermediate link in the incorporation of new members within the imperial Roman state.

[1] Dion. Hal. 9. 59. 2. Livy 3. 1. 6–7 indicates joint colonization as in 8. 14. 8, cf. below, 80.

# II

## THE SETTLEMENT OF 338 B.C. AND THE ORIGINS OF THE *MUNICEPS*

THE dissolution of the Latin League makes a convenient halting-place. The various routes along which the unification of Italy is reached, although they do not first spring into being at this point, here first clearly separate from one another. The *municeps*, the *foederatus*, and the *Latinus* up to this time are mainly found within Latium and the Trerus valley, but, with the widening of the Roman horizon that followed the wars of the late fourth century, the application and expansion of these various principles can be observed in distinct areas.

There is nothing haphazard in the choice of the methods that Rome used; when one principle has exhausted its fertility in one region it is transplanted to fresh fields, where it can and does flourish anew, its place being taken by some other form of political union whose merits have been well tested elsewhere.[1] This is particularly evident in the use of the tribal *foedus*; after the fourth century it is never again applied to groups of city-states, but is used among the non-urbanized peoples of central Italy. The separate treaty, and the peculiar bond of the 'limited' franchise, *civitas sine suffragio*, and complete incorporation within the Roman state are employed in the more urbanized areas. In another sphere, the creation of new communities, Rome has a similar variety of weapons at her disposal, and for the next two centuries skilfully employs the two types of *colonia*, with their differing bonds of loyalty, according to the demands of the situation.

For the sake of convenience it is necessary to treat of these various forms in separate sections, but they are not generically distinct types; they have not only a unity of origin but a unity of purpose. Although they differ widely in the obligations which they bring and in the privileges which they confer, their common end is to bind the peoples of Italy to Rome by links of loyalty and interest: above all, to secure for Rome the control of their military

[1] Cf. P. Fraccaro, art. cit. 207.

forces, and to carry throughout the peninsula that commonsense *modus vivendi* which Rome had already established for herself and her neighbours within Latium.

Interpreters of early Roman history are open to the danger of giving too static an account of Roman institutions. This is due to two causes, the magic of the name of Rome, and the stability of terminology. We forget that Rome was not always great. In 338 B.C. Rome was very powerful in Latium, but in Campania and Etruria there were other states in a similar stage of development which in appearance were equally strong. To the ordinary Roman farmer-soldier strange worlds lay southward beyond the Latin hills, and northward behind the mass of the Monti Cimini. The limitations of the Roman outlook are well illustrated by the stories and legends of the period—Livy tells of astonishment at the wealth of Campania, and recounts romantic adventures of Fabius in Etruria, of the 'exploratory' type.[1] Conceptions of the Roman power that are only proper after the conquest of Samnium and the Pyrrhic wars need to be set aside.

Since the limits of Roman influence expand rapidly in the half-century after 338, an exact understanding of the ever changing atmosphere of the times is the best guide to the nature of Roman dealings with this or that community. Here the second danger to historians intervenes: the institutions which Rome employs do not change their names with the change in their meaning. *Civitas sine suffragio* has suffered especially from too static a treatment, and through failure to appreciate inward changes under the cover of the same external form. We read that this or that community has been given *civitas sine suffragio*, and tend to assume that the people concerned are receiving the same treatment as some other sixty years before; yet in the interval Rome may have expanded from a provincial to a continental power.

With these warnings a more detailed examination of the various movements which culminate or originate in the period of the dissolution of the Latin League may be attempted.

## CIVITAS SINE SUFFRAGIO

### In Campania

Although Livy's references to the relationship between Rome and the Campanian peoples are at times confused, there is no

[1] e.g. Livy 7. 38. 5; 9. 36.

obscurity in his earliest statements about them. The Campani
had officially assisted the Latins in the first phase of their last
revolt, although the aristocracy, who provided the cavalry, had
refused to fight. For this, Capua as a community was punished
with fines of money and land, while the knights were rewarded
for their loyalty to Rome with the gift of what Livy calls *civitas
Romana*.[1] In the second phase of the Latin revolt Capua took
no part.[2] After this intelligent inactivity *civitas sine suffragio*, in
Livy's words, was given to all the Campani, out of respect for the
knights who had refused to fight in the previous campaign.[3] That
may be true as far as it goes, but the Campani were not alone in
receiving this *civitas*. Cumae and Suessula also were given it,
for whom the Campanian knights could do nothing, and also
Formiae and Fundi, who earned it, as Livy says explicitly,
by services rendered.[4] In 334 B.C. we are informed that the
Acerrani were 'made Romans'—*Romani facti*—by a law which
conferred on them *civitas sine suffragio*.[5] In this instance, as in that
of Cumae and Suessula, no material, or at least no military
reason, is discernible, for in the previous years Rome was
concerned only with the region north of the Liris around Cales
and Sidicinum.[6]

To these statements of Livy correspond the notices of Festus,
who defines the communities under discussion as *municipia* and
their inhabitants as *municipes*.[7] This notion is borne out by the
terms which, a century later, the Campani demanded from Hannibal as the reward of treachery: 'ne . . . civis Campanus invitus
militaret munusve faceret'.[8] These peoples were thus the original
*municipes*, but whether the term *cives Romani* could be applied to
them is another question. Festus, or his authorities, hedge, and
prefer in effect to say that their citizenship was only conditional:
they could become citizens by migration to Rome, and were
citizens in so far as they served *in legione* and thereby performed
one essential *munus* of a citizen—hence the term *municeps*.[9]

¹ Livy 8. 11. 13–16.          ² Livy 8. 12–13. 9.          ³ Livy 8. 14. 10.
⁴ Ibid., below, 48.          ⁵ Livy 8. 17. 12.          ⁶ Livy 8. 16.
⁷ Festus, s.v. 'municeps' and 'municipium'. 'Servius aiebat initio fuisse (municipes) . . . Cumanos Acerranos Atellanos.'
⁸ Livy 23. 7. 1, 'No citizen of Capua was to perform military or civil service
against his will.'
⁹ s.v. 'municeps', 'non licebat magistratum capere sed tantum muneris partem
ut . . . qui et cives Romani erant et in legione merebant'. Cf. s.v. 'municipium',
'qui cum Romam venissent neque cives Romani essent . . . post aliquot annos cives

Livy betrays an exactly similar uncertainty. In the first decade he treats them mainly as *socii* or allies, and speaks of 'spes Campanae defectionis'; the language of the third decade is much the same, e.g.: 'foedus aequum deditis dedimus' is used of them, and also the phrase 'discidium publicorum foederum'.[1] But when he comes to the punishment inflicted upon them after their revolt he consistently calls them *cives*, e.g. 'cives Romanos affinitatibus plerosque . . . iunctos', 'per senatum agi de Campanis qui cives Romani sunt iniussu populi non posse'.[2] It is not possible to escape from these apparent contradictions by maintaining that only the nobility had received the *civitas sine suffragio*, since the original statement of Livy roundly asserts the opposite. Further, the presence of the prostitute Pacula Cluvia among the *cives* is against such a view; nor is there any suggestion of such class distinction in the passage describing the final reinstatement of the Campani as *cives*.[3] The whole tone of Campanian society is too democratic.[4] The fact that by 210 B.C. 'conubium vetustum multas familias claras ac potentes Romanis miscuerat' implies not that only such unions had taken place, but that only these had an important effect on the political situation.[5]

This confusion between the terms *cives* and *socii* is not confined to the account of Capua. The Atellani are classed by Livy with the Campani as *cives*, but the story of their revolt is recorded in the list of true *socii foederati*, such as the Samnites, who revolted: 'defecere . . . hi populi . . . neque eae . . . defectiones sociorum moverunt (Romanos).'[6] Now this confusion does not originate in Livy's own mind. There is evidence to show that the current view in the fourth century was that, whatever else the acceptance of *civitas sine suffragio* implied, it meant that in some way those who took it 'became Romans'. The phrase *facti Romani* is at least as old as Ennius, and the idea is proved to be older by its connection

Romani effecti sunt', and Servius, quoted s.v. 'municeps', says 'ea condicione cives Romani fuissent ut semper rem publicam separatim a populo Romano haberent.'

[1] Livy 9. 6. 4; 7. 1; 27. 1; 23. 5. 4 and 9, 'We gave you an equal treaty when you surrendered.' 25. 18. 5, 'The break-up of public treaties.'

[2] Livy 26. 33. 3 and 10. 'The Senate could not deal with Campani who were Roman citizens except at the command of the people.'

[3] Livy 38. 28. 4; 36. 5.         [4] e.g. Livy 23. 2–4.

[5] Livy 23. 4. 7. Cf. 26. 33. 3. 'The ancient right of intermarriage had allied many notable and powerful families to Romans.'

[6] Livy 22. 61. 11–13, 'These peoples revolted, but the revolt of their *allies* did not disturb the Romans.' Contrast 26. 33. 12.

with the desperate resistance which the insignificant Aequicoli put up to Rome in 304 B.C. rather than suffer this very change of 'becoming Romans'.[1]

There can be little doubt that the institution of *municipium*, in its original form, contained both the element of partial incorporation in, and the apparently contradictory idea of alliance with, the Roman state. Such an explanation as that of the Polish scholar Z. Z. Konopka fits the various features of *civitas sine suffragio* very well.[2] He compared it to the Hellenistic isopolity. The contracting parties possess a community of social rights, especially of *conubium*, and a member of either can acquire the complete franchise of the other state by transference of domicile.[3] Until such migration the *civitas* of, e.g., the Campani is only potential. In other respects the two communities are on a par with ordinary federated allies; the special nature of this form of alliance slips out in a casual reference of Livy to the Campani as *civitate nobis coniuncti*, in addition to the more obvious *foedere coniuncti*.[4] It appears also in the distinction which he recognizes between the Roman and Campanian military contingents.[5]

The acceptance of *civitas sine suffragio* did not destroy the separate existence of the *res publica* of the folk concerned. This is the basic fact behind the statements of Festus, and is the element stressed in such a view as Konopka's. The *res publica Campanorum* existed side by side, undiminished, with the *res publica populi Romani*.[6] That is why *cives sine suffragio* were not allowed *magistratum capere*, to hold magistracies at Rome; but this limitation applied to both parties, to Romans at Capua as much as to Campani at Rome. Festus' definitions give only the Roman point of view, and hence imply that it was a disadvantage to be a *civis sine suffragio*, but the only original modification of the freedom of the Campani, apart from any obligations which could equally well have been determined by a *foedus*, is the liability *munus facere*.[7] The effect of the grant of *civitas sine suffragio* to

[1] Livy 9. 45. 5–9. Diod. 20. 101. 5. Ennius, *Ann.* fr. 5. 4. Cic. *Off.* 1. 35. Cf. Beloch, *RG* 421–2.

[2] 'Les Relations Politiques entre Rome et la Campanie', *Eos*, 32, 587 ff.

[3] Cf. above, 40 n. 9.

[4] Livy 31. 31. 11, 'Joined to us by citizenship.'

[5] Livy 10. 26. 14, 'equitatu Romano Campanisque equitibus.' *Per.* 12 and 15, 'Campana legio'. Livy 23. 4. 8, 'cum militarent apud Romanos'. Cf. Polyb. 2. 24. 14.

[6] Cf. below, 43 n. 1; above, 40 n. 9.          [7] Cf. below, 47.

the Campanian peoples was that their own citizenship coincided, or overlapped, in one section, as it were, with that of Rome. To understand the nature of *civitas sine suffragio* it is necessary to estimate the exact extent of this overlap.

It is clear from Livy's narrative of the Campanian revolt that the constitutional and political life of Capua was not seriously affected by the new link with Rome. *Meddix*, senate, lawcourts, and elections all proceed as of old, nor is there any trace of any special orientation towards Rome.[1] This is equally true of Atella, Calatia, and Cumae. The official language continued to be Oscan;[2] the name of the *Meddix Tutivus* continued to be used for the dating of public documents.[3]

The only contrary tendencies which can be discerned are associated with the obscure question of the *praefecti Capuam Cumas*, and the yet more difficult matter of the Romano-Campanian silver coinage. As for the former, Livy makes the plain statement that in the year 318 B.C. 'primum praefecti Capuam creari coepti legibus a L. Furio praetore datis, cum utrumque ipsi pro remedio aegris rebus discordia intestina petissent'.[4] He adds that this example of 'res Capuae stabilitas Romana disciplina' led the Antiates to make a similar petition. His comment is 'nec arma modo sed etiam iura Romana late pollebant'.[5] Every word is important for the proper understanding of what is happening. This is not the imposition of Roman customs upon an unwilling subject; the Roman *praefecti* were simply performing a function very familiar in Greek history—that of the international arbitrators or *diallactai*. Naturally the Roman Demonax solved the difficulties of Capua by making use of Roman wisdom. Livy does not say that the office of these *praefecti* was renewed annually. His words imply the opposite, *primum creari coepti* instead of *primum creati*. The *leges a praetore datae* should have provided a permanent solution of the troubles of the times.

In fact the course of events was otherwise. In 211 B.C. Capua

---

[1] Livy 23. 2–4; 7. 8. After the revolt, 24. 19. 2; 23. 35. 1–4 and 14. Cf. 26. 16. 6, *principes senatus* at Calatia; 23. 35. 3, *senatus Cumanus*.

[2] Cf. Livy 40. 42. 13.

[3] R. S. Conway, *Italic Dialects*, nn. 107, 117.

[4] Livy 9. 20. 5, 'Prefects for Capua first began to be created with rules of law derived from the praetor, L. Furius, when in a time of civil discord they themselves had asked for both as a cure for their political disease.'

[5] Livy 9. 20. 10, 'Affairs at Capua were set on a sound footing by Roman discipline.' 'Not only Roman arms but Roman law were gaining wide influence.'

and the majority of the other Campanian *municipia* were annihilated as communities in punishment for their defection in the war with Hannibal, and Rome began the practice of sending out prefects to Campania every year to act as resident magistrates—*ad iura reddenda* according to Livy. Velleius confirms this by saying that in 211 Capua was reduced *in formam praefecturae*.[1] In addition, an item in Festus mentions a set of four prefects who were sent out yearly to Campania, *qui ius dicerent*. That Festus is referring to the system inaugurated in 211 is proved by the fact that, first, his definition of *praefectura* is inapplicable to the original *municipia*, and, second, that the method of appointment for these prefects differs from that attributed by Livy to the original prefects of the fourth century.[2] But at the same time a difficulty arises. For Capua heads the list given by Festus, which includes Cumae and Acerrae, two places which remained *municipia* when the rest were demoted in 211. So the origin of the list must go back to the period when all these places were of the same status. The simplest explanation of the connection between the two systems is that a custom which grew up spasmodically and piecemeal in accordance with local needs during the third century was drastically remodelled in 211; Rome at that time replaced the magisterial organs of the Campanian municipalities with officials of her own, and in addition gave the new *praefecti* the oversight of the few remaining *municipia* of Campania—Cumae, Acerrae, and possibly Suessula.[3]

This solution gains some support when the reason underlying the change in the method of appointment is properly assessed. The new *praefecti Capuam Cumas* were minor magistrates elected by the people, for they were chosen from among the *vigintisexviri*.[4] But Festus mentions another and more numerous set of prefectures, for the officers of which the method of selection was the same as that of the original fourth-century prefects of Campania.

---

[1] Livy 26. 16. 10. Velleius 2. 44. 4, 'To the pattern of a prefecture'.

[2] s.v. 'praefecturae'. He defines them as places where 'erat quaedam res publica neque magistratus suos habebant'. Moreover, two of the Campanian *praefecturae* hardly existed as towns before the second Punic War, Puteoli and Volturnum, cf. Livy 24. 7. 10; 25. 20. 2.

[3] For Acerrae cf. Livy 23. 17. 7; 27. 3. Suessula turns up under *duoviri* at the end of the Republic, like other *praefecturae* which remained *municipia*, e.g. Atina, cf. Beloch, *RG* 508. But Livy 23. 17. 3 might mean that Suessula was on the Carthaginian side.

[4] Festus, s.v. 'praefecturae'.

This group includes all except the Campanian *municipia*, the prefects being simply the representatives of the praetor.[1] The Campanian set, on the other hand, is a small and closed group of peoples, mostly of inferior status, without any powers of self-government. For them the prefects are necessarily charged with wide powers of administration, and hence are minor but independent magistrates whose special creation was rendered essential by the changed situation, while the older system sufficed for the free municipalities. This distinction is implicit in the text of Festus, who says that the second type were sent out by the praetor *legibus*, that is, as Mommsen saw, in accordance with the charters of the municipalities.[2]

In the earlier period, then, prefects were sent, but not regularly, to Campania. The Campani did, in fact, complain during the Punic War of some long-standing interference which may well be attributed to the occasional appearance of *praefecti* commissioned to supervise the working of *civitas sine suffragio*, in the special sphere of *conubium*, and of *commercium*.[3] On the other hand, the main complaint was against the *munus militare* and subjection to the *imperium* of Roman magistrates. The one instance of real interference recorded by Livy is the creation of a *dictator* to inquire into an alleged conspiracy at Capua—whose powers, in fact, were never exercised.[4] The general description of political life at Capua makes it clear that such interference was very rare. The political use which Pacuvius Calavius—an anti-Roman—made of his power as judge shows this—'eas causas suscipere, ei semper parti adesse, secundum eam litem iudices dare'.[5]

There is thus clear proof that neither at the beginning nor at the end of the period in which Capua enjoyed *civitas sine suffragio* was there any deliberate suspension of the ordinary institutions of the Oscan city-state. Undoubtedly the bond of union with Rome led to the formation of close social connections, and as a consequence we may suppose that Capua, and the others too, tended to adopt various Roman laws; it was some such

---

[1] Ibid., 'quos praetor urbanus quodannis in quaeque loca miserat legibus'. See below, 52 f.

[2] Mommsen, *St. R.* iii. 582 n. 2, quoting the *lex* of Acerrae. Cf. above, 40; also the *lex* of Cumae, Livy 23. 31. 10.

[3] Livy 23. 7. 1–2; 'ut suae leges . . . Capuae essent'. Cf. Konopka, art. cit. 594 f.

[4] Livy 9. 26. 6.

[5] Livy 23. 4. 3.

process that led to the repetition of the sending of the prefects in the earlier period, if such repetition is to be treated as a fact.

The existence of the so-called Romano–Campanian coinage was once thought to cast some light upon the nature of the relations between Rome and Capua between 335 and the Pyrrhic War. It was believed to have been issued by a mint at Capua for Rome. But the numismatists point out that there is nothing specially Campanian about the coinage types; and it may be held that this series is a war coinage of Rome and Carthage, allied together against Pyrrhus, for which south Italy—and not specially Capua—provided only the artists. The existence of the coinage is thus irrelevant to the question of the restricted autonomy of Capua.[1]

Close investigation thus shows that *civitas sine suffragio* was, in its earliest form, a very peculiar sort of bond. It can only be understood by laying stress upon the term *municeps*. The conditions on which Capua went over to Hannibal make it clear that it was mainly the pressure of Roman military demands to which they objected—'ne civis Campanus invitus militaret . . .'.[2] The special advantage which led to the use of *civitas sine suffragio* was that it gave to Rome direct control of her allies' troops. 'In legione merebant.'[3] The *municipia* form a category parallel to that of the Latin states. It is difficult to see any difference between the status of *municipes* enjoying the original form of *civitas sine suffragio* and the status of Latins enjoying *conubium, commercium,* and *ius civitatis mutandae,* except that the line of demarcation between Latin and *civis Romanus* was more clearly drawn. At the time when most use was made of *municipium* the league of Italian allies, the *socii foederati,* had not yet been created, far less had it been tested or the possibility of inserting such allies into the *formula togatorum* been discovered.[4]

It was inevitable that the character of *civitas sine suffragio* should alter as the balance of power between Rome and the *municipes* began to change. The complaints of the Campanians are all the more intelligible when allowance is made for the difference between the political situation of the late third century and that

---

[1] Cf. H. Mattingly, *Roman Coins,* 6–8; *Num. Chron.* 1925, 181.
[2] Livy 23. 7. 1.
[3] Festus, s.v. 'municeps', cf. above, 42 n. 5.          [4] Below, 119 ff.

of *circa* 335. What had once been a matter of mutual advantage—self-defence against the Samnites—had become intolerable bondage for one party. The Romans, as masters of a league embracing all the peoples of Italy, being in a position to make what demands they liked, saw in the Campanians an ample supply of legionary recruits, especially of much-needed cavalry. But when three hundred of their knights were dispatched overseas to Sicily the Campani may well have felt that the equality of their isopolity was upset.[1]

At the same time it is clear that the Romans had come to regard the *municeps* as a sort of citizen not generically distinct from the ordinary *civis Romanus*. Without the conception of a mutual exchange of potential franchise, we can understand neither the Roman nor the Campanian point of view. If the Campani were *cives* why did they object to Roman demands for the fulfilment of the *munera*? If they were not *cives*, what is the explanation of the curious phrase *Romani fieri* sometimes used by the authorities in place of the more usual term *civitas sine suffragio data*? From the Roman point of view the *municipes* could if they wished settle in Roman territory and acquire the full rights of a Roman citizen, or else remain at home enjoying the political life of their own *res publica*, plus the various *iura* which they shared with Rome. The obvious parallel between the Latin Name and the *municipes* suggests that the Campanian states had formed a different idea of their status from that current at Rome. There is a clash of theories. One may be derived from a Greek source—such as Naples or even Cumae—to whose influence Campania had been open for centuries. To this the idea of *municipium* is foreign; it is a specially Roman principle, evolved in Latium during the centuries of conflict between tribal and particularist loyalties. But equally foreign to the Roman theory is the idea of a merely diplomatic exchange of citizenships, or the acquisition of a number of wholly potential 'freedoms'. This is the reason, later embodied in the principle 'duarum civitatum civis noster esse iure civili nemo potest', which made it impossible for the Romans to leave the *municipes* in their bridge position half-way between *socii* and *cives*.[2]

---

[1] Livy 23. 4. 8. Cf. Konopka, art. cit. 601 ff.

[2] 'The civil law does not allow any Roman citizen to hold the franchise of two states.' Cic. *Balb.* 28, repeated from *pro Caecina* 100.

*Municipes outside Campania*

The earliest recorded use of *civitas sine suffragio* outside Campania is contemporaneous with the grant to Capua: 'Fundanisque et Formianis . . . civitas sine suffragio data.'[1] The history of the non-Campanian *municipia* demonstrates more clearly the development of the various influences which ended by completely changing the nature of the institution. But there is also enough evidence to show that in its original form the *civitas sine suffragio* of the Volscian communities differed in no essentials from that of the Campanians. Livy tells how the Fundani, a few years after their acceptance of this status, joined with the Privernates to raid the Latin states of Setia, Norba, and Cora. When the Romans objected to this behaviour the Fundani found an excuse and declared: 'Fundis pacem esse et animos Romanos et gratam memoriam acceptae civitatis.'[2] The parallel to Capua is exact. The *res publica* of Fundi with its *populus* and senate continues to exist. The Fundani regard themselves as close allies of Rome but do not see why they should not raid non-Roman territory in the old fashion. Livy's narrative gives a precious picture of the very moment of the limitation of magisterial and municipal competence in one of the smaller *municipia*. Henceforward the *senatus populusque Fundanus* would cease to dally with such dangerous schemes and to interfere with Rome's foreign interests. But the limitation is in external policy, not in the inner life of the community.

The factor that was most to influence *civitas sine suffragio* was, here as elsewhere, the growing military power of Rome. The effect of this appears early. The consequence of the incident mentioned above was that Privernum was disciplined; her walls were destroyed and her disloyal senators exiled beyond the Tiber.[3] After this the *innoxia multitudo* was given *civitas sine suffragio* and 'became Romans'.[4] Thirty years later Anagnia and her dependents, having taken part in a rebellion, suffered similar treatment. In these instances we can discern the co-operation of two notions, that of a *foedus* and that of a merely potential citizenship. The settlement is reminiscent of the terms given, not to the *municipes*

[1] Livy 8. 14. 10.

[2] Livy 8. 19. 4–14, 'At Fundi there was peace and Roman hearts and gratitude for the gift of citizenship.'

[3] Livy 8. 20. 7–12.                    [4] Livy 8. 21. 9–10.

and *novi cives* of 338, but to the *ceteri populi Latini*. The Anagnini and their associates lose the right of *conubium* with other Hernicans, and their federal council is broken up.[1] They become *municipes*, but the later view that *municipes* were *cives* is demonstrably inapplicable to these Hernici; for if *civitas sine suffragio* implied the equation of its holder to a *civis Romanus* in all but political rights, then the Anagnini would automatically have shared in that *conubium* with the other Hernici which all *cives Romani* enjoyed.

Still more important is the partial suspension of municipal autonomy which accompanied the reorganization of the status of Anagnia:[2] 'magistratibus praeterquam sacrorum curatione interdictum'. This is the first clear indication that the Roman government was prepared to give a peculiar twist to the original conception of *municipium*. The contemporary alarm of the Aequi in fear of a Roman attempt to 'make them Romans' shows that this was not an isolated instance. On this occasion Livy describes public opinion among the Aequi in terms which go too far. The loyal Hernici had also been offered *civitas sine suffragio* in place of their former federal condition, and refused. So Livy writes: 'Hernicos docuisse (sc. Aequos) cum quibus licuerit suas leges Romanae civitati praeoptaverint; quibus legendi quid mallent copia non fuerit *pro poena* necessariam civitatem fore.'[3] The punishment consists not in the status of *municeps*, but in the supplementary measures, the destruction of the Hernican federation, etc., which are simply annexed to the grant of *civitas sine suffragio* without being implicit in it, and obviously would not have been imposed on the loyal Hernici had they accepted the Roman offer, nor on the Aequi had they not revolted.[4] Livy's interpretation of the institution is here coloured by his knowledge of its final development. Much more reasonable are the sentiments which he puts into the mouths of the Romans when they are debating about the treatment of the Privernates, who had

[1] Livy 9. 43. 24.

[2] Livy 9. 43. 24, 'Their magistrates were suspended except for the care of religious ceremonies.'

[3] Livy 9. 45. 7, 'When the Hernici used their liberty to prefer their own status to Roman citizenship, they showed (the Aequi) that where freedom of choice was not allowed the obligatory acceptance of citizenship would rank as a punishment.'

[4] Above, 42 n. 1. Arpinum and Frusino now receive *civitas s.s.* on doubtful terms, Livy 10. 1. 3.

behaved exactly as the Anagnini and Aequi did later: 'eos demum qui nihil praeterquam de libertate cogitent dignos esse qui Romani fiant.'[1]

It was only as a result of these incidents, and of certain other factors, that the status of *municeps* came to be regarded as an inferior status, and that the *municipes* came to be considered as members of the Roman state who lacked the complete political privileges of other citizens. The smaller states which received *civitas sine suffragio* at the same time as, or subsequently to, the Campanian cities tended to fall more and more into a position of dependence upon Rome, precisely because they were small and weak, and therefore were even less able than the Campani to check any usurpation at their expense. Also they were nearer to Rome in mere mileage, and their territory formed a continuous whole with that of Rome; thus, on the Appian way one passed, in the third century, from the land of the *tribus Oufentina*, through the Roman colony of Anxur, to the territory of Fundi and Formiae, north of which stretched the lands of Privernum, the *tribus Teretina*, then Frusino and Arpinum—both *municipia*. Only along the Latin way was this continuity broken by two blocks of *ager peregrinus*, the lands of Praeneste and Ferentinum, before Frusino was reached.[2] The material basis for the identification of *municipes* with *cives* was soundly laid. A cue to the date of this change is offered by the contrast between the somewhat conservative advance in the south and the bold march north-eastwards, where the lands of *cives sine suffragio* and of Roman citizens stretched unbroken along the Flaminian way, through the Sabine country, the fringes of Umbria, to Picenum and the *ager Gallicus*. This extension came later in time than the first experiments in Campania and the Volscian states. The Sabine peoples were given the limited franchise in 290 B.C., and the prefectures of Picenum cannot be prior to the final conquest of that country in 268.[3] Apart from questions of strategy and domestic politics, it is clear that the Romans, having shaped their instrument in the fourth century, proceeded to employ it more aggressively in the third, when dealing with areas that had no special traditions of autonomy or were sufficiently Latinized to encourage such treatment.

---

[1] Livy 8. 21. 9, 'Those above all whose whole soul was concentrated on liberty were worthy to become Romans.'

[2] Cf. Beloch, *RG*, maps 2 and 3.      [3] Velleius 1. 14. 6. Beloch, *RG* 474.

It is with these very areas that the later changes in the nature of *civitas sine suffragio* are connected. The Sabines were the first *municipes* to be elevated to the status of full citizens by the grant of *ius suffragi* and enrolment in a tribe; moreover, the change took place within a generation of the original grant.[1] Here also the *praefecturae* appear in large numbers in a form that departs widely, in the lack of any considerable degree of local autonomy, from the original conception of *municipium*.[2] The status of these peoples is very different from that of the Fundani or Campani. For the latter, *civitas sine suffragio* was intended to provide a permanent form of relationship to Rome; the Fundani and others remained *municipes* for a century and a half. The idea that *civitas sine suffragio* was a half-way stage in the incorporation of non-Latin peoples in the Roman state is entirely foreign to the original conception, but is closely allied to the developed form of the institution which appears on the surface of Livy's narrative, dominating the account of the Campanian rebellion, and which can be detected as the last stage in the definitions of Festus. The fact that the Sabine lands were in part occupied by viritane settlements of Roman citizens, interspersed among the *municipes*, must have helped to form this new idea of *civitas sine suffragio* as a preparatory condition. Also the growing importance of the Roman citizenship itself, which became more than local in the third century, as Rome gradually gained a pre-eminent position in Italy, would accelerate the tendency to regard *municipes* as conditional citizens.[3] Once the balance of power was upset, the fact that *civitas sine suffragio* was properly a reciprocal arrangement would naturally be obscured. Thus Festus' two definitions of *municipes* as 'those who were not Roman citizens' and as 'those who were citizens', are both correct, but belong to different periods.

It is not surprising that by the end of the third century a novel interpretation of *civitas sine suffragio* had supervened. The facts are beyond serious dispute. In Livy's well-documented narratives the Campani appear not as rebellious allies but as traitors.[4] In the story of their trial and punishment they are treated always as *cives Romani*. The procedure necessary for the punishment of

---

[1] Velleius 1. 14. 7.

[2] Below, 52 f. Festus names Reate and Nursia. *CIL* ix. 399 adds Amiternum and Peltuinum, a canton of the Vestini. Cic. *Varen.* fr. 4 gives Fulginiae. For Picenum, Caesar, *BC* 1. 15. 1.

[3] Below, 57.

[4] Livy 26. 33. 10.

citizens is followed, and the precedent invoked is that of Satricum, which rebelled in 319 after gaining Roman status.[1] The destruction of the greatest of the states that might have maintained the earlier tradition of *civitas sine suffragio* meant that henceforth the purely Roman view of the institution prevailed, and that the atmosphere was formed in which it was regarded either as a punishment or as a stepping-stone to greatness.

With this last stage in the history of *civitas sine suffragio* is connected the question of the *praefecturae*. The importance of the juridical *praefecti* undoubtedly increased when *civitas*, whether complete or *sine suffragio*, was given to communities which possessed no considerable degree of municipal machinery; it became the custom to send *praefecti iure dicundo* to market-towns and large villages in such regions, in order to provide for the administration of justice in more serious cases. These prefects appear only at a comparatively late date. As has been seen, there is a great difference between the occasional prefects sent to Campania before the Campanian revolt and the regular officials dispatched when Capua had become a simple *sedes agrestium*.[2] Festus' definition of *praefecturae* describes precisely this latter state of affairs: '. . . in quibus et ius dicebatur et nundinae agebantur et erat quaedam earum res publica neque tamen magistratus suos habebant.' This description, to which his definitions of *municipium* provide an absolute contrast, is repeated in his article on *vici*.[3] These passages, taken together, show that the importance of the prefects varied with the municipal development of the places to which they were sent. The plain mention of the term *praefectura* tells us nothing about the precise status of the community concerned. For further interpretation we need to know more about the date of the notice, the rank of the community, and its situation. Festus' own list sets side by side Caere, the Volscian states, the Samnite border states, and the hill towns of the Sabine and Aequian districts. These places, as *praefecturae*, correspond to our modern assize-towns; but the amount of interference which the visits of the prefects caused in the life of the local community is not determinable.

[1] Livy 26. 33. 10. Cf. 9. 16. 2–3.　　　　　　　　　　[2] Above, 43 f.

[3] 'Where justice was rendered, and markets held, and there was a certain communal life, though they did not have their own magistrates.' 'Sed ex vicis partim habent rem publicam et ius dicitur, partim nihil eorum at tamen ibi nundinae aguntur negotii gerundi causa et magistri vici . . . quotannis fiunt.'

The correspondence between Festus' list of *praefecturae* and the list of the early *municipia* does not completely justify Mommsen's view that every *praefectura* represents a community which entered the Roman state via *civitas sine suffragio*.[1] The institution of the *praefecti legibus a praetore datis* must have increased enormously in importance after the grant of complete franchise in the areas concerned, especially in those where the machinery of self-government was not far advanced before the act of incorporation. The existence of, e.g., the *praefectura Foroclodi* proves that prefectures were created in tribal territory populated by fully fledged Roman citizens.[2] The agrarian assignations of Flaminius must have increased the number of prefectures in the Ager Gallicus, and those of Picenum were probably of this type.[3] For while Caesar's mention of them implies that they were numerous, only one of the known communities of Picenum seems to have been a Picene folk incorporated as an early *municipium*—Urbs Salvia.[4]

Thus, it is doubtless true that in the third century the *municipes* passed more and more under the direct influence of Rome; but it is wrong to assume that the grant of the limited franchise carried with it an immediate loss of power for the local judiciary, unless this view can be supported by better evidence than the mere existence of a *praefectura*. It may be true that Festus' lists suggest an increasing tendency to interfere in the affairs of the *municipia*. But this interference must be given its proper setting, which is more likely to be the period when Rome had become the mistress of Italy, than the earlier time when she needed every possible ally to combat the power of Samnium.

## The Status of Caere

The tradition about the so-called Caerite franchise was formulated at a time when the *civitas sine suffragio* as an institution had run its course. There is the same overlaying of original meaning by later interpretation as in the story of Campania. There are two

---

[1] Mommsen, *St. R.* iii. 582 n. 1.

[2] Beloch, *RG* 562.        [3] Ibid. 475 f., 557 f.

[4] Caesar, *BC* i. 15. 1. All the other *municipia* of later times were duoviral creations of the later Republic (below, 166–7). The constitution of Urbs Salvia, *quattuorviri*, either suggests incorporation in 89 or represents an earlier Octoviral system that was later remodelled. Cf. Beloch, *RG* 505. Asculum remained federated after 268.

main traditions. Gellius says plainly that Caere was the first of the Italian states to receive *civitas sine suffragio*, and that this was a reward for the services of Caere to Rome at the time of the Gallic invasion.[1] With this statement of the facts Strabo agrees,[2] but in his interpretation follows a contrary tradition, that of the oldest Horatian scholiast. This authority, in trying to explain the term *Caerite cera* used by Horace, declares that the grant of *civitas sine suffragio* followed a defeat of Caere by Rome, and that the lack of the vote was *ignominiosum*.[3] Strabo similarly holds that the Romans were 'ungrateful' in not enrolling the Caerites in the tribes. Gellius on the contrary, writing in the second century of the Empire, says that the intention was that the Caerites 'civitatis Romanae honorem quidem caperent sed negotiis tamen atque oneribus vacarent'.[4] This statement, on any interpretation of the term *municeps*, goes too far, in ignoring the *munus militare* which it implied. It is unlikely that Gellius is doing more than repeat the learned opinion of his day.

Neither of these two accounts is to be found in Livy. He says that Rome in return for the gallant services of Caere during the Gallic invasion, contracted *hospitium* with them.[5] Later there is a war, and in 355 B.C., the Caerites being defeated by Rome, a truce of 100 years is concluded between them.[6] In Strabo and Gellius the grant of *civitas sine suffragio* usurps the place of the *hospitium*, the reality of which there is no reason to doubt. Livy in turn fails to mention any grant of *civitas sine suffragio*; but he gives a good hint of what may have happened later, in the period covered by his second decade, when he states that the success of Rome against the Latins persuaded the Falisci to exchange their temporary truce for a permanent treaty.[7]

The common element in all these tales—except only that of the Horatian scholiast—is the stress laid on the protection of the Vestal Virgins by Caere during the Gallic invasion. The belief that Caere was the first *municipium* is the consequence of the

---

[1] *NA* 16. 13. 7.   [2] Strabo 5. 2. 3 (220 C).
[3] Mommsen, *St. R.* iii. 572 n. 3. Horace, *Ep.* 1. 6. 62.
[4] Loc. cit. 'They were to have the honour of Roman franchise without its burdens and encumbrances.'
[5] Livy 5. 50. 3. *Hospitium* like the Greek *proxenia* is more a personal and individual relationship, of private rather than public friendship, though in fact generalized to apply to all citizens of both communities.
[6] Livy 7. 20. 8. Cf. 9. 36. 3. 'Caere educatus apud hospites'.   [7] Livy 7. 38. 1.

belief that the grant of this status was a reward for these services, and of the attempts to interpret the phrase *Caeritum tabulae* at a time when the original meaning was lost. Other obscurities arise from the fact that people sought to explain at a later date, when the idea of the *municeps* had changed, why the Caerites were not 'given the vote'.[1]

That Caere was a *municipium* in the strictly technical sense there is no doubt. Gellius and Strabo are supported by the appearance of Caere in Festus' lists of early *municipia*. Some confirmation of the traditional date might be found, despite Livy's silence, in the later municipal organization of the state. It retained the *dictatura* as its chief magistracy down to imperial times.[2] This probably indicates that such was the form of government existing at the time when Caere received municipal status, and retained when Caere finally acquired the *ius suffragi*. But in the present obscurity of the question of early municipal magistracies, and of the *dictatura* in particular, little can be based upon this fact. If the view that these were introduced by Rome at the time of complete incorporation were correct, there would be no evidence either for or against the traditional date; for, although the *dictatura* seems more appropriate in the fourth than the third century,[3] we have no indication of the date when Caere received the full franchise.[4] But on the far more probable view that this is the original local constitution of Caere little can be argued for or against the traditional date, since Caere may well have retained the *dictatura* as her chief magistracy down to the third century.

In an inscription of imperial date the Etruscan community of Capena is described as a *municipium foederatum*, and an attempt has been made to couple Caere with the *socii-municipes* of Campania through this *municipium foederatum*.[5] This hypothesis must remain non-proven, because there are alternative, perhaps better, explanations of this term. Capena was probably *foederata* in the sense that it was composed of a synoecism of several communities, formed at a much later date than the fourth century.[6] Also, the phrase cannot be the relic of an ancient technical term, since

---

[1] Cf. Mommsen, loc. cit.    [2] *CIL* xi, p. 534.

[3] Contrast the *praetor* at Capena, below, 68 f.

[4] This important point was missed by De Sanctis, 'La Dittatura di Caere', *Scritti in onore di B. Nogara* (Vaticano, 1937), 147.

[5] Beloch, *RG* 446.

[6] Cf. *CIL* xi. p. 570.

*municipium* in origin seems to belong to the same class of words as *conubium, mancipium,* etc., and means not a place—*oppidum*—nor a community—*civitas* or *populus*—but a right or collection of rights.[1]

The municipal status of Caere must be interpreted according to the date to which it is assigned. If Beloch is right in attributing it to the third century, and in connecting it with the revolt of Caere in *c.* 273, then there may be some parallel between the history of Caere and that of, e.g., Anagnia. Festus joins together Caere, Aricia, and Anagnia as examples of a *civitas quae universa in civitatem Romanam venit.* This phrase may cover a reference to the suspension of magisterial functions at Anagnia, and so justify the belief that the municipal status of Caere was, or eventually became, *ignominiosum.*[2]

The mention of Aricia, a Latin state, along with two *municipia* need cause no difficulty. Aricia, though never possessing the *civitas sine suffragio,* had this in common with Caere and Anagnia that when merged with Rome in 338 B.C. it retained the shell, at least, of its local identity: that is the denotation of the term *universa.*[3] This reference of Festus thus distinguishes Caere and Anagnia from communities like Capua that failed to preserve even the skeleton of their former being.

The acceptance of the traditional date would imply that Rome first came by the idea of *municeps* in her relations with her Etruscan neighbours; but this view seems very paradoxical when the general conduct of Rome towards the cities of Etruria is considered, and her shyness of entering into permanent alliances with them.[4] The existence of a strong non-Etruscan, Latin element in the archaeological remains of Caere is hardly a conclusive reason for rejecting the plain statements of Livy about the *hospitium* and the *indutiae.*[5] If Caere is to be inserted into the fourth century at all costs, but at a later date than 390–389, then there may be some truth in the statement that it was the earliest of the *municipia surviving* in Strabo's or Gellius' time, since Capua was extinguished in 211 B.C. and Tusculum had not been a *municipium* in the true sense. But it is impossible to accept *both* the

[1] Cf. Kornemann, *RE,* 'Municipium', col. 573.

[2] Festus, s.v. 'municipium'. 'A community which came as a whole into the Roman state.' Dio, fr. 33 B, Caere in 273 was pacified with confiscation of land.

[3] Cf. below, 61.                                                                                     [4] Below, 123.

[5] R. Mengarelli, 'Caere e Roma', *Atti del 3. Congresso Naz. di Stud. Rom.* (1) 115.

connection with the Gallic invasion *and* the belief that the Caerite franchise was *ignominiosum*.

What emerges most clearly from this discussion is the unwillingness of the Romans in the fourth and third centuries to incorporate non-Latin peoples completely in their body politic. In the conflicting notices about this one community the whole history of *civitas sine suffragio* can be traced till its final stage, in which it became for the early Republic what Latin rights were to the Empire. The reason for these various changes lies partly in the changing relations of the states concerned to the ever-growing power of Rome, partly also in changes taking place in the idea of Roman citizenship itself. At the close of the third century notices first begin to appear of grants of Roman citizenship to non-Italian peoples, to Sicilian and Spanish deserters from Hannibal.[1] *Civitas sine suffragio* having become the correlate of Roman citizenship, changes begin to appear in the former institution corresponding to those in the latter. While Roman citizenship gains in intrinsic worth, *civitas sine suffragio* ceases to bear a meaning in itself, and comes to be judged by the value of that to which it has become a means of approach.

Infinitely more important is the reverse effect of *civitas sine suffragio* upon the meaning of Roman citizenship. The last stage in the development of the former is summed up by Gellius thus: 'municipes... sunt cives Romani... legibus suis et suo iure utentes ... neque ulla populi Romani lege adstricti nisi in quam populus eorum fundus factus est'.[2] A particular instance is provided by Cato's statement that at Arpinum 'heredem sacra non secuntur'.[3] The meaning of all this is that, thanks to the way in which *civitas sine suffragio* developed, the Romans were able to conceive the idea that citizenship was not entirely incompatible with membership of another, secondary community. The *municipes* had been regarded in the end as *cives Romani*, yet they had undoubtedly possessed a separate *res publica*. Now the experience of the Republic throughout its earlier course was summed up in Cicero's dictum about the incompatibility of two citizenships. There is no shaking this solid testimony.[4] Only in Cicero's own

[1] Livy 26. 21. 10–11.

[2] *NA* 16. 13. 6, '*Municipes* are Roman citizens enjoying their own laws and rights and not bound by any enactment of the Roman people except such as their own legislative assembly has adopted.'

[3] Cato fr. 61.

[4] Above, 47.

day was a theory of dual *patria* being worked out.[1] But this very theory was rendered possible only because the Republic had learned in practice to retain very considerable elements of the *res publica* of those communities which Rome incorporated in herself. Had there been no *civitas sine suffragio* Rome would perhaps never have acquired the technique for the creation of a political form which ended by embracing the whole world. The essence of the Republican idea of *civitas* is that it is never a purely honorary 'freedom'. The *municipes* perform their *munera* for Rome and also perform the *munera* and enjoy the *honores* of their local *res publica*. The importance of this practical element can hardly be overstressed. In it lies the reason for Rome's success and Greece's failure to solve the problem of an imperial citizenship. Since the *municipia*, in most instances, ended up as *municipia civium Romanorum*, often after a very considerable period of time, it is reasonable to suppose that this intermediate period was of great value in securing that recognition of the secondary *quaedam res publica*, which was all-important for the future history of the Roman citizenship.

The *civitas sine suffragio* had yet another contribution to make to the unification of Italy. The *municipes* began as a special sort of ally or federate, and one may say that the *socii foederati* ended up as *municipes*.[2] The two systems of alliance by *foedus* and alliance by *civitas sine suffragio* overlap in time. It is probable that Rome found that the use of *civitas sine suffragio* involved her in more than she originally intended. Retain the *foedus*, exclude the *ius migrationis*, and there is little difference between the status of a highly privileged *socius*, even *iniquo foedere*, and that of a *municeps*. The latter serves *in legione*, the former is registered in the *formula togatorum*. Fraccaro is right in regarding the two forms, despite the chronological overlap, as successive instruments employed by Rome in the unification of Italy.[3]

## OPPIDA CIVIUM ROMANORUM

### Incorporated States

It is impossible to understand aright Cicero's statement about the incompatibility of the Roman franchise with any other unless

---

[1] Below, 154.   [2] Cf. below, 125 f.
[3] P. Fraccaro, 'L'Organizzazione Politica dell'Italia Romana', *Atti. Congr. Diritto Rom.* i. 193–208.

we discover precisely what happened to those communities which, in and after the fourth century, were completely incorporated in the Roman state. In 338 B.C. the Romans made the first large breach in the older conception of a city-state by the grant of Roman citizenship to several other Latin city-states.[1] The Livian account preserves a hint that the boldness of the new move was appreciated; for there is a stipulation that 'aedes lucusque Sospitae Junonis communis Lanuvinis municipibus cum populo Romano esset'.[2] This implies that the men of Lanuvium could be regarded as distinct from the *populus Romanus* of which henceforth they form a part.

The influence of the territorial situation is important. In 381 Tusculum, before incorporation, had been an island in a sea of *ager Romanus*.[3] Similarly, in 338 the inclusion of Aricia, Lanuvium, Pedum, Nomentum, and Antium rounded off the Roman territory on the north-east and south-west. Rome still formed a territorial unity; the essential difference between the present extension and those recorded under the kings—apart from the case of Gabii—is that the towns are left standing, not only as so many buildings, but as true communities.

On the interpretation of the term *municipibus*, in the passage of Livy quoted above, depends the question whether these Latin states were given the full *civitas* or not. Mommsen assigned to it the technical sense which the word bore at this period, and asserted that these communities were given only *civitas sine suffragio*.[4] But in this chapter, one of the most careful in the whole of Livy, the distinction between the two forms of *civitas* is most jealously observed.[5] Livy lists separately the states given the one or the other form; the categories under which he deals with the settlement are those of constitutional status, not of locality.[6] Elsewhere he admittedly fails at times to distinguish the two forms,[7] but here, where he has made the effort, the fact

---

[1] Livy 8. 14. 2–4.

[2] 'The temple and grove of Juno Sospita were to be shared by the *municipes* of Lanuvium and the Roman people.'

[3] For the credibility of this grant cf. De Sanctis, op. cit., ii. 244 n. 3. Cf. below, 64. Livy is well aware that the first incorporation was not a complete success, 8. 14. 4.

[4] *St. R.* iii. 571 n. 1, 573.             [5] Livy 8. 14.

[6] Livy 8. 14. 2–8, Latin states receiving Roman citizenship and (twice) Roman *coloni*; 9–10a, treatment of *populi* retaining *ius Latinum*; 10b–11, states, Volscian and Campanian, receiving *civitas sine suffragio*.      [7] e.g. Livy 10. 1. 3.

cannot be disputed that these states were given the Roman citizenship. This view is confirmed not only by the rapid appearance in the Fasti of Tusculan consuls of the *gens Fulvia*, but also by Cicero's remark: 'ex Latio multi ut Tusculani et Lanuvini . . . gentes universae in civitatem sunt receptae.'[1]

The only other ground for holding that the Latin states were given *civitas sine suffragio* is the inclusion of Lanuvium, Tusculum. and Aricia in Festus' lists of *municipia*. This, however, may be due to a genuine belief that all early municipalities entered the Roman state via *civitas sine suffragio*, or to a confusion of the two forms such as Livy makes. Although the coupling, in Festus, of Aricia with Caere and Anagnia suggests the former alternative, a better understanding of the nature of *municipium* excludes the possibility, even if Verrius, the source of Festus, held some such opinion.[2] Latin states would not be given *civitas sine suffragio*, because as Latini they already performed the *munera* and enjoyed the privileges which it conveyed—they were *municipes*.

The history of the Latin colonies also may be used to illustrate, as a corollary, this moderate extension of the Roman state. Here is revealed the opposite process, the equation of Romans with Latini, just as the incorporations show us the equation of Latini with Romans. Both depend upon the common ground of community of political institutions and social rights. The Latini who are brought within the Roman territory fall within that category of which Festus says, 'cum Romam venissent neque cives Romani essent . . . post aliquot annos cives Romani effecti sunt', except that here the time interval is set aside and censorial registration is replaced by legislation.[3]

The basis on which the Latin states could become capable of this change of status, apart from a voluntary process of *fundus fieri*, was the *deditio* which they made to the Romans or the yet more complete subjugation of *expugnatio*.[4] Livy several times makes clear the effect of this. The conquered 'se dediderunt in arbitrium dicionemque populi Romani . . . quosque una secum . . .

[1] *Balb.* 31, cf. *Phil.* 3. 16. Pliny, *NH* 7. 136, 'Many folk of Latium like the Tusculani and Lanuvini were taken into the Roman state as whole communities.'

[2] Cf. Cic. *Planc.* 19, 'Tu es a municipio antiquissimo Tusculano.' Cf. above, 56.

[3] Festus, s.v. 'municipium.' Cf. Livy 39. 3. 4–5. 'They came to Rome as non-citizens and became citizens after a few years.'

[4] Livy 8. 14. 2. Cf. 13. 8, 'expugnando aut in deditionem accipiendo singulas urbes'.

quaeque . . . dediderunt agrum urbemque divina humanaque utensiliaque sive quid aliud'.[1] Rome had the power to assign what status she pleased to these *dediticii*; hence the use of the phrase 'Lanuvinis sacra sua *reddita*'. Contrariwise the *populus Laurens* was not among the incorporated communities, although, like Tusculum, their territory was surrounded by that of Rome. They had come to terms earlier with Rome and renewed their *foedus*; there had been no *deditio*, and so could be no unilateral incorporation. Doubtless the Laurentes, like the Hernici later, were too much attached to their local autonomy to become Roman citizens by the process of *fundus fieri*,[2] that is, by local option.

A difficulty occurs over Aricia, which Cicero describes as 'municipium vetustate antiquissimum iure foederatum'.[3] Livy tells of nothing beyond the fact that Aricia received the citizenship along with the other Latin states.[4] Kornemann suggests that the existence of the grove of Aricia secured her special terms.[5] In view of Livy's silence it is hard to assign to this *foedus* any political value, such as the *foedus Gabinum* must have possessed. It sounds more like the special proviso that accompanied the grant of citizenship to Lanuvium.

The reason why Rome confined her earliest grants of citizenship to communities of the Latin race, and devised a looser bond of union for Volscians and Campanians, was not a merely sentimental blood-consciousness. The juridical and social situation rendered the incorporation of Latins, and only of Latins, possible without any intermediate stage. In course of time Rome changed her policy, and began to incorporate non-Latins, but only after a probationary period during which these peoples were brought under the influence of Romano-Latin discipline and culture. In the period before Rome became a continental power, there is no certain instance of the immediate incorporation in the Roman state of a distinctly foreign people. Formiae, Fundi, and Arpinum waited a century and a half for the grant of *ius suffragi*.[6] The rapid elevation of the Sabine *municipes* in 22 years to Roman citizenship provides a contrast to this, but special influences were at work

---

[1] Livy 26. 33. 13, 'They surrendered themselves to the decision and authority of the Roman people, both the men and the things which they surrendered with themselves, land, city, things divine or human, or objects of use or anything else.'
[2] Cf. Livy 9. 43. 23. Above, 27.     [3] *Phil.* 3. 15.     [4] Livy 8. 14. 3.
[5] *RE*, 'Municipium', col. 577.     [6] Livy 38. 36. 7.

here, demographic and political.[1] After the creation of the tribes
Velina and Quirina in about 241 B.C., the boundaries of the
Roman territory were not again advanced till the Social War,
despite the vast accessions of *ager publicus* that followed the Punic
Wars. The addition of the Sabine prefectures brought no great
state into the Roman system, and thus could cause no clash of
civic loyalties. The *fora* and *vici* did not exercise that centripetal
tendency which was so strong in Latium and Campania. Rome
called a halt at this point for reasons that are not hard to guess.
The common view that the city-state was already outgrowing its
size is doubtless correct, especially since *civitas sine suffragio* was
also enlarging the Roman state in a way not originally intended.

What happened to the local political life of an incorporated
community? This is the crux of the whole matter. In a lengthy
work—the most exhaustive survey of the whole question yet
attempted—Hans Rudolph has given a decisive answer. He interprets Cicero very literally, and holds that when a community
accepted the Roman franchise its separate existence was completely merged with that of the Roman state.[2] Accordingly he
lays great stress upon his attempt to prove that the local magistracies were abolished by Rome and replaced by purely administrative officials of Roman creation. In particular, holding that
there is no true municipal self-government without the possession
of some considerable degree of *iurisdictio*, he maintains that under
the Republic jurisdiction was retained entirely in the hands of
Roman magistrates or their subordinates, i.e. the *praefecti*, until
the regime of Julius Caesar, when a true municipal jurisdiction
was created.[3]

The question is not merely whether this particular thesis is
right or wrong, but whether the author has been asking the right
question. Even if it is true that Rome abolished the former
constitutions of her new boroughs, it may not follow that there
was left no shadow of a *res publica*. In particular, the possession
of extensive *iurisdictio* may not be so important on the standards of
antiquity as the maintenance of the *sacra municipalia*, or even as
those merely administrative functions, the *aedilicia potestas*, of
which Rudolph thinks so little.

[1] Velleius 1. 14. 6–7. Cf. Fraccaro, art. cit. 202 ff. *CAH* vii. 658.
[2] H. Rudolph, *Stadt und Staat im römischen Italien*, Teil 1, A, *passim*.
[3] Op. cit. 35–44, Teil 2, 224–42.

First, how did Rome in truth dispose of the pre-Roman magistracies of her fully incorporated communities? There is no serious doubt that by 90 B.C. Rome possessed a special technique for dealing with this matter. Forty years later the brief formula 'Transpadani quattuorviros creare iussi' sufficed to noise abroad Caesar's intention of giving the franchise to these people.[1] The grant of citizenship to the Italians after the Social War had likewise implied that their various types of communities had replaced their former supreme magistrates by a board of *quattuorviri*.[2] But in the fourth century there is some evidence of a possible alternative. When Rome wishes to suspend the activities of the *res publica Anagninorum*, admittedly a *municipium* and not a citizen community, the method followed was not to abolish but to limit the functions of the magistrate.[3] 'Magistratibus praeterquam sacrorum curatione interdictum.' If this was possible in a *municipium*, it was still more possible in the reorganization of an incorporated community.

The epigraphic evidence of later days shows that there was considerable variety in the type of magistracy which the incorporated communities in fact possessed. This variety can be explained in two ways. Either the communities retained their original magistracies, and the multiplicity of types is due to the multiplicity of the pre-existing forms, or else Rome introduced different types of magistracies at different periods into the incorporated states.

Rudolph maintains that the earliest group of incorporated communities were given a simple board of two aediles to perform the necessary function of minor administration and police work within the *oppidum*.[4] But this system exists only at Tusculum; at Aricia, Lanuvium, and Nomentum there were, in imperial times, not two aediles but a *dictator* assisted by either one or two aediles.[5] Rudolph attempts to explain away the presence of the *dictator* by maintaining that his functions were purely religious.[6] But further complications appear when it is remembered that at Caere also in later days there existed the scheme of *dictator* and single *aedilis*.[7] Now it is highly improbable that Caere was incorporated at the same date as the rest of this group.[8] To gain

---

[1] Cic. *ad Att.* 5. 2. 3, 'The Transpadani were bidden elect *quattuorviri*.'
[2] Lists in Beloch, *RG* 500–4.     [3] Livy 9. 43. 24.     [4] Op. cit. 32–5, 44–7.
[5] Beloch, *RG* 498. Rudolph, op. cit. 33. The epigraphic details throughout, which are not in dispute, are most conveniently collected in Beloch, *RG*.
[6] Rudolph, op. cit. 27 n. 1, 27–31.     [7] *CIL* xi. p. 534.     [8] Above, 53 ff.

support for his view of the local government of the earliest citizen communities Rudolph adds Aveia and Peltuinum, communities of the Vestini, where the two aediles appear in later days.[1] But the incorporation of these two probably belongs, as Rudolph admits, to the period 290–268, the very time when he holds that the Romans were already employing a new type of local magistracy, the Octovirate.

Admittedly at Tusculum the *dictatura*, mentioned by Livy in the fifth century, disappeared in later times. This may be due either to local causes or to the interference of Rome.[2] If the date *c.* 380 B.C. is accepted for the incorporation of Tusculum—and there is no serious reason why it should not be[3]—the difficulty disappears. The treatment of Tusculum, considered in its proper setting, is nearer to that of Gabii than to that of the other Latin states forty years later. Rome may well have tended to treat a single state, singly incorporated in special circumstances, more as a village than as a borough. But the forty years' interval should prevent the interpretation of the settlement of 338 by the light of 380 or vice versa. In 338 Rome *for the first time* had to face the problem of incorporation on a wholesale scale.

In truth the strength of Rudolph's case lies in his attempt to explain away the *dictatores* of the states incorporated in 338. If these could be proved to be the invention of Rome, then the general submersion of these places within the *res publica populi Romani* would be sufficiently demonstrated. But what Rudolph tries to do is to prove that the competence of these *dictatores* was limited to purely religious functions, that they were not magistrates but pontiffs. The only relevant evidence is what Cicero says about Milo, who was *dictator* at Lanuvium in 52 B.C.[4] His work was certainly limited, but the scope of his *stata sacrificia* was wider than Rudolph allows. Milo's journey to Lanuvium was undertaken to appoint the high priest of the borough, *ad flaminem prodendum*. To separate the religious activity of the magistrate from his administrative functions, as Rudolph does, is most improper. Further, it has been pointed out that in addition to the *dictator* Lanuvium possessed a *rex sacrorum*; thus the provision

---

[1] Op. cit. 44.

[2] A. Rosenberg, *Staat der alten Italiker*, 8–9. De Sanctis, *Riv. Fil.* 1932, 435. Beloch, op. cit. 499, thinks the office persisted *ad sacra* on the strength of a dubious inscription, *CIL* xiv, *falsae* 212, which he accepts as genuine.

[3] Above, 30; 59 ff.          [4] *Pro Milone*, 45–6, with Asconius ad loc.

of a second *sacralen Leiter* seems unnecessary.[1] Also there is no real doubt that the term *dictator* appears in a fragmentary passage of the *lex Acilia* as the first of a list of Italian magistracies, not merely priesthoods.[2] If the *dictator* was not a magistrate but a pontiff, it becomes very difficult to explain why at a later date the magisterial function of *iurisdictio* was assigned to them, and not to other officials created for the purpose.

Once it is admitted that the *dictatores* of these ex-Latin states were genuine magistrates, we are left with the fact that, in the earliest period of municipal incorporation, there were at least two types of magistracy in use, *dictatura* and dual aedileship. The view that the latter was a Roman improvisation is weakened, if it is conceded that the former was not an invention but a survival.[3] The three instances of its use—Tusculum, Aveia, Peltuinum— are too far separated to fall under a single rule or policy, especially as the two last were not communities that had reached the same stage of development as the Latin city-states, but formed subdivisions within the still distinctly tribal system of central Italy.[4] These two, in so far as their incorporation can be dated with any accuracy, belong to the group of folk to whom, on Rudolph's view, was assigned the Octovirate.[5]

*The Octovirate and the Triple Aedileship.* In the rapidly incorporated mountain districts of the Sabines and the Praetuttii another form of local magistracy appears, the Octovirate.[6] Under the accretions of later Republican terminology it is easy to discern that this office was rather a magistracy in commission than a combination of four pairs of magistrates each with different functions.[7] But that this board was 'a new creation for the special purposes of the municipalities'[8] must remain a simple assertion until the precise advantages which the Octovirate possessed over, e.g., the triple aedileship or the *praetura*—discussed below—have been demonstrated. The chief reason for accepting such a view

---

[1] Cf. R. Meiggs, *CR* 49, 236, reviewing Rudolph.

[2] l. 78, '[quei eorum in sua quisque civitate dicta]tor praetor aedilisve non fuerint'. Bruns, *FIRA*[7] 10, cited henceforth as *lex Acilia*.

[3] Cf. also De Sanctis, art. cit. 436 ff.

[4] Cf. Täubler, 'Die umbrisch-sabellischen und die römischen Tribus', *Sitz. ber. Heid. Ak.*, 1930, 6–9, 11 n. 1.

[5] For the dating cf. Rudolph himself, op. cit. 45.

[6] *CIL* ix, pp. 397, 427, 463, 485, and xi. 5621. Rosenberg, op. cit. 40–6. Rudolph, op. cit. 66–80. Beloch, *RG* 499 ff.

[7] Rudolph. op. cit. 75.          [8] Ibid. 78.

is that the group of boroughs in which this magistracy is later found contains different ethnic elements, and that the only common factor uniting them is the date at which they received the Roman citizenship. Most of the peoples concerned were Oscan,[1] and the normal upper magistracy of an Oscan community is the *meddix*. On the other hand, Plestia appears to be Umbrian, and should have been governed by *marones*.[2] The Octovirate, it is suggested, was substituted for these officers in these places.

But this is disguising ignorance. The *meddix* is found in Campania, among Samnites, Paeligni, Marsi, Aequicoli, and at Volscian Velitrae.[3] The words *octovir* and—to include Aveia and Peltuinum—*aedilis* are admittedly translations of terms to us unknown, introduced with the advancing Latinization of the peninsula. A parallel can be found in the *quinqueviri* of Assisi,[4] and perhaps the *praetor* of Capena.[5] If there were no evidence for the independent origin of the *censtur* among Oscan peoples, scholars could maintain, with arguments very similar to those of Rudolph, that the *censores* known in central Italy were all introduced by Rome.

It might be thought that at least the peculiar form of constitution possessed by the three municipalities of Fundi, Formiae, and Arpinum was a Roman creation, substituted for the pre-existing form.[6] Certainly these three were incorporated in the same year —188 B.C.[7] But equally certainly these three were of a common stock—they were Volscian.[8] This fact is as good a reason for the unity of their municipal form—a board of three aediles—as the date of their incorporation.

It has never yet been satisfactorily explained why Horace made the curious error, if it was an error, of referring to the *praetor Fundanus*.[9] *Praetura* is so far from being the normal municipal magistracy of the Augustan age that it is impossible to believe

---

[1] Amiternum, Trebula, and Nursia are 'Sabine'. Interamnia belonged to the Praetuttii. Truentum perhaps is not to be reckoned here, cf. Beloch, *RG* 500, who holds that *CIL* ix. 5158 belongs to Interamnia.

[2] Rudolph, op. cit. 67.

[3] Rosenberg, op. cit. 16–17. Add *Inscr. It. Med. Dialecticae*, no. 45, if genuine; cf. Conway, 532 n. 45.

[4] Rosenberg, op. cit. 48. *CIL* xi. 5392.                    [5] Below, 68 f.

[6] Rudolf, op. cit. 58–60.

[7] Livy 38. 36. 7.

[8] Cf. Livy 10. 1. 2. Sora—the colony planted next to Arpinum—'agri Volsci fuerat'.                    [9] *Sat.* 1. 5. 34.

that Horace used the word instead of *aedilis*, as a more familiar term. It is not necessary to upset the collegiate character of the threefold aedilate to explain Horace, since it is possible that, in addition to the three aediles, there existed a *praetor* at Fundi whose functions, like those of the *dictator* at Lanuvium, may well have been limited in scope.[1] Such a *praetor* could only be a *meddix* in disguise. It is a serious flaw in several current views about the early muncipalities that sufficient allowance is made neither for the activity of the communities themselves, in remodelling and developing their constitutions, nor for the scattered and broken character of the evidence for the municipal history of Italy. This flaw produces its evil effect especially in a tendency to elaborate extremely schematic theories. Such schematization appears in the various attempts to relate the three aediles of Fundi, etc. to the Roman aediles or the dual aedilate of Tusculum, and so on. Kornemann seems to be working on a sounder principle when he draws attention to the use of a threefold scheme in the management of *vici* and *pagi*.[2] The boards of three *magistri* found in these places cannot be an official creation inspired, in the last resort, by the Roman government. They are found in various parts of Italy at diverse periods.[3] The *vici* do not fall directly under the control of Roman magistrates in such a matter, but under the authority of their municipality. This threefold scheme is then a truly Italic form, and may well be native in the Volscian communities with the three aediles, as in the *vici* with the three *magistri*. Since an explanation has been found even for the apparent disappearance of the *meddix*, it is hardly necessary to go on believing that Rome in 188 B.C. abolished the constitutions of the states then incorporated.

*The Praetores.* There is a further objection to Rudolph's view to be derived from evidence which he neglected. He has not

---

[1] For the contrary view cf. Rosenberg, op. cit. 5, Kornemann, *Klio* 14. 199. That the 'praetura' disappeared from the constitution of Fundi—but not from popular usage—at the time of the mysterious conversion of the constitution of the sister municipality of Arpinum in 46 B.C. seems the most probable solution of this notorious crux, cf. Cic. *ad Fam.* 13. 11, and below, 205 n .2.

[2] Art. cit. 194 ff. Rudolph, 50–7, esp. 52, argues against him.

[3] Details in Rudolph, loc. cit., e.g. *CIL* ix. 3312, Paelignian, ibid. 5052, Praetuttian. The scheme of 4 at Peltuinum, *CIL* ix. 3521, and of 12 at Capua (*CIL* i. 683–8, *P.B.S.R.* 1959. 126) speaks against a unitary system invented by Rome. Also he ignores the non-Latin evidence. Cf. *Inscr. It. Med.* nos. 29, 32, where bodies of three and four men apparently act as *magistri* (= Conway, 239, 210).

fairly discussed all the forms of local government found in the *municipia civium Romanorum*. There is a small group where the *praetura* was employed even in the imperial age.[1] These are Anagnia, Capitulum Hernicum, Capena, Cumae, Lavinium.[2] No recorded unity of time, place, or nationality binds these together. It is unknown when any of them received full Roman citizenship. The two Hernican communities leave no other record of their history after the grant of *civitas sine suffragio*. Cumae was still a *municipium* proper in the second century.[3] Of Capena's incorporation nothing is known. The survival of early forms at Lavinium, a very special case, will surprise no one.[4] These instances of the retention of the *praetura* have an interest which is not connected with the date of their incorporation. Anagnia, Capitulum, and Cumae as incorporated communities enjoy the same magisterial system which they possessed as *municipia*. For the *praetura* of Anagnia can hardly be anything but the Latin praetorship, and the *praetura* of Cumae may well represent the dual but not originally collegiate office of *meddix*.[5] At Capena the *praetor* is neither a Latin nor an Oscan but an Etruscan magistrate.[6] Kornemann pointed out the strong probability that it is much the same post which in the borough of Caere and at Sutrium was translated *dictator*, and which appears again at a later date, at the formal reorganization of the league of Etruria, in the *Praetor Etruriae*.[7] So then the inscriptions which testify to the existence of a single, non-collegiate *praetor* at Capena may reasonably be connected with what little is known of the magistracies of pre-Roman Etruria.[8] The *praetor* of Capena may then be supposed to hold the same office as the *dictator* at Caere.

Certainly it would be a hard task to find a period of time to which this *praetor*-constitution could be assigned, if we are really to hold that Rome always replaced in her municipalities what had existed before by something new. There is no special reason why any of these five states should have received complete enfranchisement before the Social War, although the general uniformity of the quattuorviral system then invented suggests that they were

---

[1] This group is dismissed by Rudolph in a footnote, 222 n. 1, which practically reverses the main thesis of his book.

[2] Beloch, *RG* 498.  [3] Cf. Livy 40. 42. 13.  [4] Above, 27.

[5] Cf. Rosenberg, op. cit. 25.  [6] *CIL* xi. 3873.  [7] Art. cit. 192.

[8] Cf. Rosenberg, op. cit. 51 ff., with Beloch's caution, *RG* 231. Cf. also the *praetor* in early inscriptions of Falerii, *Inscr. It. Med.* 67, 68 (= Conway, 321, 323).

incorporated earlier. What is instructive is the marked continuity of the history of the *municipium* with that of the *municipium civium Romanorum*. It is because Rudolph limits his study to the incorporated states that he fails to see that the *municipia* were not suddenly inserted into the Roman state but rather gradually grew up into it. If it is true that a clear line separated *cives Romani* and *municipes* in the early days of the institution, and that Roman interference in the internal arrangements of a *municipium* was then unusual and improper, it is no less true that this line later became blurred; the *municipes* had gradually lost so much to Rome that special interference in their internal affairs and general reorganization were unnecessary at the time of their incorporation. The transition had been prepared beforehand; the abolition of the weakened praetors of Anagnia was required by no serious reason of policy. But this means that these communities on entering the Roman state retained their original municipal forms, however maimed and shadowy those forms might have become.[1]

The importance of these shadows is not to be dismissed with a single word. The whole error of such a theory as Rudolph's lies in the over-secular interpretation which it gives to the history of certain institutions, in the development of which such distinctions were either improper or else blurred. It was not the magistrates who were changed, but the work which they had to perform. It is doubtless true that a considerable amount of jurisdiction was transferred from the local officials to the *praefecti* sent out by the Roman *praetor*. But this does not mean that the local *res publica* disappeared completely. For that, Rome must first have destroyed the material existence of the community, as at Veii and at Capua, and marked the destruction by such measures as evocation of the local gods to Rome, or by detailed regulation of the status of the remnants of the former community.[2] Unless such a course was followed, the magistrates continued to be elected for the performance of essential services. Magisterial functions are not limited to the categories of jurisdiction and administration; e.g. the *populus Lanuvinus* had other connexions and other aspects which could not at once be merged with the institutions of the Roman state.[3] If the *praetores Volcani* of the Arulenses at Ostia were retained down to imperial times,[4] correspondingly

[1] Cf. Rudolph, op. cit. 222 n. 1.  
[2] Cf. Livy, 26. 33; 27. 3.  
[3] Livy 8. 14. 2.  
[4] J. Carcopino, op. cit. 69. Above, 12.

greater importance can be assumed for the *magistratus Lanuvinus* in the fourth and third centuries.

The fact that by the Ciceronian age the duties of the *dictator Lanuvinus* had been narrowly limited is no evidence for the situation in the fourth century.[1] The relevant contrast is not between the developed municipal system of the late Republic and its rudimentary origins, but between even the most shadowy retention of a local *res publica* in the fourth century and the complete absorption of local communities which marked the earliest period of Roman development, when, e.g., the Roman *consul* or *dictator* repaired to the Alban mount in place of the Alban magistrate. Although the *sacra* of Lanuvium were made *communia cum Romanis*,[2] their ministers had to be drawn from the place itself. It is much more important that Milo was a native of Lanuvium than that his *dictatura* was limited in scope, for in this detail lies the essence of the change which was inaugurated on a grand scale in 338, after certain preliminary trials at Gabii and Tusculum. This change set free the idea of the town within the state to develop as it would. To say that Rome 'merely' left religious duties to the incorporated boroughs obscures the fact that in this remnant lies hid the continued existence of the separate community within the Roman state.

Equally misleading is the hard distinction between the secular and non-secular powers of Italian magistrates. The close bond between *ius*, *lex*, and *fas* has been ignored by Rudolph. That the fine retained a religious tinge till a comparatively late date can be shown by colonial Latin documents. The *Lex Spoletina luci Iovis* and the *Lex Furfonensis* prove how easily the priest became a magistrate and vice versa. In the first, certain *piacula* for religious offences are to be levied by the *dicator*. 'Eius piacli moltaique dicatorei exactio estod.'[3] In the second we read: 'Sei qui heic sacrum surupuerit aedilis multatio esto.'[4] This evidence for the connection of *fas* and *lex* provides at least an analogy to the possible meaning of the early municipal magistrates, and demonstrates the way in which Latin institutions developed when left to themselves.

[1] Rudolph, op. cit. 30–1.
[2] Livy 8. 14. 2.
[3] *ILS* 4911, 'Let the collection of that pain and fine pertain to the *dicator*.'
[4] Ibid. 4906, 'Let the aedile have power to fine whoever burgles this shrine.' Cf. also 4912, *lex luci Lucerini*, 'seive *macisteratus* volet moltare licetod'.

Had municipal life been entirely limited to the due observance of certain religious ceremonies, doubtless the notion of a dual *patria* possessed by all *cives Romani* would have remained merely latent, and the municipal system would have died of inanition. In addition to the theoretic basis a broad material foundation was necessary for the erection of a sound structure. This was provided by all those activities which have been dismissed by Rudolph as 'merely administrative' and 'police work'. But the hard fact remains that, even if we accept the view that the local magistrates of the *municipia civium Romanorum* possessed no extensive power of jurisdiction, still there was plenty of work with which men might busy themselves. Livy's description of the *censura* of 174 B.C. shows how slow the Romans were to interfere in the domestic affairs of the municipalities.[1] Flaccus the censor built a temple at Fundi, but his partner regarded censorial activity outside Rome, even though in Roman territory among the colonies and municipalities, as unconstitutional. One may infer that such duties fell to the local authorities.

When the evidence is considered as a whole, and especially when the history of *civitas sine suffragio* is properly related to the study of the *municipia civium Romanorum*, the general indication is clearly that Rome did not seek to abolish the local life of her new boroughs. Certain changes in the competence of municipal magistrates became necessary, but, in however rudimentary a fashion, Rome entered at this period on the road that led to the municipal system of the empire.

One problem remains. If the account here given is correct, how did Rome acquire the technique which was successfully employed on a large scale in and after 90 B.C.? It is unlikely that the policy of replacing the local magistrates of the then incorporated states by boards of *quattuorviri* was invented out of nothing. That Roman political technique is usually the product of a long period of slow growth does not need much demonstration. The customary method of dealing with the revolt of extremely refractory states provides an example. The measures taken against Privernum, the destruction of the walls and the exile of the disloyal senators, were based on the precedent set after the revolt of Velitrae—*lege eadem qua Veliterni*.[2] Over a

[1] Livy 41. 27. 11. Cf. below, 84 f.
[2] Livy 8. 14. 5; 20. 7 and 9; 9. 16. 9–10.

century later this ancient example was recalled when Capua revolted and precisely similar measures were taken.[1]

What then was the precedent on which was based the creation of *quattuorviri* throughout the newly incorporated areas of Italy in 90 B.C.? In the survey of the earlier municipalities only the Octovirate offers serious support to the general theory of Rudolph, because only the Octovirate fulfils the two necessary and complementary conditions—unity of time and diversity of ethnic area in its employment. The attempt to prove that Rome invented new and inferior constitutions for all her new municipalities is too schematic in its insistence on theoretic unity. Equally schematic is the view that Rome sought to centralize administrative activity and to diminish the rights of local authorities. But it may well be true that in these Sabine areas, where city life was not fully developed, Rome attempted to make better provision for the local government than had been provided by the existing tribal system. It is possible to believe that the Octovirate, and possibly also, in some areas, the system of *vici magistri*,[2] was a Roman improvisation, without also accepting the view that its creation was a retrograde action. The real difficulty in believing that all the known municipal forms were Roman creations lies in the diversity of types. This diversity cannot be explained by any dissimilarity in the functions which the various bodies had to perform. Dual aediles, triple aediles, dictators, praetors, *octoviri*, all do the same work.

The study of the Octovirate ought to be related to the situation with which Rome had to deal in the Apennines. After centuries of warfare the expansion of the peoples of central Italy had at last been fettered. Henceforth the various tribal units were confined to their separate territorial limits. Some provision had to be made for the internal development of the various communities, since external expansion was barred to them. In the area covered by the Octovirate, this duty fell to Rome, and was rendered more specially urgent because Roman settlers accustomed to the various forms of the Latin municipal system were mixing with the original inhabitants. Outside the limits of Roman territory and, at a later date, within the Roman boroughs, the communities carried out necessary amplification of the organs of

[1] Livy 26. 16. 6–7; 34. 7–10.
[2] Cf. Rudolph, op. cit. 55, on the special privileges of some central Italian *pagi*.

local government by themselves, as at Bantia or in the Latin colonies.[1]

Likewise where social life was not complex, and in these areas, where, if anywhere in Italy, the importance of the rural area outweighed that of the central *oppidum*, it is easy to see that a board of eight men had special practical advantages, if in truth it was not itself native and original. There was good reason not to introduce any by-form of the Latin *praetura* or the Volscian triple aedileship; they might, and in effect did, come later with the growing complexity of municipal life and the consequent specification of magisterial functions.

The examination of the earliest forms of the Roman municipal system thus leads to the conclusion that the special characteristics of the later Roman citizenship as a dual citizenship are due to the fact that Rome in the historic period did not obliterate the local traditions of those fully developed city-states which 'came into the Roman state'. Where communities of a different kind were incorporated, Rome was so far from destroying what little already existed of a *res publica* that she sought to amplify it. At the same time it is necessary to insist upon the importance of the process *fieri Romani*. Beside the *res publica populi Romani* there remained always some residue of a secondary *res publica*, yet there never existed a secondary formal citizenship beside the Roman franchise. A compromise was thus effected. No *civis Romanus* could be a citizen of another state. The *municipes* themselves surrender to Rome the right of making war and peace with other communities when they receive the *civitas sine suffragio*. But the preparatory period, when *municipium* was a flourishing and a changing institution, left as a heritage to later generations the principle that a *civis* may also take part in the political life of his local *patria*.

## Urban Development in Ager Romanus

The Romans became accustomed to the principle of introducing Italian communities into their state without annihilating them as separate entities, at a time when the practice of creating new communities of their own people within the *tribus rusticae* was at a tentative and experimental stage. This second process lagged

---

[1] Cf. Cic. *ad Fam.* 13. 11. 3; *de Leg. Ag.* 2. 93. For Bantia, Bruns iii. 8. Below, 117 f., for the Latin colonies.

behind the former, and did not reach anything like an equal importance until the *colonia civium Romanorum* was assimilated to, and displaced, the Latin colony in the second century, for the purpose of garrisoning the peninsula and the plain of the Po.[1]

Within the narrower limits of the Roman territory the growth of true boroughs proceeded even more slowly; but as the city-land spread and the *coloni* of the rustic tribes found themselves ever more remote from the capital, and as the great roads were extended towards Ariminum and Capua, town-centres began to emerge under the titles of *fora* and *conciliabula*. In the third and later decades of Livy these begin to play an important part, levies were held, inquiries made, and edicts published *per fora atque conciliabula*.[2] There is no hint in Livy that in these places there was any trace of a true municipal organization. From the fact that he couples them with *pagi* nothing can be concluded, since he also couples them with *oppida* and *municipia*.[3] The term simply indicates the sum of forms of community found on Roman soil, apart from *coloniae*. Their character is revealed by the phrase *in agris forisque et conciliabulis et in urbe*,[4] and by the fact that their area begins *ultra decimum lapidem*.[5] They represent the natural expansion of the indigenous Roman people in the conquered territories, as distinct from the Roman citizens of the incorporated *municipia* and Latin states.

Beloch has shown that the *conciliabula* were the substitute for the earlier centres of the *tribus rusticae*, and emerged when the political structure of the latter was shattered by the arbitrary expansion of their territorial area.[6] The *fora* are distinct from *conciliabula* as being the deliberate creations of magistrates, either when building roads or when organizing newly won lands;[7] e.g. Forum Decii was built in the Sabine country, Forum Appii on the *Via* made in 312 through the newly annexed land of Privernum, the future *tribus Oufentina*.[8]

There are no signs in Livy of any political life in these places: their existence is orientated towards Rome, Roman magistrates deal directly with the citizens for whom this or that *forum* is a *sedes*. A *forum* was thus a particularly suitable seat for the later

---

[1] Cf. E. T. Salmon, 'Roman Colonization', *JRS* 26, 51–4.
[2] Livy 25. 5. 6; 29. 37. 3; 34. 1. 6; 39. 14. 7; 43. 14. 10.
[3] Livy 34. 1. 6; 39. 41. 4. With *pagi* 25. 5. 6.
[4] Livy 40. 19. 3.      [5] Livy 40. 37. 4.      [6] Beloch, *It. B.* 103–4.
[7] Ibid. 108 ff.      [8] Beloch, *RG* 584; 597.

type of *praefectura*, so that we are not surprised to hear of *praefectura Claudia Foroclodi*.[1] The inscription of Popillius Laenas
tells almost all that is known about the construction of *fora*:
'Viam fecei . . . ponteis . . . poseivei . . . forum aedisque poplicas
heic fecei'.[2] It is, however, probable that these places had some
rudimentary form of organization, like that of the *vici* and *pagi*
to which Festus, by his gloss *negotiationis locus*, equates at least
the *fora*. The *conciliabula*, since they present the focal points of
the old tribal system, must have had some institution corresponding to the *curatores tribuum* :[3] as the chief village of the group of
villages which formed the tribe, the *conciliabulum* cannot have
been inferior in organization to the *vicus* with its *magistri*. We
cannot imagine more than a minimum of local officers, sufficient
to keep the market-place in order, to watch over the *Via* on which
the *forum* was situated, and to post up edicts on their arrival from
Rome. Such duties are purely administrative; the later development of *fora* and *conciliabula*, used up and down Italy, only confirms the impression that as a form of municipality they were
rudimentary.[4] This is because, although they might have a town-
meeting, *magistri*, and even a local council, they lacked the broad
basis of a complex municipal life, the *territorium*.[5] Being subordinate to the area in which, and to supply the needs of which,
they existed, none of the juridical consequences which followed
from the inclusion of the *territorium* within the *municipium* applied
to the foundation of a *forum*. This is shown by Festus' remark on
*forum*, 'quod etiam locis privatis et in viis et agris fieri solet.'[6]

Quite apart from the vexed question of judicial powers, we
can see that in the third and second centuries the idea of the
self-governing community within the state was not an internal,
spontaneous creation, but originated from Rome's contact with
her neighbours, and from the practical necessity of incorporating

---

[1] Pliny, *NH* 3, 52.
[2] *ILS* 23, 'I made the road . . . I set bridges . . . here I made a market-place and
public buildings.'     [3] Beloch, *It. B.* 106–7.
[4] Beloch, op. cit. 106, notes that the *tabula Heracleensis* omits the titles of *conciliabula* and *fora* from the lists of boroughs where the *censura* was in the hands of the
local magistrates. But since it is uncertain how far this law embodies ancient
precedents, not much can be built on this fact.
[5] Festus, s.v. 'forum' and 'vici'. Cf. Beloch, *It. B.* 107, who sees in the *Triginta-
viri* of Castrimoenium, etc., survivals from an earlier day. But we cannot say *how*
much earlier.
[6] 'It often exists even on private property and on roads and estates.'

what it was wiser not to destroy. The influence of the idea of *municipium* upon the village system of the Roman territory was at first extremely slight; only in the first century B.C. did the Romans begin to create Roman municipalities out of tribal territory, as distinct from the insertion of allied states into it.[1]

## Growth of Coloniae

*Their place in Roman policy.* The Romans had another weapon in their armoury, the *colonia civium Romanorum*. The establishment of such colonies began to assume importance after the Latin War of 338, when the Romans founded a colony at Antium. This does not mean that the institution was invented at that time, but that the earliest of the colonies which survived to a later age was founded then. There are numerous indications in Livy and Dionysius of the establishment of small colonial settlements in the earlier centuries, and also clear indications of their destruction.[2] There is no necessity to disbelieve these stories, especially as no motive for their invention can be discovered, and as the technique of their foundation appears to be the same in all cases. But more likely they are Latin colonies in disguise.[3]

There may well be an organic connection between the ideas of *colonia*, incorporated state, and *municipium*, but it is noticeable that the Romans were shyer of the creation of citizen colonies than of acts of incorporation in this early period. This is shown not so much by the number as by the size of the colonies. From 329 B.C. until 194—perhaps 184—the number of families sent to form a colony remained fixed at three hundred.[4] This may be partly due to the strangeness of the idea of separating a body of citizens from the mother state in an artificial community. It is remarkable that this difficulty was seriously felt a century and more after the introduction and gradual transformation of the idea of the *municeps*, in so far as all the colonies founded before the second Punic War were adjacent either to Roman territory or to that of a *municipium*.[5]

[1] Below, 33 ff. For assignation of enfranchised states to *tribus* see below, 195 f.
[2] e.g. Livy 4. 30. 6; 47. 7; 5. 24. 4; 29. 3; 6. 12. 6; 21. 3. Details, such as the number of *coloni*, may be fictitious.
[3] Cf. above, 36.                                            [4] Livy 8. 21. 11; 34. 45. 1.
[5] Antium, Ostia, Terracina directly adjacent. Minturnae, Sinuessa between *ager Fundanus* and *tribus Falerna*. Sena Gallica and Aesis in *ager Gallicus*. Castrum Novum, Alsium, Fregenae adjoin *ager Caeretanus*. Cf. *R.E.* 4. 520–1.

The purpose which the *colonia civium Romanorum* served is supplementary to that of the Latin colonies. The two explain one another; the real difference between them is constitutional, and does not lie in the source from which the *coloni* were drawn, since Latins could be accepted for a citizen colony,[1] but in the lack of elaborate communal organization in the citizen colony. The *colonia civium Romanorum* has no true *res publica*; hence the *coloni* do not cease to be *cives Romani*.[2] The reason why these colonies lack full communal existence is that they are not big enough to support the life of a 'state'; thus in the last resort we must attribute the difference of status between Latin and citizen colony to the difference of function which lies behind this difference of size, and must not attribute the difference of size to the difference of status. E. T. Salmon has pointed out that the small citizen-colonies were sent to sites where there was no likelihood of the growth of an important community, and where for geographic or economic reasons certain limits were set to any development.[3] Latin colonies, on the other hand, were sent to sites of the first rank where there was every likelihood of considerable development. This is another way of saying that originally the citizen colony performed within Roman territory a modest function fulfilled by the Latin colonies in Italy on a large scale.

There was thus no motive for the enlargement of the citizen colony in the early period. Its task was much the same as that of the Athenian cleruchies, and is well indicated by the title of *coloni maritimi*, and the *sacrosancta vacatio* from military service which the colonists possessed.[4] Their sole purpose—shown by the foundation of a colony at Antium next door to the former pirate stronghold—was to control the few natural harbours and havens which lay within Roman territory at the time, and by defending the coastline from the shore to spare Rome the necessity of maintaining a permanent fleet. The *coloni* were almost entirely Roman citizens simply because the prospects were not good enough to attract many settlers from the Latin states.[5]

No break was made with this traditional division between the functions of Latin and citizen colonies until the second century. The way was perhaps prepared by the founding of five Roman

---

[1] Livy 34. 42. 6.  
[3] Cf. Salmon, loc. cit.  
[5] Cf. Livy 10. 21. 7.  

[2] Cf. E. T. Salmon, *JRS* 26, 62.  
[4] Livy 36. 3. 4–6. Cf. 27. 38. 5.

colonies out of immediate touch with Roman territory in 194 B.C.[1] But in size and purpose these obeyed the ancient rule. Then comes a sudden change. All we are told is that there was in 183 B.C. a debate at which 'illud agitabant uti colonia Aquileia deduceretur, nec satis constabat utrum Latinam an civium Romanorum deduci placeret'.[2] The decision was to found a Latin colony, but it was the last such of the epoch, and at the same time three citizen colonies were established at Mutina, Parma, and Saturnia in a style that departed entirely from the ancient pattern.[3] Two thousand families were sent instead of three hundred, and the amount of land per head was increased. The latter, however, is not a universal feature of the new type of colony.[4]

That there was a clean break in Roman policy is confirmed by the events of a few years later. The state of Pisae, much exposed to Ligurian raids, offered land in 180 B.C. for the foundation of a Latin colony.[5] The offer was accepted, and *tresviri coloniae deducendae* were appointed. Then in 177 a *citizen* colony was established at Luna, near by, by a different set of *tresviri*, the *coloni* receiving an extremely generous amount of land.[6] Later, in 168, Luna and Pisae quarrelled over some territory; a commission was sent out to settle the dispute, and was headed by Q. Fabius Buteo, one of the *tresviri* appointed for the original scheme of founding a Latin colony.[7] Clearly the Romans had changed their minds after accepting the offer of 180, and allotted the land intended for a Latin colony to a citizen colony, in *addition* to land won from other folk—*de Liguribus captus*.[8] This explains what the land was over which they quarrelled in 168. It also explains the great size of the allotments—$51\frac{1}{2}$ *iugera* according to the text of Livy. This is a strange figure in its irregularity, and hence textually suspect, but it indicates that the assignation was not on the scale normal in citizen colonies, even of the new type. Beloch had tried to show that both a citizen and a Latin colony were

---

[1] Livy 34. 45. 2–4. Salernum, Buxentum, Sipontum, Croton, Tempsa.

[2] Livy 39. 55. 5, 'They were discussing the foundation of a colony at Aquileia, but could not agree whether it should be a Latin or a citizen colony.'

[3] Livy 39. 55. 7–9.

[4] 10 *iugera* at Saturnia per man, but only 5 at Mutina, 8 at Parma; 6 were given in 194 B.C.; above, n. 1. Clearly the question of quality is relevant.

[5] Livy 40. 43. 1.    [6] Livy 41. 13. 4.    [7] Livy 45. 13. 10–11.

[8] Livy 41. 13. 5.

ounded on Pisan territory, and that Luca, a Latin colony, separated Pisae from Luna;[1] but a passage in Livy shows that in 175 Luna and Pisae were conterminous.[2] It is noticeable that Pisae, when desiring to attract a large Roman settlement to her neighbourhood, expected that it would take the form of a Latin colony, and that the Pisenses were mistaken. The change of policy was evidently recent; how recent, can be gathered from the parallel story of Aquileia.

For the future, whenever the size of a colony is mentioned, it is always of the new type, and usually it is set beyond the limits of the compact central area of Roman territory. That this change covered the deliberate assimilation of the citizen colony to the Latin, is proved by the various parallels which can be discerned between the magisterial system and general constitution of the two types.[3] This conclusion is borne out by the fact that, whatever other reasons the Roman government had for its new policy, the supply of *coloni* from their allies had not at this time dried up.[4] Undoubtedly Salmon is right in arguing that one ground of the change was to prevent further diminution of the Roman citizen body,[5] by the drafting away of numbers of citizens to Latin colonies, when new settlements were rendered necessary by the conquest of Cisalpine Gaul. The *colonia* was made more useful to Rome, and more popular with the Roman *coloni*. If the status of Latinity had become unsatisfactory to Romans of the second century, the organization of the old citizen colonies must have been even more so. For living in any but the nearest to Rome, a man effectively lost the use of his *suffragium*, and could find no substitute in the tiny round of local affairs. The new arrangement was to preserve the best features of both forms.

Life in these new colonies was bound to influence the development of the Roman citizenship. The size of the communities and their distance from Rome would encourage interest in municipal affairs; the growth of civic life would in time diminish the practical importance of the metropolitan franchise. Some of the colonies were within reach of consuls and proconsuls operating

---

[1] *It. B.* 147. Velleius I. 15. 2 puts *Luccam col.* in 177.

[2] Livy 41. 19. 1. 'P. Mucius cum iis qui Lunam Pisasque depopulati erant bellum gessit.' *Pace* the text of Velleius I. 15. 2—never a reliable quantity. For a similar general conclusion to the above, which was reached independently, cf. E. T. Salmon, 'The Last Latin Colony', *CQ* 1933, 30 ff.

[3] Below, 86 ff.     [4] Livy 34. 42. 5.     [5] Art. cit. 66.

in the Cisalpine region; but others were established in remote
southern districts where a magistrate was rarely seen. Certainly
few of the settlers could enjoy the benefits of tribunician assistance that had been at the disposal of the earlier *coloni maritimi*.[1]
But to determine the extent of the influence of the new system on
the meaning of the Roman franchise, it is necessary to gain a more
precise understanding of the growth of the municipal organization of the colonies.

*Colonia: Constitutional Development.* The citizen colony as the
perfect image and picture of Rome makes its first appearance in
our sources at the close of the domination of Julius Caesar. The
*Lex coloniae Genetivae Iuliae* reveals a complex and highly developed form of municipality for which the scanty information
in earlier sources has hardly prepared us. It is unlikely—*pace*
Rudolph—that this system came into the world at that time ready-
made and adult like Minerva from the head of Jove. The rapidity
with which the colonial system established and maintained itself
not only throughout the western world but in parts of the Greek
orient would suggest that the system was familiar, perhaps
instinctive, in its general principles and practice, to the individual Italian colonists, even if there were no scattered indications
that at least the outline of the institution was traditional. The
creation of a wholly artificial community by the removal of a
chosen number of the citizen body to another place, and the
necessary growth of certain powers of self-government, corresponding to the duties which this isolated body must fulfil, are
ideas that originated in the earlier days of the Republic.

It is usual to associate the origins of colonial self-government
with the regulation of the status of Antium as described by Livy.[2]
But the problem must have been faced before the foundation of
the colony of Antium, since this is not the first *colonia civium
Romanorum*, but merely the first which survived to a later period.[3]
The colony at Antium differs only in one particular from that
described, e.g., at Circei by Dionysius:[4] the other inhabitants of

---

[1] Livy 36. 3. 5.                                           [2] Livy 9. 20. 10.
[3] Cf. above, 76. At present it is safer to begin the list of later surviving *coloniae*
with Antium rather than Ostia owing to the difficulties involved in the traditional
account and the uncertainty of the Ostian date on archaeological grounds. Cf.
*Papers of B.S.R.* 13. 42–3, and R. Meiggs, *Roman Ostia* (1960), 16 f.
[4] 8. 14. 1, κληροῦχοι Ῥωμαίων ἅμα τοῖς ἐπιχωρίοις πολιτευόμενοι. The existence of
these dual communities has been established beyond all doubt by the excavations

the land to which it was sent were new Roman citizens. Instead of treating the *populus Antias* like the other Latin peoples incorporated at this date, a colony was sent there, which some of the Antiates, but not all, joined.[1] It is from the remnants of the *populus Antias* that the complaint came in 317 B.C., *se sine legibus certis sine magistratibus agere*.[2] Careful reading of this passage and appreciation of the circumstances make this plain. The Romans had recently regulated the status of Capua by sending a prefect thither in response to a request of the Campani.[3] The news of this, spreading *fama per socios*, reached the *populus Antias*, to whom the title *socii* might very loosely be applied (just as Livy applies it later to the Campani), since they were a very recent addition to the citizen body of Rome; but used of the *colonia civium Romanorum* the word is absurd. The difficulty of the Antiates was solved by placing them under the protection of the colony. This makes sense of the phrase *dati ab senatu ad iura statuenda ipsius coloniae patroni*, especially of the emphatic *ipsius*, which is impossible to understand on the usual interpretation that it was the colony whose status was being regulated.[4] Livy is contrasting the sending of *praefecti legibus ab . . . praetore datis* from Rome to Capua with the commission of the task to the men on the spot at Antium —*ipsius coloniae patroni*. After this Livy is able to round off his description with the general statement that *nec arma modo sed iura etiam Romana late pollebant*.[5] This phrase is absurd on the traditional view. Where else but in a body of *coloni* sent out from the city itself would one expect Roman laws to hold wide sway? It is the domination of Roman laws over the erstwhile hostile community of Antium that is remarkable.[6]

There are thus no grounds for asserting that it was demonstrably in 317 B.C., and at Antium, that some measure of

---

at Minturnae, where the *colonia* sent out in 209 B.C. is simply conterminous with the old town-centre of the Aurunci. Only at a later date was the party-wall dismantled, cf. J. Johnson, *Excavations at Minturnae*, vol. ii, part 1, 85 (Philadelphia, 1935).

[1] Livy 8. 14. 8, 'Antium nova colonia missa cum eo ut Antiatibus permitteretur si et ipsi adscribi coloni vellent; . . . Antiati populo est civitas data', above 59 n. 6.

[2] Livy 9. 20. 10, 'They were without a fixed constitution and magistrates.'

[3] Livy 9. 20. 5.

[4] 'The Senate provided patrons drawn from the colony itself to settle their constitution.' Or, 'the founders of the colony were appointed, etc.'      [5] Cf. above, 43.

[6] If the phrase 'ipsius coloniae patroni' is felt to be hard, consider the peculiar order of words in the opening sentence, 'postquam res Capuae stabilitas Romana disciplina . . . volgavit'.

self-government was first given to these *coloniae civium Roma-norum*. Rudolph remarks that between the founding of the colony at Antium and the request of the Antiates there falls the founda-tion of a colony at Tarracina.[1] It is a postulate of common sense that so distant a community 'must' have had some form of administrative machinery, however rudimentary. But there is another argument less vague and more closely based on direct evidence. The purpose of these small colonies is admittedly military, the defence of the coasts against foreign raids.[2] But this duty implies some form of military organization, of local control, and *imperium*. In the first instance the idea of local autonomy may have developed from the military rather than the civil institutions of these permanent garrisons, which were necessarily under some form of permanent command. This postulate is even more convincing than the former. These units were too small, and the military necessity too occasional, to merit the dispatch of special yearly officials from Rome.[3] Yet there must be some one always present and capable of organizing and controlling the little force of *coloni*, summoning them from the fields and leading them to battle against such a foe as Livy describes in the raid of Cleonymus on Padua.[4]

There is evidence in a passage of the Spanish *lex Ursonensis* that such powers were in the first century possessed by the magistrates of colonies.[5] The statement, which is explicit, has not yet been given its due weight, because it has been considered in isolation. The lack of reference to any control of Roman magistrates over these local magistrates and decurions in their levies and military operations is not in the least surprising, if this was the main pur-pose, or one of the main purposes, for which these magistrates

[1] Rudolph, op. cit. 142. Livy 8. 21. 11.

[2] Cf. Livy 10. 21. 7–11, 'in stationem se prope perpetuam infestae regionis non in agros mitti rebantur.' Minturnae and Sinuessa, Livy 27. 38. 5, 'supra dies xxx non pernoctaturos se esse extra moenia coloniae suae donec hostis in Italia esset'.

[3] The small size—300 families—suggests some primitive unit, *tribus, curia*, or *cohors*, to which the key is now lost.

[4] Livy 10. 2—especially ib. 7, 'maritimis Patavinorum vicis' and ib. 9, 'haec ubi Patavium sunt nuntiata . . . in duas partes iuventutem dividunt'. This instance seems to absolve the present theory from an undue indulgence in 'constructive historical imagination'.

[5] *Lex Ursonensis* 103, 'quocumque tempore coloniae finium defendendorum causa armatos educere (colonos incolasque contributosque) decuriones censuerint . . . ei IIviro idem ius eademque animadversio esto uti tribuno militum p. R. in exercitu p. R. est.'

were created. The view that these clauses were a special provision due to the unsettled character of the *Spanish* provinces is shown to be untenable by the fact that the *lex Ursonensis* speaks of a *tumultus Italicus Gallicusve*.[1] This phrase proves that the whole paragraph has been lifted bodily from the constitution of some Italian or Cisalpine colony, where reference to such a 'tumult' would be relevant. To speak of a local disturbance in Italy or Gaul as a special crisis which could excuse the suspension of local privileges and exemptions in a Spanish colony is absurd. A passage in Cicero clearly suggests the Italian origin of the clause and its antiquity, and limits the application to Italy, with the words, 'Itaque maiores nostri tumultum Italicum quod erat domesticus, tumultum Gallicum quod erat Italiae finitimus, praeterea *nullum* nominabant . . . bello vacationes valent, tumultu non valent.'[2]

This military authority did not originate in the last century of the Republic, but belonged to the Italian colonies of an earlier date; for the phrases of the *Lex Ursonensis* recall the similar provision mentioned by Livy during the war with Hannibal, when a similar though greater crisis led to a similar suspension of privileges.[3] Thus we can predicate this military authority of the *coloniae civium Romanorum* in 207 B.C. But this date precedes the expansion of these communities to the size and importance of the *coloniae Latinae*, when and where alone, on any theory that derives the local autonomy solely from the necessities of civil life, it would be reasonable to expect any considerable development in the importance of the privileges possessed by the colonial officers. If the colonies of this time had these powers, then they are the primitive powers of colonies and correspond to the primitive purpose of the *colonia*; for it is unlikely that so long as the size of the colonies was limited to three hundred families there was any great internal development. Since they continued to serve the same purpose as the foundations of the fourth century, it is likely

[1] Ibid. 62 on the *vacatio militiae* of the minor officials, 'neve quis eum eo anno . . . invitum militem faciat . . . nisi tumultus Italici Gallicive causa'.

[2] *Philipp.* 8. 3, cf. also the description of the troubles recorded by Polyb. 2. 23 as a *tumultus Gallicus* in Pliny, *NH* 3. 138, 'So our ancestors spoke of local troubles as Italic tumults, and of Gallic tumults because they were next door to us, but did not use the term otherwise . . . exemptions hold good in war but not in tumults.'

[3] Livy 27. 38. 3, 'colonos etiam maritimos qui sacrosanctam vacationem dicebantur habere . . .' especially 'cum in Italia hostis esset', Livy 27. 38. 5. Cf. Livy 36. 3. 4.

that the powers and organizations necessary to their life remained unchanged. To gain an idea of these powers one must investigate not the accidental but the essential characteristics of the *colonia*, and these are military. But it is unlikely that the exact nature of their primitive form of organization will be discovered until some satisfactory explanation has been given of the size, the 300 *familiae*, to which these settlements were limited.[1]

Once the size of the colonies was increased, so that, from small fortified villages or garrisons sometimes existing within the territory of another people, they became large quasi-states or quasi-*populi*, then there was a motive, in the growth of their municipal importance, for the extension of their *municipal* organization, because from that moment civil interests might begin to preponderate over military. The early colonies cannot have dispensed with some organization similar to that of the *conventus civium Romanorum* at a later epoch, but in such a small community the material basis, i.e. the *necessity*, for the growth of an extensive municipal organization was lacking.[2]

So far there can be no objection to the view that the earlier Republican colonies were *praefecturae*, and received their jurisdiction from itinerant prefects.[3] The displacement of the Latin colony by the citizen-colony, with the consequent enlargement of the latter, altered the situation. It is not possible that every petty assault or minor complaint in such large municipalities had to await the coming of the prefect for its adjudication. But there is no direct evidence for this view; all that can be proved is that within this period there appears an enlarged competence of colonial magistrates in matters of administration and of public works, and consequently in those limited judicial powers without which such activity becomes impossible. The evidence for this comes from a passage of Livy, which directly confirms the view set forth above that in the earlier period the civil competence of magistrates or quasi-magistrates in colonies was of very limited importance. Livy describes the activity of the censors in 174 B.C. Flaccus carries out a series of public works in Roman colonies, at

---

[1] Cf. above, 82 n. 3.

[2] It would not be wise to build upon the fact that Livy calls even the earliest of the *coloniae maritimae* 'populi', 27. 38. 4. For *conventus* cf. below, pp. 344 f.

[3] Rudolph extends Festus, s.v. 'praefecturae', to cover all the *coloniae*, op. cit. 146. But cf. above, 44 ff. and 44 n. 2, for the precise application of Festus' definitions.

Auximum, Pisaurum, Sinuessa, and Potentia.[1] He erects temples, builds markets, sewers, porches, city-gates, and walls. All this was done either with the moneys of the colony or with funds raised by the sale of *loca publica*. He clearly did not regard his authority as excluded from the boundaries of the colonies, nor did the *coloni*. Instead they greeted his efforts with great enthusiasm.[2] This was hardly due entirely to the notion that they had nothing to pay, for at Auximum it is clear that the censor merely liberated resources rather than supplied them.

Beside the provision of funds stands the activity itself, the erection of the buildings, the performance of the work, of which it would seem that the communities themselves were not fully capable. These extensive works within the colonies were apparently necessary, but had not been carried out; and yet the extra-urban activities of Flaccus were regarded by his colleague as improper.[3] This disapproval can only refer to this section of his labours, since general censorial activity *in agro Romano* had been familiar since, e.g., the building of the *Via Appia*,[4] and can only mean that here, as in the despoiling of the *Aedes Iunonis Laciniae*, the censor had exceeded his authority.[5]

Since Flaccus undoubtedly had a precedent, and since the objection came not from the colonies but from his colleague, we must look for a new factor.[6] This can only be that change of status, or of importance, which had issued from the debate of 183 B.C, when it was decided to close the long list of Latin colonies with the foundation of Aquileia, and for the future to employ an enlarged type of citizen-colony in their place. Here if ever is something epoch-making to which it is legitimate to attach other less significant but still important changes. Certainly before this period from 184 to 173 B.C. *coloniae civium Romanorum* apparently were not accustomed to any considerable degree of control over financial administration; within the period there falls a great change in the whole nature of the Roman colony; and after it, when inscriptions begin to appear, they speak of *duoviri*

[1] Livy 41. 27. 5–13.  [2] Livy 41. 27. 13.  [3] Livy 41. 27. 11.
[4] Cf. under these same censors the proposal 'ut agrum Campanum censores fruendum locarent', Livy 42. 19. 1.
[5] Cf. Livy 42. 3. 3.
[6] Livy 39. 44. 6 records similar activity ten years before of censors at Formiae—*a fortiori* then in colonies. Livy 40. 51. 1–3, 'censor . . . molem ad Tarracinam . . . locavit', 179 B.C.

who possess powers of public administration in precisely that sphere which Flaccus the censor thought still to be his preserve. A mere surmise—though reasonable—would be that the duovirate or the dual *praetura*, on the model of the Latin colonies, was first introduced into Roman colonies in fulfilment of the policy adopted after that famous debate of 183 B.C. Of the necessary *officers* of a colony before this period nothing is certain except that they 'must' have existed and that their character was more military than civil.

The great thing that happened during these years was the taking of the first step towards that assimilation of the *colonia* to the status of a *municipium*, which appears as complete only in the documents of the Ciceronian age. That the larger development of municipal autonomy began only at a comparatively late period is, after all, the material fact on which the whole character of the Roman, as distinct from the Hellenic, colony depends. The bond which connected the *coloni* to Rome was not only that sentimental and traditional affection for the mother city which Thucydides illustrates, but a real connection of law and discipline, which is best illustrated by the very title *coloniae civium Romanorum*. How close this connection is appears in the incidents of the war with Hannibal, when *colonos . . . dare milites cogebant (consules)*,[1] and of 191 B.C. when the repetition of this practice led the *coloni* to appeal to the tribunes.[2] This direct subjection to the Roman magistrates and senate, and the corresponding lack of any local *sovereignty*, established the peculiar character which the *colonia* never lost, despite the great increase in local *autonomy* of the succeeding centuries, and which led to appreciation of the *ius coloniae* under the Empire as the political form that most nearly mirrored the character of the City itself.[3] The nearest parallel to the Roman colony is the Athenian cleruchy. The special nature of the institution, in both cases, depends upon the fact that the earliest colonies were settled in small numbers on land adjacent to the territory of the mother state—Salamis and Euboea, Antium and Anxur. Only the later colonies were out of touch with their metropolis. The Roman colony, however, can claim a remoter origin than the Athenian cleruchy. It is an institution of the traditional Roman system and grows up with Rome instead of

---

[1] Livy 27. 38. 3, 'The consuls compelled the colonists to provide soldiers.'
[2] Livy 36. 3. 5.                                        [3] Below, 259, 413 ff.

being an invention of her maturity. This is the lesson of the tradition of Ostia which, though it cannot yet be vindicated in fact, contains the same moral or allegorical truth that is apparent in even the most absurd of the myths.

Once the *colonia* had received this indelible dye of a close and uniform connection with Rome it could sustain, without losing its essential characteristics, an increasing element of freedom in local government. To investigate the growth of this is the second task of an inquiry into the fundamental nature of the Roman colony. The first task must always be to find out the elements of connection and subordination, but it is impossible for lack of evidence to pursue further such questions as the relationship between a *colonus* and his family at Rome, whether he was freed from the *patria potestas*, and whether *coloni* remained eligible for *honores*. The only answers that would be important would be answers limited to the period before the colonial rights began to be assimilated to those of the *municipia*. But for these there is no distinguishable evidence.

We can recover a good deal of the constitutional forms of the colonies of the later republic. Herr Rudolph has made a great and partly successful onslaught upon this problem. His efforts would have been more fruitful if he had consulted the texts of the *CIL* a little more and its Indexes a little less, and if he had not been so dominated by the desire to refer everything to the ingenuity of Caesar. A great deal more of the later system of colonial magistracies appears in the early inscriptions than Rudolph has discovered. In the analysis of the *Lex de pariete faciundo* of Puteoli[1] he seems justified in showing that the constitution of Puteoli consisted of two *duoviri* and a senate or *consilium* of ex-magistrates or *duovirales*.[2] But the generalization of this conclusion to apply to all other Republican colonies is unwarranted, for the reason that the selection of the *lex Puteolana* as characteristic is merely accidental or wilful; in itself its testimony is in no way preferable to that of other inscriptions which name a more extensive magistracy.

---

[1] Op. cit. 134. *ILS* 5317.

[2] The argument, 136–7, against Mommsen's view that this *consilium* is a temporary committee seems very just, in view of the phrase 'qui in consilio esse solent'; and of the difference of phraseology and circumstance in the *Tabula Caeritana*, *CIL* xi. 3614. Rudolph might have added Cic. *de Leg. Ag.* 2. 93, 'hostiae maiores . . . de consili sententia probatae'.

In particular, Rudolph's argumentation against the *praetores duoviri* who appear in certain colonies is not well based. He holds, on the strength of a passage in Cicero, that the title *praetor* is merely additional or ornamental, opposing both Beloch's view that *praetor* was the original title of colonial magistrates,[1] and his natural conclusion that such a title implied an amount of local autonomy that Rudolph is unwilling to concede. In dealing with the passage from the second speech *de Lege Agraria*—perhaps the most perverse that Cicero ever produced—Rudolph forgets the necessary caution in accepting literally an orator's statements about a matter which is the centre of controversy. In the new colony, founded at Capua, though not maintained, under the regime of Cinna, the magistrates received the title *praetores duoviri*. Cicero proceeds to score a debating-point by contrasting the *superbia* of such a title with the normal appellation of *duoviri*. His statement *hi se praetores appellari volebant* is palpably tendentious, not to say false, since the magistrates took their titles in accordance with the *lex data* by which their colony was established. The element of mockery is clear elsewhere in such a phrase as, 'nonne arbitramini paucis annis . . . consulum nomen appetituros?', and in the objection to the title *conscripti* used of the local senate.[2] Yet the senate of the *municipium* of Fundi had been using this title for over two centuries, and the recent colony at Fabrateria Nova used it likewise.[3]

What this passage tells of the relation between *praetores* and *duoviri* seems to support Beloch rather than Rudolph; for it suggests that the title *Praetor duumvir* had by this time become old-fashioned, and been generally superseded by that of *duovir* alone.[4] Cicero's general statement is verbally incorrect, since inscriptions of this very epoch name *praetores duoviri* at Grumentum, Abellinum, and Telesia, and this was certainly the earliest form of the magistracy at Narbo.[5] This verbal inaccuracy, similar to that of Horace in describing the aedile of Fundi as *praetor*—if that *is*

---

[1] *RG* 492.

[2] *De Leg. Ag.* 2. 92–3, 'They wanted to be called praetors.' 'Do you not think they will seek the title of consuls in a few years?'

[3] *CIL* x. 5590, 6231.

[4] Op. cit. 93, 'cum ceteris in colonis IIviri appellentur.'

[5] *CIL* ix, p. 205, x. 1134, ix. 2221, 2220, xii. 4338; the *praetores* of Nemausus, Aquae Sextiae, and Carcaso. xii. 3215, 517, 5317, have probably a different history, *pace* Kornemann *RE*, s.v. 'Colonia', col. 585.

what he means—reminds us that Cicero felt it necessary to explain the peculiarity of the magistracy of his own *municipium* to Brutus.[1] The general principle of Cicero's remark thus remains true, that the duovirate, apart from variations of title, was the universal form of colonial magistracy in the late Republic. But the term *praetores* cannot be dismissed as a mere additional title, since it appears on the early inscriptions and tends to disappear at a later date, as at Narbo Martius; while the very form of the title suggests that it is 'duovir' that is a later addition, just as Rudolph has shown that *iure dicundo* is a later addition to a primitive title of *IIvir* or *IVvir*. Beloch has argued persuasively[2] that the date of all these colonies with *praetores IIviri* is Gracchan, because of the parallel between the surnames of the three colonies with those of the known colonies of the Gracchan or post-Gracchan period, above all Narbo, where the *praetor duumvir* also appears.[3] There is also a group of earlier colonies[4] where the magistrate's title is plain *praetor*, Castrum Novum, Potentia, and Auximum; to these examples Beloch would add as an intermediary an inscription of a *praetor IIvir* which he believes comes from Tarracina.[5]

The view which naturally suggests itself is that both these inscriptions and every detail of the invaluable passage of Cicero[6] provide a clear illustration of the modelling of the local institutions on those of Rome at a much earlier date than is admitted by Rudolph. To follow Beloch[7] and to generalize that the *praetor* was the original magistrate of the *colonia* is as unwise as to follow Rudolph's contrary generalization about the duovirate;[8] for Beloch himself admits that at Puteoli the duovirate, which appears already in 105 B.C., was original, and was perhaps the magistracy of such colonies as were within the sphere of the

---

[1] *Ad fam.* 13. 11. 3, 'is enim magistratus in nostro municipio nec alius ullus creari solet.' For the *praetor Fundanus*, cf. above, 67.

[2] *RG* 493–6.

[3] 'Col. Veneria Livia (Augusta Alexandriana) Abellinatium', 'Herculia Telesia'. Grumentum has no such title, but appears to be pre-Sullan, op. cit. 494. Cf. Narbo Martius, Minervia Scolacium, Neptunia Tarentum. Rudolph, op. cit. 143 n. 2.

[4] Beloch, op. cit. 492. Castrum Novum 290/286 B.C., Potentia 187 B.C., Auximum 157 B.C.

[5] Op. cit. 496. *CIL* x. 6320.

[6] *De Leg. Ag.* 2. 92–3, 'Lictores ... cum fascibus ... hostiae maiores in foro constitutae ... ad praeconem ... immolabantur ... patres conscripti'—in addition to the *praetores* or *praetores IIviri*.

[7] Op. cit. 492.         [8] Op. cit. 152–3.

*praefecturae*, or of the City jurisdiction itself. Further, Rudolph has shown that in certain other colonies, founded at the same period as the 'praetorian' groups, there is no trace of the praetorian constitution, although the colonies have not been disturbed by further colonization in the Sullan, Caesarean, or triumviral periods.[1]

What seems to emerge is that *coloniae civium Romanorum*, at the time of the remodelling of the whole institution of the colony, received a magistracy of the kind prevalent in the Latin colonies, to which the citizen colonies were being assimilated, either the duovirate or the *praetura*; that the duovirate became more prevalent, thought by no means universal, perhaps for those reasons of convenience and avoidance of confusion which Beloch suggests;[2] that reasons of sentiment kept the secondary form alive down to the Gracchan and even the Sullan age, after which ample scope was found for this patriotic copying of the Roman magistracies in the extension of the *lower* offices on the Roman model; then, with the growing tendency to assimilate *coloniae* to *municipia*, the duovirate, so obviously parallel to the quattuorvirate, became the predominant type of colonial magistracy.

Rudolph in his devotion to the duovirate has failed to notice that the burgeoning of the lower magistracies in the colonies cannot be confined to the post-Caesarean epoch. At Grumentum the quaestorship and aedilate appear on inscriptions firmly dated to 57 and 51 B.C. Rudolph endeavours to rid himself of this contradictory evidence,[3] apparently by referring them to an earlier community, which was (he thinks) combined with the colony and modified its constitution. But, since these aediles and quaestors are no less detrimental to Rudolph's theory of the *municipia*, this argument is not worth much. It remains certain that Grumentum had *aediles* and *quaestores* well before the date of that 'single act of organization' for which Rudolph continually makes Caesar responsible.[4]

Still more significant of the deliberate copying of the Roman constitution in the Republican period—and still more deadly to

---

[1] Rudolph, op. cit. 140, 141 n. 1, cf. Beloch, op. cit. 493. Certainly at Eporedia (100 B.C.) or Luna (177 B.C.) we might expect some trace.

[2] Op. cit. 496. 'Zur Differenzierung des municipalen von dem römischen Praetor.'

[3] Op. cit. 143 n. 2. *CIL* x. 219, 220.

[4] Op. cit. 153.

Rudolph's view of the simplicity of the pre-Caesarean magistracy
—is the appearance of the Roman censor in the citizen colonies,
exercising those powers which in the Principate appear as the
privilege of the *duovir quinquennalis*. On no view can these colonial
*censores* be attributed to Caesar. His own view of the proper
office for such duties appears clearly in the *Tabula Heracleensis*:
'qui in eis municipiis coloneis praefectureis maximum magistratum maximamve potestatem ibi habebit tum cum censor . . .
Romae populi censum aget is . . . censum agito'.[1] The *censores*
who appear, e.g., at Abellinum[2] and at Fabrateria Nova,[3] thus
belong, by origin, to a pre-Caesarean period. It is specially
instructive to note that at Fabrateria Nova the office of *censor*
later disappears in favour of the *duovir quinquennalis*,[4] although
at this very place the office had only been created at a late date,
since an inscription of the Republican period refers to 'censor . . .
a conscriptis primus factus'.[5]

In some colonies the development of the Romanized constitution had gone far beyond what Rudolph, with his insistence upon
the unitary character of all Republican magistracies, could allow.
Cicero's description of the Cinnan colony at Capua is full of
significant detail; the decurions, for example, were called *conscripti*, as at Fabrateria.[6] The colony proposed by Rullus in 63
B.C. was to be even more elaborate—it was to have a hundred
decurions, ten augurs and six pontiffs.[7] Thus there is no difficulty
in regarding a municipal career like that of M. Bivellius G. f., at
Abellinum—*aed(ilis) q(uaestor) pr(aetor) IIvir cens(oria potestate)*—
as the highest point of development reached by the colonial
magistracies under the Republic, rather than as the artificial
creation of Caesar.[8] That this complexity was universal is not

---

[1] *Tab. Her.* 143 f. 'Whoever holds the chief magistracy or authority in those
boroughs when the censor holds a census of the people at Rome is to take the census.'

[2] *CIL* x. 1130, 1134. These are of early Augustan date. Cf. 1129.

[3] *CIL* x. 5590. Beloch, *RG* 505–6, notes that the *censores* in *municipia* all come
from communities incorporated before the Social War—this perhaps confirms the
antiquity of the colonial *censura* also.     [4] *CIL* x. 5581.

[5] *CIL* x. 5590, 'the first censor appointed by the Council'. The reading, however, is not beyond doubt. Fabrateria Nova was founded in 124 B.C. (Velleius 1.
15). Mommsen's view that it was a Latin colony (*CIL* x, p. 547, s.v. Fabrateria)
has no foundation, especially since a number of apparently early duoviral inscriptions appear at a date when an ex-Latin state would have only *IVviri*. This *censor*
must be dated after 124 B.C. and before Caesar sought to transfer such activities
to 'is qui maximam potestatem habebit'.

[6] Above, n. 5.     [7] *De Leg. Ag.* 2. 96.     [8] *CIL* x. 1134.

asserted. Many colonies remained contented with their duovirate, such as Minturnae, where fresh investigation has revealed an early duoviral inscription without any mention of further diversity, and even Caesar's colony at Urso confined its magistracies to the duovirate and aedilate and dispensed with the *quaestura*.[1]

Last and least important for the history of the Republican magistracies is the question raised by Rudolph about *duoviri iure dicundo*.[2] He holds that powers of jurisdiction were only conferred upon colonial magistrates during the dictatorship of Caesar, basing his argument upon the late appearance of the adjunct *iure dicundo* in the inscriptions. His case is even harder to prove for the *coloniae* than for the *municipia*, since here, where the title *IIvir* had a more remote ancestry, it retained its primitive form much longer;[3] e.g. the Ostian *Fasti* of the second century A.D. only give the form *duoviri*, and at Fabrateria the form *duovir i. d.* is not employed in the imperial inscriptions, although *IIvir aedilis* is common.[4] What lies behind the appearance of *duoviri i. d.* in the second half of the first century B.C. is not so much the extension of the power of the *duoviri* as the completion of the process of assimilation to the status of *municipia* which was remarked earlier. The evidence for the completion of this process lies in the comprehensive formulae of the *Lex Mamilia Roscia*, of the *Tabula Heracleensis*, of the *Lex de Gallia Cisalpina*, and of the *Fragmentum Atestinum*;[5] in these laws universal rules are laid down which are to apply to *municipia* and to *coloniae* alike. The old opposition is broken down, so that both stand on a common level.[6] It may well be—though Rudolph's evidence does not prove it—that at this period the colonial magistracies increased

---

[1] *Anneé Épigraphique*, 1934, 250–1. They fall within the period 90–60 B.C. Johnson, *Excavations at Minturnae*, vol. ii, part 1, 123–4. *Lex Ursonensis, ILS* 6087, lxii, lxxi; also pontiffs and augurs, lxvi.

[2] Op. cit. 147.

[3] At Casinum, one of the new artificial *municipia* of the Ciceronian age, *duoviri i. d.* appear early, *sine cognominibus*, precisely where there was no long-established tradition of an older and simpler title, *CIL* x, p. 510, Beloch, *RG*, 508.

[4] *Ann. Ép.* 1933, 30. *CIL* x, p. 547.

[5] *Passim*—it is hardly necessary to quote; that the phrase is already reduced to initials in the *lex de Gallia* argues for the pre-Caesarean date of this assimilation. Below, 142.

[6] The other terms, *praefecturae fora conciliabula*, etc., at this time are simply alternative names for what in law is a *municipium*. Perhaps this assimilation is the best argument for the late date of the *lex Mamilia Roscia*. Cf. below, 167 f.

their judicial powers. If this is a fact it means that the close bond of real authority in every sphere which urban magistrates held over *coloniae* remained in force, in part at least, down to the Ciceronian age. But that the colonies possessed no true local autonomy because they did not possess an extended civil—as distinct from criminal—jurisdiction is not a tenable view: the decisive factors are rather the separate entity of the *colonia* from a formal religious point of view, the local military competence and the financial independence illustrated by many an inscription of the last century of the Republic. Connected with this are those necessary powers of civil coercion, shown by the incident, ignored by Rudolph, at Minturnae, when the *duoviri* arrested Marius, clapped him in irons, and nearly cut off his head. To complete, but only to complete, this structure, which in this incomplete form could already contain the *duoviri, aediles, augures, pontifices,* and *senatus* or *conscripti* named in the inscriptions, there would be added at the last that more extensive civil jurisdiction which already appears in the laws of Caesar's time, with no special hint that it was then an innovation rather than an extension of something that had already, in part or sporadically, existed before.

Evidence has been cited to show that the system of magistracies and of priesthoods revealed by the *Lex Ursonensis* was in large part anticipated and even outstripped by the experiments of the Republican colonies. This development appears to have begun in the second century, when the increase in size and the extension of citizen colonies to Cisalpine Gaul rendered necessary a complex form of local government. Of the original *colonia* few traces have been left, but if it is to be studied at all it must be as a military rather than as a civil organization. The formative period of the peculiar characteristics of the *colonia civium Romanorum* was seen to be just this long age of incubation, when the foetus did not yet possess an independent existence. Once this life began the *colonia* retained its birth-marks to the end, and multiplied them. There was developed a peculiar system of local life modelled on that of the great city to which all still belonged. For the liveliness of this imitation in the Ciceronian age and earlier there is the valuable testimony of Cicero himself, although for his own purposes he twisted all the facts. In this final form the institution of the *colonia* was bequeathed to the imperial age, to make of it what it would. But the durability of its essential

character shows it to be not a brilliant and ephemeral improvisation of Caesar but a plant of sturdy and lengthy growth, whose
roots are set centuries deep in the past.

## CONCLUSION

In the first quarter of the second century the Romans had
thoroughly accepted the principle of establishing large communities of their own citizens in remote regions, in precisely
the same fashion as formerly they had set up Latin states for
the same purpose.

By the time that the guidance of Livy fails it is clear that the
main lines of the development of the Roman territory as a collection of *municipia atque coloniae* are beginning to appear, but that
between these two classes hover a large number of diverse settlements—the *fora, conciliabula, pagi, vici, territoria*, and *loca*, which
are being held back from a true municipal development and from
assimilation to the increasing number of *municipia civium Romanorum* by two deterrents. First there is a conservative tendency
to regard the *tribus rusticae* as no more than the *territorium* of the
*urbs Roma*. The corollary of this is the system of *praefecturae*, to
which Rudolph is undoubtedly right in assigning a greater place
than has hitherto been allowed them, but wrong in failing to
distinguish between their different categories.

The second deterrent is perhaps the extreme subdivision of the
Roman territory. The *vici, pagi, castella* and the rest were not of
sufficient individual importance to form the basis, as they stood,
of a municipal system corresponding to that of the incorporated
states, each of which entered the Roman state as a large territorial
entity, with its own local traditions and history. The processes of
unification, attribution, and federation, which ended by creating
a series of *municipia civium Romanorum* throughout Italy, still lay
in the future. This is especially true of the Apennine regions of
the Roman territory which were surrounded by other Umbrian
and Oscan peoples, whose tribal organization remained so little
influenced by the town-states of the south-west, that it was
Roman policy to conclude treaties with the tribe, and not with
any subdivision such as the *populus*. The way was being prepared
in the meantime by the creation of true town-states, either Latin
or Roman colonies, on the coasts and in the heart of the mountain

regions. While Rome still felt herself as such a town-state, though the greatest of them, there was no special necessity to hasten the development of her villages into towns. But her continued policy of incorporating the *municipia*, and of founding colonies of either sort, shows that there was a definite policy fixedly pursued of encouraging municipal development, and of narrowing the circle of non-urban systems in Italy. But while the peninsula still remained under the form of federation, certain limits were set to the influence even of Rome.[1]

*Addendum.* For the evidence of a new fragment of a *Lex coloniae* from Puteoli, possibly of Augustan date, concerning the executive power of the magistrates, see below, 173.

---

[1] Somewhat similar views on the whole of this subject have been worked out by A. Bernardi, 'I *cives sine suffragio*', *Athenaeum*, 1938, 239 ff. But Bernardi, who seems not to have read the basic article of M. Konopka in *Eos* 32, 587 ff., offers an inadequate explanation of those aspects of *civitas sine suffragio* which were based upon non-Roman ideas of isopolity. Cf. below, 202 f.

# III

# ORIGINS AND DEVELOPMENT OF THE LATER LATINITY

## CHARACTER OF THE NEW LATIUM

THE institution of 'Latin rights' which at the close of the Republic and under the early Empire plays an important role, as the intermediary between peregrine status and Roman citizenship, springs directly from the settlement of 338, just as that settlement was but the natural consequence of the previous trend of the relations of Rome with the Latin states. That Latinity later became an instrument of Romanization, without the implication of any idea of race or nationality, is due to the curious character of the bond then established between Rome and the remaining 'Latin peoples', and extended to the new members of the Latin Name created during the following century and a half.

The Latins after 338 fall into two groups, the original Latin or Hernican states that remained unincorporated and the *coloniae Latinae*. What was the legal form by which these were joined to Rome is most obscure; the older name for them was simply the Latin Name, *nomen Latinum* or (*homines*) *nominis Latini*, but Livy more frequently calls them *socii nominis Latini*.[1] The clue to the understanding of the institution is that they are Rome's allies not on the ground of any treaty, but because they are recognized to possess a certain status. This recognition is a bilateral act between partners in fact unequal, one of whom is preponderant in the transaction. The members of the earlier *nomen Latinum* had severally performed the act of *deditio* to Rome,[2] and the Romans in their turn, by a process that foreshadows the treatment of the Campanians in 210, declared the various states to be 'free on certain terms'.[3] The traces of this procedure appear in Livy, who mentions specific terms such as the surrender of lands,[4] and the

---

[1] Mommsen, *St. R.* iii. 611 n. 2.      [2] Above, 60.
[3] Livy 26. 34. 7, 'liberos esse iusserunt ita ut . . .'      [4] Livy 8. 14. 9.

suspension of social relationship—'conubia commerciaque et concilia inter se', both for the Latins and later the Hernici.[1] The other course by which this recognition proceeded was the appointment of *tresviri* for the creation of a *colonia Latina* either by a law or by *senatus consultum*. It was on these declarations of status and on these charters that the duties and privileges of the Latins depended in the last resort. But these documents themselves did not exhaust the relationship between Roman and Latin in the same way as the treaty of a federated community. The *iura* which were confirmed by them formed a nexus of interpenetrating bonds far more complex than the specific obligations of a *foedus*.

Apart from Lavinium it is incorrect to speak of the Latins as *foederati*. The term is once used of them by Cicero, in a fashion which tests the rule. After casually referring to the Cassian treaty he goes on to treat the Latins of a later day as if they enjoyed the same status as the Prisci Latini. For the purposes of his case he slips in the phrase 'hanc Latinis, id est foederatis, viam . . . patere passi sunt'.[2] What better proof could there be than this rhetorical malpractice that the Latins were not *foederati* in the normal meaning of the term?

The disappearance of the *foedus* between the Hernican peoples and Rome and the assimilation of their status to that of the Latins are also apparent. At the time of the Hernican rising the loyal communities seem to have made some special act of submission to Rome, doubtless to prove their loyalty. Livy records the fact that 'tribus populis . . . suae leges redditae conubiumque inter ipsos permissum'.[3] The behaviour of Anagnia likewise necessitated a fresh settlement; for the Cassian treaty had been made not with the separate states, which probably did not then exist, but with the whole tribe, possibly under the leadership of the Anagnini, who in 307 revoked the agreement. This view is rendered probable by Livy's phrases 'concilium populorum omnium habentibus Anagninis' and 'omnes Hernici nominis . . . bellum indixerunt'. At any rate in later days the remaining *populi* appear not as special federates but as *Latini*. For example, 'novum ius a Ferentinatibus

---

[1] 8. 14. 10, cf. 9. 43. 24.

[2] Cic. *Balb.* 54, 'They left this way open to the Latins, that is, to the federated allies.'

[3] Livy 9. 43. 23, 'Autonomy was restored and intermarriage granted to the three peoples.'

temptatum ut Latini . . . cives Romani essent' is Livy's description of an attempt of the Hernici of Ferentinum, in 195 B.C., to gain admission to a citizen-colony.[1]

It is necessary to appreciate the somewhat intangible character of the bond between Rome and the Latin Name, because this explains not only much that would otherwise appear mere aggression and political interference on the part of Rome in Latin affairs, but also the far more important process by which *Latium* became the path to Roman citizenship, and almost a secondary form of the *civitas* itself. It is also well to stress the fact that no difference existed between the constitutional position, rights, and privileges of the *coloniae Latinae* and those of the few surviving members of the former *triginta populi* and those of the Hernici. When Livy mentions in one passage official letters sent *circa nomen Latinum* he means in particular Norba, Setia, Circei, and Praeneste.[2] The later entitlement of *Latini coloniarii* arose simply to distinguish ordinary Latinity from the lower status of Junian Latinity;[3] *coloniarii* was used because the majority of the states were colonies.

The main duty of the Latin Name was to supply Rome with troops, the *milites ex formula togatorum*; with the disappearance of the last shreds of the Cassian treaties the limitation of the obligation to assist only in defensive wars likewise vanished. Hiero's reported remark at the time of his offer of supplies for the war against Hannibal is important.[4] 'Milite atque equite scire, nisi Romano Latinique nominis, non uti populum Romanum.' This is not strictly true, but it demonstrates the distinction between the Latin and the federal allies of Rome. The federal allies fought on the Roman side, but her own army consisted essentially of the Roman and Latin forces, as is made abundantly clear by the military budgets in the later decades of Livy. This internal relationship in military affairs is illustrated by the contrast between the revolt of the *socii* during the Hannibalic war, and the

---

[1] Livy 9. 42. 11; 34. 42. 5, 'The Anagnini held a meeting of all their communities.' 'All folk of the Hernican Name declared war.' 'The Ferentinates sought for a new privilege, that Latins might become Roman citizens.'

[2] Livy 32. 26. 18; cf. 7–8; so 26. 8. 10 (Appiae viae municipia (!) . . . Setiam Coram Lavinium).

[3] Gaius, *Inst.* 1. 22–9, 79; 3. 56; Mommsen, *St. R.* iii. 625 n. 1. 629 n. 2.

[4] Livy 22. 37. 7. 'He knew the Roman people used only infantry and cavalry that came from Rome or the Latin Name.'

withdrawal of the forces of the twelve Latin colonies, which, despite Livy's rhetoric, was neither intended nor treated as an act of secession.[1]

This intimacy of union appears not only in the sphere of military obligation but in every aspect of Latinity; its note is heard consistently down to the Social War; afterwards it is the main characteristic of the status which was given to the Transpadane Gauls, and later its full flower is revealed in the Spanish charters of the Principate. It is largely to be explained by the fact that the greater part of the manpower of the Latin colonies was drawn from the body of the Roman citizens.[2] This proportion justified Livy in calling the colonies *Romanae*.[3] The fact is extremely important, because it enabled the Romans to trust the *nomen Latinum* to a degree which had been impossible before 338. Livy's phrase is perhaps coloured a little by Augustan views of Latinity, but there is much to suggest that the Latins held this opinion of themselves. The peculiar evidence of the early inscriptions all points this way;[4] in them the *coloniae Latinae* appear to imitate Roman institutions with riotous abandon; there are tribunes and aediles, even consuls, and *conscripti*, while at Cales and Ariminum the state is organized, like Rome, in *vici* bearing the Roman names. Cicero adds that the Latins sought to assimilate their institutions and customs to those of Rome by the adoption of *innumerabiles leges*, a statement which can only refer to the period before the Social War.[5]

This intense Romanization, with its corollary, the close political bond of Roman and Latin, emerges in full force throughout the later portion of Livy's extant narrative, from 218 to 167 B.C. These years form a period which, though terminated abruptly, presents an almost complete chapter in the history of Roman expansion; but for the internal history of Italy Livy provides rather a

---

[1] Livy 27. 9; 29. 15. Below, 104.

[2] Livy 9. 26. 4, Luceria, 'relegandis tam procul ab domo civibus'. Livy 9. 24. 15, 'plebis cuius . . . intererat tutam ubique quae passim in colonias mitteretur multitudinem esse'. Otherwise there is no indication of internal differences, e.g. Livy 10. 1. 2, 'Albam . . . sex milia colonorum scripta'. Livy 34. 42. 5 provides indirect evidence for the presence of non-Romans in Latin colonies, cf. Cic. *Pro Caec.* 98, 'in colonias Latinas saepe nostri cives profecti'.

[3] Livy 9. 23. 2; 27. 9. 10, 'admonerent . . . esse eos . . . Romanos'.

[4] Below, 117 f.

[5] *Balb.* 21, quoting the *lex Furia de testamentis* and *lex Voconia de mulierum hereditatibus*.

cross-section, in which the system established after the defeat of Pyrrhus can be seen at work and, later, modified. At this time *cives Romani atque* (*socii*) *Latini nominis* are commonly coupled together as an upper and lower division of a single class. In the Campanian decree it is provided that 'Campanos . . . liberos esse . . . . ita ut nemo eorum civis Romanus aut Latini nominis esset'.¹ In the *senatus consultum* regulating the status of Ambracia provision is made that 'portoria . . . caperent dum eorum immunes Romani ac socii Latini nominis essent'.² Very similar is the report of Duronius on conditions in Illyricum: 'multis civibus Romanis et sociis Latini nominis iniurias factas'.³ A similar conjunction appears in the text of the *S. C. de Bacchanalibus* and also in that of the *Lex Agraria*, both of which distinguish *Latini* from the ordinary Italian allies.⁴

One of the effects of this close relationship is that outside his own state the Latin falls under the care and cognizance of the Roman magistrates. The consular edict which ordered 'ut qui cives Cremonenses atque Placentini essent ante certam diem in colonias reverterentur' was no usurpation.⁵ The colonies, at least, had been established by Roman magistrates, to whom it naturally fell to maintain the numbers and very existence of the *coloni*. But the strongest indication of the narrow line which, in some respects, separated Latins from *cives Romani* at this period is shown by the acceptance of Latin volunteers for *coloniae civium Romanorum*.⁶

The territorial situation helped to create the new conception of the Latin Name. The settlement of 338 and its later development shattered for ever the territorial unity and continuity and the geographic limitation of Latium. The Latins henceforth form a

¹ Livy 26. 34. 6–7, 'The Campani were free provided that none of them should be a Roman citizen or belong to the Latin Name.'

² Livy 38. 44. 4 in 187 B.C., 'Let them collect their harbour-dues so long as Romans and Latins are exempt from them.'

³ Livy 40. 42. 4 in 180 B.C., 'Many Romans and Latin allies had suffered harm.'

⁴ *S. C. de Bacch.* (Bruns 36) 7–8, 'ne quis . . . ceivis Romanus neve nominus Latini neve socium quisquam'. *Lex agr.* 29, 'Latino peregrinoque'. Ibid. 31, 'quae pro moinicipieis colo[nieisve sunt civium Romanorum] nominisve Latini'—with no mention of the federated *socii* (Bruns 11).

⁵ 'Citizens of Cremona and Placentia were to return to their colonies before a fixed day.' Livy 28. 11. 11.

⁶ Livy 34. 42. 5–6, 'Adscripti coloni (Ferentinates) qui nomina dederant.' The later exclusion of these was doubtless due to protests of the government of Ferentinum on the score of improper *migratio*, cf. Salmon, *JRS* 1936, 63.

series of groups scattered up and down Italy. In 338 there were four groups of unequal size: the two colonies on the Etruscan borders, Nepet and Sutrium; one great tract of territory including the Hernican states, Praeneste, Cora, and the three colonies, Norba, Setia, Signia; and on the coast Ardea and Lavinium, while completely isolated—eventually surrounded by Roman territory—was Tibur. As the network of Latin colonies spread, this system developed throughout Italy; the Romans were never afraid of settling a group of conterminous colonies, such as Carseoli and Alba, or Cremona and Placentia.[1]

Since the Latin Name lacked a specific territorial unity the term was inevitably interpreted in a political and social sense alone, as meaning persons of a certain status. The separation of the geographic and political meanings of the term *Latium* is already complete in the early annalistic writers. For these Romans of the second century the presence of some *Latini* in Latium is incidental. Aulus Albinus, a contemporary of Cato, described himself as *homo Romanus natus in Latio*.[2] The phrase *in urbe Roma aut in Latio* is employed by the early writers on whom Gellius draws and comments, as a rough territorial division of the lands of the Roman state. Thus freed from geographic limitations the development of the *ius Latii* into a purely juristic concept was fairly rapid. It was the first political institution of the Roman state to be transplanted beyond the confines of Italy. It was most suitable for this purpose precisely because of this lack of any territorial connection such as bound the community of *cives Romani* to a specific area of Roman territory. By the time of the establishment of the Romano–Spanish *Partheniae* at Carteia, in 170 B.C., with the status of a Latin colony,[3] the emergence of the new concept is complete. This event also sets forth clearly for the first time the principle of connection between *Latium* and the Roman citizenship. These Spaniards who were given special Latin rights were the issue of Roman citizens on the male side. Their Latin status thus appears as a modification or diminution of Roman citizenship from which it originates and with which it partially coincides. Though conceived at this time, the principle

---

[1] Cf. maps in Beloch, *RG* ii and iii.

[2] Gellius *NA* 11. 8. 3, 'A Roman born in Latium.'

[3] Livy 43. 3. 1–4. Livy correctly speaks of a *novum genus hominum*—the institution of Latium is applied to a new situation and modified: 'Latinam eam coloniam esse libertinorumque appellari.'

had yet to go through a long period of incubation before it could issue forth as a separate form.

### THE NEW LATIUM AND ROME: EXTERNAL RELATIONS

The question is often asked, whether the Romans ever sought to reduce the privileges of the Latins. Mommsen held that in the third century there was an instance of this, arguing that the twelve Latin colonies founded in and after 268 B.C. were given a status inferior to that of the earlier settlements.[1] The basic evidence is a sentence of Cicero's, which compares the situation of Arretium in 81–80 B.C. to that of certain *duodecim coloniae* of which he names Ariminum, founded in 268.[2] 'Sulla ipse ita tulit de civitate ut non sustulerit horum nexa atque hereditates. Iubet enim eodem iure esse quo fuerint Ariminenses; quos quis ignorat duodecim coloniarum fuisse et a civibus Romanis hereditates capere potuisse?' By itself this passage is quite neutral; the words can take either a favourable or an unfavourable meaning. Cicero implies that the status to which Arretium was reduced was inferior to that of a *municipium civium Romanorum* from which it had been degraded, but as good as that of the twelve colonies; whether this latter was better or worse than that of other Latin communities he neither states nor implies. His *quos quis ignorat* may mean that these Latins possessed at least *commercium*, or equally that they possessed this and a great deal more beside.

The decision must thus depend upon what is otherwise known of the general situation in 268 B.C. Mommsen's opinion is largely determined by the desire to explain the sudden check suffered by the independent coinage of the Latin powers about this time. But better explanations of this could be offered than any desire to humble the Latins. The whole historical background of the period is completely out of tune with such a suggestion. Rome had conquered Pyrrhus through the splendid loyalty of the allies a few years before, and was still busy securing her hegemony, and tidying up the remnants of the Greek rebels. It was not a moment

[1] Mommsen, *St. R.* iii. 623 ff.

[2] *Pro Caec.* 102: 'Sulla's legislation about their civil rights was such as not to withdraw their privilege of forming contracts and receiving bequests. For he bade them be of the same status as the folk of Ariminum. And who does not know that the latter belonged to the twelve colonies and could receive bequests from Roman citizens?'

to tamper with the privileges of her staunchest supporters. Such interference is hardly conceivable till the second century, after Rome's eastern triumphs.

Beloch in turn sought to refer the passage to the twelve refractory colonies of 209 B.C. holding that their punishment in 204 was permanent.[1] His arguments against the existence of two groups of *duodecim coloniae Latinae*, each with inferior status and possibly overlapping, is sound; but the emendation of texts which he made to support his view is a desperate move when our knowledge of Republican history is so sketchy.[2] A. W. Zumpt pointed out long ago that the *duodecim coloniae* might even be the colonies of the elder Livius, a view which perhaps will not command much assent to-day.[3] There are various possibilities: one, that these *duodecim coloniae* of Cicero are something new, possibly connected with, e.g., the revolt of Fregellae; another, that these are, as Beloch says, the *duodecim* of Livy, but that Ariminum was placed in this category at some date after the termination of our text of Livy, the number being retained, as frequently numbers, such as that of the *triginta populi*, were retained long after their original significance had been partly or wholly lost.

Another interpretation has been put forward by E. T. Salmon.[4] He suggests that these are the twelve Latin colonies founded before 268 B.C., which did not refuse aid to Rome in 209 B.C., and hence did not suffer the special punishments of the refractory colonies.[5] The remaining six of the then-existing thirty he distinguishes as a separate group, all in fact founded after 268 and before the second Punic War, which in their own interests, perhaps at their own request, enjoyed only a limited form of the *ius migrationis*.[6] Salmon points out[7] that the Latins expelled from Rome in the second century for violation of the *ius migrationis* are those belonging to the two generations prior to the censorship of 204 B.C., and that some of the colonies founded in this period were not allowed to seek fresh *coloni* from Rome, i.e. were not— officially speaking—losing population by migration to Rome. He has made out a case, but his arguments are not wholly sound.

---

[1] *It. B.* 155 ff. Livy 27. 9; 29. 15.

[2] His argument that there were thirteen Latin colonies founded after 268 is untenable, since Luna was a citizen colony, cf. above, 78–9.

[3] 'De Coloniis Militaribus', *Commentationum Epigraphicarum Volumen*, 233 f.

[4] Art. cit. *JRS* 1936.    [5] Ibid. 58 f.    [6] Ibid. 60.    [7] Ibid. 57.

Livy does not in fact seem to be speaking in these passages of a section of Latins but of the whole Name, nor does he say that the two generations' test applied only to six communities.[1] Still less persuasive is the argument that colonies founded after 265 did not possess *conubium*, because they did not possess the complete *ius migrationis*, and so could not go to Rome to find wives;[2] for in, e.g., Cisalpine Gaul Latin and citizen communities existed side by side in the second century.

Whatever the exact truth about the *duodecim coloniae*, the categorical statement that in 268 B.C. a new type of Latinity was created must disappear from the textbooks. *Ius Latii* remained in its essence unchanged, whatever special arrangements might be made in the charters of individual Latin states, whether in 268 or 204 B.C.

As far as can be judged from the fairly numerous notices in Livy, down to 167 B.C. there were no special grades of Latinity. Instead, 'Old' Latins, Hernici, and *Latini coloniarii* are treated by him indifferently, especially in the discussion of constitutional privileges such as migration and the right to contract loans.[3] The only discriminatory act of which Livy knows is the sharp discipline to which his *duodecim coloniae* were subjected in 204 B.C.[4] But this punishment in no way affected the civil rights of the Twelve. Rome was concerned solely to exact the military quota from them, and to this end altered the scope of their census by compelling them to base their assessments on the Roman formularies, and to send to Rome a copy of their census rolls. The purpose of this was to enable the Romans to exact in future a larger contingent from the Twelve, who had already been bidden to provide thrice their normal quota for the current year.

Whether the Romans violated the political privileges and autonomy of these colonies by their action is another question. But the *duodecim* had after all failed to fulfil their obligations, and since their colonial constitution depended upon a unilateral act of Rome, there does not seem to be any reason why the Romans should not have modified the constitution in such a matter as the census formularies, while leaving the business of holding the census still in the hands of the local magistrates.

The examples of interference which undoubtedly appear in

[1] Livy 39. 3. 4, 'toto undique ex Latio'; 41. 8. 9, 'lex sociis Latini nominis dabat'.
[2] Salmon, art. cit. 61.     [3] Below, 108 ff.     [4] Livy 29. 15.

the early second century spring from a very different cause. They are not due to any Roman jealousy of the Latin cousins, but are the effect of the predominating position of Rome in Italy, and of the correlative fact that Rome was now beginning to govern Italy, in a sense not far removed from the modern. A gradual over-stepping of the boundaries was inevitable when the magistrates who had supreme power over the Latin military forces were also the civil heads of the Roman state, and the representatives of the power which had called the *coloniae Latinae* into existence. The steps which Rome took to deal with the affair of the Bacchanalia show how inevitable was Roman interference not only in the states of the Latin Name, but also among the *socii* proper. 'Per totam Italiam edicta mitti ne quis . . . coisse velit', 'datum consulibus negotium . . . ut . . . Bacchanalia . . . per totam Italiam diruerent', 'senatus consulto cautum est ne qua Bacchanalia Romae neve in Italia essent'.[1] Such phrases as these demonstrate how Roman control spread. Doubtless it was possible to avoid violating the forms of local independence. The *litterae hospitum de senatus consulto*[2] showed the local authorities how to act, but when the magistrates of Ardea were sent a prisoner to guard and warned not to let him escape, they were in effect being treated not as independent bodies but as administrative machinery. The very words show this—*magistratibus Ardeatium praedicendum ut . . .*[3]

This procedure recurs in a consular edict of 181 B.C.[4] which provided 'ut per totam Italiam triduum supplicatio et feriae essent'. Somewhat earlier the Romans had followed a less direct method: at the time of a slave riot in Latium the Roman *praetor* sent letters to the authorities of the Latin states asking for their assistance and co-operation.[5] This was doubtless the normal custom, and abandoned only in times of crisis and excitement. There is an example at a later date of great tact on the part of the Roman Senate in dealings with a Latin colony:[6] when Aquileia applied for assistance in the building of her city walls, the Senate by their question *vellentne eam rem C. Cassio consuli mandare?* showed

---

[1] Especially Livy 39. 14. 8; 17. 2 and 4; 18. 7–8: 'Orders were sent throughout Italy to prevent any intended conspiracy.' 'A *S. C.* provided that there should be no Bacchanalia at Rome or in Italy.'     [2] Livy 39. 17. 4.

[3] Livy 39. 19. 2, 'The magistrates of Ardea must be warned that . . .'

[4] Livy 40. 19. 5. 'a festival of thanksgiving is to be held throughout Italy'.

[5] Livy 32. 26. 18, 'ut et obsides in privato servarentur'.

[6] Livy 43. 1. 5 in 171 B.C. Cf. the *S. C. de Tiburtibus, ILS* 19. This adds nothing new.

that they required the consent of the colonial authorities before making a resolution. It is possible that the Roman magistrates gained a similar formal consent before the construction of Roman roads through the territory of a Latin colony, such as the Via Aemilia from Placentia to Ariminum, and the road from Bononia to Arretium.[1] But as these were the military measures of a consul, possibly there was no sense of interference.

The high-handed treatment of the magistrates and leading men of the *duodecim coloniae* in 204,[2] who were summoned to Rome and retained under arrest until their states had fulfilled their military obligations, is thus the exception; likewise it is only rarely, if ever, that the Latins found a consular commission knocking at their front door. But the occasions when there arrived news of *senatus consulta* and *edicta consulum*, which the local senate and magistrates were expected to adopt, were far more numerous. This process marks a change in the spirit and meaning of the Latin state, and is a great stride towards a true municipal system in which the local authorities would be the machinery for the performance of the demands of the central government. In this process Italian allies were treated much like the Latin Name, but where the Latins had so many other close connections with Rome, this is likely to have carried them further than it took the Italians, so that the *Lex Iulia* found a ready-made municipal system outside the Roman state which could be incorporated as a whole. It is worth remembering that the Latin colonies always retained the power of refusing to comply with some non-military requests of the *populus Romanus*. On almost the last extant page of Livy there is an example of such a refusal.[3] The Illyrian Gentius and his family were sent as state prisoners to Spoletium, *ex senatus consulto*. But the Spoletini refused the responsibility, and the royal family was removed to Iguvium.

The line that divided Latin from Roman may have been narrow, but still it existed. Both the distinction and the close relation of Latin and Roman are clearly marked by the arrangements which were made at various times for the division of booty. This is the heritage of the Cassian treaty, but the original 'third' is no longer maintained. Usually the Latin Name received the same amount as the *cives Romani*,[4] but once the Senate ordered

---

[1] Livy 39. 2. 10, 187 B.C.       [2] Livy 29. 15.
[3] Livy 45. 43. 9.       [4] Livy 40. 43. 7; 45. 43. 7.

a viritane land division in Cisalpine Gaul, in which the Latins received three *iugera* each, while Roman citizens were given ten.[1] On another occasion, we are told *sociis dimidio minus quam civibus datum*; that this was unusual is proved by their behaviour: *taciti ... secuti sunt currum*.[2] It is to be remembered that the Romans were strict with their own citizen-soldiers and citizen-colonies,[3] and that the Latins were usually getting more than their traditional share of booty. Certainly they were subject to the *imperium* of a Roman magistrate without appeal, but otherwise the Romans appear to have remedied grievances quickly: the consul of 193 sought to check hardships of the conscription among the Latins by providing for the raising of troops proportionately, *pro numero iuniorum*, instead, apparently, of demanding a fixed quota.[4]

In civil matters the Romans endeavoured to assist the Latins and to answer their complaints. On the two occasions when they protested against the migration of their people to Rome they received attention and relief.[5] It has been argued that the Romans left the Latins for ten years without redress from this injustice. This is not true. The first complaint, in 187, was followed by an inquiry and the compulsory return of 12,000 Latins to their homes. In the second case, in 177, Livy says that the Latins 'had worn out the censors and the previous consuls'. But since the censors concerned must be those of 179 and the consuls those of 178, there is no flagrant injustice here but normal delay. As soon as 177 substantial measures were taken to prevent any recurrence of the incidents, and all this was done at the instance of the Latins themselves. The government was clearly not interested at this time in schemes for the repression of the Latins, when it was prepared to allow them to acquire the citizenship so easily by migration. Nor were the financial regulations of 193 a blow to Latin privileges. This was an internal act of the Roman state which only concerned Latins accidentally, if their business partners happened to be *cives Romani*.[6]

[1] Livy 42. 4. 4.

[2] Livy 41. 13. 7–8, 'The allies were given half as much as the citizens; they followed the chariot in silence.'

[3] Cf. the affair of the *vacatio militiae*, Livy 27. 38. 3, in 207 B.C. and Livy 36. 3. 4–6, in 191 B.C.

[4] Livy 34. 56. 7.     [5] Livy 39. 3. 4–6; 41. 8. 6–12; 9. 9–12.

[6] Livy 35. 7. 1–5, 'in socios qui non tenerentur iis legibus nomina transcriberent ... plebes scivit ut cum sociis ac nomine Latino creditae pecuniae ius idem quod cum civibus Romanis esset.'

Apart from the inevitable extension of Roman influence which came when Rome began to exercise a general surveillance over Italy,[1] there is no policy of deliberately assailing the rights of the Latins. Instead there are a few isolated instances, of which the most important is the conduct of Postumius at Praeneste in 173. He employed the 'advisory letter' to further his private advantage, thus setting a bad example.[2] Livy is doubtless right in seeing in this affair the earliest symptom of the later deterioration of friendly relations between Rome and her allies.[3] But it is to be noted that it is not from the policy of the senate that the trouble springs, but from the abuse of the *imperium* by its holder. These incidents also served to check any gradual evolution of Latinity, any crossing of the thin line that separated the two categories of Roman and Latin, a transition which had seemed possible at the time when the Ferentinates attempted to conduct themselves *pro civibus*, but which was checked by the senate of the day. The Romans were not prepared to allow the informal assimilation of *Latini* to *Romani*. It is perhaps well that they checked the tendency, or they would have lost one of the most serviceable of many institutions for the Romanization of the western provinces.

The tendency was checked, but the Latins, with the notable exception of Fregellae, do not appear to have been embittered by the experience nor even by the harshness of the later Roman magistrates. They seem to have been somewhat unresponsive to Gaius Gracchus' attempts to enlist them in the cause of the *socii*, or to awaken them to a sense of their wrongs. In the history of the Social War, apart from Venusia, and despite the former destruction of Fregellae, which was left by fellow Latins to its doom, we hear of no Latin community voluntarily joining the Italici.[4] The Latins apparently felt themselves to be, if not Romans, at least the next best thing.

## THE IURA OF THE LATINI

Hitherto we have been considering the Latin states and their external relations with Rome rather than the precise nature of the

---

[1] Above, 103 f. Cf. Livy 42. 10. 8, 'ad . . . pestem frugum tollendam . . . praetor . . . cum imperio . . . missus'.

[2] Livy 42. 1. 7, 'litteras Praeneste misit ut sibi magistratus obviam exiret', etc.

[3] Livy 42. 1. 12, 'silentium nimis . . . modestum . . . Praenestinorum ius velut probato exemplo magistratibus fecit graviorum in dies talis generis imperiorum.'

[4] Cf. below, 136.

social and civil status of an individual Latin, and what his position meant to him. *Latium* or *ius Latii* is usually analysed as a bundle of rights possessed by the individual, but it is worth pointing out that the conception of Latin status as distinct from membership of a community attains importance only at a later date, although it appears early in embryo at Carteia in Spain. There, although the illegitimate offspring of *cives Romani* were recognized to be of a Latin status in virtue of their origin, they were immediately organized in a community, which took the form of a Latin colony.[1] Only with the creation of the *Latini Iuniani* does Latinity become merely the condition of a class within the state. Still the Latins, being individual men with private cares and interests, may be legitimately considered from this angle. As a person, the Latin possessed several rights, all more or less determined by the fact that he was a member of a certain community. Of these rights *commercium* and *conubium* are the most important, since they largely cover the sphere of social relations outside the particular community to which a man belonged. Inside that community the Latin was, of course, subject to the local laws, a free man.

That the Latins possessed *conubium* with the Romans has been disputed. Ulpian states that Roman citizens had *conubium* with Latins if it were granted specially, *ita si concessum sit*. But probably he refers only to the 'Junian Latins' of the Principate.[2] For the Republican period before the Social War there can be no doubt. The statement in Livy, 'Latinis populis conubia commerciaque... inter se ademerunt', implies that these rights persisted between Latin and Roman.[3] In the Empire provincial Latins possibly had scope enough for social life among their own people, but in the Republic the *Latini coloniarii*, in so far as they were recruited from Rome, had uncles and cousins who with their descendants always remained *cives Romani*.

There are several illustrations of the *commercium* of the Latins and Romans. The fragment of the *pro Caecina* shows that Ariminum and the mysterious *duodecim coloniae* possessed the main constituents of it, *nexa atque hereditates*,[4] while the debate over the migration problem shows that the Latins could then employ the forms of *mancipatio* in dealing with Roman citizens.[5]

[1] Cf. above, 101.  [2] *Tit. Ulp.* 5. 4, 9. Gaius 1, 56–7, cf. below, 379 n. 1.
[3] Livy 8. 14. 10.  [4] Mommsen, *St. R.* iii. 624 n. 1.
[5] Livy 41. 8. 10, 'liberos suos quibuslibet Romanis in eam condicionem ut manu

The possession of these rights was what constituted a large part of the close bond of Latins and Roman citizens. Without them it is difficult to see how that bond could have been so close or the fidelity of the Latins so intense. But once Latinity had assumed its essential character, and taken on a great deal of patriotic colouring, it would be possible to abridge some less essential portion of the rights included in *Latium*. Under the Empire, as has been said, it might only be occasionally, or accidentally, that the provincial Latin desired to exercise *conubium*. Yet in those days there was a regular number of ex-Latin *cives Romani* in every Latin community who had acquired the citizenship by holding the local magistracies, many of whose kindred and most of whose neighbours were Latins. In these circumstances it is hard to believe that under the Empire there were many *Latini coloniarii* to whom *conubium* had not been granted.

A third important part of early Republican *Latium* was the peculiar right of *migratio* to Rome.[1] We have seen that this corresponds to a very early institution of the tribal period of Latin history. How far this sank out of sight in the great days of the independent city-states is hard to tell. While the possible partial limitation of its exercise in 268 B.C. suggests that it remained lively, and the practice of *exilium* must have served to preserve it, there is no doubt that the increased value of the Roman citizenship after the second Punic War encouraged a sudden revival of the old custom, somewhat to the deteriment of the Latins themselves. Large numbers of Latins removed to Rome and by registering themselves at the census acquired Roman citizenship. Such an institution, however much Roman and Latin authorities sought to check its use, would at least keep alive the Roman traditions of the Latins, and encourage that sense of a specially privileged status second only to the Roman citizenship.

This right of gaining the franchise *per migrationem et censum* had

mitterentur mancipio dabant', i.e. before they themselves became citizens, because by that process they lost their *patria potestas*. Cf. *lex Salpensana* 22 where special provision is made 'ut qui c. Romanam consequantur maneant in eorundem mancipio manu potestate'. Also ibid. 23, 'ut . . . iura libertorum retineant'. Also Mommsen, *St. R.* iii. 629 n. 2, on *Tit. Ulp.* 19. 4, 'mancipatio locum habet inter cives Romanos et Latinos coloniarios . . . eosque peregrinos quibus commercium datum est'.

[1] Above, 34 f.; for its limitation, 103, 107.

disappeared by the time of the Social War, very probably in the interests of the Latins themselves. The view[1] that in 95 B.C. this way to citizenship was closed by the *Lex Licinia Mucia* is neither proved nor disproved by the references to this law, the essence of which was *de regundis civibus*, and consisted in checking illegal means of acquiring citizenship: 'esse pro cive qui civis non sit rectum est non licere.'[2] The censors had the remedy in their own hands where *migratio* was concerned. Nor was there much point in banning *migratio*, since the allies were at this time concerned with the rights and wrongs of their own communities, and not with securing personal preferment by change of domicile.

It is as a result of this last factor that there emerges in the period immediately before the Social War another path to citizenship. This is the acquisition of it *per magistratum*. When the Transpadane peoples were given Latin rights this element of their privilege was noted as the dominant feature. 'Cn. Pompeius Strabo . . . veteribus incolis manentibus ius dedit Latii: ut possent habere ius quod ceterae Latinae coloniae, id est ut per magistratus civitatem Romanam adipiscerentur.'[3] That Asconius is not interpreting history solely in the light of later events is shown not only by the whole story of the Social War, but by a passage in the *Lex Acilia* which presupposes the existence of the system.[4] To set the origin of the institution further back is not possible. So it was at this period that there emerged the idea of the contemporaneous exercise of a double *civitas*, partly personal and partly communal; furthermore a passage in Livy, which has been unjustly suspected, implies that before the second century the practice was unknown. The proposal of Sp. Carvilius to fill the gaps in the Senate by co-opting senators from the *populi Latini*, and in particular the words *ut . . . binis senatoribus civitas daretur* are decisive.[5] Livy and his sources knew of no Roman citizens in the Latin states, at this time,

[1] Mommsen, *St. R.* iii. 639 n. 2. A law of *c.* 180 limited it to those leaving sons, Livy 41. 8. 8–10, cited below, 127 n. 6.

[2] Cic. *Off.* 3. 47: 'it is right that those who are not citizens should not be allowed to behave as citizens.'

[3] Asconius (Clark) 3: 'Strabo gave Latin rights to the former inhabitants; they were to have the privileges of other Latin colonies, that is to get Roman citizenship by holding a magistracy'.

[4] 78. This concerns giving *provocatio* to those who '[in sua quisque⸴civitate dicta]tor praetor aedilisve non fuerint'. The implication is that in Latin states these would not yet have the citizenship *per magistratum* and might welcome some alternative reward. Since the fragment ]*tor* can only be completed as *dictator*, this part at least of the chapter refers to Latin states.
[5] Livy 23. 22. 5.

whose dignity as ex-magistrates would have fitted them even better than *senatores* for the proposed offer.

That the *ius adipiscendi c. R. per magistratum* was substituted for the *ius migrationis* is a view which receives some support from the contemporary practice of rewarding a successful prosecutor under the *Lex de repetundis* with the grant of the citizenship, to be held in his homeland.[1] The special privilege given to Marius of creating a certain number of new citizens in his colonial foundations, whether these were Roman or, as is more probable, Latin colonies,[2] shows how the Romans sought to compensate the Latins for their lost privileges; for since the founding of Aquileia, there had been no Latin foundations in which the Name could share. As a consequence, the first quarter of the last century B.C. saw the stabilization of the idea of *ius Latii* as an intermediate link between the condition of *peregrinus* and that of *civis Romanus*. The appearance of the *ius adipiscendi c. R. per magistratum* is the sign of this stabilization, which was rendered possible only by, first, the whole preceding history of the relationship between Rome and Latium and, second, a change in the conception of Roman citizenship itself. For the idea of formal passage from one status to another without change of domicile is a notion which could only emerge when the Roman citizenship began to lose some of its territorial and local associations. To gain the citizenship by *migratio* does not belong to the same level of political thought as the process *per magistratum*, since in the former the Latin changes his domicile, *solum vertit*, but in the latter enjoys his new rights in his old home. Hence the two systems, although they might in fact exist together, are not alternatives, but the one is built upon the foundation of the other.

The right of Latins resident in Rome to cast a vote in the popular assembly is another prerogative which probably belongs to the later period only.[3] But an alternative view is possible. It is in the *concilium plebis*, not in the *comitia populi tributa*, that according to Livy 'sitella lata est ut sortirentur ubi Latini suffragium ferrent'.[4] This right of voting may thus go back to a time when all Latin communities, Rome included, were divided socially into

[1] *Lex Acilia* 76, 77, 78. Cic. *Balb.* 53–4.
[2] Cic. *Balb.* 48. Cf. *CAH* ix. 169.
[3] Cf. above, 35; Rosenberg, *Hermes* 1920, 351.
[4] Livy 25. 3. 16, 'An urn was provided that they might draw lots as to where the Latins were to vote.'

*plebei* and *patricii*. Though of minor importance, this *suffragium incolarum* reappears in the Spanish charters as an element in the *Latium* of imperial times.[1]

The question remains, in what relation did the Latins stand to one another, and whether the concept of Latinity is exhausted by the charter or *lex coloniae* and the *iura* which the Latins shared with the Romans. The classical answer was that the Latin communities were isolated from one another.[2] But Mommsen, Beloch, and Gelzer are agreed that this separation was only a temporary measure.[3] In this they must be right. The clearest sign comes from the history of the loyal Hernican states which retained their ancient privilege of mutual *conubium*, and by implication *commercium* also. Livy adds the note, 'quod aliquamdiu soli Hernicorum habuerunt'.[4] This indicates that the punishment inflicted on the rebels was only a temporary measure. The growth of the Latin colony of Fregellae through the immigration of the federate allies of Rome, Samnites, and Paeligni, suggests that, if the Latins were allowed to deal thus freely with the Italian allies, they can scarcely have been forbidden similar relations with their Latin neighbours.[5] At least those Latin states which bordered on another Latin community must have possessed communal privileges, but as there were also a large number of isolated colonies, the practice of including the right of intermigration in the charter of a new Latin colony may not have been universal.

The treatment of Macedonia in 167 B.C. casts some light on the question of isolation. The Senate clearly followed principles which had been worked out in Italy and owed nothing to Greek sources.[6] Macedonia was divided into four self-governing regions, which were completely isolated from one another: 'neque conubium neque commercium agrorum aedificiorumque inter se placere cuiquam extra fines regionis suae esse.'[7] The idea of artificially isolating conterminous communities by forbidding them the use of legally enforceable contracts, was thus a leading motive in

---

[1] *Lex Malacitana* 53.         [2] On the basis of Livy 8. 14. 10.

[3] Mommsen, *St. R.* iii. 633. Beloch, *It. B.* 153, 221. Gelzer, *RE* art. cit. col. 963.

[4] Livy 9. 43. 23, 'which privilege they alone of the Hernici, for a while, preserved'.

[5] Cf. Livy 41. 8. 8, below, 127 n. 6.

[6] For the *status* of the Macedones see below, 179 f.

[7] Livy 45. 29. 10, 'It was resolved that none should have marriage rights or power to deal lawfully in land or buildings outside the boundaries of his own district.'

Roman policy of the middle of the second century. But the situation in Macedonia was very different from that of the Latin states of Italy after the expansion of the colonial system in the third century. There was no fear of treason or revolts from them. The destruction of the Council of the Latins at *Lucus Ferentinae*, and of that of the Hernici at *Circus Maritimus*, had in its time served a purpose similar to the fourfold division of Macedonia. Those *concilia* were never restored: but at a later date when the Latin Name was largely composed of ex-citizens, when Roman authority in Italy was without a rival, and when some communities at least had had their suspended rights restored, that communal isolation can have had no place in the idea of *Latium*. Some form of political association was permitted at the close of the third century, though no details are known.[1] Certainly in the first century, when *Latium* was given to large territorial areas such as Transpadane Gaul, whose peoples before the grant enjoyed normal intercourse, such artificial separation was unknown. The principle of isolation belonged not to the idea of *Latium* in itself, but to the political armoury of the Romans, who might at times associate it with *Latium* or employ it alone.

The process by which *Latium* passed from a geographical and tribal or sub-national concept to the idea of a social and political status or class was completed by the incorporation within the Roman citizenship of the last communities which were descended from the *prisci Latini*, after the Social War. Henceforth *Latium* was either the name of a district of Italy or a purely juristic term. The *ius Latii*, defined and fixed in the course of the historical adventures which we have discussed, became one of the favourite weapons in the store of Rome for the gradual elevation of provincial communities to a parity with herself. The greatest documentation of this is in the two Spanish charters, the *Lex Salpensana* and the *Lex Malacitana*.[2] An examination of them reveals how stable the conception of the Latin man and of the Latin community had become. There is the same intimate association of Latin and Roman separated by a narrow but distinct boundary. The closeness of this contact is marked by a very clear process of assimilation, not now of Latin magistrates to Roman, since the duumviral system rules unchallenged, but of law and legal practice.

[1] Livy 27. 9. 2, 'Fremitus enim inter Latinos sociosque in conciliis ortus.'
[2] *ILS* 6088, 6089.

Some instances of this may be given to show how continuous is the imperial with the republican Latinity. The chapter 'De Tutorum Datione'[1] contains the provision that 'Qui tutor hac lege datus erit, is ei cui datus erit. . . tam iustus tutor esto quam si is civis Romanus et ei adgnatus proxumus c. R. tutor esset'. Again 'De Obligatione Praedum' is remarkably explicit: 'ii omnes . . . in commune municipum eius municipi . . . obligati sunto ut ii populo Romano obligati . . . essent si apud eos qui Romae aerario praeessent ii praedes . . . essent.'[2] Somewhat less audacious is the copying of Roman electoral procedure: 'ne cuius comitiis rationem habeat qui . . . in earum qua causa erit propter quam si c. R. esset in numero decurionum conscriptumve eum esse non liceret.'[3] For here the reference is rather to municipal law, as the word *decurio* shows.

These instances drawn from official documents, which issue directly from Rome, prove that the imperial Latin like the republican was encouraged to make himself ever more quasi-Roman. Apart from these incomplete tendencies, the charters contain marks of perfected assimilation, such as the system of graded collegiate intercession.[4] But though the magisterial system differs little from that of Roman *municipia* and colonies, the intermediate status of the communities is marked by the importance of that ever-growing section of the population who gain the Roman franchise; for a large place in the fragments is occupied by the arrangements of relations between the two elements of the population.[5] Such a phrase as 'si quis municeps . . . qui Latinus erit'[6] indicates how this bridge-position of Latinity was always conscious and held in the foreground. This is the distinctive mark of the later Latinity, one that certainly does not go back far beyond the Social War, and one whose main presuppositions were created by that war, namely, that the Roman

[1] *L. Sal.* 29: 'Whoever is given as a guardian under this law is to be as proper a guardian to his ward as though he were a Roman citizen and his ward were his nearest agnate relation possessed of Roman citizenship.'

[2] *L. Mal.* 64: 'Let them all be bound to the common corporation of the borough as they would be bound to the Roman people if they were made securities before the officers of the Roman treasury.'

[3] Ibid. 54: 'Let him not take account at the elections of any person who if he were a Roman would be under a disqualification which prevented him from being reckoned among the local councillors.'

[4] *L. Sal.* 27.                                    [5] Ibid. 21–3.

[6] Ibid. 28: 'If any member of the borough who is of Latin status . . .'

state is an expanding state, with room to spare for all who are prepared to serve her and imitate her truly.

There is thus a distinction between the *Latinum nomen* of the early second century and the Latinity of the later Republic and the empire. This distinction itself arises from the change in the conception of Roman citizenship as discussed above. The earlier Republic knew of no passage from the lower status to the higher that did not involve a forfeit of local prerogatives. At some moment, possibly not before the passing of the *lex Acilia*, someone applied the developed conception of the *municeps* to Latinity. That created at a stroke the permanent form of *ius Latii*; by the exercise of its highest privileges the Latin becomes an individual or 'unattached' *municeps* retaining his place in his Latin state, whether *colonia* or *civitas*. Hitherto the Latins had formed an intermediate class between Romans and non-Romans but not a link. Henceforward they provide a passage by which non-Romans can become Romans.

This is that Latinity to which Gaius Gracchus and the younger Drusus contributed much. If it owes its form to any one man it is to Gaius. For the Latin *municeps* appears first in the Gracchan or quasi-Gracchan *lex Acilia*, and it was Gaius who first set *Latium* as an intermediate stage between that of *peregrini* and complete enfranchisement by his proposal to make citizens of the Latins and Latins of the *socii Italici*.[1] The formative period of the complete conception of *Latium* is thus the time of unrest preceding the Social War. Pliny's phrase *iactatum procellis rei publicae Latium* may conceivably refer to this important time in the history of Latin rights.[2] Even if another intepretation of the words is preferable, the fact remains that this most useful of political institutions reached maturity amid these 'storms of the republic'. Asconius' characterization of the Latinity which emerged in 89 B.C. agrees thoroughly with all we know of it from other sources. Despite minor modifications, such as the invention of *Latium maius*, the process was complete. For the imperial jurists just as for the Republican sources of Livy the world was divided into *cives Romani* and *Latini* over against the *peregrini*.

[1] Below, 136 f., 214 f.
[2] *NH* 3. 30, 'Latium tossed by the storms of the commonwealth'.

# APPENDIX

# THE INSTITUTIONS OF THE LATIN COLONIES

THE magistracies of the Latin colonies offer no real difficulties: either the constitution is of a simple *praetura* type, in which we can see only the descendant of the praetors of Latium and Latin states such as Rome, Lavinium, and Praeneste, or there is an attempt to copy the developed constitution of Rome, an attempt that is echoed by certain administrative arrangements based on a Roman model. There is no reason to imagine that there was any struggle between specially Latin separatist tendencies and a centripetal pro-Roman movement. It is probably a question of age or time. With flourishing fortune a Latin colony might well seek some more pretentious form of government than the pedestrian *praetura*. There is also the motive of administrative necessity, since in an enormous colony such as Beneventum or Venusia, the multiple lower magistracies would be a real advantage in coping with a burden of work that would have been too much for a simpler and less numerous executive.

*Praetores* appear at Cora, Signia, Setia, Cales and, according to Beloch,[1] at Interamna—all founded before 312 B.C.,[2] but also at Beneventum, Aesernia, and Spoletium—founded between 263 and 241.[3]

There are also *duoviri* known at one of these places where the *praetura* was normal, i.e. at Aesernia,[4] and several instances of *duoviri* are known at other Latin colonies, i.e. at Paestum, Ariminum, and Aquileia.[5] The fact that *duoviri* occur also at Cora[6] suggests that not all these are to be regarded as the remnants of transitory military colonies of the first century, despite Beloch,[7] but that these *duoviri* may be connected with the Romanizing tendency exhibited by the *consol pro poplo Ariminense*,[8] the tribunes and quaestors of Venusia,[9] the five quaestors of Firmum,[10] the aediles of Narnia,[11] and the censors of Copia and Beneventum.[12] This would mean that instead of copying the institutions of Rome directly, the Latins sometimes copied those of the *effigies et simulacrum*, the Roman colonies, though it is equally possible that the borrowing was the other way round in this case.[13] The *praetura* is not to be regarded as essentially Latin rather than Roman, since *Italici*

---

[1] *RG* 490.
[2] *CIL* x. 6527, 5969, 6466, 4651, 5203.
[3] Ibid. ix. 1635, 2664; xi. 4822.
[4] Ibid. ix. 2662.
[5] Ibid. x. 480; xi. 385, 400; v. 971.
[6] Ibid. x. 6517. Beloch, *RG* 491, suggests that they are *IIviri aedi dedicandae*.
[7] Loc. cit.
[8] *CIL* xiv. 4269.
[9] Ibid. ix. 438–40.
[10] Ibid. ix. 5351.
[11] Ibid. xi. 4125.
[12] Ibid. x. 123; ix. 1635.
[13] Cf. above, 90 f.

sometimes exchanged their *meddices* or other magistrates for it, when they had no motive to copy any but Roman institutions.[1] That the distinction of 'Roman' and 'Latin' in this matter is unreal is shown by the combination of *censor* and *praetor* at Beneventum, and of *duovir* and *praetor* at Aesernia—the only real issue is one of dignity, whence comes the title of *aedilis curulis* at Ariminum.[2]

In general these inscriptions, even in their *minutiae*, support the view that the bond of Latinity was the closest of all the forms known to the Roman federation.

[1] Cf. below, 129 f.        [2] *CIL* xi. 385.

# IV

# THE POSITION OF THE ITALIAN SOCII IN THE ROMAN SYSTEM

NEXT to the Latin Name and of partially similar rank stand the Italian allies, the *socii* proper, or *foederati*. It is easier to fix their precise status because the bond that links them to Rome is external and the terms of it are expressed in distinct treaties. There is not the same fusion of social status to confound the issue. The *socii* stand further off from the Roman state than the Latins, yet from one aspect, that of military obligation, there is so little distinction to be observed between them that Cicero could fuse the two together in the formula *Latinis id est foederatis*.[1] The peculiarity of the status of the Italian allies is based upon the fact that they are true 'foreigners' in language and geography, while politically their communities and institutions owed nothing to the common springs of Latium. Furthermore, except for some Umbrian and a few Apulian states, the *socii* entered the Roman alliance after considerable fighting and sometimes desperate resistance. This combination of circumstances determined the character of the Roman federation outside the territory of Rome and that of the Latin Name. The comparative simplicity of the account which can be given of the relationship between Rome and the *socii* is not entirely due to the meagreness of our information, but reflects the simplicity of the relationship itself. There is far less interpenetration of rights and loyalties than between Rome and *cives sine suffragio* or the *Latini*.

Rome emerged from the Latin period of her history with a number of political conceptions already hammered into shape, which she was able to apply schematically in the wide world of Italy. Of these the *foedus aequum*, and still more the *foedus iniquum* —the treaty between equals, and the treaty between unequal partners—served to unite under her leadership the independent states of Italy. Because of this schematic character there is nothing

---

[1] Cic. *Balb.* 54, cf. above, 97.

to be gained by surveying the history, i.e. the progressive growth in a time-series, of the federation of allies. Except in size and number there is little development, a fact which is largely responsible for the differing attitude of the *socii* and of the *socii Latini nominis* at the time of the Social War. Growth or progress in the character of the federation is limited to a tendency towards Romanization of institutions within the federated states, and the mounting ascendancy, outside, of the Roman power, built upon the broad foundation of the allies themselves.

If we ask, what, from the Roman position, was the special purpose of the *societas* as distinct from Latinity or the *civitas sine suffragio*, the answer lies in the greater looseness of the bond, such as analysis reveals to us. The view of Fraccaro that *societas* and the federal system was substituted for the system of *civitas sine suffragio*[1] is hardly correct, in so far as the two systems overlap in time. But there is no doubt that the character and purpose of *civitas sine suffragio* had changed radically by the later period of its use, so that Fraccaro's remark is justified by a survey of the whole history of the Italian federation; for the Romans avoided any further employment of *civitas sine suffragio* after the first quarter of the third century in dealing with the mainstay of their federation, the Oscan peoples, and never employed it later in Etruria. The federal system is thus easy to understand, because in its origins it closely resembles the national alliances of any other group of peoples, ancient or modern, for certain limited common purposes. It was only when these purposes were fulfilled and Rome no longer stood as merely the largest of a number of associated communities, that the history of the federation took a peculiar twist and there began that process of development which ended in the Social War.

The chief, though not the earliest, instrument in the formation of the federation of allies was the specially Roman institution of the *foedus iniquum*. Livy records what purports to be a debate between the emissaries of Antiochus Epiphanes and Titus Quinctius on international relations. The three kinds of treaties which the Greeks discuss omit what was to the Roman the most important of all, because the Greeks can see no intermediate stage between the case 'cum bello victis dicerentur leges' and that 'cum

---

[1] P. Fraccaro, 'L'Organizzazione Politica dell'Italia Romana', *Atti del Congr. Intern. di Diritto Rom.* (1), 1934, 204.

pares bello aequo foedere in pacem atque amicitiam venirent'.[1]
But such a situation 'cum impares bello iniquo foedere in pacem
atque amicitiam venirent' is precisely what the Romans faced
again and again in the period between 338 and the end of the
second Punic War. The *foedus iniquum* differs from the *foedus
aequum*—of which the Cassian treaty preserves the essential element, namely that it is a defensive alliance of equal partners—in
that one of the contracting parties is subordinate to the other : the
*socius* is bidden *maiestatem populi Romani comiter conservare*, and
is bound to assist Rome in wars where the allies' own interest is
not at stake.[2] In the Italian federation the conspicuous example
of a *foedus aequum* is that of the Umbrian Camertes.[3] Livy notes,
after giving the list of volunteers for the African campaign of 205,
that the Camertes sent a cohort, although their *foedus* was *aequum*,
'cum aequo foedere cum Romanis essent'. This is the clue to the
understanding of the federation. At an early period Livy noted
the formation of a treaty with the Teates Apuli, who were worn
out by Roman forays, 'neque ut aequo tamen foedere sed ut in
dicione populi Romani essent'.[4] This kind of arrangement
appears gradually to have become the rule, and the *foedus aequum*
the exception. After much fighting, or after some signal defeat,
the restless Sabellians send an embassy to Rome and ask for a
treaty.[5] The striking of this treaty with a submissive or defeated
people is the special mark of the Roman federation. There are
other methods of procedure when relations between the two
powers have been entirely friendly; the *foedus* of the Camertes
was one such, and another was the enrolment of the Ocriculani

---

[1] Livy 34. 57. 7 : 'The dictation of terms to the defeated.' 'When military equals
form an agreement of peace and friendship on equal terms.'

[2] 'To preserve the *"bigness"* of Rome in a friendly way.' Cf. below, 183 ff. for
a fuller discussion of *foedera* texts, for which the evidence is mainly non-Italian.
For formation of *maiestas* from the root *mag* cf. *facultas, honestas, paupertas*.

[3] Livy 9. 36. 8; 28. 45. 20. Cic. *Balb.* 46, 'Foedus omnium . . . sanctissimum
atque aequissimum'. Cf. *Arch.* 6, 'aequissimo . . . foedere', of Heraclea.

[4] Livy 9. 20. 4 and 8: 'They were not to be allied on equal terms, but to be
under the sway of the Roman people.' Cf. Conway on the text, ad loc.

[5] e.g. Livy 9. 45. 18: 'De Aequis triumphatum ; exemploque eorum clades fuit,
ut Marrucini Marsi Paeligni Frentani mitterent Romam oratores pacis petendae
amicitiaeque.' Next 'his populis foedus petentibus datum'. Cf. the advice given to
Philip of Macedon. Livy 33. 35. 5, 'quoniam pacem impetrasset ad societatem
amicitiamque petendam mitteret Romam legatos'. Later the Vestini, Livy 10.
3. 1, 'petentibus amicitiam ictum est foedus'. Then the Lucani, Livy 10. 11.
11–12. 2.

as allies by the process described as *sponsione in amicitiam accepti*.[1] But the general custom —generated by the persistent resistance to the spread of the Roman power—was the *foedus* of the lower type.[2] The peculiarity properly consists in the bilateral compact between Rome and a state which has made an act of *deditio* or surrendered itself *in fidem*. The clearest example is in the negotiations with the Lucani, who before the last struggles with Samnium urgently ask for a treaty and are prepared to give hostages for their good behaviour.[3]

The special character of the *foedus iniquum* during the period of the expansion of Rome in Italy consisted not only in a clause such as appears later in the *foedus Aetolorum*, 'If the Romans make war against others let the Aetolian people make war against Rome's enemy',[4] but even more in the introductory phrase, stressed and explained by Cicero 'imperium maiestatemque populi Romani comiter conservanto'.[5] The situation in Italy, with the Sabellian tribes ever attempting to expand into the lands of their neighbours, whether fellow-Sabellians or of other stock, was such that the Roman wars either were, or appeared to be, wars of defence. Not perhaps till the second century did the Romans need to exploit the aggressive clauses of the treaties. The instance of the Lucani shows how the federal system worked: 'ictum foedus. Fetiales missi qui Samnitem decedere agro sociorum ac deducere exercitum finibus Lucanis iuberent.'[6] Compliance being refused, Rome declared war on the Samnites. The Lucani clearly had no grounds to complain of the effects of a *foedus iniquum*. One can see how, as long as Roman expansion was confined to Italy, the obligation *maiestatem p. R. conservare*, to which all were gradually bound, was no hardship. But a time

---

[1] 'Received into friendship by guarantee', Livy 9. 41. 20. Cf. the *foedus* with the Picentes *minus cunctanter ictum*, because of the news of a *tumultus Gallicus*, Livy 10. 10. 12.

[2] Apart from the Samnites, e.g. the Marsi after the first *foedus* resisted the foundation of Carseoli, a Latin colony. Hence, Livy 10. 3. 5, 'Valerius Maximus . . . conpulsis deinde in urbes munitas . . . Marsis foedus restituit'—hardly a *f. aequum*.

[3] Above, 121 n. 5. Note the phrase *in fidem accipiant*.

[4] ἐὰν πολεμῶσι πρός τινας οἱ 'Ρωμαῖοι πολεμείτω πρὸς αὐτοὺς ὁ δῆμος ὁ τῶν Αἰτωλῶν. Polyb. 22. 15. 4. Livy 38. 11. 3. Cf. below, 185 n. 1.

[5] *Balb.* 35–7. The term *foedus iniquum* itself is directly testified in historical Latin only (it seems) in Livy 35. 46. 10.

[6] Above, 121 n. 5. 'The treaty was solemnized. Ministers were sent to bid the Samnites vacate the territory of the allies and withdraw their army from the lands of the Lucani.'

came when the essential factor which had made possible the
growth of the federation was removed by the pacification of the
Italian peóples and the establishment of friendly relations among
them all. Then, when Rome could no longer claim that her
Fetiales were 'asking things back' for her allies as much as for
herself, the whole character of the federation of the *foedus
iniquum* was changed in spirit, though not a letter had been added
or removed.

These various marks of the *foedus iniquum*, and the comparative
unimportance in the early period of the clause providing for assistance in aggressive wars, can be illustrated negatively from the
history of the Roman advance in Etruria. Here there was no
conflict of settled states and restless Sabellians to provide a motive
for Roman assistance or interference. Hence the advance of Rome
in Etruria came later. The strength of Etruria shrank but gradually even after the fall of Veii, while on the Etruscan side perhaps
the Gallic threat exhausted its main force before Rome seemed
worth consulting; or it may be that the Etruscans were as suspi-
cious of the Romans as the latter undoubtedly were of them, or
else the Etruscans were not sufficiently interested in the recovery
of their lost strongholds to invite foreign assistance.[1] The Romans
in their turn behaved far more timorously towards the northern
powers than towards the southern, once they had secured the
fortresses of Nepet and Sutrium. The early inter-state relations of
Romans and Etruscans are on a strange footing. In place of the
*foedus* providing for 'honest and eternal peace' the normal arrangement is a truce of limited period, *indutiae triginta*, or *quadraginta*,
or even *centum annorum*.[2] During the final conflagration Rome
sometimes refused even this, binding herself by no more than
an annual truce.[3] Only once according to Livy did Rome contract
a *foedus* with an Etruscan state—Falerii. He uses a curious phrase
which deliberately stresses the rarity of the event: 'the result of

---

[1] The request in Livy 5. 33. 1 came to nothing.

[2] Livy 4. 35. 2       20 years truce with Veii.

| | | | | |
|---|---|---|---|---|
| 5. 27. 6 and 15 | unfixed | ,, | ,, | Falerii. |
| 5. 32. 5 | 20 years | ,, | ,, | Volsinii. |
| 7. 20. 8 | 100 ,, | ,, | ,, | Caere. |
| 7. 22. 5 | 40 ,, | ,, | ,, | Volsinii and Falerii. |
| 9. 37. 12 | 30 ,, | ,, | ,, | Perusia Cortona Arretium. |
| 10. 37. 4 | 40 ,, | ,, | ,, | Volsinii Perusia Arretium. |
| 10. 46. 12 | *Annuae* | ,, | ,, | Falerii. |

[3] e.g. Livy 9. 41. 7.

this battle forced even the Faliscans, although they enjoyed a truce, to ask the Senate for a treaty.'[1]

This state of affairs corresponds well with the conspicuous difference between Rome's destruction of Veii in 396, and her incorporation of Tusculum in 380. In dealing with the Etruscans Rome was facing an entirely new situation. They were a people whose material culture was both older and superior and whose language and organization offered few analogies to that of Rome —whatever may be thought of the forgotten Etruscan origin of some Roman political or religious usages. But in her affairs with the Umbrians and Oscans, including the Sabellian conquerors of Campania, Rome was the more venerable, and as a Latin people, shared by race and language, though a member of a different species, the same Italic genus.

The status of the Etruscan cities when they were eventually federated with Rome is extremely obscure.[2] They certainly provided Rome with some troops, for a *Perusina cohors* is mentioned in the Punic wars.[3] But in the account of preparations for the African war of 205 the contribution of the eight cities named is entirely material,[4] a fact which recalls the war indemnities which were earlier the regular accompaniment of the *indutiae*. Apart from a reference to Volsinii as ἔνσπονδοι, 'in alliance', which could refer either to a truce or a treaty, the exile-right of Tarquinii and the revolt of Falerii in 241,[5] there is no further information. It is hardly probable that their *indutiae* were made permanent and became a form of *foedus*, yet the fact remains that there is only one example of a *foedus* between Rome and an Etruscan state.[6] The *municipium foederatum* later known at Capena has another explanation, and the grant of *civitas sine suffragio* to Caere presents no difficulty.[7] Caere was early cut off from Etruria by a ring of ager Romanus, while the population has been shown to contain a strong non-Etruscan element. When one recalls also the grave suspicion with which the Romans regarded the Etruscans throughout the second Punic War, continually maintaining a military force of usually two legions in the country, it is hard to believe

---

[1] Livy 7. 38. 1. Cf. 5. 27. 15, where *pax* with *stipendium* means *indutiae*. Also ibid. 6, 'Nobis cum Faliscis quae pacto fit humano societas non est.'

[2] Cf. Beloch, *RG* 609 ff.    [3] Livy 23. 17. 11.

[4] Livy 28. 45. 13 f.    [5] Strabo 226 C. Zonaras 8. 18.

[6] Above, n. 1.

[7] Above, 55 f.

that the states were bound by more favourable treaties than those of the Italic peoples.[1] It is scarcely necessary to enlarge upon the strength of the racial sentiment in causing this difference in the Roman attitude to two different sets of allies.

The *socius* was thus a member of a city-state or a tribal unit which, in most instances, had agreed to 'respect the majesty of the Roman people'. By this there was demanded of the *socius* a specific declaration of what remained implicit but unspoken in the relation of the Latin Name to Rome. We can trace a certain continuity in this concept which links together by community of principle the *civis Romanus*, the *Latinus*, the *civis sine suffragio*, and at last the *socius iniquo foedere*. All share in ever-increasing proportion the burden of maintaining unbroken the power and dignity of the Roman name. Here in embryo is the thought of Rutilius Namatianus.[2]

There were other more tangible obligations and privileges contained in the status of *socius*. In return for their military service, which, as Polybius' account of the Roman system makes clear, was the most important aspect of the *socius* in Roman eyes,[3] the allies might receive some share of the *iura* which the Latin Name enjoyed as a matter of course. A vague reference in Diodorus suggests that some enjoyed at least *conubium* and presumably *commercium* also.[4] This is supported by the evidence of extensive financial dealings between Romans, Latins, and other allies revealed by a debtors' crisis in 193 B.C. Although much of this business might be transacted under the jurisdiction of the *praetor peregrinus*, Livy's reference on that occasion to 'cum sociis ac nomine Latino creditae pecuniae ius' suggests that some of the persons concerned enjoyed *commercium*, that is, the right to enforce their contracts according to the ordinary forms of Roman law.[5] There is not enough evidence exactly to analyse the extent to which Italy became bound together by economic and social ties. The *lex agraria* distinguishes between the privileges enjoyed by Latin communities and those held by other Italian peoples in a way which suggests that the greater advantage tended to be with

---

[1] Cf. e.g., Livy 27. 21 ; 24.
[2] Below, 464.
[3] Cf., e.g., Polyb. 6. 21. 4; 26. 5–7; 31. 9.
[4] Diodorus 37. 15. 2 (during the Social War), συχνοὺς . . . ὁ τῆς ἐπιγαμίας νόμος (= *ius conubii*) ἐπεποιήκει κοινωνῆσαι . . . φιλίας.
[5] Livy 35. 7. 5, 'the privilege of financial transactions with the allies and Latins'.

the Latins.[1] The key to the understanding of the position of the *socii* consists precisely in this, that they are a number of nominally independent states brought by artificial means into a condition which resembles externally that of the Latins but is in fact very different, because the *socii*, while performing the same duties as the Latins, are bound to Rome only by external bonds. Their privileges are only a selection from those of the Latins, and follow not in a block from their status as a matter of course, but from individual, separate grants.

This theory is explicitly set forth not only in the later jurists but also in Polybius' discussion of *exilium*.[2] Such grants of exile-rights are recorded at Nuceria, Naples, and Tarquinii.[3] The information about the last-named makes it possible to fix the moment when *exilium* was first singled out and separated as a *ius*. Livy records the ratification in 211 B.C. by the People of the extension of this privilege to a non-Latin federated community in the words: 'Cn. Fulvius exulatum Tarquinios abiit. id ei iustum exilium esse scivit plebs.'[4] Possibly theory is only following a long current practice, but henceforth *exilium* was a distinct *ius*; it is the latest of the general *iura* evolved from the racial customs of the Latin Peoples. In the process a special influence is at work, for Cicero says: 'the right of changing one's citizenship depends not only on the laws of the state but also on the wish of the individuals.'[5] The will of both parties is concerned, 'a man is under no disability to change his citizenship provided he is adopted by the state to which he wishes to belong'. Here there emerges the effect of Rome's experience in a world which was not limited to Latium or even to Italy.

By this dual role of privilege and obligation the state of *socius* shows the strongest analogy to that of Latin and *civis sine suffragio*. The same principle applies, that the *socius* undertakes or accepts, in accordance with the explicit conditions of his treaty,[6] what was

---

[1] Above 100 n. 4.

[2] Polyb. 6. 14. 8, ἔστι δὲ ἀσφάλεια τοῖς φεύγουσιν ἔν τε τῇ τῶν Νεαπολιτῶν . . . πόλει καὶ ταῖς ἄλλαις πρὸς ἃς ἔχουσιν ὅρκια. The last phrase seems to mean 'aliis urbibus quibus hoc iure foedus intercedit cum Romanis' (Schweighäuser), i.e. not *omnibus urbibus*. Cf. 'Mancipatio locum habet inter cives Romanos et Latinos coloniarios . . . eosque peregrinos quibus commercium datum est', *Tit. Ulp.* 19. 4.

[3] Polyb. 6. 14. 8. Cic. *Balb.* 27–9.

[4] Livy 26. 3. 12. Cf. above, 34 f. 'Cn. Fulvius went into exile at Tarquinii. The *plebs* declared that it was a legitimate exile.'

[5] Loc. cit.        [6] Cf. the *foedus Mamertinorum*, Cic. *Verr.* ii. 5. 50.

implicit in the very status of the former. The sphere of the obligations or privileges is proportionally narrower for the *socius* than
for the Latin or the *civis sine suffragio*. All three exhibit the
characteristics of the *municeps* in varying degree, but the condition of the *socius* is least advanced. The more one considers the
status of the allies the more inevitable their incorporation and the
municipalization of Italy appears. At every step there are to be
found parallels and analogies to the processes which influenced
the development of the Latin states.

Nominally the Italian allies were autonomous peoples, so far as
autonomy is compatible with subordination to the foreign policy
of another power, and with the obligation to provide troops for
its wars.[1] Apart from the few *foedera aequa* this subordination is
the special characteristic of the period that opens in 338 B.C.[2] It
was a new idea at this time to the Fundani and others that alliance
with Rome entailed abstention from hostilities with other allies
of Rome. Before 338 this had not generally been so.[3] Thus 338
marks the beginning of a true period in which the new style of
confederacy takes that shape which is repeated later in the history
of the Roman federal system outside Italy.[4] The subordinate
position to which in course of time even the holders of *foedera
aequa* appear to have been reduced, by the force of circumstances
rather than by any legal alteration of status, left to the allies only
a municipal autonomy. The greater freedom which they enjoyed
in their relations with other Italian states, when compared with
the Latins, perhaps extended the limits of this autonomy. They
could, for instance, readily exchange rights of citizenship with
their neighbours,[5] and were not subject to Roman ordinances in
the matter of migration to other states.[6]

Yet the Italian states fell under the controlling influence of
Rome, much in the same way as the Latins, when in the second
century Rome began to usurp the functions of a central government in the Italian peninsula. The fact that the Senate worked
through the local authorities preserved the formalities, without

---

[1] e.g. Livy 41. 7. 8. Cf. *lex agr.* 21, 50. Sall. *Jug.* 39. 2.
[2] e.g. Livy 8. 19. 5; 10. 1. 3. Above, 48.
[3] e.g. Livy 8. 2. 13.
[4] Cf. below, 183 f.                                    [5] Cic. *Arch.* 5, 10.
[6] Livy 41. 8. 8–10. When the Samnites complain of loss of citizens to Fregellae,
the restriction *ut stirpem domi relinquerent* does not apply to the Samnites. *Legationes
socium Latini nominis* is contrasted with *Fregellas quoque Samnites . . . querebantur.*

altering the fact that the states were being gradually municipalized. The evidence is less abundant than for the Latin Name.
The precise application of such a phrase as 'consules edixerunt
ut per totam Italiam triduum supplicatio et feriae essent' is uncertain,[1] but the Italian states at the time of the Bacchanalian
scandal accepted or submitted to the consular *quaestio*.[2] Livy's
narrative, with its reference to the diplomatic messages, the
*litterae hospitum*, sent from Rome to inform the allies of the measures
proposed, suggests that up to a certain point the Senate employed the local machinery.[3] The actual *senatus consultum* supports this view. It is, as the commentators point out, a letter
sent by the consuls to the local magistrates, who are expected to
comply with its recommendations.[4] More decisive is the part
Rome or Romans played in arbitration between states;[5] for this
is the correlate of the surrender to Rome of all military independence. The invitation of Roman commissioners to settle these
disputes over boundaries, an invitation for which the initiative
lay with the Italians, shows that there was a centripetal tendency
among the allies corresponding to the inclination of Rome to
assume the government of Italy. The Italians turn to Rome
for advice and offer no resistance to her usurpations. In the affair
of Genua and the Viturii there is a particularly clear instance of
the preponderance of the central power, because the Viturii were
*attributi*, subjects of Genua, appealing against the decision of
the Genuan court to a higher authority.[6] There was of course no
formal violation of the prerogatives of Genua, since the arbitra-
tor's decision was phrased in the language of advice—an 'ought',
*oportere videtur*, takes the place of a 'must', a *iubet* or a *ne quis*.

Similar veiled interference may have occurred when the
Romans took in hand the building of roads throughout Italy. But
though from the date of the building of the Via Cassia in 177 B.C.
onwards these roads passed through much allied territory, there
is no necessity to suppose any neglect of proper formalities.[7] The

---

[1] Livy 40. 19. 5, 'The consuls ordained that there should be a thanksgiving and
festival for three days throughout Italy.' Cf. above, 105 and n. 4.

[2] Livy 39. 18. 7.                                                      [3] Ibid. 17. 4.

[4] Bruns (7) 36. The *foederati* of the opening clause clearly have nothing to do
with the 'ceivis Romanus neve nominus Latini neve *socium* quisquam', and do not
concern *socii*.

[5] e.g. Livy 45. 13. 10–11.                          [6] *ILS* 5946. 43–4, in 117 B.C.

[7] Cf. Beloch, *It. B.* 214.

formal violation of rights and the scandals recorded by Livy and Gellius are not of such permanent importance as the gradual narrowing of the sphere of interest and of the competence of the local authorities, counterbalanced at Rome by a growing sense of responsibility towards the Italian allies.[1] This appears in such acts of arbitration and police measures as have been quoted, and especially in such instances of intervention as in the serf risings of Etruria, where the Roman *praetor* restored order.[2] These two related tendencies formed the foundation for the future incorporation of the Italian states in the Roman citizenship, for which the performance of military service alone would have been an inadequate basis. The localization of the states was so complete, the penetration of Roman authority so thorough, and the performance of military *munera* so customary, that the Italian allies were not only justified in their demands, but fitted, from a Roman point of view, to receive the citizenship. They had been not only the subjects but the pupils of Rome, both in the art of war and in the conduct of public affairs.

Beloch has suggested that by the time of the Social War the constitution of each allied state was a more or less close copy of the constitution of Rome.[3] But this judgement is only partly justified by the epigraphic evidence on which it is based. The chief document of this movement is the Oscan inscription known as the 'Tabula Osca Bantiae reperta', belonging to the close of the second century B.C.[4] It contains the revised constitution of Bantia in Lucania, and reveals an intimate blending of Roman and non-Roman elements, such as makes it impossible to agree with Beloch when he speaks of the withering of the creative political spirit among the Italian allies, and of the Romanization of their institutions as mere 'imitation'.[5] The investigations of Rosenberg illustrate, what Beloch indeed admits, that the Roman influence was to amplify and enlarge ideas possessed in embryo by, at least, the Oscan-speaking peoples.[6] Their development lagged behind that of Rome because they were later in adopting an urban form of life, and had no use for some institutions, such as

---

[1] Above, 108 nn. 2, 3. Gellius, *NA* 10. 3. 3–5.
[2] Livy 33. 36. 1–3. The similar incident at Padua (Livy 41. 27. 3) was on allied territory but outside Italy proper; the interference was on request—*legati attulerant*.
[3] Op. cit. 159.          [4] Bruns (7) 8.          [5] Beloch, loc. cit.
[6] Rosenberg, op. cit. 101 ff.

the lower magistracies, until the greater complexity of city life created the need of them. Thus it is not surprising to find that the idea of the *censura* is native to the Oscans,[1] the Oscan word *kenzstur* being original and, unlike *aidil* and *kvaisstur*, not simply a transcription of the Latin. Such *kenzstur* appear in somewhat remote districts such as Bovianum Vetus and Histonium among the Frentani,[2] and justify the idea that the *censores* of Abellinum in Samnium, or of Suessula in Campania are not entirely borrowed from Rome.[3] On Rosenberg's view the *Tabula Bantina* shows the process of development or assimilation at work, the originally independent office of *censor* being subordinated to that of the new *praetor*, who exercises powers of coercion over those who fail to comply with the ordinances of the censors.[4] That there was deliberate borrowing on a large scale of Roman institutions this inscription leaves no serious doubt, especially if we may believe that the fragment of a Latin law found on the back of the Oscan *Tabula* was one adopted by the community of Bantia in the period before the Social War. If so, this is a prime example of an Italian community becoming *fundus legis Romanae*, and if Stuart Jones is right in identifying this law with the *lex Appuleia de maiestate*,[5] it would seem that the *foedus iniquo iure* directly influenced the allied communities by compelling them to interest themselves in the latest definitions of the *maiestas populi Romani* which they were bound to 'conserve'.[6]

Rosenberg, following but modifying Beloch's view, maintains that the idea of the *imperium* and the corresponding notion of true collegiality came from Rome and was not native to the Oscans, but, once accepted, considerably developed their conception of the magistracy.[7] These inductions follow from the fact that, although the Oscan states normally each possessed two *meddices* as magistrates, and though the plural form is used in the inscriptions of the type *meddices fecerunt*[8] or *meddices locaverunt*,[9] yet these two consist of one senior and one junior official, the *meddix tuticus* or *degetasius*, who frequently occurs alone,[10] and the *meddix minor*.[11]

---

[1] Rosenberg, op. cit. 31 ff.
[2] R. S. Conway, *Italic Dialects*, nn. 169, 190.     [3] *CIL* x. 1130, 1131, etc.
[4] Rosenberg, op. cit. 38; *Tabula Bantina*, 1, 20–1, Conway, n. 28.
[5] 'A Roman Law concerning Piracy', *JRS* 1926, 170 f.
[6] Ibid. 171 n. 3.                                                    [7] Op. cit. 24 f.
[8] Conway, op. cit., nn. 219, 252.     [9] Ibid.     [10] Ibid. 44, 45, 47, 94.
[11] Ibid. 117, cf. Ennius, *Ann.* 296, 'Summus ibi capitur meddix, occiditur alter.'

Furthermore when at Bantia the constitution was remodelled on Roman lines, although an attempt was made to translate *imperium* into Oscan,[1] yet the term *meddices* itself was replaced by the Latin *praetors*, a collegiate office.[2]

Both at Bantia and at Pompeii the intermixture of Oscan and Roman institutions is manifest. The aedilate when introduced at Pompeii was subordinated to the *meddix*;[3] not so the *quaestura*, for the quaestors acted apparently only *ex senatus consulto*, or *e populi sententia*;[4] but from this restriction the *meddix tuticus* was himself free.[5] Furthermore the quaestors did not form a true college, since several inscriptions name only one quaestor acting by himself.[6] At Bantia the most remarkable indication of a mixture of institutions is the provision for a *cursus honorum*: 'let no one be praetor or censor at Bantia unless he has been quaestor and let no one be censor unless he has been praetor.' Now despite the *lex Villia Annalis*, there is something more than Roman influence at work here. The fixed *cursus* may have been customary to a large extent already in Rome in the latter part of the second century, but no rule determined the holding of all the magistracies like this. However, the introduction of tribunes and their veto into public business is nothing if not Roman, and Roman of the period, too, for such interference must be 'in the interests of the commonwealth' and 'supported by a vote of the Council'.[7] There is an illustrative incident in Livy in the narrative of 188 B.C., when the proposal to complete the enfranchisement of Formiae and Fundi by a plebiscite was nearly vetoed in the interests of the Senate.[8]

To this evidence and that of the scattered Oscan aediles and quaestors of Abella, Aufidena, and such places,[9] must be added that derived from the Latin inscriptions, sometimes of a later date. Such are the tribunes of Teanum Sidicinum,[10] where the office is part of the normal *cursus*, the praetors of Herdoniae in an inscription written *litteris vetustis et pulchris*,[11] where also aediles are known, and the peculiar *dictator* of Fabrateria Vetus.[12] The list is considerably extended by Rosenberg, but has been cut down by

---

[1] *Tabula Bantina*, 14, 22.  [2] Ibid. 28.

[3] Conway, op. cit., n. 39. Rosenberg, op. cit. 104.

[4] Conway, n. 42, 43, 50.  [5] Rosenberg, op. cit. 104.  [6] Ibid.

[7] *Tabula Bantina*, 4–8, 29.  [8] Livy 38. 36. 8.

[9] Conway, op. cit., nn. 95, 178.  [10] *CIL* x. 4797.

[11] Cf. Beloch, *RG*, 502. *CIL* ix. 689, 690, 698.  [12] x. 5655.

Beloch, who assigns the *praetores duoviri* of Grumentum, Herculia Telesia, and Abellinum to colonial settlements in those places, on the analogy of Narbo Martius.[1] Against this evidence of Romanization may be set the retention of the title of the native magistracies in Umbria; the *marones* did not disappear at once with the coming of Roman influence,[2] and several inscriptions mention a quinque-virate at Assium and a decemvirate at Urvinum Mataurense, which appear to be Umbrian offices in Latin dress.[3]

The evidence is thus not strong enough to support Beloch's remarks in his early work. The influence of the Roman constitution among the allies was considerable, but it is not true that every allied state exhibited a more or less close copy of the Roman constitution, at the time of the Social War. The allies were always turning more and more towards Rome as their centre, and borrowing a great deal, but at times changing what they had borrowed. This borrowing was not inspired by the Roman government, and was no more official than the whole of the *de facto* change of the meaning of the *societas*-relationship. At the time when the Italici were beginning to demand equality with the Roman state, and using language like 'civitatis fastigium per quod homines eiusdem *et gentis et sanguinis* ut externos alienosque fastidire posset',[4] the Roman government was still contracting treaties with foreign powers that differed in no essentials from those which were still in force between the Italici and herself.[5] This is clearly the legal difficulty at the back of the Roman resistance to the demands of the Italici. The Roman state had been expanded in the third century to the very limits of the possible, if it was to remain in any sense a city-state. The relation of Rome to the *socii* was as satisfactory and normal in the first century as it had been in the fourth according to this standard. Nor was it only the Romans who felt the difficulty involved in the idea of incorporating all Italy within the Roman citizenship.[6] At Heraclea and Naples in 89 B.C. there was much hesitation over the rival claims of incorporation and *foederis sui libertas*, 'freedom

---

[1] Rosenberg, op. cit. 111. Beloch, *RG*, 493–6.                    [2] xi. 5390.

[3] Ibid. 5392. *Notizie d. Sc.* 1907, 223. *CIL* xi. 6056, 6065. Rosenberg, op. cit. 48–50.

[4] Velleius 2. 15. 2: 'The supremacy of Rome enables her to scorn men of the same blood and race as herself as though they were foreigners.'

[5] Cf. below, 183 f., except that these were usually *aequo foedere*.

[6] Below, 137 f., 144 f.

under their treaty'. The complaint of the allies, which in effect was that while performing the *munera* of citizens they were treated only as subjects, was true, but it could have been raised at many stages of Rome's history by any of her most barbarous allies.[1] In Italy it took its force largely from the geographic fact that these particular allies formed part of a territorial unit, largely administered by Rome, which was being rapidly romanized and latinized in law, speech, and custom, and from the partial overlap of the true type of ally, the *civitas foederata*, with the informal allies of the *Latinum Nomen*, who bridged the gap which at this period existed outside Italy between the *foederati* and Rome.

[1] On the grievances of the allies in the second century see further below, 214 ff.

# V

# THE AIMS OF THE ALLIES IN
# THE SOCIAL WAR

T HERE is no need here to discuss the preliminary political
skirmishes or the war itself by which the Italian allies secured
the Roman franchise; but it is necessary to discover why
the franchise was given to them, and what it meant when they
had acquired it, what differences were wrought thereby in the
political system of Italy, and how Roman statesmen and jurists
regarded the new citizens.

What emerges from the following discussion is that the aim of
the Italians was not enfranchisement in the modern sense, but the
attainment of social and political equality, that is, equality of
treatment and opportunity in the new world won for Rome with
the assistance of the allies themselves. These ideas seem to lurk
behind the first obscure scenes of the movement. The revolt of
Fregellae presumes some considerable dissatisfaction among the
Latin Name, caused by the refusal of the Senate to listen to the
proposals of Fulvius Flaccus. But the destruction of the state,
dangerously similar to that of Carthage and Corinth, shows the
increasingly domineering attitude of Rome toward her confederation at this period. The incident fits in with those lesser scandals
of the times collected by Gaius Gracchus.[1] That the desire to be
freed from this oppression rather than to gain the *civitas* was the
mainspring of the Social War, seems to follow from a careful
examination of the movement. The exclamation uttered by the
leader of the Samnite remnant before the Colline Gate sums
up the opinion of the extremists; 'nunquam defuturos raptores
Italicae libertatis lupos nisi silva in quam refugere solerent (i.e.
Rome itself) esset excisa'.[2]

The allies had no material or political advantage, in the narrower

[1] Gellius, *NA* 10. 3: three instances of abuse of *imperium* at the expense of
individual allies.
[2] Velleius 2. 27. 2, 'Never would there lack wolves to steal Italian freedom till
their wood of refuge were destroyed.'

sense, as their object. It is true that in later days the domestic nobility of the Italian boroughs swelled the ranks of the equestrian class, and doubtless drew profit from their position,[1] but Italici had been commercially active in the eastern Mediterranean long before the Social War. The Romans themselves were late-comers in this field.[2] It is true that after the war there was a scuffle over the tribal distribution of the new voters. This does not prove that the Italians fought to win the 'vote'; it only shows that they were not prepared to allow the Senate to cheat them by a trick out of the absolute equality which they had won. The question of the *suffragium* could arise only when the major issue had been solved. Since the *honores* of Rome were open only to a narrow ring of families even among 'true blue' Romans, and since the Italians before the war had taken no part in Roman political life, the vote could have had but an indirect and occasional interest for the allies.

What they disliked was their improper subjection to the undivided and unchecked *imperium* of Roman magistrates, and the exploitation of themselves by the power for which they had won the Empire. This is why the right of appeal, the *ius provocationis*, was from the beginning regarded as a possible alternative to enfranchisement.[3] These forms of oppression touched the whole people, even as the military levy fell on all alike. Hence there is no sign of persistent divisions within the various communities that rose against Rome. A state was either for her or against her. Had there been more material objects at stake, there would have been class divisions within the ranks of the secessionists, rich against poor or aristocrats against the masses, as in the Second Punic War. Although the conflagration was set ablaze by interference with the vested agrarian interests of the allies, this affair appears only as the last in a long series of provocative incidents that roused the Italians to protest. They cared more, according to Appian, for the citizenship, that is, for the question of equality, than for their lands.[4]

The view that the main complaint of the allies was against inequality of privilege is demonstrated by the part played by the Latins themselves in the long contest. Although the movement

---

[1] Cf. the instances in Cic. *ad Fam.* 13. 11–14, 33, 43, 45, 56, etc.

[2] T. Frank, *Economic Survey of Ancient Rome*, i. 274, 278.

[3] Below, 136.          [4] *BC* i. 87 (V). Cf. below, 141 f., 214 f.

began with the rising of Fregellae in 125, few Latin states joined the secessionists in the war of 90. Apart from a vague reference in Florus,[1] the only Latin colony known to have gone over to the rebels is Venusia. Elsewhere the Latins put up a stout resistance to them,[2] and are known to have received the citizenship under the first of the enabling laws,[3] that which offered it to states which had not yet taken up arms against Rome. The 'Latin actor' in Diodorus saved himself from the Picentes by reminding them that *even* Latins were subject to the Fasces.[4] Whether this was strictly true or not, the complaints of the Latins, who were already the most privileged members of the Confederation, and so were best prepared for absorption, were more easy to solve by the grant of the citizenship than those of the essentially Italic, largely non-romanized peoples of central Italy. In general the fiercest resistance came from those same Oscan peoples who, having most often rebelled in the days of the conquest, possessed the most unfavourable treaties, or who had suffered diminution of rights after the Hannibalic war. In Etruria where, at least in the earlier period, the levy had not been so common,[5] and in Umbria where one state, if not more, held a *foedus omnium aequissimum*, and where the Romans had recently been generous of individual *viritim* grants of citizenship,[6] there was less support given to the rebellion. It was also in Umbria and Etruria that the enemies of Drusus found an element among the allies prepared to object to one of the Livian laws.[7]

The formula which was proposed for the solution of the problem of the allies was not originally the simple extension of the citizenship to all Italy. Fulvius Flaccus, and later the elder Drusus, offered the *ius provocationis* to those who were unwilling to exchange their rights for Roman citizenship.[8] Gaius Gracchus, and the younger Livius Drusus, when they dealt with this problem,

---

[1] 2. 6. 7, *omne Latium* is absurd. For Fregellae, Livy, *Ep.* 60.

[2] App. *BC* i. 182 (V) Aesernia, 'Ρωμαΐζουσαν. Ibid. 204 (V) Firmum, cf. Livy, *Ep.* 72, 'Auxilia deinde . . . Latini nominis missa populo Romano'. *Contra* Venusia App. i. 175 (V); 190 (V). Cf. Sall. *Hist.* i. 17 (Dietsch).

[3] Gellius, *NA* 4. 4. 3, drawn from S. Sulpicius, and Velleius, 2. 16. 4.

[4] Diod. 37. 12. 3. It might seem from the incident at Novum Comum in 51 B.C. that the proposal of the elder Drusus was eventually carried out, cf. Cic. *ad Att.* 5. 11. 2. But Hardy, *Some Problems in Roman History*, 146, denies this, on good grounds —for if the man possessed *ius provocationis*, why did he not use it?

[5] Cf. 139 n. 2.                                              [6] Cic. *Balb.* 46.

[7] App. *BC* i. 163 (V).                    [8] Plut. *C. Gracch.* 9. Val. Max. 9. 5. 1.

seem at first to have suggested the elevation of the Latins to the *civitas*, and of the *socii Italici* to Latin status.[1] The expedient proposed by Fulvius Flaccus was even put into operation on a small scale, since a precisely similar proviso was included in the section of the Gracchan law which regulated the rewards of successful prosecution for extortion.[2]

Thus although the champions of the allies ended by proposing their complete enfranchisement, they showed in the development of their policy that they knew that neither side regarded this as the ideal solution, and that there was a time when the Italians might have been better satisfied with a great deal less. However the bitterness of the political struggle led the allies into an extremist position, some demanding complete enfranchisement and others seeking total separation from the Roman state; although neither corresponds exactly with their real grievance, either would provide them with the relief which they needed and something else beside.

The account of the organization of the allies themselves during the Social War confirms the view that the citizenship was valued by the Italici as a guarantee of equality, and that it was regarded as an essentially supplementary citizenship from which purely political interests were excluded. The new Italia, of which all became citizens without abandoning their former urban or cantonal arrangements, embodied the ideal reorganization of the Roman Confederation which was the goal of the allies' efforts, but which the Senate refused to admit. The sources make this clear. Corfinium is to be 'a city common to all the Italiots in place of Rome'.[3] Beside the new semi-federal constitution and officials stand the ordinary magistrates of the separate communities, of whom Herius Asinius, *praetor Marrucinorum*, that is *meddix tuticus*, is an example.[4] It is true that the new Italia contained also a central political element. But that is due to the necessities of war: there had to be some unity of authority. How much of this was intended to be permanent we cannot say, but the whole

---

[1] For the original form of Gaius' proposals see *CAH* ix. 51. 78–9. The well-informed chapter in *de Viris Illustribus* 66, indicates that in this matter as in that of the juries Drusus followed the plan of Gaius closely, ibid. 4, 'Latinis civitatem permisit', 11, 'ut Latinorum postulata differet'.    [2] Cf. above, 111 n. 4.

[3] Strabo 5. 4. 2 (241 C.) App. I, 181 (V). Velleius 2. 16. 4, 'caput imperii sui Corfinium'. Diod. 37. 2.

[4] Livy, *Ep.* 73. Appian, loc. cit. στρατηγοὶ καὶ κατὰ πόλεις ἕτεροι.

course of the war shows how much stronger were the separatist than the centripetal tendencies. The latter view is borne out by the dual language of the coins, the refusal of Pinna to assist, the attempt of Judacilius to save his own city, and the lack of effective co-operation among the allies.[1]

Although the war was a revolt from Roman authority, and although the allies maintained the privileges of their separate units and states, yet they asserted the sentiment of Italian unity, and the need for a common form which should join all *Italici* together. This sentiment, which had been felt earlier by Cato and expressed in the scheme of his *Origines*, was voiced again by Tiberius Gracchus in his speech about the Italian Race, in which he spoke of the Italians as kinsmen of the Romans.[2] The phrase appears later in the propaganda of the movement for enfranchisement, and the principle received a practical demonstration in a scene of fraternization between the opposing armies during the war itself.[3] But this sentiment did not imply the desire to be completely engulfed in the political system of Rome. The hesitation of Naples and Heraclea to accept the franchise, when it was finally offered to them in 90 B.C., is here important. It was not only their Greek traditions which caused this hesitation. The Hernici, among others, had behaved in the same way centuries before, and the various offers of *ius provocationis* were intended to provide for just such reluctance, and show that it was expected.[4]

An accommodation of the two forms of *civitas*, national and local, was being sought—just the renewal on a large scale of that accommodation which Rome had discovered two and a half centuries before. The importance of the Social War in the history of antiquity lies just here—Rome was forced by the war to renew the practice of an earlier day that had been resting too long in disuse, and to adjust the Roman conception of the citizenship to the ideas that her allies were forming about it. The sources indeed, drawing upon Roman, aristocratic writers, give prominence to the question of the *suffragium*, which for the statesmen

---

[1] Cf. below, 149. Diod. 37, 19–21. App. *BC*. I. 207–8 (V).

[2] App. I, 35 (V); cf. 99 (V). Cf. Sall. *Hist.* 1. 14 and below, 155 n. 1.

[3] Diod. 37. 15. Cf. Vell. 2. 15. 2, 'homines eiusdem et gentis et sanguinis'.

[4] Cic. *Balb.* 21, 'magna contentio Heracliensium et Neapolitanorum fuit, cum magna pars in iis civitatibus foederis sui libertatem civitati anteferret.' Cf. above, 49 n. 3.

of the *comitia* continued to be of great importance in the post-Gracchan period. But the Italici themselves were not thinking of that when they demanded incorporation in the Roman state as a means to gaining equality with their exploiters.

## SOME MODERN THEORIES

The most constructive recent discussions of the enfranchisement movement have been those of Gabba, Badian, Brunt, and Salmon.[1] The difference between the attitude of the allies in the Gracchan phase (126–122 B.C.) and that in the 90s has been emphasized by Brunt, who stressed the gap of a generation between the two phases. Noting the apparent absence in the 90s of any proposal for those alternatives to the Roman citizenship which were offered earlier, he suggested that a new generation of Italian leaders, for whom the Cimbric wars had demonstrated anew the vital dependence of Rome on Italian manpower, was now ready to sacrifice local autonomy to the advantages of the Roman citizenship. This case is strengthened by Badian's demonstration that the enfranchisement bill of Gaius Gracchus, unlike that of Drusus in 91, never proposed more than the full enfranchisement of the Latin allies and the grant of Latin status to the *socii Italici*.[2] But certain counter-indications are largely underestimated or ignored in this view—the existence of a dissident element among the Italians in 90 B.C. whose object was to secure not the Roman citizenship but independence, the implications of the federal character of the new 'Italia', and the possibility that Livius Drusus at one stage merely revived the bill of Gaius Gracchus.[3]

[1] E. Gabba, *Le origini della guerra sociale* . . . (Pavia, 1954). P. A. Brunt, 'Italian aims at the time of the Social War', *JRS* 55 (1965), 90 ff.—a concentrated discussion of all issues, but somewhat one-sided. E. T. Salmon, *Samnium and the Samnites* (Cambridge, 1967), chs. 9, 10. E. Badian, *Foreign Clientelae* 264–70 B.C. (Oxford, 1958), chs. 8, 9, clarifies details, but treats the agrarian issue of 129 as the sole grievance of the allies instead of the proximate cause.

[2] Brunt, art. cit. 93, 105. Badian, op. cit. 299, improving on Last, *CAH* ix. 49 f. Badian, op. cit. 218 f. disposes of the argument, based on App. *BC* i. 36. 163, that Umbrians and Etruscans opposed the enfranchisement bill of Drusus: the context refers to his agrarian bill.

[3] For Drusus' bill see above, 137 n. 1. It is not clear from the sources that his enfranchisement bill was ever passed or even promulgated in final form before his death, though admittedly only one source suggests any content other than enfranchisement for all. See esp. Velleius 2. 14, App. *BC* i. 35. 155, *de Vir. Illustr.* 66.

The development of the enfranchisement movement in the 90s would be clearer if there were adequate evidence for the suggestion of Badian that Marius and his associates between 103 and 96 underlined the claims of the allies by assisting their individual enfranchisement in a variety of ways—awards 'for valour' on the battlefield, surreptitious enrolment of *Italici* on the census lists of 97–96 B.C., and the inclusion of a proportion of allied veterans as citizens in the colonial settlements envisaged by the *leges Appuleiae*.[1] One way or another the latter laws drew attention to Italian claims, either by the omission or by the inclusion of Italian soldiery in the rewarding of their Roman comrades. Finally the role of the *lex Licinia Mucia* of 95 as the proximate cause of the Social War has been clarified by the demonstration that it was concerned not with the bodily expulsion of resident aliens from Rome—which was not a legitimate grievance—but with the cancellation of the illicit registration of *Italici* as Roman citizens whether at the recent census or otherwise.[2] This law, which revealed the animus of Roman policy, would begin to bite when the new censors of 92 B.C. set to work: an anecdote speaks of ten thousand persons facing disfranchisement at their hands. Hence the crisis of 91 and the proposals of Drusus.[3]

The recent writers agree in general that by 91 B.C. the Italian allies, or the majority of them, had decided that the acquisition of the Roman franchise was their only effective means of securing equality of treatment within the Roman system. Such indeed is also the consensus of the sources, so far as they are specific. But the modern scholars differ in their definition of the precise advantages of the Roman citizenship that the Italians had in mind. Gabba, whose contribution is the most original, argues

[1] Badian, op. cit. 203 f., 211 f.

[2] Ibid. 297 n. R, with earlier citations. Asconius 60 C is basic—'cum . . . magna pars (Italorum) pro c.R. se gereret . . . ut in suae quisque civitatis ius . . . redigeretur . . . ita alienati animi sunt principum Italorum populorum'—with Cic. *de Off.* 3. 47, cited above, 111, where Badian's view was anticipated. Brunt justly dissents from Badian's interpretation of Asconius that the *principes* themselves had been thus infiltrating, as being too conspicuous to remain undetected. Besides, the notion that before the *lex Licinia Mucia* censorial registration was a valid form of enfranchisement, without a supporting *Lex*, is contrary to the direct evidence, discussed below, 314 n. 4.

[3] Diod. 37. 13. 'Those who feared the probation' march to protest at Rome, and are checked by one 'Gaius Domitius', surely none other than the censor of 92, Gnaeus Domitius. The *praenomen* Gaius is unknown among the senatorial Domitii. Cf. T. S. R. Broughton, *Magistrates of the Roman Republic*, ii. 560.

that the Italian gentry wanted the *suffragium* so as to secure
control over Roman external policy, which both in Italy and in
the provinces had neglected or abused Italian economic interests.
He starts from the connection that Appian makes between the
activity of the Gracchan land commissioners in taking *ager
publicus* away from Italian occupiers and the offer by Fulvius
Flaccus in 125 of the Roman citizenship as a *quid pro quo*.[1] He
extends this argument by drawing attention to the great role of
Italian businessmen, drawn from the regions of Italy that were
foremost in the Social War, in the exploitation of Roman provinces, documented most notably at the trading centre of Delos
down to its destruction in 88 B.C.[2] The case can be supported by
a number of occasions during the second century (apart from the
agrarian question) when the Senate took unilateral decisions
without consulting Italian interests—the suspension of mining in
Italy, and of viticulture in southern Gaul, the condonation of the
malpractices of Jugurtha in Numidia and later of Mithridates in
Paphlagonia and Galatia, lands where the *Italici negotiatores*
operated. To protect their interests the *Italici* needed the political
influence that would flow from possession of the *suffragium*.[3]
Gabba also argued from the number of former *Italici* who can
eventually be detected holding Roman magistracies, that the
Italian gentry, possibly encouraged by the example of Marius of
Arpinum (as others have suggested), were determined to secure
direct control of the Roman administration and membership of
the Senate.

Gabba's first suggestion is only an extension of what the sources
twice say about voting rights, in 122 and in 88 B.C., but his second
rests on no direct evidence, though Cicero dilates at times on the
energy shown by the Italian municipalities in supporting local
candidates at Roman elections.[4] That the Italians had reason to

[1] Art. cit. 53 ff. App. *BC* I. 21. 86–7.

[2] Art. *cit.* 56 f. drawing largely on J. Hatzfeld, *Les trafiquants italiens dans l'Orient
hellénique* (Paris, 1919), 242 ff. See now also A. J. N. Wilson, *Emigration from Italy in
the Republican age of Rome* (N.Y., 1966), 85 f. Note that the identifications depend
mainly on family names and are not personal; cf. Gabba, art. cit. 55 n. 4, and
below, 142 n. 3.

[3] Gabba, op. cit. 18 f. Cf. Salmon, op. cit. 330 f., for Roman disregard of
Italian economic interests. But the evidence points both ways.

[4] Notably App. *BC* I. 23. 99; 34. 152–4; 49. 214–15; 53. 231; 55. 242. Cf.
Brunt, art. cit. 104, citing Cic. *Verr.* I. 54, *Mur.* 47, *ad Fam.* 13. 4. 1; 7. 4; for
Marius as exemplar, Brunt, art. cit. 105–6. For ex-Latin and Italic senators in the

be dissatisfied with the rate of expansion of the Roman empire and the manner of its exploitation is doubtful. The worst failure of Rome to protect her own people—the Mithridatic massacre of Italian and Roman businessmen in Asia—lay in the future, while Gabba himself has shown that Italians rather than Romans had the lion's share in the exploitation of the Oriental kingdoms, where both were known by the common designation of 'Roman folk' to the Greek populations. Rome frequently supported the interests of the Italian *negotiatores* during the second century, and as late as 102–100 B.C. the energetic measures taken against the Cilician pirates benefited all parties.[1] J. Goehler suggested that the agrarian legislation of the Gracchi envisaged the settlement of both Italians and Romans; though few accept this for the original *lex Sempronia*, it may well be true of the colonies of Gaius Gracchus and of Marius.[2] Certainly the agrarian question disappears from the Italian arena after 125 B.C. down to the tribunate of Livius Drusus, and hence cannot be held responsible for the Italian agitation of the 90s. A greater objection to the thesis of Gabba is that the hard core, if not the whole, of that agitation came precisely from those people, the Sabellian high-landers of the central and southern Apennines, who have least connection with the *negotiatores Italici* hailing from Campania and the seaports of southern Italy. It is true that when the war came Pompeii and the adjacent Oscan townships were won over to the Italian cause, and supported it to the end. But the initiative and the leadership came, as Gabba admits, from the land-owning gentry of the highlands.[3]

late Republic and early Principate see R. Syme, *Roman Revolution* (Oxford, 1952), 81 f., 89 f., 358 ff., T. P. Wiseman, *New Men in the Roman Senate 139 B.C.–A.D. 14* (Clarendon Press, Oxford, 1971), 19 ff.: they become more frequent in the period after 49 B.C. Cisalpines and ex-rebels are very rare till the Principate. Q. Varius Geminus (c. A.D. 14) may be characteristic: 'is primus omnium Paelignorum senator factus est et eos honores gessit.' For the more rapid advancement of actively pro-Roman *Italici* cf. Velleius 2. 16. 3.

[1] Gabba, op. cit. 21, cf. Badian, op. cit. 152; the *lex de piratis* refers to the pro-tection of *Latini* and *socii Italici* throughout Anatolia, cf. Brunt, art. cit. 98 n. 55. *FIRA* I². 9. B 6.

[2] J. Goehler, *Rom und Italien* (Breslau, 1939), 70 ff. Cf. H. M. Last, *JRS* 30 (1940), 83, and below, pp. 217 f. On colonies, Badian, op. cit. 206. For Carthage, App. *BC* 1. 24. 104, with Solinus 27. 11. Cf. Gabba, *Appian* ad loc.

[3] By Sabellian I mean those speaking Oscan itself and Oscan dialects. Cf. Salmon's discussion (op. cit. 340 f.) of the allied *populi* listed by App. *BC* 1. 39. 175, Diod. 37. 2. 6–7. *Negotiatores* with Oscan names may hail from Roman Campania

For Brunt also the Italian motive was narrowly political, though he is sceptical of the commercial purpose. The Italians required the *suffragium* as a means to political power, primarily through the control of legislative assemblies, and to a lesser extent for the election of Italian magnates to Roman magistracies, as the only guarantees of equality. A weakness of both explanations is that though valid for the Italian leaders, who with their retainers alone could afford to frequent Roman political assemblies, they fail to account for the solid and intransigent support which the masses gave to their leaders during the grim and disastrous Social War. Brunt particularly insists that by the 90s no alternatives, such as the *ius provocationis*, were acceptable, though the evidence shows that such alternatives were still being offered, and possibly that Livius Drusus had them in mind.[1] Hence more than passive benefits were being sought: the citizenship or nothing.

The value of the *suffragium* to the more wealthy and politically active allies was somewhat underestimated above.[2] Recent theories equally fail to realize the passive value of the Roman citizenship. Apart from its protective function, which as Verres showed in Sicily was not always reliable outside Italy for the common man, the Roman citizenship automatically opened channels of advantage to Italians of all grades.[3] On military service, which remained a prime grievance down to 90 B.C., they would as Romans be on equal footing with other citizens in matters of discipline, pay, and booty, and in the new type of veteran colonization in provincial territory introduced by Marius. Equally the new style of voluntary recruitment of needy proletarians would be substituted for the irksome conscription of

rather than Samnium. Only the Egnatii from Delos fairly connect with a Samnite leader, Marius Egnatius, and the only trading families that certainly hold magistracies at home are the Granii of Puteoli and Messii of Capua; both were Roman territory long before 90 B.C. Cf. Gabba, op. cit. 16 n. 4, 19 n. 1, 20 n. 1. The father of the best-known Italian operator of later days, P. Sittius of Nuceria, kept his city on the Roman side; cf. Salmon, op. cit. 344 n. 8, Cic. *Sulla* 58.

[1] But cf. above, 137 n. 1, and text. Alternatives to the citizenship were still on offer *c.* 105 under the latest extortion law; cf. *Epigraphica*, 9 (1947), 3 ff., Cic. *pro Balbo* 54.                     [2] Above, pp. 134 f.
[3] Cf. Cic. *Verr.* ii. 5. 139–63 for violations of the rules *de provocatione*. Brunt, art. cit. 104–5 briefly conceded specific benefits connected with voting-rights and military service.

the landed peasantry. The Italian or Latin *negotiator* could compete with Roman capitalists for the profitable contracts of the Roman financial system, including the plums of provincial tax-farming, reserved for Roman citizens by the method of censorial auctions at Rome. All this would accrue without active participation in Roman politics. So too in the provinces at the tribunals of Roman proconsuls, the interests and pressures of *negotiatores Italici* would carry the full weight of citizen status, with the underlying threat of judicial sanctions at Rome, where equestrians from the new municipalities could be effective on the juries of the political courts.[1] Within provincial cities the resident *Italicus* would now benefit from the remarkable freedom from local liturgies enjoyed by the *civis Romanus*.[2] All this too would accrue without direct political activity. As for the *suffragium*, the fact that the issue of equal voting rights provoked a crisis in the politics of Rome in 88 B.C., when politicians unexpectedly tried to devalue the Italian vote, does not prove that the *suffragium* was the primary objective of the Italian agitation beforehand, rather than one of several desirable advantages.[3]

## THE SECESSIONISTS

The various writers take too simple a view of a complex matter, and have left the purpose of the Social War itself in some ambiguity. It was suggested briefly above that some of the Italian insurgents were fighting to secure not the Roman citizenship but independence. Salmon in his history of Samnium wavers between treating the rebellion as a bid for citizenship and as a bid for independence.[4] Brunt sought to re-establish the doctrine of the *Cambridge Ancient History* that the underlying object of the rebels

[1] Cic. op. cit. 147, 155, 158, 161, 168, makes much play with the names of equestrian *negotiatores* in Sicily against Verres, by whom no *eques* was maltreated. Cf. the malpractices of Romans against provincials in the courts of Cyrenaica under Augustus. (*FIRA* I². 68. 1)    [2] Cf. below, 295 ff.

[3] The *suffragium* was not as crucial even in 88 as Brunt makes out (art. cit. 103). Sulla initiated the civil war not because of the *lex de suffragiis* (to which he withdrew his objection) but because of the transfer of his command *after* he left Rome. Cf. Cic. *Phil.* 8. 7 confirming App. *BC* 1. 56. 248–51. Cic. *Phil.* 12. 27 is irrelevant: Sulla and Scipio were discussing not Italian votes but the powers of the popular assemblies at Rome.

[4] Above, 134 f. Salmon, op. cit., ch. 10 does not distinguish the contradictory elements; he regards the new *Italia* as permanent in form, yet as an expendable substitute for the Roman citizenship, ibid. 360–1.

throughout was to secure the Roman citizenship.[1] Though all of these views can be justified from some of the evidence, a critical examination of the historians concerned, who are all epitomators, and often of an extreme brevity, shows that they do not distinguish between the cause of the revolt, which lay in the Roman refusal of the Italian request for the citizenship, and its purpose, which was a break-away aimed at independence. The more explicit writers make this clear. Strabo saw that 'when the Italians failed to secure the freedom and citizenship which they desired they *broke away* from Rome',[2] ἀπέστησαν. So too Appian, the longest source: 'When they had no hope left of securing the citizenship by any means they determined to *break away* from the Romans and to fight with them for the mastery.' For Diodorus too, the earliest of the historians, it was a 'break-away'—he uses the same term for the recent servile revolt in Sicily, the Greek word which is reserved from Herodotus and Thucydides onwards to indicate rebellions aimed at independence.[3] When the Ionians or the Samians 'break away' from Persia or Athens, or the Sicilian serfs from their masters, we do not imagine that they were merely seeking better terms of subjection. But of course not all Italians 'broke away' from Rome. When Appian says that under a law of late 90 B.C. 'the allies secured the citizenship which they nearly[?] all desired', he is referring precisely to the Umbrians and Etruscans, who had not joined in the 'break-away' of the Sabellian peoples.[4] When the late Latin epitomators, who speak of *bellum* and *defectio*, neatly contradict one another over causes and

[1] R. Gardiner, *CAH* ix. 185, 187, though he concedes the dissident element among the Samnites, ibid. 200. Brunt's Section II is devoted to a formal rebuttal of the theory of independence, and his Section III demonstrates the growing Romanization and unification of Italy, much as described above, 128 ff., in support of this. He briefly concedes (pp. 92, 97) that the allies as a last resort were obliged to seek a different solution, but like Salmon regards *Italia* as expendable.

[2] Strabo 5. 4. 2. He equates this with κοινωνία; cf. Justin's *consortium*.

[3] Appian, *BC* 1. 38. 169. So too after Asculum (ibid. 39. 177) 'they gave up thought of these things and turned to war.' Ibid. 49. 271, Umbrians and Tuscans are incited to 'break away'. Cf. Diod. 37. 2. 1, 11; 19. 4; and of the Sicilian slaves, 36. 4. 1, 3, 4, 6. Cf. Herodotus 5. 35. 1–4, Thucydides 1. 98. 4; 99. 1–3, for origins.

[4] App. *BC* 1. 49. 212. Whether μόνον or μόνον οὐ is read makes little difference; but the emendation is historically more accurate, cf. above, 137. Eutropius 5. 3. Justin 38. 4. 13. Orosius 5. 18. 2, 'spe libertatis . . . inlectos . . . in arma excitavit [sc. Drusus]', combines both motives. For *civitas* was only one mothod of securing *libertas*. The Epitomator of Livy 72 has merely *defecerunt*. Velleius 2. 15, Val. Max. 8. 6. 4, Asconius 19, Florus 2. 6, speak of a *bellum* against Rome with the refusal of *civitas* as its cause.

aims, Justin is as correct in describing the Italians as demanding 'not freedom but citizenship and a share of power', as Eutropius in asserting that 'they began to demand independence.' The point of reference differs. Livy devoted a large part of his Book 81 to the motives and plans of the allies.[1] No more survives, but his ultimate epitomators indicate that motives were decidedly mixed: not even all Sabellians supported the break-away, despite the general solidarity of the tribal communes.[2]

There may be cited against this view the four colloquies which took place at various stages of the war between the leaders of the opposing armies on the theme of 'peace and citizenship', as representing the original purpose of the war. Yet two at least took place in the second and third or fourth year when the Italians were losing or had lost the war, and it is noteworthy that all failed as much through the intransigence of the Italians as through that of the Romans, who took the initiative on three of these occasions.[3] Even in 87 B.C. the Samnite remnant facing final defeat refused an offer of citizenship, because it did not entirely restore their *status quo ante*. Yet more determined were the Lucanian rebels who at this time made a desperate attempt to seize Sicily rather than come to terms.[4] Cicero, reporting as an eyewitness the colloquy of the consul Strabo and the Marsian Scato, nicely reveals two different formulations of Italian objectives through the verbal ambiguity of the word *civitas*: 'They were not seeking to take over our state but to be received into our citizenship.' Earliest of all witnesses, the *Auctor ad Herennium* takes it for granted that the Italian purpose was precisely to take over the Roman imperial position.[5]

---

[1] Livy 71 recounted the 'speeches and plans' of the allies at length after the narrative of Drusus' tribunate (cf. *Epitome*).

[2] Brunt, art. cit., 95 rightly objects to my statement (above, 135) that there were *no* internal divisions within any Italian communes, but it remains true that there were very few fluctuations of loyalty once a decision was taken, and the vast majority showed great persistence, as his citations show.

[3] Diod. 37. 15: Marius and the Marsi in 90; Marius made the first move. Frontinus, *Strat.* 1. 5. 17: Sulla, caught in a defile before Aesernia in 90, made the first move, but 'sine effectu agitabat'. Cic. *Phil.* 12. 27: Pompeius and the Marsi, initiative not stated. Licin. p. 20 F, Dio, fr. 100. 7: Metellus and the Samnites in 87, initiative of Metellus *ex S. C.* Brunt, art. cit. 96, attributed the intransigence to the Romans bent on securing unconditional surrender.

[4] Diod. 37. 2. 13–14. The Lucanian leader had served earlier against the Sicilian rebels, ib. 36. 8. 1.

[5] 'Non ut eriperent nobis socii civitatem sed ut in eam reciperentur', above n. 3. Cf. *Auctor ad Her.* 4. 13, at some length.

The attempt to explain away the federal organization set up by the allies as merely an arrangement for managing the war, rather than as an indication of their objectives, is inept, because on any view it shows the type of organization that the Italians preferred when left to their own devices. This was not so similar to the centralized Roman system as Diodorus and some moderns allege. The sources show that it contained local and federal authority at the command level. The large Council of five hundred delegates—described as σύνεδροι, the usual term for members of similar federal councils in the Greek world—bears little relationship to the Roman Senate of 300 ex-magistrates.[1] It had ample room for representatives of all the Allied communes, and was vested with positive administrative control that the Roman Senate lacked. It goes beyond the evidence to speak of the Italians *merging* their local communes in the *unitary* State of Italia. The federal officers, the 'consuls' and 'praetors' of Diodorus, appear only as military commanders, and no evidence implies the abolition of local autonomy. H. D. Meyer sought, in a reassertion of the unitary view of Italia, to water down the role of the Council and to exalt that of a general Assembly of citizens. This is based on a misunderstanding of phrases in Diodorus and Strabo. Diodorus does not say that 'rulers' and 'wise deliberators' were to be 'selected as an executive committee' from the Council, but that those capable of this would be 'brought forward' or 'produced' within the Council, which was to have supreme power.[2] Equally Strabo does not say that the allies 'held political assemblies' but that they 'mustered their troops' at Corfinium. There is in fact no direct evidence for a primary assembly of citizens at all.[3]

It has been urged that the Italian insurgents proved their desire for complete independence by continuing the war after the

---

[1] Cf. above, 137. Diod. 37. 2. 5. Strabo 5. 4. 2. For σύνεδροι see citations in LSJ s.v. Salmon, op. cit. 348 compares *Italia* to the contemporary Thessalian league, a Graeco–Roman model.

[2] H. D. Meyer, *Historia*, 7 (1958), 74 f. Diodorus, l. c. ἐξ ὧν οἱ . . . ἄξιοι προαχθήσεσθαι ἔμελλον . . . τούτοις ἐπέτρεψαν . . . τὸν πόλεμον αὐτοκράτορας ποιήσαντες τοὺς συνέδρους. οὗτοι δὲ ἐνομοθέτησαν . . . On any view the σύνεδροι who are 'autocratic' and 'pass laws' in the following sentence can only be the members of the Five Hundred, while the 'promoted ones' hold executive power.

[3] Strabo, loc. cit. τοὺς συνεπομένους ἀθροίσαντες. He is describing both political and military arrangements of the allies. The only remaining trace of a popular assembly lies in the 'large forum' of Corfinium in Diodorus.

*lex Julia* or the *lex Plautia* offered the citizenship to 'those who laid down their arms in good time'.[1] Some think that this offer did not refer to the committed rebels who had been fighting strenuously for twelve months, but to the half-hearted or to those who had already been defeated. The question concerns the precise formulation of a clause of the law. The peculiar word used by Velleius—*maturius*—should refer to a clause defining a time within which resistance was to cease, like the clause of the *lex Plautia* that allowed *adscripti municipiis* sixty days within which to register as citizens. It is less likely to mean merely 'before the passing of this law', for which more appropriate adverbs were to hand. Appian hints that the offer was conditionally open to insurgents who could now 'hope for the same' as the still faithful allies, to whom the offer was immediately open.[2]

The thesis that enfranchisement was the single purpose of the Social War requires evidence that the allies presented an ultimatum demanding the citizenship under threat of war. But this is lacking, and for a good reason. The rebellion was precipitated by an unplanned incident, the massacre of the Roman mission at Asculum. After that it was too late for anything but a deputation to Rome that tried to blame the Asculan affair on the intransigent attitude of the Romans.[3] Senatorial opinion, that had largely supported the proposals of Drusus a few weeks earlier, hardened against the allies.[4] The severity of the Roman reply left the Italians no alternative but to struggle for independence, while no

---

[1] 'Qui arma aut non ceperant aut maturius deposuerant'. Velleius 2. 16. 4, App. *BC* 1. 49. 212. Sherwin-White, *JRS* 45 (1955), 169. *Contra* Brunt, art. cit. 95, Salmon, op. cit. 361. Whether Velleius refers to one or to two laws by his *aut . . . aut* is unclear.

[2] Strictly, Appian describes a *S. C.* preceding the *lex Julia*, not the law itself. Brunt presses Appian to imply the total exclusion of active rebels from the *lex Julia*. But if Appian describes the same measure as Velleius, then the allies were covered conditionally. For Cicero the *lex Julia* was the sole general law of enfranchisement for all allies (*Balb.* 21). Possibly it was applied to doubtful cases, as ultimately to the recalcitrant Samnites, by *S. C.* Cf. below, 153, 155 n. 5.

[3] App. *BC* 1. 39. 176: 'The emissaries put the blame on the Romans because they did not deem the Italians worthy of their citizenship . . .' If Appian is to be pressed, this mission did not present any request at all. How could it after Asculum?

[4] For the dates cf. Brunt, art. cit. 107. The invalidation of Drusus' legislation must follow the death of Crassus on 20 Sept. Till then Drusus had (it seems) the support of a majority in the Senate. Brunt presses Diod. 37. 2. 2 to mean that the Senate formally approved an enfranchisement measure during 91. But Diodorus may be generalizing from the role of Drusus as *patronus Senatus*, cf. above, 139 n. 3.

suggestion of compromise was possible for the Romans until they began to gain the upper hand. There is no intrinsic improbability in the notion that the peoples of the central and southern highlands and plateaux of the Apennines, who alone continuously sustained the great rebellion, should withdraw altogether from the Roman system after such discouragement. The geographical and ethnic limitation of the movement is significant: it was a Sabellian affair. The Latin Name stood aloof, and though at the end of the first season's fighting, in which the allies had great successes, some Umbrian and Etruscan peoples joined the rebellion, their resistance was not extensive or prolonged.[1] But southwards the Samnites were able to spread the revolt among the Oscan-speaking peoples of southern Campania and of Lucania, where the resistance continued beyond the end of the third season.[2] The element of Oscan nationalism is well documented in the symbolism of the insurgent coinage, and in certain historical anecdotes which underline the irreconcilable hatred of Romans and Samnites. The significance of neither is diminished by being labelled 'propaganda'. Equally the gradual spread of Romanization among the Italians, whether in language, dress, legal usages, or civic government, during the previous century, in which some find the clue to the Italian attitude to Rome, is no proof that they did not object to Roman domination, or that the Social War was not a protest against Roman centralization, though often so regarded. In modern experience of 'colonialism' it is precisely among the 'westernized' elements that the nationalist reaction begins. When the supposedly Romanized, or half-Romanized, Samnites sent a mission to seek aid of Mithridates, the arch-enemy of Rome, their move, akin to Capua's support of Hannibal, was not calculated to 'win the citizenship'.[3]

[1] Livy, *Ep.* 74, Orosius 5. 18. 7, taken with App. *BC* 1. 49. 211; 50. 216, suggest that a limited rebellion (involving Faesulae and Ocriculum, cf. Florus 2. 6. 11), which failed to link up with the southern rebels, was crushed by the praetor L. Cato late in 90, before the passing of the *lex Julia* by the consul returning to Rome belatedly for the consular elections (cf. App. *BC* 1. 44. 196). But an earlier date for both events is not quite excluded.

[2] Salmon, op. cit. 341, 358, 369–70, 373–4. Note also his suggestion, p. 346, that Italian reserves in demobilized men were especially ample *c.* 91, and hence victory not impossible, though nominally contradicted by *Auctor ad Her.* 4. 13.

[3] Brunt, art. cit. 96–7, dismisses the coin evidence as 'not amounting to much'; so too the stories of Romano–Samnite hatred (Velleius 2. 27, Plut. *Sulla* 29. 4, Strabo 5. 4. 11). But *propaganda* exploits *beliefs.*

# VI

# THE POLITICAL UNIFICATION OF
# ITALY AND CONSEQUENT CHANGES

## THE PRINCIPLES OF THE ENFRANCHISEMENT

### Incorporation as Communities

It was as communities and not as individuals that the Italian allies were eventually incorporated in the Roman state, under the various enabling laws. It is important to emphasize this fact, because it is a link in the continuous development of that idea of the Roman citizenship which began in the earliest days, and was still vital at the time of the *Constitutio Antoniniana*.[1] The communities which now entered the Roman body politic retained a great deal of the character which they had possessed before enfranchisement. When they ceased to be states, they became self-governing *municipia*.[2] But the fact has been challenged, both by external and by internal arguments; some hold that the grants of citizenship to the Italians were made not to communities but to individuals, while others seek to show that the former self-government of the new *municipia* was largely annulled, and not replaced till Caesar created a new system out of his own head.

Doubtless at the height of the crisis generals were empowered to secure the loyalty of the allies by making offers of the franchise *ad hoc*, and to reward devotion on the field of battle in the fashion revealed by Pompeius Strabo's inscription: 'virtutis caussa equites Hispanos ceives (Romanos fecit in castr)eis apud Asculum . . . ex lege Julia.'[3] There is, however, no doubt about the method prescribed in general by the *lex Julia*. 'Ipsa denique Julia . . . lege civitas est sociis et Latinis data, qui fundi populi facti non essent civitatem non haberent.'[4] All those states which persisted in the war received the citizenship in a similar manner.

---

[1] Below, 383.       [2] Below, 159 ff.       [3] *ILS* 8888.
[4] Cic. *Balb.* 21. 'Finally, by the Julian law citizenship was given to the allies and Latins on condition that those peoples which did not adopt the law did not gain the citizenship.' For the meaning of *fundi ... facti* see below, 159.

The record in the epitome of Livy leaves no doubt about this. The various *populi* made their *deditio* to the Roman commanders,[1] and after a considerable interval of time the Epitomator of Livy says that 'Italicis populis a senatu civitas data est'.[2] This statement is borne out by a particular instance known from a fragment of Sisenna, and is paralleled in Granius Licinianus by the words 'dediticiis omnibus a senatu civitas data'.[3] Since *deditio* is a term not of personal but of constitutional law, and the act implied is the act of a community, it is clear that these allies also entered the Roman state as *populi*. The language of Velleius and Appian is too vague to assist here,[4] but the strength of the verbal argument is supported by the general accuracy of Livy in these matters, once he is past the mythical period, and by the incident, during the war itself, when Sulla allowed his troops to plunder Aeclanum because the place was not *dedita* but *capta*.[5] This shows that attention was paid to constitutional niceties.

The question remains whether a different procedure was introduced by the *lex Plautia Papiria*. The current interpretation of this law is derived from a statement of Cicero: 'data est civitas (i.e. Archiae) Silvani lege et Carbonis: si qui foederatis civitatibus ascripti fuissent, si tum cum lex ferebatur in Italia domicilium habuissent et si sexaginta diebus apud praetorem essent professi'.[6] These words are usually explained in the way that the Bobbian scholiast suggests: 'ut omnes qui essent ex foederatis populis civitatem Romanam consequerentur si modo illo tempore quo lex lata esset', etc.[7] But Cicero is here speaking not of all *foederati* but of Archias alone, who having become a member of the State of

---

[1] Livy, *Ep.* 75, Vestini, 76, Marrucini, more cantons of the Vestini, Paeligni, Marsi; Appian, who seems to use ὑπηγάγετο and παρέλαβεν as meaning 'in deditionem accepit', records the *deditio* of Hirpini Marsi Marrucini Vestini Poediculi, 1. 222 (V) ff.

[2] Livy, *Ep.* 80. 'The citizenship was given by the Senate to the Italian peoples.'

[3] Sisenna fr. 119, below, 153 n. 3; Granianus 15; Mommsen, *History* iii. 527 n. 1.

[4] App. I, 212 (V); 231 (V). Velleius, 2. 16. 4, 'recipiendo in civitatem' recalls Festus, s.v. 'Municeps', 'Municipium', and Cic. *Balb.* 31, 'gentes universae in civitatem sunt receptae'. These phrases are more appropriate to communities than to individuals.

[5] App. I, 223 (V).

[6] *Pro Archia*, 7. 'Citizenship was given [to Archias] by the law of Silvanus and Carbo: whoever were members by ascription of federated states, and resided in Italy at the time of the passing of the law, and declared their names before the praetor within sixty days. . . .'

[7] p. 353 (= Stangl, ii. 175). 'All members of federated states should gain the citizenship provided that at the time of the passing of the law, etc.'

Heraclea by 'ascription', was not living at Heraclea in these years, but at Rome.[1] Since Heraclea acquired the citizenship not by the *lex Plautia Papiria* but by the *lex Julia*,[2] it follows that Cicero was quoting a special provision which affected *ascripti* and not summing up the whole scope of the law. This special clause was inserted in the *lex P. Papiria* to remove an anomaly which had been overlooked in the passing of the *lex Julia*. The anomaly consists in the fact that *ascripti* of the type of Archias, not resident in their adoptive *patria*, were unable to benefit by the *lex Julia*. There is proof of this in a letter of Cicero: 'L. Manlius est Sosis. Is fuit Catinensis sed est una cum reliquis Neapolitanis civis Romanus factus decurioque Neapoli; erat enim adscriptus in id municipium ante civitatem sociis et Latinis datam.'[3] This Sosis was a resident of Naples, as is shown by his decurionate. The scope of the clause quoted by Cicero is now clearly defined—to enable non-resident *ascripti*, who were, however, domiciled in Italy, to share the benefits of the *lex Julia*.[4] The procedure would be very strange if it intended that all those allies who had been excluded from the offer of citizenship under the *lex Julia*, that is, those who had not desisted from revolt in good time, were to make their way to the praetor at Rome. During a civil war this would be out of the question, and hardly possible in time of peace. The main administrative officials must have been the *imperatores* directing the campaigns. This clause makes good sense only if it refers to men like Archias, persons resident in Rome for whom it was simple to apply to 'the praetor'. There is a negative element latent in the clause, which has been framed to exclude some *ascripti*. The Romans were not prepared to allow a host of provincials to creep into the fold on the plea that at some time they or their ancestors had been given the freedom of some Hellenic city in the south of Italy.[5]

---

[1] *Pro Archia* 9.  [2] *Balb.* 21.

[3] *Ad Fam.* 13. 30. 'This is L. Manlius Sosis. He was of Catina but became a Roman citizen along with the other inhabitants of Neapolis, and a councillor. For he was ascripted to that municipality before the citizenship was given to the allies and Latins.'

[4] Cf. *Pro Archia* 6, 'ascribi se in eam civitatem voluit'. For the technical meaning of this term cf. Livy 8. 14. 8; 31. 49. 6; 32. 7. 3, etc. Normally it is used of colonies, cf. Festus s.v., and describes an artificial relationship created by law, and is not the definition of an already existing state of affairs, e.g. Cicero could not be described as *ascriptus municipio Arpinati*.

[5] Cf. *Arch.* 3, 5.

Very little is known about the content of either the *lex Julia* or the *lex P. Papiria*, and even less about the *lex Calpurnia*, third of the enabling laws. The two former were probably hasty war measures designed in the first place to reduce the number of the insurgents.[1] It is unlikely that they provided a final settlement of the status of the new citizens, or that the second measure set up a form of procedure entirely different from that employed both before and after it. What happened later in the way of acts of settlement is even more obscure. It is reasonable to believe that there was some general law passed that fixed the necessary details, or at least the principles, of the municipal reorganization. Whether or not the *lex Calpurnia* which provided for the establishment of two new tribes—never actually carried out—is to be identified with such a law must remain uncertain.[2] But the method generally followed in the execution of these various laws must have been that indicated by the fragment of Sisenna: 'Tudertibus senati consulto et populi iussu dat civitatem.'[3] The senate's part would perhaps be to decide what communities fell under the scope of particular enactments, and how the details of reorganization were to be carried out.

It is not merely an academic point that is at issue, but one that influenced the whole development of the Roman view of *patria*. Since it was the former city-states and not so many individuals that entered the Roman Commonwealth, each new citizen had a double existence, but these two lives were bound together by the most intimate of bonds, which is expressed by the Epitomator's statement: 'Italicis populis data civitas.' So too in the areas of central Italy where the forms of the city-state were not yet established, the tribal and sub-tribal communities retained their corporate existence and remained the basis of political organization after the Social War; for the new *municipia* are the old tribes. The tribe of the Marrucini, for example, continued to exist thinly disguised as the *municipium* Teate—the central *oppidum* of the old tribe[4]—and individual Marrucini and others continued

[1] Cf. Velleius 2. 16. 4, and Sisenna, fr. 120 (Peter).
[2] Sisenna fr. 17, 120.
[3] Ibid. 119. 'He gives citizenship to the men of Tuder in virtue of a *senatus consultum* and the will of the people.'
[4] Cf. the lists in Beloch, *RG* 502. The quattuorviral system was introduced throughout the tribal areas. Below, 165.

to employ the old tribal designations, so strong were the forces of local patriotism.[1]

On the alternative view the importance of municipal life in the following period must be seriously underestimated, and must rank only as one of the activities in which a man may indulge at his pleasure, such as membership of a *collegium*. But this view is flagrantly untrue.[2] It amounts to a denial of the doctrine of *communis patria Roma*, to the development of which the Social War gave a great impetus. This theory, as we know it, was worked out by Cicero, after obvious pondering. In his forensic writings he emphasized the principle that no Roman citizen could hold the franchise of another state while retaining that of his own.[3] In the *De Legibus* he draws the necessary conclusions from the history of the unification of Italy.[4]

Omnibus municipibus duas esse censeo patrias unam naturae alteram civitatis. Ut ille Cato cum esset Tusculi natus in populi Romani civitatem susceptus est, itaque cum ortu Tusculanus esset, civitate Romanus, habuit alteram loci patriam alteram iuris. . . . Sed necesse est caritate eam praestare qua reipublicae nomen universae civitatis est, pro qua mori et cui nos totos dedere et in qua nostra omnia ponere et quasi consecrare debemus. Dulcis autem non multo secus est ea quae genuit quam illa quae excepit.

The upshot of this is that while a man was a member of only one sovereign state, he was attached as *municeps* to a secondary community, his municipal *patria*, which, though not on the same scale as the state, imposed its obligations and offered its honours to him. The doctrine which Cicero expounds and canonizes in the *De Legibus* is the full development of what was expressed more crudely in a document belonging to the period of the Social War:

---

[1] Cf. *ILS* 932, 'Q. Vario . . . Gemino leg. divi Aug. . . . Is primus omnium Paelign[orum] senator factus est.' *CIL* iii. 4060, 'Marrucinus'. *ILS* 6533, 'sevir Aug. Marsis'.

[2] Cf. below, 165 ff.          [3] *Balb*. 28. Cf. Nepos, *Atticus* 3. 1.

[4] *De Legibus* 2. 2. 5. 'I hold that all members of boroughs have two fatherlands, one in nature, one in the state. Even as the great Cato was born at Tusculum and received into the community of the Roman people, so, though he was a Tusculan by origin, he was yet a Roman and had one local and one legal fatherland. . . . We must prefer in affection that one which is called the state and the whole community for which we must be ready to die, and to which we must surrender our whole being and in which we must place all our hopes, and to which we must consecrate all that is ours. But the fatherland which begot us is not much less beloved by us than that which adopted us.'

'If I become a citizen by the law of Drusus I will consider Rome as my native land.'[1] Whatever the origin of this fragment, it illustrates the ideas of the times and adds to the effect of, e.g., the constitution of the new Italia. If it is drawn from *anti*-Drusan propaganda, the contrast with Cicero's view shows how far Roman political feeling had changed in the following half century.[2]

## The Enrolment of the Dediticii Populi

There has been a somewhat profitless discussion of the time and manner of the final enfranchisement of those Italian peoples who fought on until total defeat and surrender.[3] Their incorporation was delayed by the violent dispute over the tribal distribution of the new citizens, intended to limit the effectiveness of their voting power, which erupted into the civil war of 88–87 between the optimate and radical factions.[4] The epitomators give dates in both 87 and 84 for the grant of what is variously described as 'citizenship' or 'the vote'.[5] The first date has been connected with the agreement recorded between the still-resistant Samnite remnant and the Cinnan faction, after the optimates had refused to grant the Samnites the citizenship on special terms.[6] But all that is certain is that the enfranchisement was completed by 84, after which year no more references to enfranchisement or tribal distribution occur, and that the attempt to limit the new citizens to a small group of new tribes was abandoned. It has escaped notice that the sources do not mention new laws *de civitate danda*, but arrangements made by decrees of the Senate. It was a question of applying the provisions of the legislation of 90–89, the *lex Julia* and the *Plautia Papiria*, to particular groups by

---

[1] ἐὰν γένωμαι πολίτης τῷ Δρούσου νόμῳ πατρίδα ἡγήσομαι τὴν 'Ρώμην. Diod. 37. 11.

[2] Cf. H. J. Rose, 'The Oath of Philip', *Harvard Theo. Rev.* 30, 165 ff.

[3] Cf. Badian, op. cit. 241, 297 n. T. Brunt, art. cit. (1965), 107–8. Taylor, *V. D.*, 102 f. These add little to the substance of p. 153 above.

[4] Since the proposal to limit the new citizens to eight tribes (Velleius 2. 20, Appian *BC* 1. 49. 214) was cancelled by the legislation of Sulpicius and Cinna, and never renewed after 87 (Appian, *BC* 1. 55. 242; 56. 249; 64. 287. Cf. Cic. *Phil.* 8. 7), it had no permanent effect.

[5] Livy, *Ep.* 80, 'Italicis populis a senatu civitas data est' (in 87). Licinianus p. 21, 9–10 'dediticiis omnibus civitas data' (in 87). Livy, *Ep.* 84, 'novis civibus senatus consulto suffragium datum est' (in 84), which Taylor would connect with tribal registration.

[6] Cf. above, 146. In Licinianus the transaction precedes the grant (pp. 20, 21).

administrative action.[1] It seems that in 87 the Senate was prepared to enfranchise the bulk of the *dediticii* thus, but drew the line
at the remnant who had refused to make the act of formal surrender. To bring the new citizens into the political machinery of
the Roman state also required their technical registration by tribes
and centuries on the censorial rolls. Little headway was made
with this by the censors of 86–85, who registered only some 25
per cent more citizens than in the last surviving record dated to
115. It is only in the censorship of 70–69, restored after an interval
of fifteen years, that an effective registration was made of some
900,000 male heads.[2]

Somewhat more illuminating is the re-examination by L. R.
Taylor of the actual tribal distribution of the Italian and Latin
*municipia* as it appears from later epigraphical evidence.[3] The
enfranchised communes were distributed throughout all thirty-
one of the old *tribus rusticae*, but in somewhat irregular fashion.
Two principles seem to have been followed. The peoples loyal to
Rome in 90–89 were distributed in small numbers through a wide
range of tribes, while the rebels, especially those organized in
large ethnic groups, were mostly assigned *en bloc* to single tribes.
Thus a group of seven tribes received a preponderance of ex-
rebel Italici,[4] while, so far as is known, twenty seven of the former
*coloniae Latinae* were distributed through sixteen *tribus rusticae*,
which excluded the seven reserved for the blocks of ex-rebels.[5]
No tribe received more than three Latin communes, and similarly
most of the peoples of Etruria and Umbria were distributed
through two groups of some twelve overlapping tribes, but less
evenly.[6] There are exceptions to these rough rules: some ex-rebels

[1] Cf. above, 150 n. 5, and 153, on the fragment of Sisenna (17. 119), 'Tudertibus senati consulto et populi iussu dat civitatem.'
[2] Livy, *Ep.* 63, for 115–114 gives 394,336 persons, while Jerome, *Chron.* for
86–85 gives 463,000, with possibly 491,000 in Phlegon. The figure for 70–69 is
900,000 in Livy, *Ep.* 98, confirmed sufficiently by the 910,000 of Phlegon (fr. 12).
[3] Taylor, op. cit. ch. 8.
[4] Cf. Taylor, op. cit. 111 f. Notably Voltinia for Samnites, Sergia for Marsi and
Paeligni, and Arnensis for Frentani and Marrucini. Some of the tribes thus used
may have been associated earlier with these regions through Roman viritane
colonization and the enfranchisement of *cives s.s.* (ibid.).
[5] Cf. ibid. 109 f., where it is suggested that these tribes were associated with the
Latin colonies before 120, to accommodate Latins enfranchised *per honorem*.
[6] Ibid. 114, 115. In Umbria a large group of communes, possibly identical with
the rebels of 90, were assigned to the Clustumina, while numerous others were
distributed through some twelve tribes. The new *municipia* of Etruria were assigned

were assigned in isolation to the tribes of the loyalists, and some related groups of loyalists were assigned *en bloc* to single tribes.[1] Altogether the arrangements, which were made or completed by the radical leaders who had espoused the Italian interest after the Social War, do not seem to be malicious or partisan.

## Enfranchisement of Gallia Cisalpina

It has been widely assumed that in the north of the peninsula the Roman citizenship was extended to all allied communities between the Apennines and the river Po in 89 B.C.[2] This is an inference from the existence of *municipia* in southern Gallia Cisalpina before 49 B.C., and from the fact that Latin status was given to the Celtic peoples north of the river by a *lex Pompeia* of 89.[3] The southern plains had been intensively colonized with Latin and Roman colonies and viritane settlements during the early second century, while tribal groups of Ligurians survived in the highlands between Genua and Bononia from the systematic war of conquest in that period.[4] The enfranchisement of the old *coloniae Latinae*, such as Placentia, to which Cicero specifically refers, is not in dispute. But in a detailed study of the Romanization of the Cisalpine region, Miss Ewins has reaffirmed the view of Beloch that the wild men of the hills did not receive the citizenship before Julius Caesar extended it to Transpadane Gaul in 49. Her main argument is that if all the Cispadanes became Romans in 89 they should have been treated as 'part of Italy', and been placed under the authority not of proconsuls but of the urban magistrates of Rome.[5] This ignores the clearly marked distinction in the sources between Gallia and Italia. The need

to about fourteen tribes, some of which may be connected with viritane colonization and *municipia* enfranchised before the Social War.

[1] e.g. the Hernican communes all appear in the *Publilia*, though only Anagnia antedates the Social War, cf. Taylor, op. cit. 51, 114.

[2] e.g. E. Hardy, *JRS* 6 (1916), 65. A. Ferrua, *Inscr. Ital.* ix. 1. 1, p. xiii. *CAH* ix. 195.

[3] Asc. *in Pis.* 3 C (cited 111 n. 3) with Pliny, *NH* 3. 138 (cf. below, 356 n. 5). For the *municipia*: Placentia, Cic. *In Pis.* fr. 10 with 53; Lucca, *ad Fam.* 13. 13, in 46; Caesar, *BG* 8. 50. 1, 3; 51. 1, in 50. The role of *Gallia togata* (as Hirtius calls it) in Roman elections (*BG* 8. 50–2, Cic. *ad Att.* 1. 1. 2); and the agitation of the Transpadani *alone* for the franchise in 70–50 B.C. are less conclusive.

[4] Cf. Toynbee, op. cit. ii, Map 2.

[5] U. Ewins, 'Enfranchisement of Cisalpine Gaul', *BSR* 23 (1955), 77 ff., seemingly accepting 'urbanization' as a necessary condition, for which there is no ancient evidence. Beloch, *RG* 621 ff.

for a regular military zone in northern Italy to deal with the hostile Alpine and Dalmatian neighbours had not diminished since the troubles of 120–100 B.C., and there was no necessity to change provincial arrangements of proven worth.[1] It is probable that the *lex Julia* had formally defined its recipients in a formula like that used in the agrarian law of 111 covering 'all Latins and allies from whom the Romans exact soldiers *e formula togatorum*'.[2] The Ligurians are found providing regular cohorts like the other *Italici* in the Numidian wars of 112–105, and may well have qualified under the *lex Julia*.[3] There was no reason to refuse the franchise to loyal tribesmen who had taken no part in the Italian insurrection, and who had long been hemmed in by Roman settlements, when much less friendly 'tribesmen' were receiving it in the central Apennines. The Ligurians can hardly have received less than the cantons of Celtic tribes in Transpadana. Since Asconius implies that only the Transpadanes received Latin status under the *lex Pompeia* it should follow that the Ligurians were fully enfranchised. It is unlikely that they alone of the old Roman alliance in the peninsula emerged with no promotion at all. They are to be distinguished in this from their western neighbours, the Ligurians of the Alpine foothills north-west of Genua. The conquest of that people had only begun in the last quarter of the second century with the incipient subjection of Transalpine Gaul, and they had no claims in 89.[4]

A special law was necessary to provide for the Celts of Gallia Transpadana, who were neither former *Latini* nor allies of the

[1] In the early second century the assignation of Italia and Gallia as provinces was quite distinct, and 'Ligures' was frequently distinguished from Gallia: cf. esp. Livy 41. 5. 4–9; also id. 39. 1–2; 3. 1; 40. 1. 1–2, 6.; 41. 14. 6–8; 19. 2; 42. 1. 1–3. After the pacification, Gallia and 'Ligures' form a single province which became the base for the Alpine, Dalmatian, and Cimbric campaigns of 119–101: cf. esp. for 119–115, Livy, *Ep.* 62, *De viris ill.* 72, *Fasti Tr.* for 117, 115; for 113, App. *Celt.* 13; for 101, Livy, *Ep.* 68, Florus 1. 38. For Italia see below, 158 n. 3.

[2] *FIRA* i². 8. 21, 50, 'sociumve nominisve Latini quibus ex formula togatorum milites in terra Italia imperare solent'.

[3] Sall. *BJ* 38. 6; 77. 4; 100. 2. Sall. *Hist.* 1. 20 (M), defines the scope of the agitation for the franchise in 95–90 as concerning *omnibus citra Padum*.

[4] Beloch, *RG* 627, inferred from evidence for the late enfranchisement of some *western* Ligurians (Cic. *ad Fam.* 8. 15. 2, Pliny, *NH* 3. 135) that *all* the Ligurians received merely Latin status in 89, like (possibly) the sub-Alpine Bagienni. But Pliny groups these (loc. cit.) with those Alpine peoples promoted to Latin rights by Claudius and Nero (cf. below, 371 f.). So too other Alpine tribes, the so-called *attributi*, later included in the *regiones* of Italy, were excluded from the promotions of 89 and 49, below, 356 f.

*toga*. In Transpadana there was a living Celtic tradition, penetrated by colonies only at Cremona, Eporedia, and distant
Aquileia. The consul of 89 ingeniously applied to the Transpadane Gauls the formula devised by Gaius Gracchus for the non-
Latin peoples of Italy. This gave the Celtic cantons the status of
*coloniae Latinae*, and opened a narrow door to the enfranchisement
of their gentry through the holding of local office.[1] Forty years
later the unification of the whole peninsula was promoted by the
extension of the full franchise and Roman municipal status to
these Latin colonies in turn, and to any surviving enclaves of
*foederati* south of the Po.[2] The assimilation of the Cisalpine zone
to Italy was completed by the abolition of its provincial status in
42 B.C. From this time onwards in Roman usage *Italia* came to
mean the whole territory of the peninsula from the straits of
Messana to the Alpine foothills. Earlier *Italia* had ended where
'Ligures' and Gallia began.[3] This Italy was now identical with
the Roman State, which after a period of cultural and social
fusion provided the closest parallel found in antiquity to a large
national state in the modern sense, with a universal language and
a single system of local government and civil law. The emergence
of this uniformity is best seen in the development of the municipal
system during the last half-century of the Republic. All else
rested on this.

### The Reorganization and Development of Local Government

It is possible to form a picture of the actual process that took
place when the *populi Italici* entered the Roman state. This will
help to clarify the relationship between *patria naturae* and *patria
civitatis*. First of all the *populus* in its proper assembly formally
adopted the Roman law that offered the franchise.[4] This act
turned the *populus* into a *municipium* directly subject to Roman law
and Roman magistrates. It was now possible to regulate the
system of local government directly, without the mediation of the

---

[1] Asconius, *in Pis.* 3 C., cited p. 111, with Pliny, *NH* 3. 138; cf. below, 216.
[2] Dio 41. 36. 3, Strabo 5. 1. 1 (210 C.) with implications of *lex de Gallia Cisalpina*
(*FIRA* i². 19) 22, 23. Ewins, art. cit. 91 f., argues unconvincingly for the retention
of allied status by Ravenna after 89, from Cic. *Balb.* 50, *ad Fam.* 8. 1. 4.
[3] Appian, *BC* 5. 3. 12, Dio 48. 12. 5, with Strabo l.c., confirm the view that the
Romans did not regard Gallia Cisalpina as Italic until this time. So too Pliny,
*NH* 3. 138. Cf. Cic. *prov. cons.* 34, 36, and below, 317 f.
[4] Cic. *pro Balbo* 21.

local assembly, by a *lex*, *plebiscitum*, or *senatusconsultum*.[1] Cicero's phrase 'erat rumor de Transpadanis eos iussos quattuorviros creare', sums up the situation.[2] Any further change could proceed in accordance with an enabling act. The famous inscription of Padua provides an instance—'iv vir aediliciae potestatis e lege Julia municipali.'[3] After the first reorganization the local authorities themselves could be the agents of change.[4] Cicero speaks of such an event at Arpinum in 49 B.C., 'nam constituendi municipi causa hoc anno aedilem filium meum fieri volui'.[5] The provisions contained in the *tabula Heracleensis* clearly depended upon similar local initiative to put them into effect.[6]

The only period when an agent of the central government could be required was in the period after the incorporation or establishment of a new municipality and before the election of its first magistrates, i.e. before the new constitution was in full working order. The last section of the *tabula Heracleensis* provides a probable instance of such commissioners and the execution of a *lex data* at a *municipium*—Fundi.[7] A similar instance occurs in the *lex municipi Tarentini*, the only probable example of a *lex data* of this type.[8] This law probably regulates the fusion of two communities into one, a *colonia Neptunia* founded by the Gracchan commissioners and the old Greek city; certainly the mention of *duoviri* in the law next to *quattuorviri* supports this view: the law simply names the pre-existing officials of both communities.[9] That the interference of the central authority was exceptional in the reorganization of municipalities, once a general enabling act had been passed, is thus confirmed by the evidence of this document. Once the new or newly modelled borough has been set on its feet, it can function without external aid, absorbing the laws and edicts of the central authority and giving effect to them through its own machinery.

In Cicero's theory of dual *patria*, although Rome is preponderant, the local *germana patria* means a great deal. To assess its

---

[1] *Fr. Atest.* 1. 10–15.    [2] *Ad Att.* 5. 2. 3.

[3] *ILS* 5406. Cf. the *iv vir lege Petronia* at Aesernia, ibid. 6518. Also ibid. 6125, 6468, 6469.

[4] Below, 165 ff., for later reorganization.

[5] *Ad Fam.* 13. 11. 3. 'I wanted my son to be aedile this year to settle the constitution of the borough.'

[6] Bruns, (7), 18, 83–158, *passim*.    [7] Below, 167.    [8] Bruns, (7) 27.

[9] Rudolph, op. cit. 122 ff.

importance exactly, it is necessary to define the extent of the powers of self-government which were granted to the new municipalities after 89 B.C. This is debated ground. Rudolph, in his treatment, the fullest yet attempted, of the status of *municipia* in the period between 89 B.C. and the dictatorship of Caesar, has tried to reconstruct the municipal history of Italy without paying enough attention to the practical presuppositions, geographic and historical, of the subject. His view is that in 89 B.C. the former jurisdiction of the local magistrates, and all their functions save those of minor administration, were abolished, and that all Italians came, for purposes of juridical activity, directly under the Roman city courts.[1] He sees an annihilation of local independence which was only ended by Caesar, who created out of his own head the system of devolved jurisdiction, performed by *ii viri iure dicundo*, etc., which is familiar under the Principate.[2] As a corollary he holds that the functions of the *ivviri*, the magistracy admittedly installed in the new boroughs, were limited, along with those of the colonial *iiviri*, to such matters of building-contracts, etc., as one can see illustrated by the *lex de pariete faciundo* of Puteoli.[3]

Rudolph seriously underestimates the importance of the other functions of this type that fell to the local magistrates—the care of public works, games, ceremonies, finance in general—in a deliberate revulsion from the views of Liebenam; but the latter has after all the support of the ancients themselves in setting foremost the financial functions of government. This appears as much in the letters of Cicero as in those of Pliny. The first thought of the Atinates, Atellani, and Volaterrani is for their *vectigalia* and lands.[4] Yet to judge by the distribution of subject-matter in the extant charters, the theory of Rudolph at least halves the importance of local politics and public life within the republican *municipia*. It implies that incorporation completely changed the political orientation of the *populi Italici*, and conferred a degree of judicial dependence not testified in the copious evidence of the late Republic.

Rudolph has not sufficiently considered the conditions that ruled in these states before their incorporation, the whole fabric of political life which even our fragmentary sources permit us to reconstruct. A great part of this would be swept away, on his

---

[1] Op. cit. 230, 238, 239, sum up his views.    [2] Ibid. 119, 218.
[3] Rudolph, op. cit. 105–7, 109. For the *ivviri* cf. below, 163.
[4] e.g. Cic. *ad Fam.* 13. 4; 7; 11. Pliny, *Epp.* 10. 18. 3, 23, 38, 43.

view. His main argument is the flimsiest, that the inscriptions of *ivviri* and *iiviri* with the qualification *iure dicundo* only begin to appear after the death of Caesar; particularly weak is the belief that the presence of any inscriptions in the first volume of the *Corpus of Latin Inscriptions* sufficiently proves that they belong to the earlier period and system.[1] To wreck such an argument it would suffice to find a single example of a *ivvir i.d.* dated before the time to which Rudolph assigns the law which he deduces from this evidence. Nor are possible examples lacking.[2] But this is not really the point. That Caesar is an important figure in the re-organization of Italy is not denied. To this subject Rudolph has in other matters contributed much. But it is not possible to draw from the data this particular conclusion about the restoration of local *iurisdictio*. All that could be proved, if the data were un-disputed, would be that after 47 B.C.—to which year he assigns his law—a greater degree of specialization was introduced into the functions of the quattuorviral boards, and that this was marked by their division into two colleges of *ivviri iure dicundo* and of *ivviri aedilicia potestate*. If the historians of Italy correctly assert that in this century its commercial, industrial, and agricultural activity reached proportions unknown before,[3] this specialization of duties among those whose task it was to regulate the modes and formal expression of this increased activity is just what one would expect to find, and Caesar is perhaps just the man to whom such changes might be attributed. But conclusions more radical than this cannot be dragged from the testimony.

To argue from formal title to function in this manner could be valid only if the new form *displaced* the older. But in fact there is no such break. In some places the simpler title even remained in normal and official use in the second century A.D.[4] If, however, Rome, in changing the type of local magistracies, as she did by substituting the *ivviri* for the *meddices*, etc., changed also their

[1] Op. cit. 108–9.
[2] Cf. Stuart Jones's review of Rudolph in *JRS* 1936, 270, quoting *ILS* 5706, 5729, 6356, 6358. *CIL* i², 1721, 1727, 1728, 1730. Absolute certainty in dating these examples to the *aetas Sullana*, however, depends upon an investigation into questions of building material on which opinions still differ. The failure of Rudolph to deal with the plain statement in the *lex Mamilia Roscia* 'quicumque in . . . municipio iure dicundo praeerit eius magistratus de ea re . . . iurisdictio esto' is also to be remarked, since this precedes his *lex Julia* by several years (below, 167).
[3] Cf. T. Frank, *Economic Survey*, i. 352 ff., 363.
[4] e.g. in the *Fasti Ostienses*, *Année Ép.* 1933, n. 30.

functions, and withdrew minor jurisdiction from the local courts, one may well ask what provision was made for this necessity of daily life? That the great lawsuits would go before the central courts is not disputed. But so they did in the heyday of the Empire. What, however, happened to the hundred small cases of a market town that could not suffer such delay or such expense? Nothing further is now heard of the *praefecti* of earlier days. They are last mentioned in a passage of a law of 100 B.C., and, though the prefectural system was possibly retained in the old city territory after 89 B.C., there is no sign of its extension to the new municipalities.[1] In neglecting the other functions of the local magistrates Rudolph loses sight of the fact that these functions presuppose the possession of some powers of coercion, sufficient, e.g. *ad vectigalia visenda pecuniasque exigendas*, to collect tithes and rents, where such lay within their own territory.[2] This implies at least the powers of a police court. Already in 58 B.C. the aedile of the *vicus Furfonensis*, a person far below the dignity of a municipal *ivvir*, held, as the complement of his duties of managing the local finances, the right of exacting fines, and that too *quanti volet*. Rudolph would dismiss these powers as different in kind from the later jurisdiction, and attach the label of 'a necessary right which was not limited to the municipalities'.[3] But this gives away the very point at issue. This necessary right is the very basis of the idea of a self-governing community. If allowed to a *vicus*, it cannot be denied to other and greater municipal units of the new Italy.

Further evidence comes from the fragments of the municipal laws and charters of late Republican date. The impression given by their arrangements for local jurisdiction is not that of a sudden innovation or improvisation, but that the purpose of, e.g., the *Lex Rubria de Gallia Cisalpina* was to extend throughout that area a system that had long been in practice elsewhere. A sentence of the Atestine law seems to deny Rudolph's thesis explicitly. '. . . in quoque municipio colonia praefectura . . . ii viri eiusve qui ibi lege *foedere* plebeive scito senatusve consulto *institutove* iure dicundo praefuit.'[4] This passage does not stand alone. In the *tabula Heracleensis* one reads: 'Qui minor annos xxx

---

[1] *FIRA* i². 9. 11. 12; cf. 7. 31. Dio 54. 26. 7 dates abolition before 13 B.C.
[2] Cic. *ad Fam.* 13. 11. 1.
[3] *ILS* 4906, 15. Rudolph, op. cit. 232.
[4] *Fr. Lex. Atest.* 11. 'In any municipality the *iivir* or whoever is in charge of jurisdiction there by law, treaty, plebiscite, senatus-consultum, or custom.'

natus est . . . nei ' . . quis eorum . . . magistratum petito . . . nisei
. . . ei vacatio rei militaris legibus plebeive scitis exve foedere
erit.' At a much earlier date in the *lex agraria* also: '. . . facere
licebit Latino peregrinoque . . . ex lege plebeivescito exve
foedere.'[1] The chain is complete. The language is technical, and
the meaning of the terms is clear. These phrases mean that in the
local judicature, as in other spheres of public life, there is continuity with the system that prevailed before the incorporation of
the *municipia*, despite the introduction of a Roman or at least a
Latin form of collegiate magistracy. In the Atestine fragment the
words *ex foedere . . . institutove* mean that the local magistracy is
continuous with what had been there before.

Nothing more is known about the limitations of the functions of
the original quattuorviral boards than that they were not known
as *quattuorviri iure dicundo*. But the omission is not significant, for
the very documents that contain most information about municipal jurisdiction generally omit the additional title.[2] Normally
the function is only mentioned in the case of substitutes for the
magistrates; only the *lex Rubria* among Republican charters once
uses the form *ivvir i.d.*, while in other instances it employs phrases
which suggest that the notion of jurisdiction is latent in the term
*quattuorvir* alone. For the phrase 'iv vir quive ibi iure dicundo
. . . praeest' is exactly parallel to the description of the Roman
magistrate in the same document as 'praetor isve qui . . . Romae
iure dicundo praeest'.[3] The addition of *iure dicundo* is simply
explanatory.

The evidence thus seems to justify Mommsen's view that these
powers are a remnant of the former sovereignty of the Italian
states.[4] That the universal supremacy of the local courts was
modified, is not in dispute. The provision for *revocatio Romae*
in the laws and charters proves this.[5] But there is no support in
them for Rudolph's sweeping generalization. The importance of
the extension of the franchise in 89 B.C. lies in the consequent fresh

---

[1] *Tab. Her.* 90–5. *Lex Agr.* 29.

[2] *Tab. Her.* uses the forms *iivirei ivvirei*, 83–105, 135–40. *Lex m. Tarentini* uses the
same, also *magistratus*, 8–15, 35–40. *Fr. Atest.* uses *iivir eiusve*, etc. *Lex col. Gen.* uses
*iivir* alone except for the form *quive*, etc., in 61. *Lex Rubria* uses *iivir ivvir praefectusve*
in 19, 20; *is qui ibi i.d.p.* in 22, 23; and *iivir i.d.p.* only in 20, l. 42.

[3] *Lex Rubria* 22, l. 30, l. 45.

[4] Mommsen, *St. R.* iii. 812 ff. Rudolph *contra*, op. cit. 225 ff.

[5] *Lex Rubria* 21; 22. For criminal jurisdiction over *municipes* at Rome cf. Cic.
*pro Clu., Rosc. Am.* generally.

contribution made by the newly incorporated states to the meaning of the citizenship. Hence the interest of the discovery that the Roman government did not wipe the slate clean in the reorganization of Italy.

That there was considerable development of the municipal system during the Ciceronian age is, however, not to be denied. It is a reasonable surmise that the *quattuorviri* were less concerned with local jurisdiction in the days before the addition of *i.d.* to their title than afterwards. At the very least the change implies greater specialization of function, and the splitting up, as Rudolph says, of the unitary college into two pairs of senior and junior magistrates, to cope with an increased burden of administration. The development of the system in this way has left a clear mark in the sources. The *lex municipi Tarentini* does not contain the elaborate detail in the paragraphs devoted to judicial arrangements which is notable in the later documents. After a *ne quis* the law-giver is satisfied to provide briefly that 'si quis adversus ea faxit . . . pecuniam municipio dare damnas esto eiusque pecuniae qui volet petitio esto. Magistratus qui exegerit dimidium in publicum referto.'[1] The contrast with, e.g., *lex Rubria* XXI–XXII suggests that those are right who, like Liebenam, see in finance the primary sphere of municipal autonomy.[2]

## THE MUNICIPALIZATION OF ITALY AND ITS CONSEQUENCES

The incorporation of the Latin and allied states, and the establishment of general uniformity among them by the introduction of the quattuorvirate, were accomplished by 80 B.C. at the latest.[3] This change was carried out uniformly not only in those parts, like Etruria and the Hellenized south, where the city-state was normal, but throughout the tribal areas of central Italy. The Umbrian and Oscan peoples were uniformly reorganized as *municipia* with *quattuorviri* as magistrates.[4] As a consequence of this enormous preponderance of *municipia* within the Roman state,

---

[1] Bruns (7) 27, 34 ff., cf. 5 f. 'Whoever acts contrarily is to owe a fine to the borough and may be prosecuted by anyone at will. The magistrate who exacts the fine is to pay half into the treasury.'

[2] Liebenam, *Städteverwaltung*, 296.

[3] Cf. Rudolph, op. cit. 94. Cic. *pro Clu.* 25 and 94, *ad Att.* 10. 13. 1.

[4] Beloch, *RG* 502 f.

the position of the municipally undeveloped areas of the older territory of Rome was rendered anomalous. It became necessary to equate the prefectures of central Italy and Campania with the new municipalities. Otherwise, though all Italians south of the Po were now Romans, there would remain a distinction between two sorts of Roman citizens, those with an *origo municipalis* and those registered in the City. So long as large areas of Italy were directly attached to Rome this distinction could persist. At some time in the middle of the first century these lands were divided up and shared out as *territoria* to the more important villages and market towns. This meant the assimilation of these rural communities to *municipia*. Occasionally the former titles such as *forum* or *praefectura*, like the tribal names of the new Oscan municipalities, persisted to a later date, to prove the strength of the superseded system; but the former chaos is no more.[1] The importance of this reform is that by the introduction of real uniformity throughout Italy, extended in 49 B.C. to the Alps, and by the removal of the *territorium* of the City, the distinction between urban and municipal Romans, still echoed by Cicero, was gradually forgotten, and the unification of Italy into one nation greatly forwarded.[2]

To date this change exactly is not easy. Sulla began the process by municipalizing at least part of the city territory in Latium. The *conciliabula* in the immediate vicinity of Rome are described by Cicero as municipalities, and in two instances, Castrimoenium and Bovillae, the local magistracy is known to have been the quattuorvirate, a fact which agrees with the date given by the rather weak authority of the *Liber Coloniarum*, which attributes their foundation to Sulla.[3] But the Sullan innovation did not extend beyond Latium, and probably did not complete the work even there.[4] Yet by the end of the Republic the prefectures and market towns of Campania, the Sabine country, Picenum and the Ager Gallicus, had all—excepting those few places where the Octovirate already existed—become municipalities whose local

[1] Above, 63 ff.

[2] Cf. above, 154, and the gibes at Cicero as a foreigner, *pro Sulla* 22–5.

[3] Beloch, *RG* 162 f. Rudolph, op. cit. 96. Cic. *pro Planc.* 23. *de Har. Resp.* 20. Liber Col. 231. 233.

[4] Veii and Fidenae belong to the later system, their magistracy being the duovirate. Beloch, *RG* 163. But Cures, ibid. 504, an old Sabine *municipium*, has the quattuorvirate.

magistrates, instead of being *quattuorviri*, were known as *duoviri*.[1] An indication of the date at which the new system was inaugurated is given by Caesar's reference to the transformation of Cingulum in Picenum, one of the duoviral boroughs.[2] This was a recent event in 49 B.C. Given this terminal point it is very probable that the view sponsored by Rudolph is correct, namely that the changes were carried out in virtue of the *lex Mamilia Roscia* quoted by the *agrimensores*, and that this law was passed in 55 B.C., under the aegis of the Triumvirate.[3] This *lex Roscia*, which is a colonial and municipal law, is the first known text to envisage the creation of artificial *municipia*, and the asssimilation of the various forms of *oppida* to municipalities by the assignation of *territoria*.

To what extent Caesar as dictator implemented the *lex Roscia* by other legislation for this particular purpose, it is not possible to determine. All that is certain is that by 44 B.C., the date of the *tabula Heracleensis*, the process of assimilation had been completed, since the formularies of the later document recognize no differences but those of title between the various types of municipality, new and old, normal and artificial.[4] Rudolph's further speculations about a *lex Julia municipalis* that, as he believes, completed the work of the *lex Roscia*, are not well grounded. The occasional hints in the letters of Cicero about Caesar's municipal activity have no bearing upon this particular point;[5] but the basis of Rudolph's view is an untenable identification of the new duoviral boroughs with a class of *municipia fundana*, to which the notorious last clause of the *tabula Heracleensis* is supposed to refer. These *municipia* are then explained as being made up of *fundi*—the farmlands of the viritane settlers in Rome's older territory—and thus are easily identified with some—but not all—of the new municipalities.[6] But the *tabula* is not speaking of a class of municipalities at all,[7] or of more than one municipality, while the phrase *municipes fundani* which it employs is not parallel to

[1] Beloch, *RG* 508 f. For the Octovirate cf. above, 65 ff.

[2] Caesar, *BC* 1. 15, 'quod oppidum Labienus constituerat suaque pecunia exaedificaverat'. Cic. *ad Att.* 10. 13. 1 is not decisive, *pace* Rudolph, op. cit. 97.

[3] Rudolph, op. cit. 197 ff. For the text, Bruns (7) 15.

[4] Bruns (7) 18, 83 cc.

[5] *Ad Fam.* 6. 18. 1; 13. 11. 3.

[6] Rudolph, op. cit. 176 ff.

[7] *Tab. Her.* 159–63. Cf. 160, 'municipibus eius municipi'. Also H. Stuart-Jones, *JRS* 1936, 271, and A. von Premerstein, *Ƶ. Sav. St.* 1922, 68 ff.

such a term as *Latini coloniarii*. Adjectives other than place-names are not normally attached to *municeps* except in a non-technical sense. The *lex Salpensana*, for example, does not speak of *municipes Latini*, but uses a periphrasis, *si quis . . . qui Latinus erit*.[1] Since Arpinum also, with whose fortunes those of Fundi had been linked at the time both of the grant of *civitas sine suffragio* and of incorporation, had its constitution remodelled in these years, it is reasonable to suppose that the *tabula* is speaking of the *municipium Fundanum*, and not of a group of *municipia fundana*.[2] The last clause of the law was in fact simply tacked on to a bill of mixed content.

It is possible to detect in the language of Cicero some signs of this withdrawal of the remaining city territory from the direct supervision of the urban magistrates, and of the consequent 'capitalization' of Rome. One passage, written a year before the proposed date of the *lex Mamilia Roscia*, marks the half-way stage. Cicero is summing up in an exhaustive list the various forms of association that constitute the Roman people: 'erat igitur in luctu senatus, squalebat civitas publico consilio . . . nullum erat *Italiae* municipium nulla colonia nulla praefectura, nulla *Romae* societas vectigalium nullum collegium aut concilium aut omnino aliquod commune consilium.'[3] Two years later he describes the *praefectura* of Atina simply as a *municipium*.[4] The same threefold division of *municipium colonia praefectura* appears in the *tabula Heracleensis* as an alternative to the fivefold division of types. In other accounts of his return from exile Cicero uses a variety of phrases: 'omnes ex omnibus agris atque oppidis cives',[5] 'qui e municipiis venissent'[6] 'celebritas oppidorum',[7] 'motus municipiorum et coloniarum',[8] 'municipiorum et coloniarum et totius Italiae'.[9] The phrases of the *pro Sestio* are the most careful; they do not disagree with the others but supplement them, and suggest a country in which, beside a great majority of *municipia et coloniae*, other types of community exist that are gradually being translated to the more complex form.[10] Already in Sallust, who

[1] *ILS* 6088. 28.                                   [2] Cic. *ad Fam.* 13, 11, 3, above, 66.
[3] *Pro Sestio* 32. 'The Senate was in mourning, the state with its national Council was showing its grief. No borough of Italy, no colony, no prefecture, no tax company at Rome, no club, no group, nor any common gathering at all.'
[4] *Pro Plancio* 8. 19–9. 23.          [5] *Post Red.* 9. 24.          [6] Ibid. 11. 27.
[7] *Ad Quirites* 1. 4.          [8] Ibid. 4. 10.          [9] *De Domo* 28, 75.
[10] Cf. also *pro Sulla* 7, 23, as early as 62 B.C.

belongs to the generation of Caelius rather than that of Cicero, the older idea of *municipium* is unfamiliar. He uses it in the later, general sense, less exactly than Cicero.[1] The older terminology was soon to pass out of use except for place-names, in which sphere phrases like *municipes Foroclaudienses* shadow forth the late imperial use of such terms as *respublica municipii, respublica civitatis.*

This municipalization of Italy has sometimes been disguised as the municipalization of Rome; but the situation is that the city-state of Rome has disappeared while the city remains. In the Social War the city-state, though overgrown, existed in a very real sense, politically and geographically, and fought a war with its neighbours. By the close of the Republic there is a complete change. *Municipia et coloniae* means Italy, apart from Rome; and Urbs Roma stands either literally for so much brick and mortar and stone, or else for an idea.[2] In the *de Legibus* Cicero says, in effect, that before the Social War the Romans had regarded the lands and communities which had been Roman since the fourth and third centuries as the *territorium* of their *urbs*, but that after 89 B.C. such language was felt to be inapplicable to the new situation.[3] Anomalies whose harshness was not felt when the municipalities could be counted on a man's fingers became insistent when they covered the whole peninsula. After 89 the *municipium* ceased to be the exceptional and became the typical basis of the Roman citizenship since the City no longer *materially* balanced the municipalities. It is precisely because of this change that Rome was able to serve as the formal *patria* of all, wherever born or living, who had received the Roman citizenship.

Behind this change lies a considerable growth of the idea and importance of the *municipium*. Among the municipalities of the Principate are many that would not have been recognized as such even in the Ciceronian age. *Municipium* came to mean any Roman municipality, irrespective of place or origin, though historically it meant an Italian *populus* which had entered the Roman state. This change covers the gradual equalization of all citizens in privilege and reputation. The process began even before the

---

[1] Sall. *Cat.* 30, 7, 'uti . . . familiae Capuam et in cetera municipia distribuerentur'.

[2] Cf. Horace, *Ep.* 1, 10, 11, 14, *passim. Carmen S.* 11, 'possis nihil urbe Roma Visere maius'. For *municipia et coloniae* in the Principate, cf. below, 238.

[3] Above, 154.

Social War. The *lex agraria* of *c.* 111 B.C. speaks of *pro moenicipis* beside true *municipia*.[1] This is the first stage only, for another passage of the same law shows that the idea of artificially creating a *municipium* out of an area of Roman territory with its inhabitants was not yet accepted.[2] Mommsen suggested that in this document the phrase 'coloniae seive moinicipia seive quae pro moenicipiis coloniisve sunt' is the equivalent of the longer exhaustive catalogues of the later documents.[3] This would mean that *conciliabula*, etc., were already being equated with *municipia* at the date of the *lex agraria*. That is certainly not so. The law is simply naming those communities which were capable of holding *ager publicus*; only in this respect does it link Roman *oppida* together with *municipia*, and so provide the first indication of the future assimilation of the various municipal units.

If the *Tabula Heracleensis*, which combines measures about Rome and about *municipia*, contains disparate proposals issued in one bill by Antonius after Caesar's death, a fairly clear account can be given of Caesar's later municipal plans.[4] After the completion of the municipalization of Italy by the carrying out of laws like the *lex Mamilia Roscia*, it was the intention of Caesar to establish a reasonable uniformity of procedure, though not necessarily of titulature, in the varied hotch-potch of local government as it then was. The *tabula* contains, amid some unrelated matter, fragments of his plans which were never put into effect as a whole during his lifetime. It is possible that the new uniformity was to be established partly by the issue of particular *leges municipales* for particular boroughs, such as the *lex Julia municipalis* of Padua, and partly by the issue of general legislation such as the *lex Rubria de Gallia Cisalpina*, and the clauses of the *tabula* concerning the local censorship, which were intended to apply to all Italy.[5] But once the *tabula* is regarded as a *lex satura*, it ceases to offer any support to the notion that Rome was reduced to the level of a municipality. In fact this was not true even in the Augustan age. The only puzzle left is to decide why the clauses affecting the local administration of Rome were published at Heraclea, for this fact is the basis of the notion of the municipalization of Rome.

[1] Bruns, *Fontes* (7) 11, 31.
[2] Ibid. 22, 'quo in agro iiivir . . . *oppidum* coloniamve ex lege constituerit deduxit conlocavitve.'
[3] Mommsen, *St. R.* iii. 792.     [4] Cf. citations in 167 n. 7.
[5] Above, 167 f., *Tab. Her.* 142 cc.

A fair parallel is provided by the publication at Bantia, at the close of the second century B.C., of a Roman law concerning *maiestas*.[1] Bantia was then remodelling her constitution on that of Rome, and the discovery of the *tabula* at Heraclea, and of these clauses in particular, suggests a similar Romanization of that place, much more than the degradation of Rome.

The importance of Julius Caesar in the municipal history of Italy has been much magnified, thanks largely to the luck of epigraphic discovery, and to the influence of the misleading inscription of Padua in particular. In Italy Julius was not an innovator, but completed the work begun by others. To imagine that the municipal system was left incomplete for half a century, and then was perfected at a stroke by the genius of one man, is only possible if the extreme complexity of the system as manifested in the surviving charters is ignored. Such complexity is the product of accumulated experience. That Caesar improved the system is not in dispute, but his method was in accordance with established tradition.[2] The arrangements for the taking of the census, set forth in the *tabula*, show a strict respect for tradition, being based, directly or indirectly, upon a precedent of the third century.[3] The improvements made by Caesar in all departments, including jurisdiction, must have been in the same spirit of loyalty to tradition. Otherwise it would be hard to explain their permanence, their success, and the lack of any reference in contemporary writers to drastic changes.

More valuable than the attempt to make Caesar the cause of everything is the reconstruction of the growth of local autonomy from modest beginnings to the elaborate system of later days. It emerges that the extension of the competence of the local authorities kept pace with the extension of the Roman citizenship. Here lies the importance of Rudolph's investigation into the specialization of the functions of the *ivviri*.[4] In the Ciceronian age there is sufficient material to assess the balance of loyalty between the two *patriae* of a Roman citizen. The impression given by the laws and charters agrees very well with Cicero's remarks in the *de Legibus*, when one reckons that Cicero's attitude is that of a prominent public man. For the ordinary Italian the part played by the *curia* in the life of Cicero is filled by the army; the essential

[1] Above, 129 ff.                           [2] Cf. above, 163 f.
[3] *Tab. Her.* 142 cc. Cf. Livy 29. 15. 9–11; 37, 7.        [4] Above, 161 ff.

*munus* of the plain man is to serve his country—the *patria civitatis pro qua* mori *debemus*—as a soldier. It was only the Empire, but not the Empire of Augustus, that saw the loosening of this bond.[1]

The limits to the competence of local magistrates in civil jurisdiction are another expression of the subordination of the *patria naturae* to the Roman state.[2] While the Roman citizenship was confined to Italy the possibility of *revocatio Romae* kept alive the real contrast between the scope of the local and that of the national citizenship. The charters illustrate this amply, but the reality of the Roman citizenship would remain, in the sphere of jurisdiction, only so long as there was a constant stir of important litigation.

The last mark of the balance between Rome and the municipalities lies in the disposition of the local census in accordance with a formula published at Rome.[3] By themselves these regulations, with the sending of the lists to Rome, suggest a preponderance of Rome over her units. Exactly to determine the accuracy of the balance is not possible, since it would vary with the circumstances of peace and war, poverty and wealth. Possibly so long as the citizenship was confined almost entirely to Italy the *patria naturae* must have remained secondary. But in the very period under discussion the Roman franchise was spreading in Africa, Gaul, and Spain. While this migratory movement of the citizenship was still nascent the balance perhaps swung away from the borough to the City. The *Tabula Heracleensis* provides one illustration of this inevitable preference for Rome within Italy. 'Qui plurubus in municipiis coloniis praefecturis domicilium habebit et is Romae census erit, quo magis in municipio censeatur . . . hac lege nihilum rogatur.'[4]

Above this minor question the major issue rises clear. Over against the local divisions of Italy, the fulfilment of the task begun by Gaius Gracchus and finished by Caesar set not a force, not another state, but an idea. This fruitful principle could not be *established* until a series of reforms covered the peninsula with a

---

[1] For the importance of the *munus militare*, cf. *Tab. Her.* 89–125. Horace's line 'Dulce et decorum est *pro patria mori*' is more than an inane platitude.

[2] *Lex de G. Cisalpina* 21, 22. Fr. Atest. 15–20.

[3] *Tab. Her.* 145–55.

[4] Ibid. 155–60. 'Whoever has his residence in several boroughs and is registered at Rome, that he should be registered in his borough rather than at Rome is not required by this law.'

municipal system which 'finally withdrew from Rome her sole control and gave back to the Italian peoples in large part the government of the land'.[1] Here was solved the riddling difficulty of preserving within the unity of Rome the essential value of the Italic city-states. At this moment of the late Ciceronian age both seem to be safe, caught up in the Ciceronian formula. Those Roman knights known from the letters of Cicero, who on returning from the wars busy themselves with the concerns of their native boroughs, are a lively illustration of the principles of the *Tabula Heracleensis*, men to whom both *patriae* are real.[2]

*Addendum.* Recently a notable section of the *lex coloniae* (it seems) of Puteoli, and a badly damaged fragment of a similar *lex* from Cumae have been published: L. Bove, *Rendiconti Acc. Arch. Lett. Belle Arti di Napoli* 41 (1966), 207 f.

Since the orthography suggests a date no earlier than the known Caesarean documents, and probably Augustan rather than Julian, these cast no direct light on the evolution of municipal jurisdiction between 89 and 49. But it is remarkable that the law of Puteoli is concerned with detailed arrangements for the execution of prisoners after local magisterial sentences, and other condign punishments. It is not clear whether any limitation of *personae* was imposed. If not, the *duoviri* possess an unexpectedly high power of *coercitio* without appeal to another tribunal, like the imperial *praefectus urbi* at Rome. For Puteoli cf. above, 87, 89.

[1] Rudolph, op. cit. 219.
[2] *ad Fam.* 13, 11; 12, 1. Cf. *ad Q.f.* 2, 12, 3; both concern *trib. mil.*

# VII

## POPULI LIBERI AND FOEDERATI

### DEVELOPMENT TOWARDS A WORLD STATE
### OUTSIDE ITALY

THE negative influence of the existence of a provincial empire upon the content and extension of the Roman citizenship under the Republic can only be studied indirectly, yet that influence continually suggests itself, when the complicated pattern of the Roman hegemony is examined. E. Täubler has endeavoured to represent the latter as a series of concentric circles with Rome at the centre, but the matter is more complicated than that. The Romans, in and after the great wars of the second century, built up for themselves a series of dependencies and alliances which tended, with the continual increase in the material power of Rome, to become more and more a part of the internal structure of a world-state instead of remaining the junior partners of a federal system. The very generation that saw Rome deliberately refuse opportunities of provincial annexation saw the conversion of the forms of *civitas foederata* and of *civitas libera*, the federated ally and the free state outside Italy, into something like a type of subjection to Rome. It is true that the Romans of the Republic, especially those for whom Cicero speaks, refused to draw the last practical conclusions from this process, but still the change is one of the first steps towards the conception, which becomes common in the second century A.D., of the Roman world as consisting of τὰ ἔθνη, 'the peoples', irrespective—before the Constitutio Antoniniana—of their precise status or civic privilege.[1]

The study of the Roman confederation outside Italy is all the more important because it has not yet been undertaken as a whole since Marquardt and Mommsen sketched the outlines of the problem. The invaluable work of Henze, Täubler, and Horn, while often exhaustive, if not final, as far as it goes, has been mainly directed to the separate and special study of the main features of the

---

[1] Below, 437 ff.

problem, and has perhaps suffered a little from its very speciality. It is possible to make a synthesis of their results, and perhaps to add a little more, by treating these constitutional forms not only together, but over a somewhat longer period than was attempted by Täubler or Horn, at least for the *civitas libera*.

There is little doubt about the origins of the two institutions. The solemn treaty of alliance between two independent powers is too common and necessary a feature of a civilized world to call for special comment, though it is well to notice that the group of extra-Italian *foederati* is not to be regarded as an extension of the Italian federation.[1] Rome had entered into alliance with non-Italian powers such as Carthage and Massilia long before the Italian federation was completed.[2] There is even a notable difference between the two systems, in that the *foedus iure iniquo* is considerably less common outside Italy, especially in the Hellenistic East, than within. The circle of the *formula togatorum* remained closed to Asiatic, or to other European *foederati*, till a period at which the *foedus* had largely lost its original purpose and value.[3]

It is the *civitas libera* which excites attention by the unfamiliarity of the conception in modern days, especially since in the later history of the Republic and under the early Empire it is of infinitely greater importance than the *civitas foederata*. The assimilation of the two forms, which has been often noticed, has been interpreted rather as implying the deterioration of the position of the *civitas foederata* than as suggesting that the senatorial government deliberately abandoned the use of the treaty-form in favour of the declaration of freedom by *senatus consultum* in its dealings with the more civilized states of the ancient world.[4] The latter view by no means contradicts the general interpretation of *foedus* and *libertas* which has been established by Mommsen and his successors, but results from the comparison of phenomena which they studied separately.

The practice of declaring a community to be 'free', whether in a wider or more limited sense of the word, is one that Rome first

---

[1] Cf. H. Horn, *Foederati*, 14.    [2] Ibid. 19–22.    [3] Ibid. 82.
[4] Horn, op. cit. 52, justly remarks that the only important group of *foederati* under the early principate are certain peoples of *Gallia Comata*. For a more recent discussion of the evolution of *Libertas* in the Hellenistic policy of Rome see E. Badian, *Foreign Clientelae*, ch. ii.

learned from the Greeks, and then twisted in most Roman fashion to her own purposes. Her first experiment was innocent. Having defeated Philip of Macedon, Rome inserted into the treaty of 197 B.C. a clause that guaranteed the freedom of those Greek states which had in fact been, of old, nominally free from the intervention of the Macedonian kings.[1] In doing this Rome was only following the tradition of Artaxerxes and Polyperchon.[2] Her next step took her further, when at Corinth Flamininus declared the freedom of those Greek communities whose fate Rome could claim to decide by right of conquest, that is to say, the subjects or allies of Philip.[3] This is the category of states among which the institution of 'freedom' was most widely spread by Rome not only in the succeeding half century, but until the consolidation of the *Orbis Romanus* was complete.

If the current view is true that at this period the Roman government was trying to avoid a policy of provincial annexation, it seems a little surprising that such a method was followed in preference to the conclusion of formal treaties, which is a more normal method of regulating inter-state relations. The explanation lies partly in the obvious advantages of a unilateral arrangement of which the interpretation lay only with the senior partner,[4] but also in the political situation of the majority of the states that Rome declared to be free: they had been the subjects of a Hellenistic king.[5] Rome's contact with them was only indirect. The juristic grounds for the conclusion of a treaty did not exist, since a treaty can only be struck between independent communities. Conceivably after the declaration that X was to be free a regular treaty might have been made, nor are possible examples lacking.[6] But where Rome acquired sovereign powers over a community through the conquest of its overlord, the immediate possibility of

---

[1] E. Täubler, *Imperium Romanum*, 432–3. Polyb. 18. 27 (44). 2.

[2] Täubler, op. cit. 434–6. Badian o.c. 37 dates invention of *libertas* to grants to five Sicilian cities c. 241 B.C. But Diod. 23. 4. 5, Zon. 8. 9, Cic. *II in Verr* 3. 13 do not confirm this origin; see S. Calderone. *Kokkalos*, 1964–5, 93 ff. Cf. *libertas* granted to *Campani dediticii*, below, 211 n. 5.

[3] Täubler, op. cit. 437–8. This is explicit in the phrase of the declaration. Pol. 18. 29 (46). 5, καταπολεμήσαντες βασιλέα . . . ἀφιᾶσιν ἐλευθέρους . . . Κορινθίους.

[4] Cf. E. W. Henze, *De Civitatibus Liberis*, 6.

[5] Cf. Pol. 18. 27 (44), 5, quoted below, 178 n. 1. Cf. at a later period the freedom granted to the *civitates* of the kingdom of Cyrene bequeathed to Rome by Ptolemy Apion, Livy, *Ep.* 70; and Strabo 16. 2. 8 (751), on Seleucia Pieria, ἐλευθέραν αὐτὴν ἔκρινε Πομπήιος ἀποκλείσας Τιγράνην.

[6] e.g. Utica, *lex agr.* 80, Cic. *Balb.* 51, cf. below, 181 n. 5.

a *foedus* with the subject state was absent. In fact the notable treaties made by Rome in the East are with great powers, such as the Aetolian or Achaean league, or with small communities whose independence is either known or possible. Cibyra, for example, the earliest in date of the minor federated states of Asia, was, a little before the time of the treaty, an independent power ruled by a local dynast.[1]

The Roman adaptation of the declaration of freedom thus preserved the rights of conquest, without involving Rome in the encumbrance of provincial government. That the Greeks did not observe the subtlety of this adaptation of their own custom is proved by the fact that even Polybius identifies or confuses the two distinct processes, Rome's guarantee of the continued freedom of the original independent states and her act of declaring free the subject states of Philip.[2]

Täubler has analysed the process by which Rome's benevolent protectorate over the original category of 'free states' quickly changed to the control of a master,[3] but he has not probed further into the history of the institution. In European Greece and the Islands the Romans acted indirectly; partly they limited the external political freedom of the original category of free states by securing control over the European policy of their powerful neighbours, such as Antiochus,[4] but partly also they proceeded to make treaties with the most powerful of the Greeks themselves, such as the Achaean and Aetolian leagues.[5] The number of fully independent states sank, leaving the *civitates liberae*, whose freedom depended entirely upon Roman favour, to dominate the scene.

Apart from the legal foundation, there does not seem to have been any difference in quality between the various categories of 'free states' as recognized by Rome at the opening of the second century. Henze, although he does not place the fact in its right historical setting, notes that 'freedom' may mean 'freedom from a king'.[6] But this is in fact the essence of the matter in the days before the world-wide supremacy of Rome removed all the 'kings'

---

[1] Livy 38. 14. 3, cf. Dittenberger, *OGIS* 762 n. 1.
[2] Cf. Täubler, op. cit. 439; cf. Pol. 18. 29 (46). 15, with 27 (44). 2, 29 (46). 5. But Badian, o.c. 73 ff., denies any *arrière pensée* on Rome's side at this stage.
[3] Cf. Täubler, op. cit. 440–5.
[4] Ibid. 443.        [5] Ibid. 448.        [6] Op. cit. 1.

of importance.[1] The words 'they are to be free', ἐλευθέρους ὑπάρχειν, of the original *senatus consultum* are expanded, in the solemn formula of the herald at the Isthmus, into ἀφρουρήτους ἀφορολογήτους κτλ. 'they are to be free from garrisons and tribute, etc.'[2] The states are to be free from every form of royal domination. In addition, they are to enjoy their own laws and constitution. While this latter stipulation always remained as part of the content of *libertas*, autonomy in itself is at no period the sole privilege of the 'free states', nor the privilege of the free states alone, and forms no criterion by which to judge the relation of the free states to Rome. It is by Rome's attitude to the old royal prerogatives of exacting tribute and imposing garrisons, that one can decide whether or not she is respecting the full original freedom of the communities concerned. When Rome makes a distinction between freedom and immunity, an attempt to bring certain communities into a close dependence is to be suspected. And when, as under the early Principate, there ceases to be any connection between the two,[3] it is certain that *libera* is but a title of courtesy, and that the communities, whatever their rank, have all become something like 'subordinate members of an imperial State'. But the original form of the institution was far different.[4] Freedom means freedom from a king, and the sign of this freedom is the abolition of the royal tax and the withdrawal of the royal garrison.

It is often stated that the *civitas foederata* and the *civitas libera* represent in theory the maximum and the minimum of sovereign rights which Rome recognized among her allied communities, and that the two forms were assimilated to one another by the reduction of the privileges of the first class and the increase of those of the second.[5] That this was the final position in the fully developed Empire is not to be disputed, but it is not true of the original relationship between the two forms in the earliest years of the second century, and is in fact the result of a long process, and above all of the provincialization of the Orbis Terrarum by Rome. However, corruption soon began. The means by which

---

[1] Cf. Pol. 18. 27 (44). 5, περὶ δὲ τῆς τῶν Κιανῶν ἐλευθερώσεως Τίτον γράψαι πρὸς Προυσίαν.

[2] Comparison of Polyb. 18. 27 (44), 2 with ibid. 29 (46). 5.

[3] Cf. Henze, op. cit. 4.

[4] Cf. Jos. *Ant.* 17. 9. 4, quoted by Henze (at a somewhat later period): ἐπιθυμοῦντες ἐλευθερίας καὶ ὑπὸ Ῥωμαίων στρατηγῷ τετάχθαι.

[5] e.g. Täubler, op. cit. 448–9. Horn, op. cit. 51. Hardy, *Six Roman Laws*, ed. 1, 95.

it was effected consisted in the addition of special conditions to the simple 'declaration of freedom' of earlier times.[1] The process began by the analysis of the conception of 'freedom' into its component parts. These, as time goes on, tend to be confirmed individually, instead of being granted in a block, and thus the way was open to withhold some of them, and to add further special conditions that were unknown to the original conception of 'freedom'. The passage from the precise analysis which the Romans characteristically made of 'freedom' in 197 B.C. to the addition of special conditions was accomplished within ten years. For in 187 B.C., when the Senate settled the status of Ambracia, a condition was added to the declaration of freedom: 'ut . . . portoria quae vellent terra marique caperent dum eorum immunes Romani ac socii nominis Latini essent.'[2] Twenty years later the Romans took the great step of separating *immunitas* from the conception of *libertas*. The fact emerges clearly from Livy's plain account of the establishment of the new order in Illyricum and Macedonia in 167 B.C.[3] The peoples of these two countries are to be 'free', but are to pay tribute to Rome,[4] except for a specially privileged class, of whom it is said 'non solum liberos sed etiam immunes fore'.[5] There is, in addition, a tremendous list of special conditions for the future arrangement of the two countries, the whole proceeding being summed up as *formula dicta*. Here is a strong contrast with the simple statement of a Roman consul to the city of Heraclea-by-Latmos, some twenty years before: 'We grant you freedom like the other cities . . . you are to control your own affairs and your constitution is to be in accordance with your own laws'.[6] Instead, the whole external liberty of at least the Macedonian communities is hedged and confined in every possible manner, not merely in relation to powers outside Macedon but to the

[1] e.g. in Xen. *Hell.* 5. 1. 31; Diod. 18. 55. 2.

[2] Livy 38. 44. 4. 'They could collect what customs dues they liked by land or sea provided that Romans and Latins were not made liable to them.'

[3] Livy 45. 26. 12-15, and 29. 4. Thus the separation of *immunitas* which characterized the later *libertas* goes back to an early precedent. Pompey, if it was he, thus contributed to the development not of the theory, only of its practice. Cf. Mommsen, *St. R.* iii. 659 n. 1, 683 n. 4.

[4] Livy 45. 26. 14, and 29. 4.

[5] Livy 45. 26. 13. 'They were not only to be free but were not even to be liable to taxation.'

[6] *SIG* iii³. 618, συγχωροῦμεν δὲ ὑμῖν τήν τε ἐλευθερίαν καθότι καὶ ταῖς ἄλλαις πόλεσιν . . . ἔχουσιν ὑφ' αὑτοὺς πάντα τὰ αὑτῶν πολιτεύεσθαι κατὰ τοὺς ὑμετέρους νόμους.

other districts of Macedonia. In what then did their 'freedom' consist? Simply, according to Livy, in the withdrawal of the Roman garrisons and in the fact that the Romans did not propose to occupy the throne of Perseus.[1] In his explanation of the motivation of this settlement Livy makes this abundantly clear, and distinguishes explicitly between the 'free states' and those subject to kings.[2]

The Romans thus perfected in the short period of thirty years a new political device which contained elements new and old, and whose great advantage was that it enabled them to secure the political control of large areas of the Hellenistic world, without alienating the friendship of the various communities and without the necessity of governing them directly. The declaration of freedom is simply a method of regulating the status of *populi dediti* from which Rome does not wish to demand the supply of troops, a procedure that would perhaps render necessary a treaty, but over whom she wishes to preserve some form of control. In its final form the system of *libertas* recalls the method used in the re-establishment of the Latin Name in 338 B.C., but difference of circumstances prevented the two types of relationship from developing on parallel lines.

The only further change that modified the institution is that which was a consequence of the extension of the provincial system. The effect of this was to improve the position of the *civitas libera* in relation to its less privileged neighbours, but at the same time still further to reduce the meaning of the term *libera* by restricting the title under which the community held its lands. In 167 B.C. the Macedonians were bidden to enjoy freedom and the possession of their cities and lands.[3] The tribute that they were ordered to pay was only a continuance of the practice of the Macedonian kings—and the sum was cut by half. It was not at this time brought into any special connection with the land of the communities as *tributum soli*; but when, about 70 B.C., the status of Termessus Major was being regulated, although numerous privileges

[1] Livy 45. 26. 12, 'praesidia . . . sese deducturum' immediately follows 'Illyrios esse liberos iubere'.

[2] Livy 45. 18. 1–2, 'liberos esse placebat Macedonas atque Illyrios ut . . . appareret arma populi Romani . . . servientibus libertatem afferre ut *et in libertate gentes quae essent* tutam eam sibi . . . sub tutela populi Romani esse *et quae sub regibus viverent* . . . mitiores eos . . . habere se crederent.'

[3] Livy 45. 29. 4.

were granted, a reservation was made on her territorial rights.[1] This interpretation of the *lex Antonia* becomes less difficult when the history of the *civitates liberae* is regarded as a whole; it is the natural conclusion of the process of 167 B.C. whereby some *liberi* enjoyed possession of their land and also paid tribute in an unspecified form.[2]

The connection of the great series of declarations of freedom in the first half of the second century with the isolated *civitates liberae* of the later Republican period is finally secured, by considering one of the last important groups of free states whose freedom was declared in a block. These are the seven African states, as they appear in the *lex agraria* of 111 B.C.[3] This is the earliest instance of the extension of the system to the non-Greek world, and is doubly interesting because it follows the formation of the province.[4] The complete lack of *civitates foederatae* in Africa at this period,[5] when the relationship of Rome to the old Carthaginian territories was being remodelled, shows how thoroughly the Romans had appreciated and accepted, as an instrument of empire, the tool which the Greeks first taught them to use, and how they preferred it to the treaty wherever their choice was not limited by special circumstances.[6]

---

[1] *ILS* 38. Cf. Bormann in *Festschrift Hirschfeld*, 439 on ll. 1. 27–35 of the *lex Antonia de Termessibus*: 'publica preivatave praeter locata . . . omnia habere liceto'; also the situation of Selge in Strabo, quoted below, n. 6.

[2] The contrary view held, e.g., by Hardy, op. cit. 97, and 72, 78 n. 27, is weakened by the consideration that in the *lex agraria* the land of the *c. liberae* is treated along with other categories where the title is not absolutely perfect, e.g., the *ager colonicus* assigned in accordance with the *lex Rubria*, 'since repealed'. In no case can it be maintained that the communities held anything or any land *suo iure*, since all depended upon a Roman law or *S.C.* Only the *civitas foederata* had rights whose basis was independent of Rome.

[3] Bruns, *Fontes*, 11. *lex agr.* 75 and 79, 80.                         [4] Ibid. 79.

[5] Cic. *Balb.* 51, mentions Utica in passing, as *foederata*. This may be an instance of the conclusion of a treaty with a *c. libera* after the declaration of freedom, or may be a slip of Cicero's; in any case it is irrelevant to the period under discussion.— In the Jugurthine war Leptis became *foederata*, Sall. *BJ* 77. 2.

[6] Cf. Livy, *Ep.* 70 for a later example of the policy in Cyrene, 'eius regni civitates senatus liberas esse iussit'. They paid some form of tribute *before* the creation of the province in 74 B.C., Henze, op. cit. 78. More surprising is the refusal to make a *foedus* with the people of Selge, Strabo 12. 7. 3 (571), οὔτε πρότερον οὔτε ὕστερον . . . ἐπ' ἄλλοις ἐγένοντο (i.e. in the time of the Seleucids and Ptolemies) πρὸς δὲ τοὺς Ῥωμαίους ἐπὶ τακτοῖς τισι κατεῖχον τὴν χώραν· . . . νῦν δὲ ὑπήκοοι τελέως γεγόνασι. They were clearly *liberi* at first, and later provincialized. Another example under the late Republic appears in the *S.C. de Tabenis* (*OGIS* 442), with which compare Cic. *de Off.* 3. 87, 'quas civitates Lucius Sulla . . . ex senatus consulto liberavisset'.

This sketch of the history of the *civitates liberae*, down to the time when the features of the institution seem to have been permanently fixed, has shown that 'free states' were gradually changed into subject states. In this, their history is parallel to that of the *civitates foederatae*, although the path followed was not exactly the same. It was the overwhelming military supremacy of Rome that led to the disruption of the federal relationship between herself and the Greek states.[1] But the growth of the system of *libertas*, though based on the military conquests of Rome, took place without any violation of formal rights. For Rome was always entitled to make what stipulations she chose when dealing with her *dediticii*. There can be little doubt that in this difference lies the reason why the Romans preferred the system of the one-sided declaration to that of the bilateral treaty.

The important question for the present inquiry into the growth of the *Orbis Romanus* is that of the meaning of the statement that *civitates liberae* and *civitates foederatae* became subject-states. To say this is not to say that these *civitates* became 'part of the Roman State'. The able German studies of the question have not been entirely conclusive because, while admirably demonstrating the gradual process by which these communities became *Reichsangehörige*, as they put it, they have not always pointed out that there is nothing that exactly answers to this conception in the jurisprudence of the Romans. The various tests that can be applied—existence of *postliminium*, *ius exili*, subjection to Roman laws, freedom from magisterial influence, absence of the circuit court of the governor, the *conventus iuridicus*, possession of military authority—never clarify the situation as a whole, but only qualify the condition of a given state in a certain aspect.[2] The reason for this is very simple: it is the great strength of the spirit of local autonomy in the ancient world. The question thus takes the following shape: 'how far did these communities which enjoyed a high degree of autonomy regard themselves as also subjects of the Roman state? And how far did the Romans consider that these communities were their subjects? And what is the meaning of the term "subject" in this connection?'

---

[1] Cf. Horn, op. cit. 27, 38–9, 51, 63. Täubler, op. cit. 447–9.

[2] e.g. Horn, op. cit. 45. His view, based on the *pro Balbo*, is curiously opposed to the conclusions drawn by Vogt in *Ciceros Glaube am Rom*, 67–8, and 89–93. See below, 187 ff.

Dr. Horn's study of the historical development of the non-Italian *foederati* has made it abundantly clear that Mommsen's analysis[1] of the position of these states in the Roman Empire as subject-states, dependent in external politics for all practical purposes upon Rome, is indeed true for the latest period of the Republic and the early Principate, but is not to be reflected back into the period when Rome first began to enter into alliance with states outside Italy.[2] That Rome's early relations with powers like the Aetolian and Achaean leagues, Rhodes, Massilia and Pergamum were entirely normal, either party retaining an absolute sovereignty while agreeing 'to help the other side if attacked', appears from the plain narrative of the sources.[3] In the first treaty with the Aetolians it was rather the Greeks than the Romans who had the upper hand, because in the particular political situation it was Rome that had need of the Greeks rather than the opposite.[4] The independence of the Greek states allied to Rome is determined far more by the relative political power of the two parties than by the actual form or content of their treaties. Rome's interference in the politics of, e.g., the Achaean league takes place despite the *foedus aequum*, the maintenance of which was the real cause of the final Achaean war.[5] At the same time there was a tendency for the states concerned, or a pro-Roman party within them, to submit to this interference, or to seek out Roman approval of their policy, in a manner highly detrimental to the maintenance of their true sovereignty, precisely because they felt that anything was better than a political clash with the greatest military power of the Mediterranean world.[6]

The grounds for the disfavour with which Rome came to regard the treaty as an instrument of empire, at least in her dealings with the Greek world, thus lie in the difficulty which she experienced in bending the more important of the *foederati* to her will. The final solution of her problem, in areas which Rome did not desire to provincialize, was found, not so much in the substitution of the

---

[1] *St. R.* iii. 650.                              [2] Horn, op. cit. 15–16.
[3] For Massilia, op. cit. 15, 16, 20, 21. But Cicero's reference to it as an *exemplum imperii amissi*, *de Off.* 2. 28, means that M. lost its dependencies, not its autonomy; cf. Strabo 4. 1. 5 (181) cited in part below, 189 n. 2. For Aetoli, Horn, 24–5. For Achaei, 35–8; for Rhodes, 62, which had no formal treaty until 165 B.C.
[4] Ibid. 23–4.                    [5] Ibid. 37 ff. Cf. Täubler, op. cit. 447.
[6] Täubler, op. cit. 448. Cf. Horn's remarks on Rhodes, op. cit. 61 and 63, and on Achaea, 38.

*foedus iniquum* for the *foedus aequum* after a military conquest, as in the development of the institution of the declaration of freedom discussed above. The Aetolian league, the earliest of her allies to quarrel with her, was subjected to the *foedus iniquum* in accordance with the technique acquired in the formation of the Italian hegemony, but the experiment was not repeated, nor does the Aetolian treaty seem to have survived long after 146 B.C.[1] The treaty-form, whether *aequo* or *iniquo iure*, was not sufficiently useful or pliant for dealing with these powers. Rome broke the power of the Greek *foederati*—apart from actual wars—by unconstitutional or extra-constitutional means, such as the weakening of Rhodes by the declaration of the free port at Delos, and afterwards abandoned the general use of treaties within the Empire.[2] Thus the list of *foederati* which can be formed for the later period consists, apart from the Gallic tribes, entirely of unimportant little powers, mainly individual city-states in Asia or in Spain; nor is it surprising, after a review of the history of the earlier *foederati*, that where actual texts have been preserved, the form seems to have been that of the *foedus aequum*. For Rome had little to fear from states such as Astypalaea, Cibyra, and Epidaurus; *they* were not likely to defy the *domina gentium*, until some champion like Mithridates arose to encourage them.

Nothing shows more clearly that it was not by constitutional means that the Romans reduced their *foederati* to a subordinate position than this collection of treaties with cities of minor importance, among which there is no absolutely certain example of a *foedus iniquum*. In Italy, and perhaps in the western provinces, the clause *maiestatem populi Romani comiter conservanto* played an important, though not an exclusive, part in reducing the independence of the federated states. Its omission from these eastern documents suggests something like contempt for the Greeks.

The evidence is fairly clear on this point, despite the imperfect condition in which some of these epigraphic texts have been found. The treaty of Cibyra, dated about 188 B.C., and a whole group of treaties which belong to the period 130–90 B.C.—those of Methymna (129 B.C.), Astypalaea (105 B.C.), and Thyrrheum (94 B.C.) contain clauses relating to a simple defensive alliance with Rome, and lack any trace of the *maiestas* clause. Only under

---

[1] Cf. Horn, op. cit. 30–1.
[2] Ibid. 52. Cf. below, 187.

the Principate of Augustus does this, or any trace of it, appear in the treaties of Cnidus and Mytilene.[1]

The treaty as a form of political relationship was clearly sliding into a neglect at the close of the second century B.C. from which it was only recalled for special service in Gaul, and then in a somewhat restricted form.[2] Except for the Mytilenean and Cnidian treaties, of which the former certainly,[3] and the latter in all probability,[4] was a renewal of an earlier alliance, all these treaties belong to a period before 90 B.C., and many of them can be carried back to a much earlier date; that of Gades, for example, goes back to the year 206 B.C.[5] The comparison of the short list of *foederati* in the index of Horn, not all of whom existed contemporaneously, with the vast series of *civitates liberae* established by Henze, most of which flourished together under the early Principate, illustrates how the one institution waxed while the other waned. The last step, not so much in the degradation as in the metamorphosis of the treaty, came when the Romans began to treat it exactly like the charter of a free state, by inserting special conditions into the very text of alliance. Among the epigraphic texts this appears first in the treaty of Mytilene,[6] though Cicero

---

[1] This conclusion is reinforced by the presence in three of these treaties, in so far as they are preserved, and by the apparent absence from the somewhat mutilated treaties of Mytilene and Cnidus, of the clause of the type ὁ δῆμος ὁ τῶν δεῖνα τῷ δήμῳ τῷ 'Ρωμαίων βοηθείτω ὡς ἂν εὔκαιρον ᾖ ἐκ τῶν συνθηκῶν καὶ τῶν ὁρκίων τῷ δήμῳ τῷ τῶν δεῖνα καὶ τῷ δήμῳ τῷ 'Ρωμαίων φαίνηται (and vice versa). This clause, whether, as Dittenberger (*OGIS* 762 n. 4) thinks, it refers to *other* treaties by which either party was bound, or not, clearly shows that both parties to the treaty are regarded as sovereign states. The contrast with the parallel clause of the *foedus iniquum* of the Aetolians makes this clear, ἐὰν πολεμῶσιν πρός τινας 'Ρωμαῖοι πολεμείτω πρὸς αὐτοὺς ὁ δῆμος ὁ τῶν Αἰτωλῶν. (Polyb. 21. 30. 15.) It is impossible to decide to which type the treaties of Elaea (?) and Epidaurus belong. Nor is the restoration of the 'maiestas' clause' in the treaty of Cnidus certain.

The *foedus Callatinum* from Thrace, of the second century, is too fragmentary to decide its nature (*Année Ép.* 1933, n. 106) with certainty, but the numerous repetitions of the words *poplus(o) Callatinus(o)*, and *poplus(o) Romanus(o)*, suggest rather the bilateral arrangements of the *foedus aequum* than the one-sided provision of the Aetolian treaty quoted above.

For the texts, see: *SIG* ii³, 693, Methymna. 694, Elaea(?), 732, Thyrrheum. *OGIS* 762, Cibyra. *IGRR* iv. 33, Mytilene. 1028, Astypalaea; also 'Εφ. 'Αρχ. 1918, 117 for Epidaurus, and Täubler, op. cit. 450, for Cnidus.

Neither Aphrodisias nor Stratonicea, *OGIS* 453–5, 441, is more than a *civitas libera*—the special proof that they are *socii foederati* is to seek; cf. Horn's remarks on the necessary criterion, op. cit. 12, and Henze, op. cit. 6.

[2] Horn, op. cit. 53, cf. below, 186 n. 1.      [3] *IGRR* iv. 33 b 20–5.
[4] Cf. Täubler, op. cit. 454.      [5] Cic. *pro Balbo*, 15. 34.
[6] Horn, op. cit. 73 f.

mentions it at an earlier date for the Gallic treaties.[1] This means the reduction of the *foedus*, bilateral act though it is, to the level of the *lex* of the free states, and is a final proof of the great profit the Romans drew from the use of the latter institution.

It is now possible to deal with the relation of these various communities to the Roman state, in the form of the question posed above. After this sketch of their history it is clear why all these peoples alike were called by the Romans *socii* or *socii et amici*. Horn's investigations have shown how loosely this title of *socii* was applied to every category of non-citizen provincials from the *stipendiarii* upwards.[2] Thus the Roman government, however seriously it interfered with the freedom of the *foederati* and the *populi liberi*, was always able to draw a line of demarcation between Rome and her subjects. The very law that disposes with sovereign voice of the *publica privatave* of the Termenses Maiores declares 'liberei amicei socieique populi Romani sunto'.[3] It is not sufficient to describe the ever-lengthening inroads made by Rome upon the external freedom and administrative autonomy of her various subjects, because while with one hand she treats them as *Reichsangehörige*, with the other she sets up a record of their independence. Nor is it enough to dismiss this as a 'concession' to local feeling. Was it not also a concession to Roman feeling? The period in which this deterioration of the position of *civitates liberae* and *foederatae* was accomplished is also the period in which the exclusiveness of the Roman state over against the Italian peoples reached a maximum. The insistence that allies and subjects alike must remain formally outside the Roman state, while submitting to a varying degree of actual control is only a device, from one point of view, to insure the Roman government against the defective character of its own administrative machinery.

There were three methods by which these various communities were brought to a certain extent 'within the state'. First, the original charter of the *liberi* might lay down *any* conditions, both specific obligations to perform certain services,[4] and general provisions that the community concerned should be subject to further laws or *senatus consulta* of Rome.[5] Second, *liberi* and *foederati*

---

[1] *Pro Balbo*, 32.

[2] Op. cit. 9 ff., 'socius ist alles was nicht civis und nicht hostis ist.'

[3] *ILS* 38.

[4] Cf. *lex Ant. de Termess.*, *ILS* 38. 2. 34–5, or *S.C. de Stratonicensibus*, *OGIS* 441, in general.        [5] Ibid. 11, 'nisi senatus nominatim . . . decreverit.'

were influenced alike by the establishment of Roman provinces. Horn has shown how federated states situated within a province had lost many of their financial and political privileges in the Ciceronian period and later, being subject to such requisitions as *frumentum imperatum*,[1] and, in Gaul, eventually to the tribute[2] and to the establishment of permanent military camps upon their territory.[3] Third, while Roman interference could be, and often was, achieved by the mere right of force,[4] which Roman magistrates excused with the Marian plea *inter armorum strepitum silere leges*, there can be no doubt that the proper method of influencing the decision of a free or federate state is that adopted by Augustus in his letter to Cnidos.[5] It is the method of advice: 'I think you would do well if you followed my advice about this.'[6] Such are his words, and they secure acceptance because Rome had a much more subtle claim upon the loyalty of her allies, of all categories, than that based on force, or even upon law. They have all come into her 'trust', *in fidem*.[7] For the states bound by *foedus iniquum* this relationship is made explicit by the undertaking *comiter conservare maiestatem populi Romani*. Thus when Horn argues that Cicero in the *Pro Balbo* is claiming that (some) Roman laws are binding upon the *foederati*, and that this is the effect of the preponderance of Roman power in the Mediterranean world, and that the Romans did not, in effect, distinguish between the 'foreign office' and 'home affairs', it seems that he is barking up the wrong tree.[8] It is not so much that the ancient world knew no proper *Völkerrecht*,[9] as that the Romans possessed a conception which no longer exists, that of the *clientela*. Here is to be found the essence of the peculiarity in the relation of Rome to her allies of the higher grades. The doctrine, which had been worked out in the unification of Italy, is declared explicitly by the Senate at the time of the settlement of Macedon.[10] 'In libertate gentes quae

---

[1] Op. cit. 42.     [2] Ibid. 55–6, 58, 59.     [3] Ibid. 59.
[4] Ibid. 40, cf. *SIG*³ ii. 664.     [5] *SIG*³ ii. 780.
[6] Ἀλλὰ νῦν ὀρθῶς ἄν μοι δοκεῖτε ποιῆσαι τῇ ἐμῇ περὶ τούτων γνώμῃ προνοήσαντες.
[7] Cf. Vogt's treatment of the general relationship of the Roman world to Rome, as viewed by Cicero, op. cit. 89–93. Cf. Cic. *de Off*. 3. 22. 87. for dependence of *civitates liberae* on *fides*, based in the last resort upon their *deditio*, direct or indirect.
[8] Horn, op. cit. 45–6.
[9] Ibid.
[10] Livy 45. 18. 2. Cf. above, 122. 'The peoples which enjoyed freedom would have it guaranteed to them by the guardianship of Rome.'

essent tutam eam sibi . . . sub tutela populi Romani esse.' It is the existence of this conception of clientship that made it possible for Rome to combine increasing interference in the affairs of her *liberi* and *foederati* with the continual recognition of their position outside the Roman state. The attempt to limit this client relationship to a particular set of allies has had the effect of withdrawing the attention of scholars from the fact that it is a general notion,[1] that colours the attitude of Rome to all her allies.[2] To speak of 'client states' is to use a metaphor. It is not a term of international law for the Romans. There are in fact no client states. The term is one that belongs to personal law and custom; but the *clientela* was the obvious expression for the relation between the strong and the weak, and, since in many instances these *liberi* and *foederati* had once been 'surrendered into trust', *dediti in fidem*, clientship and patronage came to form the background of the Roman attitude towards them.

Dr. Horn seems to see a contradiction between the degraded condition of the *liberi* and *foederati* of the late Republic, when they seem to him to be as good as *Reichsangehörige*, and such evidence for their continued sovereignty at the same period as the possession of rights like *postliminium* and *exilium*, and the necessity of the process *fundus fieri*.[3] Yet in their proper setting these phenomena are not contradictory. We cannot characterize the people of Gades as *reichsangehörig*, in the sense of 'within the

[1] Cf. the language of the *Res Gestae*, 32. 3, 'Plurimae . . . gentes expertae sunt populi Romani fidem . . . quibus antea cum populo Romano nullum extiterat . . . amicitiae commercium', where the reference is to *extraneae gentes*.

[2] It is bound up with the notion of Rome as a 'benefactor' of the allies, cf. Cic. *Balb.* 20–4; for the mutual relationship cf. ibid. 37. 'Potest esse ulla denique maiestas si impedimur quo minus . . . beneficiorum . . . tribuendorum potestatem imperatoribus nostris deferamus?'

[3] Horn, op. cit. 45–6. He argues from the phrase (Cic. *Balb.* 38) 'huic generi legum fundos populos fieri non solere' that Cicero is treating Gades as subject to Roman law, and hence at least partly 'within the state'. This is by no means so. The longer discussion in 19–22 shows that Cicero merely means that this was a purely internal law that concerned non-Romans as individuals only, not as states, 'ut cives Romani sint ii quos Cn. Pompeius . . . singillatim civitate donaverit'; cf. 22, 'de nostra . . . republica . . . fundos populos fieri noluerunt'. Its purpose was 'elicere ex civitatibus . . . fortissimum quemque . . . ad subeunda pro salute nostra pericula'. The doctrine of the *pro Balbo* is that a man is free to change his *civitas* as he wishes (27; 29–30). This law merely offered something to the *socii* as a gift from outside. Balbus by accepting it ceased to be *Gaditanus*. To speak of this *lex* as binding upon Gades is thus an error based on a misunderstanding of Cicero's point of view.

state', until a law of 49 B.C. incorporated Gades in the *civitas Romana*. Caesar, for instance, had at an earlier date respected their local, though limited, sovereignty.[1] The insistence of the ancient authors upon the importance of self-government, αὐτονομία, as meaning freedom from the interference of provincial governors, is not to be dismissed lightly.[2] Despite the preponderant power of Rome, it is difficult to see how any of these *civitates* could ever have become truly a 'part of the Roman state' except by travelling the road that the Gaditani followed, and except for the appearance, under the Principate, of a new factor, devotion to the emperor and to Rome.[3] It was this latter that finally destroyed the balance of elements within the little, free or federate, autonomous communities of the Roman world. Until the sense of opposition between Roman and local sovereignty was destroyed, and the two were recognized as compatible, thanks to the mediation of a new notion (though one latent within the phrase *maiestatem populi Romani comiter conservanto*), there was no reason why the *civitates* here under discussion should not have lain for ever at the threshold, and only at the threshold, of the Roman state. Täubler remarks that by the time of Trajan the treaty of Amisus was regarded by that prince as a mere *beneficium*; yet Trajan respected the autonomy of Amisus, in the spirit of the old *foedus*.[4] In truth, though it was Rome's brutality that reduced the independence of the *foederati* and *liberi* to a nominal and conditional freedom, it was her generosity in a later age that finally brought them 'within the state'.

[1] Cf. *pro Balbo* 43. 'Caesar . . . in Hispania praetor . . . iura ipsorum permissu statuerit'. For the law, cf. Dio 41. 24. 1.

[2] e.g. Strabo, p. 181, 4. 1. 5, on Massilia after the loss of her *imperium*, τὴν αὐτονομίαν ἐφύλαξαν (οἱ ἡγεμόνες) . . . ὥστε μὴ ὑπακούειν τῶν εἰς τὴν ἐπαρχίαν πεμπομένων στρατηγῶν. This echoes the language of the contemporary official document affirming the freedom of Chios. *SIG*[3] ii. 785.

[3] Below, 402 ff.

[4] Op. cit. 449. Pliny, *Ep.* 10, 93. 'Si concessum est . . . possumus . . . non impedire . . . in ceteris civitatibus quae *nostro iure obstrictae* sunt res huiusmodi prohibenda est', i.e. Trajan does not regard Amisus as properly *Reichsangehörige*.

# APPENDIX

## SOME RECENT THEORIES ABOUT *LATINI,* *MUNICIPES,* AND *SOCII, ITALICA*

### I. EARLY LATIUM[1]

A. ALFÖLDI in an audacious reconstruction of early Roman history, which utilizes much recent work, violently attacked the annalistic tradition of Rome's relations with the Latin peoples.[2] His reconstruction of the history of the Latin League in the fifth and fourth centuries amplifies that given in the first part of this book without greatly differing from it. But there is a notable divergence in the handling of the earliest phases. Alföldi denies the existence of small local leagues in early Latium, holding that there was always a single league of 'Thirty Peoples', of which the leadership, and the location of the federal sanctuary, passed in time from Alba to Lavinium and Aricia, and thence eventually to Rome at the end of the fifth century. He rejects any Roman hegemony in Latium, even within an equal league, before that time, when it resulted from the weakening of the Latins in the Aequian and Volscian wars, and from the territorial expansion of the Roman state from five to seventeen *tribus rusticae* in the late fifth century. Hence in particular he rejects the Polybian date for the first Carthaginian treaty, with its implication of a hegemony of Etruscan Rome over Latium, and assigns it, as many others have done, to the Livian date of 348 B.C.[3] He also rejects the annalistic account of the *foedus Cassianum,* and of the early *tribus rusticae,* which mark the first expansion of Roman territory in Latium.[4]

Yet Alföldi's version of the evolution of the League of the Thirty Peoples implies that the Latiar itself was once only a district league. He holds that the group of thirty vanished small communities, listed by Pliny as those 'that took meat on the Alban mountain', was eventually replaced by a group of larger historical states, such as those listed by Dionysius in his account of the Cassian treaty.[5] But those cover all

---

[1] Throughout this section I owe much to the constructive suggestions and the learning of Mr. A. Drummond.

[2] A. Alföldi, *Early Rome and the Latins,* Jerome Lectures, 7th ser. (Michigan, 1964–5), esp. chs. i–iii and viii. The lengthy discussions of R. Werner, *Der Beginn der r. Republik* (Munich, 1963), are more conventional, cf. below, 193 n. 3.

[3] Op. cit. 350 ff.                                      [4] Ibid. 113 ff., 296 ff.

[5] Ibid. 13 ff. Pliny, *NH* 3. 69. Dion. Hal. 5. 61. 3. It is assumed from the number and the names that Pliny's list is intended for the primitive Thirty. He lists separately in *s.* 68 twenty other vanished communities including the trans-Anio communes and some from southern Latium which were still independent in the fifth century (Pometia, Satricum, Norba).

Latium beyond the boundaries of the seventeen *tribus rusticae* of the Roman state which had come into existence on any view before 400 B.C. Only six names are common to both lists, and of these at least two come from within the zone of the seventeen tribes.[1] Some five peoples on the list of Dionysius could represent communes absorbed into the Roman tribal territory before the fourth century.[2] Pliny's list omits all the well-known cities of Latium (except Pedum), such as the members of the early League of Aricia, and seems to consist largely of small communes no longer independent in the fifth and fourth centuries, which did not cover more than a section of the Latin territory of any period.[3] They mostly lay in the coastal plain or on the flank of the hills from Aricia to Praeneste, or within the territory of the rustic tribes.[4] The comparison suggests that the Latiar was originally organized as a restricted league for the communes of inner Latium, a number of which were early incorporated into the Roman territory. The remarkable discovery of a formal line of thirteen large archaic altars,

[1] Internal: Forcti, Querquetula, possibly Bubentum. External: Corioli, Pedum Tolerii. Many names are garbled in the text of Pliny, and many are unknown or unplaced. Cf. Alföldi, op. cit. 13, mostly following A. Rosenberg's surmises (*Hermes* 54 (1919), 121 f.). He adds improbably Nomentum out of Numienses, from beyond the Anio, and Carventum out of Cosuetani, too far south of Tusculum.

[2] Bubentani, Cabani, Fortini (i.e. Forcti), Querquetulani, Tellenenses. Cf. Alföldi, op. cit. 14. For Tellene cf. R. M. Ogilvie, *Commentary on Livy 1–5* (Oxford, 1965), 136–7.

[3] For Aricia, above, 13.

[4] Aefula (out of *Aesolani*), Alba, Corioli, (Castri-)moenium, Longula, Pollusca (out of *Pollustini*, a necessary emendation since Politorium occurs in s. 68), lie in the south-western zone around Tusculum, Aricia, Ardea, Antium. Cf. Ogilvie, op. cit. 318–19. Aefula is shown by Livy 26. 9. 9 to lie nearer Rome than Monte S. Angelo beyond Tibur, despite *RE* i. 475–6. Bola and Pedum lie between Tusculum and Praeneste, while Vetelia (Vitellia) and Tolerii are placed speculatively beyond Praeneste in the upper Liris (Tolerus) valley; cf. Ogilvie, op. cit. 332–3. Dion. Hal. 8. 17. 4 places Tolerii south of Bola. The list notably excludes all the communes of Livy's *Prisci* beyond Anio incorporated under the kings (above, 9), cf. 190 n. 5. It includes Fidenae, beyond Anio, held in the fifth century by Veii, but listed as an Alban colony in Diod. 7. 5. 9. On the Forcti, Querquetulani, Latinienses in the tribal zone cf. Alföldi, op. cit. 13–14. The term *prisci* or *casci* should not be applied specifically to those or any group of *populi Latini*, cf. above, 9. Ancient writers use it variously to distinguish any phase of early Latium from the post 338 Latin Name; Cf. Livy 1. 3. 7, Pliny, *NH* 34. 20, Festus s.v.

R. Werner, op. cit. 415 ff., adjusts Pliny's text to include all known participants in the Alban festival to the total of thirty, and regards this as its composition down to the Etruscan domination of Rome. But Pliny is listing only defunct *populi*, which survived merely as *pagi*, in 3. 69, and his items may total 31 rather than 30: he adds another 22–3 in s. 68, ambiguously described as *cum iis carnem . . . soliti accipere*. The number thirty in the tradition refers to the colonies of Alba or Lavinium or to the members of the group based on Lucus Ferentinae (Dion. Hal. 5. 61). The Alban colonies of Diod. 7. 5. 9 (Eusebius) mostly appear in Pliny's *first* list (s. 68), so that the combination of the two lists into a single total may be correct.

dated to the sixth century, outside the urban precinct of Lavinium, confirms the notion of restricted leagues. They probably formed the sanctuary of the federal cult shared between Lavinium, Ardea, and other Latin peoples, barely mentioned by Strabo, the extent of which was not previously known.[1]

The diversity of the deities of the leagues also indicates the plurality of contemporaneous leagues. The league of Aricia kept the cult of Diana, the Alban federation that of Juppiter Latiaris, while the Lavinian group observed the archaic *pater* or *Juppiter indiges* and *penates* under the form of the Dioscuri.[2] The Lavinian cult still operates in 339 B.C. when special provision is made for its formal continuance on behalf of the Latin Name.[3] Hence it had always coexisted with the Latiar. So too the council of the Latins at Lucus Ferentinae continued its activities down to the dissolution of all such groups in 338.[4]

The rejection of even a partial hegemony of Rome over Latium under Tarquinius Superbus, such as was suggested above, seems to conflict with Alföldi's own account of the dominant Etruscan element in Rome and Latium in the sixth century, which aimed especially at the control of the coastal route from Rome to Campania through those very cities which are listed in the first Carthaginian treaty of Polybius.[5] The argument is that the first and second treaties given by Polybius belong close together and reflect the situation of 350–340 B.C., when Rome claimed a general dominion over all Latium, and when Rome and Carthage needed each other's help against the contemporary menace of Syracusan sea-power, whereas *c.* 500 B.C. Rome had no seaboard, no maritime interests, and no hegemony in Latium.[6] But in

---

[1] Cf. above, 12 n. 4. Alföldi summarizes the reports, with bibliography, op. cit. 265 f. Plate 16: the altars are dated by associated finds; otherwise this might be the sanctuary of the league in its final form of thirteen cities (Strabo 5. 3. 5 (232)).

[2] Cf. Alföldi, op. cit. 255 ff., for the connection between the *penates* and *sacra principia* of Lavinium with the dedication found in the new sanctuary: 'Castorei Podloqueique Curois'; S. Weinstock, *JRS* 50 (1960), 117 n. 58. Strabo adds 'Venus'.

[3] The annual renewal of the *foedus* with Lavinium (Livy 8. 11. 15) is perpetuated together with the cult of the *sacra principia* in the Claudian document *ILS* 5004. Alföldi, op. cit. 264–5, oddly fails to see that this militates against his 'single league' theory.

[4] Cf. Festus cited above, 13 n. 6, with Livy 7. 25. 5; 8. 3. 9–10.

[5] Alföldi, op. cit. ch. v, esp. 186 f., 193 f., 202 f. He quotes no direct archaeological evidence for the land route by the Liris valley to Campania, though insisting on its importance (against p. 16 above). Etruscan finds are now documented at Capua, Cales, and between Cales and Teanum in the seventh century, though not yet in the Liris. See briefly H. H. Scullard, *Etruscan Cities and Rome* (London, 1967), 190 ff. and n. 130. P. Gierow, *Iron Age Culture of Latium* (Lund, 1966), i. 503 argues for the inland route; *contra* M. Pallottino, *Parola del Passato*, 11 (1956), 81 ff.

[6] Polyb. 3. 22–4. Alföldi, op. cit. 350–4, with bibliography of the extensive controversy over the Carthaginian treaties, which is well surveyed by A. J. Toynbee, *Hannibal's Legacy* (Oxford, 1965), i. 518 ff. Alföldi follows especially A. Aymard,

fact neither treaty is concerned with military alliance at all: both lack the normal clause of mutual assistance found in later treaties. This occurs as an addition in the third Polybian treaty, which was a military alliance against the threat of Pyrrhus.[1] They also fail in two ways to reflect the circumstances of 348–343 B.C., to which years Alföldi dates them. At that time Rome was becoming active in Campania. The Carthaginian mission of 343 in Livy's narrative follows and was prompted by the Roman treaty with Capua and the Roman victory in Campania. Yet, as Polybius noted, the treaties restrict Roman interests to the coast of Latium.[2] So too the mention of Antium in the first treaty as a Latin city under the suzerainty of Rome does not fit the Livian treaty of 348, made at a time when Antium had long been in Volscian hands and was actively hostile to Rome.[3] The first of Polybius' two treaties, which he said were both unknown to Roman antiquarians, makes sense as reflecting the claims of the Etruscan overlords of Rome to a limited hegemony in coastal Latium; the absence of Aricia fits the evidence, stressed by Alföldi, of its opposition to Etrusco-Roman power in Latium. The recent discovery of a Punic dedication in the port of neighbouring Caere, dated to the early fifth century (it seems), provides, with the Etrusco-Punic alliance of *c.* 475–470, a context of Punic maritime intervention for the first treaty.[4]

*Rev. Ét. Anc.* 59 (1957), 277 ff., usefully criticized by Toynbee, op. cit. 536. For the Syracusan menace cf. Alföldi (op. cit. 343 f.) stressing the raids of 349 in Livy 7. 25–6.

[1] Polyb. 3. 25. 3–5.

[2] Livy 7. 38. 2. Cf. chs. 30–1, pact with Capua; 37. 4–17, battle of Suessula; 38. 4–10, Romans winter in Campania. Polyb. 3. 23. 6: 'The Romans make a covenant about the Latin land, but do not mention the rest of Italy which did not fall under their power.' Cf. also Toynbee, op. cit. 522, who with others would date the second treaty after 354 close to the Livian date (cf. below, n. 3), when Rome was making 'written treaties' with non-subjects such as the Samnites, Caere, Tarquinii, though Rome may well have had such a treaty with Tibur and Praeneste much earlier; cf. above, 28.

[3] Livy 7. 27. 2, set within an account of Antiate aggression, 27. 1 and 5–7. Cf. Werner, op. cit. 297 ff., who also argues that the first treaty by implying Carthaginian control of Sardinia, Sicily, and the coast west of Carthage, with Carthaginian absence from Spain, fits the situation *c.* 480–470. Though he abandons the annalistic chronology based on consular *Fasti* beginning in 509, his reconstruction of the history of the Latin League agrees largely with this book: he accepts an Etrusco-Roman hegemony of sorts over Latium in the sixth century, and merely lowers the dates of the first Carthaginian treaty and of the 'Cassian' treaty by a generation; cf. below, 194 n. 6.

[4] Polyb. 3. 22. 11. For Aricia, Alföldi, op. cit. 47 ff. Cf. J. Heurgon, *JRS* 56 (1966), 1 ff., Scullard, op. cit. 103–4, for a survey of the Pyrgi evidence: the alliance of the Etruscans of Caere-Agylla with Carthage, testified by Herodotus (1. 166–7) at Alalia *c.* 546, recurs at Cyme in 474 according to Pindar, *Pyth.* 1. 70–5, unnoticed by Heurgon and Diodorus (11. 51). The ingenious unpublished suggestion of Mr. Drummond that Polybius' term ὑπήκοος, used to distinguish subject-allies

The second treaty must be earlier than the Roman control of Campania, but reflects a wider area of Roman action than the first. Further, there are wide differences between the two treaties which the school of Alföldi ignore. The first treaty, unlike the second, expects no Roman forays on the seas or any colonizing activity outside Latium.[1] The arrangements for commercial activity differ in the two texts. The first subjects Latin commerce in African territory to formal public control —'with scribe and herald under public guarantee'. But the second treaty establishes reciprocal rights in Africa and Latium for both parties under the civil law, in a phrase that may have been applied in the first treaty to transactions in Sicily.[2] Further, Polybius' remark about the archaic character and unintelligibility of the first treaty tells against the proposal of Alföldi to date them close together.[3]

Alföldi rejects the text of the 'Cassian' treaty in Dionysius as irreconcilable with the view (which he shares with this book) that the renewal of the alliance after Regillus was on equal terms.[4] He holds that Rome simply returned to membership of the Council of Ferentina as one among many equal partners. Some clauses in the tradition may belong to a later period, though the treaty of the bronze column known to Livy and Cicero can hardly be later than the end of the League in 338 B.C. But Alföldi somewhat misunderstands the text of Dionysius. The main clauses established peace and a mutual defensive alliance between Rome and the Latins. They do not anachronistically forbid internal wars between the Latins themselves. The relevant phrase is a definition of the preceding clause about peace: the two parties are neither to fight one another directly nor to let third parties attack the other through their territory.[5] This ties in with the recent intrigues of Aricia, Rome, and Porsenna which Alföldi elsewhere stresses.[6] These clauses fit the evidence of Livy on a later occasion that

of Rome in the first treaty, is an interpretative mistranslation of *socius*, would neatly solve most problems by reducing Rome's role to that of a federal leader of Latium. But Polybius uses σύμμαχος (sc. 'socii') elsewhere of the Latins in both treaties, and presumably found a different term where he or his source used ὑπήκοος, perhaps some equivalent of 'qui in dicione sunt'.

[1] The clause of the second treaty, forbidding to the Romans plundering and founding of strong places (24. 4), is absent from the first, which solely concerns trading operations of Rome and the Latins. Both treaties forbid the taking of strong places by the Carthaginians.   [2] Compare ibid. 22. 8–10 with 24. 12.

[3] Ibid. 22. 3.   [4] Alföldi, op. cit. 113 ff. Cf. above, 22 f.

[5] Dion. Hal. 6. 95. 2. The term ἀλλήλοι in the text formally refers to the two contracting parties. The text is a good deal more than a Greek invention in Hellenistic terms, on any view. Cf. Werner, op. cit. 455 ff., who connects the treaty with the Volscian menace of *c*. 465–460.

[6] Cf. Alföldi, op. cit. 47 ff. The clause about jurisdiction cited by Festus, s.v. *nancitor*—'pecuniam quis nancitor habeto'—is only anachronistic if *pecuniam* is taken to mean coined money. The clause about the *equal* sharing of booty is only

the Latin treaty allowed the Latins to make war on whom they wished —other than Rome—and they do not contradict the resumption by Rome of membership of the Council of Ferentina in Alföldi's sense.[1] Yet at some time Rome acquired more than a rotating share in the military leadership of Latium—the clash between the two parties in the fourth century is otherwise inexplicable. Equally the Council of Ferentina certainly operates with an independent organization of its own and without Roman participation in the fourth century.[2] These facts suggest that at some later date, if not in 493, a bipartite agreement was made, exactly as in the 'Cassian' treaty, giving Rome more than a rotating share in the hegemony of Latium, but not exclusive control.

## Latium and the Tribus Rusticae of Rome

Alföldi has based his thesis of the restricted role of Rome in Latium down to the end of the fifth century on certain assumptions about the size of the Roman state. In this book no attempt was made to connect Roman relations with Latium with the extension of her territorial 'tribes', because of the extreme obscurity of all but the barest facts about the expansion of the tribal system, and the great uncertainty of the boundaries and even of the general location of most of the thirty-five tribes in their original form, especially those created before the conquest of Veii. The recent work of L. R. Taylor has rendered the subject somewhat more manageable.[3] But Alföldi rejects the annalistic tradition, which she accepts, that the Roman territory extended to seventeen *tribus rusticae* by 495 B.C. with an estimated area of some 800 square kilometres. Instead he posits a 'little Rome' with a territory of only five rural tribes down to the conquest of Fidenae in 426 B.C., extending east of the Tiber in an arc around the city some five miles wide, and covering an estimated third or quarter of the later area. For this restricted territory, usually attributed to the early regal period, there is some evidence in the location of certain boundary festivals of great antiquity.[4]

partly inaccurate for the early period; cf. above, 24 n. 1. Besides, it is doubtful whether Rome shared captured land *equally* in the fourth century when dividing conquests between Roman tribes and Latin colonies. Cf. below, 199.

[1] Livy 8. 2. 13.

[2] Cf. above, 23, with Livy 8. 3. 9–10, and the perhaps anachronistic episode in Dion. Hal. 3. 34. 3; 5. 50. 2, implying that the original *foedus* required the summoning of *Concilia* by formal notice (accepted by Alföldi).

[3] L. R. Taylor, *The Voting Districts of the Roman Republic* (Rome, 1960), esp. chs. 4 and 5.

[4] Alföldi, op. cit. 296–318, with fig. p. 297. For the areas cf. Taylor, op. cit. 38 n. 8, Alföldi. op. cit. 303. Cf. for an early date G. Lugli, *Mélanges Carcopino* (Paris, 1960), 641 ff.

The boundaries of the first seventeen rural tribes of the annalistic tradition have been very roughly established, with scraps of evidence, in relation to the independent townships of inner Latium, as extending around Rome in an irregular arc some ten to fifteen miles wide south and east towards Lavinium, Aricia, Tusculum, Pedum, and Nomentum, with a narrow enclave west of the Tiber into the territory of Veii.[1] Livy refers to the completion of this system in 509 and 495 B.C. by the addition of the *tribus Claudia* and apparently the *tribus Clustumina*, both north of the Anio river.[2] Alföldi puts this great extension of 'little Rome' in the late fifth century and mostly after 426 B.C.

Alföldi's only substantial argument is that the eight tribes— Claudia, Aemilia, Cornelia, etc.—which draw their names from great patrician families ought to belong to the period of the dominance of the patriciate.[3] But his dating fits very badly with the skeleton of fifth-century history which he accepts. He attributes a great expansion of Roman territory, at the expense of her Latin neighbours, to the period when they were conjointly engaged in the lengthy defence of Latium against the pressure of the Volscian and Aequian invasions, and when there is no hint of any Roman warfare in the area of the supposed annexations except for the capture of Fidenae.[4] In this respect the annalistic tradition about the tribes is in itself quite consistent. After the consolidation of the gains of the regal period in 495 B.C., no new tribes are added during the period of defensive wars. Townships or areas regained from the invaders are re-established as *coloniae Latinae*, joint foundations of the Latino-Roman alliance, not annexed to Rome as *tribus rusticae*. This happens as late as 418 even in an area so close to Rome as Labici, at the time and in the zone of Alföldi's supposed annexations, when Labici was recovered from the Aequi.[5]

---

[1] Taylor, op. cit. 36 ff. for detailed evidence, such as it is. The diagram facing p. 35 wrongly includes Lavinium within the boundary of the seventeen tribes. Alföldi, op. cit. 288 f., argues that the Roman territory did not reach the sea at any point in the sixth century.

[2] Taylor, op. cit. 35 f. Livy 2. 16. 4–5 is specific for the *Claudia*. The rejection of the annalistic date for the arrival of Attius Clausus does not by itself invalidate the date of the tribal creation, *pace* Alföldi; but rather vice versa. Livy 2. 21. 7, *tribus una et viginti factae* follows the capture of Crustumeria in 19. 2. 'The tribes became twenty-one', not 'twenty-one tribes were created [sc. at once].' Cf. Livy 6. 5. 8.

[3] Alföldi, op. cit. 315–16. For the patrician tribes cf. Taylor, op. cit. 35, 282 f.

[4] Op. cit. 317. Livy 4. 17–22.

[5] Cf. above, 24, 36. Cf. Alföldi, op. cit. 392 ff. and Toynbee, op. cit. i. 391 ff., following E. T. Salmon, *Phoenix* 1953, 98 f., who elaborated my point that the *coloniae* settled around Latium down to 338 B.C., were all federal colonies of the League under Roman leadership, though frequently called *coloniae Romanae* by Livy. Cf. the refounding of Ardea mainly with Rutuli as settlers, Livy 4. 11. 3–7. Velleius 1. 14 records no citizen colony before Tarracina (332). For Labici, Livy 4. 47. 4–7.

In the tradition tribal extension begins again in 389—coupled with the foundation of Latin colonies—only after the successful Roman aggression against Veii, with the additions of four new tribes beyond the Tiber, and continues through the fourth century, as Roman dominance increases, at the expense of the Latins, Volscians, and Aequians, and finally breaks new ground in Campania.[1]

The place-names in the later regal wars indicate annexations in the outer zone of the seventeen tribes, particularly in the extreme south-west towards Ostia, Lavinium, and Bovillae, where Ficana and Tellene mark the frontier, and in the north-east beyond the Anio towards Nomentum, where the final conquest of Crustumeria in 499 precedes Livy's statement of the completion of the roll of the twenty-one tribes.[2] The absence of any indication of wars or rebellions within this tribal zone in the fifth century tells against the hypothesis of Alföldi. Even in the wars of the earliest period the place-names come either from beyond the Anio—on any view the latest part of the zone of the seventeen rural tribes to be annexed—or from the periphery of the rest of the area.[3] This suggests that the expansion of Rome from the fifth to the tenth or twelfth milestone belonged to a very early period. The analogy of Athens—where the unification of Attica in the time of 'Theseus' remains unchallenged—may be recalled.

The theory of a 'small Rome' in the regal period that expands later in time when her power in Latium is seen to increase, has some attractions. But the great extension of territory and manpower through the acquisition of the broad lands of Veii, which accommodated four extensive *tribus rusticae*, is enough to account for the altered balance of power in the fourth century. Alföldi's theory rests on too many vicious arguments, such as the assumption that the patrician clans, who gave names to many of the seventeen tribes, lacked power under the kings. It also assumes an inexplicable falsification of the tribal record, and a surprising substitution of the kings for the great houses of the middle Republic as the founders of the tribes. This is too refined a defamation even for Fabius Pictor, the supposed author of such falsifications, especially as the only tribal forefather to be named in the tradition is the progenitor of the Claudii—the arch-enemy of the Fabian house.

So far the rural tribes appear simply as an organ of the Roman state, a territorial subdivision useful in the civil organization, but not contributing to the special quality of the Roman citizenship in its

---

[1] Veii, Livy 6. 5. 8. Taylor, op. cit. 47 f.

[2] Above, 9 f. For Ficana and Tellene cf. Ogilvie, op. cit. 136–7.

[3] Antemnae was near the mouth of the Anio and Caenina beyond it, possibly near Fidenae, cf. Ogilvie, op. cit. 67–8 citing Strabo 5. p. 230. In the south-west Ficana and Tellene recur. Politorium is not located, Ogilvie, op. cit. 136.

extension to outsiders. The role of the fourteen new tribes created between 387 and 241 B.C. appears somewhat more positive in the light of L. R. Taylor's studies.[1] The creation of new tribes did not primarily increase the number of Roman citizens, though by giving land to the proletarian element it increased the numbers of the landowning peasantry and their capacity for raising families, and hence added to the military potential of Rome.[2] But twice Livy states that new tribes were created 'for new citizens', first of the four tribes in the lands of Veii (387 B.C.) and later of the Maecia and Scaptia in the Volscian coastal zone (332 B.C.).[3] The Veientane tribes included deserters and Roman supporters from Capena, Falerii, and Veii, who received land and were presumably enfranchised among the mass of Roman settlers as full citizens.[4] The Maecia seems to have been created for the citizens of Lanuvium enfranchised in 338, and the Scaptia for new Roman settlers and for the remnant of the Velitrans oddly described by Livy as already citizens (presumably *sine suffragio*) in 338.[5] Otherwise 'new citizens' are not mentioned, though the incorporation of remnants of the Sabine peoples in the Quirina (241) has been inferred from the later nomenclature of the region.[6] It may be suspected elsewhere. The enfranchised survivors of rebellious Privernum, which never recovered its autonomy, may be sought in the *tribus Oufentina* (318), which took the greater part of their land, though they may have been separate as *cives s.s.* for some time.[7] Some of the Aurunci, whose territory was wholly engulfed by Latino-Roman colonization between 313 and 296, may have survived within the Teretina (299).[8] This tribal incorporation of conquered peoples seems to have been a means of dealing with the remnants of shattered communities, which the Romans were bent on erasing and replacing by Latin and Roman colonization, and which were too weak to become *municipia* in the heyday of *civitas sine suffragio*.

The tribal expansion of the Roman territory was contiguous down to the incorporation of the lands of Veii. Beloch held that it was always so, but the investigations of L. R. Taylor suggest that some of the later tribal settlements were made on detached lands, separated from the

[1] Op. cit. ch. 5.

[2] Cf. Livy 5. 30. 8: 'ut agri Veientani . . . dividerentur . . . vellentque in eam spem liberos tollere'.

[3] Livy 6. 5. 8; 8. 17. 11.

[4] Livy 6. 4. 4; cf. Taylor, op. cit. 48.

[5] Op. cit. 53–5, citing Livy 8. 14. 5–7. For the existence of a commune of *cives s.s.*, dimly implied by Livy's *veteres cives Romanos* see below p. 212 n. 4.

[6] Taylor, op. cit. 60 n. 50.

[7] Taylor, op. cit. 56. Cf. Livy 8. 1. 3; 20. 9; 21. 10. Listed as *praefectura* by Festus s.v., who also records an addition to the original Oufentina s.v. Cf. above, 48.

[8] See below, 199 n. 2.

central Roman territory, and from each other, by surviving allied communities, and by newly created Latin colonies. Though it is often hard to establish the original location of the new tribes, which were greatly expanded in later times, this separation is clear in the case of the Pomptina, established in 358 B.C. on the territory of Pometia, and hemmed in by Latin Norba and Setia.[1] For three other tribes the evidence is also clear. In 318 the Oufentina was founded beyond Setia on part of the territory of Privernum, and in yet greater isolation the Falerna was settled also in 318 beyond the territory of the submissive but still independent Aurunci, on Campanian land south of the Volturnus, while in 299 the Aniensis was set in the upper Anio valley beyond the Latin state of Tibur.[2] The tribal settlements seem, however, to be connected in most instances with the foundation of a *colonia Latina* in the same or adjacent districts: Setia (382) for the Pomptina (358), and for the Oufentina, which also had Fregellae (328) in its rear, Sora and Alba (303) for the Aniensis (299), Cales (334) for the Falerna (318), and Suessa for the Teretina (313, 299).[3] As the Latin colonies of this period were increasingly Roman in foundation and composition, the military and political isolation of the new tribes was much reduced, and mostly disappeared within a generation through the creation of other *tribus rusticae*, through the extension of *civitas sine suffragio* to their neighbours, and through the settlement on their coasts of the new style of *coloniae civium Romanorum*.[4] After the founding of the Teretina in 299 B.C. in the lowland zone, between the Oufentina and the Falerna, the continuity of Roman tribal territory from Latium to Campania along the Via Appia was apparently unbroken, though reduced to a narrow neck between the Latin colony of Suessa Aurunca and the coast.[5] But in the inland zones, from Latium through to the upper Liris and upper Anio valleys, the tribal territory continued to be fragmented by the lands of various Latin communes down to the Social War.[6]

The pattern repeats itself in the third century in the Apennine territories north-east of Rome, annexed after the wars of 290 and 268

[1] Taylor, op. cit. 50.
[2] Ibid. 55–6. The Auruncan zone of Minturnae and Vescia-Sinuessa, which separates the *ager Falernus* from the *municipium Formiae*, was not colonized until 296, after the settlement of the *tribus Teretina* in 299, though the *gens* was conquered in 314 and the hinterland became a Latin colony in 313. Cf. Livy 9. 25. 4–9; 28. 7; 10. 21. 8; Taylor, op. cit. 57–8. To avoid this gap Beloch (*RG* 82) oddly inferred from the earlier *deditio* (Livy 8. 15. 2) that the coastal Aurunci became *cives s.s.* in 340.
[3] Taylor, op. cit. 49, 50, 53, 56, 58. Cf. Livy 6. 5. 8 with 21. 4, and 10. 1. 3 with 9. 14.　　　　　　　　　　　　　　　　　　　　　　　　[4] Above, 48 ff., 76 ff.
[5] Cf. maps in Taylor, op. cit., facing p. 47 and at end of volume.
[6] Ibid. 63, with maps.

B.C. There the Quirina and the Velina were belatedly established in 241 B.C. in areas controlled by the Latin colonies of Hadria (286 B.C.) and Firmum (264 B.C.), Narnia (299 B.C.) and Spoletium (241 B.C.). But the original location and limits of these tribes, which later covered a great part of that territory, remains obscure.[1]

Thus the fourteen tribes created between 387 and 241 B.C. acted in some degree as integrating elements between the Roman State and the communes of its semi-citizen dependants, whether *cives sine suffragio* or of Latin status, and also between Roman settlers and enfranchised natives within the tribal territory.[2]

## II. *CIVITAS SINE SUFFRAGIO*

Though much has been written about *civitas sine suffragio* and its holders (*municipes*) since 1938, scholars have been mostly concerned with minor adjustments and criticism of earlier views, and with the investigation of particular difficulties. No general reinterpretation has appeared, and several historians have taken a more limited and literal view than that advocated above. The most original contribution has been that of three Italian historians who, starting from the definitions of Festus and Gellius, have suggested that the status originated in a very early period, as the personal and individual privilege of foreigners from particular states temporarily resident in Rome, enjoying social rights, and performing civic duties like Athenian metics.[3] So E. Manni and A. Bernardi. Improving on this M. Sordi sought to connect the 'Caerite franchise', through the grant of *hospitium* attributed by Livy to the nexus of events in 390 B.C., with the provision in the second Polybian treaty of Rome and Carthage (c. 350 B.C. or earlier) for reciprocal rights between individuals transacting business in each other's city, and with the *immunitas* and other privileges tacked on to the treaty made with Massilia in the same period.[4] These are then connected with Gellius' explanation of the

---

[1] Cf. Taylor, op. cit. 59 ff., Toynbee, op. cit. i. 377 ff. for the controversy.

[2] Cf. the events at Antium, above, 80 ff.

[3] A. Bernardi, '*I Cives sine Suffragio*', *Athenaeum* 16 (1938), 238 ff. E. Manni, *Per la Storia dei Municipi* etc. (Rome, 1947), ch. 1. M. Sordi, *I Rapporti Romani-Ceriti e L'Origine della* Civitas sine Suffragio (Rome, 1960), esp. chs. V–VI, stressing the importance of Caere as the maritime outlet of Rome in the early fourth century.

[4] Cf. above, 193 f., for the dates. Polyb. 3. 24. 12. 'Let the Roman at Carthage do and sell whatever a citizen may do or sell, and let the Carthaginian do likewise at Rome.' For Massilia, Justin 43. 5. 10. They also receive the right to seats at public festivals, which suggests the distinguished *hospes*. Sordi, op. cit. 94, also cites the privileges given to Timosthenes of Lipara (Diod. 14. 93. 45) and the *immunitas* granted to certain Roman settlers in Sardinia in 378–7 (Diod. 15. 27. 4). For an instance of a Roman *hospes* at Caere cf. Livy 9. 36. 3. For the dating of the second treaty with Carthage before 348 see above, 193 n. 2.

status of the Caerites as that of persons who 'held the Roman citizenship but were free from all its burdens'.[1] Noting a remark of Aristotle about the inter-state jurisdiction on commercial matters practised by Etruscans and Carthaginians, Sordi argued that *civitas sine suffragio* was developed from Carthaginian and Etruscan models in the fourth century B.C. as a personal status for alien residents.[2] But the reconstruction is spoiled by the literal acceptance of Gellius' definition in order to cover the instance of Massilia. This cannot be reconciled with the evidence of Festus' republican sources, which insist that *municipes* resident at Rome were liable to *munera*: they cannot be identified with a group of *immunes*. The version of Gellius is derived from Hadrian and his advisers, who, as J. Pinsent has argued, for reasons of ad-administrative policy were concerned to prove that the status of *municipium* was more honourable than that of *colonia*, and used some very doubtful arguments to do so.[3] Hence Gellius cannot be preferred on this issue to Festus.

Sordi's theory is improved by abandoning the connection with *immunitas*. The analogy between the judicial provisions of the Carthaginian treaty, the *hospitium* granted to Caere in 390, and the status of individual *municipes* resident at Rome is strong. But a straight identification of *municipes* and *hospites* will hardly do. Earlier scholars suggested something similar from the etymology of *municeps*, taken to mean originally a 'taker of gifts', and hence a guest-friend or *hospes*, and only subsequently an 'accepter of duties'. But no historical evidence supports this etymology, and philologically it seems that *muni*, *munia*, and its derivatives always have the primary sense of service and duties, while only *munus*, *munera* bears the sense of 'gift'.[4] It does, however, seem reasonable to regard the gifts exchanged by guest-friends as the token of the obligation of mutual protection which they bind themselves to provide. Only so far may a direct connection exist between *hospitium* and *municipium*.

Surprisingly no one has noticed that evidence exists for the notion

---

[1] For Gellius and Festus, above, 40 n. 9, 54.

[2] Ar. *Pol.* 3. 9. 1280ᵃ, illustrated by the immunities granted to a Sidonian merchant visiting Athens (M. Tod, *Greek Historical Inscriptions* (Oxford, 1948), ii. no. 139).

[3] J. Pinsent, *CQ* N.S. 7 (1957), 89 ff. The definition of *municipes* as *muneris honorarii participes* and the gloss of Gellius 'qui . . . c.R. honorem . . . caperent sed negotiis . . . vacarent' are equally false whether applied (as intended) to Republican *municipia civium Romanorum*, or to the historical *cives s.s.* Pinsent suggests that *honorarii* agrees with *participes* taken as a noun: a reference to *munus honorarium* in its contemporary meaning would not have helped Hadrian's case. Cf. also below, 363.

[4] Cf. J. Pinsent, *CQ* N.S. 4 (1954), 158 ff. Ibid. 162 n. 1, he cites Karlowa, *RRG* i. 288 for the notion of *municeps* as a permanent *hospes* performing *munera*, and Mommsen's rejection of this (*St. R.* iii. 231 n. 1).

of *municeps* and *municipium* as a status of individuals rather than of communities in the personal grant of *civitas* (sc. *sine suffragio*) to the *equites Campani*, which in Livy's account precedes the grant to the whole *populus Campanus*.[1] In the conditions of the fourth century this first grant can be nothing but such a combination of *isopolity* and classical *hospitium* as Sordi suggests for Caere in 390. The grant of communal *civitas sine suffragio* to Caere is then best connected with the rebellion of *c.* 272 B.C. and the following surrender of territory to Rome, on which at least three citizen colonies were settled between 264 and 245 B.C. This condition would then resemble the treatment of rebellious Volscians in 338 and 318–315, while the enigma of the *Caeritum tabulae* may be solved with Sordi and others by regarding these as an official register of Caeritan *hospites* at Rome who after 272 were catalogued anew as *municipes*.[2]

## Campania

The status of Capua and the other Campanian peoples after the grant of *civitas sine suffragio* in 338 (or 334) B.C. has been discussed at length by A. Bernardi in two articles and by J. Heurgon in his *Capoue préromaine* in a somewhat paradoxical fashion.[3] Both stress the full retention of local autonomy, much as in this book. This fulfils the Servian definition of *municipes* as those who 'become Roman citizens with the proviso that they always preserve their communal organization separately from that of the Roman people', and distinguishes the Campani from the category of communes such as Anagnia, where a suspension of local autonomy accompanied the grant of *civitas sine*

---

[1] Above, 40. The omission of this from the brief summaries of Velleius 1. 14. 3 and the Oxyrhynchus *Chronicon* (Jacoby, *FGH* ii. B. 255) does not disprove its historicity, despite J. Heurgon, *Capoue préromaine*, 178 f.

[2] For Caere in 272 see Dio, fr. 33 B. Cf. Beloch, *RG* 562, 607: Castrum Novum 264 (Velleius 1. 14. 8), Fregenae (245), Alsium (247), possibly also Pyrgi. Inland lay the *Praefectura Foroclodiensis*, evidently a citizen settlement built on the Via Clodia (225), later a 'duoviral' municipality. L. R. Taylor, *The Voting Districts of the Roman Republic*, Papers Am. Ac. Rome (1960), 48, places it in the former territory of Veii and the original *tribus Arnensis*, improbably, since none of the metropolitan *tribus rusticae* had or needed a *praefectura*, being under the immediate jurisdiction of the praetor. Sordi also attributed the supposedly 'punitive' status of Caere to the rebellion, but transferred this for complex reasons from 272 to 293, rejecting the Livian rebellion of 353 (and the truce of a hundred years, above, 54), as an 'anticipatory doublet'. But there is no motive for falsification. For the Volscian *municipia* see below, 212 n. 4.

[3] A. Bernardi, art. cit. *Athenaeum* 16 (1938), 238 ff. (barely noted above, p. 95); 'Roma e Capua', ibid. (1942) 86 ff. (1943), 21 ff., J. Heurgon, *Capoue préromaine* (Paris, 1942). A. J. Toynbee, *Hannibal's Legacy* (London, 1965), i, ch. 3, sections 6–7, summarizes most usefully a wide range of modern literature. The difference of dating between Livy and the Velleius tradition does not affect the interpretation of *civitas s.s.*, since both put the grants after the Roman victories.

*suffragio*: 'quorum civitas universa in civitatem Romanam venit'. Yet both scholars regard the Campanian *municipes* as being in all other respects ordinary Roman citizens, consider their communes as 'normal citizen communities with no unusual privileges', and discount Livy's application of the terms *socii* and *foedus* to their status.[1] Bernardi, in his first article, stressed the relative independence of Capua, and minimized the extent of Roman intervention, which Heurgon attributed largely to Roman support of the governing class of *equites Campani*, who were at loggerheads with the common folk, rather than to direct Roman interests.[2] But in his second article Bernardi rejected the evolutionary view of *civitas s.s.* advocated in this book, and to which his first article independently inclined. Instead he insisted on the subordinate and purely 'Roman' status of the Campanians from 338 onwards, though the main evidence for this comes from the period *c.* 211 B.C. and later.[3] He objected somewhat literally to the comparison of *civitas sine suffragio* with Hellenic isopolity, partly because of the equality of parties in isopolity, which does not hold good between Rome and Capua, but also because Hellenic isopolity emerges in its full form only in documents of the third century B.C., *after* the Roman invention of *civitas s.s.*[4] In this book isopolity was not identified with *civitas s.s.*, but was suggested merely as a formative influence: the basic concept of an exchange of potential or actual civic rights occurs in Greek usage as early as the offer of Athenian franchise to the Samians in 404 B.C., and in the amalgamation of Argos and Corinth in *c.* 390 B.C., when, as Xenophon puts it, 'Corinth became Argos, and the Corinthians acquired the citizenship of Argos and . . . became like metics in the city.'[5]

Heurgon and Bernardi stress peculiarities in the situation of Capua which seem not to support their case. While the Campanian man-power was included in totals given for Roman citizen numbers, they were classified separately, and the Campanian cavalry served in separate units, like the *socii Italici*, as also did their infantry in so far as its use is recorded; some evidence even suggests that the Romans did not normally mobilize the Campanian infantry.[6] Both historians reject the

---

[1] Heurgon, op. cit. 194, 198, 243. Bernardi, art. cit. (1942), 89 f.

[2] Bernardi, art. cit. (1938), 246 f., 251, 277; Heurgon, op. cit. ch. XI, esp. 255 ff.

[3] Bernardi, art. cit. (1942), 89 f., cf. Heurgon, op. cit. 194. They stress the evidence of Ennius (above, 42 n. 1), Livy 26. 33. 10, Val. Max. 2. 7. 15.

[4] Bernardi, art. cit. (1942), 98 ff.

[5] M. Tod, *Greek Historical Inscriptions* (Oxford, 1948), i. 96. Xenophon, *Hell.* 4. 4. 6; 5. 1; 5. 1. 34. Cf. G. T. Griffith, *Historia* 1, 245 ff. The argument above, 42 ff. was not (*pace* Bernardi loc. cit.) based on Dionysius' unreliable use of ἰσοπολίτης for *municipia* and incorporated communes.

[6] Heurgon, op. cit. 195 ff. Bernardi, art. cit. (1943), 29 ff. Separate forces, Dion. Hal. 20. 1. 2 (contingents of Campani are listed in 279 with Latini, Sabini,

appointment of *praefecti iuri dicundo* for Campania in 318 B.C. as incompatible with the then existing local autonomy, or else limit their function to jurisdiction over the Roman settlers in the new *tribus Falerna*.[1] Thus their literal view of the Roman status of the Campanian *municipes* as citizens merely lacking the positive political rights does not quite square with their account of the Campanian peculiarities. While Bernardi held that the obligation of military assistance was unilateral to the advantage of Rome—which ignores the whole background of Campanian fears of Samnium—Heurgon suggested that the intervention of Rome at Neapolis beyond Capua in 326 was instigated by Capua.[2] That the Campani interpreted their status differently from the Romans is suggested by the conditions they demanded of Hannibal: 'ne ... magistratus [sc. Poenus] ius ullum in civem Campanum haberet neve civis Campanus invitus militaret munusve faceret.'[3]

Festus implies that *municipes* who migrated permanently to Rome could secure the political rights of Roman citizenship. Heurgon combines this with the surmise of Münzer that there was a series of Campanian gentry established at Rome who secured numerous consulships in the period 335–255 B.C., and especially during the years 258–255.[4] Apart from P. Decius Mus, the mysterious consul of 340 B.C., the very year of the grant of citizenship in Livy, and his son, thrice consul between 312 and 297, these are all members of the *gens Atilia*, some of whom bear local *cognomina*, Calenus, Calatius, or Caiatius. But these names are equally explicable as commemorations of victories, while the tribal affiliations of the *gens* with Pupinia and Aemilia hardly support a Campanian connection.[5] A strong objection also lies in the silence of the Roman tradition, when Livy records the fictitious request of the Campanians for access to the Roman consulship in 212 B.C.,[6] or when he records the consulships of the Decii in his

Volsci—both largely *cives s.s.*—and Umbri, Marrucini, Paeligni, Frentani, separately from the Roman legions). Livy 10. 26. 14, 29. 12; 23. 4. 8, cf. below, 207 n. 1. The term *legio Campana* (only in Livy, *Ep.* 12, 15) may mislead, cf. Heurgon, op. cit. 203. Totals: Polyb. 2. 24, 273,000 for both Romani and Campani in 225, compared with *c.* 270,000 in census of 234–3 (Livy, *Ep.* 20). Apparent absence of Campani from Caudine Forks and Cannae: Livy 9. 6. 4–8; 23. 5. 15.

[1] Bernardi, art. cit. (1938), 246 f., (1943), 30. Heurgon, op. cit. 180 f., 237 f.
[2] Livy 8. 22. 7; 23. 10. Heurgon, op. cit. 283.    [3] Livy 23. 7. 1, cf. above, 46.
[4] Heurgon, op. cit. chs. 12–13. Beloch *contra*, *RG* 338–9, cf. Taylor, *VD* 194–5. Heurgon (op. cit. 287) with Münzer (*Adelsparteien*, 57) discounts Atilii listed as consular tribunes in the earlier *Fasti* (444, 399, 396). The Decii Mures, *coss.* 340, 312, 307, 297, have no predecessors.
[5] Taylor, loc. cit. Note also the *cognomen* Nomentanus of L. Atilius, a mintmaster *c.* 130–120 (ibid.).
[6] Livy 23. 6. 6, 'ut alter consul Campanus fieret'. Livy doubts this.

annalistic list. So notable an invasion of the *Fasti* should have been remembered somewhere in the ancient sources, along with the first consulship of the Fulvii of Tusculum. But Heurgon's application of Festus circumvents the objection of Beloch to the political probability of such families ever migrating to Rome. It remains possible that *cives s.s.* were in the original conception at once 'allies' and 'citizens', but not of a normal sort.

### *Municipia outside Campania*

Bernardi distinguished two classes of *municipia civium sine suffragio*, much as in this book—those which secured the status in more or less friendly circumstances and retained full local autonomy, principally in Campania and Volscium, and those on which the status was thrust or whose status was altered after rebellion, reconquest, and confiscation of lands. These latter were allowed only a reduced measure of autonomy, or none at all (as at Privernum and Antium), their existing magistracies being frequently limited to priestly functions.[1] This second group contains (for Bernardi) all the *municipia* except the Volscian triad, the Campanian cities, and originally Caere.[2] This view, that Campania was the main focus of the more privileged form of *civitas s.s.*, reflects the bias of the surviving evidence. But there are some indications in the Latin tradition that this form was disseminated as early and as widely in the Volscian zone as in Campania. Apart from the faithful triad of Arpinum, Formiae, and Fundi, promoted in the same period as Capua, Livy implies that Velitrae and Satricum received the status *before* their rebellions (338, 315), while the extension to Antium (338) and Privernum (318–317) after rebellions is documented at length. The tradition concentrates on the Volscian rebellions, and hence stresses the penal consequences. Yet autonomy survived at Velitrae, which later has its *meddices*. It is possible that the Campanian form of *civitas s.s.* was originally normal throughout Volscium.[3]

The emergence of a less privileged form of *civitas s.s.* is however clear. It remains uncertain what was the number and extent of *municipia* of this type, created between the end of Livy's first decade in 292 and the

---

[1] Bernardi, art. cit. (1938), 267 ff.

[2] Ibid. 255 f. He argues that the triple aediles of Fundi etc. include the *meddix tuticus*—Horace's *praetor Fundanus*—and hence were as autonomous as Capua's. Heurgon, op. cit. 232 f., takes *meddix summus* in Ennius (as distinct from *superior*) similarly to mean 'one of three'—following S. Weinstock, *Klio* 24 (1931), 235. This improves on the suggestion, above, 67, that the *meddix-praetor* was additional to the aediles, which hardly fits Cic. *ad Fam.* 13. 11. 3.

[3] For Privernum and Antium cf. above, 50, 81; for Satricum and Velitrae below, 209 n. 6, 212 n. 4.

resumption of the Livian record in 218 B.C., after which no fresh grants of *civitas s.s.* are recorded. This problem can only be discussed in terms of the lists of *praefecturae* given by Festus and compiled from other sources, which were not fully explored above. Since many *municipia* of both sorts appear in Festus' list of *praefecturae* outside Campania, the identification of all *praefecturae* with *municipia s.s.* has been suggested. But it is clear from the lists themselves, and accepted by most scholars, that the *praefectura* system was also used to provide jurisdiction for distant settlements of Roman citizens in *tribus rusticae* and *coloniae maritimae*, created out of confiscated lands, notably in Picenum, Etruria, and the *Ager Gallicus*.[1] Since *civitas s.s.* covered the whole territory of a community, while colonization, whether 'Latin' or 'Roman', was generally limited to only a proportion of even the confiscated lands,[2] the sorting out of *praefecturae* of Roman citizens from 'municipal' *praefecturae* of *cives s.s.* greatly affects the distribution of Roman territory in central Italy, which may have been far less continuous than it appears in some modern maps and descriptions.

There is not much doubt that the apparently numerous *praefecturae* of Picenum are the *fora* and *conciliabula* of Roman citizens of the *tribus Velina*, first created in 241 B.C., which much later were administered by municipal *duoviri*. L. R. Taylor has, however, argued against the assumption that seemingly large *tribus rusticae* at their creation covered all the communes later found within their central territory.[3] This is relevant to the question of the Sabines. It was accepted above that the evidence of Velleius means that the Sabine communes from Cures in the Tiber valley through Trebula Mutuesca to the *praefecturae* of Reate, Nursia, and Amiternum, all received *civitas s.s.* in 290 and full citizenship in 268, together with the Vestinian *praefecturae* of Aveia and Peltuinum—mainly because the latter five communes all appear later in the *tribus Quirina* (created with the Velina in 241).[4] But Cures and Trebula Mutuesca belong to the tribe Sergia, while Nursia, Reate, and Amiternum appear with Caere in a list of *socii Italici* proper, who made voluntary contributions to the African campaign of Scipio in 203 B.C. Hence it is argued that these were no more than

---

[1] Cf. above, 43 f., 51 f. Bernardi, art. cit. (1938), 271 f. similarly. Heurgon, op. cit. 237 f., oddly assumed that *praefecti* took over the whole administration of their *municipia*. Toynbee, op. cit. 239 f., identified *praefecturae* with *municipia c.s.s.* of the less autonomous sort and those fully incorporated; this does not fit Cumae and Acerrae.

[2] Cf. Taylor's discussion of the Pomptina, Falerna, Velina, Quirina (*VD* 50, 55–6, 59, 66–7).

[3] Above, pp. 53, 167. So too Bernardi, art. cit. (1938), 271, Taylor, op. cit. 64. For the *duoviri*, Beloch, *RG* 509; for their tribes, Taylor, op. cit. 275.

[4] Above, p. 65.

*cives s.s.*, or even *foederati*, down to that date, and that the grants of status in 290–268, were limited to the Sabines of Cures and Trebula adjacent to Roman territory. The assumption is that Velleius used *Sabinus* in a restricted and archaic sense.[1]

The title *praefectura* and the survival of the octoviral magistracy would suggest that the rest of the Sabines secured citizenship in some form before the Social War. But there is no reason to assume that the Quirina was created in 241 for their enfranchisement, rather than for Roman settlers on their lands. Reate indeed, like Urbs Salvia and Asculum in Picenum, has the municipal quattuorvirate instead of the octovirate or the duovirate in later times. But so too has Cures. Hence the magistracy does not prove that Reate and Urbs Salvia remained federate allies, like Asculum, till the Social War.[2]

It is noteworthy that the duoviral magistracy does not occur later in the communes outside Campania listed as *praefecturae* by Festus, though the evidence for them is admittedly incomplete.[3] But it is found in Campania at Suessula and in other *praefecturae* and adjacent municipalities in Picenum, the *Ager Gallicus*, the Samnite border zone, and the isolated Etruscan *Praefectura Statoniensis*.[4] At none of these is there any direct evidence of a grant of *civitas s.s.* The duovirate does, however, occur at three municipalities of the former Aequi-Aequicoli, not known as prefectures, of which at least Trebula Suffenas, and possibly all, received *civitas s.s.* after a savage conquest and the confiscation of the greater part of their land.[5]

The evidence for the Samnite prefectures is in all respects unsatisfactory, except for the title itself. This is testified on the territory of the Pentri at Casinum, Allifae, Venafrum, and Atina, in the Volturnus-Liris region, and possibly at distant Aufidena, while the duovirate occurs at Casinum, Atina, and Aufidena. All of these were eventually

---

[1] Taylor, op. cit. 59 ff., citing Livy 28. 45. 19, where the immediate context suggests that Sabini are *socii* rather than *cives s.s.*: '...Clusini, Rusellani...Umbriae populi et praeter hos Nursini et Reatini et Amiterni...Marsi' But for *cives s.s.* as *socii* see above, pp. 41 f. P. A. Brunt, *Coll. Latomus* 102 (1969), 121, argues for the traditional explanation of Velleius. Cic. *Off.* 1. 35 is neutral.

[2] Above, 65, and below, 212 n. 6.

[3] The later magistracies of Allifae, Venafrum, Frusino are unknown, and Saturnia became a *colonia c.R.*

[4] Above, 167. For Visentium, within the *Praefectura Statoniensis*, cf. Beloch, *RG* 510, 566. Suessula apparently remained loyal in 213–210, like Cumae; cf. above, 44 n. 3 and Livy 26. 34. 6–11.

[5] Trebula Suffenas, Cliternia, Respublica Aequicolorum, cf. Beloch, *RG* 508–9. After the war two Latin Colonies, Alba and Carseoli, and the *tribus Aniensis* were settled on Aequian land between 303 and 298: Livy 9. 45. 5–9; 17–18; 10. 1. 1; 9. 14; 13. 1. In the context the Trebulani who receive *civitas s.s.* in Livy 10. 1. 3 are clearly those of Aequian Trebula Suffenas, *pace* Beloch, *RG* 425; cf. Taylor, op. cit. 56 n. 35. For their earlier refusal of it cf. above, 49.

registered in the *tribus Teretina*, except Aufidena.[1] But the duovirate also appears at adjacent Cubulteria, Caiatia, and Telesia in Caudine Samnium south of the Volturnus, where the tribal registration is different and there is no trace of *praefecturae*, and at other communes of northern Samnium.[2] It is commonly assumed that the Samnite prefectures received *civitas s.s.* after the last Samnite wars in *c.* 290 or 270. But the only indication is very indirect—the foundation of a Latin colony at Aesernia beyond this zone in 268, which implies land confiscation[3]. There was viritane settlement on unspecified land in Samnium (and Apulia) in 200, probably in the disloyal south, but so far as is known no *tribus rustica* was established then or earlier on Samnite lands.[4] The extension of the Teretina to accommodate the Samnite prefectures after final enfranchisement need not precede the Social War.

The situation in Samnium is very different from that of the Sabine area and Picenum, and recalls the treatment of the Etruscan territory taken from Volci and Volsinii after the war of 280. The Latin colony of Cosa (273) and the later Roman colonies of Saturnia (183) and the undated Heba occupied much of this, while the remainder formed the

[1] Beloch, *RG* 472, Taylor, *VD* 92 n. 39, 275, 276. Venafrum, Allifae in Festus s.v.; Atina, Cic. *Planc.* 21; Casinum depends on *CIL* x. 5193, 5194: 'C. Futius. [pra]ef. [C]asinat[ium]'. But the evidence for Aufidena—on which Salmon (op. cit. 290) bases Roman annexation in 270—is far from definitive: *CIL* ix. 2802. Since Aufidena later has the Roman tribe (Voltinia) of the northern Samnites enfranchised after the Social War it probably remained *socius* till then. For the *duoviri*, Beloch, *RG* 509.

[2] Beloch, *RG* 508–9: Vibinum, Fagifulae, Saepinum, Tereventum. The analysis of A. Degrassi, *Quattuorviri in colonie romane* etc., Atti Acc. Naz. Lincei, A. 346. Ser. 8, vol. II, fasc. 6, 326–7, shows that as in other instances the 'quattuorviri' of these duoviral communes were junior magistrates (*aedilicia potestate*). That Saepinum was refounded in *c.* A.D. 2 (*CIL* ix. 2483) confirms the suspicion of a late date for all these duoviral communes in Samnium (cf. above, 167). For the survival of Caudine Caiatia, Cubulteria, and Telesia as *socii* down to *c.* 216–210 cf. Beloch, *RG* 511, citing Livy 23. 14. 13; 39. 6; 24. 20. 5. Taylor, op. cit. 90 n. 32, disagrees. For Caiatia and Telesia in the *tribus Falerna*, cf. Taylor, loc. cit. and 113 n. 31; Mommsen, *CIL* x, p. 444. The *duoviri* of Telesia may be due to a Gracchan colony (Beloch, loc. cit.).

[3] Salmon, *Samnium*, 277–8, 290, hesitates between 290 and 270 for the *Praefecturae*, but infers from coins attributed uncertainly to Venafrum that it may have remained independent longer. The foundation date of Aesernia makes a date post-270 more probable than post-290 for any grant of *c.s.s.*; cf. the Latin colony settled at Beneventum in 263 on Hirpine territory (Beloch, *RG* 450, 472). The only evidence for *civitas s.s.* given to Samnites is Velleius 1. 14. 3 on the grant in 334 to *pars Samnitium* in Campania.

[4] Livy 31. 4. 1–3; 49. 5. Bernardi art. cit. (1938), 274 connected this with the Pentrian prefectures, but Taylor, op. cit. 92, rightly notes that the disloyal Hirpini are more probable victims. Mommsen (*St. R.* iii. 187) suggested that the *tribus Voltinia* (the tribe of Aufidena) was extended into northern Samnium at this time.

*Praefectura Statoniensis.* No grant of *civitas s.s.* to the latter is recorded; its township of Visentium in later time is 'duoviral' and has the same tribe as Saturnia.[1] The treatment of the Caerite territory after 272 is similar, with the unconfiscated remnant forming the *praefectura* of Festus' list. But here the survival of the antiquated type of magistracy proves an earlier origin or stage of development.

There is some unsatisfactory evidence in the *Liber coloniarum* for prefectures in Lucania and Bruttium, at Atina, Consilinum, Grumentum, Potentia, and Paestum, most of which retained 'allied' status down to the Social War, and became 'quattuorviral' municipalities after it.[2] The duovirate appears elsewhere in the region later, and Grumentum may have been a Roman colony of the Gracchan period.[3]

It is apparent how fragile are the grounds for depicting huge areas in the central Apennines, Samnium, and Lucania as territory inhabited solidly by Roman citizens, whether *s.s.* or not, as is done in the maps and plans of Afzelius and Toynbee. These combine the maximum possible extension of the *civitas s.s.* with the audacious speculations of Beloch about the boundaries and territorial extent of the Italian communes. The date and precise status of the Samnite prefectures at least must remain uncertain. Perhaps a grant of *civitas s.s.* in the half-century preceding 218, unaccompanied by formal Roman settlement, is the likely guess.

The latest grants of *civitas s.s.* would seem to be those to Caere, in the final reorganization of its status *c.* 272, and to the Samnite border states, if these prefectures stem from *civitas s.s.*[4] This carries its latest use beyond the period of the Sabine and Picene wars suggested as its limits above.[5] After this its extension was abandoned, but not because it had failed, as some think.[6] Even Campania remained loyal for a hundred years, and its final secession to Hannibal is over half a century after the last extension of *civitas s.s.* There is no sign of disloyalty in the third century among the numerous *municipia* from the

---

[1] Cf. above, 207 n. 4. Beloch, *RG* 455, 565, 608. Taylor, op. cit. 86. For Cosa, Pliny, *NH* 3. 51, Velleius 1. 14, 7; Saturnia, Livy 39. 55. 9. The *praefectura Statoniensis* (Vit. 2. 7. 3 only) may have overlapped with the *praef. Saturnia* of Festus.

[2] *Lib. col.* c. 209, cf. Beloch *RG*, 503, 593. Paestum as *colonia Latina*, Elia as federate ally, cannot be such.

[3] Ibid. 508, 593 f.: Aceruntia, Blanda, Eburum.

[4] Cf. above, 202 n. 2.                                                          [5] Above, 50–1.

[6] So Toynbee, op. cit. i. 206, largely due to his belief (*passim*) that *civitas s.s.* was from the beginning a penal condition imposed by force. Apart from the later Campanian revolt, and the solitary early instance (Livy 9. 12. 5, 26. 33. 10) of Satricum, there is only the preference of the Hernici and Aequi for federal status (cf. above, 49). His rebellious 'Auruncan municipia' derive from a figment of Beloch, *RG* 382, concocted out of the *deditio* of the *gens* in 337 (Livy 8. 15. 2; 9. 25); cf. Taylor, op. cit. 58.

Volscian zone through the central Apennines to Picenum and southern Etruria, while the Caerites and Sabines were even volunteering help to Rome after the war with Hannibal.[1]

### The Enfranchisement of the Municipia

The loyalty of the *municipia* would indeed be explained if, as A. J. Toynbee coolly surmised, they had nearly all been fully enfranchised before 218 B.C. by the formal grant of *ius suffragii*.[2] The date of the ultimate promotion of the various *municipia* was not discussed above, because there is no direct evidence except for the grant to the 'Sabines' in 268 and that to the three Volscian communes—Arpinum, Fundi, Formiae—eighty years later.[3] Opinion fluctuates. Some attribute a general promotion of *cives s.s.* to the period between the Volscian grant and the Social War.[4] Others hold that many survived unpromoted down to the Social War, or even that the promotions of 188 were the last before the Social War.[5] Arguments are indirect. The absence of *cives s.s.* from the groups of discontented allies in the agitations of 125–90 B.C. is invoked to prove their previous and universal promotion. But *cives s.s.*, who enjoyed tribunician protection, would be protected against the grosser abuses from which the *socii Italici* suffered,[6] their gentry had access to the full citizenship and in rare instances even to office at Rome,[7] and the silence of the thin, late, and often garbled accounts of the enfranchisement movement proves little.[8] An early enfranchisement of the Appennine *municipia* is inferred by Toynbee from the creation in 241 B.C. of the *tribus Velina* and *Quirina*, in which many of them are known to have been ultimately enrolled, and from the extensive colonization of Picenum under the *lex Flaminia* of 232.[9] These certainly could have provided an occasion for the promotion of the native population in the area, including the Sabines discussed above. But *tribus rusticae* were created primarily for the

---

[1] Above, 207 n. 1.    [2] Op. cit. 403 ff.    [3] Above, 61.

[4] So Brunt, allowing no exceptions, *JRS* 55 (1965), 93.

[5] Cf. Kornemann, *RE* xxi col. 584. His theory that the *lex Mamilia Roscia* (*FIRA* i. 12) reorganizing *municipia* belongs to 109 and dealt with *municipia c.s.s.* must yield to its modern identification with a law of five tribunes or praetors of 55 or 49; cf. above, 167, and below, 212–13. Bernardi, art. cit. (1938), 263, argued that Roman intransigence began with the expulsion orders of 187 and 177. But these were due to pressure from the allies, cf. above, 107; a better indication is the abolition of Latin colonization, above, 78.

[6] Bernardi, art. cit. (1938), 265, cf. Livy 26. 33. 10 with reference to capital jurisdiction.

[7] Cf. Bernardi, art. cit. (1943), 27–8, based on Festus s.v. *municipium* cited above, 40 n. 9. Also cf. 204 above.

[8] Cf. above, 134 ff. The earliest sources are the Augustan Diodorus and Strabo; cf. the obscure passages in the longest, Appian, *BC* 1. 23. 99; 24. 104; 29. 132; 49 214.    [9] Toynbee, op. cit. i. 386, 403 f.

agrarian settlement of existing Roman citizens in new areas, not for the accommodation of new citizens.[1] So there is no proof.[2] The assumption of Toynbee that Rome could not have depended for her own manpower in the war with Hannibal on a citizenry of which nearly half lacked political rights, is merely an expression of surprise at the pattern of the Roman state; the great mass of citizens from Campania and the adjacent Volscian and Samnite prefectures were certainly *sine suffragio* at that time.

The fact that Livy's full narrative from 200 to 167 mentions only the full enfranchisement of the Volscian triad in 188 is the main stumbling-block. If for twenty years after 188 there were no more promotions, it is unlikely that there were many between 167 and 125 when Roman attitudes were becoming increasingly egoistic and intransigent in all external spheres.[3] Hence it is suggested that Livy omitted many instances, and only included the Volscian case because it involved a political intervention by the tribunes.[4] But the context shows that Livy included it along with other facts which had no political overtones, as part of the *acta censorum* of 189–188, a feature of his annals for which he regularly scrapes up what information is available. Hence his silence carries weight. At the same time some of the Campani, who had been disfranchised in 211 and reduced to the status of *liberi homines* lacking a *res publica*, were allowed a relaxation by the grant of *ius conubii* with Roman women.[5] This has been represented as a restoration of their former *civitas s.s.* in full, and as proof of Roman generosity towards *cives s.s.* in general,[6] and even as a presage of the *ius suffragii*. But Livy says nothing about 'citizenship' of any sort or its restoration. On the same occasion the Campani as stateless men were required to register at the Roman census because there was nowhere else for them to do so; though expelled from Campania they could hold land elsewhere and were liable for military service. Presumably they were listed in a special category such as the *Caeritum tabulae*—but not as citizens.[7]

---

[1] Cf. Taylor, op. cit. 66. See also above, 198.

[2] Toynbee's theory requires the acceptance of Taylor's hypothesis that the grants of 290–268, were limited to Cures, cf. above, 206 f.

[3] For Roman foreign policy in general cf. A. E. Astin, *Scipio Aemilianus* (Oxford, 1967), 41 f., 49 f., 147 f. For attitude to allies cf. above, 128, 134 f.

[4] Livy 38. 36. 7. Taylor, art. cit. 93, followed by Brunt, art. cit. 93.

[5] Livy 38. 36. 5–6, 'petierunt ut sibi cives Romanas ducere uxores liceret et si qui prius duxissent ut . . . nati . . . iusti sibi liberi heredesque essent.' Cf. Livy 26. 34. 6, 'Campanos omnes . . . liberos esse iusserunt ita ut nemo eorum civis Romanus aut Latini nominis esset.'

[6] Brunt, loc. cit.

[7] Livy 38. 36. 5. It is not clear which of the various groups of demoted and exiled Campani—some *ultra Tiberim*, others *cis Lirim* or *cis Volturnum*—are here

The ambiguous evidence of the *pro Plancio* has been invoked to date the incorporation of the *praefectura* of Atina to the late second century. Cicero describes it as a 'not very ancient' municipality, in comparison with Tusculum, traditionally dated to 380, and mentions the election of its first Roman curule magistrate, evidently *c.* 100–90.[1] But he also describes the forebears of his client Plancius as having been *equites Romani* for the three previous generations, a technicality which may or may not carry the incorporation of Atina—and perhaps the neighbouring prefectures—far back into the second century.[2] Velitrae too has had its full status dated back to before the first appearance of the Velitran *gens Octavia* in the Roman *Fasti* for 231.[3] But the forebears of Octavian with their Latin *nomen* are more likely to derive from the Roman settlers of 324 than from the Oscan *municipium*, testified possibly by an inscription of the third century which mentions *meddices*.[4]

It is sometimes held that all former *municipia s.s.*, which later have magistracies other than the quattuorvirate instituted for those enfranchised in 89 (and the subsequent duovirate), must not only have acquired these magistracies but have been promoted to full citizenship before 90.[5] This can hardly be proved or disproved from the existing evidence. Sabine Cures and Reate, enfranchised, one certainly, the other probably, in 268, and the neighbouring Fulginiae, alone among known *municipia c.s.s.* and *praefecturae*, have the quattuorvirate in later time. This may be explained away as a later mutation of the original octovirate found in the other *municipia s.s.* of this region, and hence need not be attributed to the general reorganization after 89.[6]

There remains the group of former *praefecturae* and *municipia s.s.* at which the duovirate, probably instituted by the *lex Roscia* of 55 or 49,

concerned. They were all allowed conditionally to hold substantial property (Livy 26. 34. 9–10.)

[1] A. Afzelius, *Die römische Eroberung Italiens* (1942), 25. Cic., *pro Plancio* 19.

[2] Ibid. 32. Earlier *cives s.s.* served in their own units, cf. above, 111. Cicero implies that the Plancii were registered as *equites Romani*.

[3] Toynbee, op. cit. i. 405, cf. Suet. *Aug.* 1. Taylor, op. cit. 239.

[4] Taylor, op. cit. 55, connects the Roman settlers (Livy 8. 14. 7) with the establishment of the *tribus Scaptia* (later the tribe of Velitrae, ibid. 221) in 332 (Livy 8. 17. 11). The grant of *civitas s.s.* (before 338) is an inference from Livy's obscure *veteres cives Romanos* (8. 14. 5), but may be as genuine as that equally indirectly recorded for Satricum (above, 209 n. 6). The Oscan inscription is neutral evidence (Conway, *Italic Dialects*, i. n. 252), but the later *praetores*, if *CIL. x.* 6554 is genuine, would suggest a pre-90 *municipium s.s.*

[5] e.g. Taylor, op. cit. 82 f. Cf. above, 63 ff. for the magistracies.

[6] Scholars follow Beloch, *RG* 504; cf. 505 also, for the *ivviri* of Urbs Salvia; at Plestia both *ivviri* and *viiiviri* appear. Cic. *ad Att.* 10. 13. 1, a general summons to municipal magistrates as *ivviri*, does not prove that those of Cumae who appeared in reply were *ivviri* rather than the *praetores* of *CIL* x. 3685, 3698.

appears instead of the quattuorvirate.[1] This includes the Samnite, Picene, and Etruscan prefectures, and the Aequian communes. While some of these were townships of *tribus rusticae*, others, such as Campanian Suessula and Aequian Cliternia, certainly originated in a grant of *civitas s.s.*, made in some cases to fragments of formerly integral *gentes* and *populi*.[2] If these owed their magisterial organization to the legislation of the late Republic, they must have existed previously as insignificant village communities dependent largely upon the itinerant Prefects, down to the Social War and throughout the next generation, without any change of internal administration. Hence no group of former *municipia s.s.*, whatever the date of its *ius suffragii*, is likely to have had its magistracy altered or instituted in the 80s. The continued existence of the Roman *praefecti* is documented in legal texts of 123 and 100, and implied in the 50s by Cicero's stress on the title of *praefectura* at Fulginiae, Reate, and Atina; the special *praefecti Capuam Cumas* continued to be elected until their formal abolition in 26 B.C.[3]

The survival of the system after 89 does not mean that *praefecturae* were always fully enfranchised towns, as L. R. Taylor supposed, or hence that all had been enfranchised before 89. For the system was not extended to the new incorporations of 89, and it certainly originated with communes that lacked full Roman status.[4] Nothing can be inferred from the title *praefectura* about the date of any grant of *ius suffragii*. The *praefecturae* overlap but are not identical with *municipia c.s.s.*, and the system continues until municipal reorganization, and colonization, as at Capua in 59, made it unnecessary.

There are two direct indications that some *municipia* survived *sine suffragio* down to the decades before the Social War. The *lex agraria* of 111 lists *moenicipia* and *pro moenicipiis* together with *coloniae* and *pro colonieis* as holders of *ager publicus* which are to have their rights safeguarded.[5] At that time the term *municipium* should refer technically to a self-governing commune of *cives s.s.*, while the *pro municipiis* should be either fully enfranchised *municipia* and *oppida c.R.* or else the category of small communes just discussed as duoviral prefectures, formed out of mere fragments of former *populi* and *gentes*. Brunt, while admitting this, yet dismisses the formula as probably out of date and

---

[1] Above, 167 ff. and 207–209 nn.

[2] Cf. 205. For Suessula cf. above, 207 n. 4, and below, 214 n. 3.

[3] *FIRA²* i. 7. 31, 'in oppidis foris conciliabulis ubi iuri dicundo praeesse solent'. Ibid. 9. 11–12. Cic. *pro Plancio* 19, 32, *pro Scauro* 27, *pro Vareno* 4.

[4] Cf. above, 43 f.

[5] *FIRA²* i n. 8. 31 '[si quei colonieis seive moi]nicipieis seive quae pro moinicipeis colo[nieisve sunt civium Romanorum] nominisve Latini poplice deve senati sententia ager fruendus datus est', and below '[queiv]e pro colonia moinicipiove prove moinciipieis fruentur'.

'tralatician'.[1] If it is tralatician, whence was it transferred? The original could only be the *lex Sempronia* of 133, the first of a new pattern of agrarian laws dealing with *ager publicus* as a whole, to which the law of 111 constantly refers as its starting-point. So *municipia s.s.* still existed in 133 B.C.

A more ambiguous reference to *municipia* is given in the same historical context by Appian's account of the opposition to the proposals of Tiberius Gracchus by 'a mass of men from the colonies and the cities with equal civic rights which had holdings of public land'.[2] Nominally this phrase could be merely a translation of the much later formula common in texts of the imperial period, 'municipia et coloniae', for the sum total of Italian communes. But in 133 it should refer precisely to the existing colonies, which were mostly *coloniae Latinae*, and to the existing *municipia*, in the technical sense, just as in the formula of the law of 111.

If *municipia c.s.s.* still existed in 133 it is unlikely that they received the *ius suffragii* in the period of extreme intransigence that began with the opposition to the proposals of Fulvius Flaccus in 125. The most probable group to survive unpromoted are those that later had the duoviral magistracy.[3]

### III. GRIEVANCES AND BENEFITS OF *SOCII ITALICI* AND *LATINI*

There have been several studies of the Roman treatment of the allies in the well-documented period of the later third and second centuries, which either reproduce or develop certain aspects of the

---

[1] Brunt, art. cit. 93 n. 21. *Pace* Brunt this document takes excessive care in definitions that were of the utmost importance for property rights. The nominal implication of the first citation, if pressed, that there were *municipia nominis Latini*, is no objection because not real. That *municipia* in the later sense did not yet exist is indicated by the absence of this term from the compendious formula for Roman communes in s. 22 '[i]d oppidum coloniamve ex lege . . . constituit deduxitve conlocavitve.' Contrast *lex Mamilia* 3: 'quae colonia hac lege deducta quodve municipium praefectura forum conciliabulum constitutum erit.'

[2] Appian, *BC* 1. 10. 41: ἐν ταῖς ἀποίκοις πόλεσιν ἢ ταῖς ἰσοπολίτισιν. Cf. ibid. 1. 21. 87: τοὺς ὑπηκόους σφῶν ἰσοπολίτας εἰ ποιήσονται. This neatly renders *municipes* into Greek.

[3] Bernardi's suggestion (art. cit. (1938), 251) that Cumae, Acerrae, and Atella were cited by 'Servius' (Festus, s.v. *municeps*, above, 40 n. 7) as *municipia s.s.* surviving down to his own age, is invalidated by the inclusion of Atella, which shared the fate of Capua in 211. Even if permanently taken over by the 'ally' Nuceria (Livy 27. 3. 6–7) it ceased to be a *municipium s.s.* Cf. Toynbee, op. cit. i. 410 n. 4. It is remarkable that Cumae, still *s.s.* in 180 (Livy 40. 42. 13), has a pre-89 magistracy (above, 212 n. 6), but Suessula, though not connected with the Campanian revolt, has the later duovirate (above, 207, and 44 n. 3). Unfortunately the later magistracy of Acerrae, the peer of both, is not known.

account in this book without materially altering the picture.[1] Badian
has taken a somewhat more cynical view of Roman goodwill in the
second century than is always justified by the evidence. It is not clear
why he holds that the acquisition of the Roman status by Latin allies
through migration to Roman territory totally ceased in 177 after the
establishment of the rule limiting this procedure to persons who left
a son behind in their colony of origin.[2] By underestimating the new
Latin privilege of gaining Roman citizenship through holding the
magistracy of one's colony, which was established in or before the
Gracchan period, he distorts the attitude of Rome, ungenerous as it
was, to the enfranchisement of the Latin aristocracy.[3] Göhler, however,
while rightly rejecting the notion of an earlier age that Roman policy
in Italy was based on a conscious rule of *divide et impera,* took an over-
optimistic view of Roman beneficence. He tried to explain away obvious meannesses in the division of land and booty,[4] and exaggerated
the importance of the privilege that allowed Latins present in Rome to
vote in a single tribal unit, as though this conveyed significant
political power.[5] Badian conceded with Göhler that the soldiery of the
allies benefited greatly from their share in the considerable booty of
the imperialist wars in Spain and the East in the early second century,
even if their leaders did not acquire the vast fortunes gained by the
Roman commanders. This benefit, not found in the barren wars with
the Spanish tribes of later years, was renewed with the sack of Carthage
and Corinth in 146, and the exploitation of southern Gaul in the last
two decades of the century.

An ingenious attempt has been made by two scholars to date the
Latin privilege of acquiring Roman citizenship *per honorem,* that is by
holding the magistracies of their colonies, much later than the
Gracchan period, placing it either after the Social War or after the
end of the Republic. This runs clean counter to the evidence of two

---

[1] Especially: J. Göhler, *Rom und Italien* (Breslau, 1939), contemporary with *RC*
and independent. A. H. McDonald, 'Rome and the Italian Confederation', *JRS*
34 (1944), 11 ff. E. Badian, *Foreign Clientelae* (Oxford, 1958), ch. 6. E. T. Salmon,
*Roman Colonization under the Republic* (London, 1969) synthesizes his various articles.
P. A. Brunt, 'Italian Aims at the time of the Social War', *JRS* 55 (1965), 90 ff.,
surveys the second century. A. Toynbee, *Hannibal's Legacy* (Oxford, 1965), ii, ch. iv
synthesizes modern literature at length.

[2] Badian, op. cit. 150: 'Henceforth the gulf between *cives Romani* and their
subjects is fixed.'

[3] Ibid. 179, 189, but 221 is more balanced. For the date see below; G. Tibiletti,
*Rend. Ist. Lombard.* 86. 54 dated this privilege (much as above, 111, 137) after the
revolt of Fregellae.

[4] Göhler, op. cit. 50–2. Cf. *contra*, H. M. Last, *JRS* 30 (1940), 81 f., Badian, op.
cit. 150, citing e.g. Livy 41. 13. 7 f., 42. 4. 4.

[5] Göhler, op. cit. 80, 135, etc. Last, art. cit. 84. *contra.*

documents.[1] First, it had previously been widely accepted that the *lex Repetundarum* of Gracchan date, which offered a group of Roman privileges as an alternative to the Roman citizenship to persons from Latin states who had not held their local magistracies, proved that both these alternatives were offered to the magistrates themselves. It is objected with excessive sophistication that the text only proves the grant of the select privileges *per honorem*, and that the citizenship is mentioned only because it was offered separately as a reward by the *lex Repetundarum* itself to successful prosecutors. But this ignores the implication of the select privileges themselves: *provocatio, muneris publici vacatio*, and a right of choice between local and Roman jurisdiction. These form the main benefits of the Roman citizenship for persons resident outside the Roman state, and only make sense as an alternative to an offer of the citizenship.[2] Since such an alternative choice was already put forward in the enfranchisement bill of Fulvius Flaccus in 125 B.C., there is nothing improbable in its use in other contexts at this time. Further, Asconius states that the Latin privilege of gaining Roman status *per honorem* existed in 89 B.C., when it was extended with *ius Latii* to the Transpadane Gauls. There was no reason at that time to invent the privilege specially for the benefit of the Gauls, who had not agitated for the franchise, and who had at one time objected to the enfranchisement of their tribesmen. Hence the attempt to explain away the implication of the *lex Repetundarum* 78–9 is otiose.[3]

Afzelius has cast new light on the condition of the Italian and Latin allies by his detailed study of the Livian figures for the annual enlistment and distribution of Rome's military forces.[4] During the great wars of the first quarter of the second century Rome made heavy demands on the allies, whose contribution continued at much the same rate as during the war with Hannibal. No account was apparently taken of the devastation of their communes during the long war, or of the extensive confiscation of territories from secessionist allies, with consequent loss of manpower, after it. Allied troops tended to be

---

[1] D. W. Bradeen, *Cl. J.* 54, 221 f., H. B. Mattingly, *JRS* 60 (1970), 163 f. The evidence of *lex Repetundarum* 78–9 and Asconius, *in Pis.* 3 C, is quoted in part above, III nn. 3–4. The choice of jurisdiction appears also in the *Tabula Tarantina* I. 5 (*Epigraphica* ix. 7): 'ioudicium Romae certet sei Romae veolet.' The incident at Comum (Cic. *ad Att.* 5. 11. 2) is ambiguous, and can be used to support either view, cf. above, 136 n. 4. Cf. my forthcoming article in *JRS* 62 (1972).

[2] Cf. ch. XIII, below, 296 ff.

[3] Cf. Cic. *pro Balbo* 32: 'Cenomanorum, Insubrium, ... in foederibus exceptum est ne quis eorum a nobis civis recipiatur.' They coolly reject Asconius.

[4] A. Afzelius, *Römische Kriegsmacht*, Acta Jutlandica 16. 2, (Copenhagen, 1944). The table on pp. 78–9 summarizes the statistical evidence of Livy. Toynbee, op. cit. ii. 128 f., exploits Afzelius with additional points; cf. briefly, Badian, op. cit. 149.

retained on active service for longer periods than the Roman legions, and to be assigned disproportionately to the formidable battle zones in Spain and north Italy where military losses were highest.[1] But faced by a manifest decline in the manpower of the Italian communes, the Senate in the decade after 176 at last reduced its rate of demand by about a third, so that the allied contribution was numerically on a par with the Roman: a Roman legion with a nominal strength of 5,200 men was balanced by a complement of 5,000 allied infantry *e formula togatorum*.[2] Which side provided the greater proportion of troops in relation to its potential is left uncertain by the lack of demographical statistics about the allies, and by the inadequacy of information about the precise boundaries of the Roman tribal and 'municipal' territories at this time. But comparison with the ratio which Polybius gives for the third and second centuries of five Italian infantrymen to four Roman, in the heyday of Italian prosperity, suggests that the burden of conscription pressed more heavily on the allies than on the Romans even after the reductions of 176.[3] It is likely that the second bout of bitter warfare in Spain, from 154 to 132, made demands as heavy and as unequal as those of the previous war. The Roman peasantry by violent protests and with tribunician help were able to extort some concessions from the Senatorial government that mitigated the severity of the demands made on them.[4] But the Latin and Italian allies lacked the political means of redressing similar injustices.

Just before the end of the Spanish war Tiberius Gracchus proposed his agrarian scheme for the recolonization of Italy. This is commonly thought to have been limited to the distribution of *ager publicus*, confiscated in an earlier age from the various Italian peoples, to Roman citizenry alone. Hence there was a new grievance for the allies, which precipitated the isolated revolt of Fregellae, a Latin colony, in 126, and led to the proposals of Fulvius Flaccus and Gaius Gracchus for the enfranchisement of the allies. Göhler sought to counter this common opinion by arguing that the *lex Sempronia* proposed the distribution of land to landless Romans and Italians alike. His argument is against the main indications of the somewhat ambiguous evidence, and he has found few followers.[5] Yet it would be in line with the custom of the age

---

[1] Cf. Toynbee, op. cit. ii. 134–5.

[2] Cf. Badian, op. cit. 150, Toynbee, op. cit. ii. 132.

[3] Cf. Toynbee, op. cit. i. 433, 481, at length, ii. 107, 132; Polyb. 2. 24. 3–4, 9, 13; 6. 26. 7–8; 30. 2. Afzelius, op. cit. 13, notes that the Roman census total for 169 is higher than Polybius' manpower total for 225, and though *coloniae Latinae* have increased in number since then, the total for *Italici* must have diminished, as a result of the loss of e.g. 16,000 cavalrymen formerly supplied by intact Apulia (Toynbee, op. cit. 132 n. 3; Polyb. 2. 24. 11). For boundaries cf. above, 209.

[4] Cf. A. E. Astin, *Scipio Aemilianus* (Oxford, 1967), 167 f.

[5] Cf. Last, art. cit. 82 f., Badian, op. cit. 169 ff. Even Appian only speaks of

to which Tiberius harked back for his precedents to include at least
the Latin allies in the division of land and settlement of colonists.[1]
Appian certainly represents Tiberius as making a famous speech
'concerning the military prowess of the Italian race and its kinship to
the Romans', and as claiming to have restored all the peoples of
Italy, while elsewhere he consistently regards the *lex Sempronia* as
concerned with the restoration of all Italy.[2] This language cannot be
explained away, with Badian, as due to the bias of a 'pro-Italian'
source of late Republican date.[3] Such misrepresentation of the facts
about Tiberius would be a pointless exercise unless Tiberius were also
represented, like Livius Drusus, as the victim of an anti-Italian faction.
Besides, Appian's adjacent account of Gaius Gracchus, Livius Drusus,
and the causes of the Social War is fair rather than partisan towards
the Italians. Yet there is no direct evidence that the *lex Sempronia*
distributed any land to *socii Italici*, and some ambiguous indications
that it did not.[4] So perhaps Tiberius and his associates were unable to
free themselves from the exclusive attitude towards the allies that had
become established in the previous generation.

distribution to 'the poor', while Plutarch confines the beneficiaries to citizens
(Badian, op. cit. 171 nn. 1, 2). The implication of *lex agraria* 3 and 15 for or against
the exclusion of *socii* from viritane allotments is ambiguous; cf. the discussions cited
by Last and Badian (loc. cit.) of the interpretation, originally proposed by Mommsen, that the law was not exclusive. The relevance of Cic., *de Rep*. 3. 41 (with 1. 31)
—'Tiberius Gracchus perseveravit in civibus, sociorum nominisque Latini iura ac
foedera neglexit'—may not be as decisive as some have thought; the context
suggests that Cicero is referring to the failure of Tiberius to appease the enraged
allies, and may not exclude a minor redistribution of lands to landless Latins. For
Mommsen, cf. *GS* i. 98, 104.

[1] Cf. above, 36 f., 76 f., 99 n. 2. The last known distribution to Latins was in
173–172 (Livy 42. 4. 4).
[2] Cf. App. *BC* 1. 9. 1; 11. 1; 12. 7; 13. 3, for Tiberius' Italian outlook. So too
7. 4, 6; 8. 1 stress *Italia* and *Italici*, as in 19. 1, 5. 21. 2; 22. 3; 34. 4; 35. 1; 36. 2.
Appian's Ἰταλιῶται undoubtedly means *Italici*, except possibly in the ambiguous
passage 29. 4; cf. Göhler, op. cit. 76 f., 100 f. For the colonists of Gaius cf. App.
*BC* 1. 24. 3. Badian rightly dismisses Velleius 2. 2. 2, 'pollicitus . . . Italiae . . .
civitatem', for the attitude of Tiberius; that issue did not arise before the events of
129–126 stirred it up. Cf. App. *BC* 1. 20. 1–3; 21. 2; 34. 4–5.
[3] Badian, op. cit. 172.
[4] Above, 217 n. 4. The reference to *Italici* as 'kinsmen' in the speech of Tiberius
may well conceal a mention of *Latini coloniarii*, who were largely of Roman
derivation. Gaius Gracchus also called them 'kinsmen', App. *BC* 1. 23. 2.

# PART II

# THE PRINCIPATE AND
# THE CITIZENSHIP

# INTRODUCTION

THE Principate of Augustus marks the opening of a new period in the history of the Roman Empire and of the subject of this study in particular. The many threads and lines of development can, of course, be traced far back into the Republic: there was a fictitious *colonia Latinorum* in a western province,[1] and temples for the adoration of Rome in eastern cities,[2] in the early part of the second century; indeed, the whole story of the unification of all Italy within the Roman state is only a violent and tempestuous harbinger of the Constitutio Antoniniana. But at a precise moment, in truth after the victory of Actium, a new factor was added that changed the whole situation, and called forth ideas and motives that had only been latent and dimly felt before. This factor is the *Pax Augusta*, and the establishment of a government with a more permanent and consistent policy than had marked the provincial administration of the Senate in the later Republic.

In the western provinces perhaps this date does not so certainly mark a turning-point, but it was the Roman peace, the *Pax Augusta*, that made possible the unification of the Empire as a whole and the reconciliation of the Greek Orient to the rule of Rome.[3] The Romanization of the West might have been possible without the Principate, though not without the *Pax*; a study of Baetica and Narbonensis, where the less continuous peace of the Republic had already encouraged considerable development, will make this clear.[4] But in the East the later *Romania* finds its origin in the double combination of Peace and Principate; the first satisfied the material hopes and desires of men, and the second provided scope for political speculation in the resurrection of the old but not forgotten spirit of the Greek Kingship.[5] Even in the West the idea of the Princeps provided a focus or centre of radiation, stimulated the processes of Romanization, and encouraged loyalty.[6]

It is, then, a true historical period, and not merely a period of

[1] Above, 101.  [2] Below, 399 n. 3.  [3] Below, 402 ff.
[4] Below, 226 ff., 336 f.  [5] Below, 406 f.  [6] Below, 415 f.

convenience, that opens after Actium. There are other reasons for making a break at this point. The spread of the Roman citizenship begins to follow new channels under the Principate. First the connection of citizenship with Italian birth or origin, and later its connection with Latin culture, is gradually loosened. At the same time the value and meaning of the franchise change; it becomes a *passive* citizenship, in Mommsen's phrase, and is sought no longer for its political significance but as an honour, or out of sentiment; the old privileges and duties of *civis Romanus* are effaced, and the extension of the citizenship becomes the sign of the unification of the Empire within one abiding system of law, within *victuras Romana in saecula leges*.

This change in the character of the citizenship is thus clearly connected with the establishment of the *Pax Augusta*, which alone rendered possible its extension over non-Italian areas and areas not deeply Latinized. Where these two qualifications are lacking there will always be found a third, loyalty to Rome, which is perhaps the most important of the new elements that appear under the Principate. Since this loyalty often emerges quite separately from the desire for the citizenship, a method of study becomes necessary that is different from, and wider than, that followed in the first part of this investigation. Loyalty to Rome is marked in the West and in the Danubian provinces by a process which, though commonly called Romanization, is really self-Romanization; in the hellenized East loyalty takes a less material form, its conspicuous characteristic or badge being devotion to the emperors. These various processes must be followed, in order to understand what the complete incorporation of the *Orbis* within the *Urbs* really meant, and how it was rendered possible. But the investigation can no longer be limited to a discussion of the former topics, such as the municipal system, the various *iura* or the legal obligations and duties of citizens and their corporate bodies, the municipalities and colonies. It is also necessary to consider both the material and psychological conditions of the non-Roman provincials of East and West, and their attitude towards what is henceforward increasingly known to all men of every status as 'The City'. But this attitude is expressed in many forms, sometimes in terms of respect for the ruling house, sometimes in the deliberate adoption of Latin or Roman ways by peregrine communities, sometimes it may even be traced—though this is the most dangerous method—by the evidence of bricks and mortar, pots and pans.

There are two strands to be unravelled, the somewhat intangible expression of the sentiment that the peregrine provincials are as much 'Romans' as the *cives Romani* themselves, and the more easily traceable extension of the Roman citizenship in the provinces through the *municipia* and *coloniae*, the grants of Latin rights and the various forms of viritane donation of citizenship. Then, to understand the complex whole, it is necessary to assess the importance of both strands in the political thought and practice of the later Empire, where alone there is direct evidence for the attitude of men towards the completed *Orbis Romanus*.

The investigation falls naturally into two sections. A study of the attitude of the emperors towards their subjects and especially of their policy of extension of the citizenship comes first. The nature of this inquiry is determined by the nature of the evidence, which is drawn either from the *Digest* or from other sources, epigraphic or literary, of a corresponding nature; it is essentially *formal*, and only comes to life when supplemented by material of the second class—that which reveals the attitude of the subjects towards Rome and the emperors. In this latter section appears all the richness of detail, the variety of daily life and practice, whereas all that can be discovered of the emperors is that they permitted such a practice, or refused such a privilege. Thus the first part will follow the development of policy and law, the skeleton of the empire, essential to its being but still only the bones; and the second will touch the flesh, the colourful practices and even irrational sentiment of what the later writers call τὰ ἔθνη.

These two sections thus largely correspond with the division of the subject into a study of the extension of the citizenship as imperial policy, and a study of Romanization. This division again answers to both the nature of the evidence and the nature of the fact; for the evidence of the existence of, e.g., a *municipium civium Romanorum* in Dacia is evidence that some emperor made a special grant, whereas the self-Romanization of the provinces is no such proof of imperial activity. The two sections will also tend to overlap, since some forms of expressing loyalty to Rome need official sanction, while grants of privileged status to citizen communities can be made only where the community is fit for such treatment. But in general it is easier to trace the growth of the municipal system in terms of imperial policy, and the growth of Romanization in terms of popular sentiment.

# VIII

## THE ITALIAN PERIOD

UNDER Caesar and Augustus comes the first large-scale extension of the Roman citizenship in provincial areas. This extension is based upon the firm foundation of a genuine Italian immigration, either of legionary veterans or of farmers, merchants, and businessmen. Beside this stands the extensive grant of *ius Latii* in the more Romanized areas of Spain and southern Gaul. Again and again, where a Julian or an Augustan colony or *municipium* or, in Pliny's phrase, *oppidum civium Romanorum*, is concerned, a settlement can be traced either of legionaries or private citizens from Italy—*colonia civica*—or else a previous *conventus civium Romanorum*, dating back to Republican times,[1] or sometimes where the evidence is more vague, as in Africa, there are signs of viritane settlement. But the grant of civic rights to a purely native community is rare. In this respect doubtless Caesar was more lax than Augustus; yet when allowance has been made for the necessities of the civil wars, which compelled political leaders to bind communities and even provinces to themselves by generous grants of privileges, the general rule seems to emerge for both Caesar and Augustus—who could afford after Actium to be strict—that the extension of Roman citizenship within the provinces is limited to areas where there is a solid foundation of Italian immigration, and that communities where the native element preponderated were favoured with a grant of Latin rights rather than of the citizenship.

The extent of this Italian immigration must be traced and its limits compared with those of the growth of the provincial municipalities. Voluntary immigration certainly took place during the last half-century of the Republic, and can often be deduced from the existence of a *conventus civium Romanorum*. An example of the process is given by Narona, which appears in the earliest

---

[1] *Conventus* are the unofficial organizations in which Roman businessmen domiciled in provincial towns grouped themselves for the administration of their own affairs. Cf. in general Kornemann, art. 'Conventus', in *RE*.

inscriptions as a community of Roman citizens administered by a board of two *magistri* and two quaestors.[1] Soon Narona supplies soldiers to the Roman legions,[2] and later it has all the appearance of a normal *municipium*, governed by *ivviri*.[3] This is an instance of what happened in numerous other places where *municipia* or *coloniae* are attested for this period. Kornemann had pointed out how the *conventus civium Romanorum* were absorbed, in the more municipalized of the western provinces,[4] and only remained as a conspicuous feature in the frontier provinces, the *Tres Galliae*, and in the Orient under the Principate, where the municipal system of Rome made little headway.[5] This list of such absorbed communities of the Republic provides a clue to the understanding of Pliny's phrase, *oppida civium Romanorum*, which he abandons only in his account of Baetica in favour of the more technical word *municipium*.[6] If any serious difference of status lies behind this difference of terminology, it is one that confirms the view indicated above of the principle upon which the extension of the municipal system was based at this time; for the difference can only be that at the date of Pliny's source the assimilation of the *oppida civium Romanorum* of the provinces had been completed in Hispania Ulterior alone,[7] that is, in the oldest of the greater provinces of the Empire. The reasonableness of this view is supported by the fact that Agrippa, who is generally taken to be the source of Pliny's lists, had himself, with Augustus, played a large part in the reorganization of Spain; in the other provinces where *oppida civium Romanorum* are numerous there is no sign of any civil reorganization undertaken by the greatest men of the Empire, and in Sicily, where they certainly were at work, they have left a mark, though of a somewhat different kind, upon the organization of the island. Further support for this view of

---

[1] *CIL* iii. 1820.                                    [2] Ibid. 1812, 1813.

[3] The statement of Pliny that Narona was a colony, *NH* 3. 142, receives no confirmation from the inscriptions, though Kornemann retains it. *RE* s.v. 'Coloniae', col. 530.

[4] *RE* s.v. 'Conventus', col. 1183.                   [5] Ibid., col. 1187.

[6] Ibid., col. 1183. In Sicily: Halaesa, Syracuse, Panormus, Lilybaeum, Agrigentum. In Africa: Carthage, Utica, Hadrumetum, Thapsus, Forum Thysdri, Vaga, Cirta. In Spain (ulterior): Corduba, Italica, Hispalis; (citerior): Cartagena, Tarraco. In Gaul: Tolosa. In Illyricum: Lissus, Narona, Salonae, Nauportus. In Noricum: Julium Carnicum.

[7] Pliny, *NH* 3. 7; also the single *municipium*, ibid. 4. 117, of Lusitania, Olisipo. Cf. Kornemann, *RE*, s.v. 'Municipium', cols. 594–5.

Pliny's *oppida* might be found in the manifest apology which Claudius makes for extending the phrase *municipia et coloniae* to provincial communities.[1]

Pliny's lists of *oppida civium Romanorum* may thus extend the evidence supplied by the known instances of *conventus* for Italian immigration.[2] Lissus, which possessed a *conventus* under the Republic, is such an *oppidum* in Pliny. Conversely, certain Sicilian towns[3] where a *conventus civium Romanorum* once existed are listed as *oppida* or *civitates stipendiariae* by Pliny, but at a later date within Augustus' reign acquired municipal status. It seems reasonable to hold that an *oppidum civium Romanorum* is a provincial community which, having long possessed a kernel of citizens, receives the rights of citizenship for all its registered inhabitants, and that a provincial *municipium* is such an *oppidum* that had been equated in legal status with an Italian *municipium*, probably by the regulation of its magistracies and the ordering of its *territorium* according to the principles of Roman municipal law.[4] The clearest instance under Augustus of the extension of citizen rights to the native population of a place where a citizen community of Italian extraction already existed comes not from a *municipium* but from a colony: at Carthage the Punic *civitas* which existed before the foundation of the Augustan colony was, at an early date during the rule of Augustus, merged with the colony to form a single unit.[5]

If these are the stages of development it is clear that for success everything depends upon that original core of immigrant Italians, who are the intermediaries for the transmission of their political culture to the natives. Any view, such as Heitland's, which denies that there was any such considerable influx of Italian settlers, especially in the rural districts, is extremely dubious.[6] Broughton, who has collected the evidence for Africa,

[1] *ILS* 214, cf. below, 238 n. 5.    [2] Above, 226 n. 6.
[3] Pliny, *NH* 3. 90–1. *RE* s.v. 'Municipium', col. 593 f. Halaesa, Agrigentum, and Lilybaeum became *municipia*. Panormus, a *conventus*, then a colony. Cf. the *oppidum c. R.* at Stobi, the sole example in the East. As a great road-centre it was probably similar to the *oppida c. R.* of Dalmatia, which were demonstrably *conventus* by origin, Pliny, *NH* 4. 34; *RE* s.v. 'Colonia', col. 549.
[4] So enfranchised Gades (233 n. 2) is *municipium* on coins (Heiss, *MAE* 350).
[5] Tertullian, *de Pall.* 1, with Appian, *Pun.* 136, Dio 52. 43. 1.
[6] W. Heitland, 'A Great Agricultural Emigration from Italy', *JRS* 8. 34 ff. It is not who they were that matters, since veterans and casual immigrants were equally peasant by origin, but where they settled. In Africa at least they did not confine themselves to the towns of the littoral. Cf. T. Frank, *Am. J. Phil.* 1926, 61 ff.

points out that the process had begun early with the official settlement of Gracchan and Marian *coloni*, and continued throughout the troubled times of the civil wars.[1] One might add that when Marius fled to Africa the reason of his choice must have been that he expected, like Octavian in later days, to raise an army from his veteran settlers; but it is also worth remarking that Virgil's line:

At nos hinc alii sitientes ibimus Afros

presupposes such a condition as familiar to his readers, as a part of the life of the times.[2] The African settlements are important because, where they did not supply the basis of municipal development in the Augustan age, they were responsible for a deep diffusion of Latin culture in the country areas,[3] where they formed certain peculiar double communities of which more must be said later.[4]

To trace the settlement of legionary veterans is a far easier matter, since they have usually left abundant traces of themselves in their personal inscriptions or in the titles of their colonies.[5] Apart from the general statements of Augustus in the *Res Gestae*, a lengthy list of the veteran colonies of Augustus and of Caesar before him can be compiled. To this very definite evidence can be added a number of passages in Strabo and Dio which refer to the settlement of pretorian or legionary veterans or of civilians in formal colonies.[6] The colonies of civilians are extremely

[1] T. S. R. Broughton, *The Romanisation of Africa Proconsularis*, 19, 25, 31 ff., 39 ff. 53. Cf. T. Frank, *Am. J. Phil.* 1937, 91 ff., for a new Marian settlement in Africa.

[2] *Eclogues* 1. 64. 'But the rest of us will go hence to thirsty Africa.' Cf. the expatriations in Italy that led to colonial settlement in Macedon, Dio 51. 4. 6. For examples in Africa, at Utica, Hippo, Thuburnicum, and Thunusuda, cf. Broughton, op. cit. 77 ff.

[3] Cf. Broughton, op. cit. 83.

[4] Cf. ibid. 32 ff.; below, 270.

[5] See Kornemann, *RE* 'Colonia', esp. for Narbonensis, where a very complete list has survived, cols. 528–9; see also Corduba, Acci, 527–8, Emerita, 541, Patrae, 549, Antioch, 531, Berytus, 552. For Mauretania: Gunugu, Cartenna, 559. At all these places the names of the military units concerned are preserved.

[6] Strabo 3. 141. Corduba 151, Pax Augusta, Emerita. 161, Caesaraugusta and Celsa. 168, Pollentia (?) in Balearic Isles. 4. 206, Augusta Praetoria. 6. 270, Syracuse. 272, Panormus. 8. 387, Patrae. 12. 542 and 546, Heraclea Pontica and Sinope. 577, Antioch *in P.* 13. 593, Troas. 17. 833, Carthage. For references to Roman or Italian settlers of an earlier period see 4. 205 ff., in NW. Cisalpina, and 17. 832, Utica as μητρόπολις . . . καὶ ὁρμητήριον of the Romans. Dio Cassius 51. 4. 6. Itali sent to Macedon in 30 B.C.; 53. 26. 1, legionaries sent to Emerita, and 53. 25. 5, Augusta Praetoria.

interesting because they were apparently regarded as exceptional among the great number of veteran colonies. At least they receive a distinctive title. Caesar's colony at Urso had been called *colonia Genetiva Urbanorum* and recalls those colonies which he either completed or planned at Corinth and Carthage. In Italy itself such a one appears in Brixia, *colonia civica Augusta*.[1] How many of those colonies of Augustus whose origins remains anonymous were of this type it is impossible to guess, but the very existence of such a title as *colonia civica* suggests that there were not many such. The title could only be used at a time when it was the rule for a colony to consist of veterans and when the original term *colonia civium Romanorum* had dropped out of use. Thus it seems likely that under Caesar and Augustus the traces of casual immigration are to be sought in the *oppida civium Romanorum*, and those of the formal settlement, mainly, but not entirely, of veteran soldiers, are to be found in the extremely large-scale extension of colonies throughout the Roman world.

It is rather surprising to find so many colonies of Augustus in the oriental provinces, when we are accustomed to regard him as essentially the champion of Latinity and of the western world.[2] Some of these eastern colonies—those in Pisidia—are explained by military necessity, but hardly those at, e.g., Berytus and Heliopolis. The probable explanation is that Augustus had to make the most of his opportunities, and that land was available in those places. But there is something lying behind the fact that in the eastern provinces there are so many colonies and only a single *oppidum civium Romanorum*—at Stobi in Macedonia—despite the numerous examples of *conventus civium Romanorum*.[3] This something is simply the fact that in the hellenized areas it was impossible to create anything like an Italian *municipium* out of a few dozen, or even a few hundred, Romans and a large number of 'Hellenes', but it was possible to set down a closed community of *cives Romani* as a *colonia*, the most definitely Roman of all the forms of corporations and constitutions known to Rome, and to trust that this *effigies Romae* might survive among Greek neighbours. The absence of the *municipium* from the East seems to indicate that Augustus clearly understood what was at this time

---

[1] *RE* 'Colonia', col. 536.    [2] *RE*, art. cit., cols. 550–1.
[3] Those in Macedon, *RE*, art. cit., col. 549, are explained by Dio 51. 4. 6 as due to a necessity of another sort, to settle somewhere the dispossessed Italians of the 18 cities of Italy. For Stobi cf. above, 227 n. 1.

possible and what was not; the presence of *coloniae* shows that, where necessary or unavoidable, he made the best of a bad job.

The activity of Caesar and Augustus, and any deliberate policy of theirs, appear more in the colonies which they founded than in the provincial *oppida* which they may or may not have organized. In the latter task they were but registering and normalizing the effects of a spontaneous movement, which was perhaps coming to a standstill in the days of Augustus; but in the establishment of colonies, although this too was forced upon both of them by the necessity of rewarding their troops, they had some control of the direction which the stream of official emigration was to follow. It seems that, as far as they could, they set the stream towards Africa, the Spanish provinces, Narbonensis and what had once been Cisalpine Gaul; but there was hardly a province of the empire that could not show a notable colonial foundation of Julius or Augustus.

So far only the general agreement of the policy of Caesar and Augustus has been considered. That there are certain points on which they differed is not to be denied, but the view commonly put forward, that Caesar and Augustus represent fundamentally different attitudes towards the spread of the Roman citizenship, needs much modification and definition.[1] In their policy of permitting or encouraging the Latinization and Romanization of the western provinces the only real difference between them is one of time. Augustus, since he comes later, appears rather to have the task of organizing and completing the somewhat chaotic work of the pioneer Caesar. There is a true divergence in their attitude towards the hellenized subjects of Rome and—which comes to much the same thing—towards freedmen. But even here some caution is necessary. Augustus appears from Pliny's lists to have rescinded the incorporation of Sicily within the Roman citizenship, but this grant had been due to the corrupt activity of Antony and not to Caesar, who with a reasonable moderation had granted the Greeks of the island only the *ius Latii*. Cicero makes this perfectly plain.[2] Instead of a wholesale grant Augustus permitted gradual extension of citizenship to the Sicilian communities, and fortified the process by the foundation of colonies.[3]

---

[1] e.g. Kornemann, *RE* s.v. 'Municipium', cols. 591 ff.

[2] *Ad Atticum* 14. 21. 1.

[3] See *RE*, art. cit. col. 593, for Augustan municipalities later than the supposed

In a similar fashion Augustus seems to have followed up Caesar's extension of the citizenship to the Transpadanes by the establishment of colonies in the border valleys at Turin and Aosta. Since the discovery of the inscription which proves that Augustus included the remnants of the Salassi in his colony at Aosta,[1] there is less reason to challenge the view that it was Augustus rather than Caesar who regulated the status of certain tribes of the Alpine border by granting them *ius Latii*, or by attaching them as *attributi* to a neighbouring *municipium*.[2]

The belief in a cleavage between the policies of Caesar and Augustus depends upon three undisputed acts of Caesar.[3] One, the grant of *Latium* to Sicily, has been discussed. Although Sicily was in the great part a Greek island, still it was the oldest of the provinces: it had been the centre of activity for Italian and Roman agents of all sorts for two centuries,[4] and contained at least four *conventus civium Romanorum* in the later Republican period.[5] The grant of *Latium* was hardly a more alarming step than the incorporation of the Greek states of southern Italy in the Roman state had been half a century earlier.

The second constitutional peculiarity of Caesar is the mixed character of his colony at Comum. According to Strabo, he granted to five hundred distinguished Greeks—τῶν Ἑλλήνων οἱ ἐπιφανέστατοι—a place in the colony and 'citizenship'; but, he adds, they did not settle there, though they gave their name to the place.[6] The passage is, at least, obscure. If the text of Strabo is not corrupt, this is an example, on a small scale, of what Caesar practised on a larger scale in Sicily when he became the sole ruler of the Roman world. If the text is at fault, then the reference may

date of Pliny's source. The Sicilian Diodorus, writing under Augustus, ignores any cancellation (13. 35. 3), perhaps rightly, cf. below, 341.

[1] *ILS* 6753.

[2] Ibid. 206, 'Edictum Claudii de civitate Anaunorum.'

[3] The question of the 'Gallic Senators' is not relevant to the question of the material extension of the *civitas* but belongs to the discussion of the quality of the *civitas* of the new citizens from, e.g., the Latin states, below, 234 ff.

[4] Cf. T. Frank, *Am. J. Phil.* 56. 61 ff. on the migration of Romans to Sicily.

[5] *RE* s.v. 'Conventus', col. 1183; above, 226 n. 6.

[6] Strabo 5. 213 C. οὐ μέντοι ᾤκησαν. What these 'Hellenes' were doing in Transpadane Gaul is beyond conjecture. They are hardly freedmen because they are ἐπιφανέστατοι. The phrase τοὔνομα τῷ κτίσματι κατέλιπον suggests the view put forward in the text, 'Novi Comenses' is not particularly applicable to these Hellenes. For Caesar Comum was a citizen colony, cf. Hardy, *Some Problems of Roman History*, 135 ff. Does Strabo think Comum means κώμη?

be to some experiment in attribution, perhaps of a local tribe, to which the key is lost.

Less dangerous ground is provided by Dio's plain statement that Caesar, after various successes in Spain, 'gave citizenship to some and to others the name of Roman colonists'.[1] Is the reference here solely to Roman citizenship or does it include *ius Latii*? That Caesar was responsible for the Latinization of Narbonensis is certain, and at this date some of the Gallic states which received the *ius Latii* followed the precedent of Transpadane Gaul and called themselves *coloniae*, i.e. Latin colonies.[2] It is also certain from Pliny's lists that there had been a considerable extension of *ius Latii* in both Spanish provinces during this period.[3] Strabo refers to this process in two passages which are illuminating for an understanding of what was happening here and in Narbonensis. The Turdetani in Hispania Ulterior, he says, 'have completely gone over to the Roman fashion and do not now remember even their language. Most of them have become Latins.'[4] So much so that, with the Roman colonies, practically all this part of Spain was 'Roman', and the inhabitants gained the name of *togati*. In the second passage he says the same thing about the Volcae in Narbonensis,[5] and goes on to describe the grant of Latin rights to Nemausus, 'so that those elected to be aediles or quaestors became Romans'.[6]

These passages make it clear that the situation in Narbonensis and in the civilized parts of Spain was similar; if Caesar was the author of the Latinity of the one province he may well have been responsible for it in the other. Or else, if the lack of the title of a Latin *colony* in Spain suggests that here the grant was later and due to Augustus, then the general agreement of the policy of the two is demonstrated. But the sentence of Dio quoted above, especially the reference to titular colonies, does seem to cover an extension of *Latium* in Spain similar to that in Narbonensis, though Kornemann sees also a reference to the colonial

---

[1] Dio 43. 39. 5. ἔδωκε . . . πολιτείαν τέ τισι καὶ ἄλλοις ἀποίκοις τῶν Ῥωμαίων νομίζεσθαι.

[2] Jullian, *Histoire de la Gaule*, iv. 243 ff. *RE* s.v. 'Colonia', cols. 517–18. e.g. Julia Apta, *CIL* xii, 1114, 1116, etc.

[3] Pliny *NH* 3. 7; 18. 4, 117; thirty-eight *Latina oppida* in all.

[4] Strabo 3. 151 C. τελέως εἰς τὸν Ῥωμαίων μεταβέβληνται τρόπον, οὐδὲ τῆς διαλέκτου τῆς σφετέρας ἔτι μεμνημένοι· Λατῖνοί τε οἱ πλεῖστοι γεγόνασιν.

[5] 4. 186 C.

[6] 4. 187 C.

status of Tarraco where no traces of any other veteran or civil settlement at this date can be found.[1] In any case, the illuminative passages from Strabo show that Caesar was not engaged in any dangerous or revolutionary activity in the extension of *Latium*, or of Roman citizenship; for in these provinces there had been a cultural self-Romanization which fitted them for some promotion of status. Caesar was more cautious than is usually admitted, and followed the policy, initiated by Pompeius Strabo, of inserting a preparatory period of Latin status before the elevation of purely foreign communities to the full citizenship. The condition of a grant of Latin rights appears to have been the possession of a certain degree of Latin or Roman culture. Of the general elevation of non-Italianized communities to Roman status there is no trace. Only Gades, Emporiae, Utica, and Tingi are known to have received the full citizenship from Caesar or Octavian.[2]

The general agreement of Caesar and Augustus about the method by which the advancing Romanization of the western provinces was to be recognized in law corresponds to the general agreement of their colonizing policy. They seem to part company only on the question of the necessary limits to the extension of the franchise. That Caesar thought of any Alexandrine amalgam of races is not proved, but his liberality to Greeks and freedmen[3] certainly contrasts with Augustus' policy of slow, conservative advance in Sicily, and with the creation of an intermediate class of freedmen—the Latini Juniani, if that institution is really Augustan. The true importance of Caesar is that he first exported *Latium* and the colonial system *in bulk* to *transmarine* provinces, having first seen that the ground was well prepared. He carried out on a large scale beyond the geographic limits of Italy what was formerly normal within those limits and only exceptional and occasional beyond them. He drew the logical conclusion from the policy forced upon the Senate in 89 B.C. within the area of Cisalpine Gaul. The work of Pompeius Strabo, and Caesar's own completion of it in Cisalpina, set the model for municipal development within provincial areas. Cicero in 44 B.C. calls Cisalpine Gaul the flower of Italy, and speaks of the 'consensus municipiorum coloniarumque provinciae Galliae'.[4] Antony in

[1] *RE*, 'Colonia', col. 528.
[2] Cf. Dio 41. 24. 1; 48. 45. 3; 49. 16. 1. Livy 34. 9. 3.
[3] e.g. at Urso, Carthage, Corinth. *ILS* 6087, cv; *CIL* x. 6104; Strabo 8. 381 C.
[4] *Phil.* 3. 13, cf. 2. 76.

the same year speaks of Cisalpina as *Gallia togata*.[1] The process might have stopped there and produced not the *Orbis Romanus*, but nothing more than that true nation of Italy in the modern sense which Augustus sought to create. But since part of Italy, of both her peoples and her culture, had already fled abroad, Caesar and Augustus sent the orderly forms of Roman citizenship and *Latium*, of *municipia* and *coloniae*, following after them. Thus before the Principate was established the Roman state had already burst its geographic bonds and made its westward leap. But to divide the honours, to decide who first saw the possibility and the necessity of the assimilation of the citizen abroad to the citizen at home, of the *oppidum civium Romanorum* to the Italian *municipium*, is not permitted by the evidence in our possession. Possibly the crown here belongs to Augustus, especially as where Caesar's activity in municipal reform can be traced it seems to be confined to Italy. At a time when the regulations revealed by the *tabula Heracleensis* could only be roughly drafted it is unlikely that a provincial municipal system was devised.[2]

After the material extension of the *civitas* at this period its quality and its meaning to its possessors call for discussion. In the late Republican and Caesarian epoch the *civitas* retained its positive obligations, especially those of military service, for its holders.[3] Likewise, the Augustan age, though it is the threshold of the period during which the positive political aspects of the citizenship were to fade into a sentiment, is rather the time of great wars of conquest fought by true citizens. The continual appearance among municipal magistrates of *tribuni militum* reflects the military activity of the ordinary middle-class Roman citizen at this period.[4]

Evidence for the position of provincial *cives* and especially their claim to the so-called *ius honorum*, the right to seek office at Rome, is somewhat rare. Caesar's experiment with the Gallic senators is notable, but there remains considerable doubt as to who these men really were.[5] The popular songs identified them with the defeated princes of Gallia Comata; but there is no certainty that they were not respectable Latinized gentry of Narbonensis, or even of Transpadane Gaul.[6] At some time the question

---

[1] *Phil.* 8. 27.    [2] Above, 170.    [3] Above, 171–2.
[4] Cf. *CIL* xi, p. 611 and 4183a, 4184, 4189–94. These, of course, are Italian.
[5] Suet. *Julius* 80. 2. Cf. *CAH* ix. 730.    [6] Cf. Cic. *in Pisonem* 53.

had to be raised whether, when Roman citizenship was bestowed
—as it was through the *ius Latii*—upon non-Italian peoples, it
carried with it the full status of the older order of Roman citizens.
This problem, however, had been settled in principle in the
period before the dictatorship of Caesar. The Italian peoples
who were incorporated after the Social War, especially the
Etruscans and Greeks, were as much foreigners to the elder
Romans of the Ciceronian age as were the partly Romanized
Spaniards and Gauls to the contemporaries of Augustus; but
there is no sign that in the Ciceronian age any citizen was
barred on the ground of foreign extraction from office or honours.
Cicero in the *pro Sulla* discusses this question of *cives peregrini*
in a way that makes it clear that the old aristocratic families had
to put up with the rivalry of influential upstarts from all over the
country, 'ex tota Italia delecti'.[1] The family of Velleius Pater-
culus may illustrate the type: an ancestor was given the citizenship for services rendered in the Social War, and *his sons* reached
the praetorship.[2] Even before the Social War Q. Varius was not
prevented by a provincial origin, that gained him the cognomen
of Hybrida and enabled his enemies to dub him *Hispanus*, from
reaching the tribunate.[3] The obstacles that hindered ambitious
Italian provincials from achieving a *status dignitatis*, as it was
called, were political and social rather than any exact legal disqualification.[4] The notion that there was such a thing as an
official *ius honorum*, like the *ius conubi*, is due to a mistaken interpretation of the phraseology of Tacitus. He uses this term to
describe the request made by the Gallic *primores* for admission
to senatorial rank and office, privileges which depended upon the
grant of the *latus clavus*. But Tacitus is a writer who deliberately
avoids the use of technical terms.[5]

It is, then, doubtful whether Caesar or Augustus ever posed

---

[1] *Pro Sulla* 24. Cf. R. Syme, 'Caesar, the Senate and Italy', *BSR* 14. 1 ff.

[2] Velleius 2. 16. 3. Cf. above, 141 n. 4.

[3] Val. Max. 8. 6. 4, 'propter obscurum ius civitatis Hybrida cognominatus.'
Ascon, *in Scaur*. 20. 'Q. Varius Hispanus M. Scaurum principem senatus socios in
arma ait convocasse.' Probably he was born of parents long settled abroad, or of
a mixed marriage of dubious legality.

[4] Cf. especially Sall. *Cat. Coni*. 35. 3.

[5] Tac. *Ann*. 11. 23. Cf. ibid. 14. 50, 'venditata . . . munera principis et adi-
piscendorum honorum ius', decisive for the equation with *latus clavus*. For his
avoidance of technical terms cf., e.g., *praefectus remigum*, *Ann*. 13. 30. 2; *praetura
functus*, *Hist*. 2. 63. Cf. below, 239, for Claudius.

the question about the admission of provincials to *honores* in the form in which it has been set by most modern scholars. Since it was even more difficult for provincial citizens to secure *honores* in competitive elections at Rome than for Italians, the question of technical bans did not arise. The problem was rather how to manage their admission. The custom of granting the *latus clavus* to indicate imperial approval of the candidatures of 'new men' was an established method before the time of Claudius.[1] Caesar and Augustus were interested in the extension rather than the limitation of privilege, Augustus maintaining what Caesar had practised on a larger scale than had been known before, namely, that any Italian was as good as another for any post to which his *dignitas et fortuna* entitled him.[2] Extra-Italian provincials were, for the most part, not so much excluded from, as not yet employed in, high office.

There was not any formal defect or flaw in the rights of such provincial citizens; simply their names were not accepted by the magistrates at the elections, and later the *latus clavus* was not in fact given to them. It is in this respect that the Augustan age ushered in the period in which the material importance of the *civitas* began to decline. The characteristic mark of the time is that the development of the municipal system among communities composed, or mainly composed, of Italian emigants was balanced by the conversion of large numbers of the provincial subjects themselves into Roman citizens, especially through the machinery of *ius Latii*. These various sources supplied the Roman army with its necessary recruits, while from Italy was drawn the ruling class of the *orbis terrarum*, the *flos coloniarum ac municipiorum*. Although within this Augustan system the germ of future development was already beginning to sprout, Augustus was able to assert for his time the primacy of Italy.

[1] Suet. *Vesp.* 2. 2. Dio 59. 9. 5, under late Tiberius and Gaius.

[2] For the connection cf. Cic. *Phil.* 1. 20. The statement in Dio 51. 17. 2 that Augustus refused to admit Egyptians to the Senate is wildly anachronistic; at most it is an absurd deduction from the peculiar status of 'Aegyptii'—who were incapable of receiving even citizenship—inserted for rhetorical effect. Cf. below, 319. Dio 59. 9. 5 indicates that Gaius first formally approved the assumption of the *latus clavus* by provincial knights seeking *honores*.

# IX

## THE CLAUDIAN PROBLEM AND VIRITANE GRANTS

CLOTHO speaks: 'Ego mehercules pusillum temporis adicere illi volebam dum hos pauculos qui supersunt civitate donaret. Constituerat enim omnes Graecos Gallos Hispanos Britannos togatos videre; sed quoniam placet aliquos peregrinos in semen relinqui, et tu ita iubes fieri, fiat!'[1]

These famous and much-discussed words seem to open the last period in the history of the extension of the Roman citizenship, which from the time of Claudius appears to develop without a break until the issue of the *Constitutio Antoniniana*. Sufficient evidence has now accumulated to make possible an assessment of the part that Claudius played in this movement. The view which seems to commend itself is as follows. After the activity of Caesar and of Augustus in the earlier part of his reign, the process of formal development slowed down to a snail's pace under Tiberius; the first forty years of the Christian era form a period of incubation during which the assimilation of Latin culture and the material development of the western provinces went on without ceasing, until Claudius saw that the time had come for a fresh advance. He resumed what was the traditional policy of Rome in her wiser moments—the policy which had been vigorously asserted by Caesar and prudently defined by Augustus. The importance of Claudius does not lie in any revolutionary reforms or proposals actually carried out, but in the reassertion of the general principle, in a modest and conservative advance, which served to check an attitude among the ruling class of the day which was not dissimilar to that of the Senate in the time of the Gracchi and Drusi.

In this view Claudius' remarks, recorded in the Tabula Lugdunensis, are taken at their surface value. Claudius does not

---

[1] *Apocolocyntosis* 3. 'Lord, I wanted to give him a little time till he could make citizens of the few that remain. He had made up his mind, you know, to see all the Greeks, Gauls, Spaniards, and Britons in togas. But as the powers would have a few foreigners left for propagation purposes, and your will commends it, so be it.'

say anything very original on the subject of *civitas* in this speech.[1]
He has even been accused of borrowing most of it from Livy,
and the arguments are certainly somewhat hackneyed and were
so already in the time of Dionysius and Livy. But this is precisely
their importance; this very fact proves that at least in his theories
Claudius was not the magnificent innovator that Rostovtzeff
makes of him.[2] The policy of Claudius seems to fall into two
sections. First, he proposes to make fuller use in the service of
the state of those provincial citizens of Rome who are the
descendants of the new citizens of the Caesarian and Augustan
period. Second, he views with favour, or is represented as view-
ing with favour, some further extension of the citizenship to
peregrine communities.

The evidence for the first proposal is fairly straightforward.
Claudius proposes to enlarge that custom of Augustus and
Tiberius, which he describes by the phrase: 'Sane novo more et
divus Augustus avunculus meus et patruus Ti. Caesar omnem
florem ubique coloniarum ac municipiorum . . . in hac curia esse
voluit.' Those who have interpreted this to refer to both provincial and Italian citizens[3] have been misled by the cunning of
Claudius himself, who slips in the word *ubique* in order to assist
his case by rendering his expression a little vague. That the
phrase *municipia et coloniae* means *Italia tota*, as it always seems
to do in Tacitus,[4] is borne out by the very document of this same
period which is often adduced to prove the opposite—the *edictum
Claudii de cursu publico*. Here an apology or explanation is made
for the extension of the phrase to provincial communities.[5] What
Claudius is recalling is explained by the arguments of Claudius'
opponents, preserved in Tacitus:[6] 'An parum quod Veneti et
Insubres in curiam inruperint?' And this again seems to refer
in part at least to the old affair of Caesar and the Gallic senators.
Claudius replies to the objection by saying that it would be
absurdly old-fashioned (*sane novo more*) to object to the senators

[1] *ILS* 212. Cf. P. Fabia, *La Table Claudienne de Lyon*, 71 ff.; Livy 4. 3. 13; 4. 7.
[2] *Social and Economic History*, 82 f. Cf. A. Momigliano, *Claudius*, 16 f.
[3] e.g. Fabia, op. cit. 93 ff. 'It was I suppose a new custom when my uncle the
divine Augustus and my other uncle Tiberius wanted to see the whole flower of
the colonies and boroughs *everywhere* in this assembly.'
[4] Cf. H. J. Cunningham, 'Claudius and the *Primores Galliae*', *CQ* 8. 132.
[5] *ILS* 214. 'Colonias et municipia non solum Italiae verum etiam provinciarum.'
[6] Tac. *Ann.* 11. 23, 'Is it not enough that the Veneti and Insubres have burst into
the Senate?'

drawn from North Italy, *Italici senatores* whom Augustus and Tiberius welcomed and whom the opposition had long tolerated,[1] and that the Gallic aristocracy, the *primores Galliae*, are just as desirable and useful. The identification of the nobility of Cisalpine Gaul with the *flos ubique municipiorum et coloniarum* in the *Tabula* is somewhat supported by Cicero's use of similar phrases to describe the communities of Cisalpine Gaul: *flos Italiae, firmamentum imperii p. R., ornamentum dignitatis*.[2]

The view that under Augustus and Tiberius—his faithful imitator—the senate was mainly limited to *senatores Italici* agrees well with the former's general policy of encouraging everything Italian. It also explains the precise bearing of Claudius' words: 'Sed ne provinciales quidem si modo ornare curiam poterint reiciendos puto', and his promise 'hanc partem censurae meae adprobare coepero'.[3] This speech of Claudius deals almost inadvertently with a good deal more than the request of the *primores Galliae* for the *ius honorum*. A few lines below Claudius introduces a request for a special honour for an equestrian official, L. Vestinus,[4] and in the words quoted above Claudius seems to be defending something which he has either already done or is going to do, whatever the *patres* think of it—something quite separate from the request of the *primores Galliae*. This was perhaps the adlection of a fair number of new senators from the provincial municipalities and colonies. In addition to this he also supports the request of the *primores Galliae*, which was not for admission to the senate but for the *ius honorum*, i.e. the possibility of adlection or election. This point was finally conceded through the grant of the *latus clavus* to the Aedui.[5]

Claudius is able to show that, despite the general view, there have been examples of provincial senators, although he does not quote a large number. He mentions only three at the most, although he speaks vaguely of senators from Vienne and Lugdunum.[6] Of these three one is Cornelius Balbus of Gades, the first provincial consul, whom even the Elder Pliny regarded as

---

[1] Cf. the *Tabula*, col. ii, 'non Italicus senator . . . potior est?'      [2] *Phil*. 3. 13.
[3] Col. ii. 6–8, 'I think that not even provincials should be rejected provided they are an ornament to the Senate.' 'I will begin to justify this section of my acts as censor.'
[4] Ibid. ii. 10–15.           [5] Cf. above, 235–6 for the terminology.
[6] Tac. *Ann*. 11. 24, the summary 'Balbos ex Hispania nec minus insignes viros e Gallia Narbonensi', and their progeny.

a rare bird.[1] Since the death of Augustus provincial senators had become less rare: notably some three future consuls, Domitius Afer, the orator from Nemausus, Valerius Asiaticus, grandee of Vienna, and young Annaeus Seneca, the genius of Corduba, enter under Tiberius.[2] The innovation of Claudius consists in making considerable use of these precedents and at the same time encouraging the suit of the *primores Galliae*. Thus the older discussions of this subject seem to have asked the wrong questions. They assumed that Claudius' proposal was limited to the introduction of the *primores* into the senate, and then sought to explain the earlier exclusion of these men by the lack of a municipal system in the *Tres Galliae*.[3] But a close examination of the text of the *Tabula* and of Tacitus suggests that Claudius was dealing not only with the demand of the *primores*, but with a general opposition to the recruiting of the senate outside the boundaries of Italy.[4] The only qualifications that Claudius names as necessary are those of loyalty and wealth—*boni viri et locupletes*—together with a respectable degree of Latin culture.[5] There is no demand for any special type of domicile or *origo*; in fact Claudius does not distinguish between different sorts of provincials in any way. Closely connected with his adlection of provincial senators is the provision mentioned in the course of the next year, 'ut senatoribus (provinciae Narbonensis) non exquisita principis sententia . . . res suas invisere liceret'.[6] That this rule had not been relaxed before is an indication that before the censorship of Claudius and Vitellius the number of senators from this province was extremely small. After this time families like the Boionii begin to appear in high office. but it is notable that great senatorial officials drawn from the *Tres Galliae* in the first century are extremely rare; Julius Vindex is the only one who has left a conspicuous mark in the history of the times.[7]

[1] 'The first foreigner, aye, the first of those born on the coasts of the ocean, to hold that honour.' Pliny, *NH* 7. 136. Cf. 5. 36. Dio 48. 32. 2.

[2] For the subsequent steady increase cf. R. Syme, *Tacitus* (Oxford, 1958), ii. 589 ff.    [3] Cf. Fabia, op. cit. 95, n. 2, for bibliography.

[4] Esp. Tac. *Ann.* 11. 23, 'non adeo aegram Italiam', etc.

[5] Col. ii. 3–4 and 35: 'immobilem fidem obsequiumque', cf. *Ann.* 11. 24: 'iam moribus artibus adfinitatibus nostris mixti aurum et opes suas inferant potius quam separati habeant.'

[6] Tac. *Ann.* 12. 23. 'Senators of Narbonensis might visit their estates without asking for the permission of the emperor.'

[7] Cf. B. Stech, *Klio*, Beiheft 10. 176 f. Below, 260 nn. 2–3.

In this affair Claudius' policy does not appear to be very sinister or dangerous. His chief concern is to transfer to the service of Rome all good elements, *quod usquam egregium fuit*, especially in the province of which the Elder Pliny wrote some time later that it was *Italia verius quam provincia*; and doubtless he promoted the notable families of Spain also. This idea of extending the recruiting-ground for the senatorial service to Gallia Comata did not come from Claudius, but was the suggestion of the Gauls themselves.[1] This suggestion Claudius adopted when he had examined the question carefully, and had decided that the loyalty of the *Tres Galliae* was to be trusted. Claudius himself is responsible for establishing the respectability of provincial senators, rather than for any vast increase in their numbers; his work here was to challenge the Augustan idea of the essential primacy of Italy, but he only took the first step.

Parallel to this modest advance is what can be traced of Claudius' extensions of citizenship and of *Latium*. In the Lyons oration Claudius explained his general attitude towards the extension of citizenship to those who had it not, as well as towards the extension of its special privileges to those who already possessed it. He reaffirmed the belief that the greatness of Rome depended upon her pursuing a course opposite to the policy of the Greek city-states, which he sums up as *quod victos pro alienigenis arcebant.*[2] But the available evidence provides no support to the sarcastic phrases of the *Apocolocyntosis*, or to any modern view that Claudius showered the citizenship broadcast upon peregrine communities. In the two most debated cases—the *edictum de Anaunis*, and the inscriptions of Volubilis—there were very special circumstances which influenced his decision. The edict from Trent can speak for itself and needs no discussion.[3] The situation at Volubilis was no less peculiar. There had been colonial warfare, *bellum adversus Aedemonem*. In this the community of Volubilis had suffered, and its great man, Valerius Severus, had rendered useful services to the Romans.[4] The circumstances recommended Volubilis to Claudius, and *on request*

---

[1] Tac. *Ann.* 11. 23, 'cum primores Galliae . . . ius . . . honorum expeterent'.

[2] Op. cit. 11.24, 'they barred their subject peoples from their polity as foreigners.'

[3] *ILS* 206. Claudius allows tribal subjects of a *municipium* to retain the *c.R.* which they had usurped in good faith, thereby entering the Roman service.

[4] *ILA* 634 (*FIRA.* I². 70). Cf. Pliny, *NH* 5. 11. *CRAI* 1924, 77 f.

of the Volubilitani[1] he granted them not only citizenship but
a whole series of exceptional privileges. Charlesworth describes
this as 'an act of political liberality which can scarcely have been
isolated'.[2] Perhaps not, but the record of Claudius' activity in
provincial municipalization is modest. In this sphere he seems
to have set in motion again the lively advance that had been at
a standstill, according to the evidence, for forty years, but there
is nothing spectacular. Certain important colonies were founded,
and it is remarkable that they are nearly all in the newer provinces; the military and political importance of the *colonia* had
not yet been forgotten.[3] Claudius planted no colonies in the older
provinces of the West; there, at least, he cannot be accused of
breaking with tradition.

There are hardly any traces of Claudian activity in the heavily
Romanized or Latinized provinces;[4] instead, he busied himself
with the border-land of northern Italy. He created five Roman
municipalities in Noricum, which must have included a great
part of the population.[5] Complementary to this are the grants
under him and Nero of *Latium* to a large number of tribes of the
mountain valleys, of which possibly the majority were due to
Claudius.[6] These events are but the sequel to the long history of
the unification of Italy. Claudius acts here, as also in Mauretania,
on the plan of supplementing grants of *civitas* in one district with
grants of *Latium* in another.[7] As Noricum and the *Mauretaniae*
are the only provinces in which Claudius founded a number of
*municipia*, it seems reasonable to refuse to apply inferences from
the inscriptions of Volubilis to lands outside the limits of the
*Mauretaniae*.[8] Within these two provinces there is no evidence

---

[1] *CRAI* 1924, 77 f.　　　　　　　　　　　　　　　　[2] *CAH* x. 675.

[3] Cf. *RE* s.v. 'Municipium', cols. 597–8 and s.v. 'Colonia', cols. 543–5; 551; 559.
In Britain: Camulodunum. In Gaul: col. Agrippinensis. In Dalmatia: Aequum.
In Pannonia, Emona and Savaria. In Thrace: Apri. In the *Mauretaniae*, four
colonies. Also 3 oriental colonies—with evidence for *deductio veteranorum*.

[4] *RE* s.v. 'Municipium', loc. cit.

[5] Ibid. 598. Pliny, *NH* 3. 146: 'oppida Claudia'. Pliny names no other *civitates*
there except Flavian *Solva*. They may be of Latin status, cf. below, 373.

[6] Cf. *RE*, art. cit., col. 599, Pliny, 3. 135, certainly the *Octodurenses* and *Ceutrones*
with their *Fora Claudia*, perhaps also the *Euganeae gentes*, Pliny, 3. 133. The grant to
the *Cottianae civitates* had to wait for the death of the king-prefect, Suet. *Nero* 18,
with Tac. *Ann.* 15. 32.

[7] *RE*, art. cit., col. 598.

[8] Elsewhere apparently only Verulamium, Britain; in the *Mauretaniae* three,
apparently two *m.* of citizens, one Latin, *RE*, loc. cit.

that citizenship was granted to people who were unfitted to hold it. The peculiar mention in the inscription of *incolae* granted to Volubilis does not support the latter idea; the *incolae* are settlers from other parts who were called upon to take their share of civic burdens, not remote tribal peasantry who were being merged with Romanized inhabitants of the *oppidum*.[1] Gradation of status and Latinization of the natives can certainly be traced in the grant of *Latium* to Tipasa, of *conubium cum peregrinis mulieribus*—and not *cum peregrinis hominibus*—to the *municipes Volubilitani*, and of citizenship to Rusucurru, all in Mauretania.[2]

The evidence from Noricum and Mauretania reveals the point of the gibes of the *Apocolocyntosis*.[3] They are recruits to the ranks of the *provinciae togatae*, the term applied (in Greek) by Strabo to the Spanish provinces,[4] by Cicero and Antony to Cisalpina, and, in effect, by Pliny to Narbonensis.[5] The method of the *Apocolocyntosis* is manifestly that of exaggeration;[6] on the basis even of what is known of Claudius' practice and still more of what is recorded of his theory, which—to judge by the *Oratio Lugdunensis*—he was obviously fond of discussing, it appears that the gibe, though ridiculous, as it was meant to be, was shrewdly aimed. The *Oratio Lugdunensis* itself, if pressed, means that Claudius saw the possibility that a day would come when the *Urbs* would comprise the *Orbis terrarum*; a passage in Seneca[7] suggests that it was fashionable in these times to discuss such possibilities as 'Si princeps civitatem dederit omnibus Gallis', though the magnificence of the conception savours more of Nero than of Claudius. For, wherever the details are known of Claudian grants of citizenship or Latin rights, there are apparent both wisdom and moderation. Claudius stands as the direct successor of the Caesarian and Augustan plan, and is very loyal to it. A good example of this sedulous devotion to the best in Roman tradition will be found by comparing the colonial settlements of Claudius with the colonies of Augustus in Lusitania; the identity

---

[1] The meaning that the *incolae* were to share in the *munera* of the *municipium* is secured by the fact that the word occurs between the grant of *immunitas* and that of the *bona vacantia*. Cf. De Sanctis, *Riv. Fil.* 53. 372 ff. For *incolae* as resident aliens cf. *Lex Mal.* 53, 69. *Lex Urs.* 126 (cf. 98).

[2] Because the wives reside at Volubilis. For Tipasa etc., cf. Pliny, *NH* 5. 20.

[3] Ch. 3.     [4] Above, 232.     [5] *Phil.* 8. 27 f. Pliny, *NH* 3. 31.

[6] *Passim*, but e.g. ch. 6, Claudius is a *Gallus germanus*, and ch. 12, 'quis nunc iudex toto lites audiet anno?'

[7] *De Beneficiis* 6. 19. 2. 'If the *princeps* gives the citizenship to all the Gauls'.

of purpose—defence of the border-lands of the newly settled areas, and the consolidation of Romanization at key positions in the country—is remarkable.[1]

Promotion in status as the reward of service or loyalty is the mark of the period; and, though it is nothing new in Roman policy, it led to the development of one innovation which had the most important consequences later. This is the grant of honorary titles, especially that of *colonia*, to municipalities. In origin this practice is only a development of what was latent within any grant of *civitas* or *Latium* to a community, and it goes back, in germ, not only to Caesar but to Pompeius Strabo. The immense popularity and importance of the honorary title in the second century as a badge of loyalty will be demonstrated later, but it is worth noting that the institution makes its first important appearance in the time of Claudius and in Gaul. In the *Tabula* there is a reference apparently to the elevation of Vienna, a purely native community, from Latin status to that of a Roman colony, without any suggestion of the settlement of colonists there.[2] Even more interesting is the elevation of the central towns of the Gallic states to colonial rank, which, in four instances, is associated with Claudius, though not always with absolute certainty.[3] The use of this honour, though not specially Claudian in origin, is perhaps a characteristic development of the period.

Last comes a question that is more relevant to Claudius' reputation. Was there at this period an unduly generous distribution of individual grants of *civitas*, especially in those provinces of the Hellenistic world where the predecessor of Claudius had adopted

---

[1] Cf. *RE* s.v. 'Colonia', col. 541; a map makes the argument clear. Emerita, Scallabis, Metellinum, Pax Julia, and Norba form a clear system that rivets the Roman hold of the land between the Tagus and Anas rivers, and of their valleys. Claudius' Danubian colonies, though less numerous, are similarly important (list above, 242 n. 3).

[2] Cf. Fabia, op. cit. 108 ff. 'Antequam colonia sua solidum civitatis Romanae beneficium consecuta est.' The alternative interpretation, that this means *ius Italicum*, only reinforces the argument in the text, for that *ius* is the very peak of privilege. But there is no certain example of the grant of *ius Italicum* to a community of peregrine origin at this period, except where it is a question of rearranging the Italian frontier, Plin. *Nat. Hist.* 3, 25 and 139. Cf. Premerstein, *RE* s.v. 'Ius Italicum', col. 1239. Vienna is known as *Colonia Romana* to Pliny, *NH* 3. 36, but not to Strabo 4. 186.

[3] *RE* s.v. 'Colonia', col. 544. Colonia Vellavorum, c. Treverorum, c. Sequanorum, c. Lingonum. Jullian, *Histoire de la Gaule*, iv. 261 f., thinks these were *coloniae Latinae*, but there is no proof of this.

a more cautious policy? In other words, why does the author of the *Apocolocyntosis* add 'Graecos' to the list of the peoples whom Claudius wished to see wearing the *toga*?

This will be a convenient place to discuss the whole question of viritane donations of citizenship, their importance and their purpose, since there is more definite and suggestive evidence connected with Claudius than with any other emperor. The gift of honorary citizenship to individuals in return for services rendered was a long-established practice among the Romans. The earliest instances which can be trusted appear in the course of the second Punic War;[1] but it is only with the establishment of the Roman world-power, and more especially of the direct government of the provinces, that this honorary and individual citizenship began to acquire a positive importance outside Italy,[2] i.e. to assure its holder of certain privileges in his own country, such as exemption from the summary jurisdiction of the Roman governor. Under the Republic two factors tended to reduce the value of the honour, the Roman principle that 'duarum civitatium civis noster esse iure civili nemo potest', and the exemption from the authority of the provincial governors of the most favoured states, as *civitates liberae*, etc., which were precisely those where such gifts of citizenship were most likely to be frequent. Not until the imperial period did it become normal for a man of peregrine origin to make a real use of his citizen status without surrendering his connection with his original home. Already in the time of the Triumvirate *civitas* and *immunitas* began to be separated,[3] but explicit evidence for the abandonment of the Ciceronian principle comes only in the Cyrenean Edicts of 7–6 B.C.[4] Thus, early in the Principate numbers of Roman citizens appear who enter the imperial service, and even hold important posts, without being attached to any *municipium* or *colonia*.[5] It is especially through service in the auxiliary forces of the army that the number of unattached citizens increased. An early instance is the *Decretum Cn. Pompeii Strabonis*, by which in

---

[1] Above, 57. Cf. Cic. *pro Balbo* 51.

[2] H. Box in *JRS* 22, 183, puts the earliest grant of *c. R.* to a Greek not before 102 B.C., possibly not before 62 B.C. for an oriental, Cic. *pro Archia* 24, but cf. ibid. 10.

[3] P. Roussel, *Syria* xv, 'Un Syrien au service de Rome et d'Auguste', 51 f.

[4] Below, 271. Cf. A. v. Premerstein, *Zeitschr. Sav.-St. Röm. Abt.*, 1928, 470 f.

[5] Cf. below, 247 n. 1.

89 B.C. a group of Spanish cavalrymen received the citizenship *virtutis caussa*.[1]

Such grants as these provided nuclei of Roman loyalty in the provinces; but the charge that is brought against Claudius is that he was lavish with such grants in the wrong part of the empire, that he planted the citizenship in unfertile soil. It is true that in the eastern provinces, more especially in the old province of Achaea, the very heart of Hellas, there are numerous instances of Greek *cives Romani* who bear the Claudian *nomina*,[2] although some at least of these are likely to be due to Nero;[3] there are other isolated cases such as Claudius Lysias in the Acts, who acquired the citizenship 'for a great price'; there has also come from Egypt a papyrus text which records a grant to a man and his sons, who were apparently, contrary to the rule, not even citizens of Alexandria.[4] This Egyptian *apographē* is written in Latin, a fact which reminds us that Suetonius, on this question of viritane grants, gives Claudius an excellent character for maintaining the distinctions and dignity of the Roman franchise.[5] Dio Cassius not only confirms this but adds, quoting an example, that Claudius held 'it was not proper for a man to be a Roman who had no knowledge of the Roman tongue',[6] and that Claudius deprived 'unworthy men' of their Roman status, i.e. men without any Latin culture.[7] After this, it is true, comes a vague and lengthy charge of the very opposite kind, that Claudius allowed the citizenship to be bought and sold indiscriminately.[8]

What was Claudius attempting by this apparently contradictory policy, traces of both parts of which are continually turning up? The first notable thing is that he did not grant citizenship to 'whole groups' in the eastern provinces. There are no *municipia Claudia* in the Orient. The second is that Claudius held some view about the unity of the Roman Empire. He admitted Greeks to the equestrian order and, after military

---

[1] *ILS* 8888.      [2] Walton, *JRS*, 1929, 42.

[3] Also H. Box, 'Roman Citizenship in Laconia', *JRS* 21, 209 f., points out that in *saec.* A.D. I–II the *nomina* of proconsuls as well as of emperors appear among the *c. R.* of Laconia.

[4] *PSI*, 1183. 'Idem professus se et filios civitate donatos esse a Ti. Claudio Caesare domo Aegypto nomo Oxyrhyncho,' of A.D. 45. Cf. *P. Lond.* 1178, 30. Acts 22: 28.

[5] *Claudius* 25. 3. 'Peregrinae conditionis homines vetuit usurpare Romana nomina dumtaxat gentilicia. c. R. usurpantes . . . securi percussit.' Cf. *ILS* 206 *ad fin.*

[6] 60. 17. 4.      [7] Ibid. 5.      [8] Ibid. 6–8.

service, to the imperial procuratorships,[1] and he regarded the two languages of Greek and Latin as *uterque sermo noster*.[2] The third peculiarity is that there is apparently no evidence of any large gift of citizenship to any *Galli*—at least of the *Tres Galliae*—or to any *Britanni*. This is probably where the military diplomata make their contribution. A considerable number of these documents exist, forming a series, starting from the time of Claudius, onwards to the third century.[3] Any argument from silence in the history of the empire is dangerous, unless it can be strongly supported by indirect positive evidence; but it is very tempting to assign to Claudius the credit for first regularizing and systematizing the practice of presenting auxiliary veterans with the citizenship upon discharge. If the arguments brought forward below are conclusive, it becomes apparent that Claudius was following a definite plan, which had a special place in his theory of the evolution of the Roman world. In addition to his activity in promoting the already Latinized and Romanized portions in the manner that has been discussed, he proposed to sow in those vaster areas, where in his time nothing grandiose could be done, a crop that others would reap, i.e. he meant to establish little groups of Roman citizens up and down the provinces,[4] which one day would form the basis for a large-scale extension of the citizenship, even as the dispersion of Italian *cives* under the Republic had formed the basis of the Romanization of Narbonensis and of Baetica. Thus the equation of the *Apocolocyntosis* turns out to mean that in return for the military services of the Galli, Hispani, Britanni—precisely the people who appear most frequently on the diplomata—and in return for the civilian services of the Graeci—provided always that they had imbibed some understanding of Latinity—he was prepared to distribute the citizenship as a reward.[5]

---

[1] Cf. Ti. Julius Alexander, *OGIS* 663, C. Stertinius Xenophon, *SIG*[3] ii. 804. C. Julius Dionysius, *P. Lond.* 1912; Suidas s.v. Dionysius. C. Julius Spartiaticus, *Ann. Ép.*, 1912, n. 2.

[2] Suet. *Claudius* 42. 1.

[3] Now collected in *CIL* xvi; the earliest date from A.D. 52, 61.

[4] Compare Aelius Aristides' remarks, *Or.* (ed. Keil) 26. 64: πολλοὶ ἐν ἑκάστῃ πόλει πολῖται ὑμέτεροι . . . τὰς ἑαυτῶν πατρίδας ὑμῖν φυλάττουσιν.

[5] Relevant are Claudius' remarks in Dio 60. 11. 7, on his obligations to those who 'cheerfully help to bear the burden of government', though applied here to senatorial governors. Also the 'Rewards of the Freedmen', Tac. *Ann.* 11. 38; 12. 53, especially the words 'quod . . . veterrimam nobilitatem usui publico postponeret'.

Octavian as *triumvir* had rewarded Seleucus of Rhosus for his military services with citizenship and other privileges also.[1] The style of Octavian's letter suggests by the extreme length of the formulae that the technique was yet incompletely fashioned. Another document of the Triumvirate shows closer approximation to the Claudian type of Diploma, but the generosity of its terms, including wholesale immunity from taxation, *immunitas omnium rerum*, suggests that not yet had the process of rewarding auxiliaries been regularized.[2] Such regulation of what had long been the occasional practice of the Romans precisely fits the character of Claudius' government. His importance in other spheres is very largely this activity of putting things in pigeonholes, and of creating departments. There is evidence that Claudius occupied himself in a similar fashion with military *administration*.[3] A passage of Dio, which either refers directly to these diplomata or else to something very closely allied, runs: 'The men serving in the army, since they could not legally have wives, were granted the privileges of married men.'[4] This may just as well refer to auxiliaries as to legionaries,[5] especially as the greatest 'privilege of married men' is that retrospective 'conubium cum uxoribus . . . dumtaxat singuli singulas', i.e. the legitimization of their offspring, which is the main feature, next to the grant of citizenship, of these documents.

Claudius' attention may well have been drawn to the auxiliaries at the time of the Britannic war.[6] The idea of rewarding their services with citizenship agrees extremely well with the principles of the *Tabula Lugdunensis*,[7] with the very definite example of such a policy at Volubilis, and with a passage in Tacitus' paraphrase of the *Tabula*, where Claudius says: 'specie deductarum per orbem terrae legionum *additis provincialium validissimis* fesso imperio subventum est.' This refers to a policy of including native elements in the veteran colonies, as was done by the incorporation of the Salassi in Augusta Praetoria, and of the Punic

---

[1] Cf. P. Roussel, *Syria* xv, 51 f. (*FIRA* I². 55).

[2] Wilcken, *Chrestomathie*, n. 462 (*FIRA* I². 56).

[3] e.g. Suet. *Claudius* 25. 1: 'equestris militias ita *ordinauit*'.

[4] Dio 60. 24. 3.

[5] Cf. ibid. τοῖς στρατευομένοις.

[6] For a mention of *cohortes* in Britain under Claudius see Tac. *Ann.* 12. 40.

[7] e.g. col. ii. 3–8, Tac. *Ann.* 11. 24, *passim*, though of course this refers in the first instance to men already *cives*.

population in Augustan Carthage.[1] On any interpretation, the readiness of Claudius to assimilate citizen-soldiers and peregrine troops is manifest.

A last argument in favour of Claudius as the author of this regulation can be drawn from the fact that, while Tiberius, the other possible candidate, had considerable trouble with his auxiliary troops,[2] under Claudius there is no such record, but rather the opposite; for in the *bellum adversus Aedemonem* the valiant Severus, who obtained citizenship for his homeland, was *praefectus auxiliorum omnium*. Short of the fatal discovery of a pre-Claudian diploma of the normal type and formula—since all that is suggested is that Claudius normalized and universalized this practice—the case for Claudian authorship seems to be very strong.[3]

A comprehensive idea of the history and importance of the citizenship in the time of Claudius can now be formed. There is a plurality of processes in operation at the same time, which corresponds to the diversity of conditions in the Empire itself. While the material achievement of Claudius is neither trifling nor grandiose, but bears the signs of patient care and forethought, his great importance is more in the theory of the thing, in that he broke through a prejudice of his time, and shattered the opinion that the Roman state knew boundaries determined by any other consideration than her own power of absorption and attraction. In this period a balance is maintained between the citizenship as a reward for services and as the ground of duty; the material content and the dignity of the *civitas* do not suffer, although the tendency, due to the enthusiasm of the provincials themselves, that created degrees of honour within the citizenship, a sort of *civitas*-within-*civitas*, is just beginning to appear. The connection with Latin culture is maintained; although Claudius is a *princeps* who understands and deliberately promotes the unity of the Roman world, Eastern and Western alike, yet he

---

[1] Tac. *Ann.* 11. 24. Cf. *ILS* 6753. 'The weary empire was relieved by the fashion of settling legionaries in colonies throughout the world, *along with the strongest elements among the provincial peoples.*' Cf. above, 227 n. 5.

[2] Both Tacfarinas, Tac. *Ann.* 2. 52, and the Thracians were auxiliaries, ibid. 4. 46–51; there is no mention of any compensation given for the services of the Thracians; the fact that they were under a client king doubtless added to the difficulty—the Romans gave them little in return. Tacfarinas does not seem to have been a *c. R.* Cf. Tac. loc. cit.

[3] Cf. *CIL* xvi, p. 148.

clearly understood the necessary limits of his day.[1] In the lampoon the 'Graeci' held but a fourth place, and this is perhaps some indication of their position in the practical policy of Claudius, who, after all, was mainly interested in the West.

[1] Cf. Pliny, *NH* 33. 30, on this period: 'provinciis ad . . . munus (iudicandi) admissis servatum . . . in hodiernum est ne quis e novis civibus . . . iudicaret', i.e. *in the first generation* new citizens were not admitted to the titular honour of jury-service, although provincial citizens were not disqualified as such. For instances later of provincials serving on the Roman *decuriae iudicum* cf. *ILS* 6764, 6863a, 6932, 6936, etc., mostly from Spain, Narbonensis, and Africa. For equestrian procurators of provincial origin from Claudius onwards see now H. G. Pflaum, *Les Procurateurs équestres* (Paris, 1950), 173, 177 f., 183 f., 191 f., listed by their periods. The earliest known oriental recruits are Ti. Claudius Balbillus of Alexandria (or Ephesus), military tribune in 43 (*AE* 1924, n. 78) and C. Julius Aquila of Amastris, *praefectus fabrum* in *c.* 45 (Tac. *Ann.* 12. 15; *ILS* 5883). Gessius Florus, the Neronian procurator of Judaea, came from Clazomene (Jos. *Ant.* 20. 11. 1). For consular senators from Baetica and Narbonensis under Claudius and Nero see now R. Syme, *Tacitus* (Oxford, 1958), ch. xliv. G. W. Bowersock, *Augustus and the Greek World*, Oxford, 1965 ch. 3, somewhat misprises the role of Greeks in the imperial service of Augustus. Before the gradual establishment of the equestrian procuratorial system a few Greeks managed estates and libraries and held adminstrative posts in Egypt; afterwards, these duties are confined to equestrian ex-officers from Italy; cf. ibid. 41 n. 5, and my 'Procurator Augusti', *P.B.S.R.* 1939, 1 ff.

# X

## THE FLOOD TIDE

WHEN it is next possible to take an official view of the Roman Empire, the impression is as though a great machine were at work to stamp with the seal of a formal recognition all that has been done or is being achieved in the way of what is called Romanization. The intervention of Claudius had been effective; henceforth there is no opposition; it is understood that successive *principes* must register, with the mark of promotion suitable to each, the varying stages of the growth of the Roman world, here bestowing *Latium* or there establishing a Roman *municipium* according to the necessity of time and place.

The nature of the evidence for the period which opens with the Flavians renders the study of the imperial attitude to the various questions of policy extremely formal and official. There is no disinterested geographer, no Strabo or Pliny, to indicate the living core that must once have lain beneath the official phrases of inscriptions and of panegyrists, on which we are almost entirely dependent. The writings of Tacitus, especially the *Histories*, give a brief but fragmentary view of the Empire, and of what men thought of it and of Rome at the opening of the second century; but apart from a few personal grumbles and the detailed and valuable analysis of the state of Gallic society about A.D. 70, Tacitus tends to join hands with the Greek writers of the second Sophistic. Thus it here becomes necessary to make a separate study of what was the official view and policy, what the emperors thought or wanted men to think of Rome, and what they wished to make of their world, in so far as this is set forth by contemporary writers and illustrated by the dry, epigraphic sketch which can be built up of the processes of development; after this one can proceed to a further study of the people themselves in their various communities, discover separately their attitude to Rome, and then compare the two views and try to estimate their relation to each other.

The study of official policy comes first. There was a pause

during the principate of Nero, who in this respect bears the same relation to Claudius as Tiberius does to Augustus, and continued a time of peaceful subterranean development with few outward changes.[1] Activity is renewed under the Flavians and never ceases till the bad times of the third century. This is the greatest age of the municipalization of the Roman world; the process has often been treated, whether as a whole in Kornemann's great article in Pauly–Wissowa, or in the numerous discussions of separate provinces. Here it is necessary to demonstrate the mechanical nature of the process, and to separate out any new features which show some change in the relation of the various parts of the Roman world to each other, and to discuss the consolidation of certain provinces.

This consolidation is very much a feature of the times. The Flavians complete the work of centuries in Spain. 'Universae Hispaniae Vespasianus imperator . . . Latium tribuit.'[2] This is the machine at work; a short passage of Pliny seems to reproduce its regulated beat: 'Oppidum . . . Caesarea . . . a divo Claudio coloniae iure donata; eiusdem iussu deductis veteranis oppidum Novum et Latio dato Tipasa, itemque a Vespasiano imperatore eodem munere donatum Icosium.'[3] It is not necessary to follow every detail of such a system. But by estimating the consolidation of various provinces it is possible to assess the new historical feature of this period, the elevation of the provinces first to the same level as Italy and later even above it. The activity of the Flavians was not confined to Spain.[4] This is the time when the *fines imperii* seem ever to be farther and farther removed from Rome. Thus Pannonia under the Flavians begins to assume a partially urbanized and municipalized aspect; at least seven *municipia Flavia* are known.[5] Communities begin to move from their hills to the plains. During the civil war Dalmatia seemed

[1] Cf. Tac. *Ann.* 15. 46: 'haud alias tam immota pax'. Apart from the possible effects of the Grecian tour (e.g. Suet. *Nero* 24), the grant of *Latium* to the Maritime Alps suggests that Nero's reign is but an appendix to the Claudian period. Cf. above, 242 n. 6.

[2] Pliny, *NH* 3. 30. For details see R. K. McElderry *JRS* 8 (1918) 53 ff.

[3] Ibid. 5. 20. *RE* s.v. 'Municipium', col. 601. 'The town of Caesarea was given colonial status by Claudius, who also ordered the foundation of a veteran colony at Novum and gave Tipasa Latin rights, while Vespasian in turn gave Icosium the same status.' For the mechanism of grants see below, 360 ff.          [4] Ibid.

[5] Neviodunum and Andautonia on the upper Save above Siscia, Solva and Scarabantia farther northward. Ibid., col. 602. The colony at Siscia belongs to the same system. *RE* s.v. 'Colonia', col. 546.

to produce a legion overnight.[1] Likewise, in the conterminous areas of Dalmatia and Noricum municipalization continued.

In the rest of the Danubian provinces the Flavians and Trajan had a different task to perform. It is difficult to distinguish by epigraphic evidence alone the various stages of development; but the period of consolidation in these provinces comes later in the second century and appears to be marked by the growth of the 'honorary colonies'. The surest proof that the period of the Flavians and Trajan is still a time of constructive groundwork is to be found in the fact that these are the provinces where the latest *coloniae deductae* are to be found. There is a curious statement in the skeleton epitome of Victor: 'deductae coloniarum pleraeque'.[2] Why he should single out this as a special feature of Trajan's reign is not very clear, unless it is to mark the end of an epoch, the epoch of the *deductio coloniarum*. After Trajan such activity is extremely rare, if it does not cease altogether. But the Flavians and Trajan were still occupied with the task of establishing towns and settlements of trustworthy men at the key-positions of the Danubian provinces. Scupi, a road-centre at a critical point of the first route that penetrates the Balkans from north to south, received a Flavian colony.[3] In these provinces we seem to slip back to an earlier age;[4] it was not till the principate of Hadrian that the rate of municipalization was accelerated; the change is then marked by the growth of *municipia* along the very banks of the Danube, where formerly there had been only armed camps and colonies and castles.[5] The method is revealed very fully, as in some detailed miniature, by the history of Roman Dacia, and within a remarkably short period of time. First comes the Trajanic colony at Sarmizegethusa, together with the official encouragement of immigration.[6] Under Hadrian the more important centres are ready to become *municipia*. Hardly is this stage reached when they are given the honorary title of *colonia*; by the third century only places of secondary importance remained *municipia*.

[1] Tac. *Hist.* 3. 50.
[2] *Liber de Caesaribus* 13. 4. 'Several colonies were founded.'
[3] With true *deductio*, *CIL* iii. 8195–7.
[4] *RE* s.v. 'Colonia', col. 547. Cf. Ratiaria, Oescus, in Moesia, Trajanic colonies, or Vespasian's Palestinian colony at Caesarea. Pliny, *NH* 5. 69.
[5] *RE* s.v. 'Municipium', col. 603–4; e.g. Carnuntum, Brigetio, Aquincum.
[6] Ibid., cols. 604–5.

This impression of a perfected technique possessed by the Roman government, of something almost mechanical which ordered and regulated the formless enthusiasms of the provincial populations,[1] is abundantly confirmed by even the most superficial study of Roman Africa.[2] It has often been noted that the general development of the province, corresponding to that of the Danubian lands, comes later than in the provinces which were romanized earlier; in the Flavian and Trajanic periods it is possible to notice all stages of development. In the far south, by the Aures mountains, there is still the stage of roads, camps, and colonies, with the usual phenomena of growing veteran-communities.[3] In other parts this is the period in which numerous *municipia civium Romanorum* begin to appear within purely native areas.[4] This is the consequence of the material encouragement given by the conversion of nomad peoples into settled agriculturalists, which followed the Julio-Claudian policy of delimitation and road-building. In such instances the part played by the government is purely material in the first instance, and later is confined to the registration of facts, when the time appears to be ripe for such registration by advance in status. Elsewhere again there is evidence of a more intensified romanizing spirit among the longer-established urban communities, with the appearance of the colonial title at places like Hadrumetum and Lepcis.[5]

These various processes rise to a veritable fury of activity in the middle of the second century;[6] from Hadrian to Commodus there is a continuous flow of new *municipia* revealed by the inscriptions, and a spate of titular colonies, while at the smaller centres there is continuous development of various types of village communities into self-governing *civitates*, thus providing a basis for still further developments of *municipia* under the Severan dynasty.[7]

Where the history of single communities can be followed in detail, the same impression of something mechanical and regular

---

[1] Summed up by Pliny, *Pan.* 37. 3, 'novi seu per Latium in civitatem seu beneficio principis venissent'.

[2] Cf. Broughton, op. cit. 95 ff., 119 ff., 136 ff. *RE* s.v. 'Municipium', col. 606; s.v. 'Colonia', col. 554.

[3] Broughton, 120 f.                                           [4] Ibid. 127 f.

[5] *RE* s.v. 'Colonia', col. 555. Broughton, 130.

[6] *RE* s.v. 'Municipium', col. 606; s.v. 'Colonia', col. 555–6.

[7] Broughton, 142–3, 186–8, 194–5. *RE* s.v. 'Municipium', cols. 607–8.

is felt. For example, the *canabae* township of Lambaesis passes from the stage of *municipium Latini iuris* to that of Roman status and titular colony in about a hundred years.[1] The part that the government plays, once the period of military settlement and the establishment of order is past, becomes the passive examination and approval of petitions for the advancement of status; but though this is a passive part, the health of the empire largely depends upon the wisdom with which it is performed.[2] This, after all, is the point of the gibe against Claudius in the *Apocolocyntosis*.

Upon the solidity of these *provinciae togatae* would depend the power of the empire to stand any shocks, or assaults, or dangers that might—and did—attack it in later days. There can be no doubt that the emperors were conscious of this. One proof lies in an invention of the period, *Latium Maius*, whereby citizenship was given not only, as in ordinary Latin states, to the magistrates, but also the the local councillors.[3] Those who see in this evidence that the empire was already failing have fallen into the error of illuminating an institution by the light of a later age.[4] *Latium Maius* fits the perspective of its own and not of another time, and this time appears to be the principate of Hadrian, a time when the seeds of municipal decay and curial oppression cannot be found in the African province. The Gigthenses in particular made a deal of fuss to secure the special privileges of the *Latium Maius*; the initiative was theirs, not the emperor's.[5] It is not possible to regard such circumstances as evidence for an imperial plan to make the *honores* of municipalities more attractive. The alternative is to regard the new form of *Latium* as an attempt either to speed up the development of the Roman world, or to fit the status of communities more exactly to their real condition by permitting here a more rapid, there a slower, completion of the enfranchisement of peoples.

All the evidence that is brought forward to support the contrary view of *Latium Maius* as a palliative of intolerable municipal burdens is tainted with the same error—which is really an error

---

[1] Broughton, 138. *ILS* 6848, *CIL* viii. 18256. *RE* s.v. 'Colonia', col. 558, colonial rights under Gordian? Cf. promotion of Uchi, Thugga, below, 413, 415.

[2] Cf. below, 413 ff.

[3] Cf. 'decuriones cives Romani et municipes Thisiduenses', *ILS* 6781. Gaius, *Inst.* 1. 96.          [4] O. Hirschfeld, *Kleine Schriften*, 307 ff.

[5] *ILS* 6780. Cf. below, 414. For the Hadrianic date, cf. *RE* s.v. 'Ius Latii', col. 1270.

of historical method—of failing to interpret the dry bones of
political institutions, which carry practically no positive content
by themselves and may be forced to bear any meaning, in the
light of their own times. The root of the error lies in that paragraph of the *lex Malacitana* which deals with the compulsory
nomination of candidates for the municipal magistracies.[1] This is
usually explained *in deterius*, to mean that the shadow of the later
curial system had already fallen on Spain before there were any
*curiales*. What then is to be made of that provision in a Republican law which offered freedom from the service of their state,
*muneris publici vacatio*, to members of Latin colonies, as a privilege no less desirable than Roman citizenship itself?[2] Clearly the
common view of the universal enthusiasm and competition for
municipal honours has been a little over-emphasized; though it
is generally true that there was a steady stream of candidates for
these offices, the lawgiver, in a world where a very great deal of
administrative government depended entirely upon the local
authorities, had to provide against any possibility of accident due
to whatever cause, whereby for some years there might come
a gap in the governmental system. It is possible to imagine
a variety of such causes, with the solid evidence of the *Digest*
in support. The likely men might be away on a legation, or hold
some special *vacatio* for that year, or be absent on imperial service
in army or state. Still more relevant is the fact that there is
absolutely no proof that this clause was first added to the charter
of Latin towns in the particular document from which it is known.
The opposite view is vastly more probable: the distribution of
Latin status had become a mechanical process by the Flavian
period, and there is a close relationship between these charters
and the civil institutions of the late Republic.[3]

The argument drawn from the *lex Malacitana* was at least
relevant. Those taken from the correspondence of Trajan and
Pliny, which refer entirely to the state of affairs in the cities of
Bithynia, are not. Even the appearance of financial commissioners
to control municipal affairs, *curatores civitatium*, does not support
the gloomier interpretation of *Latium Maius*, since their purpose
was to restrain the enthusiasm of municipalities rather than to
bolster up a failing system. It is then proper to see in *Latium*

[1] *ILS* 6089, li.    [2] *Lex repetundarum*, Bruns⁷. 10. 78.
[3] Above, 115 ff. Cf. the fragments of other charters, Bruns 31, 33a.

*Maius* proof of the delicate care with which the emperors of the second period performed their duty of regulating and controlling the growth of the Roman world.

Another glimpse of this care, and of the precise part played by the government, is offered by what Gellius records of Hadrian's oration *de Italicensibus*. This fragment[1] makes it clear that the growth of the honorary colony, so striking a feature of the period, is in origin a *popular* movement, which the *princeps* permitted, and perhaps encouraged by a pretended reluctance, or deliberate caution, in granting the title. The atmosphere of the speech agrees with the preceding interpretation of *Latium Maius*; the two form part of one policy, the deliberate extension of an ever-increasing degree of privileged status to communities that are not only fitted but eager to receive it. This alacrity adds a new note to the theme of imperial development, one that ends by becoming the very diapason of Roman loyalty. When the *primores Galliae* sued for the *ius honorum* they seemed to be seeking some personal advantage. The municipal petitions of the first century and a half of the Principate are mostly concerned, where they can be traced, with financial advantages.[2] The initiative in grants of *Latium* or citizenship comes from the *princeps*,[3] and is a *beneficium* rather than an instance of *indulgentia*: petitions for citizenship seem largely to be confined to individuals in the earlier period.[4] Under Claudius comes the first known example of a community petitioning—and that only in special circumstances —for a grant of citizenship and municipal status. In the second century this seems to become the universal rule; at least it is the form which all the evidence takes, so that Dio,[5] in describing the principate of Marcus, speaks of envoys coming from τὰ ἔθνη to supplicate for the *civitas*, whereas Tacitus describes the initiative as coming in the first century from the *princeps*.[6] It is true that

---

[1] 'Hadrianus . . . mirari se ostendit quod et ipsi Italicenses et quaedam item alia municipia antiqua in quibus Uticenses nominat . . . in ius coloniarum mutari gestiverint', *NA* 16. 13. 4. Cf. Tac. *Ann.* 14. 33. 1, 'Londinium . . . cognomento quidem coloniae non insigne'.

[2] e.g. Vespasian's letter to Sabora, *ILS* 6092, or *ad Vanacinos*, *CIL* x. 8038.

[3] Cf. 'Edictum Claudii de c. Anaunorum', *ILS* 206 *ad fin.*, and below, n. 6.

[4] *ILS* 1981. 'municipes Igabrenses beneficio imp. Caesaris Aug. Vespasiani civitatem Romanam consecuti cum suis per honorem.' Cf. Suet. *Aug.* 40. 3–4, with *ILS* 1977 as an example. Contrast Volubilis under Claudius, above, 241.

[5] 72. 19. 1.

[6] Tac. *Hist.* 1. 78: 'Lingonibus universis civitatem Romanam . . . dono dedit (Otho); nova iura Cappadociae, nova Africae, ostentata'. Cf. Pliny, *NH* 3. 30:

the emperors of A.D. 68–9 would tend to make exceptional offers, but the form which the offers took was likely to be traditional. The important thing is that in the second century the initiative in the settled areas of the empire seems to pass largely over to the community, or at least the communities take matters more and more into their own hands.

It did not escape the notice of contemporaries that the Roman state, and its formal expression, the Roman citizenship, were undergoing an extensive transformation. Their attitude towards this change varies. Tacitus, as the sentimental Republican, speaks, with a mild disgust for the situation in his day, of certain Gallic nobles to whom the citizenship had been given: 'olim . . . cum id rarum nec nisi virtuti pretium esset'.[1] Pliny the Younger mentions the phenomenon with an interesting absence of all personal comment; the lack of special enthusiasm in a panegyric oration shows how much a matter of routine the extension of the citizenship had become.[2] He is much more interested in the minor privileges, which the *princeps*, as it were, threw in with the citizenship, than in gifts of citizenship itself. He refers almost incidentally to 'novi seu per Latium in civitatem seu beneficio principis venissent'. All the stress of his argument falls on the *iura cognationis*, i.e. exemption from death-duties, without which 'maximum beneficium vertebatur in gravissimam iniuriam'. Pliny allows himself to speak of it as surprising that men should welcome the citizenship at such a price.[3] Even for a panegyric the language is curious, and is obviously based upon a thought akin to that of Tacitus, that 'the citizenship is not worth much nowadays'. Echoes of the thought reverberate still in a phrase of Victor, where he states that under Marcus 'data cunctis promiscue civitas Romana'.[4]

Universae Hispaniae . . . Latium tribuit.' Tac. *Hist.* 3. 55: 'Latium externis dilargiri (Vitellius).' Cf. 1. 8: 'Galliae super memoriam Vindicis obligatae recenti dono Romanae civitatis'. Tac. *Ann.* 15. 32: 'Caesar nationes Alpium maritimarum in ius Latii transtulit.'

[1] Tac. *Ann.* 3. 40. 'Long ago, when the grant was rare and only made as the reward of valour', one of the numerous phrases in Tacitus which reflect the feeling of his day rather than the atmosphere of the time of which he writes. Cf. his numerous sneers at freedmen and slaves, and, e.g., *Ann.* 2. 52; 4. 15, introduced by *etiam tum.*        [2] *Pan.* 37. 2–5.

[3] Ibid. 5: 'Inveniebantur tamen quibus tantus amor nominis nostri', etc. 'New citizens who gained their status either via Latin rights or by the gift of the emperor.' 'A great benefit was turned to a deadly injury.'

[4] *Liber de Caesaribus* 16. 12. 'Roman citizenship was given blindly to all.'

A somewhat different attitude is expressed by writers less closely identified with Italian interests, the orators of the second Sophistic, above all Aelius Aristides. His panegyric on Rome reveals, in a way which the Latin writers bound by the old terminology never do, how far the empire had already travelled away from the conceptions of the Augustan age towards the thought and ideas of the late empire. Quite apart from the famous passage where the former division of Hellenes and Barbarians is replaced by that of Romans and non-Romans,[1] the whole speech is permeated by the idea of an *Orbis Romanus* in which even this distinction of citizen and non-citizen is being effaced; and the theme of Rome as the ἄστυ κοινόν, the commonwealth of nations, receives considerable elaboration.[2]

His idea of the Roman citizenship is a form of unity which includes existing differences and distinctions without effacing them; this is marked by a notable tendency to conflate the *imperium Romanum* with the whole body of Roman citizens.[3] The circumstances of the oration suggest that it gives expression to what may be called the official policy of the Roman government, or at least forms a reasonable account of such a policy from the viewpoint of the provincials. Many of the ideas are demonstrably Roman. His ἄστυ κοινόν is simply *communis patria*, and the Greek form of the principle which Claudius re-established is easy to recognize—ξένος οὐδεὶς ὅστις ἄξιος, i.e., ὠφέλιμος, 'No one is a foreigner who is worthy'.[4]

In such a document as this, which marks the consummation of the provinces, especially of the *provinciae togatae*, Italy has no place, and the City itself is less the material Rome than an idea. It is possible to trace the process by which such a situation arose in the emergence of certain tendencies, which all serve to illustrate both the phrase just quoted, and the way in which the primacy of Italy disappeared as the provinces were raised to her level.

The increased recruiting of the Senate, and in particular of the personnel of those branches of the civil and military administration which were reserved for senators, from the most able of the provincial nobility provides the clearest evidence. It was Vespasian who decisively promoted the principles established by

---

[1] Aelius Aristides, *Orationes* (ed. Keil) 26. 63.
[2] The panegyric is discussed at length below, 425 ff.
[3] Cf. below, 427.
[4] Aristides, op. cit. 26. 60; 74. Cf. below, 428.

Claudius. The researches of Stech, Walton, and Lambrechts have made much clear here.[1] It appears that this process began, as one might guess, under Claudius and Nero; it received a considerable impulse under Vespasian, and was mounting high under Trajan. A considerable number of the new senatorial families in this period come from the Spanish provinces, especially Baetica and Narbonensis, with Africa a bad third, Dalmatia and Sicily being barely represented.[2] The *Tres Galliae* can show only two senators, despite the noise Claudius made about the *primores*. It is especially noticeable that these families come from a very limited set of municipalities.[3]

The evidence is mainly epigraphic, and perhaps a little suspect of accidentality; yet sixty-five names are known. The proportion of men to provinces so exactly answers to the conception of the Romanization of these provinces which can be formed from other sources,[4] that the arguments based upon these figures seem trustworthy; the main view which they suggest is that the period of the Flavians is a preparatory period, in which the generalizations of Aristides are inapplicable, but that under Trajan provincial recruitment began to account for a considerable proportion of new senators.[5] Certainly it is under Trajan, and not, as was formerly believed, under Hadrian, that the aristocracy of the Greek Orient began to take an important place in the Roman state.[6] The post-Trajanic princes continue to embrace with eagerness the best which the Greek world could offer. In this subsequent period the Orient makes a very definite bid for the favour of the West, and the seeds that had been sown under Trajan bear a rich crop.[7] Despite the modest place which the Greek provinces held within the fold of the Roman citizenship,

---

[1] B. Stech, *Klio*, Beiheft 10, especially *De senatoribus ex provinciis ortis*. C. S. Walton, *JRS* 19, 'Oriental Senators in the Service of Rome', 381 ff. P. L. Lambrechts, *Ant. Cl.* 1936, 'Trajan et le recrutement du sénat', 108 ff.

[2] Stech, op. cit. 176–7; maximum figures: Spain 23, Narbonensis 19 (cf. Baetica 15), Africa 6, Dalmatia 2, Sicily 1, Tres Galliae 1.

[3] Stech says one—omitting Vindex. Fifteen *municipia* and *coloniae* in Spain and Narbonensis account for the senators drawn from these provinces. See now R. Syme, *Tacitus* (Oxford, 1958), chs. xlii–xliv. M. Hammond, *JRS* 1957, 74 ff.

[4] e.g. the later appearance of Africa in the field. Cf. Stech, 170.

[5] Lambrechts, art. cit. 111 f. For the corresponding recruitment of Knights from the East, beginning under Claudius, cf. above, 247, 250; below, 410, 411 n. 1.

[6] Ibid., correcting the view of Walton, art. cit. 54 ff., and Stech, 179–82.

[7] Evidence still accrues, e.g. a Trajanic centurion from Attalia 'first and only from his city', father of a Roman quaestor. *SEG* xvii. 584.

it was in the earlier period that the government began to feel the
necessity of somehow bringing the Greeks within the inner orbit
of the Roman state. The success with which the task was performed, without sacrificing the valuable characteristics of the
Latin or Roman forms of political life and government, is best
estimated by contrasting the tone of the speeches of Dio Chrysostom and that of the panegyric of Aelius Aristides. Dio, labouring
for a reconciliation of the Hellenistic and the Roman worlds,
is all the time conscious of the difference between 'Greek tricks'
and Roman gravity.[1] But by the time of Aelius Aristides the solution, either in theory or in practice, appears to have been found.[2]

The principate of Trajan marked the turning of the scale in
favour of the provinces in other more emphatic ways; for Italy
was still the main source for the supply of senators, although not
of emperors, at this time. Trajan forbade the levy of troops from
Italy.[3] This, though perhaps only the recognition of a fact, was
a profoundly important moment in the theory of the Roman
citizenship; it meant a further loosening of the connection of the
idea of Rome from that of Italy. The material strength of Rome
passed from Italy to the provinces for ever. The only reminder
of the special position of Italy in the world is the legal privilege
of the *ius Italicum*. Aristides' version of these changes must have
made his audience a little uneasy.[4] Military service is unpleasant,
and is not 'worthy' of 'those from the city'; the Romans show
their wisdom by leaving it to more suitable peoples, drawn from
the newer provinces. It is only another aspect of this decline of
Italy when Trajan endeavours to check the rot by making provincial senators acquire estates within Italy. Yet all his numerous
efforts to revive the life of Italy, though doubtless sufficiently
successful, could not make Italy again the dominant element in
the Roman world. The long roads which Trajan built or repaired
only emphasized the fact that, for the future, Italy was merely
the land in which Rome happened to be situated.[5] Here probably
lies one root of that peculiar confusion which runs through all

---

[1] Ἑλληνικὰ ἁμαρτήματα. Dio Chrys. *Oratio* 38, 148 R; below, 423.

[2] Cf. below, 236 ff.

[3] SHA, *Marcus* 11. 7. Except praetorians? Dio 74 (75). 2. 4.

[4] Aristides, op. cit. 26, 74, 86.

[5] Paribeni, *Optimus Princeps* ii. 120. Cf. SHA, *Marcus* 11. 8; *Severus* 4. 5. Severus
originally only had an *aedes brevissimae* in Rome and *unus fundus* in Venetia. Cf. Dio
76 (77). 2. 1 'When I am in Italy'. Pliny, *Epp*. 6. 19. 4: Rome as Senate's hotel.

the later references to Rome, whether panegyrical, poetical, or historical, the confusion of the idea of the all-embracing *civitas* with the material form of the glorious city upon the Tiber.[1]

Under Hadrian the many tendencies of the preceding period come to a head; what has been but a steady march becomes a gallop. It is a one-sided view of his policy which dismisses him as the *Graeculus*. His philhellenism was more obvious, and perhaps more interesting, to the circles from which most of the literary people who have recorded these things were drawn. But throughout the times that are commonly regarded as the Golden Age, with a Hellenic revival as one of its characteristics, there is discernible much more seriousness of purpose than is commonly allowed. The oriental provinces with their loquacious inscriptions have imposed a somewhat partial view. In the other scale are to be set the less noisy records of the municipal development of the Roman world in Africa, in the Danubian provinces, and in Spain. If the creation of new Greek cities and a care for the old are the criterion, Trajan must share the title of *Graeculus*.[2]

The truth is that these and other events, Trajan's Parthian wars as much as the imperial journeys of Hadrian, testify to a growing consciousness of that unity of the Roman world which includes *partes* both *orientales* and *occidentales*, the differences between Trajan and Hadrian being largely a matter of degree. His official interests must be judged not only by the favours shown to Opramoas,[3] but by his careful interest in the discipline and defence of the whole world, especially such expressions of it as the fragments of the speech at the general inspection of the African soldiers stationed at Lambaesis.[4] The enthusiasm of Aelius Aristides in the time of Marcus is not confined to Greeks and is not original; the substance of what he has to say was anticipated by Tacitus in certain passages of the *Histories*, where he speaks of that 'urbem quam victi victoresque eodem iure obtinemus',[5] and of the overwhelming dignity of Rome and of the loyalty which she inspired in her subjects.[6] This was perhaps

---

[1] Below, 461 f.

[2] Paribeni, op. cit. i. 330–4, the Greek cities of Thrace; ii. 135, Trajanopolis of Syria. Jones, *Cities of the Eastern Roman Provinces*, 18 f.

[3] e.g. *IGRR* iii. 739, c. 28; below, 410.      [4] *ILS* 2487.

[5] Tac. *Hist.* 4. 74. 'The City which conquered and conquerors enjoy on equal terms.'

[6] e.g. ibid. 1. 9, the remarkable words 'A. Vitellius aderat, censoris Vitellii ac

a new thing in Tacitus' day.[1] One cannot fix periods for what was
a continuous process, but it seems clear that Hadrian extended
on a large scale a policy that had been pursued by his predecessor,
who in turn took it over from the Flavians. A Roman world; that
is the idea that became increasingly evident to the imperial chan-
cellery of the second century as the goal of the empire, but by
that phrase was not meant the confusion of all distinctions in a
medley of heterogeneous institutions. Hadrian himself was well
versed in the meaning of Roman municipal forms; there is not
only the evidence of Gellius, for a passage in the *Vita*, which
there is no reason to doubt, records that Hadrian held various
ancient offices in the Italian municipalities.[2] The taste for anti-
quities during this reign was not limited to those of Hellas,
witness the *Noctes Atticae*. Such is the mental background of the
*princeps* under whom new forms, like the *Latium Maius* and the
honorary *ius coloniae*, make their first prominent appearance; his
energy was clearly devoted to the promotion of the interests of
the empire as a whole, whether by founding Roman municipalities
on the Danube or a Greek city in the valley of the Nile.

ter consulis filius: id satis videbatur'. 1. 76, 'longinquae provinciae . . . penes
Othonem manebat non partium studio, sed erat grande momentum in nomine
urbis ac praetexto senatus.' Cf. 2. 32.

[1] Cf. ibid. 4. 69, for the more material grounds of loyalty at the beginning of the
Flavian period, which are summed up as *vim Romanam pacisque bona*!
[2] SHA, *Hadrianus* 19. 1. 'In Etruria praeturam . . . egit. per Latina oppida
dictator et aedilis et IIvir fuit.' The letter to Plotina reveals a normal understanding of a particular problem in the relation of *c. R.* to *homines iuris peregrini*. *ILS* 7784.

# XI

# CHARACTERISTICS OF THE ROMAN CITIZENSHIP IN THE AGE OF THE ANTONINES

AFTER Hadrian any attempt to analyse particular policies must be abandoned until the time of the Severi. Under Pius and Marcus there seem to be no new features, but only the normal working of the machine at the accelerated pace which Trajan and Hadrian had regulated. It was possible to stress the particular contributions of various single emperors to what is really, after Claudius, an undivided process, because the very immensity of the task, of controlling and promoting the unification of the empire, meant that particular problems fell to the special care of individual rulers, one man being incapable of everything. Thus Trajan fights wars and builds roads, while Hadrian personally inspects the provinces and completes a plan for the defensive boundaries of the empire. But after Hadrian the evidence makes it impossible to select moments within the oecumenical process. Instead it is better to attempt to discover what the Roman citizenship had come to mean by the middle of the second century, and so prepare the way for the proper study of the Constitutio Antoniniana.

The citizenship in the fullest sense, as it appears in the political and forensic writings of Cicero, has a double aspect. It affects both a man's public and his private life; politically it brings the exercise of the *honores* and *munera* of the Roman state, and socially the various *iura* by which private life was regulated. The new citizen enters into the contacts and contracts of daily existence under the guidance and protection of Roman law. It is apparent that the analysis of the citizenship into political rights leaves its fundamental content untouched, so that, e.g., the *cives sine suffragio*, the *municipes* of the rising Republic, are not to be regarded as half-citizens; they were—at least in the later form of the institution and from the Roman point of view—much more than that. There is no period of Roman history in which the *honores* were, in practice, open to the whole community; financial qualifications always, oligarchical tendencies at most periods, made the magistracies of the Roman state the privilege of a class, or of a clique. But I do not cease to be a British citizen because I am not, and am not capable of becoming, the Duke of Norfolk. The Roman view of the matter was broader yet. The positive activity of the *ius suffragi ferendi* was not an essential characteristic of the citizenship. This was not only the Augustan view of the matter, as it appears in the writings of Livy and Velleius, but that of the late Republic, since it agrees with the articles in Festus, which are drawn from Verrius, and earlier yet with the suggestive phrase of Ennius—'cives Romani facti sunt Campani'—who hardly invented the thought. The essential marks of the citizenship are the civil status of its holders and their liability to service *pro patria*, i.e. liability to the *munera*. *Ius suffragi*, and the so-called *ius honorum*, are special additional graces, but never essential.[1]

For these reasons it is not possible to follow C. Jullian in his view that, under the empire, the only persons who exhibit the complete picture of a Republican citizen are the members of the senatorial order.[2] He has asked the wrong question. Not how many people held the *ius honorum*, etc., but to how wide a circle may the diverse offices of the state be opened, is the criterion. Tiberius gave the answer in his pun about a certain senator who had risen to the highest posts from a lowly origin, 'Curtius Rufus videtur mihi ex se natus.'[3] There can be no doubt that under the empire office was open to a wider circle through the favour of the emperor, *principis suffragio*, than ever in the free Republic.[4] If fresh blood or ripe experience was wanted a way was always found, the elevation of new men becoming an ever quicker process as time advanced. But for the present subject all this is comparatively unimportant. The genuine character of the Roman citizenship is not to be judged by the chances which men had of reaching senatorial rank and privilege. The fact that, e.g.,

---

[1] Cf. above, 235 f., 239. Compare the hesitation about granting the *ius suffragi* to the *populi dediticii* after the Social War, above, 155. Also the limited rights in these two matters of *liberti*, cf. Last, *CAH* ix. 9; 203. Cf. above, 250 n. 1.

[2] C. Jullian, *Histoire de la Gaule*, iv. 267. Cf. below, 409.

[3] Tac. *Ann.* 11. 21. 'Curtius Rufus seems to be self-begotten.'

[4] Cf. above, 238 ff.

Vespasian 'amplissimos ordines . . . supplevit . . . honestissimo quoque Italicorum ac provincialium allecto',[1] proves that there was no difference of quality between provincial or Italian citizens; both might, subject to certain conditions, become senators without it being the right of any and every citizen, however humble, to sue for such honours. In other words, the *latus clavus* and the *angustus clavus* are alike indifferent to the question. Granted the citizenship, then to reach the *amplissimi ordines* is, as Vespasian put it, a matter not of *libertas* but of *dignitas*.[2]

What happens to the citizenship during the Principate is a further specialization of function, marked by a partial severance of the essential connection of *civitas* with *munera*, more particularly the duty of military service. This was a change more of practice than of theory. To the sophist Aristides it is a remarkable feature of the Roman system that the army is recruited from special areas; he gives a non-technical description of the method, as it appeared to him: 'You visit the whole (of your) empire and choose thence those that shall perform military service . . . and give them your franchise.'[3] This specialization never became an absolute rule, but the plain fact is that, ever since voluntary enlistment had become usual, this separation of the *munus militare* from the list of essential characteristics of the citizenship had been growing through the mere effect of practice. With the limitation of the legionary army, the necessity of exercising the latent power of compulsion disappeared, except in times of great crisis, and even then Augustus himself seems to have preferred voluntary freedmen to forced *ingenui*.[4] This practice began to affect, if not theory, at least the ordinary attitude of the vast majority of men to the citizenship.[5] Military service, like the *iura publica*, came to be regarded as an adjunct of Roman status which may or may not

---

[1] Suet. *Vespasianus* 9. 2. 'Vespasian filled up the highest grades of society by promoting the most distinguished Italians and provincials.'

[2] Suet. loc. cit., paraphrased by Suetonius, 'utrumque ordinem non tam libertate inter se quam dignitate differre'. Cf. Pliny on *novi cives* in the *decuriae*, above, 250 n. 1.

[3] Aristides, op. cit. 26. 75. ἐλθόντες ἐπὶ πᾶσαν τὴν ὑπήκοον ἐσκέψασθε τοὺς λειτουργήσοντας τήνδε τὴν λειτουργίαν . . . καὶ τὴν ὑμετέραν αὐτῶν πόλιν ἀντέδοτε αὐτοῖς.          [4] Dio 55. 31. 1.

[5] e.g. Tac. *Ann.* 4. 5, limits the levy of praetorians to Italy, even to certain parts of Italy, at a time when there is epigraphic evidence to the contrary, e.g., *ILS* 2024, 2025, 2027. Dio, speaking of his own times, 74 (75). 2. 4, refers to the raising of praetorians in Italy, while Marcus held an *Italica adlectio*, SHA, *Marcus* 11. 7, on which see R. Syme, *JRS* 54 (1964) 47. Cf. above, 261.

fall to this or that man's lot. This is especially true of the second century, when Trajan and Hadrian for divers reasons encouraged the limitation of the areas of recruitment. The practical disappearance of the military duties of the Roman citizen meant that for the Roman municipalities the term *munus* was confined in meaning to the service of the local *patria*. It is in this sense that the *munera civilia* are discussed in the *Digest* by the jurists of the second and third centuries;[1] in fact Gellius' explanation of the term *municipes*, 'muneris tantum cum populo Romano honorarii participes',[2] fits better the imperial *municipes* than their ancestors of the third century B.C.

By the middle of the second century the content of the citizenship, as far as concerns public duties or public honours, had been whittled down. A man can be a Roman without the exercise of these *publica iura*. They are, indeed, a possible consequence of citizenship; Paulus speaks of a form of *'capitis deminutio* quae salva civitate accidit, per quam publica iura non interverti constat'; here his meaning is plain—if this *deminutio* carried with it *amissio civitatis*, it would carry also the loss of the *publica iura*.[3] He has just said that there is a form if *deminutio* which does entail the loss of citizenship, and consequently the loss of *publica iura*. There should be left, as the core and heart of the citizenship, the social status which it conferred, the *iura privata* affecting the family and its uniform subjection to Roman law, and so forth. But even here some inroad appears to have been made upon the distinctive marks of the citizenship, not so much by the direct diminution of the *iura privata*, as by some assimilation of the rights of non-Roman persons and communities to those of Roman citizens, and by the increasing co-operation, within a community, of Roman and non-Roman elements of the population.

This phenomenon is most conspicuous, as it was most inevitable, within the Latin municipalities, but it appears also in Africa and in the Danubian provinces, where certain peculiar

[1] e.g. *Dig.* 50. 1. 17, Papinian. 50. 4. 1, Hermogenian.

[2] 'Sharing only duties of distinction with the Roman people', 16. 13. 6. Cf. 7 on the Caerites, 'ut civitatis R. honorem quidem caperent sed negotiis tamen atque oneribus vacarent'. *Munus honorarium* means simply *honores*, public office.

[3] *Dig.* 4. 5. 5 f. 'Reduction of civil rights not involving loss of citizenship, by which it is agreed that public rights are not annulled.' The terminology is a little surprising, since one would expect the *publica iura* in this sense to be affected first. But the passage continues 'nam manere magistratum vel senatorem . . . certum est'.

double-communities are found. Since the *ius Latii* was intended to mediate the transformation of *peregrini* into Roman citizens, and since in each Latin state the Latins and Romans were by all ties of family origin and history members of that particular state, the government was bound to devise some means of their living together, without any unnatural severance or division, within what was one community. The two surviving charters of Latin towns reveal numerous traces of such assimilation of Latin and Roman legal practice;[1] convenience is clearly the reason for the provisions in the two rubrics, 'ut qui c. R. consequantur maneant in eorundem mancipio manu potestate', and 'ut qui c. R. consequentur iura libertorum retineant'. Phrases like 'eadem condicio esto quae esset si civitate mutatus non esset' indicate the processes of accommodation and assimilation that are at work,[2] complementing and extending *commercium* and *conubium*.

Something similar appears in the freedom with which the emperors granted not only the citizenship but *conubium* with foreign wives—*cum uxoribus quas tunc habuissent*—to their auxiliary troops. They will not give the women the citizenship, but they do not refuse to regulate their legal status. There is a notable extension of this practice in the diplomata of the Flavian period and onwards. The praetorian troops, who were Roman citizens before they became soldiers, are concerned. To these men the Princeps states: 'ius tribuo conubii dumtaxat cum singulis et primis uxoribus ut etiamsi peregrini iuris feminas matrimonio suo iunxerint proinde liberos tollant ac si ex duobus civibus Romanis natos.'[3] It is evidently in the spirit of the age to do everything to enable men to live in all comfort of legal harmony, in those parts of the world where there is considerable mixture of personal status within the same communities. The privileges granted by these diplomata must have been of considerable practical importance in those areas of the Empire, especially in Gaul, where the municipal system was not introduced, or where, as in the Moesian provinces, it was still rudimentary. It became

---

[1] Cf. above, 114 ff.

[2] *ILS* 6088, 22; 23. 'Those who gain Roman citizenship are to remain under the power and authority of their former relations.' 'Such persons are to retain their rights over their freedmen.' 'His status is to be the same as if he had not changed his citizenship.'

[3] 'I give them the right of legal marriage with one wife (the first only) so that though they marry women of foreign status they may raise up children born as it were of two Roman citizens.' Cf. *CIL* xvi, p. 156 and nn. 18, 21, etc.

the normal thing to have mixed groups of Roman citizens and of *homines peregrini iuris* living in the same village or canton and exercising communal authority jointly. Such a situation must have meant a considerable decline in the positive importance of the citizenship, when it was seen that the possession of it left men in much the same position as before, in relation to their neighbours, as far as power or privilege was concerned.

The Danubian provinces provide documentary evidence for this view in the form of corporate inscriptions of the type 'cives Romani et Bessi consistentes vico', or 'cives Romani et Lai consistentes vico'.[1] The known examples are nearly all dated, and they appear mainly in the second and early third century. Sometimes the variation 'veterani et cives Romani et Bessi' appears. The military diplomata of the period help to reconstruct the situation. These inscriptions, of the *consistentes* type, seem to record the activities of village communities composed of, e.g., Bessi, some of whom have acquired the citizenship by military service, and some of whom have yet to serve, and so acquire citizenship in their turn. This is made certain by the fact that the *magistri* of these communities for a single year include men with Roman and men with native names.[2] But it is to be remarked that these communities retained their original titles, at a date when it is certain that all concerned possessed the citizenship. Twenty years and more after the Constitutio Antoniniana the 'cives Romani et Lai consistentes' turn up again.[3] This suggests that the existence of the title is no proof, even in the second century, that all the *consistentes* were not *cives Romani* already, except where a native *magister* or *quaestor* appears. For it is notable that under Hadrian a large number of the auxiliary units were drawn from among peoples who already possessed the citizenship, especially in the Spanish provinces.[4]

---

[1] *CIL* iii. 3505, 7533, 14214 (26). 'Romans and Bessi living together in the village.' *Année Ép.* 1924, nn. 142–8. The earliest is dated A.D. 140, the latest A.D. 246, op. cit. 1934, n. 166.

[2] e.g. *Année Ép.* 1924, n. 144. 'Curantibus magistris Aelio Bellico et Mucatralo Doli [filio] et quaestore Dotuzi Nebti.'

[3] Ibid., n. 148 in A.D. 237. Pârvan in *Dacia* ii, 1925, p. 243, recognized that the Lai are simply the Λααῖοι of Thuc. 2. 96, in a Latin dress, and have no connection with *Laeti*.

[4] e.g. *CIL* xvi. 69, in A.D. 122 contains 'ala', or 'cohors' Vetton. Hispan. c.R. Gallor. Petriana c.R.—Vardulorum c.R.—Cugern. c.R.—Vascon. c.R.—Vocont. c.R.—Afrorum c.R.

In these communities, which are the best guide to what was taking place in the second century up and down the non-urbanized provinces, the status of Roman citizen is a matter of honour and titular distinction. It does not separate off its possessors from their fellows, as a privileged class or special clique. The form of the community—that of a *conventus* or else of a *collegium*—is Roman, but within it, as far as can be seen, *veterani, cives Romani*, and natives stand on the same level, without any political advantage attaching to any particular grade. That this phenomenon is parallel to the development of the Latin towns is clear. There the *Latini et cives Romani*, all of whom are, e.g., *Malacitani*, form a single community; here the *cives Romani* and *peregrini*, all of whom are, e.g., *Bessi*, form likewise a single community. In such circumstances the thing that mattered would be the charter of the individual borough, the *lex cuiusque civitatis*,[1] while the Roman citizenship would become something like a form of imperial unity.

The numerous examples of this type of double-community which are now known in the Danubian provinces render it easier to understand the analogous institutions of Africa. There are some settlements which are precisely similar to the Danubian villages. Such a one is the 'conventus civium Romanorum et Numidarum qui Mascululae habitant'. In this inscription, the earliest instance of the type found anywhere, and probably of Tiberian date,[2] the name of the *Numidae* is cut in much smaller letters than the words *civium Romanorum*, a fact which suggests that the Romans regarded themselves as the important men of the place.[3] There is an explicit example of the second century from Rapidum, where the unity of the two elements is asserted by the words *intra eundem murum habitantes*.[4] But more numerous and more peculiar to Africa is another kind of municipal irregularity, where two separate communities existing side by side, one of *peregrini*, the other of Roman citizens, join together from time to time in some form of united activity. This type is known as the *pagus et civitas*. Its genesis may take one or two forms: either, in a district which forms a territorial and perhaps

---

[1] *Dig.* 50. 4. 1. 2.

[2] *ILS* 6774; it is set up to honour *Divus Augustus*.

[3] Cf. also 'Afri et c. R. Suenses', *ILS* 6776.

[4] *ILS* 6885, 'dwelling within the same town-wall'; also, ibid., 'veterani et pagani consistentes', *circa* A.D. 167.

an ethnic unit, the central *oppidum* is promoted in civic status separately from the country areas; or else—as is more common— a nucleus of Roman citizens, normally Italian immigrants or their descendants, form a self-administering group or *pagus* under the tutelage of the nearest Roman municipality, while the rest of the local population, the *civitas*, is left at an earlier stage of development. The process continues *pari passu*: e.g. native *civitas* and Roman *municipium* form the next stage, or else there may be an ex-native *municipium* and a *pagus c. R.* side by side. Sometimes both communities end by coalescing at the highest grade of development into a single municipality.[1] Much is still obscure in the history of these communities, largely because of attempts to explain them all on one plan. But of the duality itself there is no doubt.[2] The difference between these African and the Danubian communities is that here there are two separate bodies, each with some form of corporate organization, but standing on different levels of status, although at times the two combine for special purposes into a single body corresponding to their real geographic unity;[3] whereas in Moesia the difference of status exists within the single *vicus*.

The process by which Roman citizens and provincials gradually became linked together is indicated by the evidence of the Cyrenean Edicts. In this province there was, under Augustus, a sharp conflict between the local Roman citizens and the Greeks. These Romans, from the enmity which they exhibit towards the Greeks, must be *Italici*.[4] Between the two groups stands a third, composed of provincials who had been given the Roman citizenship.[5] These naturally are not likely to support the immigrant Romans against their own folk.[6] Furthermore, these provincial citizens retain their original place within the Greek community. There is a special provision that explains their position

---

[1] Kornemann, *Philologus* 1901, 402 ff. Merlin, *Les Inscriptions d'Uchi Maius* (Paris, 1908), 17 ff. Broughton, op. cit. 210 ff.

[2] Kornemann, art. cit. 421. Cf. *ILS* 6795, 6822, Thaignic; 541, 6796–7, 9399, 9404, Thugga; 6827, Agbia. Cf. at Uchi the *pagus* under *magistri* about A.D. 126, and the *res publica* with an *ordo* already under Nerva, cf. Merlin, op. cit. 21. *CIL* viii. 26241, 26252–3.

[3] But the dual *colonia* and *municipium* at Thuburbo Maius of *ILA* 244 disappears by revision of text in *I.L.T.* (1944) 699. Cf. below, 351.

[4] *JRS* 17. 34. i. 7. συνωμοσίας ... ἐπιβαρυνούσας τοὺς Ἕλληνας (= *FIRA* I². 68).

[5] Ibid. 35. i. 39. Ῥωμαιότητι τετιμημένος.

[6] Cf. ibid. 35. i. 38 f.

unambiguously: 'My ordinance is that, if any have been honoured with the Roman citizenship, they are to perform the services due by them in the community of the Greeks just the same, except such as have been granted immunity as well as citizenship.'[1]

This third element must have been the link of mediation, not only in Cyrene, but wherever communities of Italian Romans and communities of peregrines stood side by side. In Cyrene, as a Greek province, doubtless the sense of division was sharper than in lands where there was less opposition of rival cultures, and where these dual communities seem to grow up under the guidance of *Concordia* rather than of *Eris*.[2] At least it is certain that these mixed settlements were a fairly common feature of the Roman world in the second century, and that their development contributed to the decrease in the practical importance of the Roman citizenship, and to the growth of an attitude that made of the *civitas* a form of unity or a badge of loyalty. Even in the time of Augustus the citizenship of the Cyreneans is treated in this fashion. It is regarded as a mark of dignity, which carries no special political privileges with it, but leaves a man, for the purpose of daily life and local politics and the payment of taxes, very much where he stood before. This is precisely the language which Gellius uses in his analysis of the term *municeps* and which he applies to the *municipia* in general,[3] whereas Augustus only uses such phrases of ex-Greek citizens. This extension sums up the development which has been in process during the intervening century and a half.

Amid the welter of evidence which suggests the decline of the practical content of the citizenship, and its acceleration during the second century, it is not to be forgotten that its grant still brought men directly within the sphere of Roman law, especially in those areas where the spread of the citizenship is accompanied by the municipalization of the province concerned. Here numerous problems arise about the maintenance of the provincial status of

[1] εἴ τινες . . . πολειτήαι τετείμηνται τούτους λειτουργεῖν οὐδὲν ἔλασσον ἐμ μέρει τῷ τῶν Ἑλλήνων σώματι κελεύω ἐκτὸς τούτων οἷς . . . ἀνεισφορία ὁμοῦ σὺν τῇ πολιτήαι δέδοται. *JRS* 35. iii. 56 ff. Cf. above, 245 f.

[2] For an instance of the syncretism of Roman and Punic elements in African double-communities, see Merlin, *Le Forum de Thuburbo Maius*, 47. Cf. Merlin, *Les Inscriptions d'Uchi Maius*, n. 2. The *ordo civitatis Bencennensis* sets up an offering 'Concordiae . . . quod indulgentia Augusti nostri Colonia . . . Uchi . . . promota . . . sit', *CIL* viii. 15447. See further below, 304 f.

[3] Above, 267.

promoted communities, or about the conversion of native custom into Roman law, continuous with the extension of the Roman state, or about the countenance given to local peculiarities within organized Roman provincial communities, or about the conversion of native institutions into Roman institutions. But for the period under discussion there is one document, the Rule-Book of the Comptroller of imperial lands in Egypt, which indicates that in the second century the status of a Roman citizen was, in private law, as clearly fixed and defined as ever it had been.[1]

Likewise the right of appeal remained as part of the practical meaning of the citizenship. The value of the *ius provocationis* to the allies and subjects of Rome had first become prominent in the Gracchan age, but under the Principate St. Paul was certainly not the only citizen of the eastern provinces to protect himself against the summary jurisdiction of a provincial governor by the plea of citizenship, *civis Romanus sum*. Other known examples are rare, but an indirect instance is provided by the punishment of the free state of Rhodes for the execution of Roman citizens.[2] It is, however, possible that the right of appeal was more lively in the East, where the citizenship spread only by individual grants, than in the West, where wholesale extension of it must have led to some practical limitation of a right, which would have become a nuisance when universalized. On the other hand, the benefits of the *tribunicia potestas* must have been extended beyond the ranks of Roman citizens in the imperial provinces, where its chief holder was in any case the ultimate court of appeal. The trials of the 'pagan martyrs' before the *princeps* at Rome exemplify this tendency.[3] So in this respect too there may have been some assimilation of the rights of *peregrini* to those of citizens.[4]

However, certain changes in the formulae of the military diplomata suggest that in general the distinctions of civil law were fully maintained. Thus in A.D. 139 the emperors ceased to

[1] P. Meyer, *Juristische Papyri*, n. 93, e.g. 18. 56; 23. 70; 24. 73; 27, 80, etc., regulations affecting *conubium, commercium*, etc.

[2] Dio 60. 24. 4 f. Cf. also Eusebius *H.E.* 5. 1. 207 for exemption of Romans *c.* 177.

[3] Cf., e.g., *P. Oxy.* 1. 33. *BGU* 511. Possibly also Plin. *Ep.* 2. 11. 8, is relevant, the judicial murder of a Roman knight by the governor of Africa. Pliny as advocate apparently did not invoke the *leges Porciae* against Priscus, but cf. *contra*, ibid. 10, 96, 4, Roman citizens sent for trial on capital charges from Bithynia to Rome.

[4] Cf. A. H. M. Jones, 'Another Interpretation of the Constitutio Antoniniana', *JRS* 1936, 234. and Mitteis, *Chrestomathie*, n. 371 for possible confusion of *honestas* with *civitas* in appeals. See below, 313.

grant the citizenship retrospectively to the offspring of soldiers begotten during service; such children, to gain the citizenship, must serve like their fathers.[1] At the same time the full privileges continued to be granted to the marines and sailors because the fleet was the unpopular service.[2] Also *conubium* continued to be granted by diploma to the praetorian and urban troops till the time of Diocletian.[3] These dodges of the recruiting-office bear out the general conclusion.[4] Another consideration lies in the centralizing tendencies that are visible in this century in every department of imperial administration of which any adequate account can be given. It is relevant to note that Gellius' discussion of the local rights and independent status of the *municipia* ends with the statement that these were in his day *obscura oblitterataque iura*.[5] This means that the *leges municipales*, of which the jurists speak, were probably all formed on some common model, with only minor local differences, a view that is certainly supported by what is known of the Latin charters.[6]

The essence of the problem is after all contained, not in any negation of the original character of the citizenship, but in the vast accumulation of extraneous matter that was being assimilated. The earlier elements remained, but they receded in importance when they were no longer the sole occupants of the conception of citizenship, when to be a *civis* one must be so much else beside—e.g. not only a citizen, but an *Hispanus* and a *municeps* too. The newly found *Tabula Banasitana* clearly indicates both that the Roman citizenship was, in the remoter regions, still a privilege granted only with selective discrimination even to the leading men of loyal 'tribes', and that its personal content was adjusted to local law, in the late second century.[7]

---

[1] Cf. *CIL* xvi, pp. 160 f.    [2] Ibid., p. 161.    [3] Ibid., p. 156 and n. 156.
[4] Cf. Hadrian's letter to Plotina, above, 555 n. 6.
[5] *NA* 16. 13. 9. 'Dim and confused privileges.'
[6] *Dig.* 50, 4. 18. 27; 6. 6. 1; 9. 6.
[7] See below, 312, 393 (text cited).

# XII

## THE UNION OF EAST AND WEST UNDER THE SEVERI

THE dynasty of Severus seems, in the state of our knowledge, to form a decisive point in the constitutional history of the Empire. Doubtless the course had been set by the Antonines, but it is only Severus who rounds the last mark and drives straight for the complete balance and equalization, and even the fusion, of the Greek and Latin elements of the Roman world. The severance of the connection between Latin culture and Roman status had doubtless been long prepared by such means as the increasing adlection of oriental senators,[1] or the continual bestowal of the franchise on auxiliary troops drawn from the less civilized parts of the Empire.[2] Even in Trajan's day appeared the sinister figure of Lusius Quietus, 'the Man of Qwrnyn'.[3] But with the elevation of Severus we touch something more firm and solid. His policy takes visible shape in the bestowal of the *ius coloniae* and the *ius Italicum* on city-states and principalities, some of which are not so much Greek, in their life and thought, as Semitic. No one had done such a thing before. The Roman colonies in the eastern provinces had been, without exception, based upon veteran settlements. Any other form of city-building had been after the fashion and law not of Roman *municipia*, but of Hellenic city-states. Now comes Severus, annexes his new province of Mesopotamia, and gives to the old town-centres like Nisibis the titles of a Roman colony.[4] Where one can trace the character of the troops that formed the garrisons of the province based upon these *coloniae*, they are not legionaries but auxiliaries, as at Doura-Europos, a colony of Caracallus or Alexander Severus, where was stationed a Palmyrene cohort.[5]

---

[1] Above, 260 f.  [2] Above, 261, 269.
[3] J. Carcopino, 'Lusius Quietus', *Istros*, 1934, 5 ff.
[4] Cf. Kornemann, *RE* s.v. 'Colonia', col. 552 f.
[5] Cf. *Excavations at Doura-Europos*, Third Season, 161 f. Fourth Season, 204, with legionary detachments. A. H. M. Jones, *Cities of the Eastern Roman Provinces*, 443 n. 10.

Similar is the list of cities which at this time received the *ius Italicum*, a privilege which implied complete assimilation to the status of Italian colonies and, in particular, a general immunity from taxation.[1] The statements of Ulpian and Paulus set out the facts in a clear light. In the East the *ius Italicum*, whatever is made of the privileges which it brought with it, was given to Tyre, to Laodicea, to Emesa, to Palmyra, and to Heliopolis, by Severus or Caracallus.[2] It is a somewhat barbarous list, saving Laodicea. Where the ground of the grant is stated, it is mainly the reward of service to the Roman state, in the person of Severus himself.[3] It is true that the *ius Italicum* brought with it a great practical advantage, freedom from the land-tax, *tributum soli*, and apparently also from the poll-tax, *tributum capitis*.[4] Undoubtedly the fact that *ius Italicum* could not be granted without this immunity accounts for the rarity of the grant. Cities had to fulfil a double condition before they were given it, whereas the title of *colonia* cost the imperial government nothing. But there is more yet in the desire for *ius Italicum* that needs explanation. Of the earlier examples of *coloniae iuris Italici* part are the largest cities of the province concerned, the rest being eastern foundations of Caesar or Augustus, where it was perhaps desirable to emphasize the non-Greek character of the community.[5] C. Jullian has already suggested that the importance of this status to the Gallic cities at Cologne, Vienne, and Lyons was one of sentiment rather than of finance.[6] As the title of *colonia* began to spread among the *civitates* of the Gallic provinces, these three desired to 'go one better'. The rivalry of Vienne and Lugdunum at least is

---

[1] Cf. v. Premerstein, *RE* s.v. 'Ius Italicum', col. 1239 f.

[2] *Dig.* 50. 15. 1; 8. Cf. the list in Kornemann, art. cit., cols. 580 f.

[3] *Dig.* loc. cit. 1, Tyre (1), 'ob egregiam . . . fidem'. Laodicea (3), 'ob civilis belli merita'. Only the grant to Palmyra (5), 'prope barbaras gentes . . . collocata', suggests less of opportunism.

[4] Ibid. 8. 4–5 and 7 make this certain. 'Antiochenses colonos fecit salvis tributis' is meant to contrast with the preceding instance of Tyre, i.e. Antioch was not given the *ius I.* The group named in 7 and 8 are colonies which possess the material content of *ius I.*, without having been formally granted the *ius* itself. What Titus said ('solum immune factum interpretatus est') was simply that the Caesarienses held this immunity; he avoided stating in so many words that they were *iuris Italici*. Else why the circumlocutions of Paulus? Again, in 8, 1, *immunes* is used as an alternative.

[5] e.g. ibid. 1. 1, Berytus. 1. 10, Apamea, Sinope. 8. 10, Troas, Parium, Antiochia in Pisidia. Also those of Macedon, 8. 8, where the Italians dispossessed by the *Tresviri* settled. Cf. Premerstein, art. cit. 1239.

[6] Op. cit. iv. 263.

notorious.[1] There is a parallel in the competition among the Asiatic cities for titles like 'First City' or 'Temple-Holder'. A similar explanation is possible for the grant of *ius Italicum* to the three African cities, to which Severus and Antoninus gave it.[2] Carthage was the capital city of the province; Utica had eagerly sought the title of *colonia* from Hadrian for purely sentimental reasons; Leptis Magna would score off her ancient rival Oea.[3] The close connection between this title and that of *colonia* supports the view that a sentimental value was attached to the *ius Italicum*, in addition to its practical advantages, which could be given separately, although they could not be withheld once *ius Italicum* was granted.[4] But the rarity of the grant suggests that the fiscal benefits which it conferred were always the first consideration. Because of them *ius Italicum* could not be given away lightly by the central government, and hence could only become a reasonable object of municipal ambition in exceptional circumstances.

The degree to which the pursuit and veneration of the title of *colonia* were accepted and approved by the emperors is revealed, somewhat absurdly, by the name of *Colonia Commodiana* that Commodus is said to have given to Rome.[5] The almost universal connection of the title with an imperial name only shows how thoroughly the state was at this time being identified with the person of the emperor, and how effectively the imperial cult had done its work of encouraging loyalty throughout the Roman world.

In the Severan period there is thus an extension to the Greek-speaking provinces of what formerly had been confined to the Latin provinces. This universal penetration of loyalty and fervour for the Roman state and its institutions is a finger-post to the Constitutio Antoniniana. But, before that enactment, it is worth discussing the encouragement which Severus appears to have given to the development of municipal or quasi-municipal life in Egypt.[6] This tendency is important because it suggests that the granting of honorary titles and the wholesale extension of citizenship are not all eyewash and humbug, that there was an attempt to set the provincial peoples in a position where the

---

[1] Cf. Tac. *Hist.* i. 65.   [2] *Dig.* loc. cit., Carthage, Utica, Leptis Magna.
[3] Cf. Tac. *Hist.* 4. 50.   [4] *Dig.* loc. cit. 8. 5.
[5] Dio Cassius, *Ep.* 72 (73). 15. 2.
[6] P. Jouguet, *La Vie municipale d'Égypte*, 269 f., 345 ff. A. H. M. Jones, *Cities of the Eastern Roman Provinces*, 329 ff.

Roman franchise would have some meaning for them, and where at least they would be something better than serfs. The subject is still under dispute, largely owing to the difficulty of distinguishing government officials from true municipal or quasi-municipal officers, in a land where the word 'liturgy' had largely lost its true meaning; but in general the conclusion seems to be established that the decentralization of the governmental system under the Romans prepared the way for a sort of municipal life in the capitals of the Nomes,[1] and to a smaller degree in the villages,[2] where there had always been a skeleton of a closely delimited local administration,[3] supervised by the central authorities or subject to their interference.[4] An important change was wrought by the introduction under Severus of urban councils, βουλαί, to the metropoleis of the Nomes; but this period saw only the opening of the process by which the Nomes became the *civitates* of the late empire.[5] Still there is an indisputable growth, in a small way, of local autonomy in Egypt during the third century, both in villages and metropoleis, and this appears to have received its main impulse from the reforms of Severus.[6] This development can also be viewed as the influence of the rest of the empire upon Egypt,[7] especially when the assimilation at this time of the three cities of Egypt to the normal type is considered. There is a sign, in the middle of the previous century, that the rigid separation of Egypt from the rest of the empire, and of the classses within Egypt from one another, was already slightly slackened.[8] This appears in the right of intermarriage with the native Egyptians which Hadrian granted to the citizens of his new city Antinooupolis, by a deliberate departure from the charter of Naucratis, which he had otherwise followed in his new creation.[9] Another explicit indication of such a policy of educating the *Aegyptii* in something like city life is found in Caracallus' edict *De Reditu*, dated a few years after the great *constitutio*.[10] Here special exemption is granted to such *Aegyptii* as visit Alexandria, among other causes 'for the sake of a more

---

[1] P. Jouguet, *La Vie municipale d'Égypte*, 454 f.
[2] Ibid. 221, 271.
[3] Ibid. for the villages, 61 ff., 217 f.; for the nomal capitals, 292 ff.
[4] Ibid. 313 f. Cf. 357.         [5] Ibid. 345 ff.         [6] Ibid. 386.
[7] Ibid. 398.                                               [8] Ibid. 454 ff.
[9] Ibid. 184. *A. and J.* n. 184, l. 19, κατ' ἐξαίρετον (Wilcken, *Chrestomathie*, n. 27).
[10] Ibid. n. 193 (Wilcken, op. cit., n. 22).

civilized life',[1] and special attention is called to the difference between country folk and those that have had the benefit of living in a city.[2] Even in Egypt the ground was not unprepared, although it was a special preserve and treasure-house of the emperors; but the preparation of the Egyptians for the *civitas* was the spread of Greek rather than Latin culture. In the land of the Ptolemies this was doubtless inevitable. At least it is certain that even in this strange field, where men had no great reason to bless the Roman Empire, and where the capital city seemed to be permanently opposed to any devotion towards *S.P.Q.R.*, there had been some effort to till the soil. The grant of a Council to Alexandria, a petition so long and perhaps so often refused, was one of the wisest of the acts of Severus.[3]

All these details seem to fall in place as part of a scheme which in turn was but part of the vast process through which the *Orbis Terrarum* had been passing for two and a half centuries, once it is agreed that the final act itself, the Constitutio Antoniniana, can be summed up in the three words of the writer of the *Vita Severi*, *civitatem omnibus datam*. This subject has been somewhat unnecessarily complicated by discussion since the discovery of *P. Giessen* 40, containing a document which has been taken for a Greek text of the *constitutio* itself. The document has added little to the understanding of this act of Caracallus, which can be evaluated independently of the papyrus.

There can be no doubt that every province of the empire was scattered with multitudes of men, organized into every possible type of community, who possessed the citizenship, while some provinces such as Baetica, Narbonensis, or Africa were now very solidly Latin or Roman. Where the citizenship was lacking, there is abundant proof of a real enthusiasm for the empire and the idea of Rome. Possibly the only important exceptions to these statements would be provided by some Jewish and Christian communities, and some sections of the Egyptian population.[4] Still, the old division remained of *peregrini* and *cives Romani*, and there were numerous communities, which were nominally *Latini iuris*, where the greater part of the upper classes had become in fact Roman. These distinctions were now swept away; the world

---

[1] πολειτικωτέρας ζωῆς ἕνεκεν. Ibid. l. 25.
[2] ἀναστροφὴ πολειτική. Ibid. *ad fin.*      [3] Cf. below, 423 f.
[4] Cf. below, 422 f.

that had long been regarded as the *Orbis Romanus*, first in the sense that it was subject to Rome, then in the sense that it was subject to Roman government and Roman laws,[1] now became such in a real sense, even from the aspect of constitutional law, because its inhabitants were all, with the most modest of possible exceptions, Roman citizens. The *constitutio* thus is the last great act of the emperors in their function of registrars. The world became ready, and Caracallus had only to affix the official seal.

It is beyond dispute that Caracallus gave the franchise to all or nearly all the free inhabitants of the empire ;[2] the idea that it was reserved for city-dwellers has been put out of court by the accumulation of contrary evidence. Such a principle could never have applied in the Three Gauls or Britain, where the importance of the city was minimal. From the aspect of personal law the *constitutio* thus swept away a number of what had come to be anomalies, and simplified the relationship of all the members of what a contemporary writer calls 'the world of Rome'.[3] There was a completion or assimilation or unification,[4] if we may take a hint from the attempts to complete the last sentence of *P. Giessen* 40, of the personal status of the individual members of the empire, but only in the narrowest sense.[5] The various grades of communities remained unchanged, from the smallest *vicus* or *castellum* to the *colonia iuris Italici*, except in so far as all tend to fall under the heading *civitas*.[6] This latter tendency towards a general assimilation appears already in the writings of the Severan jurists, and was encouraged by the fact that all the communities of the higher grades were, or formed, a *res publica*.[7] But as within the urban organization of the empire the Roman citizenship was only supplementary to the local *patria*, so also in the rural areas the administrative status of *Aegyptii* or imperial

---

[1] Cf. below, 429 ff.

[2] For Egypt, Jouguet, op. cit. 353 ff., but more full and decisive is E. Bickermann in *Das Edikt des Kaisers Caracalla*, 27–34 (Berlin, 1926). For Asiatic provinces, the humble 'Aurelii' of an imperial estate in Phrygia, *BSA*, 1911–12, 63, and Bickermann's comment, op. cit. 37. See Dio 77 (78) 9. 5, Ulpian, *Dig.* 1. 5. 17.

[3] ἡ οἰκουμένη αὐτῆς (i.e. Ῥώμης). Dio 78 (79). 26. 1.

[4] ἐξάπλωσις or ὁμάλωσις or ὅλωσις, below, 282 n. 2.

[5] The suggestions fit the C.A. itself, cf. below, 282, 286.

[6] For an example see *A. and J.* n. 137, where the privileges of Aphrodisias as a *ivitas libera* were confirmed and extended by Alexander Severus.

[7] Cf. *Dig.* 50. 12. 8 for an early instance.

*coloni* remained the same as before.[1] Any development of municipal institutions in Egypt, where perhaps the decree had the greatest numerical effect in creating new Romans, was due not to Caracallus but to Severus, as far as it owed anything to a single man rather than to almost impersonal forces.

The practical effect of the decree was at the time nominal. The only motive that Dio assigned to the measure was a possible extension of the inheritance tax,[2] a motive which is somewhat weakened by the consideration that in Egypt at least this tax had always existed.[3] Under Trajan tax and citizenship went hand in hand,[4] but it is highly probable that by the time of Caracallus the majority of the great fortunes of the empire were already within the fold.[5] One modern authority even goes so far as to build on this fact—if it is a fact—the hypothesis that the decree was to subject the great fortunes, in the eastern provinces, to the municipal *munera*;[6] but since the time of Augustus the possession of citizenship no longer enabled the millionaires to avoid these.[7] Such a hypothesis, which is based upon the by no means proven theory that the municipalities of the Eastern provinces were bankrupt, would at the best be cogent only within a limited section of the empire, and leaves the main problem, the extension of the citizenship throughout the rural, non-urbanized areas, untouched. Nor is Wilcken's suggestion, based on a restoration of *P. Giessen* 40, any more helpful, that Caracallus desired to extend the imperial cult which was already universal.[8]

The only help, other than Dio's, which is offered by the remains of antiquity to interpret the measure are the panegyrical passage in the *Civitas Dei*, and *P. Giessen* 40. St. Augustine's remarks are vague enough—'ut . . . esset omnium quod erat paucorum ( ! )' etc.[9]—but they agree with the general tone of the papyrus, so far as its meaning can be recovered without accepting tendentious readings. It records after all *some* grant of *civitas*,

---

[1] Cf. the *Edictum de Reditu* quoted above, 278.

[2] 77 (78). 9. 5.

[3] Cf. Jouguet, op. cit. 356. S. L. Wallace, *Taxation in Egypt* (Princeton, N.J., 1938), 234.

[4] Plin. *Pan.* 39.

[5] Cf. the list of Asiarchs and High Priests of Asia, all *c. R.*, in V. Chapot, *La Province romaine proconsulaire d'Asie*, 482 ff.

[6] Abbot and Johnson, *Municipal Administration in the Roman Empire*, 549.

[7] Cf. above, 272.         [8] *Archiv für Papyrusforschung*, v. 426 ff.

[9] *De C. Dei*, 5. 17. Cf. below, 462.

even if it is not the *constitutio* itself. The most profitable comment so far has been Stroux's remark about the connection between this scheme of *civitas omnibus data* and other vast conceptions of Caracallus, the enormous size of his buildings and the generality of his thoughts, wherever his *ipsissima verba* have survived.[1] In this papyrus three of the leading ideas are of this type. Caracallus stresses both the greatness of the gods who have preserved him, the necessity of a similarly great recompense, and the greatness of the Roman people. The dominant note of the papyrus is one of *maiestas*. There is certainly no suggestion that Caracallus was aiming at any practical benefits.

The proposed restorations of the last sentence are helpful here, especially as they fit either of the current views of the document; the readings all aim at the same meaning, which in plain Latin is 'hoc edictum explebit maiestatem populi Romani'.[2] It is necessary to put this into the Latin, in which presumably the document was originally written, because the Greek translation is very bald, the words 'the greatness of the Roman people'[3] do not in Greek carry the same atmosphere as the Latin formulae, centuries old and containing within themselves the very essence of Roman history.[4] It is important to notice that it is the *maiestas populi Romani*, and not the *magnitudo imperii*, with which Caracallus is concerned. Aelius Aristides has some peculiar remarks, in which he compared Rome to the sea that is fed by many rivers but never changes in size.[5] The greatness of Rome is in this respect a quality—*maiestas*. Every one knew that in fact Rome ruled an empire of a certain size, which had grown from small beginnings, and contained a certain number of provinces that had not always belonged to the empire. Tacitus speaks of a time, 'M. Porcio consule magnis quidem iam populi Romani rebus nondum tamen ad summum elatis, stante adhuc Punica urbe et validis per Asiam regibus'. That is *magnitudo*, an attribute of the *imperium* rather

[1] *Philologus* 1933, 'Die Constitutio Antoniniana', 279. As in *Dig.* 50. 2. 3. 1, 'cuicumque aut quacumque causa', etc.; also *de Reditu, A. and J.*, n. 193, l. 17, πάντηι πάντως (Wilcken, *Chrestomathie*, n. 22).

[2] e.g. Stroux, art. cit. 295, ἐ[ξο]λώσει [τὴν] μεγαλειότητα [το]ῦ Ῥωμα[ίων δήμου μετὰ τὸ τὴν ἴσην δύναμι]ν περὶ τοὺς [ἄλλο]υς γεγενῆσθαι ἧπερ διὰ [τὴν εὐγένειαν Ῥωμαῖοι τετίμηνται].

[3] μεγαλειότης τοῦ Ῥωμαίων δήμου.

[4] For the Latin original cf. the use of the word (δεδ)ειτικίων.

[5] *Or.* 26. 62, ἐξιόντων καὶ εἰσιόντων ἴση οὖσα ,and οὐδὲ τῇδε ὑπὸ μεγέθους οὐδὲν ἐπίδηλον.

than of the *urbs*.[1] For these two ideas there is only one Greek word, μεγαλειότης. In the following two centuries it was not the *magnitudo imperii*, but the *maiestas populi Romani* that was important. The empire would be convulsed, broken, shattered, partially or totally, time after time, but still there would remain a conception of the unity and of the grandeur of Rome, that inspired men to put the shreds together again. The importance of Caracallus is that, by completing the processes of a century, he set the *maiestas populi Romani* upon the widest possible basis. The unifying element that held together the very diverse constituents of the empire was their common interest in Rome, and Caracallus' edict identified the whole population of the empire with Rome, thus providing the juridical foundation for the development of the later idea of *Romania*. It was perhaps an odd thing to do at the time, perhaps a little premature, certainly grandiose; but the importance of it appeared in the time of the invasions, when men, contrasting themselves with the barbarians, could know that they were truly *Romani*, and not merely such by courtesy.[2] Before this time came, certain circumstances prevented the meaning of 'Romanus' from degenerating into a polite word for 'subject'. There still existed men within the Roman world who were not Roman citizens; there were left at least slaves and *Latini Juniani*;[3] and it is very probable that there was a third class, but this depends upon the reconstruction and interpretation of the much disputed central sentence of the papyrus known as *Giessen* 40, δίδωμι τοί[ν]υν ἅπα[σιν ξένοις τοῖς κατὰ τ]ὴν οἰκουμένην π[ολιτ]είαν Ῥωμαίων [μ]ένοντος [παντὸς γένους πολιτευμ]άτων (or ]ατως) χωρ[ὶς] τῶν [δεδ]ειτικίων.[4] Who are the *dediticii* that they are debarred from citizenship, and what sort of document is this papyrus? These two questions must be taken together, since the answer to the first largely depends upon the answer to the second. If the papyrus contains the text of the Constitutio Antoniniana, the *dediticii* lose their interest since they can then be identified

---

[1] Tac. *Ann.* 4. 56. Cf. 4. 5, 'regibus qui magnitudine nostra proteguntur adversum externa imperia'. 'In the consulship of M. Porcius when the importance of Rome had increased greatly but had not yet reached its zenith, since the city of Carthage still stood and the kings were strong in Asia.'

[2] Cf. below, 451 ff.

[3] *Cod. Just.* 7. 6. 1. 6.

[4] 'So I give to all foreigners in the world Roman citizenship, provided that the status of all communities remains unchanged, except the *dediticii*.'

with the class of criminals *qui in dediticiorum numero sunt*, to whom it was but right and proper to refuse the citizenship.[1] But if Bicker-mann were right in holding this to be a supplementary decree granting citizenship to certain categories of immigrant barbarians, 'strangers' or 'foreigners' to the Empire, then the document would begin to assume a fresh importance; it would provide an additional explanation for the attachment and respect which was felt for the Roman Empire by even those barbarians who did much to destroy it, and it would show that an attempt was made to assimilate the *barbari*, in the same way that the various peregrine peoples had been assimilated earlier.

The third possibility, that by the *dediticii* of the papyrus are meant the inhabitants of the ordinary provincial communities of the lowest grade, the *civitates stipendiariae*, has now been effectively disproven together with its various corollaries.[2] It is a suggestion that should never have been made, since the status of *dediticius* in the original sense is purely temporary, and re-mains only pending the assignation to the peculiar *populus dediticius* of a particular and permanent position within the Roman system, i.e. until the Senate or Roman people or *Princeps* has given the new subjects *leges et iura*.[3] A refinement of this view was put forward by A. H. M. Jones.[4] He holds that under the Principate the native inhabitants of Egypt, and possibly of Cappadocia, *remained dediticii* because they never had any civic organization conferred upon them. In this status he finds the reason why no *Aegyptius* was capable of becoming a Roman citizen directly. Tacitus' description of Egypt as *insciam legum ignaram magistratuum* confirms Jones's general view, which is not in itself impossible.[5] Unfortunately the consequences which he draws from this view depend upon a reading of the text which is paleographically improbable.[6] He holds that the *Aegyptii* of the villages were to be excluded from the new 'nomal' cities lest the

---

[1] Stroux, art. cit. 284 f. But exclusion of Junian Latins is also required.

[2] For Egypt, cf. Bickermann, op. cit. 15 ff.

[3] Cf. above, 60 f., 96 f., 151 f.; also A. H. M. Jones, *JRS* 1936, 'Another interpretation of the Constitutio Antoniniana', 229 f.

[4] Jones, art. cit. 223 ff.

[5] Tac. *Hist.* 1. 11. 'Without knowledge or experience of charters and [self] government.' Cf. *Annales* 11. 19, 'senatum magistratus leges imposuit'—of the organization of a normal province. So too Jos. *c. Ap.* 2. 4.

[6] Jones accepted Wilhelm's μένοντος [οὐδένος ἐκτὸς τῶν πολιτευμ]άτων etc.

village administrative personnel should be drained off to the latter, and the village system collapse. But if, in the text, χωρὶς τῶν δεδειτικίων goes with the genitive absolute it cannot also go with the main verb δίδωμι.[1] So they get the citizenship. Jones has proved that conferment of the citizenship, indeed of any civic status or local autonomy, of *leges et iura*, annulled the condition of *dediticius*. The populations of the villages could hardly continue to be known as *dediticii* after the Constitutio Antoniniana.

The condition of *dediticius* was a continual possibility, even within the empire, as is shown by e.g. the Jewish revolts of the second century, but it was not a normally permanent category in the original sense. A new meaning, however, or a new application, has been proposed for the term by Bickermann, who sees in the *dediticii* a characteristic of the age, the large masses of conquered barbarians settled within the empire by Marcus and his successors, and sometimes known as *laeti*.[2] Bickermann holds in effect that Caracallus proposed to give the citizenship to barbarians who were attracted to the empire and ready to serve in the *militia armata*—the new *foederati*—but was not prepared to make Roman citizens of the *laeti* and the rest, who had been forcibly settled there. If this theory were true, it would provide a valuable link between a most characteristic practice of the later empire and the last period of the Principate, and help to clarify a little more of the lost history of the third century, and the various causes that led to the production of men like Stilicho. Unfortunately Bickermann is forced to base his view, apart from the short clause discussed below, upon evidence that is only relevant to the fourth century.[3] The attractiveness of this theory, which has received considerable support,[4] consists in the historical importance given by it to *P. Giessen* 40, which otherwise remains formal, rather than

---

[1] Mr. C. H. Roberts estimates that the gap can only be of 18–19 letters. His view, privately communicated, is that 'the break on the left-hand side of the papyrus is vertical, so that the amount of space to be filled is the same for each line, and in a hand of such a formal and regular character the number of letters in a given space hardly varies. In ll. 1 and 2 where the supplement may be regarded as certain, 18 letters are required to fill the gap: in l. 9 Wilhelm's restoration assumes 23 letters for a gap of the same extent. Consequently the reconstruction of which this line is the crux must be regarded with suspicion.'

[2] E. Bickermann, art. cit. 23 f.; for the positive scope of the Edict, cf. ibid. 13 f.

[3] Ibid. 24.

[4] e.g. from A. Segré, *Rivista di Filologia*, 1926, 471 ff. and De Sanctis, ibid., more enthusiastically, 497 f.

practical, in its immediate effect. If Caracallus was seeking to bring the *foederati*, or some of them, within the range of the citizenship, he was doing something which contributed directly to the perpetuation of the idea of the Roman empire, right down to the days of Charlemagne. But for the present this view of *P. Giessen* 40 must remain an hypothesis unless it can be proved from the text itself. Too much has perished from the records of the third century for us safely to connect directly with Caracallus the customs of the days of Theodosius, or even of Constantine.

Yet, after all, this document can hardly be the Constitutio Antoniniana itself, however cleverly restored by Stroux and Wilhelm. 'Whenever they migrate to my people', ὁσάκις ἂν ὑπεισ-έλθωσιν εἰς τοὺς ἐμοὺς ἀνθρώπους, is given in the sentence preceding the grant of citizenship as a definition of the persons affected; the meaning of this can only be understood as the Greek version of something like *quotiens ad nostros immigraverint*.[1] The *nostri* must be the Roman empire as a whole, and the preceding phrase seems to refer to men entering the empire from outside. But a wider question is, whether a measure capable of being described as *civitas omnibus data*[2] can have been effected by the three lines which this document, taken in that sense, assigns to it. Apart from the disputed reading in line nine the definition of status can hardly have been dismissed in eight words and a genitive absolute, whereas if the reference is only to one particular category of new citizens, and if there had been a previous decree explaining the general principles of an earlier and vaster grant of citizenship, the eight words and the genitive absolute may have sufficed. The document is not necessarily a specific enactment. In general style, all words and little matter, it resembles the discursive edict of Caracallus *de reditu Aegyptiorum*, and differs markedly from enactments like the *constitutiones* which granted the citizenship

---

[1] Stroux, art. cit. 275 f., it is true, avoids this pitfall—he makes ὁσάκις mean *quot*, and ὑπεισέλθωσιν a translation of e.g. *censentur* or *numerantur*. But the normal meaning of the verb in late papyri is 'to enter upon an office', 'to undertake a task', cf. Preisigke, *Wörterbuch*, s.v. Even so, can he escape the conclusion that the subject of the verb is *not* identical with what follows—εἰς τοὺς ἐμοὺς ἀνθρώπους? For the use of *noster* referring to the empire and emperors rather than to a portion of it see, apart from the phrase in SHA, *Niger* 4. 2 (*nostri* contrasted to *Sarmatae*), the phrase of the early second century *nec nostri saeculi est*, Pliny, *Ep.* 10. 97. Dio 73 (74). 1. 5, speaking of his own times, uses ἡμεῖς to mean the senatorial order; similarly ὑμέτερος is used by Aristides of the emperor–subjects relationship, below, 427 n. 11.

[2] SHA 10. 1. 2.

to the retired auxiliaries of particular provincial armies, listed in their units, or from Caracallus' own edict *de decurionibus,* about a specific problem of local government.[1] The document suggests a general proclamation of policy, or even the abstract of a speech introducing the formal *constitutio.* Δίδωμι τοίνυν sounds more like 'accordingly I propose to give' than the formula of the military diplomata *imperator . . . civitatem . . . dedit.*

The unsatisfactory condition of *P. Giessen* 40 has been sufficiently indicated. It is, however, undisputed that Caracallus was thinking in terms of sentiment, was even inspired by a grand boastfulness, rather than aiming at some material change in the circumstances of his time, when he made the world Roman. At all events, he finally stripped the citizenship of any specific content; the claim to it was based neither on Latin nor on Greek culture, nor on any service done for the state, nor on the existence of urban organization in some form, although there is proof that he, like his father, was not unaware of the importance of these things.[2] Henceforth a man was a Roman citizen simply because he was a free inhabitant of the civilized world.

---

[1] *A. and J.,* n. 193, n. 195 (*P. Giessen* 40, col. ii, *P. Oxy.* 1406).
[2] Above, 276, 278.

# PART III

# TECHNICAL PROBLEMS OF ROMAN STATUS

# XIII

## EXTERNS: DUAL CITIZENSHIP AND THE ENFRANCHISEMENT OF INDIVIDUALS

SIDE by side with the grant of Roman citizenship *en bloc* to communes in the late Republic and the Principate, Roman status was given extensively to individuals from provincial communities which remained peregrine. In the early Republic this occurs, if at all, in a carefully delimited form of *civitas sine suffragio*, which placed the recipient as a *municeps* in a special relationship towards Rome but left him otherwise in full enjoyment of his local citizenship. That he was not a member of the Roman body politic is shown by his lack of *suffragium* and of tribal affiliation, and by his inability to hold office at Rome.[1] It is not certain at what date the Romans began to grant the full franchise to individuals who did not settle within the Roman State. Livy records the grant of some form of citizenship to Carthaginian deserters who then settle in Sicily, in the late third century. The term is ambiguous, and no more than *civitas sine suffragio* may be meant, but the latest of these, who took the Roman names of his patron in the style normal in later times, may be the first instance of the full enfranchisement of a foreigner resident outside the Roman state. He was given a house at Rome, according to Asconius, but it is not clear that he settled in Italy.[2]

---

[1] Above, 40 f. On the development of viritane enfranchisement see especially E. Badian, *Foreign Clientelae* (Oxford, 1958), 152 ff.; earlier C. E. Goodfellow, *Roman Citizenship* (Bryn Mawr, 1935) collected information.

[2] Sosis, Moericus, and his companions receive *civitas* land, and a township in Sicily. Muttines is *factus civis Romanus*, a term applied to *cives s.s.* (cf. 42 n. 6), and gets a house at Rome (Livy 26. 21. 11–13; 27. 5. 7; 27. 8. 18; 38. 41. 12. Asc. *in Pis.* 12 C). Later in a list of Delphian *proxeni* (*SIG* 585, 32 f.) he and his sons appear as Valerii with Roman *praenomina*, and entitled 'Romans', while Muttines retains his personal name as a *cognomen*. Livy omits his Roman names and later calls him 'the Numidian'. There is no record of tribal affiliation for any of these, and the first group should be *municipes* rather than full citizens, since they reside in Sicily. If Muttines settled at Rome he rates with the Greek doctor who received *ius Quiritium* and a shop at Rome in 221, as a resident citizen, not an extern (Pliny, *NH* 29. 12). Cf. a rejected offer of *c.R.* to Praenestini in 216, Livy 23. 20. 2.

That grants of the full franchise remained rare in the following century is shown by the scanty record of particular instances before the age of Marius available to Cicero in his *pro Balbo*, and elsewhere, and by the formality of the procedure by which, down to the Social War, a separate legislative act was required on each occasion to enfranchise the priestesses of Ceres recruited regularly from the Greek cities of southern Italy.[1] The earliest organized categories of externs, newly enfranchised foreigners resident in alien communities, are the citizens of Latin colonies who secured the Roman status by holding their local magistracies, and those provincial or Italian persons who secured it as a reward for a successful prosecution under the *lex repetundarum*. Both these groups originate in the time of Gaius Gracchus (*c.* 125–122 B.C.). The section of the law of 123 which provides for this enfranchisement uses the term 'iusti cives Romani sunto', and specifically regulates the tribal enrolment and the voting right of such persons.[2] The formula implies the existence at the time of its invention of another grade of less perfect citizenship, which it replaces, and which can only have been the *civitas sine suffragio*.

The rarity of such grants before the age of Marius may be connected with the attitude towards citizenship revealed by the primitive concept of *postliminium*.[3] This was a legal procedure by which the Roman who either through *force majeure* of piracy or war, or of his own free will, has settled in the territory of another state, recovers his status as a Roman citizen on returning to the Roman territory. Such a person was regarded, surprisingly to modern thought, as ceasing to be a Roman citizen through the change of domicile. The concept is evidently archaic, and can be connected with the interchange of civil rights in early Latium which survived in the *ius migrationis* of the Latin colonies down to 177 B.C., by which the colonists obtained Roman citizenship

[1] *Pro Balbo* 55. The urban praetor of *c.* 96 proposed 'nominatim . . . ut ea civis Romana esset'. But note that in *pro Balbo* Cicero is nominally limited to those from *civitates foederatae*, which were rare outside Italy.

[2] Above, 111; for the date, 215–16. *FIRA* i². 7. 77, 'in eam tribum suffragium erunto inque eam tribum censento militiaeque eis vocatio esto, etc.'

[3] Cf. above, 34; below, 302 nn. 3, 5. Pomponius cites the actual words of Q. Mucius (*Dig.* 49. 15. 5. 1), while Festus s.v. cites Aelius Gallus; Cic. *pro Balbo* 28, *Topica* 36–7 (citing Scaevola and Servius on etymology), *de Or.* 1. 181–2. Later *Dig.* 49. 15. Cf. *RE* 22. 1. cols. 864 f. A. Watson, *Law of Persons in the Later Roman Republic* (Oxford, 1967), 237 ff. For *ius migrationis*, above, 103, 107.

on removing to Roman territory. The underlying thought is that a man can only be a political member of the community in which he resides, and that when he leaves it he ceases to belong. The antiquity of *postliminium* is shown by the fact that two juris-prudents in the age of Marius discussed it as a term of which the philological derivation was uncertain. Its active reality throughout Roman history appears from the fact that the classical lawyers of the Severan age were still expounding it at length in terms that differ only slightly from the earlier defini-tions. The effectiveness of such concepts in the Republican period is shown by the whole history of *civitas sine suffragio*, and in later times by the formal insistence of Cicero on the incom-patibility of the Roman citizenship with that of any other state, even in his own day, when the rule was beginning to be dis-regarded by certain privileged persons. He repeats this doctrine in two speeches separated by an interval of some fourteen years, and since the earlier passage is an aside not particularly relevant to his argument, its basic truth is established.[1] Hence it is not surprising that the Romans in the earlier period were slow to adopt the notion of granting the full franchise, with social and political affiliation, to externs residing outside their territory. This chariness has its analogy in the reluctance with which the settlement of colonies of Roman citizens in territory outside Italy was admitted by senatorial opinion in the age of Marius.[2] A technicality about the enfranchisement by manumission of the interpreter Menander, in the second century, confirms the im-pression that the Romans still regarded the enfranchised extern as a person liable to resume his former status, like the earlier *municipes*, if he returned to his native city.[3]

[1] Cic. *pro Balbo* 28, repeats the statement of *pro Caecina* 100: 'cum ex nostro iure duarum civitatum nemo esse possit, tum amittitur haec civitas denique cum is qui profugit receptus est in exilium.' For non-observance by Roman residents at Athens cf. *pro Balbo* 30, and for the refusal of Atticus, Nepos, *Att.* 3. 1.

[2] Velleius 1. 15. 1; 2. 7, 6–8, indicates that the objection to extra-Italian colonies at Carthage (123) and Narbo (118) was social as well as partisan: 'vires refovendae magis quam spargendae', 'cives Romanos ad censendum ex provincia in Italiam revocaverunt.'

[3] Cic. *pro Balbo* 28. A special law was required to ensure 'ut is Publicius si domum revenisset et inde Romam redisset ne minus civis esset'. As a Greek by origin the freedman was thought liable to revert to his former status if he returned to his *patria*, even though on Roman service. It is clear that the loss of citizenship by change of soil was originally regarded as automatic. None of the certainly Republican texts suggests that the *intention* of the emigrant was relevant. The

Only at the end of the second century do viritane grants begin to proliferate. Cicero in the *pro Balbo* lists numerous grants made by proconsuls as rewards for service to Rome, ranging from Marius down to Sulla and Pompeius, but can quote not a single instance before Marius. Badian, cataloging the known instances from the later Republic quotes no other before Marius.[1] The absence of enfranchised Greeks from outside Italy before the civil wars, in the same lists, confirms the impression, while Sulla's Greek sea-captains received every privilege *except* the Roman citizenship.[2] The most notable early instances are the enfranchisement of two whole cohorts of Umbrian infantry by Marius in the Cimbric War, and that of a squadron of Spanish cavalrymen by Pompeius Strabo in the Social War.[3] Strabo and some later proconsuls were given the power of enfranchisement by enabling laws, a fact which accounts for the frequency of such grants in the following period.[4] The *nomina* of provincial citizens in the inscriptions of the Principate continually reveal the activity of the late Republican proconsuls.[5] Badian has argued from the plea of Marius in excuse of his enfranchisements—'the clash of arms silenced the voice of law'—that Marius had no such enabling law, and that the system begins with the *lex Julia* of 90 under

---

*animus remanendi* first appears at the end of Pomponius' discussion of Q. Scaevola's doctrine (*Dig.* 49. 15. 3). Here it is very doubtful (*pace* Watson, op. cit. 242) whether Pomponius is still summarizing Scaevola, whose objections are based on the binding oath taken by Regulus (sc. not to return) rather than his personal intention, or giving learned opinion in general.

[1] Cic. *pro Balbo* 46–51, 55. Badian, op. cit. 302–8, adds only T. Didius (*cos.* 94) to Cicero's list of enfranchising proconsuls, and doubtfully.

[2] Cf. *S.C. de Asclepiade*, etc., *FIRA* i². 35. Seleucus of Rhosus received all this and the citizenship as well from Octavian a generation later; cf. *FIRA* i². 55, and below, 296 f. For the first enfranchisement of Sicilian Greeks see below, 306 f.

[3] For Marius, *pro Balbo* 46, Val. Max. 5. 2. 8, Plut. *Marius* 28. Strabo's decree preserved in a bronze tablet (*ILS* 8888) states 'Cn. Pompeius Sex. f. . . . virtutis causa equites Hispanos cives Romanos fecit . . . ex lege Iulia', etc., and adds a list of thirty persons. Archias' friends could not help him till 89 (*Arch.* 5–7).

[4] Cf. Sisenna fr. 120 P: 'milites ut lex Calpurnia concesserat virtutis ergo civitate donari' (c. 90 B.C.). Cic. *pro Balbo*. 19, on the *lex Cornelia Gellia* of 73: 'qua lege . . . esse sanctum ut cives Romani sint ii quos Cn. Pompeius de consili sententia singillatim civitate donaverit'. The later enfranchisements of Pompeius and Caesar suggest that this power was included in the *leges de imperio* from the *lex Gabinia de piratis* onwards. It was conferred on the members of the Second Triumvirate by a *lex Munatia Aemilia* (*FIRA* i². 55. 2 pref.). Cf. below, 310 n. 3

[5] Cf. the lists in Badian, op. cit. 309–10, 'Names of early Republican *gentes* in Spain, Gaul and Africa', 311–21, 'Members of the Roman *gentes* known to have served in Spain, Gaul and Africa'.

which Strabo acted.[1] Hence viritane enfranchisement made no great headway earlier. Cicero indeed generalizes about provincials from Africa, Sardinia, and Sicily becoming Roman citizens after these early conquests, but gives no precise dates.[2] An objection may yet be urged that among the common *nomina* of provincial citizens of later times in the lists of Badian, the names of proconsuls of the pre-Marian period play a notable part. Narbonensis can provide some eighty Domitii and fifty Fabii, names connected with the proconsuls who first conquered the area, Domitius Ahenobarbus (*cos.* 122) and Fabius Maximus (*cos.* 121), and whose descendants hardly ever operated there.[3] If the Pompeii of the western provinces are thought to derive their citizenship directly from grants made to their forebears by Pompeius Magnus, the same should hold good in some instances for the earlier imperators. Against this Badian rightly remarks that names alone do not prove the acquisition of Roman citizenship, since many provincials in all later periods adopt Roman names without authority, and that before the long-resisted enfranchisement of Italy any extensive enfranchisement of ordinary provincials is improbable.[4]

With the proliferation of viritane enfranchisement questions arose about the precise status of such externs in relation to the Roman State and to their former civic communities. It was argued above that the Ciceronian principle, set out at some length in the *pro Balbo*, of the incompatibility of the Roman citizenship with that of any other community, was gradually abandoned in favour of the notion of dual citizenship, combining the Roman franchise with that of a local *patria*, after the end of the Republic.[5] The theme has been examined in greater depth by F. de Visscher in a series of articles in which he proposed the paradoxical doctrine that already in the middle Republican period the Ciceronian principle applied only to 'Romans by

---

[1] Above, 294 n. 3, cf. Badian, op. cit. 206, 259 f.

[2] *Pro Balbo* 24, 'stipendiarios ex Africa Sicilia Sardinia . . . multos civitate donatos'; ibid. 40–1, 'si Afris si Sardis si Hispanis agris . . . multatis virtute adipisci licet civitatem'. These were provinces acquired before 140 B.C.

[3] Cf. Badian, op. cit. 309, 313, 314.

[4] Ibid. 256, 259. For provincial Pompeii see below, 308 ff. The three Hispani in *ILS* 8888 with Roman *nomina* probably took these at the time from members of Strabo's *consilium*, and not before enfranchisement, though before the tablet was engraved (cf. Badian l.c.).

[5] Above, 245 f., 271 f.

origin', whom he eventually defined as citizens inhabiting the territory of the Roman State in Italy. Enfranchised persons from outside the Roman boundaries were free, he held, to retain and exercise their local citizenship in private and public spheres if the 'city' concerned permitted them to do so. The doctrine is paradoxical because of the logical objection that, when enfranchised, the new Roman citizen should be bound in all respects by Roman legal usage. De Visscher was constrained to admit that in matters of personal status, succession, and testamentary disposition, the enfranchised person resident in his place of origin followed Roman civil law, but he sought to show that in other activities such persons lived according to local usage and took part in the public life of their former 'city'.[1]

The case was largely based upon a close examination of the edict of Octavian granting Roman franchise and other privileges to Seleucus of Rhodes in *c.* 41 B.C., and of the edict of Augustus made in 7–6 B.C., limiting the local immunities of the enfranchised Greeks of Cyrenaica.[2] The argument is that the status of Seleucus and of others enfranchised by the same enactment represents the norm of Republican usage rather than a recent innovation. The edict granted Seleucus a general freedom from the liturgies and fiscal obligations explicitly of the Roman State, and perhaps conditionally from those of his 'city', but allowed him to retain his local honours and priesthoods if he wished, and to exercise a choice of jurisdiction when a defendant either in a criminal or in a civil suit: he could appear either before the local courts of Rhosus, or before a Roman proconsular tribunal, or he might (apparently) demand the arbitration of an independent 'free city'. Finally in the event of a capital prosecution at Rhosus he was given the right of appealing by private embassy to the Senate at Rome or to a Roman provincial governor.[3] Though at

---

[1] For the original thesis see F. de Visscher, *Les Édits d'Auguste* (1940), 108 ff.; *Ant. Class.* 13 (1945), 11 ff., 14 (1946), 29 ff.; *Bull. Ac. Roy. Belg.* (1947), 50 ff.; *CRAI* 1939, 111 ff.; for his supporters cf. A. Wilhelm, *Anz. Ak. Wiss. Wien* (ph. hist. Kl.), 1943, 1 ff.; L. Wenger, *Mélanges de Visscher*, R.I.D.A. (1949), 521 ff.; E. Schönbauer, *Anz. Oest. Ak. Wiss.* 1954, 18 f. *Contra* esp. V. Arango-Ruiz, *Riv. Fil.* 1930, 222 f. H. F. Jolowicz, *Historical Introduction to the Study of Roman Law*[2] (Cambridge, 1952), 542 ff.

[2] *FIRA* i[2]. 55. 1–3; 68. 3. For a full bibliography see R. Sherk, *Roman Documents from the Greek East* (Baltimore, Md., 1969), 294.

[3] So much seems reasonably certain. I omit here the suggestion, hotly debated, that Seleucus was offered a choice not only of tribunals but of legal systems, i.e.

first sight this all seems to mean that Seleucus was no longer an ordinary citizen of Rhosus, it is argued that apart from these exceptions Seleucus remained subject to the civic laws of Rhosus as a local citizen. The Senate had granted somewhat similar privileges *without* the Roman franchise in 78 B.C. to three navarchs of Greek origin, who certainly retained their local status otherwise, while earlier the *lex repetundarum* did much the same for those who refused *civitas*. Hence it might seem that the immunities of Seleucus are independent of the grant of Roman franchise.[1] Externs, it is argued, may receive these special privileges as an extra reward for their services, setting them free from their local ties, but without them they remain subject to the laws and duties of their local citizenship. In neither case are they automatically and totally deprived of their local citizenship by acquiring that of Rome.[2]

Clearly the edict reveals an attempt to adjust the status of 'externs' to fit their practical circumstances. There are many ambiguities in the somewhat fragmentary text, of which some clauses are totally lost. But it does not consistently favour the hypothesis of de Visscher. The clause about the permissive retention of local offices implies that without it Seleucus would forfeit

Greek or Roman law. This depends on conjectural restorations (cf. Sherk's app. crit.). The document (*FIRA* i². 55. 2) is badly damaged, and the precise meaning of many of its clauses is much less certain than scholars maintain. But there are close similarities with the edict of Octavian *de veteranis* (298–9). The grant of fiscal immunity, ἀνεισφορίαν τῶν ὑπαρχόντων comes in the first two sections of the edict (2. 1–2), which are concerned solely with the grant of Roman citizenship itself (*census*, tribe, freedom from *munus militare* and *m. publicum*). So too the edict *de veteranis* specifies both *immunitas omnium rerum* and *muneris publici fungendi vacatio*, in the clause granting citizenship *optimo iure*. Next in the edict of Seleucus (2. 3) comes the clause about the permissive retention of local offices. After a missing section, apparently concerned with *conubium*, the edict deals (2. 8) with the local judicial privileges of Seleucus. These may be limited to prosecutions under criminal law, but a short phrase—[κρίσ]ιν τε συνίστασθαι—is commonly interpreted to refer to *litis contestatio* in civil actions. The beginning of s. 3 may have granted exemption from local civic dues and duties to him only if he had this previously (cf. 299 n. 3).

[1] *FIRA* i². 35. 10–15. They are to be free from civic taxes and obligations— ἀλειτούργητοι . . . καὶ ἀνείσφοροι—in their native cities, Carystus, Miletus, Clazomene, and to have a choice of jurisdiction in civil courts, together with an unrestricted right of petition *de rebus suis* to the Roman Senate. For *lex repetundarum* see 300 f.

[2] De Visscher also stressed Octavian's reference to Seleucus as 'my admiral and your citizen' in the later letter. But this refers to Seleucus' career *before* he received the Roman citizenship, and the language is diplomatic rather than technical.

this part of his former status on becoming a Roman citizen. So too the clauses about jurisdiction are permissive: they allow him to plead locally if he likes. Those clauses should be related to the fact that Rhosus was a 'free city'.[1] Even in the Principate free cities occasionally abused their independence at the expense of Roman citizens.[2] These clauses are only concerned with the position of Seleucus as a defendant. They may be intended to make explicit the privileged judicial position which a Roman citizen should enjoy even in a free city, throughout the Roman world.

The edict about Seleucus resembles in its effect a *lex Antonia* of 40 B.C. granting citizenship to certain gentry of Cos—unpublished and fragmentary—and, more informatively, the later and briefer edict of Octavian granting citizenship and 'immunity' to certain veterans in Egypt.[3] They receive the Roman citizenship together with a general immunity from dues on property and from the 'public' liturgies and military service of the Roman state. The text also lists a number of local civic liturgies which they cannot be required to hold against their will, in a clause not found in the extant part of the Seleucus edict. Like that it also grants the enfranchised veterans the right to maintain their previous civic honours and offices.[4] But unlike that text it grants no privileges in local jurisdiction nor any special protection against capital prosecution, which though desirable in a free city were nominally unnecessary in a Roman province. The comparison of the two texts shows a common pattern, but also shows

---

[1] The autonomous status of Rhosus in underlined in the letters of Octavian, though Pliny, *NH* 5. 80 does not list it as a *civitas libera*.

[2] Cf. Dio 60. 24. 4, Tac. *Ann.* 12. 58. 2.

[3] *FIRA* i². 56. The text though virtually complete is careless and ungrammatical, but there is little difficulty about its general meaning. Its Latin terminology is parallel to the Greek of the Rhosian edict, and its clauses about citizenship, tribal assignation, and census rights are similar. It contains a grant both of Roman and of municipal 'immunity' (ll. 5, 8–11, 15–16), and also a clause about freedom from billeting absent from the extant part of the Rhosian edict (cf. 296 n. 3).—For the *lex Antonia*, of which only the preamble appears to be relatively intact see R. Herzog, *Historische Zeitschrift* 125 (1921–2), 212 n. 3, who noted similarities with the *S.C. de Asclepiade*. It proves that the Seleucus document was not isolated. I owe this reference to the vigilance of Miss. S. M. Sherwin-White.—Whether Caesar's grants of *civitas* with *immunitas* to oriental Greeks (*FIRA* i². 68. 3, cf. Jos. *Ant. Jud.* 14. 137, to Antipater) anticipated the formula of these documents is quite unknown.

[4] It is not to be assumed that the veterans concerned were all domiciled in Egypt, where cities and civic honours in the strict sense were rare.

that the conditions of such grants were tailored to the local circumstances.

De Visscher did not plumb the implication of the clauses in the two edicts of Octavian about *immunitas rerum*, exemption from fiscal dues on property. This occurs in both edicts as part of the section that grants the citizenship and other privileges within the Roman state. It can refer only to remissions from Roman taxation, and hence proves nothing about dual status.[1] Neither text in its present condition clearly includes a general remission of local civic liturgies and local tax obligations. But the edict *de veteranis* contains a second clause about *immunitas*, obscurely worded, in a separate section which is otherwise concerned with local privileges.[2] The clause seems to mean that the veterans are to retain local immunity if they possessed it previously. A similar reference to local immunity was restored by Arango-Ruiz at the beginning of the similar section of the edict of Seleucus dealing with the retention of local privileges.[3] The wording of this section in the edict *de veteranis* is noteworthy. It does not use the language of command but that of permission, appropriate to dealings with provincial communes that were nominally autonomous in their internal affairs. The implication is that the cities could refuse to receive the externs back into the fold which they had abandoned: as Roman citizens they have no claim to the *beneficia* of their former *patria* such as *immunitas rerum*, just as it has no claim on them for the performance of liturgies. The Roman citizenship does not create a special advantage for the externs as resident foreigners—it cancels any claim to local immunity that they formerly possessed unless this is preserved by a special enactment, which the edict in fact presses upon the city authority. Such *beneficia* can be restored at the wish of both parties. This is the opposite of what is commonly said about *immunitas*, because *immunitas* has not been sufficiently distinguished, as it is

---

[1] *FIRA* i². 55. 2. 1–2 deals with *vacatio militiae*, tribal assignment, voting rights, and *census*, as well as *immunitas rerum*. So too ibid. 56. 1–14. Cf. K. M. Atkinson, *Studies presented to V. Ehrenberg*, (Oxford, 1966), 21 ff., for a similar view.

[2] *FIRA* i². 56. 16–22. 'item quemadmodum veterani immunes essent eorum esse (sc. immunes) volui. quaecumque sacerdotia quosque honores . . . habuerunt item ut habeant . . . permitti do. invitis eis neque magistratus ceteros neque laegatum neque . . . emptorem tributorum esse placet . . .'

[3] The supplement is necessarily uncertain, but the rest is closely parallel. Note the more certain restoration of the suggestive phrase: . . . τὸ] δίκαιον ἐὰν χ[ρῆ]σθ[αι] [θέλῃ ἐξεῖναι].

distinguished in all the Republican documents, from *muneris vacatio*, or its Greek equivalents, and freedom from Roman taxes has been confused with freedom from local dues.[1]

The general conclusion is the opposite to the theory of de Visscher: without the special exemptions the extern would be totally sundered from his former *patria*. De Visscher had difficulty in proving that the modified status of externs revealed by the edict of Seleucus was older, as his view required, than the date of the edict. The general argument that the notion of dual citizenship had already been introduced into the Roman state by the development of *civitas sine suffragio* and by the growth of the *municipia* in the middle Republican period is not relevant, because these forms of communal status had ceased to correspond to the Roman notion of an autonomous *civitas* long before the Ciceronian age,[2] while the *municipes* of the late Republic were for major matters under the direct government and jurisdiction of the consuls and praetors at Rome.[3] Individual instances of externs in the earlier period, such as Ennius of Rudiae, are too ill documented to prove their precise condition.[4]

Precise evidence about the status of externs, to which too little attention has been paid, exists in the *lex repetundarum* of 123 B.C., and in the *pro Balbo* of 56 B.C. The former offered a reward to successful plaintiffs in an alternative form. They could receive either the Roman citizenship together with exemption from

---

[1] The edict de Seleuco separates ἀνεισφορία τῶν ὑπαρχόντων from λειτουργίας δημοσίας πάρεσις. That de veteranis separates *immunitas omnium rerum* from *liberi militiae* and *muneribus publicis fungendi vacatio*. In the *S.C. de Asclepiade (FIRA* i². 35. 10–15) the term ἀλειτούργητοι is distinct from ἀνείσφοροι, which is related to the payment of contributions ἐκ τῶν ὑπαρχόντων. It is clear from the *lex Antonia de Termessibus (FIRA* i². 11. 30–5) that Roman citizens of all classes were not usually exempt from the *vectigalia* of provincial communes; cf. *S.C. de Mytilenaeis (IGRR* iv. 33) on local ἀτέλεια. The *S.C. de Aphrodisiensibus (FIRA* i². 38) uses ἀτέλεια instead of ἀνεισφορία for freedom from Roman taxes. Thus exemption from local dues was an extra privilege granted separately, as in the Triumviral edicts (296–8 nn.), not included in the immunity from Roman taxes.

[2] *Édits d'Auguste*, 110 f.; *Ant. Class.* 14. 55 f. He also invokes the much abused statement of Hadrian in Aulus Gellius, *NA* 16. 13. 4, which is irrelevant to externs *viritim c.R. donati* like Seleucus, Cf. above, 201 n. 3, 363 n. 1.

[3] Cf. the indictment of Cicero's clients, Roscius of Ameria and Cluentius of Larinum, recently enfranchised municipalities, before Roman courts on capital charges, and the civil suit of Caecina, concerning municipal estates at Volaterrae. For *cives sine suffragio* and *municipes* cf. above, 45 ff.

[4] Cf. above, 291 n. 2. For Ennius see *RE* 5. 2589–90 on Cic. *Arch.* 22, Nepos, *Cato* 1. 4.

military service, or the *ius provocationis* together with a dispensa-
tion both from military service and from the civic liturgies *of
their own states*. The second alternative combines two main
advantages of the Roman status, *ius provocationis* and immunity
from local liturgies, with the extra privilege of *militiae vacatio*,
which is common to both alternatives, while leaving the benefits
of local status otherwise intact. It follows that the provincial
notables who accepted the first alternative were automatically
freed from local civic obligations by becoming Roman citizens.
Nothing is said about *immunitas rerum*, fiscal immunity, precisely
because like *militiae vacatio* this was not inherent in the grant of
citizenship itself, though a later law adds this too. This evidence
takes the rule of incompatibility back to later second century B.C.[1]

In the *pro Balbo*, delivered only fifteen years before the edict
about Seleucus, Cicero makes it plain that Cornelius Balbus
ceased to be a citizen of Gades after his acquisition of the Roman
citizenship. This is stated explicitly in connection with the compact of *hospitium* or 'guest-friendship' that Balbus made with his
former citizens, a relationship which by itself implies that the
two parties are from different states.[2] Cicero also refers to the
process of *repetitio* which would have been necessary if the city
of Gades had wanted to 'claim back' its former citizen, and quotes
a recent instance of such a suit by the city of Messana.[3] Cornelius
Balbus, who was enfranchised by Pompeius in about 73 B.C., and
after 61 B.C. held Roman appointments, clearly did not retain
his local citizenship as an extern.[4] Cicero nowhere suggests any

[1] *FIRA* i[2]. 7. 76–9. The restoration of 'militiae munerisque poplici in su[a
quoiusque ceiv]itate [vocatio esto]' is not in doubt. Possibly this section also included a choice of jurisdiction as one of the supplementary benefits alternative to
the Roman citizenship, s. 86: 'de ea re eius [optio est]o utrum velit vel in sua
ceivitat[e . . .' This appears among the rewards of the *lex repetundarum* from
Tarentum, possibly the lex Servilia of *c.* 106/5 B.C., which also seems to include
*immunitas omnium rerum*, which appears here for the first time combined with
*civitas*. See *Epigraphica* IX (1947) 33 f. for the text. Cf. above, 216 n. 1.

[2] Cic. *pro Balbo* 42: 'hospitium fecit ut et civitate illum mutatum esse fatere-
tur'; 43: 'defendunt amore ut suum civem, testimonio ut nostrum, officio ut ex
nobilissimo civi sanctissimum hospitem'. Cf. the tablets of *hospitium* collected in
*ILS* 6093–6100.

[3] *Pro Balbo* 38, 52. M. Cassius is *ex hypothesi* not a double citizen, though whether
he resides at Messana or at Rome, where he was prosecuted in 64 under the *lex
Papia*, is not clear.

[4] He served as *praefectus fabrum* with Caesar in Spain in 61–60, and in Gaul after
59 (ibid. 63), and also conducted a public prosecution at Rome (ibid. 57). For the
date of his first arrival in Rome see 302 n. 7.

distinction between kinds of citizens to whom the rule of incompatibility did or did not apply. He talks simply of *nostri*, and
elsewhere, in the context of loss of status, argues that there was
no distinction between 'new' and 'old' citizens.[1]

In a later paper de Visscher modified his theory to take account
of the history of Balbus.[2] Noting the stress that Cicero lays on
the formal change of domicile (*solum vertere*) in the procedures of
voluntary change of citizenship by *dicatio* and recovery of it by
*postliminium*, he ingeniously suggested that the extern did not
forfeit his local citizenship until or unless he moved from his
native community, his *patria*, to the territory of Rome.[3] He has
here uncovered the primitive basis of the doctrine of incompatibility: a man cannot be in two places at the same time.[4] But
Cicero no longer holds the primitive doctrine. He distinguishes
the formal change of *civitas*, the act of *dicatio*, from the antecedent
change of domicile, which no longer by itself affects the status
of a man unconditionally.[5] Hence Cicero does not support de
Visscher's view of Republican externs. It may well be true that
in practice externs who remained in their native land continued
to exercise their local rights, especially in Greek cities, which
were accustomed to the notion of isopolity and multiple citizenship.[6] The evidence of the *pro Balbo* for the career of Balbus, on
the usual interpretation, suggests that he ceased to be regarded
as a Gaditanus before he left Gades for Rome in the company
of the C. Julius Caesar in 60 B.C.[7] Besides, the amended view
fails to explain why it was necessary in the edict of Octavian to
assert the right of Seleucus to retain local civic privileges as a

---

[1] *Pro Caec.* 101.

[2] *Bull. Ac. Roy. Belg.* 40 (1954), 49 ff.

[3] *Pro Balbo* 28; 'neque solum dicatione . . . cum hanc ante amittere non potuis-
sent quam hoc solum civitatis mutatione vertissent, sed etiam postliminio potest
civitatis fieri mutatio.'                                   [4] Cf. above 292, and n. 3.

[5] In *pro Balbo* 27, 28, 30 (cf. above, n. 3) it is the *dicatio* and *adscitio*, not the
change of soil, that effects the *civitatis mutatio*. His account of *postliminium* (ibid. 28,
30) suggests that originally the change of soil effected the change of status, which
was reversed by the process of *postliminium* when the expatriate returned.

[6] Cf. *pro Balbo* 30, *Arch.* 5, and below, 304 n. 3.

[7] Cf. 301 nn. 2, 4. It is commonly assumed that young Caesar first met Balbus
at Gades when quaestor of Further Spain in 68 (cf. *pro Balbo* 63, Suet. *Iul.* 7) and
that he renewed the acquaintance in 61 as propraetor, after which Balbus returned
with Caesar to Rome in 60. Hence the act of *hospitium* 'many years before this
time' (i.e. 56, *pro Balbo* 41) should precede Balbus' emigration from Gades to
Rome. But this is uncertain. Cf. *RE* iv. 1269 f.

resident of Rhosus, since he should only lose them if he ceased to reside there.

There is supplementary evidence for the exclusive principle in a clause of the provincial statute of Bithynia drafted seven years before the prosecution of Balbus. The *lex Pompeia*, which introduced several other Roman usages into the municipal charters of Bithynia, to the detriment of Hellenistic democracy, laid down that no city in Bithynia might co-opt citizens from other cities in Bithynia. The bar was adjacency; a man might be tempted to serve two masters. That the rule was not effectively observed in the time of Trajan underlines its alien character.[1]

It would seem that de Visscher's demonstration holds good only from the Triumviral period onwards. The edicts of Octavian reveal an attempt to strike a balance between the privileged position of an extern freed from all civic obligations to his place of residence, and a dual citizenship in which both elements are active. But de Visscher must be right in holding that the new pattern was not a sudden innovation—elements of it are discernible in privileges granted to Latins by the *lex repetundarum* of 123 and to Asclepias in the Sullan period, while Cicero reveals that in his age even Roman citizens from Italy ignored the formal rule of incompatibility by holding municipal offices in provincial cities.[2] Yet Cicero's formal pronouncement in two widely separated speeches seems absolute. More attention might be paid to its wording: 'duarum civitatum civis noster esse iure civili nemo potest'.[3] He explains later that the great difficulty lay in the *varietas iuris* that would ensue under dual or multiple status. In a similar discussion in the *pro Caecina* he makes it clear that he uses *ius civile* in this connection to denote the law of property and persons rather than public and political rights. Status and the bequest of property can only be regulated by a single system of private law. But a single person can at different times hold public office and perform public duties in different cities or

---

[1] Pliny, *Epp.* 10. 114. 1: 'lege . . . Pompeia permissum Bithynicis civitatibus adscriberes ibi . . . cives dum ne quem earum civitatum quae sunt in Bithynia.' Cf. originally E. G. Hardy, *Correspondence of Trajan* etc., ad loc.

[2] *Pro Balbo* 30. Cf. the offer to Atticus of Athenian franchise and office which he refused on Cicero's ground; Nepos, *Att.* 3. 1.

[3] *Pro Balbo* 28. He here repeats the statement made fourteen years earlier in *pro Caecina* 100, where it is certainly to be taken literally, since it does not serve the immediate forensic argument: 'cum ex nostro iure duarum civitatum nemo esse possit, tum amittitur haec civitas denique cum is qui profugit receptus est in exilium'.

states without legal confusion, and can manage his property under different local codes.[1] Hence the possibility of moving towards a dual citizenship, as in the Principate, in which a man's public life lay in his local *patria*, while his status and property were determined by the rules of the Roman state. This is very different from the situation in Cicero's analysis of the dual *patria* in the *de Legibus*, in which public life and civil law are determined by the *patria iuris*—the Roman state—and the municipality is merely one's *patria naturae* and has no legal claim. The edict of Seleucus has barely initiated the transition from this regime to the dual citizenship of the later Principate. Both it and the edict *de veteranis* affirm that the beneficiaries are to be *cives Romani optimo iure immunes*. This implies the very opposite of de Visscher's theory; they are equated with Roman citizens of Italy, the true 'Romans by origin', who were *immunes* simply because they had been exempt from tribute since its abolition in Italy in 167 B.C.: the *immunitas* is not part of the citizenship, and was added or withheld at will.[2]

It is often forgotten that law and its enforcement are very different matters. No one at Rome was interested in preventing the enfranchised peregrine or the itinerant Roman from holding the public offices or using the local courts of the city of his domicile if it suited him. The power of such persons can be seen from the virtual dictatorship that the elder Balbus and his son later exercised at Gades, and from the dominant position held at Utica and other provincial cities by resident Italians in incidental stories of the late Republic.[3] An issue arose only if the privileged status of individuals conflicted with the interests of the Roman state. Such a conflict is revealed by the third edict of Augustus from Cyrene, dated to 7–6 B.C. A numerous body of externs claimed exemption from certain duties in the cities of Cyrenaica.

---

[1] *Pro Balbo* 31, 'dissimilitudo . . . civitatum varietatem iuris habeat necesse est'. Cf. *pro Caec.* 97: 'lege agant et suum ius persequantur et omni iure civili . . . utantur'; ibid. 101–2, *nexa et hereditates* are the core of Roman status retained by the demoted Volaterrans; similarly *pro Arch.* 11. For the local use of Greek civic law by resident Romans in *civitates liberae* see A. J. Marshall, *GRBS* 10 (1969), 255 ff. on *SIG* ii⁴. 785, Cic. *pro Flacco*, 70–83.

[2] For Cic. *de Legg.* 2. 2. 5, see above, 154. For *cives immunes*, above, 296 ff.; below, 334 f.; for the disjunction in the early *lex repetundarum*, cf. above, 301.

[3] Cic. *ad Fam.* 10. 32. 1–3, after Gades became a *municipium*; cf. also *pro Balbo* 43, For Utica etc. cf. below, 344 n. 3; see also Cic. *Verr.* ii. 4. 15, 19, for an extern of Messana continuing in local politics.

Augustus replied by cutting down the immunities in question. The document, which gives only the reply of Augustus, though entire, is obscure in its precise meaning at a crucial point. On the most literal interpretation of the main sentence, all externs who had not received *immunitas omnium rerum* together with the Roman citizenship were required henceforth to perform local liturgies, apparently, in the Greek cities.[1]

The literal meaning of the document, however, involves a curious illogicality and a surprising confusion of *immunitas rerum* with *muneris publici vacatio*, in Latin terms. The liability to local liturgies is inferred nominally from the liability to imperial taxes. It is possible that the Greek text has incorrectly rendered the original decision of Augustus, and that the edict merely rejected a false claim of ordinary externs to *immunitas rerum*, either local or imperial or both. If so, it adds nothing to what is known from the earlier edicts of Octavian. De Visscher and others have argued that it treats the externs as retaining their local franchise in full, and hence that it recognizes a completely dual citizenship. But nothing is said in the edict about the rights of externs in other matters—such as liability for local magistracies or exemption from local jurisdiction, detailed at length in the earlier edicts. This edict, as it stands, breaks the rule of incompatibility solely in the area of liturgies. The liturgical duties of externs are inferred from their lack of *immunitas rerum*, and nothing else is laid down.

De Visscher remarked that this edict left the incompatibility of his 'Romans by origin' untouched. But only just. The text concerns externs of two grades, those who have and those who have not been given *immunitas omnium rerum* with the Roman citizenship. The former belong to the category of *cives Romani optimo iure immunes*. Augustus does not hesitate to restrict their privilege to property owned at the time of their enfranchisement. How long before a limit is imposed on the immunity of the original *cives Romani optimo iure*, the immigrants from Italy, who were numerous in Cyrenaica?

The final conclusion from all this evidence should be that it was a special privilege, and very far from normal, in the Republican period, for the extern to retain the formal right to exercise his local citizenship, and that this privilege was limited

[1] See below, Appendix 334 f. For the text, *FIRA* i².  68. 3.

to a select number of *cives Romani optimo iure immunes*. The Augustan edict of 6 B.C. remains the earliest evidence for the compulsory submission of externs to some of the duties of local citizenship in varying degrees—unless after all it is solely concerned with the payment of Roman taxes.

## ENFRANCHISEMENT OF GREEKS

The evolution of the rights of externs is closely connected in the documents with the enfranchisement of Greeks from the eastern provinces. It is relevant to inquire when this began. The practical effect of the rule of incompatibility is seen in the rarity of the enfranchisement of transmarine Greeks even in the last generation of the Republic. Few can have become Romans except as manumitted slaves before Sulla's dictatorship. No Greek 'allies' are recorded to have been honoured like the Carthaginian deserters 'for valour' in the wars of the second century, which increasingly involved the suppression of Greek liberties, with the creation of Greek provinces in Achaea, Macedonia, and Asia, rather than the extension of privileges. Cicero cites no transmarine Greeks in his account of provincial enfranchisements in the *pro Balbo*, while his client Archias, though a native of Syrian Antioch, had secured Roman status as an incorporated townsman of Italian Heraclea.[1] The first group of Greek externs would seem to be some Sicilian gentry, enfranchised for services to the Sullan cause during the Sicilian operations of the young Pompeius in 82 B.C. The lengthy account of Sicilian affairs in Cicero's *Verrines* shows that while the vast majority of the numerous notables of this ancient Roman province who suffered from the depradations of Verres were plain provincials, some nine were Roman citizens, whose status is noted by Cicero as unusual. Of these nine, five bear the family names of Pompeius, and six, including three of the Pompeii, are stated to have received the citizenship in fairly recent years, including one 'for valour' and another on the authority of Sulla, though not on his initiative.[2] Other sources add five names in the following twenty

[1] Above, 151–2; *pro Balbo* cites only a Greek of Massilia, Italici, and the men of Messana in 50–2, 55, who like the Percennii (ii *in Verr.* 4. 25) are Campanian, not Greek, by name.

[2] For the Pompeii, ii *in Verr.* 2. 23, 102; 4. 25, 48, with indications of date ('civis Romanus . . . iam diu', 'qui nunc Pompeii sunt', 'Philo qui fuit'). Q.Caecilius Dio

years, including another family of Pompeii.[1] But the sea-captains from Asia and Achaea who had assisted the Sullan cause received as their reward in 78 instead of the Roman citizenship a bundle of positive privileges in their own cities, which the Roman citizenship would have conferred upon them, such as exemption from local liturgies and the right to claim jurisdiction outside their local courts: these benefits closely resemble those conferred earlier upon Italian gentry of Latin status 'who did not wish to change their citizenship'.[2] Evidently citizens of eastern Greek cities were not expected to welcome the grant of Roman status at this time, and were not allowed the opportunity. Equally, when L. Flaccus proconsul of Asia in 62–61 was arraigned for extortion, none of the Asians involved in the case were Roman citizens, while Badian in his catalogue of late Republican externs can list only a single free-born Asian, apart from three characters of dubious status.[3]

The alienation of Greek feeling revealed by the Mithridatic wars goes far to explain the prolongation of the natural Roman reluctance to extend their citizenship in any form to distant and alien Greeks of Achaea and Asia. Indeed on Cicero's showing Romans were becoming Athenians before any Athenians became Romans.[4] By the Triumviral period the attitude of both parties has changed, so that the sea-captains of Octavian and Antonius

(ibid. 2. 20) and Q. Lutatius Diodorus (4. 37) gained their status through the consuls of 80 and 78. A. Clodius Apollonius (4. 37) is a new citizen. C. Heius (4. 3. 15, 19) may be included, and 'Diocles Popilius cognomine' (4. 35) excluded, by the forms of their names. Nothing in Cic. *Div. in Caec.* 4 and 20 suggests that Q. Caecilius, the rival prosecutor and a senator, was more than a resident of Sicily by economic connection (cf. pseudo-Asconius 98 'domo Sicilia') or remote servile origin (Plut. *Cic.* 7. 6). Verres' two professors of arts were of Asian origin, not Sicilians: Cicero firmly rejects their status as irregular ('quorum civis Romanus nemo erat . . . repente Cornelii') though accepting that of A. Clodius Apollonius (3. 69; 4. 37).

[1] Cic. *pro Balbo* 51, 52, *ad Fam.* 13. 2; Suet. *Gramm.* 29 (Clodii and a Pompeius).

[2] Above, 297, 300.

[3] Cic. *pro Flacco* 34–58, 72–4; the 'complaints of Roman citizens' come from *negotiatores Italici* (70–93). Badian, op. cit. 302–8, in his catalogue of viritane enfranchisements lists three enfranchised Asians with servile origins, Nicias Porcianus from Cyprus (post 58), Cornelius Alexander (Miletus, Sullan), and Curtius Nicias (friend of Pompeius); cf. also Murena's manumission of the scholar war-captive Turannio, Plut. *Lucullus* 19. 8. For Verres' two Asian artists see 306 n. 3 above.

[4] Cic. *pro Archia* 25 notably omits *Graecos* from Sulla's other enfranchisements, 'cum Hispanos et Gallos donaret', though Sulla was responsible for those of his legate Pompeius in Sicily and other individuals (n. 3, 308 n. 2). For Athens, cf. *pro Balbo* 30, above, 303 n. 2.

now receive the Roman citizenship on terms which allow them to retain as much of their local status as they desire. But when did the breakthrough occur? It might be expected that Pompeius, who had been liberal to Sicilian Greeks in his early years, would initiate the enfranchisement of oriental Greeks on a generous scale during his six years of action and organization in the Hellenistic East. It is recorded only that he enfranchised his protégé and historian, Theophanes of Mytilene.[1] But others did as much, or as little.[2] One might expect to detect his enfranchisement of other oriental magnates in the inscriptions of provincial Pompeii of later times, just as the numerous Antonii, Julii, and Claudii of the eastern provinces record through their names former grants of citizenship to their forebears by the dynasts of the Second Triumvirate and early Principate. Such Pompeii emerge in the inscriptions, but they are rare.[3] A judicious examination of the indexes of personal names in the great collections of oriental inscriptions reveals that the *nomen* Pompeius was not widespread among Roman citizens with Greek by-names in the eastern provinces, and is often rarer than other proconsular names of the late Republican period.[4] Only in the Aegean islands

---

[1] Cic. *pro Archia* 24, Strabo 13. 618 C, Ditt. *SIG* 1. 752–5 nn. The enfranchisement was formal 'in contione militum', as if *virtutis causa*; cf. *ILS* 8888.

[2] Cf. *pro Archia* 6, assistance of M. Lucullus to Archias; Sulla's manumission of Alexander Polyhistor (Servius *ad Aen.* 10. 388, Suidas s.v.), who like Turannio (above, 307 n. 3) was probably a prisoner of war; Caesar and Theopompus of Cnidos, Ditt. *SIG*⁴ 761 C, nn., cf. Strabo 14. 656 C, Plut. *Caes.* 48. 1. So too Verres and his artists, 306 n. 2 above. Cf. Goodfellow, *Roman Citizenship*, 35, 38, 94.

[3] Much caution is necessary. Many provincial Pompeii bear *praenomina* other than those of the consular Pompeii, and may include descendants of obscure Italian emigrants. Some are demonstrably enfranchised veterans or freedmen of the Principate taking their names from imperial officials with the name Pompeius, themselves possibly descendants of men enfranchised by Magnus. Strictly only Gnaei and Sexti Pompeii with Greek *cognomina* should be reckoned in the count. Yet the descendants of Theophanes were known as M. Pompeius Macer or Macrinus (Strabo 13. 618 C, *PIR* s.v.).

[4] In the following summary, which is suggestive but not definitive, the references are to the indexes of personal names in the cited books. More detailed analysis is required of this evidence. *IGRR* iv, covering Roman Asia, against 14 columns of early imperial *nomina* (Julii 4, Claudii 7, Flavii 3) has sixteen Pompeii other than Roman officials, of whom six are gentry of Mytilene. *IGRR* iii, covering the other Asiatic provinces and Syria, yields seven Pompeii of whom only the freedwoman of a procurator is not a Roman official (unless the consular Pompeius Falco is counted as Asian); yet it has numerous other persons with Roman Republican *nomina*, including ten Domitii with Greek *cognomina*. *MAMA* iv–vii with wider coverage in rural areas produces two Pompeii (including another Falco). *Inscr. Gr. Lat. Syrie* (L. Jalobert, R. Moutarde, Paris, 1950–9) and *Inscr. Creticae* i–iv

of Cos, Chios, and especially at Mytilene, and at Ephesus on the mainland, is there fair evidence for the enfranchisement of several local magnates who bear the name of Pompey. Otherwise such personages are rare, and come sometimes from surprising places—a family from Asian Philadelphia, a single notable each from Syrian Seleucia, from Crete, and from Cyrene[1]—while a dynast like Pythodorus of Tralles, though a friend of Pompey, secured his family's citizenship later from the triumvir Antonius.[2] So it seems that Pompeius was sparing in the enfranchisement of oriental Greeks. He initiated it, but on no lavish scale.

Instead, it was the stresses of the civil wars after 49 B.C. that led to liberal offers of individual enfranchisement in the East, just as they led to communal grants of Roman status in the West. This surmise is confirmed by the presence of a minor concentration of Pompeii in later times among the gentry of the Peloponnese, notably at Sparta and Argos, several of whom bear the *praenomen* not of Magnus, like most of the Sicilian Pompeii, but of his son Sextus, who ruled the Peloponnese under the Second Triumvirate.[3] This fact, with the pullulation of Antonii among the

(M. Guarducci, Rome, 1950) each yield a single notable or family. Pompeii are absent from: *Didyma* II (A. Rehm, Berlin, 1958), *Lindos* II (C. Blankenberg Berlin, 1941), *Inschriften von Pergamum* (M. Frankel, Berlin, 1895), *Milet* I. 3 (Th. Wiegand, Vienna, 1914), and *Tit. As. Min.* II (Lycia). For Cyrene, *SEG* ix gives one Pompeius in some five hundred Roman inscriptions, including a long list of ephebes (A.D. 224–5, no. 128). See also below, n. 3. By contrast, in *IG* xiv Sicily has 12 Pompeii, and they abound in Narbonensis, *CIL* xii, and southern Spain, *CIL* ii.

[1] The six gentry from Mytilene mostly connect with Pompeius Theophanes. Chios (*IGRR* iv. 934) and Cos (ibid. 1101) each have a priestly or magisterial personage, though the latter (*praenomen* Quintus A.D. 2) is the sole Pompeius among 52 annual priests of Apollo with Roman *nomina* at Halasarna between 30 B.C. and A.D. 103; Philadelphia, ibid. 1643. For Crete. *IGRR* i. 987–8, 993 (A.D. 112–13, *praenomen* Marcus). For Cyrene, *SEG* ix. 278, a Pompeius Granius Magnus (!), priest. For Syria, *Inscr. Gr. Lat. Syrie* iii. 1185, 1213 (*praenomen* Gnaeus, A.D. 191). At Ephesus, *Forschungen Ephesus* ii. 69, iii. 38 (Vienna, 1912, 1922) give three notables from two families (*praenomen* Gnaeus, second century), and *SIG*[4] ii. 820 adds a fourth (*praenomen* Lucius, A.D. 83–4). *SEG* viii adds a Gn. Pompeius of 'strategic' rank (n. 527) from Egypt.

[2] For Pythodorus of Tralles whose kinsmen were Antonii see Goodfellow, op. cit. 98–9; Strabo 12. 578 C, 14. 649 C.

[3] The Peloponnesian Pompeii appear first in the index of the antiquated *CIG*, where (excluding Italians) about one third of the total comes from the Peloponnese, especially Sparta and Argos, with five or six from the Asian provinces. More recently the consolidated index of *SEG* xi–xx (1950–64) adds a group of ten Peloponnesians (five or six from Sparta) out of fourteen. Both groups include two or three Sexti Pompeii (cf. *SEG* xi. 529, 598, 849).

Greek citizenry of the East, who must include many descendants enfranchised by the rival of Octavian, since no other Antonius was in a similar position of power, goes far to prove that enfranchisement in the East became common only with the Second Triumvirate.[1] Hence it is no accident that such offers appear in the edicts of Octavian and Antonius, defined with the detail of an innovation.[2]

The frequent enfranchisement of oriental gentry by the emperors of the first century A.D. raises the question of method. Its rarity even in the late Republic is partly due to the fact that only the great commanders, and not the normal proconsuls, had this power.[3] The emperors had it, but how did they exercise it? In the century after Augustus only Nero and Vespasian spent a few months of their rule in an eastern province, down to Trajan's three years of campaigning beyond the eastern frontiers. So the personal presence of the Princeps is not a decisive factor. Yet there is no known institution by which the eastern gentry could acquire Roman status automatically, like the annual magistrates of Latin municipalities in the West, or the barbarian peasantry who secured it by long service in the provincial militia. It is probable that the provincial councils, composed of representatives of the self-governing cities and communes, assisted the enfranchisement of their members.[4] They provided a regular link between the local aristocracies and the Roman governors, who

[1] In *IGRR* iv the Antonii, mostly with the *praenomina* Marcus or Lucius, double the number of Pompeii. For proven individuals see Goodfellow, op. cit. 97 f. In the priestly *Fasti* of Halasarna (above, 309 n. 1) there are four Antonii to a single Julius and Pompeius. The list of Asiarchs in D. Magie, *Roman Rule in Asia Minor* (Princeton, N.J., 1966), 1604 f., gives five Antonii to one Pompeius.

[2] The numerous Julii are not chronologically helpful since their enfranchisement can seldom be precisely distributed between Caesar, Augustus, Tiberius, and Gaius. Goodfellow, op. cit. 93 f., attributes some five Asiatic enfranchisements with fair certainty to Caesar. G. W. Bowersock, *Augustus and the Greek World* (Oxford, 1965), casts no light here.

[3] Badian, op. cit. 303, 304, 306, assumes that any proconsul could enfranchise in the late Republic. This is improbable, since special powers were conferred on the imperators of the social and civil wars and later for this purpose (above, 294). Cicero cites only such persons in *pro Balbo* 50–2 and *pro Archia* 24–6, where he notably does not suggest that Archias could have secured enfranchisement directly from the proconsul L. Lucullus. In *Verr.* ii. 4. 37 he notes that Lutatius Catulus secured the enfranchisement of Diodorus through Sulla, while in 2. 20 Q. Metellus Pius, also cited for enfranchisement in *pro Archia*, could do this himself, by 70 B.C. (*nunc*) probably, like Pompeius in Spain, thanks to the *lex Gellia* of 72. Hence the enfranchisement of Verres' henchmen was invalid (above, 306 n. 2).

[4] For the provincial Councils see briefly below, 405 f.

might have regularly commended the 'High Priests' or presidents and other officials to the Princeps for a grant of Roman status. But there is no evidence for the enticing suggestion that this was regularly given to such personages *ex officio*; though most Lyciarchs and most high priests of Asia appear to be Roman citizens, exceptions exist.[1] Alternatively it was a matter of individual approach. The provincials could request such promotion by a written petition to the Princeps, with the sponsorship of highly placed Roman friends or officials. The method is documented in the various letters in which the consular Pliny recommends his friends of high and low estate to the emperor Trajan for promotion in office or in civic condition, including Roman status.[2] Either way it is evident that from the principate of Augustus onwards it was fully acceptable to both sides that the gentry of Greek cities should combine an active career in local politics with the personal acquisition of Roman citizenship.

## INDIVIDUAL PRIVILEGES IN THE LATER PRINCIPATE

How long any residue of the doctrine of incompatibility survived is hard to determine. There is evidence from the Julio-Claudian period onwards for externs holding their local magistracies and proceeding to enter the public service of the Roman state.[3] At a lower level the priority that St. Paul assigns to his status as a citizen of Tarsus—'no mean city'—over his Roman franchise is characteristic.[4] But evidence about the domestic condition of externs is scarce. The edict of Domitian concerning legionary veterans separates the grant of citizenship from that of fiscal and local immunities in the Augustan manner, while nothing is said of the other privileges granted to the Augustan beneficiaries.[5] This document stood alone until the discovery of

---

[1] For lists see Magie, op. cit. ii. 1601–12.

[2] Cf. my *Letters of Pliny, An Historical Commentary* (Oxford, 1966), 1. 19; 2. 13; 10. 5–6, 11, 87, 106–7 nn. Cf. also *Tab. Ban.* below, 336.

[3] Cf., e.g., E. M. Smallwood, *Documents . . . of Gaius, Claudius, and Nero* (Cambridge, 1967), nn. 260, 262–4.

[4] Acts 21. 37–9; 22. 3. Cf. my *Roman Society and Roman Law* (Oxford, 1963), 179 ff.

[5] *FIRA* i². n. 76, dated A.D. 88. The fiscal immunities here cover both civic and imperial dues, as in the edict of Octavian *de veteranis*, cf. above, 296 n. 3, 298 n. 3.

a remarkable text at Banasa in Mauretania in 1961.[1] It concerns the grant of Roman status in *c.* A.D. 168–77 to a barbarian chieftain and his family under a condition summarily defined as *salvo iure gentis*. This clearly preserves the man's status as a *princeps gentium Zegrensium*, and it is in turn limited by a phrase that protects the financial claims of the imperial treasury: 'sine deminutione tributorum et vectigalium populi et fisci'. The Roman status is being steadily reduced in significance, and here takes a minor place beside the man's local and provincial obligations. Perhaps the idea of incompatibility of citizenships survives longest in the rule of the early Empire that a man was liable for civic *munera* in the place of his origin rather than that of his domicile. This rule, though manifestly unfair to the interest of the cities, yielded only gradually to the contrary principle.[2]

The question merges in the later Empire into the wider question of the application of Roman private law to enfranchised persons, whether externs or communally promoted *municipes*, the survival of local law, and the amalgamation of the two. The legal historians disagree, and the debate continues.[3] But it is certain that for the period before the *Constitutio Antoniniana*, throughout the second century A.D., in matters of personal status and basic property rights, marriage, descent, and succession, the extern employed the *ius civile*. The formal demonstration of this can be found in the document known as the *Gnomon* of the *Idios Logos*, which applies the strict rules of Roman Law to the status of all Roman citizens in Egypt.[4] Equally the Roman status retained its distinction in the privilege that even humble Roman citizens

---

[1] W. Seston and M. Euzennat made the preliminary publication in *CRAI* 1961. For the full text see below, 336.

[2] Texts of Gaius, Paulus, and later jurists show that it was only during the second century that the principle was established that liability to *munera* depended not on *patria* but on *domicilium*, and that *incolae* of an alien city came to be freed from the *munera* of their *patria*, while the definition of *incola* long remained under dispute in texts from Caius onwards. Cf. *Dig.* 50. 1. 17. 6, 20, 22 pr., 27, 29, 37 pr.; 4. 3 pr.; 6. 5.

[3] The standard treatment is still L. Mitteis, *Reichsrecht und Volksrecht.* etc. (Leipzig, 1891); for modern interpretations see the articles of de Visscher and Wenger cited, above, 296 n. 1, also many articles cited by Jolowicz, op. cit. 545 nn. 4–5, and Sherk, op. cit. 307 n. 27, including R. Taubenschlag, *Studi . . . Bonfante* (Pavia, 1929) i. 369–440, and V. Arango-Ruiz, *L'applicazione del diritto romano . . . dopo la C.A.*, (Napoli, 1947).

[4] Cf. de Visscher, *Ant. Class.* 14. 54. For the *Gnomon* see the selections in *FIRA* i². n. 99. Its clauses are largely concerned with the application of the Augustan social legislation to Roman citizens in Egypt from the fiscal aspect. For *ius civile* cf. the reference to marriage by *coemptio* ibid. 33.

could claim before the criminal law when faced by a capital penalty or by arbitrary punishment. It has been suggested that this position had been virtually replaced by the emergence of the new privileged class of the *honestiores*, the upper classes of the cities, during the second century.[1] The *honestiores*, who would mostly be Roman citizens, retain and extend their privileges, while the *humiliores* of Roman status are reduced to the condition of ordinary provincials. But this theory depends upon legal texts edited in their present form at a period when the distinction between citizens and non-citizen inhabitants of the Empire no longer existed. Hence it is not certain whether the texts about *humiliores* earlier than the *Constitutio Antoniniana* included or excluded proletarian Romans in their original form. Certain legates assumed that Christians who were Roman citizens were exempt from their capital jurisdiction, while the humble tenants of the imperial estates in Africa show in their appeal to Commodus that the exemption of all Romans from physical punishment without proper trial was still regarded as valid seventy years later, and the contemporary classical lawyers continue to recite the relevant clauses of the *lex Julia de vi* concerning this.[2]

These documents argue against the serious diminution of the prestige and even of the practical value of the Roman citizenship in the later second century. They confirm the impression made by the fact that the citizenship continued to be offered as a reward to auxiliary soldiers, and by the ambitious pursuit of 'colonial rights' on the part of peregrine and Latin communes throughout the period. The maintenance of their titular distinctions by local associations of *cives Romani* in the provinces of northern Europe even after the *Constitutio Antoniniana* adds to this impression.[3] So too Aelius Aristides makes a great fuss in his panegyric of Rome about the grant of the Roman citizenship to 'the better sort of men', who are precisely the *honestiores*.[4]

---

[1] Cf. A. H. M. Jones, *Studies in Roman Government* (Oxford, 1960), 64–5. The basic discussion is by G. Cardascia, *Rev. Hist. Dr. fr. étr.* 1950, 305 f., 461 f. For a new view see P. Garnsey, *Social Status . . . in the Roman Empire* (Oxford, 1970), who stresses the universality of this Roman attitude from an early period.

[2] Above, 273. *FIRA* i². n. 103: 'cives etiam Romanos virgis et fustibus effligi iusserit.' For *provocatio*, Ulpian, *Dig.* 48. 6. 7; Marcian, ibid. 8, and *Sent. Pauli* 5. 26. 1–2; cf. my *Roman Society and Roman Law*, 57 ff., Garnsey, op. cit. 260 ff.

[3] Below, 387.

[4] *Pan.* 59, below, 390 n. 3. The *Tab. Ban.* stresses the rarity of such grants, above, 274 n. 7.

## THE REGISTRATION OF CITIZENSHIP

Within the territory of the Roman state, at Rome or in the municipalities of Italy, the proof of citizenship rested originally upon the act of parental recognition. The Roman father acknowledged his legitimate child by picking him up after birth.[1] The only documentation in the Republican period was the registration of the young adult citizen in the tribal lists that were drawn up and revised at Rome by the censors every five years.[2] Municipalities kept their own local lists also, which acquired the validity of censorial lists when a law of 44 transferred the census to the magistrates of the Roman municipalities, who were required to register the citizen population with their full names, patronymics, and tribes, and with a schedule of their property.[3] The purpose of this was fiscal and administrative. The lists were the basis of taxation and military service, and of the composition of the political assemblies. Such registration was the only regular documentary evidence of personal citizenship in the Republic, and censors would on occasion strike off the rolls the names of spurious claimants to the citizenship. But inscription on the rolls provided only a presumption of citizen status. It was not a proof in itself. That depended normally on evidence of birth, or for new citizens either on the text of the law which authorized each communal or individual enfranchisement, or on the existence of a traditional claim, such as the migration of a Latinus, or the manumission of a slave, or the *postliminium* of a prisoner-of-war. The role of the *lex populi* in the enfranchisement of foreigners makes it improbable that the censors had the direct power of enfranchisement, as some have suggested. Like the magistrates who preside over the manumission of slaves in the *vindicta* process, they recognize rather than create the right to Roman status.[4]

[1] For the dependence of citizenship on membership of a *gens* and hence of a family cf. Mommsen, *DPR* iv. 35 f. Hence the necessity of a *lex populi* to authorize the admission of new citizens into the gentile community, ibid. 148 f.

[2] For censorial registration cf. Mommsen, op. cit. iv. 35 ff.

[3] *Tab. Her.* (*FIRA* i². 13), 142 ff.: 'omnium municipium . . . quei c.R. erunt censum agito eorumque nomina praenomina patres aut patronos tribus cognomina et quot annos quisque eorum habet et rationem pecuniae . . . ab ieis iurateis accipito [s.c. quei in eis municipieis . . . maximum magistratum . . . habebit].' These lists were then registered in the municipal *tabulae publicae* and copies sent to Rome. Cf. earlier, Cic. *pro Clu.* 41, for censorial *tabulae* at Larinum, primarily a property schedule, cf. *leg. ag.* 1. 4.

[4] Cf. *pro Archia* 11; 'census non ius civitatis confirmat . . . indicat eum . . . se iam

Within the limits of a municipal society direct proof would not be hard to establish. But with the steady extension of the citizenship by individual grants to provincials isolated in peregrine communes, and with the informal settlement of large numbers of Italian immigrants in the provincial territories, a more effective means of registration became necessary. Formal documentation of the grant of the citizenship to provincial soldiery appears first in 89 B.C., in the shape of a bronze tablet recording the decree of a proconsul enfranchising a unit of Spanish cavalrymen in the Social War, who are all named in a general list.[1] Presumably each soldier received a copy. The cities of persons of higher status enfranchised by Octavian in *c*. 40 B.C. received a copy of a decree detailing all the privileges of their new status, while his auxiliary veterans could acquire copies of the enabling edict that enfranchised them.[2] But it is only with the regularization of the grant of citizenship to all time-expired auxiliaries by Claudius that a standardized document appears. This is the small bronze diptych known as the *diploma civitatis*, containing a brief and uniform formula conferring the Roman citizenship on the holder and his descendants, who is indicated by his name and military unit.[3] These documents were not normally used for civilians, who received instead a copy in *libellus* form of the brief imperial warrant authorizing the registration of their enfranchisement in the archives at Rome.[4]

*Diplomata* and *libelli* provided for new citizens. For the mass of the citizenry, for whom censorial registration at five-yearly intervals was an inefficient instrument, adequate provision was finally made by the creation of an official system of compulsory birth registration under the social legislation of Augustus (A.D. 4). The researches of F. Schulz into the documents of birth registrations

---

tum gessisse pro cive.' The censor of 101 removed the name of Equitius from the civic lists when Cornelia testified that he was not the son of Ti. Gracchus; Cic. *pro Sest.* 101, Victor, *DVI* 73. For laws *nominatim* and general, cf. above, 291–2 nn., 294 nn. 3–4, and earlier, e.g. Livy 8. 17. 12; 21. 10; 26. 33. 10–14; 38. 36. 7–9. For manumission see below, 322 ff.

[1] *ILS* 8888, cited above, 294 n. 3.

[2] *FIRA* i². 55, 56.

[3] The *diplomata militaria* are collected and discussed in *CIL* xvi; cf. also *FIRA* i². 223 f., and above, 247 f., 273 f.

[4] Cf. Suet. *Nero* 12. 1 for the exceptional issue of *diplomata civitatis* to Nero's dancers. For *libelli* and *commentarii principis* cf. Pliny, *Epp.* 10. 6. 2, 105, 107 with notes in my *Letters of Pliny* (Oxford, 1965), ad loc, and now *Tab. Ban.* below, 336.

from Roman Egypt have clarified this.[1] The Roman citizen was required to register the birth of his children within thirty days before a Roman official, and he received a wooden diptych recording the declaration, which acted as a certificate of citizenship for the child for the rest of his life. Like the military *diplomata* this contained the names of seven witnesses, and provided a presumptive proof of citizen status. But complete validation of a claim depended in disputed cases on confirmation by the witnesses that the document was a true copy of the official archive in which the enfranchisement or birth was formally registered. Similarly the enfranchisement of freedmen, which depended upon a formal act, was recorded in a documentary *tabella manumissionis*.[2] Citizens of diverse origins thus came to have some form of documentary evidence of their status.

### IUS ITALICUM

The origin of this privilege was not investigated above, where its role in the Severan period was defined as a status symbol sought after by *coloniae civium Romanorum* as the height of civic prestige. It first emerges as the condition of certain veteran settlements of the Julian period, mainly in the eastern provinces where Roman colonization was a novelty, probably to compensate the settlers for the remoteness of their environment. This explanation may also serve for the few Julian colonies in the western provinces which received *ius Italicum*.[3] It was not given universally to colonial settlements, and was not reserved for especially favoured groups, since the dispossessed Antonians of Italy whom Augustus settled in Macedonia held it, but the great Julian colonies of Corinth and Carthage did not.[4] Its later extension in the colonization of Dacia by Trajan and Hadrian may have had the practical purpose of encouraging settlement in an exposed region

---

[1] F. Schulz, 'Roman registers and Birth Certificates', *JRS* 32 (1942), 78 ff., 33 (1943), 55 ff. For a selection of texts, *FIRA* ii². 1–4.

[2] Ibid. 6, 15–20. For checking of documents, ibid. 5–7.

[3] Above, 276 nn. 3–5. For the standard account of *ius It.* see von Premerstein, *RE* x. 1238 ff.

[4] Dio 51. 4. 6. Cf. Vittinghof, op. cit. 134–5 (n. 1). M. Grant, op. cit. 175, 177. The lists of Ulpian and Paulus (*Dig.* 50. 15. 1, 8) are intended to be complete (cf. ibid. 1. 3. 6) and imply comparative rarity. Thus Carthage, Utica, and Lepcis, the three great metropolitan colonies of Africa Proconsularis, receive *ius Italicum* only from the Severi, while neither Mauretanian capital is 'Italic'.

of the northern frontier, while the Severan dynasty used it as a reward for political support in civil war.[1]

Its precise origins are obscure. The term appears first in the Elder Pliny in the sense of a communal privilege, which he does not explain, and afterwards in legal texts of the late second and third centuries concerning *coloniae*, while Agennius Urbicus indirectly refers to its most material privilege as if it were confined to colonies. Hence it might be regarded as a communal grant reserved for Roman colonies, though two of the communes listed in the *Digest* were probably not yet colonies at the time of the grant.[2] But an inscription from Didyma in Asia, dated to the late first or early second century, records a Roman citizen of recent origin, with no colonial connections, as a person 'of the Italian status'.[3] There is a possible parallel in a papyrus from Syrian Dura which lists certain Roman soldiers as *Italici*.[4] Hence an individual form of *ius Italicum* has been posited, though it is not certain that the inscription is technically exact. A simpler explanation is to hand. Two edicts of Octavian and Domitian, a century apart in time, granting the citizenship to veterans resident in the eastern provinces, use the formula 'let them be Roman citizens of the highest grade and condition exempt from taxation'. Their property likewise was to be held *optimo iure*. Citizenship which secures a man's property and personal status on these conditions closely resembles the later *ius Italicum*, which thus need have no essential connection with colonial status.[5]

There are two clues to its first definition. First, the Macedonian colonies of dispossessed Italians may well have been granted all

[1] *Dig.* 50. 15. 1–8.

[2] Pliny, *NH* 3. 25, 'ius Italiae', 139, 'ius Italicum'. Gaius (below, 320 n. 1) is the earliest juristic source. Agennius, *de contr. agrar.* B 39 (Thulin). For Stobi and Selinus see below, 318 n. 2. Strabo 4. 1. 9 C 184, τῶν Ἰταλιωτίδων ἐξετάζεται, means not that Antipolis, west of the Varus boundary of Italy, has the *ius Italicum* as a provincial city, but that it was included in Italy, whereas Nicaea east of the Varus was in Narbonensis. This resulted from a judicial decision, which evidently promoted Antipolis from the Latin status recorded by Pliny, *NH* 3. 35. This is not evidence for a Latin municipality holding *ius Italicum*.

[3] Cf. J. Triantophyllopoulos, *Iura* 14 (1963), 108 f. A. Rehm, *Didyma* II (1958), n. 331. Claudia Polla, wife of Gaius and mother of Julia, is described as Ἰταλικοῦ δικαίου. One T. Flavius Lyciscus is also mentioned. The names imply a date *c.* A.D. 70–120. For δίκαιον = *ius* cf. *FIRA* i². 55. 2. 1, iii. 171 (a).

[4] *P. Dura* 456. Possibly the *Italicenses* of Spain, SHA *Hadr.* 12. 4, also.

[5] Cited above, 296, 311: 'optimo iure optimaque lege cives Romani immunes sint.' Atkinson, a.c. 31 make this connection, briefly. Cf. also above, 158–9, for origins.

aspects of their former privileges as Roman citizens of Italy. Secondly, the Elder Pliny applies *ius Italicum* to certain communes of Dalmatian Liburnia, beyond the frontier of Italy, which he also lists with the rest of Liburnia as lying within the Tenth Region of Italy.[1] None of these were *coloniae*, and their status as *municipia* is not firmly documented. The most probable explanation of this puzzling doublet is that these Liburnian communes secured the Roman citizenship on the same terms as the rest of Italy when the citizenship was extended to the whole of adjacent Transpadane Gaul in 49 B.C., and were later excluded from Italy when Augustus finally fixed the boundary of the Tenth Region at the Arsia river, but were allowed to retain the status, known later as *ius Italicum*, which they shared with the Transpadanes.[2] The incorporation of Transpadana in Italy, first by its enfranchisement in 49 and later by the abolition of its provincial status in 42, provided an occasion for the definition of the legal status of this great block of enfranchised persons and communes lying beyond the previous bounds of Italy, in terms similar to those of the veteran edicts.[3]

The substantial fragments of the municipal laws that survive from northern Italy at this period indicate that the procedures of Roman civil law were regularized and established in the local courts, and that the jurisdiction of these was equated, within certain financial limits, with that of the praetorian court of Rome, and was freed from the intervention of any magistrate

---

[1] *NH* 3. 130, 139–40. Before the Augustan conquest Illyricum was not a defined territorial province.

[2] Cf. R. Thomsen, *Italic Regions* (Copenhagen, 1947), 23 ff.; U. Ewins, *PBSR* 23 (1955), 89 f.; J. Wilkes, G. Alfoldi (op. cit. below, 347 n. 4) provide variant solutions. Pliny lists only a select few of the fourteen *civitates* of Liburnia as having *ius Italicum*, so that the whole of Liburnia cannot have been enfranchised in 49. Hence Ewins (art. cit. 90) and Alfoldi (op. cit. 88), followed by Wilkes (op. cit. 487), suppose that these few secured both *ius Italicum* and later the municipal status from Augustus or Tiberius. But the evidence for this promotion is only that of Roman tribal attributions and municipal officers in the later Principate (cf. 348 n. 1). Alfoldi seems to conceive *ius Italicum* as merely a combination of citizenship and *immunitas*. No other ordinary provincial *municipium* is known to have had it, since Stobi, a *municipium* till the Severan period, may have originated from dispossessed *Italici* like the Macedonian colonies, or have acquired the *ius* at a late date with colonial status; cf. *Dig.* loc. cit. 8. 8, *RE* (2) 4. 49, 54. The status of Selinus Trajanopolis, apparently given the *ius* in memory of Trajan's death in the city, remains obscure and anomalous (cf. *RE* (2) 2. 1308 f.).

[3] Cf. Ewins, art. cit. 89 f., for the extensive reorganization of Cisalpina after 49 B.C., and above, 159.

or proconsuls of the Roman State.[1] Thus their status was identified with that of the municipalities of Italy. The new citizens of the Transpadane region were in effect secured the freedom from arbitrary jurisdiction which in the past has been the prerogative of the Roman citizens of Italy, and the full exercise of the *ius civile* both in their native townships and in Rome. They would also hold their property *ex iure Quiritium*, a term used by the Roman lawyers to denote especially the earlier usages of the law of property, many of which were valid only within the bounds of Italy.[2] This was a distinction rather than an advantage, since other and simpler legal forms of universal validity were taking the place of those *ex iure Quiritium*: citizens throughout the greater part of the Roman world managed without either *mancipatio* or *in iure cessio*. Other more practical advantages in matters of civil law and personal status existed or were later created under various statutes that applied only to Roman citizens of Italy, quite apart from the material advantage of freedom from direct taxation (*immunitas*) that had existed in Italy since 167 B.C.[3]

All these advantages should accrue to the provincial holder of Italian status, in addition to the plain citizenship, through the legal fiction which it created. The impression that it principally conveyed *immunitas* is due to the accidental fact that *ius Italicum* is mostly known from its citation in two long excerpts of Ulpian and Paulus about the *census*, for which this was the relevant aspect, and from the distinction in Agennius between *ager Italicus* and provincial *ager colonicus* for which again *immunitas* was the decisive point. The accidental bias of the sources should not lead to the undervaluing of the brief indications of citations from Gaius and Ulpian, who though not primarily concerned with provincial

---

[1] Cf. *lex de Gallia Cisalpina* (*FIRA* i². 19) 20. 23 f., 33 f., 50 f.; 21. 4, 19; 22. 28, 40 f.; 23. *Fragmentum Atestinum* (ibid. 20) 17 f. For the dating cf. Riccobono, op. cit. 170, 176.

[2] Cf. esp. Gaius 2. 14–15, 19–21, 31, 40–6, 63, 194, 196; 4. 36. *Tit. Ulp.* 19. 1. *Mancipatio, in iure cessio usucapio*, were technically valid for real estate only in Italy. Hence ownership *in bonis* and transfer of ownership by *traditio* replace that *ex iure Quiritium* (Gaius 2. 40–1, 65). Similarly legacies *per vindicationem* applied only to property held *ex iure Quiritium* (ibid. 196). In 1. 54 he comments on the possible insufficiency of ownership based on *nudum ius Quiritium*. Cf. Triantophyllopoulos, art. cit. 131. *RE* x. 2. 1290–1.

[3] e.g. certain rules of the *lex Julia de maritandis ordinibus*, including advantages in the *ius liberorum*, and the *lex Furia* concerning *sponsio*, were only valid in Italy, cf. Gaius 2. 63; 3. 121–2. Ulpian, *Fr. Vat.* 191–2, Paulus, ibid. 247. For the early combination of citizenship with *immunitas* see above, 300–1.

civil law, indicate that the benefits of the Augustan social legislation applied to the provincial holders of *ius Italicum*, however
this was defined at that date.[1] The term itself cannot have come
into existence until the identification of Italy with the Roman
state and its citizenship was a commonplace. It serves with Pliny
and the classical lawyers as a convenient portmanteau term
summarizing the long formulae of the personal edicts and
municipal laws which defined it in detail. It is notably absent
from the lengthy disquisitions of Gaius' *Institutes* on personal
status, though he employs the parallel *Latium*, which has a dual
connotation of personal and municipal standing. This suggests
that unlike the term *ius Quiritium*, which he uses for two aspects
of personal standing, *ius Italicum* was primarily concerned with
communities.[2] Earlier the Emperor Claudius apparently eschewed
the use of the later term when he referred to Vienne on the
Rhône, by that time a Roman colony with Italian status, as
having acquired 'the complete privilege of Roman citizenship'.[3]

It has been suggested that *ius Italicum* conferred a special
degree of municipal autonomy, and of freedom from the intervention of provincial governors.[4] But the statutory independence
of municipal jurisdiction, within certain limits, and of local
administration, was common to all Roman or Latin colonies
and municipalities under the detailed regulations of their permanent charters or *leges*. Strabo gave this as a characteristic of
the Latin municipalities of Narbonensis. There is no apparent
difference in this respect between the effect of the Julian *lex*

[1] A brief excerpt from Gaius (*Dig.* loc. cit. 7) notes the possession of *ius It.* by
three provincial colonies in connection with the *lex Papia Poppaea*, which must have
referred to the registered *coloni* or *municipes* of Roman provincial communes equated
with those of Italy. Cf. 319 n. 3. Nearly all the *Digest* evidence comes not from
general treatises of *ius civile* but from monographs (*de censibus, ad legem P. Poppaeam*).

[2] Gaius 1. 32–5, 65; 3. 72–3; *Tit. Ulp.* 3. 1–6, equate the acquisition of *ius
Quiritium* by a Latinus Junianus with that of *civitas Romana*, i.e. full freedman status
(cf. Pliny, *Epp.* 10. 104). Both primarily have residents of Rome and Italy in mind.
For ownership *ex iure Quiritium* cf. 319 n. 2 above. For Latium, Gaius 1. 95–6.

[3] *ILS* 212. 2. 16–17, 'solidum civitatis Romanae beneficium'. Cf. 352 n. 1 for
an alternative view. The grant of *ius It.* may possibly be due to Galba, cf. Tac.
*Hist.* 1. 65.

[4] Cf. H. M. Last, *CAH* xi 455, following Premerstein, *RE* x. 1248 f., who stresses
Seneca's remark about Lugdunum, 'ornamentum . . . provinciarum quibus et
inserta erat et excepta' (*Epp.* 91. 10), and the claim of Apamea to have a *privilegium
. . . arbitrio suo rem publicam gerere* (Pliny, *Epp.* 10. 47), though no similar objection
seems to have been raised with Pliny by Sinope, also a colony with *ius It.* (ibid. 10.
90, *Dig.* 50. 15. 1. 10).

*coloniae Ursonensis* and of the Flavian *lex municipii Malacitani,* though neither is of the Italic standing.[1] Certainly that gave no exemption from the capital jurisdiction of Roman governors, though the absence of tribute meant practical freedom from the attentions of fiscal agents of the government.[2]

The *ius Italicum* serves in the later Principate as the highest category of communal privilege or *beneficium,* reserved for special occasions or unusual merit. Hence its erratic distribution in time. Rare in the Julio-Claudian period, its use revives in the crises of the Flavio-Trajanic and of the Severan period. Hence too its close association with the status of *colonia civium Romanorum,* the pre-eminent civic status of the later Principate. Only the doubtful instance of Selinus suggests that it was ever given separately from colonial status in that period. The anomalies in Liburnia and Macedonia belong to the origins of the institution. But in the eastern provinces there were numerous individuals holding a similar status, with no 'colonial' connections, descended from the privileged categories known from the edicts of Octavian and Domitian. If the latter may be pressed, those provincials of peregrine status who were not infrequently enfranchised on initial recruitment into Roman legions, especially in the eastern provinces, thus received the equivalent of the *ius Italicum* as a bonus at the end of their military service.[3] This served to

---

[1] Strabo 4. 1. 12. 187 C.: 'on account of this [sc. *ius Latii*] this people is not subject to the commands of the proconsuls.' Pausanias says something similar about the *libertas* of the colony of Patrae in Achaea (7. 18. 7). They give the viewpoint of the unprivileged provincial. Cf. for actual limitations above, 318–19 and *lex Mal.* 69, cited 379 n. 4.

[2] Cf. the *cognitio* of the governor of Lugdunensis dealing with the Christians of Lugdunum, who included both natives and peregrines, whom Eusebius carefully distinguishes (*Hist. Eccl.* 5. 1). Pliny, *Epp.* 4. 22 does not state whether the dispute between the magistrate and the Council of Vienna came to the Princeps's tribunal from the proconsul or directly. Premerstein, art. cit. 1250, notes the intervention of the legate of Dalmatia in a dispute involving an 'Italic' commune of Liburnia in A.D. 69 (*ILS* 5951). Major civil jurisdiction likewise, under the rule known from *lex de Gallia Cisalpina* 21, 22, goes to the provincial governor. The old theory that statues of Marsyas widely erected in municipal *fora* or depicted on colonial coins, are a proof of *ius Italicum,* is no longer held (cf. Premerstein, art. cit. 1251).

[3] For Selinus, Liburnia, Stobi cf. above, 318 n. 2. For enlistment of peregrines in legions see H. M. Parker, *Roman Legions,* (Oxford, 1928), 181 f., G. Forni, *Il reclutamento delle legioni* (Milan, 1953), 103 ff. The evidence is mostly indirect, since Aristides' loose generalization about 'soldiers receiving the Roman citizenship' may refer only to his own times, or only to the well-known reward of auxiliaries. (*Pan. in Romam,* ed. Keil ii. 112–13). Lists of legionaries from Egypt and Africa (e.g. *ILS* 2483, *CIL* viii. 18084) indicate widespread recruitment in mainly

distinguish them and their descendants from the more numerous provincials of the auxiliary regiments, who received only the unadorned citizenship as their reward. The papyrus record of a Prefect of Egypt in A.D. 63 refers tantalizingly to the distinction between the citizen rights of legionary veterans and those of other veterans as familiar, but fails to elucidate.[1]

## CITIZENSHIP BY MANUMISSION

Throughout the Roman Republic the freed slaves who on manumission regularly secured not only liberty but the status of citizens were a vastly more numerous group than the enfranchised externs of free birth. This enfranchisement of slaves was unique in the Graeco-Roman world, and drew an admiring comment from Philip V of Macedon, who assumed that it aimed at the increase of the military strength of the State.[2] It contrasts with the usage of Greek cities which kept their freedmen in a sub-ordinate position akin to that of resident foreigners. Enfranchise-ment through formal manumission was never called in question in the Republic, although the growing numbers of freedmen at Rome itself gave rise to political concern at their influence in the voting assemblies and to social prejudice against the class.[3] There were attempts both to limit and to extend this by manipulating the tribal distribution of freedmen from the censorship of 312 onwards, especially in the last century of the Republic. The most drastic proposal, that of the censor Ti. Gracchus in 169, to deprive

peregrine areas of Asia Minor, but do not prove that the persons listed were all or mainly *peregrini* in origin. Only Domitian's edict (311 n. 5) seems decisive for certain veterans of the *Legio X Fretensis*, unless the clause about citizenship is meant only for the wives of the veterans, like the similar proviso in the *diplomata* issued to praetorian guardsmen, who were normally Roman citizens by birth. The affir-mation of an Egyptian legionary—'[se] natum ingenuum et civem Romanum esse et habere ius in legione militandi' is ambiguous: Barns, *Chron. d'Égypte* 48 (1949), 296. For pretorians, e.g. *ILS* 1986 ff.

[1] *FIRA* iii.² 171 (a). In the *diplomata* the auxiliary veterans receive only *civitatem Romanam sibi ipsis liberisque* and *conubium cum uxoribus*.

[2] *SEG* ii.⁴ 343; iv. 30–5. So too the Greek Dionysius under Augustus, *Ant.* 4. 22. 3–4.

[3] S. Treggiari, *Roman Freedmen during the Later Republic* (Oxford, 1969), with the older book of A. M. Duff, *Freedmen in the Early Roman Empire* (Oxford, 1928), and H. M. Last, 'The Social Policy of Augustus', *CAH* x. 429 ff., now cover the evolution of freedman status from the regal period to the Antonine age. See also A. Watson, *Law of Persons in the Later Roman Republic* (Oxford, 1967), 184 ff.

the freedmen altogether of their votes, was commuted into the limitation of them apparently to a single tribe, and subsequently to the four *tribus urbanae*, which became the prevalent arrangement in the later Republic.[1] This liberal attitude towards the enfranchisement of slaves contrasts with the reluctance of the Romans in the second century to grant their citizenship to externs, which was not lessened by the growing dislike of high society for the increasing proportion of alien freedmen in the city population themselves externs by origin, recruited into slavery from the foreign wars of the period.[2]

In their origins there is a link between the two forms of enfranchisement, which even the latest study of freedmen in the Roman Republic has not identified. The motives commonly alleged to explain the Roman liberality in manumission are unsatisfactory because they apply equally well to the grant of freedom without enfranchisement: the gratitude or affection of masters, the recognition of services, the incentive to servile industry.[3] But in Roman usage all types of formal manumission conveyed citizenship, and the rule was of great antiquity.[4] Livy in a prototypal story dates manumission with enfranchisement 'by the rod' to the first year of the Republic, Dionysius carries manumission by registration at the census back to the regal period, and the Twelve Tables document manumission by testament.[5] It has often been noted that the Roman attitude might be due to the fact that in the earlier ages most slaves originated as prisoners of war (if not as citizen debtors), and hence were fellow Italians with kindred language and culture. But this applies equally to the origins of slavery in Greece with different results. It is more relevant that the earliest enemies of Rome in the most archaic period were not merely 'Italians' but fellow Latins. The notions underlying *postliminium* and the exchange of citizenship by transfer of domicile between Latins of different communes explain very simply the enfranchisement of freedmen

[1] Treggiari, op. cit. 38 ff., esp. 45–7; for 169, Livy 45. 15. 1–7.

[2] Treggiari, op. cit. 163, 167; cf. the derogatory remarks of Ap. Claudius and Scipio Aemilianus (142, 131 B.C.) in Plut. *Paulus* 38. 4; Velleius 2. 4. 4; Val. Max. 6. 2. 3.

[3] e.g. Treggiari, op. cit. 11 ff.

[4] Cic. *Topica* 2. 10; 'si neque censu neque vindicta nec testamento liber factus est, non est liber.'

[5] Treggiari, op. cit. 20 ff. Livy 2. 5. 9. Dion. *Ant.* 4. 22. 4. *Tit. Ulp.* 1. 9, 2. 4, where the Tables specify *libertas* rather than *civitas*.

in early Rome. The freed slave may return to the *populus Latinus* from which he was taken, and recover his original status as a Tusculan or an Arician, or he may remain at Rome and secure registration as a *civis Romanus* before a magistrate, like any other Latin. The influence of time and precedent may explain the extension of this usage to freedmen of non-Latin origin, Etruscans, Volscians, and Samnites, to whom Cicero may refer when he speaks of *postliminium* applying to freedmen from *populi foederati* who return to their original homes.[1]

The magisterial sanction, which is distinctive in the Roman procedure, was essential for establishing the civic status of the freedman. Without it there could be no citizenship, even when tardily it came to be accepted that informal manumission created a kind of freedom. Thus the consul or praetor presides over manumission 'by the rod', and the quinquennial censor registers the manumission *censu*. Manumission by will is no exception, though at first sight it might seem so. The earliest form of Roman will was a public act authorized at sessions of the archaic *comitia calata* under the presidency of a magistrate. When this procedure was replaced by testation *per aes et libram*, the role of the state was maintained by the nuncupatory formula preserved from the earlier process, 'Vos Quirites testimonium mihi perhibetote', addressed to the five citizen witnesses, who thus represent the *populus* in its assembly. The will itself with its legacies and manumissions only takes effect when the praetor grants the Roman form of probate—'bonorum possessionem secundum tabulas'. When late in time the Augustan *lex Aelia* created a new form of full manumission this only took effect through a formal declaration before a magistrate or pro-magistrate.[2]

It has been convincingly argued that in the Republic freedmen suffered no statutory limitations to their political rights and duties as Roman citizens, but that social prejudice effectively excluded them and their sons from certain functions. Freedmen certainly served in the Roman legions in times of crisis, in so far as their age permitted, and more frequently as marines, though they seem not to have been regularly enlisted at the annual

---

[1] For *ius migrationis* cf. above, 14 ff., 34 ff., 110. For *postliminium* of freedmen, Cic. *de Or.* 1. 182, *pro Balbo* 28, cf. Dion. *Ant.* 4. 22. 4, and above, 293 n. 3.

[2] For the magisterial role 330 nn. 1-3, 333 n. 4 below, and for manumission *censu* also *Fr. Dos.* 17. For the history of wills, Gaius 2. 101-4.

legionary levies.[1] There was no absolute bar against servile personnel, since in the Hannibalic war *volones* were in frequent use, who were slaves purchased from their masters and later liberated by the state. The more limited use of ordinary freedmen as soldiers was probably due to their age, as Livy hints, since few freedmen would be found in the younger age-groups, and also to their poverty, since many may have been too poor to qualify for service in the military *classes*.[2] While freedmen themselves are not known ever to have secured public magistracies at Rome before the fall of the Republic, their sons managed to hold the lesser Roman magistracies from time to time, from the fourth century onwards, though none surpassed the success of the prototype, Flavius the former *scriba*, or treasury clerk, who became curule aedile in 304. The recorded instances are confined to the plebeian tribunate, and mostly belong to the last century of the Republic. Only in the Triumviral period are there instances of servile persons who secure, or try to secure, the praetorship. Admission of freedmen's sons to the Senate has much the same history.[3] So too with equestrian positions. Freedmen were tacitly excluded from service on the political juries created in the late second century, for which the letter of the law required free birth. This rule admitted the sons of freedmen, who, as a single instance seems to indicate, were not prohibited from acquiring formal equestrian status as *equites equo publico* if any censor was prepared to enrol them.[4] Instances are rare even in the Triumviral period, when freedmen are found also in the office of

---

[1] Treggiari, op. cit. 67–8, citing Livy 10. 21. 4; 22. 11. 8; App. *BC* 1. 49, for legionaries, and for marines Livy 36. 2. 15; 40. 18. 7; 42. 27. 3; for *volones* cf. Treggiari, op. cit. 68 n. 2.

[2] Livy 10. 21. 4, 'seniorum etiam cohortes factae libertinique centuriati'; id. 22. 11. 8, freedmen with families are conscripted; id. 45. 15. 2 implies that few freedmen belonged to the First Class.

[3] Treggiari, op. cit. 52 f., combats the widely held notion of Mommsen (*St. R.* iii. 451 f.) that freedmen and their families were nominally excluded from holding public office. Cn. Flavius (Livy 9. 46. 1) had no certain successor until the tribunate of A. Gabinius in 139, who was probably the grandson of a freedman (cf. E. Badian, *Philol.* 103 (1959), 87 on Livy, *Per. Ox.* 54), and P. Furius, L. Equitius, tribunes in 100–99 (App. *BC* 1. 32. 1; 33. 2; *de V.I.* 73; Cic. *Rab. Perd.* 20). On the transitory freedmen senators of 312, and their successors in the post-Sullan period cf. Treggiari, op. cit. 54 f., 60 f., Livy 9. 46. 10, Cic. *Clu.* 131, Dio 40. 63. 4; the rest are Triumviral, with the freedmen praetors of Dio 48. 34. 4; *Dig.* 1. 14. 3, *Suda* s.v. Barbios Philippikos.

[4] Cf. Treggiari, op. cit. 64 f., 67 n. 2, on *lex repetundarum* s. 15 (*FIRA* i.² 7), Dio, fr. 93. 2 (P. Furius as *eques*).

*tribunus militum*, which by origin was a minor magistracy and may have required equestrian standing.[1] For this a high financial qualification was necessary, many times that of the First Class of the centuriate system, which in the middle Republican period may have greatly exceeded the scope even of prosperous freedmen.[2]

In the municipalities of Italy it was public opinion rather than public regulations that prevented freedmen from holding office during the late Republic. The general rules of Caesar's municipal legislation did not specifically bar freedmen from the decurionate. At certain colonies outside Italy, which having been recruited from the urban population of Rome contained a high proportion of freedmen, a new rule was necessary. Hence the charter of Urso in Spain makes an exception in favour of freedmen. Their status is not to be alleged as a bar against their holding the decurionate 'for the cause of unworthiness'.[3] The phrase suggests that elsewhere it was censorial prejudice rather than the letter of the law that excluded freedmen.

If the Republic restricted the political rights of freedmen in some degree, they enjoyed a large measure of equality of private rights under the *ius civile*. The Roman freedman had the *ius Quiritium* and in matters of property and personal relationships could do everything that a free-born citizen could do, including testamentary disposition of his estate, though this freedom was restricted in the age of Sulla by the severe qualification that the *patronus* had a claim to half the estate of the freedman who left no 'natural heirs'.[4] It has been much disputed whether there

---

[1] Military tribunes and prefects cannot be assumed to be technically *equites equo publico* in the Triumviral period, cf. Treggiari, op. cit. 65. On the distinction between *equites Romani* and *equites equo publico* in the Principate cf. M. I. Henderson, *JRS* 53 (1963), 61 ff., P. A. Brunt, *JRS* 51 (1961), 76 f., confirmed by Pliny, *Epp.* I. 19. 2 (cf. A. N. Sherwin-White, *Letters of Pliny*, ad loc.).

[2] The equestrian census of S. 400,000, testified from 67 B.C., was ten times the Livian figure for the First Class; cf. A. Stein, *Römische Ritterstand* (Munich, 1927), 23 nn. 1–2. For poverty of many, cf. Treggiari, op. cit. 105–6, 142 ff.

[3] *Tab. Her.* 94–5. *Lex Urs.* 105. Cf. Strabo 8. 6. 23 (381) on Corinth. Duff, op. cit. 66 n. 3. The law did not specify disqualification but provided for a trial 'si quis quem decurionum indignum loci aut ordinis . . . esse dicet'.

[4] Treggiari, op. cit. 79, 81. A. Watson, op. cit. 231. Freedmen also owed the performance of sundry *operae* to their patrons, but these various and heavy servitudes were contractual, not mandatory, being based on an agreement made at the time of manumission; for a discussion cf. Treggiari, op. cit. 68 ff., Duff, op. cit. 44 f.

were any legal bars on intermarriage with free-born Romans, as a text of Livy appears to imply. But the clear wording of the Augustan law on marriage indicates that there were no bans on intermarriage between any of the social classes until that law vetoed marriages between senators and freedwomen. It was social prejudice that effectively limited such intermarriage in the Republic, though it did not entirely prevent it.[1] Since Augustus placed no other veto on the marriages of freedmen it is likely that there was no general ban earlier.

Legal bans appear with the Principate, which was both liberal in its general attitude towards freedmen and manumission, and strict in its precise regulations. Inscriptions and legal evidence of the post-Augustan period indicate that freedmen were now barred from the annual magistracies and the decurionate of most municipalities, whether Latin or Roman in status. The rule of the Flavian *lex Malacitana* which bars freedmen from the civil offices of this Latin municipality, is echoed in other documents and claims a Roman model.[2] In compensation the minor office of *sevir*, concerned with certain civic festivals, was open to freedmen in many Italian and provincial municipalities, and a civic corporation, the *ordo Augustalium*, was created by Augustus for their dignification.[3] This general differentiation towards freedmen may be due likewise to Augustus, whose legislation sought to lessen the frequency of manumission, and invented the specific ban on intermarriage with senators. Yet it was not otherwise restrictive towards freedmen's rights, and positively encouraged marriage and procreation between freedmen and free-born citizens in general. The main concern of Augustus was to lay down strict rules for the modes of manumission so as to limit it to the deserving.[4] Though the rules of the *lex Aelia Sentia* (A.D. 4)

[1] Treggiari, op. cit. 83, stresses, with others, the formal implication of the text of the *lex Julia de maritandis ordinibus*, cited from Paulus in *Dig.* 23. 2. 44, that the Augustan innovation was not the validation of mixed marriages in general but the veto of those between senators and freedwomen, against the opposite suggestion of Dio 54. 16. 2; 56. 7. 2, and Celsus in *Dig.* 23. 2. 23. She explains Livy's account of the reward of Faecennia (39. 19. 5, 'utique ei ingenuo nubere liceret neve quid ob id . . . fraudi ignominiaeve esset') as protection merely against censorial action, though this may not suffice for *fraudi*.

[2] Cf. Duff, op. cit. 66, 69 f. *Lex Mal.* 54. *ILS* 6914, 'omnibus honoribus honorati quos libertini gerere potuerunt', also from a Spanish municipality. The *lex Visellia* excluded freedmen from the decurionate (Just. *Inst.* 1. 5. 3).

[3] Cf. G. Chilver, *Cisalpine Gaul* (Oxford, 1941), 198 f., improving on Duff, op. cit. 133 f.   [4] Cf. *CAH* x. 432 f; and above, n. 1.

were designed to check the lavish manumission of young slaves and the undue generosity of young masters, it approved of such manumission 'for a just cause'. This was interpreted broadly and was concerned more with personal relationships than with merit in isolation. Favoured categories covered kinsmen in servile status, personal retainers, and regular marriage with a female slave: only one category of practical utility is mentioned by Gaius.[1] You could free your old nurse, but not your cook or your butler.

The most restrictive of the Augustan laws was the *Fufia Caninia*. This limited manumission by will, a common practice in Roman society, to a maximum of one fifth of *familiae* numbering between one and five hundred persons, with an absolute maximum of one hundred persons to be freed. These large 'families', so extravagantly set free for purposes of social ostentation, were not the sweating gangs of rustic slaves working on great estates, but the household establishments of the great palaces of Rome, where servants were numbered by the score, and acted as consumers rather than creators of wealth.[2] The weight of formal manumission particularly touched the population of Rome itself, where the urban domestics would mostly remain after manumission, rather than the municipalities of Italy where formal manumission was subject to practical limiting factors that did not apply at Rome.[3] Italy may have been more affected by the creation of a new category of freedmen, the *Latini Juniani*, invented by a *lex Junia* of uncertain date.

This remarkable innovation, which may be attributed chronologically either to Augustus or to his successor Tiberius, provided a special status for a type of freedman whose numbers had been increasing rapidly (it seems) in the later Republic.[4] These were

---

[1] Gaius 1. 19, 39. Ulpian in *Dig.* 40. 2. 13 extends the list of personal relationships, and ibid. 16 defines the *iusta causa* as *ex affectu*. Paulus ibid. 15 adds only life-saving service. No ordinary household duty is listed outside the nursery and schoolroom.

[2] Cf. Gaius 1. 42–6. *Tit. Ulp.* 1. 24–5. Sent. Pauli 4. 14. *CAH* x. 432 f. Duff, op. cit. 31–2. The criticism of testamentary manumission in Dion. *Ant.* 4. 24. 4–7 implies urban *familiae* in many details, such as attendance at the master's funeral, and expulsion from Rome. Cf. Gaius 1. 27, 160, and *Sent. Pauli* 4. 14. 1, *opsonatores* and *ancillae*. The consular Pedanius had a *familia* of four hundred persons in his Roman palace on the day of his murder (Tac. *Ann.* 14. 43. 4).

[3] Cf. below, 330 nn. 1–2.

[4] For the dates see below, 332 n. 2–3, 333 n. 1. On Junian Latinity in general there is little to add to Last, op. cit. 432 f., Duff, op. cit. 75 ff., and Steinwenter *RE* xii. 1. cols. 910–23. The main evidence comes from Gaius 1. 22–3, 28–35, 41, 66–71, 80; 3. 56–72. *Tit. Ulp.* 1. 10, 12; 3. 1–6; 7. 4; 20. 14; 22. 3 and *Fr. Dos.* 5–14.

ex-slaves whose masters substituted an informal declaration of freedom (*manumissio inter amicos*) for the formal act which had alone hitherto been recognized as conferring both freedom and Roman status on a slave. This class previously had enjoyed merely a precarious status of freedom without specific civil rights. Though praetors would recognize and protect this freedom if disputes came to their attention, such persons had no precise status in law; they were what Ulpian elsewhere terms 'cives nullius certae civitatis'.[1] By a fine distinction which has other analogies in Roman law they were slaves under the older concept of *ius Quiritium* and free men under the praetorian edict on which so much of Roman law depended.[2] For these persons the *lex Junia* provided a civil standing, based on the old *ius Latii*, now extinct in Italy. This secured for Junian Latins most of the property and procedural rights of citizens, but for their lifetime and their personal gains only, since at death their property passed to their former masters in its entirety, and they lacked the right of inheritance, unless they had secured a further promotion to full citizen status. At the time of its creation Junian Latinity must have been a clear gain to its holders, the informally freed slaves. The law blended justice towards a meritorious class with caution against excessive manumission, and protected vested interests. But the unfavourable contrast with the condition of full freedman citizenship made the Latin status appear restrictive in later times. Though channels of promotion to citizen status were soon opened to Junian Latins either through the birth of a single son under a special form of legitimate wedlock, or through various activities in the service of the Roman state, the latter were all connected with the life of the city of Rome itself, and the former until about the year 75 were confined to those freed under the age of thirty.[3] Hence outside Rome Junian Latins

---

[1] *Tit. Ulp.* 20. 14. Such persons have no 'leges civitatis suae'.

[2] Gaius 3. 56: 'olim ex iure Quiritium servos fuisse sed auxilio praetoris in libertatis forma servari solitos'; cf. id. 1. 22 'olim servi viderentur', *Fr. Dos.* 5,'praetor . . . non patiebatur servire'. Cf. e.g. Gaius 1. 54 for the distinction between ownership *ex iure Quiritium* and *in bonis*. The *i.Q.* represents the oldest stratum of *ius civile*, cf. above, 319 n. 2–3.

[3] Gaius 1. 29–34. *Tit. Ulp.* 3. 1–6, listing service in the *vigiles*, corn-shipment to Rome, house-building at Rome, keeping a bakery at Rome (later). Full citizenship could also be secured by *principis beneficium*, or by a second manumission ceremony (*iteratio*), but these required the initiative of others (Pliny, *Epp.* 7. 16. 4; 10. 104. Gaius 1. 35. *Tit. Ulp.* 3. 2, 4). For the Aelian form of marriage see below, 333 n. 4.

must have constituted a numerous group of under-privileged half-citizens in the municipalities of Italy and the western provinces, where only the 'benefit of paternity' could secure the citizenship for some of them by their own initiative.

A prevalence of Junian Latins outside Rome is the more likely in that formal manumission in its commonest type (*vindicta*) required the presence of a Roman magistrate with *imperium*. This normally limited its use in Italy to the city of Rome, where such manumission was possible at frequent intervals, and to the capital cities and assize centres of the provinces during the periodic visitations of Roman governors.[1] Hence in the late Republic, after the unification of Italy, and throughout the Principate, factors of distance encouraged the spread of informal manumission. This need not have become common if municipal magistrates had been competent to preside. But the silence of the lawyers excludes them, while a letter of Pliny indicates that a magnate of Comum could only secure his formal manumissions through the chance presence of a proconsul travelling to his province. Though the rules of the Latin municipality of Salpensa in Spain allow the *duoviri* to preside over the formal manumission of slaves whose masters had normal Latin rights, so that the slaves became 'Latin freedmen of the best condition', such municipal enfranchisement was not available for the slaves of Roman citizens anywhere.[2] The same limitation applied to the promotion of Junian Latins through the 'benefit of paternity', which likewise required the presence of a Roman magistrate with *imperium*.[3] The strictness with which the advancement of slaves to Roman status was guarded, and the neglect of the interests of the gentry of municipal Italy, is remarkable.

The serious complaints about the disadvantages of Junian status are all late, listed in *RE* art. cit., col. 915. Tac. *Ann.* 13. 27, 'vinculo servitutis' is not a complaint.

[1] Cf. Gaius 1. 20, 'in provinciis . . . id . . . fit ultimo die conventus sed Romae certis diebus . . . vel in transitu . . . cum praetor aut proconsule in . . . balneum eat.' Cf. *Tit. Ulp.* 3. 3, 'apud praetorem vel praesidem'. Citations in *Dig.* 40. 2 confirm this in detail, stressing the difficulty in Italy (15. 5), and the special warrant given to the Prefect of Egypt under Augustus for this function (21). Gaius in another context remarks (2. 25) : 'quod . . . ipsi per nos praesentibus amicis agere possumus, hoc non est necesse cum maiore difficultate apud praetorem aut apud praesidem provinciae agere'.

[2] Cf. above, n. 1. Pliny, *Epp.* 7. 16. 4: 'vindicta liberare quos proxime inter amicos manumisisti'. *Lex Mal.* 28., cf. *RE* art. cit., col. 915. *Fr. Dos.* 17 shows that manumission *censu* was available only at Rome, and not before municipal *quinquennales*.          [3] Gaius 1. 29, cf. below, 333 n. 4.

If the *lex Junia* belongs to A.D. 15 or 19, as its full title of *Junia Norbana* suggests, it may be connected with other legislation of the period which is similarly restrictive towards newly enfranchised persons, yet generous to the idea of liberation. A *lex Junia Petronia* of 19 encouraged liberality by giving the benefit of the doubt, in cases of disputed status, to the claim for freedom when evidence was evenly poised. A *lex Visellia* of A.D. 23 created the first allowance of Roman status to Junians for public service, but it also implemented a senatorial decree of the previous year, excluding the children and grandchildren of freedmen from the privilege of wearing the 'golden rings', which were a distinctive emblem of equestrian status, even though possessing the necessary property qualification.[1] The implication is that equestrian status itself was now barred to persons in these degrees, though no source states as much. The *lex Visellia* contained a clause which allowed the Princeps to dispense grants of the 'golden rings' to the unqualified, but the emperors were criticized by aristocratic opinion for doing so, and the rule was otherwise enforced with severity.[2] A similar rule, apparently formulated under Gaius Caesar, while encouraging wealthy provincial Romans to exercise equestrian privileges, excluded those of the first generation from service on the jury panels at Rome.[3]

[1] For the *lex Junia Petronia* cf. *Dig.* 40. 1. 24; 48. 8. 11. 2. For the *S.C.* and the *lex Visellia* cf. Pliny *NH* 33. 32: 'ne cui ius id esset nisi qui ingenuus ipse ingenuo patre avo paterno HS CCCC census fuisset et lege Iulia theatrali in quattuordecim ordinibus sedisset'. *Tit. Ulp.* 3. 5; *Cod. Iust.* 9. 21, summarizes the provisions of the law against usurpation by freedmen of the privileges of *ingenui*, its only interest for the *C.J.*, and the dispensatory power of the Princeps. A similar definition occurs in a *S.C.* of A.D. 19 protecting the equestrian order against infamous women (Tac. *Ann.* 2. 85. 1–2). There is no foundation for the widely held view that the *lex Visellia* modified the *S.C.* of Pliny. The texts down to Trajan's time clearly associate the rings with equestrian status (e.g. Martial 8. 5; 14. 122. Suet. *Aug.* 74. Dio 48. 45. 7; 53. 30. 3; cf. Treggiari, op. cit. 66 f.). The later stress on the grant of the *ius anulorum* as a symbol of fictitious *ingenuitas* derives from the qualification given by the *S.C.* This was its practical value to freedmen, but does not disprove association with equestrian status. The *ius* did not confer the actual standing of a Knight, but the *ornamenta* of one, like the grant of senatorial *ornamenta* to equestrian procurators in e.g. Tac. *Ann.* 12. 21. 2. For modern views see Duff, op. cit. 214 ff., Henderson, art. cit. 67 ff. The *ius* was steadily devalued during the second century until Severus in 197 allowed it to all legionary soldiers (Duff, op. cit. 215, cf. *Dig.* 40. 10. 6, Herodian 3. 8. 5).

[2] Pliny, *NH* 33. 33 records the prosecution of four hundred freedmen for illicit use of the rings. Tac. *Hist.* 1. 13, 2. 57; *Ann.* 12. 53. 2–5; Pliny, *Epp.* 8. 6. 4, animadvert on grants to freedmen.

[3] Pliny, *NH* 33. 30 (cited above, 250 n. 1), clarified by Dio 59. 9. 5, suggests that

## THE DATE OF THE LEX JUNIA

The chronology of this law does not greatly affect the understanding of the policy towards manumission in the early Principate. But the later dating fits the conservative attitude of Tiberius and his advisers, which appears not only in the legislation just discussed, but also in their lack of initiative towards the general extension of the citizenship.[1] Hence certainty about the date of the *lex Junia* would clarify the history of enfranchisement from Augustus through to Claudius. The evidence of the title would be regarded as decisive for A.D. 15 or 19 according to the normal custom of naming laws after the magistrates holding office in the year of their proposal, since only in these two years are a Junius and a Norbanus known as consuls in the same year, but for the detailed evidence of Gaius.[2] This appears to date the *lex Junia* firmly before the passing of the *lex Aelia Sentia* of A.D. 4, by stating that the latter created the 'benefit of paternity' for certain Junian Latins. A passage in the epitome of Ulpian supports Gaius, though others assert or imply a date after the *lex Aelia*.[3]

provincial Romans of the second generation were admitted to equestrian status and jury service by the initiative of Gaius Caesar.

[1] Cf. above, 237.

[2] Just. *Inst.* 1. 5. 3 is the only evidence for the double title. Doubts about the reading have been reaffirmed by M. de Dominicis, *Tidjschrift voor Rechtsgeschiedener*, 1965, 556 f. on textual grounds. The intended year can as well be A.D. 15, when an *ordinarius* and a suffect consul had these names, as A.D. 19, when they were held by the two *ordinarii*. The Augustan laws *Papia Poppaea* and *Fufia Caninia* take their names from two suffects or from mixed pairs of consuls. Any year with suffects as yet unknown before A.D. 23 (*Tit. Ulp.* 3. 5) is possible, e.g. 6, 7 B.C. The exemplary discussion of the legal evidence by H. M. Last, *CAH* x. 888 f., in favour of an Augustan date before A.D. 4 against Steinwenter's argument for A.D. 19 (*RE* art. cit. cols. 911 f.), seems to have silenced but not settled the controversy. I hope to show elsewhere that the neglected *statim* in Gaius 1. 29 (cited below, n. 3) in its context decisively favours a Tiberian date.

[3] Gaius 1. 29 is primary: 'Latini multis modis ad civitatem Romanam perveniunt. Statim enim ex lege Aelia Sentia minores triginta annorum manumissi et Latini facti si uxores duxerint . . . et filium procreaverint . . . datur eis potestas . . .' Gaius consistently attributes this 'benefit of paternity' to the *lex Aelia* (cf. 1. 66. 68, 71, 80) and is supported by the substance of a Hadrianic *S.C.* which he cites in 3. 73. Against this *Tit. Ulp.* 3. 3 attributes the 'benefit of paternity' directly to the *lex Junia* without mention of the *lex Aelia*. Less certainly *Tit. Ulp.* 1. 12 implies that the *Latini Juniani* were unknown, and 7. 4 that they were known, to the *lex Aelia*. Gaius 3. 74–6 seems to be a discussion of a topic involving sections of the *lex Aelia* and of the *lex Junia* in the terminology of his own times, and hence not to illuminate the direct wording of the *lex Aelia*. Steinwenter, *RE* art. cit. 912–13 explains away all these references as additions or interpretations of Gaius or Ulpian.

Further, the double title of *Junia Norbana* is unknown to Gaius and Ulpian. Hence recent historians have eitherly accepted the masterly analysis of the legal evidence by H. M. Last in favour of the early date, or left the question open, though preferring the later date on the evidence of the title.[1] It is relevant to add that a series of amendments, clarifying the status of Junian Latins or extending their opportunities for full enfranchisement, begins in A.D. 23 with a clause of the *lex Visellia*, and continues with four measures down to 65.[2] This suggests the amendment of a recent and imperfect statute rather than the revival of interest in a law passed some forty years earlier.

If the *lex Junia* could be firmly dated to the time of Tiberius it would follow that the 'benefit of paternity' created by the *lex Aelia* for those informally manumitted under the age of thirty was a first step in improving the condition of a class of persons who were 'informally free', and who later became Latins under the *lex Junia*, since Gaius consistently attributes this 'benefit' to the *lex Aelia* in several passages.[3] It is possible that the *lex Aelia* stabilized the previous guarantee of freedom under the pretorian edict, since it created a special kind of *conubium* between its beneficiaries and persons of Roman status with whom they contracted a form of marriage.[4] This implies that they were now permanently free persons, not nominal slaves. Augustus would then be responsible for initiating the solution finally perfected in the *lex Junia* under Tiberius.

It is remarkable that this clause created an escape route from the inferior status for persons who at the time of their manumission were excluded from the full citizenship because a 'just cause' could not be alleged for them. The 'just cause', however, was based on personal relationship as much as on merit.

---

[1] Cf. J. Crook, *Law and Life of Rome* (London, 1967), 296 n. 29.

[2] Gaius 1. 31–4; 3. 63: Tit. Ulp. 3. 5–6.

[3] Above, 332 n. 3. Cf. Steinwenter, art. cit.

[4] Gaius 1. 80. Such *conubium* applies only to persons who contract marriage *ex lege Aelia*. The beneficiary was required first to register his marriage to a Roman or to another beneficiary before seven witnesses as being *liberorum creandorum causa*, and later to prove the existence of a child of twelve months before a magistrate, in order to establish his claim to the Roman citizenship. Marriages of Junians and Romans on other terms did not have the effect of *conubium* for their children until Hadrian allowed this (Gaius 1. 29–30. *Tit. Ulp.* 3. 3). Steinwenter (art. cit. 913) regards the *conubium ex Aelia lege* as a short-lived anomaly with no further implications.

Subsequent extension of promotion for Junian Latins was based on service to the state: the less your potential the smaller your chance of advancement. Hence the 'over thirties' remained excluded from the benefit of paternity for seventy years after the *lex Aelia*.[1] The vicious slave was the subject of another section of the *lex Aelia* which relegated slaves who had bad personal records, whether freed formally or informally, to a new category of free persons with minimal civil rights, styled *in numero dediticiorum*, and ordained their permanent exclusion from Rome and its environs in a circuit of a hundred miles. It is clear from these arrangements that the status of Junian Latinity, which was not open to those *in numero dediticiorum*, was not concerned with the degradation of the unworthy, and also that the manumissory legislation of Augustus was concerned primarily with the population of the capital itself rather than with the people of Italy.[2]

# APPENDIX

## THE PROBLEMS OF THE THIRD AUGUSTAN EDICT FROM CYRENE

THE difficulty lies in translating the principal clause: τούτους λειτουργεῖν οὐδὲν ἔλασσον ἐμ μέρει τῷ τῶν Ἑλλήνων σώματι κελεύω, and in the relationship of this to what follows: ἐκτὸς τούτων οἷς ... ἀνεισφορία ὁμοῦ σὺν τῇ πολιτήαι δέδοται. Formerly the phrase τῷ ... σώματι was taken to refer to the totality of Greek communes in Cyrenaica, as meaning e.g. 'the enfranchised Greeks are none the less to perform liturgies turn in turn for the community of Greeks'. De Visscher (in *Édits*, supported by Wilhelm, art. cit., and in other articles cited above, 296 n. 1) denied that σῶμα could have the required meaning, and suggested that σώματι should be taken with λειτουργεῖν to mean: 'They are to perform the personal duties of Greeks in their turn.' This rests on the well-documented distinction in earlier Greek and later Roman usage between duties arising from personal status (*personae*, σώματα) and those attached to real property (*patrimonium*, χρήματα).

[1] Cf. above, 328 n. 1, 329 n. 3. A *S.C.* of *c.* A.D. 75 extended the benefit to those over thirty when freed.

[2] Gaius 1. 13, 15, 25–7; 3. 74–6, *Tit. Ulp.* 1. 11; 20. 14; 22. 2. For the meaning of *in numero dediticiorum* cf. below, 335, 391 n. 1.

But this meaning is extracted from the text only with some difficulty. Wilhelm improved matters by taking τῷ τῶν Ἑλλήνων with ἐμ μέρει, in the sense of 'in the role of Greeks', or *vice Graecorum*. He cited usages of ἐν μέρει with the genitive in papyri from Pape (*Handwörterbuch* s.v.) but no precise parallel. The phrase is better connected with its use in Edict 1. 9, where there is no dependent genitive and the meaning is simply *in vicem*. The difficulty over σώματι has been intensified by the doubtful insistence of certain scholars that the edict was drafted in Greek and not translated from a Latin original. This does not exclude the probability that the original instructions of Augustus were given in Latin. The simplest solution is that σώματι represents the not unfamiliar phrase *in numero*, used by Gaius and others in a precisely apposite sense to indicate a category of persons to whom a different category is being assimilated without total identification. Thus the *lex agraria* of 111 B.C. (ss. 66–9) distinguishes *coloni* from 'qui in coloni numero est' (*FIRA* i.² 8). Such were the freedmen who were *in numero dediticiorum* (Gaius 1. 68, below, 391 n. 1.), and the *Latini coloniarii* reckoned *in numero peregrinorum* (id. 1. 79). Here the externs are to perform duties *in numero Graecorum* though they are not *Graeci*. The term Ἕλλην is used in the Cyrene edicts, as in other documents from the eastern provinces, to indicate the most privileged category of local citizens within the various cities, as notably in Egypt; cf. *FIRA* i.² 99. 18, *CAH* x. 297–8, *OGIS* 458 n. 24, Jos. *Ant.* 18. 9. 9. The term σῶμα does not occur in de Visscher's sense in any of the Republican and Triumviral documents, which consistently use only *immunitas rerum* and *muneris vacatio* or their literal Greek equivalents; cf. 297–300 nn. The Hellenes of Cyrene may be connected with the 'citizens' of the Ptolemaic constitution; cf. G. de Sanctis, *Documenti di Cirene Ant.* (*Riv. Fil. CL.* 1928), 240 f.

But the greatest difficulty lies in the use of λειτουργεῖν, and it is made worse by construing this with σώματι. The logic of the documents requires not λειτουργεῖν but, e.g., εἰσφέρειν. As it is, Augustus makes the grant of ἀνεισφορία, which should here be the equivalent of ἀνεισφορία and of *immunitas rerum* in the veteran edicts (above, 300 n. 1) i.e. freedom from imperial taxes, include πάρεσις λειτουργίας (*muneris vacatio*). The externs are to be subject to *munera* because they lack not *muneris vacatio* but *immunitas rerum*. Yet all previous documents clearly distinguish between the two privileges (above, 300 n. 1). The emendation of J. H. Oliver (*Hesperia* 29 (1960), 324 f.) would solve all these difficulties by expanding the text to read χρήμασι καὶ σώματι to be taken with λειτουργεῖν: 'The externs are to be liable to both real and personal obligations if they lack real immunity.' This ingeniously restores logic and technical credibility, but unfortunately the emendation is not acceptable because the text requires the plural σώμασι, 'they are to serve with their bodies', instead of the singular, which stands on the stone and should not be altered to fit a conjectural supplement, although the five Cyrene edicts certainly contain many minor errors and omissions elsewhere in what is a single inscription. The existing text must be taken to mean that Augustus justified the cancellation of the externs' freedom from *munera* by a sharp argument.

K. M. Atkinson (art. cit. 31) suggested that the disputed phrase referred specifically to *militiae vacatio*, from which only *cives optimo iure immunes* were exempt. But this is not so; the texts always distinguish *militiae vacatio* as a separate grant from the condition of *cives o.i. immunes* (300 n. 1, 301 n. 1). Besides, provincial Romans did not serve in a civic militia, as Atkinson interprets ἐμ μέρει τῷ τῶν Ἑλλήνων, but in the legionary army.


# ADDENDUM

The full text of the Tabula Banasitana was finally published by its editors in *CRAI* 1971 (Paris, 1972), 468 f. Since this document is unique its substance is given here. It contains two letters addressed by the joint emperors to successive procurators who supported the requests. The first states: 'Libellum Iuliani Zegrensis litteris tuis iunctum legimus et quamquam civitas Romana non nisi maximis meritis provocata indulgentia principali gentibus istis dari solita sit tamen cum eum adfirmes . . . nostris rebus prompto obsequio fidissimum. . . . quamquam plurimos cupiamus . . . ad aemulationem Iuliani excitari, non cunctamur et ipsi Ziddinae uxori item liberis . . . civitatem Romanam salvo iure gentis dare'. The second letter repeats most of this and adds an excerpt, dated 6 July 177, from the *commentarius civitate Romana donatorum* (pertaining to all emperors from Augustus to Marcus except Otho and Vitellius). This lists the names of the enfranchised persons and adds: 'Rogatu Aureli Iuliani principis gentis Zegrensium per libellum suffragante Vallio Maximo per epistulam, his civitatem Romanam dedimus salvo iure gentis sine deminutione tributorum et vectigalium populi et fisci'. To stress its importance it is sealed by twelve members of the imperial *Consilium*. Two distinct persons are concerned, at ten years' interval, seeking citizenship for their wives and children.

# XIV

## THE DIRECT ENFRANCHISEMENT OF PROVINCIAL COMMUNES

I T was maintained above that from the time of Caesar onwards Roman privileges were commonly given to native
provincial communities in the form of Latin rights rather
than the full citizenship, which was generally reserved, with the
status of *municipium civium Romanorum*, for communities that contained a substantial element of immigrant Italians organized as
*conventus civium Romanorum*, and indicated in the provincial lists
of Pliny, dating in the main from the Augustan period, as *oppida
civium Romanorum*.[1] Latin status itself was treated as a bridge-
status, both for the individual members of the upper classes, who
through it secured the Roman citizenship by holding their local
magistracies (*per honorem*), and for the communities themselves,
which eventually secured the status of a full Roman *municipium*
after an intermediate period as a *municipium Latini iuris*.[2]

These notions have been developed, amended, or rejected in
four main ways. F. Vittinghoff suggested briefly that Latin
municipalities were seldom or never promoted to full Roman
status, because the primary interest of the central government
and of the local aristocracies were fully secured by the admission
of the upper classes to the Roman citizenship, which won their
loyalty to Rome.[3] L. Teutsch has argued at length that Pliny's
*oppida civium Romanorum* have nothing to do with the enfranchisement of native communes. H. von Braunert has suggested that
the communal status and organization of a *municipium* was a
subsequent development distinct from the initial grant of either
Roman or Latin citizenship to a provincial community. And,
most radical of all, C. Saumagne has argued at length that the
Roman government in the late Republic and the Principate was
never so rash as to incorporate alien and barbarian communities

---

[1] Above, 232, 251 ff.  [2] Above, 115, 233, 254–5.
[3] F. Vittinghoff, *Römische Kolonisation und Bürgerrechtspolitik unter Caesar und
Augustus* (Wiesbaden, 1952), 29–30, 47. For Teutsch and Braunert see below, 340
n. 4 and 360 n. 1.

directly into the Roman polity: there were no *municipia civium Romanorum* outside Italy at any time; the term *municipium* in documents of all sorts concerning the provinces always refers to communes of Latin status, which alone was given to peregrines.[1]

Saumagne's theory, if accepted, is a discovery of considerable importance. His starting-point is the fact—not sufficiently emphasized previously—that in the public documents of provincial municipalities no distinctive term is ever used to indicate that a community possessed the Roman rather than the Latin status. Plain *municipium* is used by all and sundry, despite the notorious ambition of the municipalities to make much of their distinctions. Hence even those inscriptions which name an emperor as *conditor municipii* do not prove the elevation of the community to full Roman status, and the mere appearance of such a title as *municipium Julium* or *Aelium* at a former peregrine commune indicates no more than the grant of Latin status by an emperor with that name. Saumagne underlined the fact that after the accession of Vespasian, though documents refer to the acquisition of Latin Rights by formulae such as *Latium impetratum*, or imply it indirectly by reference to the gaining of citizenship *per honorem*, no text refers with certainty to the promotion of a peregrine community to the status of a *municipium* by means of a block grant of the Roman citizenship.[2]

Saumagne cites passages from the *Institutes* of the lawyer Gaius, and from the *Panegyric* of the consular Pliny, written under Hadrian or Pius and in A.D. 100 respectively, to prove that peregrine provincials were promoted to Roman status by two channels only, either indirectly through the working of Latin rights (*per honorem*) or directly by individual grants characterized as *beneficium principis*.[3] He maintains that Gaius and Pliny here

[1] C. Saumagne, *Le droit latin et les cités romaines sous l'empire* (Paris, 1965). This book has many strange errors about the citizenship in the Republican period, which do not, however, affect its main thesis. Cf. *JRS* 58 (1968), 269.

[2] The grants of citizenship to unspecified Gauls and to the Ilurcones (or Lingones?) by Galba and Otho (Tac. *Hist.* 1. 8, 78) seem to be the latest known examples. But Saumagne ignores the grant of colonial status to peregrine communes, discussed below, 350 f. The assumption that most *municipia* are Roman leads even G. Alföldi into many minor difficulties in his reconstruction of the civic history of Dalmatia (cited 347 n. 4) e.g. 86 n. 156, 75 n. 50, when peregrines appear as officers of a *municipium*.

[3] Gaius 1. 93, 95. 'Si peregrinus sibi liberisque suis civitatem Romanam petierit ... item si quis civitate Romana donatus sit ... alia causa est eorum qui Latii iure cum liberis suis ad civitatem Romanam perveniunt.' Pliny, *Pan.* 37. 3; 39. 1–2.

speak of these channels exhaustively, and that there did not exist a third method of promotion by a block grant of citizenship to the status of *municipium civium Romanorum*. But first it is to be noted that Saumagne identifies the phrase used by Gaius 'si . . . peregrinus . . . sibi civitatem Romanam petierit' with Pliny's briefer 'seu beneficio principis venissent [sc. in civitatem Romanam]'. Gaius does not here use the term *beneficium principis*, though he certainly refers to Latium in the same way as Pliny. Next, Gaius in his passage is concerned not with a general treatment of promotion but solely with the effect of individual naturalization upon the *patria potestas* of those concerned. Even so he here omits the large category of auxiliary veterans, who secured their citizenship by an unsolicited grant, though he mentions them elsewhere in connection with *patria potestas*.[1] So the omission of block grants by Gaius is not decisive; they were in fact irrelevant to the point at issue, which arose from the isolated nature of individual grants.[2]

The passage from Pliny seems more decisive, since the context, which concerns the exemption of new enfranchised persons (*novi cives*) from the inheritance tax, requires that all forms of naturalization should be indicated.[3] But the assumption that Pliny's term *seu beneficio principis* refers only to individual grants is not correct, though the term naturally can be used in that connection. The following formula indicates a wider range: 'municipes Igabrenses beneficio . . . Vespasiani civitatem Romanam consecuti cum suis per honorem'.[4] The *beneficium* here is the grant of Latin status which subsequently secured the automatic promotion of these personages to the Roman citizenship. After all, any grant of communal privilege rates as a *beneficium*.

To maintain his theory that in the provinces municipal status is always 'Latin', Saumagne had to dispose of certain refractory statements in the Elder Pliny and Cassius Dio.[5] Pliny in his summary of the communes of Baetica and Lusitania used the

[1] Gaius I. 57. The auxiliary veterans did not solicit the citizenship, but received it at the end of their service by an automatic *beneficium principis*.

[2] Gaius is here concerned solely with viritane grants. He remarks in I. 95 that promoted Latins secured *patria potestas* automatically, just as is laid down in the extant charter of Salpensa s. 22 (*FIRA* i². 23). So too with a block grant of citizenship the conditions could be laid down in detail by the local *lex municipii*, if the difficulty could arise where all were *Romani*.　　　　　[3] Cited above, 258.

[4] *ILS* 6781.　　　　　[5] Saumagne, op. cit. 71 f., 79 f., 101.

term *municipium civium Romanorum* instead of *oppidum civium Romanorum*, which he has in all his other summaries and lists.[1] This was explained as the error of a learned commentator or scribe, who wrongly altered Pliny's original text, just in these two places—necessarily, because it is not possible to reject the evidence of a senior imperial administrator who had actually served in the Spanish provinces. But Pliny uses the term not only in these numerical summaries. He goes out of his way to apply it to Olisipo in the detailed list. It is more reasonable to take this evidence as Pliny's own correction of the provincial lists made through his own knowledge, than as a learned alteration of the prototype manuscript at this one point.

With Dio the case is less ambiguous. He states categorically that the 'citizenship' was given by Caesar to all the people of Gades, and by Octavian to those of Utica and Tingi (38–36 B.C.).[2] In these passages he uses the term 'citizenship' or 'citizens'. In numerous other passages it is apparent that by this word, without the specific addition of 'Roman' or 'of the Romans', Dio means the Roman franchise.[3] Saumagne is compelled to maintain that in these three instances it refers to Latin rights. It is possible that Dio failed on occasion to distinguish between Roman and Latin status, a term for which he has no Greek equivalent. There are ambiguities in other evidence above Tingi which suggest that possibly it was originally a *colonia Latini iuris*, like many of the communes of Narbonensis.[4] But the epitomator of Livy confirms the grant of full citizenship to Gades, which had the title of a *municipium* under Augustus, and there is explicit evidence for the status of Utica as a *municipium civium Romanorum*, a full Roman borough, in an oration of Hadrian cited by Gellius.[5]

---

[1] Pliny, *NH* 3. 7; 4. 117–19.

[2] Dio 41. 24. 1; 48. 45. 3; 49. 16. 1

[3] e.g. Dio 43. 39. 5; 60. 17. 4–8; 72. 19. 1.

[4] Cf. L. Teutsch, *Das Römische Städtewesen in Nordafrika* (Berlin, 1962), 206–8. Some of its Augustan coins give it the title *Iulia* and both *quattuorviri* and *duoviri* as chief magistrates (cf. *Inscr. Lat. Maroc.* 2). Pliny, *NH* 5. 2, attributes its colonial status to Claudius while wrongly giving it the by-name of Iotsa (*Iulia Traducta*). For the Narbonensian situation see below, 365 n. 1). A. Degrassi, *Quattuorviri in colonie Romane* etc., Atti dei Lincei mem. sci. mor. (1950), ii. 6. 337–8, suggests that Tingi was promoted from *municipium* to *colonia* before 27 B.C. M. Grant, *From Imperium to Auctoritas* (1946), 177, assumes only titular changes.

[5] Livy, *Epit.* 110, as elsewhere, refers only to the Roman franchise. Gades, entitled Augusta or Augustana and Julia in Pliny, *NH* 4. 119, calls Augustus *parens municipii* on coins; Cf. Vittinghoff, op. cit. 75. It had Roman municipal

Saumagne neglects the evidence of Cicero that Caesar's recent grant of Latin rights to Sicily was converted by Antonius after Caesar's death to an offer of the full franchise. Antonius in practical effect gave the citizenship to the Sicilians as peregrines contrary to Saumagne's views of Roman policy. There is no direct evidence for the modern view that Augustus revoked the grant of Antonius, and two Sicilian cities use the term *municipium* on coins of the triumviral period (44–43 B.C.).[1] There remain the plain statement of Pliny, not noticed by Saumagne, that Mauretanian Rusucurru was given the citizenship by Claudius, and the inscriptions that indicate a similar grant to Mauretian Volubilis in A.D. 44.[2] Saumagne made an ingenious effort to explain away the evidence of these inscriptions.[3] He distinguished between the title of *municipium*, granted to Volubilis on his view with Latin rights in the first year of Claudius' reign, and the grant of Roman citizenship and other privileges made three years later to a select group of local inhabitants, who had assisted the Romans during the recent rebellion of Aedemon.[4] This interpretation would hardly be probable even if the main thesis of Saumagne about the citizenship were well documented. It is against the clear meaning of the Latin texts and the supporting evidence of other documents.

There are three inscriptions. The first was set up to honour Claudius in A.D. 44–5 by the *municipium Volub(ilitanum) impetrata civitate Romana et conubio et oneribus remissis*.[5] By itself this can only mean that the commune acquired all these privileges, as e.g. in an inscription from Lambaesis: 'res publica Gemellensium . . . Latio . . . impetrato dedicavit.'[6] Next a long inscription was set up, after Claudius' death, in which the local Council (*ordo municipii*) honours Valerius Severus, local magnate and military

---

magistrates by 43 B.C. (Cic. *ad Fam* 10. 32. 2), first *quattuorviri*, later *duoviri*, cf. Degrassi, op. cit. 331. For it as *oppidum civium Romanorum* see below, 347

[1] Above, 230–1 ; Cic. *ad Att.* 14. 12. 1. See below, 365 n. 1. For the early date of the coins of Panormus and Henna cf. M. Grant, op. cit. 190–1 (44–43 B.C.).

[2] *NH* 5. 20, 'Rusucurium civitate honoratum a Claudio'. Saumagne's attempt to equate *civitas* and *Latium* through Suet. *Aug.* 47 (*civitate vel Latinitate*), contrary to the usage of authors of this period, is a desperate device.

[3] C. Saumagne, 'Volubilis municipe latine', *Rev. Hist. Dr. Fr. Étr.* 1952, 388 f.

[4] Cf. above, 241–2.

[5] *Inscr. Lat. Mar.* 56 (= *AE* 1924, n. 56) 'When it acquired at its request the Roman citizenship and intermarriage and the remission of burdens'.

[6] *ILS* 6848.

leader against Aedemon, 'on account of his services to the community'.[1] These consist in his activity in securing from Claudius the benefits summarized in the first inscription.[2] They fall into two detailed groups, one concerned with status, the other with financial relief, just as in the earlier document. Saumagne maintains that the first group, which are akin to the rewards granted to certain auxiliary veterans by imperial edict, was limited to the soldiery of Valerius, mentioned in the first part of the inscription, though he cannot deny that the last two fiscal benefits were given to the whole community.[3] But in fact the document simply assigns both groups of benefits to 'the people of Valerius': 'suis impetravit'. Saumagne requires *suis* to mean two different things, the auxiliaries of Valerius and the whole people of Volubilis. But in contemporary and later inscriptions of Volubilis *sui* is used as an alternative to the term *cives sui* or *municipes sui*, regularly used elsewhere.[4]

The third inscription was also set up after the death of Claudius in his honour by *Volubilitani civitate Romana ab eo donati*.[5] This is taken by Saumagne to refer to the individual men of Volubilis who benefited from the Claudian grants, including those enfranchised *per honorem*. But its wording recalls the language in which Pliny records other Claudian promotions in Mauretania: 'Iol . . . coloniae iure donata . . . et Latio dato Tipasa . . . Rusucurium civitate honoratum'.[6] The use of the proper name by itself in other municipalities designates the commune, as in an early inscription of Sicca: 'divo Augusto conditori Siccenses'.[7] Thus Saumagne's tortuous interpretation leaves us with three

---

[1] *I.L. Afr.* 634 = *Inscr. Lat. Mar.* 116.

[2] 'Civitatem Romanam et conubium cum peregrinis mulieribus immunitatem annorum X incolas bona civium bello interfectorum quorum heredes non extabant suis impetravit.'

[3] For the privileges of veterans other than those of the *diplomata* cf. *FIRA* i. 28, 55–6, 76, discussed pp. 296 ff. They include *immunitas*, which Saumagne here claims for his first group. But the veteran *immunitas* was perpetual, whereas relief from taxation for a number of years was regularly granted to cities in distress; cf. Tac. *Ann.* 2. 47; 12. 58. 2; 63. 3.

[4] *Inscr. Lat. Mar.* 128, 'ordo Volub . . . ob merita suorum statuam decrevit.' Ibid. 129, ' in municipio Vol. erga suos piissimae'. 'Men of Volubilis presented by him with the Roman citizenship'.

[5] Ibid. 57.

[6] *NH* 5. 20. 'Iol was given the status of a colony, Tipasa received Latin rights, and Rusucurru was given the distinction of citizenship.'

[7] *ILS* 6773, cf. ibid. 6779; 'imp. Caesari . . . conditori municipii Gigthenses publice'.

public inscriptions about civic promotion at Volubilis, none of which celebrates what in his view was the most important benefit of all—the grant of Latin rights to the commune itself. This should have been mentioned at least in the dedication of A.D. 44.[1]

Saumagne was led to deny that the Romans ever incorporated provincial peoples directly into their citizenship, partly by a curious misunderstanding of Strabo's description of Gades,[2] which he wrongly took to mean that the little island housed a population nearly as big as that of Rome, and hence flinched at the vast scale of enfranchisement—a million Semites at a stroke.[3] He also invoked the reluctance of the Republican government to tolerate the enfranchisement of Italy. But the situation was very different in the Caesarean period from that of the age of Marius. Unlike the Italian 'allies', the enfranchised citizens of Utica and Gades were no threat to the political machinery of Rome or to the privileged inhabitants of the capital.

What emerges is not that peregrine communes were never directly enfranchised, but that this type of promotion, which had never been predominant, fell out of normal usage in the post-Claudian period. The grant of Latin rights became the general practice, as in the grants made by Claudius and Nero to certain Alpine peoples, in the great benefaction of the Flavians to Spain,

---

[1] Saumagne maintained that the grant of municipal (i.e. Latin) status preceded the revolt of Aedemon, apparently because in the list of Severus' offices the military post follows his magistracies. He assumes that Severus secured the citizenship *per honorem* between 41 and 44. But his tribe Galeria is not the regular tribe of Volubilis, which was the Claudia (*Inscr. Lat. Mar.* 84, 90–3, 99, 100, 106–7). Hence it is probable that Severus became a Roman citizen *before* the promotion of Volubilis, which was the reward for its services in the war under the leadership of Severus. The revolt of Aedemon seems to have started soon after Gaius murdered king Ptolemy (in 40), and was left for Claudius to suppress. Cf. Pliny, *NH* 5. 11. Dio 59. 25. 1.

[2] Saumagne, *Droit latin*, 71 f. Strabo 3. 5. 3, 168–9 C.

[3] Strabo compares Gades to Patavium, which he reckons the largest city in Italy apart from Rome. He mentions only the fact that both had five hundred men of equestrian standing, evidently at a late Augustan census; for the knights of Gades, cf. Cic. *ad Fam.* 10. 32. 2. This is decisive for the Roman status of Gades. Only Roman colonies and boroughs were included in the census of the Roman State. Besides, the operation of the system of promotion *per honorem* could hardly produce five hundred Roman citizens so soon when allowance is made for the limiting factors—the procession of the same men and the same families through the four or six posts of the local *cursus honorum*. After the first two decades there might not be two new citizens created a year by this method, and sometimes none, with or without children.

and in the separate grants of Latin status documented in Africa later.

## THE STATUS OF *OPPIDA CIVIUM ROMANORUM*

Whether direct enfranchisement had ever been a common form of promotion depends upon the interpretation of the *oppida civium Romanorum*, the towns of Roman citizens, listed in the provincial descriptions of Pliny, notably for Spain, Africa, and Dalmatia. It has been suggested above that these communes represent an amalgamation of immigrant Roman citizens from central Italy, who formed 'conventual' associations within the native townships, and of the enfranchised native inhabitants, and that these *oppida civium Romanorum* in or after the Augustan period were formally organized as *municipia civium Romanorum*.[1] This process would have secured an extensive enfranchisement of provincials in the western empire. But this view, which has been widely held, has been seriously challenged by the findings of the scholarly Teutsch, who minutely investigated the evidence for the province of Africa, and independently by Saumagne's shorter examination of the same material.[2] This area is of special interest because it is better served than any other western province for evidence about the composition of the Roman townships. Passing references in the writings of Caesar and his followers reveal the existence in the late Republic of politically organized associations of Roman citizens—*conventus civium Romanorum*—consisting of businessmen and landholders of Italian origin, in several native townships of the coastal zone. The clearest evidence concerns Utica, where the Roman *conventus* with an upper crust of three hundred leading men dominated the native community and its 'senate'.[3] Inscriptions from the Augustan period onwards speak of similar associations, and especially of certain *pagi civium Romanorum*, found in inland areas within the towns and territory

[1] Above, 225 ff.

[2] Teutsch, op. cit. 23–65, is extremely thorough. Saumagne, op. cit. 81–119, reached similar conclusions from a part of the same material, but is more speculative than Teutsch, whose book he had not apparently read.

[3] *Bell. Afr.* 36. 2, Thysdrus; 97. 1–2, Zama, Thapsus, Hadrumetum. For Utica, *Bell. Afr.* 68. 4; 87–90; *Bell. Civ.* 2. 36. 1. Cf. Livy, *Ep.* 88; Plut. *Cat. Min.* 59. 3; 61. 1. For earlier *conventus* cf. Sall. *Bell. Jug.* 26, 63. 5. For a discussion see A. J. N. Wilson, *Emigration from Italy in the Republican Age of Rome* (New York, 1966), 42 ff., which fully documents the once disputed fact of extensive emigration.

of native communes. These can be connected with the agrarian settlement of the veteran soldiery of Marius in informal groups about 100 B.C., through their later use of *Marianus* as a civic title. Nearly all of Pliny's *oppida civium Romanorum* that can be identified come from the area of the Marian colonization in Numidia, and two of them, Uchi Maius and Thuburnica, claim the connection with Marius, while in the documents from Uchi a native *civitas* and a *pagus* exist side by side.[1]

Teutsch suggested that all fifteen of Pliny's *oppida c. R.* were once of this type. Further, he argued convincingly that Pliny's African lists, about which there are notorious difficulties on the assumption that they are of Augustan origin, should be dated before the Augustan reorganization of African Proconsularis. Hence they reveal the status of communes of the Triumviral period at latest, and cast no light on the later extension of Roman citizenship or of municipal status to the African communities.[2] The evidence about these *oppida* is, however, far from complete. Some five of them were transformed into Roman colonies by veteran settlement (so far as is known) in the Caesarean or Augustan period.[3] Seven are either unidentifiable or have produced no solid evidence of their later status, while two or three contain a peregrine commune in the Principate.[4] Only Utica is known to have received the Roman citizenship for its inhabitants and to have had the status of a *municipium civium Romanorum*, from the time of Tiberius at latest to that of Hadrian.[5] Only at

---

[1] Above, 270 f. For the Marian titles cf. Teutsch, op. cit. 14 f., 23–5; e.g. *AE* 1951, no. 81 (Thuburnica, hailing Marius as *conditor coloniae*), *ILS* 1334 (Uchi Maius), 6790 (Thibari, dated *c.* A.D. 289). Also Saumagne, op. cit. 82 f. The Marian settlements only became formal *coloniae* in later times.

[2] Teutsch, op. cit. 27 ff., 37 f., 79 f., 87 f. For his chronology see below, 353 n. 3.

[3] Certainly Simitthu, *col. Julia Augusta*, *ILS* 6823. Thabraca, *col. V.P.* (*Urbs Patricia?*) *Julia*, *ILS* 5976. Assuras, *col. Julia*, *AE* 1913, no. 40. Thuburnica, *col. Augusta*, *CIL* viii. 14687 with *ILS* 2249. Cf. Teutsch, op. cit. 42, 119, 172, 175.

[4] Teutsch, op. cit. 30–7; apart from Uchi, 'Chiniavenses peregrini' appear in *CIL* viii. 25450, and Thibica is still a *civitas* ruled by *sufetes* under Pius, *CIL* viii. 765. Cf. Saumagne, op. cit. 96–7.

[5] Coins of Utica only issued under Tiberius with the title *mun. Iul. Utic.* (Grant, op. cit. 182) confirm Dio (above, 340 n. 2), while Hadrian in his speech about *municipia* which sought colonial status cites Spanish Italica, and Italian Praeneste with Utica as communities of the same rank; cf. above, 257 n. 1 and below, 363 n. 1. The parallel is decisive for the Roman status. Since Hadrian could find no material advantage in such promotion, none of them can be merely 'Latin'. There is no evidence to clarify the *beneficium Iuliae legis* of Utica in *Bell. Afr.* 87. 3, commonly referred to as a grant of Latin status under a law of 59 B.C.

two of Pliny's *oppida*, at Utica in the time of Caesar and at Uchi Maius in the inscriptions of the Principate, is there external evidence for a *conventus* or *pagus* of Roman citizens, while three cities where there is Caesarean evidence for a *conventus* appear in Pliny's lists as 'free townships' of peregrine status (*oppida libera*).[1] The conundrum is underlined by the fact that on present evidence the title of *municipium*, so common in second century Africa, is rarely documented in the Julio-Claudian period.[2]

After this, doubts must arise about the status of the Roman *oppida* recorded by Pliny outside Africa, notably in the Spanish provinces and in Dalmatia.[3] For Hispania Tarraconensis the evidence of the local coinages shows that out of the twelve such *oppida* listed by Pliny no less than six or seven, including all of the five Roman *oppida* of the region of Caesaraugusta, had the title of *municipium* under Augustus and Tiberius. An eighth, Saguntum, has the machinery but not the title of a *municipium* on Tiberian coins, and possesses both in later inscriptions. But only at Emporiae, where Livy describes the unification of peregrine community and Roman settlers by a grant of Roman citizenship, is it certain that the *municipium* had Roman and not Latin status. There are other indications that some of these townships included a strong native element. When Pliny describes Ilerda as commune both of Romans and of the 'tribe of the Surdaones', he would seem to mean that Ilerda, a *municipium* on its coins, was an enfranchised Spanish community including a former conventual settlement of Romans from Italy. His listing of Emporiae, 'this twin township of indigenous inhabitants and

[1] Pliny, *NH* 5. 25, 30. Thysdrus, Thapsus, Hadrumentum. Cf. above, 344 n. 3. Coin evidence may suggest early colonial or municipal promotion at Hadrumetum and Thapsus; cf. Grant, op. cit. 226–7, *Sylloge Nummorum Graecorum, North Africa* (Copenhagen, 1969), Pl. 3, nn. 51–5, and below, 350 n. 2.

[2] The title *municipium* appears early, apart from Utica, only at Hippo Regius, where *m. Augustum* is probably of Latin status (below, 351 n. 3), and possibly at the recently documented *municipium Iulium Aurelium* of Musti (unknown to Pliny), near Thugga in the area of the Marian settlement, if the Julian title commemorates more than the former settlement of a *pagus*; cf. *AE* 1968, nos. 593, 601, discussed at length by A. Beschaouch, *Karthago* 13 (1965–6), 118 ff. The title does not appear indisputably on any of the coins which Grant (op. cit. 178–89) sought to identify from magisterial titles as the foundation-coins of four otherwise undocumented Augustan *municipia*. Of these Simitthu and Thuburnica are excluded by other evidence (above, 345 nn. 1, 3). For Hadrumetum see above n. 1

[3] *NH* 3. 18–24, 144. Tarraconensis and Dalmatia have substantial lists of *o.c.R.* Single instances occur in Sardinia and other islands, ibid. 3. 77, 85, 88, 93, and in Mauretania, ibid. 5. 19.

of Greeks', as also a Roman township, can hardly mean that the 'twin peoples' were *excluded* from the Roman community, even if the evidence of Livy did not prove the opposite.[1] But ambiguity remains, because the communes of Spain that have Latin rights in the lists of Pliny also have the title of *municipium* on early coins and inscriptions.[2] In Baetica, where Pliny uses the term *municipia civium Romanorum* in his summary instead of *oppida c.R.*, only two, Gades and Regina, are specified in the lists themselves, where the term used is *oppidum c.R.* Of these two, only Gades is independently known to have had the full citizenship to match its title of *municipium*; Italica also had both, but Pliny does not denote its status.[3]

In Dalmatia Pliny records eight Roman *oppida*, of which Lissus is known in the late Republic as a conventual settlement, while a strong Italian element is found later at Risinium.[4] There is

---

[1] Vittinghoff, op. cit. 79 f., 107 f., studies the formal colonization of Tarraconensis, but is not much concerned with the *oppida c.R.* Of these, Ilerda, Osca, Calagurris, Bilbilis, and Turiasso (in the *conventus* of Caesaraugusta) appear as *municipia* on Augustan or Tiberian coins (A. Heiss, *Description Générale des Monnaies antiques de L'Espagne* (Paris, 1870), 133, 157, 182–3, 193; Grant, *From Imperium to Auctoritas* (Cambridge, 1946), 154 ff.). For the identification of Dertosa with *mun. Hibera Iulia Ilercavonia*—i.e. 'of the Ilercaones'—on the coins of which its name also appears cf. Vittinghoff, op. cit. 107, Heiss, op. cit. 129–30, Grant, op. cit. 158. The coins of these *municipia* mention *duoviri, aediles*, and *decuriones*, but not apparently *quattuorviri* (except at Latin Carteia, cf. Heiss, 332. At Ilerda a wolf symbol from the pre-municipal coinage reappears on the Augustan issues. An Augustan coin from Osca has the Celtiberian Pegasus (Heiss, op. cit. 157 n. 8). But Bilbilis is once styled *municipium Italicum*: Heiss, op. cit. 182 n. 8, *CIL* ii, p. 941. Emporiae has a single issue with *mun[icipium]*; Heiss, op. cit. 100, n. 54, Grant, op. cit. 155, Pliny, *NH* 3. 22, Livy 34. 9. 3. For Saguntum, Heiss, op. cit. 219, *CIL* ii, p. 511, Grant op. cit. 161.

[2] Cf., e.g., Ercavica, Graccurris, Castulo; Heiss, op. cit. 172–3, 175, 285. For Castulo cf. *AE* 1958, nos. 4–8; *decuriones, duoviri, ordo*.

[3] Gades and Italica, Heiss, op. cit. 350, 379, Grant, op. cit. 171 f. Italica is called *municipium* by implication already in *Bell. Alex.* 52. 4, despite the doubts of Wilson, op. cit. 38 n. 9, and Grant, loc. c. For its Roman status see 345 n. 5; cf. Vittinghoff, op. cit. 72. For Gades, above, 340 n. 5. Only pre-municipal coins with Celto-Latin types are known from Regina, Pliny's second *oppidum c.R.* (Heiss, op. cit. 365).R. Thouvenot, *Essai sur la province romaine de Bétique* (Paris, 1940), 191 f., briefly identifies nine of the *municipia* without questioning their origin and status. For native population at Julia Traducta Iotsa and Ulia Faventia, which may be Roman *municipia*, cf. Strabo 3. 1. 8, *Bell. Hisp.* 3. 3; Vittinghoff, op. cit. 103–5. For casual Roman immigration see A. J. N. Wilson, op. cit. 29 ff., citing, e.g., Caesar, *BC* 1. 86. 3; 2. 18. 4; 19. 3; 20. 5.

[4] *NH* 3. 144, 152; see Wilson, op. cit. 68 f. G. Alföldi, *Bevölkerung und Gesellschaft der r. p. Dalmatien* (Budapest 1965) 142–3, and now J. J. Wilkes, *Dalmatia* (London, 1969) 298 f., for Italian immigrants.

some evidence from the later Principate for the institutions or the title of a *municipium* at three or four of these *oppida*, and another acquired the title of *colonia* at some time, but only the name of Julium Risinium proves an early foundation.[1] The development of the Roman *oppida* can be seen at Narona, which became a Julian colony. A pre-colonial inscription shows first the conventual officers, *magistri* and *quaestores*, replaced later by *quattuorviri*, a title which apparently replaced the normal duovirate in some Dalmatian colonies.[2] Latin status is most clearly indicated in the inscriptions of two communes where no *oppidum civium Romanorum* is known: Rider, or Municipium Riditarum, where many of the inhabitants have Latinized names of barbaric origin, yet do not seem to use the triple Roman style, and Scardona, known from inscriptions as a Flavian *municipium*, and from Pliny as a peregrine commune.[3]

The conclusion is neither that of Saumagne and Teutsch, that *oppida civium Romanorum* were all conventual communes of Italian immigrants which excluded the native population and had no connection with *municipia*, nor is it that they all cover the enfranchisement of native communes as *municipia civium Romanorum*. As so often in the Roman empire one finds diversity of types. Many of Pliny's Roman *oppida* disappear from view or become Julian or Augustan *coloniae civium Romanorum*, and in a few

---

[1] Lissus (*CIL* iii. 1704), Acruvium (1711), Risinium (12695). Alföldi (op. cit. 141 n. 78) and Wilkes (op. cit. 254 ff.) make these and other settlements to be of Julian date on flimsy grounds, notably the possession of the *tribus Sergia*, which actually recurs at Flavian Scardona (Wilkes, op. cit. 218). In *CIL* iii. 12695 Risinium is distinguished from three other communes as lacking the title of *colonia*. Of the rest of Pliny's *oppida c.R.* Tragurium and Issa were included in the colony of Salona, and Scodra eventually appears as a *colonia* also (*CIL* iii. 12695), while there is no evidence for Olcinium and Butua (cf. Alföldi, op. cit. 105 f., Wilkes. op. cit. 229 f., 317 n. 3), since *CIL* iii. 8783 is referred now to Bistua.

[2] *CIL* iii. 1820; Wilkes, op. cit. 247 f.; Alföldi, op. cit. 134. Degrassi, op. cit. 319–20 refers the *quattuorviri* of Narona, Salona, and Aequum to previous or adjacent *municipia*, replaced later by colonial *duoviri*. But since Flavian or later *ivviri* appear at Narona (A. J. Sasel, 'Inscr. Lat. Jug.', *Situla* 5 (1963), 117), probably they are all 'colonial', cf. Wilkes, op. cit. 223 f., 247 f., Alföldi, op. cit. 102. Salona developed like Narona from a *conventus c.R.* to a Julian *colonia*, cf. Wilkes, op. cit. 229 f.

[3] Rider, *CIL* iii. 2774 f., 9865, e.g. 'Apludius Statius'; Sasel nos. 171–98, dated to the second century, id. p. 72. Cf. Alföldi, op. cit. 97–8, Wilkes, op. cit. 240 f., who recognizes no other Latin *municipium*. Scardona, *CIL* iii. 2802, Flavian *municipium* from *civitas peregrina* in Pliny, *NH* 3. 141; cf. Wilkes, op. cit. 218. See also below, 374 n. 1.

instances the arrangement persists of a Roman *conventus* organized within a native commune. A fair proportion of the remainder, even in the present state of knowledge, emerge later as *municipia*. Of these some four or five, which can be dated to the Julian or Augustan periods, include the native population and have the full Roman status. Further, the evidence of the Spanish coins could be pressed to suggest that most of the Plinian *oppida civium Romanorum* in Spain were reorganized, as suggested in this book, as full Roman municipalities in the time of Augustus.[1]

A possible simplification of the problem has been provided by the suggestion of E. Schönbauer that Pliny always uses the term *oppidum* in its primary meaning of township or strong place, without any implication of status or community, so that *oppidum civium Romanorum* means just what it says, a township inhabited by persons all or most of whom happen to be Roman citizens, while the town might technically be the urban centre either of a *municipium*—whether Latin or Roman—or of a peregrine commune.[2] Sometimes Pliny makes it clear that his *oppidum* means no more than that, as when he mentions the six *oppida* of the Arevaci, or refers to Cenomelum as the 'township of the commune of the Vediantii'.[3] But he is far from consistent. Though careful in his use of *colonia*, he does not firmly distinguish between *civitas*, *populus*, or *gens*, the normal Latin terms for separate communes, and *oppidum*. In his African lists, in which *oppidum* predominates, he occasionally substitutes *civitas* for no clear reason. In the account of Hispania Tarraconensis he uses *oppidum* exclusively in the coastal regions for communes of all grades (except *coloniae*), while in the inland districts he uses *populus* for all grades, including what he elsewhere calls *oppida civium Romanorum*, and uses *civitas* as a frequent variant for peregrine communes only. In Baetica he uses only *oppidum*, and in Lusitania he slides from *populus* to *oppidum*. In the brief list of the Baliaric peoples he uses *oppidum* for the privileged communes and *civitas* for the others.[4] Probably Pliny only uses *oppidum* where the

[1] Some of the coins are Tiberian, but Tiberius as Princeps is not known to have promoted any Spanish borough.

[2] E. Schönbauer, '*Municipia* und *coloniae*' etc., *Anz. Oesterr. Ak. Wiss.* 1954, 18 f., followed rigidly by Alföldi, op. cit. 71 n. 19, and Wilkes, op. cit. 227.

[3] *NH* 3. 27, 47, '. . . oppido Vediantiorum civitatis Cemenelo'.

[4] Ibid. 5. 21, *civitates Timici*, *Tigavae* in isolation. Africa, ibid. 5. 30, 'oppida libera xxx . . . ex reliquo numero non civitates tantum sed . . . nationes', and ibid. 27 *civitas Oeensis* in isolation. Tarraconensis, ibid. 3. 9–22, *oppida*; 23–8, *populi* with

township is the prominent feature of the boroughs which he lists, as in the Mediterranean zones of Africa and Spain. But equally his lists of *oppida*, like those of *populi* and *civitates*, are meant for a catalogue of communes by status. Terms like *oppidum liberum* or *oppidum Latinum* make sense only as implying *civitates* or *municipia* of the indicated grade. So his *oppida civium Romanorum* may be taken to imply Roman municipal boroughs in some instances, though external confirmation is required for certainty.

### PROMOTION TO COLONIAL STATUS

The notions of Vittinghoff that Latin boroughs were not normally promoted to the full Roman status, and of Saumagne that peregrine communes were not admitted to Roman status directly, ignores the abundant evidence from the later Principate in the African provinces for the grant of colonial status to *municipia*, which may have been mostly of Latin grade, and also to mere peregrine *civitates*, in the second and early third centuries. This was always a well-documented phenomenon, but its significance is enhanced by the new hypotheses. Thugga, after the amalgamation of its dual community into a *municipium* under Septimius Severus, ends as a *colonia* under Severus Alexander.[1] The *civitas libera* of prosperous Hadrumetum, despite the presence of an organized *conventus civium Romanorum*, apparently retained its independent status until Trajan made it a Roman colony. So too the obscure Thaenae passed directly from *civitas libera* to *colonia Aelia*. No fewer than eight such promotions of 'free cities' have been noted by G. Picard, though not all are sufficiently documented to exclude the possibility of an intermediate stage of Latin rights.[2] Among less exalted communes the *pagus et*

*civitates* intermittently in 26–8. Lusitania, ibid. 4. 117–18, 'tota populorum xlv in quibus . . . stipendiaria xxxvi . . . oppida'. Baliares, ibid. 3. 77, 'oppida habet c.R. . . . Latina . . . et foederatum . . . civitates habet . . .' The pundits have not noticed the *populi civium Romanorum* in 3. 23, 24, or the hybrid *populi . . . oppidani Lati veteris* in 25.

[1] Below, 415. The complete development of Thugga, promoted to *municipium* in 205 (*I.L. Afr.* 525) can now be traced in the Index of *CIL* viii (1957).

[2] Hadrumetum: *conventus, Bell. Afr.* 97; *libera*, Pliny, *NH* 5. 25; *col. Ulpia* in *CIL* viii. 11138 with 2968 and vi. 1687. Teutsch, op. cit. 145. No inscriptions of the first century A.D. The tile seal with 'CIH' cannot be turned against this evidence to mean *col. Iulia Hadrumetum*, cf. Teutsch, op. cit. 145, 185. Yet *iiviri* appear on coins, *SNG* Plate 3, n. 60. P. Quoniam, *Karthago* 10 (1959), 77–8, suggests a previous

*civitas* of Uchi moved straight to colonial status under Alexander Severus.[1] Thuburbo Maius in central Proconsularis remained peregrine until Hadrian made it a *municipium Aelium*, which two generations later received colonial rights from Commodus.[2] Hippo Regius, one of the Latin *municipia* of the Augustan period, trod the same path in due course.[3] Then there is the ambiguous case of Lepcis Magna, the prosperous caravan city of Tripolitania and an unprivileged state in Pliny's list, which either passed directly to Roman status as a *colonia* under Trajan or received an intermediary grant of Latin status earlier from Vespasian.[4]

These colonies were not merely titular. The evidence of their official documents and magistracies shows that in the second century, as Vittinghoff insisted, the title conferred all the privileges and structure of a 'Roman colony'. The speech of Hadrian quoted by Gellius about these promotions makes the same point.[5] No actual settlement of new colonists seems to accompany any of these promotions, though the foundation of veteran colonies was still in use elsewhere, and the technical term of *deductio* is sometimes employed for these formal promotions, as in an inscription of Uchi.[6] This then was the most frequent form of promotion for a Latin *municipium* in the later Principate, and it provided a new form of promotion for 'peregrine' communities that had special claims. Tacitus hints at the new usage when he notes with surprise that the principal town in Britain lacked the distinction of colonial rank.[7] The procedure can possibly be traced back to the promotion of Vienna in Narbonensis, chief township of the Allobroges, through Latin rights—given by

*municipium Iulium*. For the list of *coloniae*, G. C. Picard, *Karthago* 8 (1957), 153. For Thaenae, cf. *CIL* vi. 1685, Teutsch, op. cit. 137.

[1] Uchi still as plain *civitas* in A.D. 179, *pagus* with *magistri* in A.D. 177: *CIL* viii. 26250, 26254; *colonia*, ibid. 26262.

[2] Teutsch, op. cit. 130 ff., *ILS* 498, *I.L. Tun.* 699, *I.L. Afr.* 240. The by-name Julia appears first under Caracalla, *I.L. Afr.* 268, *ILS* 498.

[3] Apparently peregrine in Pliny, *NH* 5. 22; *mun. Augustum*, *ILS* 5976 *a* with *senatus* instead of *ordo* in A.D. 42–3 (*AE* 1935, n. 32); *municipium* in A.D. 78, *AE* 1949, n. 76; then plain *colonia Augusta*, *AE* 1958, n. 141.

[4] Pliny, *NH* 5. 27. For its coins, Teutsch, op. cit. 130 f.; for its peculiar development see below, 363.             [5] Above, 257, n. 1; below, 413.

[6] *CIL* viii. 26262; '[colonia Alexandri]ana . . . eius nomine . . . deducta per Caesinium . . .' So too at Vaga in 209, ibid. 14395.

[7] Tac'. *Ann.* 14. 33. 1; 'Londinium . . . cognomento quidem coloniae non insigne'. Cf. ibid. 27. 2, 'ius coloniae et cognomentum' at Puteoli without *deductio*. See below, 370 n. 1.

Caesar or Octavian—to full colonial status by the time of Claudius, at latest, without any certain indication of external colonization.[1] The number of such promotions in Africa alone, under Trajan, Hadrian, and Pius, often of communes of moderate size, is not insignificant.[2]

A link between the new system and the old method of formal Roman colonization can be found in the custom of the Julio-Augustan period, mentioned by the Tacitean version of a speech of Claudius, by which a proportion of the dispossessed native population, probably limited to the local nobility, was included in the Roman foundation.[3] Once only, in the exceptional circumstances of the foundation of the veteran settlements at and around Numidian Cirta by the adventurer Sittius and his private army, in and after the time of Caesar, there are indications that a large body of non-Romans acquired Roman status under the mantle of the colony.[4]

[1] Vienna, listed by Pliny, *NH* 3. 36 as a *colonia Romana*, was earlier one of those Latin communes of Narbonensis which have the *tribus Voltinia* and *quattuorviri* as magistrates and use the title *colonia* (below, 365 n. 1). The *ivviri* are replaced during or after Tiberius' reign by *duoviri*. One inscription of Claudian or Neronian date attests the title *col. Julia Florentina* (*ILS* 6995; cf. *AE* 1935, n. 5), and Vienna received the *solidum civitatis Romanae beneficium*, in the words of Claudius, between A.D. 35 and 46 (*ILS* 212). Hence two possibilities—the replacement of the Latin commune by a veteran colony of Augustan date which later receives the *ius Italicum* from Gaius or Claudius, or the promotion of the *colonia Latina* to Roman status by Gaius with a new title. There is no necessity to identify the *beneficium* with the grant of *ius Italicum* known from *Dig.* 50. 15. 8 (above, 320 n. 3). Since the Roman colony later administers the whole tribal territory (below, 369 n. 1) the second alternative is more probable. On either view a Celtic canton, or a section of it, travelled via Latin rights to Roman colonial status. For diverse opinions see Vittinghoff. op. cit. 65 n. 1; *RE* viii. cols. 2114 f.; *CIL.* xii, p. 218; A. Oltremare, *Genava* 11 (1932), 109 f.; Degrassi, op. cit. 305 f., who links the supposed foundation of Roman *coloniae* by Augustus at Nemausus and Vienna with his building benefactions at both *c.* 16 B.C. (*CIL* xii. 1850 with 3151). But neither *colonia c.R.* is certain. It is disputed whether any Augustan foundations after 27 B.C. ever bear the title Julia instead of Augusta or Julia Augusta; Vittinghoff, op. cit. 133 n. 2; Teutsch, op. cit. 116 f.

[2] Cf. the list in J. Baradez, *Lybica, Archéologie, Épigraphie*, 4 (1956), 271, n. 12, which adds Zama Regia under Hadrian, and Mauretanian Tipasa under Pius, both ex-municipalities (cf. *AE* 1955, n. 130, 1958, n. 128). Mactar, *col. Aelia Aurelia*, may be a promoted *municipium*; Teutsch, *RIDA* 349. But see below, 364 n. 1.

[3] Tac. *Ann.* 11. 24. 3, cited above, 245. Cf. the incorporation of local people in the *colonia Julia* at Carthage, below, 354 n. 1, and that of the remnants of the Salassi at Augusta Praetoria, *ILS* 6753.

[4] Teutsch, op. cit. 69–70, argues that the extremely numerous Sittii known from the imperial inscriptions of the Cirtan region—some three hundred in all, of whom over ninety come from the territory of Cirta—can only be the descendants of

## DUAL COMMUNITIES AND DUAL MUNICIPALITIES

Some stress was given above to the role of certain dual communities of Roman citizens and ordinary provincials, especially
in the African provinces, in the cultural and political Romanization of the native peoples, and hence in their promotion to
Roman status. The presence of informal colonies, *conventus* and
*pagi*, of Roman citizens within peregrine communities is well
documented from the second century B.C. to the Antonine period.[1]
But certain scholars developed a more extensive theory of dual
municipalities—again mainly from African evidence—consisting
of organized settlements of Roman emigrants, either *municipia* or
*coloniae*, in the same localities as peregrine *civitates*. This theory,
briefly accepted above, has been under heavy fire. It arose
largely from attempts to reconcile the evidence of Pliny's lists of
African communes with that of coins and inscriptions, which
indicate the existence of an Augustan or Julian municipality or
colony at places defined as peregrine townships in Pliny, or
conversely of peregrine communes at places where Pliny lists
*oppida civium Romanorum*. Pliny indeed records only six African
*coloniae* out of some fifteen or more that existed in the Augustan
period.[2] Some of these difficulties disappear when it is understood that the term *oppidum civium Romanorum* need only refer to
a 'conventual' settlement of informal character. But many arose
from the acceptance of an Augustan date for the bulk of Pliny's
material, which made the notion of dual municipalities a necessary solution. The situation has been altered by the work of
L. Teutsch, whose careful analysis of the Plinian lists leads to the
probable conclusion that the date of the bulk of the material is
pre-Augustan, and possibly pre-Caesarean, with a few later
additions which give an incomplete account of the Augustan
arrangements.[3]

enfranchised native supporters of Sittius. His account, op. cit. 65–7, of the Sittian
settlement in this Wild West of Roman Africa illuminates the theme of Roman
immigration and its consequences.

[1] Above, 225 f., 269 f., 344–5.
[2] L. Teutsch, op. cit. 152, and 'Gab es Doppelgemeinden in röm. Afrika?'
*RIDA* 8 (1961), 282 n. 1, gives the older bibliography. Cf. T. R. S. Broughton,
*Romanization of Africa Proconsularis*, 210 f. For the total of colonies, cf. Vittinghoff,
op. cit. 82 f., 111 f.
[3] *Städtewesen*, 27 ff., 77 ff., 82. The core of his complex argument is that the lists
in *NH* 5. 29–30 of *oppida libera* and *oppida c.R.*, in which the names of townships are

Other supposed instances of dual municipalities arose from the ambiguities and inaccuracies of local terminology in inscriptions. Known *municipia* appear on occasion as *civitates*, and even *coloniae* may feature as *municipia*, and *coloni* as *municipes*.[1] Difficulty arose from the anachronistic employment or revival of the title *Julia*, like that of *Mariana*, in the later second century by *coloniae* which on other evidence appear to be of recent origin. The justification of such titles cannot always be divined, though sometimes an Augustan *beneficium* or the existence of a previous *municipium Iulium* may be inferred. But not every *colonia Iulia* dates back to Caesar or Octavian, and hence the last of the dual municipalities of Africa, such as Thuburbo Maius, can be eliminated.[2] But Teutsch goes against the evidence when he argues that no dual municipalities of any sort ever existed in the Roman

given in adjectival form (e.g. *Assuritanum* instead of Assuras) and in alphabetical instead of regional order, differ in this from all the other provincial lists in Pliny, and hence do not come from the Agrippan survey. Teutsch then argues that the lists were compiled before the total destruction of Vaga by Juba in 46 B.C., because each of Pliny's lists includes a Vaga; cf. *Bell. Afr.* 74; Strabo 17. 3. 12. In addition to *NH* 5. 29–30 there is a list of communes including *o. libera* and *o. civium Romanorum* in the coastal survey of 22–8, complementary to 29–30. No names are duplicated, and the sum of items in all the lists corresponds exactly to the totals of each category given in 29. Teutsch did not observe that this means that, apart from the few Julio-Claudian additions, Pliny's source combined lists of all the *oppida libera* and *o. civium Romanorum* of both Africa Vetus, annexed in 146 B.C., and of Africa Nova, formed *after* 46 B.C. by the annexation of Juba's kingdom. Most of the *oppida c.R.* in 22–7 and 29, and some of the *o. libera* in s. 25, though none of those in 30, belong to Africa Nova. Hence Pliny's source should be later than the creation of Africa Nova, but perhaps earlier than the unification of the two provinces by Octavian after 36 B.C., since the list in s. 30 covers only Vetus. Pliny in fact refers to the obsolete distinction in s. 25. But the thesis of Teutsch still stands in the main as the best explanation of the gaps in Pliny's information for the Julio-Augustan period, which contrasts with his more up-to-date account of Mauretania.

[1] e.g. Mactar, *col. Aelia Aurelia*, appears as *civitas* in A.D. 170 and once has *municipes* instead of *coloni*, cf. *CIL* viii. 11799, 11811. Cf. *municipes coloniae* at Sicca, *ILS* 6818. At Lepcis Magna 'genio municipii' and 'genio coloniae' are used interchangeably; *I.R. Trip.* 286–8. Cf. Teutsch, op. cit. 345–9. At Timgad. where there is no other trace of dualism, *patrono coloniae et municipi* in *ILS* 1178 may mean 'patron and citizen of the colony'. At Carthage the evidence for the survival of an enfranchised peregrine commune beside the Julian colony, rejected above, 227, is better interpreted as referring to the incorporation of the local element at the foundation of the colony. Cf. Teutsch, op. cit. 102 f., 158, on Appian, *Pun.* 136, Tertullian, *de Pall.* 1 ('toga oblata'), Dio 52. 43. 1. The coins with KAR VENERIS and *sufetes* in their legend found near Sardinian Caralis, do not concern Carthage; cf. Quoniam, *Karthago* 10 (1959–60), 70, Grant, op. cit. 149.

[2] Cf. P. Quoniam, art. cit. 67 ff. The title Julia appears late at Thuburbo Maius (above, 351 n. 2), Utica (*CIL* viii. 1181, above, 345), and Thysdrus (*CIL* vi. 3884).

empire.[1] The description in Livy and Pliny of the bipartite or tripartite commune of Emporiae in Spain is explicit, and according to Tacitus the *civitas Ubiorum* and its *oppidum* seem to have continued to exist in close contiguity with the *colonia Agrippinensis* on the Rhine. Pliny's *oppidum geminum* even provides a formal term for such a community. Certain of the Roman colonies of Caesar in Asia Minor are described by Strabo as sharing the territory and the town of a Greek city with the Greek community, notably at Heraclea and Sinope, while Apamea may have retained this arrangement into the time of Trajan. There is also the possibility that a veteran colony and a native commune with Latin rights coexisted at and around Vienna Allobrogum in the Augustan period.[2] It is partly a matter of definition, as Schönbauer remarked. Such communities would be adjacent rather than intermixed.[3] The techniques of the Roman surveyor would ensure that the distinction of territories was clearly marked, and the fine distinction of personal status in Roman law would secure a separation of jurisdictions.

Teutsch also tried to eliminate the independent character of the *pagus* element in the dual communities of *pagus et civitas* type, the existence of which he could not dispute, by reducing the role of the *pagus civium Romanorum* to that of a private association, existing only to represent the private interests of its members.[4] The officers of such *pagi* are *magistri*, the term used for the annual presidents of social clubs (*collegia*) and of commercial associations (*societates*). But equally this term is used for the annual officers of the constituent parishes and villages (*pagi*, *vici*) of Italian municipalities, which had an official if subordinate role in municipal affairs. In at least two dual communes of Africa the *pagus* had its own set of councillors or *decuriones* and passed 'decrees' long

---

[1] Originally in art. cit. *RIDA* 8 (1961), 281 ff., and later with refinements in op. cit. (*Städtewesen*), 152 ff. E. Schönbauer criticized his rigid rejection of all dual communities in art. cit. 13 ff., with similar arguments to those urged here.

[2] Emporiae, above, 347 n. 1; 'geminum hoc veterum incolarum et Graecorum' in Pliny corresponds to Strabo's description (3. 4. 8.). Livy 34. 9 proves that the Greek community coexisted with the Roman until it was absorbed by a grant of Roman citizenship. For Asia, Strabo 12. 3. 6 (C. 542); 11 (C. 545); 4. 3 (C. 564); Dio, *Or.* 41. 5–6. Cf. Schönbauer, art. cit. 28. For *oppidum Ubiorum*, see below, 371 n. 5. For Vienna see above, 352 n. 1.

[3] Schönbauer, art. cit. 25; earlier Broughton, op. cit. 210: 'two communities fortuitously located at or near the same site'. But note 80 n. 1 above, and *ILS* 5671.

[4] Op. cit. (*Städtewesen*), 152 f., art. cit. *RIDA* 288 f.

before the establishment of a unified *municipium*.[1] In the late Republic conventual settlements of Romans in Africa and Dalmatia had been active in the organization and defence of their localities, dominating and even setting aside the native authorities.[2] But it is probable that the *magistri* of such settlements exercised no civil jurisdiction over the territory of the *pagus*, for which they were dependent, not on the magistrates of the adjacent *civitas*, but upon itinerant judges from a more distant Roman *colonia*.[3]

This brings up the custom of *attributio*, ignored by Teutsch. By this, communes of inferior status, while retaining some degree of local self-government, were subordinated to the authority of an adjacent Roman municipality. The evidence of *attributio* has been studied anew by Ugo Laffi, who distinguishes this type of 'attribution' from similar relationships between non-Roman communities under Roman rule, and also from *contributio*, which means the synoecism of two adjacent Roman boroughs into a single community.[4] Attribution in the restricted sense is found in use along the Alpine borders of northern Italy, where certain tribal peoples were put under the controlling authority of the municipalities of Cisalpine Gaul, after its reorganization by the *lex Pompeia* of 89 B.C. and after the Augustan conquest of the Alps.[5] Some of them continued in this condition down to the time of Pius. The attributed folk either remained *peregrini*, or acquired Latin status, and they paid certain taxes to their patron city, which supervised their local government, though they could not hold its magistracies.[6]

---

[1] For Italy cf. above, 74–5, and the material in *ILS* Index 3. 2, p. 662; e.g. nos. 5575, 5643, 6703, and the well-known *magistri vicorum* of Rome. For decurions of the *pagus* at Thugga cf. *CIL* viii. 26498, 26526, *I.L. Afr.* 524, 556 (A.D. 136); at Numlulis viii. 26121 (A.D. 170); at Suttu, ibid. 26418.

[2] Notably at Utica, Caesar, *BC* 2. 36, *Bell. Afr.* 89–90; cf. Plutarch, *Cato Min.* 59. 2–3. Cato and the *conventus* bundle the native *senatus* out of the town. For *conventus* in Dalmatia see Wilson, op. cit. 70 f.

[3] Below, 358.            [4] U. Laffi, *Adtributio e Contributio* (Pisa, 1966).

[5] The basic evidence is the list of tribes such as the Trumplini *adtributi municipiis . . . lege Pompeia* in Pliny, *NH* 3. 134 and 138, together with inferences from the Claudian edict *de Anaunis* (etc.) and an Antoninian city decree of Tergeste about the Carni and Catali (*ILS* 206, 6680). Brixia is indicated by *ILS* 266, 6713, as the patronal city of the Trumplini and their associates. Cf. Laffi, op. cit. 21–36. The date after Augustus' conquest of the Alps for these attributions inferred from Pliny (above, 231) is too late for those made by the *lex Pompeia*.

[6] Pliny notes that the *Euganeae gentes*, which include the Trumplini and Camunni, had Latin status, but gives no date. The privilege given by Pius to the Carni and

In a wider sense attribution is a fairly common phenomenon in the Roman empire from an early period. The subordination of one provincial community to another was often tolerated, approved, or initiated by the Roman government in its own interest.[1] The most explicit example is that of Genua and the Langenses in northern Liguria, known from a long document of 117 B.C.[2] This association might form the prototype for the Cisalpine attributions under the *lex Pompeia*; the magistrates of Genua collect taxes from the Langenses and enforce the collection with jurisdiction and severe penalties.

It is uncertain to what extent attribution to Roman boroughs was used in other regions. Laffi admits only the instance of Nemausus, the central township of the Volcae Arecomici of Narbonensis. This had Latin status and controlled the other twenty-four *pagi* or *oppida* of the Volcae, which were 'subordinate' and 'paid taxes' to Nemausus. A similar arrangement may be found in the early Principate at Vienna and Vasio, in the great tribal cantons of the Allobroges and Vocontii, and later in the relationship between the colony of Aventicum and the Helvetii.[3] But none of these is quite parallel to the Cisalpine usage. Nemausus, Vienna, and possibly Aventicum were component sections of the tribal cantons which they ruled, even if of superior status; they were not separate entities like the boroughs of Cisalpine Gaul. However, the relationship between the *colonia Latina* of Nemausus and the twenty subordinate townships was described as *attributio* by Pliny.

Catali at Tergeste may imply that they lacked Latin rights. The late Augustan *princeps Trumplinorum*, Staius, *Esdragassi filius*, was a peregrine (*ILS* 847). The Camunni appear organized as a *civitas* in the early Principate (*ILS* 5525), and later have *iiviri*; cf. below, 371 ff.

[1] For attribution between other non-Roman provincial communes see Laffi, op. cit. 46 f.

[2] Bruns, *FIR*[7] 184. Despite Laffi, op. cit. 55 f., the Langenses were clearly not incorporated into Genua.

[3] For Nemausus, Strabo 4. 1. 12 (p. 186), Pliny, *NH* 3. 37; see below, 368 n. 1. Vienna (above, 352 n. 1), Lucus Augusti, and Vasio, were Latin communes that may have developed separately from the rest of their tribe. Pliny, *NH* 3. 37 is oddly ambiguous; 'Vocontiorum civitatis foederatae duo capita [sc. sunt oppida Latina] oppida vero ignobilia xviii sicut xxiv Nemausiensibus adtributa.' The latter phrase may either summarize the peregrine communes of the province or mean that Vasio and Lucus conjointly had eighteen attributes. Cf. below, 368, and Laffi, op. cit. 62 f., 65 f. The magistrates of Vienna control all the territory of the Allobroges, whereas the Vocontii control Vasio rather than vice versa; below, 368 n. 4. For Aventicum see 370.

Elsewhere the evidence is often inconclusive. But there are firm indications that Carthage exercised some kind of supervision over certain of the dual communes of central Africa. Notables of Carthage, magistrates or ex-magistrates, including *praefecti iuri dicundo* or deputy magistrates, are frequently honoured at such places as Thugga and Uchi Maius, where it is possible that they provided local jurisdiction for the Roman citizens of the *pagus*, who are not likely to have been satisfied with the authority of the native *sufetes* of the adjacent peregrine commune.[1] There is an instance in about 36 B.C. of a magistrate of Carthage who acted as a justice of the peace and taxation officer for a group of eighty-three villages. The same man, it seems, but lacking a title, appears again at Uchi Maius, where he divided the civic territory between the Roman settlers and the native inhabitants.[2] It is uncertain from these inscriptions whether the eighty-three villages belonged to the territory of Carthage itself, or whether they comprised distant *civitates* and *pagi* 'attributed' to Carthage, though some have always held that the *pagi civium Romanorum* were within the colonial territory. A recently published inscription suggests that the whole region of the distant *pagi et civitates* belonged to the *pertica Carthaginiensium*, the assignment of land made at the foundation of the colony, which thus may have included the numerous native townships, though these enjoyed a tolerated autonomy.[3] This adds to the probability of the suggestion that the *praefecti iuri dicundo* of Carthage acted in the isolated *pagi* for the benefit of the Roman citizens. But this is not the *attributio* of the *lex Pompeia*. The various African communes, *pagi, castella, civitates*, were either incorporated in the colonial territory or separated from it by intervening territories, while the inhabitants of the *pagi*, being Roman citizens, had the same personal status as those of Carthage.

---

[1] Cf. Saumagne, op. cit. 85 n. 91, 86 n. 94, and e.g. *ILS* 9404. The area of activity of the *praefecti* is never indicated.

[2] *ILS* 1945, 'praef. i.d. vectig. quinque locand. in castellis LXXXIII'; nothing limits his jurisdiction to Carthage, *pace* Laffi. *CIL* viii. 26274.

[3] *AE* 1963, n. 94 (*c*. A.D. 102–14), a civic decree (*ex.d.d.*) from Thugga, honours a senator who had acted as 'defensor immunitatis perticae Carthaginiensium' in the interests of Thugga. This suggests that Thugga, *pagus* and *civitas* alike, lay within the *pertica*. The difference of tribe between Thugga (Quirina) and Carthage (Arnensis) is not decisive against this suggestion, despite Teutsch, art. cit. *RIDA* 305. Cf. G. Picard, *CRAI* 1962, 55 f. In *CIL* viii. 26121 a decurion from Carthage names Numlulis as his *patria*; Arnensis is used by some men of Thugga, cf. *CIL* viii Index, s.v.

What is thus known of the working of different forms of 'attribution' suggests that there were various ways in which a native *civitas* might be associated with a Roman or Latin borough, even if this is less common than was once believed. The normal pattern is one of subordination. The coexistence in one area of two self-governing communes of differing status on equal terms is a rarity. But it may be added to the preceding discussion, which concerned provincial communes under the Empire, that in Italy under the Republic formal colonization certainly created a number of dual communities sharing the same territories and town centres. The Gracchan colony of Neptunia was settled within the federal state of Tarentum, which survived a partial confiscation of land and was enfranchised after 90.[1] Some time afterwards, as Pliny explicitly affirms and the Lex Municipi Tarentini documents, the colony was fused with the enfranchised *municipium*.[2] Elsewhere colonization, early or late, had similar effects, testified with varying clarity at Interamnia Praetuttiorum, Faesulae, and Puteoli. At the first of these the evidence is unambiguous: 'Q. C. Poppaei Q.F. municipi et coloniai patroni municipibus colonieis incoleis hospitibus . . . dant'.[3] Hence there is no intrinsic improbability in the existence of such arrangements elsewhere and at other times in the Roman world.

[1] Livy 27. 21. 8, 25. 2, 35. 16. 3, 44. 16. 7. These passages prove that Tarentum did not suffer the fate of Capua. For Neptunia, Vell. Pat. 1. 15. 4, Strabo 6. 3. 4. Cf. U. Kahrstedt, *Historia* 8 (1959) 206.

[2] Pliny *N.H.* 3. 99. 'In recessu hoc intimo situm (sc. oppidum Tarentum Laconum) contributa eo maritima colonia quae ibi fuerat.' Cf. above, 356. The *lex mun. Tar.* (*FIRA* i². 18) sets up a *municipium* which combines *duoviri* and *quattuorviri* as senior magistrates.

[3] *ILS* 5671. For Sullan *coloni* at Faesulae and the survival of the native *municipium*, cf. Licinianus p. 34. F. Cic. *Cat.* 3. 14, *Mur.* 49; *ILS* 1429, *CIL* xi. 1610.

# XV

# LATIN RIGHTS AND MUNICIPAL STATUS

THE problem raised by Saumagne about the meaning of the term *municipium* in the Romanized provinces has been solved in another fashion by Dr. von Braunert.[1] He suggests that in the Principate the grant of Latin rights affected only the status of persons, not that of communities, and that the promotion of a commune to the rank of *municipium* by the grant of a detailed charter was a later and distinct process, a frequent but not a necessary sequel to Latin status. The essence of this was the conversion of a group of peregrines into *cives Latini*, a term used in the charter of Malaca, whereby they secured a similar position to that of Romans in civil law and the prerogative of acquiring the Roman franchise *per honorem*, by holding the magistracies of their local communes, whether these were *municipia* or not. Such local magnates encouraged the local adoption of Roman municipal usages, widely testified in the western provinces, which prepared the way for the formal grant of the status of *municipium*. Of this there was only one form, which was neither 'Roman' nor 'Latin', but was granted to communes of Roman citizens and to those of Latins alike in the same terms: hence the absence of any titular distinction between Latin and Roman *municipia* in provincial inscriptions.

The evidence for this neat solution comes from certain peculiarities of the Spanish charters. Twice, in clauses about the grant of Roman citizenship *per honorem*, the *lex Salpensana* refers to an edict of Vespasian, Titus, or Domitian as authorizing this procedure, in addition to 'this law', whereas all the arrangements for local administration are described as laid down simply 'in accordance with' or 'after this law'.[2] There is also a chronological argument. The two extant charters were issued under the hand of Domitian between his accession in 81 and his assumption of

---

[1] Von Braunert, 'Ius Latii', *Corolla Memoriae E. Swoboda*, (Graz, 1966) 68–83.

[2] 'Qui ex h.l. exve edicto . . . Vespasiani . . . c.R. consecutus . . . erit'. *Lex Sal.* 22, 23. Braunert catalogues the references *ex lege*, op. cit. 72 f.—Note that the term 'charter' is used for convenience only: no analogy is intended with medieval usages.

the title of Germanicus in 83-4.[1] But the grant of Latin status to the Spanish province was made by Vespasian, before or during his censorship in 75.[2] The ten years gap is usually explained as administrative delay due to the huge task of preparing and issuing charters to some three or four hundred communes. But Braunert argues that the edict of Vespasian, confirmed and reconfirmed by Titus and Domitian, simply conferred Latin rights as a personal status on the provincials of Spain, and that the charters clearly imply that individuals had been securing the Roman franchise *per honorem* for some ten years before their cities were finally promoted to municipal status and received their charters.[3]

The alternative and older explanation is that the edict of Vespasian represented only the first stage of Latinization—the grant of the personal status to the local inhabitants and of municipal status to their commune together with a brief instruction like that issued to the inhabitants of Transpadane Gaul in 49 B.C.—to 'elect *duoviri*', or as happened at Salpensa, *duoviri*, aediles, and quaestors.[4] Then in course of time the *lex municipii* amplified the arrangements in detail. Braunert's thesis requires the evidence of examples where a great interval of time intervened between the grant of Latin rights and that of municipal status, or where a Latin community never became a *municipium*. Most of the evidence points the other way. In Africa at Gigthis the mission to Pius which asked for Latin rights is followed by a dedication to him in his lifetime as 'founder of the municipality'.[5] At Thisiduo a fragmentary inscription seems to indicate the same close connection under Hadrian.[6] In Spain at Igabra the

---

[1] *Lex. Sal.* 22, 25. *Lex Mal.* 59, Braunert, op. cit. 70 n. 15, 74 n. 29.

[2] Braunert, art. cit. 70 f. The date is based on dedications of sundry *municipia Flavia* to Vespasian and Titus as *censores*, sometimes posthumously. The grant should have been made soon after A.D. 70 if it was intended to quieten Spanish opinion after the civil war, as Pliny suggests ambiguously, *NH* 3. 30.

[3] *Lex Scl.* 26 distinguishes between magistrates already in office at the time of the issue of the *lex*, and those subsequently appointed *ex hac lege*, while cc. 22-3 imply that the former had been receiving the citizenship since the edict of Vespasian. The argument would be stronger if the text read 'qui ex edicto . . . c.R. consecutus *est*' instead of *erit*.

[4] Above, 160. *Lex. Sal.* 26.

[5] *ILS* 6779, 6780. Saumagne, op. cit. 121 f. argues rightly that these two inscriptions refer to the same promotion. No evidence directly connects Hadrian with this, though *CIL* viii. 22736 connects the early career of the agent of Gigthis with him.

[6] *ILS* 6781. But not at Gemellae where only *res publica* is mentioned, *ILS* 6848.

term *municipes* is used within three years of Vespasian's grant of Latin rights,[1] while at Munigua there seems to be some few years' delay between the two stages of promotion, though there, as also at Sabora, edicts of Vespasian and Titus mention the magistrates but not the title of a *municipium*.[2]

Braunert could produce only one instance of an *oppidum* from the lists of Pliny which after the Flavian grant still remained a *pagus* in the second century. To this can be added one or two communes in the Bracaran region denoted merely *civitates* in the second century.[3] Braunert limited his discussion to Spain. In the wider survey that follows better evidence for his view will be found occasionally in other western provinces. In the districts of the western Alps which received Latin status from Claudius and Nero the inscriptions suggest that the use of Roman or Latin municipal forms spread only slowly. Here the title of *municipium* is not documented until the later second and third century. Though this may be due to the accidents of archaeology, there are some indications that the tribal peoples were not suddenly or totally converted into *municipia* and that tribal identities survived to a late age.[4] But this is part of a peculiar pattern found in all Celtic lands that requires special discussion. In other areas the institution of *Latium maius*, whereby all local decurions became Romans, hardly fits the theory of Braunert.[5] It depends upon the complicated Roman device of the local quinquennial census and the co-optation of local councillors from the upper classes by the censors. Hence the implementation of *Latium maius*, at least, seems inseparable from full municipal status.

Braunert and others have connected Latin status with the remarks of Hadrian about *municipia* and *coloniae*, quoted by Gellius.[6] Hadrian was surprised that boroughs which could have continued to enjoy their own local usages and laws were eager to exchange these for the straitjacket of colonial status with

---

[1] *ILS* 1981, A.D. 76.

[2] For Munigua, *AE* 1962, no. 287, plain *civitas* under Claudius; *ILS* 256, *municipium*, to Vespasian as *censor*; *AE* 1962, no. 288, *quattuorviri, decuriones*; *CIL* ii. 1052, *promotor sui iuris*, of Titus. Sabora, *ILS* 6092.

[3] Carbulo, Braunert, art. cit. 77: Pliny, *NH* 3. 10 with *CIL* ii. 2322. The *civitas* of the Aravi in 119, *AE* 1954, no. 87, cf. *CIL* ii. 429; 'civitas Limicorum', in 132/141, *CIL* ii. 2516–17. Cf. the detailed study R. K. McElderry, *JRS* 7 (1918), 53 ff.

[4] See below, 372.                                                [5] Above, 255.

[6] For the text of Gellius, above, 257, 274. Cf. Braunert, art. cit. 81 f., Saumagne, op. cit. 50 f.

its highly standardized pattern of local government. This is widely taken to refer to all the new *municipia* of the imperial period, whether Roman or Latin, which (it is inferred) combined their former native system with that laid down by the *lex municipii*, if they did not dispense with a *lex municipii* altogether. But the text is misapplied. Hadrian was talking only about the most ancient boroughs of the Roman system—Spanish Italica, African Utica, and Praeneste in Italy, which were all communes of Roman citizens, not of Latins, created or promoted in the last age of the Republic or during the triumviral period.[1] Gellius in any case adds that the privileges under discussion were obscure and obsolescent by his time. That could hardly be said of the Spanish *municipia* created by the Flavians or of their successors elsewhere, promoted by Hadrian and Pius, that posted along the highway from *municipium* to *colonia*.

Some would see an illustration of Hadrian's remarks in the peculiar and well-documented cases of Lepcis Magna and Mactar in Africa. Lepcis was a plain *civitas* in the early Principate, ruled by magistrates with the Punic title of *sufetes*. Other 'Punic' pecularities appear in its organization as late as A.D. 91–2, and some of its public documents in Latin are followed by a summary in neo-Punic.[2] Yet dedications made in the name of the proconsul of Africa in A.D. 77–8 and 91–2 refer to the community as a *municipium*, a title otherwise absent from its inscriptions.[3] All this might suggest that Lepcis, between its peregrine period and its promotion to a full Roman colony by Trajan, possessed Latin status but lacked the *lex municipii* which would have remodelled the local organization after the style of Malaca. Yet the *sufetes* known before A.D. 90 mostly lack the Roman triple names, which suggests that they were not enjoying the Latin privilege of securing citizenship *per honorem*.[4]

The history of inland Mactar, in central Proconsularis, resembles that of Lepcis. Its institutions are Punic, and its citizens

---

[1] Cf. above, 257. Vittinghoff, op. cit. 35–6. Hadrian's words are frequently used to prove something which he did not say; he is talking either about *municipia c.R.* of the late Republic (above, 345 n. 5) or about the earlier *cives sine suffragio* (cf. 54).

[2] For a summary of the epigraphical evidence see *IRT* pp. 79 f. Lepcis was a plain *civitas* in A.D. 6, ibid. 301; cf. ibid. 330, A.D. 36. The earlier term *senatus* (ibid. 615) yields in the Flavian period to *ordo*, normal in *municipia*. The title *quattuorvir* occurs on an undated inscription, presumably pre-colonial, unless it is merely *aedilicia potestate* (ibid. 305). For neo-Punic cf. ibid. pp. 10 f.

[3] Ibid. 342, 436. For the colonization, ibid. 353, p. 81.          [4] Ibid. p. 80.

conspicuously peregrine in status and nomenclature in the Flavian period. Later a forum is dedicated to Trajan, Roman citizens appear, and titles of officials are translated from neo-Punic into Latin, but the commune is styled only *civitas* in a dedication to Marcus Aurelius. It is never entitled *municipium*, but was elevated to full colonial status apparently under Commodus.[1] There has been speculation about the existence of a class of 'quasi-*municipia*' to explain Lepcis and Mactar. But what happens in these two places is only unusual in an African context —the process of self-Romanization of municipal terms and usages, in anticipation of formal promotion, is familiar from the cantons of northern Gaul. Lepcis may be a half-assimilated Latin commune in the sense of Braunert, or it may be wrongly arrogating the title of *municipium*, but there is no reason to regard Mactar as other than a peregrine commune before its elevation, like that of other *civitates liberae* at that time, to colonial status. Lepcis does not represent the norm of municipal usage in Africa, which is shown by the bountiful evidence for the prevalence of the standardized municipal pattern throughout the rest of the African municipalities. In other localities such as Thugga and Gigthis, where there is evidence for the survival of Punic influences in the religious sphere, the native elements disappear from the local administration with the advent of municipal status, whether Latin or Roman.[2]

Braunert did not consider the earlier history of Latin rights in Italy and the provinces. Vittinghoff has usefully tabulated the evidence which shows that the communities which received Latin status from Caesar or Augustus in Spain and Sicily— Pliny's *oppida Latina*—have the title of *municipium* and are mostly governed by *duoviri*, but that those in Narbonensis have the title of *colonia* and are mostly governed by *quattuorviri*, though they

---

[1] See C. Picard, 'Civitas Mactaritana', *Karthago* 8 (1957), 77 ff. In a lengthy inscription (ibid.) listing the members of a *collegium iuventutis* the Latin names are all peregrine in type, and largely non-Roman and neo-Punic or translations from neo-Punic in derivation. For the later officials, replacing a triple *sufetatus* by *tresviri, decuriones,* and *quinquennales,* cf. *CIL* viii. 630, 11827, 11811 (*municipes*); *civitas,* A.D. 170, ibid. 11799; *AE* 1951, 43–4; *col. Aelia Aurelia,* ibid. 1949, 47, *CIL* viii. 11801. Picard identifies Mactar with Pliny's *oppidum Melizitanum* (*liberum*). Perhaps his *o. Materense* is more probable (*NH* 5. 30).

[2] For semi-Romanized titles in northern Gaul cf. e.g., *ILS* 7040, 7042, 7045. For Gigthis and Thugga cf. *CIL* viii, Index s.v. *Res Municipalis, Dei deaeque.*

can precede the promotions in Sicily by only a few years.[1] These Narbonensian *coloniae Latinae*, which are quite clearly distinguished by several particulars from the veteran settlements of Caesar and Augustus, may find their prototype in the grant of Latin rights to the peoples of Transpadane Gaul in 89 B.C. described by Asconius. 'They thereby secured the status of Latin colonies, without any settlement of colonists, and the privilege of securing the Roman citizenship by election to a local magistracy.'[2] The grant of Latin status to the two populations and the conversion of their communities to *coloniae Latinae* is similar. It was prescribed in 89 B.C. by a single legislative act, the *lex Pompeia*. This historical context helps to explain the origins and development of the complex charters of Latin municipalities as they appear in the Flavian documents. These can be connected through the *lex Pompeia* with whatever form of *lex coloniae* was used in the

---

[1] Cf. Vittinghoff, op. cit. 43–4, 76, 79 f., for Spain; 64–5 n. 1, for Narbonensis. The title *municipium* does not appear in Narbonensis, except at Dinia which was added to the province only in A.D. 68–9 (cf. 372 n. 1). The veteran colonies of Julian date which are listed by Pliny have *duoviri* as magistrates and *Teretina* as their tribe, while the *oppida Latina* of Pliny which later bear the title *colonia* or *c. Julia* have *quattuorviri* and the tribe Voltinia (except Aquae Sextiae, which has the tribe only). Degrassi (op. cit. 308), who did not notice the tribal evidence, took all seven (or ten) of the Latin communes to be Roman colonies which retained the quattuorvirate from a previous 'municipal' status, but does not explain why so many Roman colonies should fail to adopt their appropriate form of magistracy. Vienna, the only commune of this sort which certainly became a Roman colony, dropped the quattuorvirate for the duovirate (cf. 352 n. 1). Even Dea, a dependant township within Vocontian territory, calls itself *colonia Augusta* (*ILS* 6990, cf. 6992). Some *oppida Latina* not known as *coloniae* have the combination of quattuorvirate and Voltinian tribe, notably Alba and Antipolis (Degrassi, art. cit. 311, 316–17, 319 n. 3). Twice *praetores* appear with names indicative of recent enfranchisement; *CIL* xii. 517 (Aquae), 5371 (Carcaso). Degrassi produces too many *coloniae c.R.* of unknown origin, and no specific designation for the Latin communes. The grant of *ius Latii* to Sicily, converted by Antonius to Roman citizenship in April 44, belongs to Caesar's last acts, above, 230. Coins of Panormus, Henna, and Halaesa of *c.* 44–3 and of Lipara of *c.* 36 B.C. already have *duoviri* or the title 'municipium' (Grant, art. cit. 190–1, 195). Degrassi, art. cit. 314–15, rightly contests the view that Augustus later revoked the action of Antonius, which is based on the assumption that Pliny's list is of Augustan date: it includes only two *oppida c.R.*, three Latin communes, and five *coloniae c.R.* among the sixty-eight *civitates* of Sicily (*NH* 3. 88). Latin or Roman, municipal or colonial, the Sicilian magistracy was always the duovirate, which also preponderates in the pre-Flavian *municipia* of Spain. Cf. Degrassi, art. cit. 314–15, 332 and above, 347 nn. 12. The construction by Grant and others (above, 230) of the gradual re-enfranchisement of Sicily after 12 B.C. is called in question by the work of Teutsch on Pliny. Dio 49. 12. 5, Diodorus 13. 35. 3, say nothing about disfranchisement.

[2] Above, 111, 138–9.

Latin foundations of the third and second centuries B.C., though they doubtless assimilated many of the provisions laid down for *municipia civium Romanorum* in the documents of the late Republic. A link between the Latin *coloniae Iuliae* of Narbonensis and the *lex Pompeia* may be provided by Lugdunum Convenarum in Aquitania. This was a settlement of uprooted and stateless men, the flotsam of the Sertorian wars, organized by the young Pompeius in *c.* 71 after his campaigns in Spain, possibly on the model of his father's fictitious colonies in north Italy. In later days it had Latin status, the title of *colonia*, and much the same internal establishment as the Latin colonies of Narbonensis.[1]

The chronology of the Julian grants of Latin rights in Spain remains obscure.[2] A case can be made out for either Caesar or Augustus (before or after 27 B.C.). It matters little, except that the change of title from *colonia* to *municipium*, and of magistracy from the quattuorvirate to the duovirate, must be connected with the similar arrangements in Sicily, for the promotion of which Caesar was certainly responsible. The change suggests a decision to differentiate between the colonial settlements of the master-race and the up-graded communities of their most favoured subjects. The former *lex coloniae Latinae* could now serve in a revised form for the new 'Latin' *municipia*, and pass on as a standardized text to be issued and reissued at need in later times.

Braunert isolated the Flavian evidence from the earlier history of Latin rights. A simpler solution can be offered for the peculiarities of the Spanish evidence on which his case rests. The text of Pliny does not say that Vespasian 'gave', i.e. 'effectively conferred', Latin rights to all Spain, but that he made an allowance, assignment, or offer of it: 'tribuit'. The term recalls a phrase of Tacitus referring to the same period: 'nova iura . . . Africae ostentata'.[3]

---

[1] For its origins and Latin status cf. Strabo 4. 2. 2, p. 191; Hieronymus, *adv. Vigilantium* 2. 357, citing Sallust, in *CIL* xiii, p. 5; *AE* 1938, 171; 1941, 153–4; 1957, 4, testify to *ivviri*, the Voltinian tribe, and *colonia*. But *CIL* xiii. 254 has *civitas Convenarum* in a Claudian dedication, possibly distinct from the *colonia*, like Aventicum and the Helvetii, cf. below, 370.

[2] Vittinghoff, op. cit. 76 n. 8, 79, criticizes M. I. Henderson, *JRS* 23 (1942), 5 ff. for assigning all the Julian *oppida Latina* to Caesar, who had (he holds) no motive for rewarding Hispania Ulterior. Her likely suggestion that Augustus abolished the title of *colonia* for Latin communes in Spain cannot be proved. For the universality of the duovirate cf. *CIL* ii, Index 1066, 1168.

[3] *NH* 3. 30, cited 252. Tac. *Hist.* 1. 78. The distinction, though often narrow, is clear in the instances cited in *Thesaurus L.L.* s.v. Cf. above, 257. 'New privileges . . . were put on show for Africa.'

The inscriptions show that not all Spanish communes were able to take up the offer at once.[1] Implementation required positive action by the provincial communes, either a mission to Rome or at least a deputation to the provincial governor. In Spain, the effect was not so 'universal' as the very laconic text at first sight suggests. Some *civitates*, slow off the mark, may have remained peregrine until the *Constitutio Antoniniana*. There is a singular lack of post-Flavian creations in Spain.[2]

## LATIN STATUS AND THE CELTIC CANTONS

There remains the question of the precise effect of the grant of Latin status on provincial communes of alien culture. It is easy to see how effectively the system known from the charters worked in the comparatively small communes of Spain with their restricted territories and numerous townships. Southern Gaul, when it was gradually converted into a Roman province between 122 and 62 B.C., was a land of great tribal cantons with an aristocratic and feudal pattern of government, just as in the northern territories that Caesar conquered in the 50s. But unlike the north, where the population dwelled scattered through the countryside in hamlets and manors, *dispersi ac rudes* as in Britain, the southern Gauls, living in a Mediterranean climate, perforce adopted the Mediterranean pattern of rural habitation predominantly in large townships, *oppida* or *castella*, except in the mountain fringes, where a more open pattern was possible.[3] The Elder Pliny in his list of the Latin townships of Narbonensis frequently catalogues the numerous *oppida* with their tribal territories in the form *Avennio Cavarum, Tolosani Tectosagum*, or *Nemausus Arecomicorum*.[4] It is left uncertain whether the Cavae, Tectosages, and Arecomici as a whole share in the Latin status of their chief townships. Pliny distinguishes twenty-four other townships of the Arecomici from Nemausus as *oppida adtributa*, 'attributed settlements', and (it seems) another eighteen *oppida* of the Vocontii from their two capital communes, Lucus Augusti

---

[1] Above, 302 n. 31.

[2] Cf. the indexes of *CIL* ii for the lack of *municipia Ulpia* etc.

[3] For the human geography of Gaul see briefly *CAH* ix. 537 ff.; T. Rice-Holmes, *Roman Republic*, ii. 1 ff. The distribution of the tribal cantons can be recovered easily from Pliny, *NH* 3. 31–7 and Strabo 4. 6, pp. 202–4.

[4] Pliny, *NH* 3. 36–7.

and Vasio, which both had Latin rights. Strabo clarifies what Pliny left ambiguous: 'Nemausus has Latin rights and rules over twenty-four other communes of the Arecomici as tributaries.' He also says that the Vocontii had the same communal regime as the Arecomici of Nemausus, and in his account of Vienna he implies that it had a somewhat similar predominance within the canton of the Allobroges.[1]

If Strabo is rightly informed, the situation reflects the well-known division of the tribal cantons into territorial clans or *pagi*. The *pagus* within which the chief township lay may receive Latin rights and become a *colonia Latina*, while the other *pagi* remain peregrine either as parts of a separate tribal *civitas*, or under the supervision of the *colonia* as 'attributees'; in a few instances a tribe may have been split between two such *coloniae*, as when Pliny lists two Latin communes for the Volcae Tectosages or the Vocontii.[2] Alternatively, the whole tribal territory and its population may have constituted a colonial borough, and have shared equally in its Latin status. The texts of Pliny and Strabo do not absolutely exclude this solution, and the inscriptions from Narbonensis do not clarify the problem sufficiently. While certain *pagi* are administered by prefects appointed by the Latin boroughs, it is not clear whether the *pagi* are component parts of the tribe or of the borough. There is evidence for the survival of the old Celtic magistrates of the tribes, Latinized into aediles and praetors.[3] Among the Vocontii the tribal authorities seem to retain the predominance, controlling the *pagi* by their prefects, while even at Vasio, which manifests some of the activities of a municipality, the chief power seems to be in the hands not of an independent *quattuorvir*, but of a *praefectus*, and neither *municipium* nor *colonia* occurs as a title in inscriptions of the Vocontii.[4] But

---

[1] Pliny l.c. cited 357 n. 3. For attribution see above, 356. Strabo 4. 1. 11, C. p. 186, οἱ μὲν ἄλλοι κωμηδὸν ζῶσιν οἱ δὲ ἐπιφανέστατοι . . . βίενναν . . . κώμην ἔχοντες πρότερον . . . μητρόπολιν τοῦ ἔθνους . . . κατεσκευάκασι πόλιν. For Vocontii, id. 4. 6. 4, p. 203; above, 357 n. 3. Nemausus id. 4. 1. 12, p. 186, ὑπηκόους γὰρ ἔχει τέτταρας καὶ εἴκοσι . . . συντελούσας εἰς αὐτὴν ἔχουσα καὶ τὸ καλούμενον Λάτιον. (The reading ἐχούσας is stylistically improbable with the preceding συντελούσας.)

[2] For a similar view cf. E. Schönbauer, art. cit., 24 f.

[3] For *pagi*, cf., e.g., *ILS* 6989, *Vardenses pagani* to a *iivir* of Julia Apta; *ILS* 6988, *pagus Lucretius* subordinate to the Roman colony of Arelate. A *praetor Volcarum* (*CIL* xii. 1028), and a *quattuorvir praetor* of Nemausus (*ILS* 6976) may combine municipal and tribal offices, disguising the title *vergobret*.

[4] A *praetor Vas. Voc.* (*CIL* xii. 1369, 1371, 1586), also *ordo* and *aediles* of the Vocontii, (*ILS* 5614, 6992–93; *CIL* xii. 1375) and subordinate *pagi*. Vasio, the Latin *oppidum*,

the extensive territory of the Allobroges was administered cen-
trally by the colonial magistrates of Vienna, organized in the
conventional style first of a Latin and later of a Roman colony.
The Allobroges as such disappear from the inscriptions, and even
so distant a *vicus* as Geneva remains subordinate to Vienna.[1]
The early use of Latin name-patterns may suggest that the clans-
men of the *pagi* had Latin status,[2] but there are no indications of
their personal grade being affected by the later promotion of
Vienna to full Roman status, or of their dependent communes
being later advanced to independent municipal status as in the
territory of Carthage in Africa.

How far these patterns of promotion were applied to the
cantons of northern Gaul remains unclear. The policy of Augustus
was to leave the northern peoples to themselves, while encouraging loyalty to Rome by devices such as the establishment of the
provincial Council at Lugdunum, and the development of cantonal capitals with imperial titles like Augustodunum, but
apparently lacking privileged status.[3] It is possible that some of
these capitals received Latin rights after the model of Nemausus,
and designated themselves similarly by a local archaism as
*coloniae*. This would explain the occasional use of the title *colonia*
in northern Gaul at places where there is no other evidence of any
promotion such as the adoption of an imperial name to denote
its author.[4] If so, the supposed problem of the 'titular' colonies
disappears, and there is no reason to imagine that whole tribal
cantons in northern Gaul came to be organized as *coloniae civium
Romanorum*. Possibly this is what Tacitus had in mind when he
styled the head township of the Treviri, Augusta Trevirorum,
a *colonia*, though the canton still calls itself *civitas Trevirorum* in a

is *respublica Juliensium*, not *colonia* (so far), and its officers are a *praefectus* and *seviri*
(*ILS* 2709, 6991, *CIL* xii. 1375) Lucus, twin of Vasio in Pliny, has no known
magistrates (*CIL* xii, pp. 161–2). For Dea as *colonia* see 365 n. 1. Tac. *Hist.* 1. 66
is technically incorrect in calling Lucus a *municipium*, unless it developed later.

  [1] Cf. E. Howald, E. Meyer, *Die Römische Schweiz* (Zurich, 1940), 219–20, 235,
and nos. 91–103; its *pagi* and *vici* make dedications to the colonial magistrates both
of the Latin and the Roman period, cf. *ILS* 6998, 7001–4.
  [2] Cf. the stemma of P. Decius Esunertus, first Roman citizen of his family,
Howald–Meyer, op. cit. n. 124, dated 8 B.C. His father Trouceteius Vepus, coeval
of the grant of Latin rights, used the *duo nomina*, while his grandparents Troucetes
and Cobrovillus merely Latinized their single names.
  [3] Cf. Vittinghoff, op. cit. 102.
  [4] Cf. above, 244 n. 3; Vittinghoff, op. cit. 27, argued rightly that the title always
imples technical status, cf. above, 351.

document of *c.* A.D. 161–9, and when he expressed surprise that Londinium in Britain lacked the *cognomentum coloniae*.[1]

The well-documented situation of Aventicum and the Helvetii, and of Colonia Agrippensis and the Ubii is relevant here. In the Julio-Claudian period the Helvetii formed a unitary tribal *civitas*, subdivided into *pagi* with several townships or *vici* of which Aventicum was the chief. After the accession of Vespasian, Aventicum, for services rendered in the civil war against the Vitellian cause, and through a connection with the Flavian family, was promoted to colonial status with a long list of titles, of which the items *Constans Emerita* ambiguously suggest either a veteran settlement, of which there is no other trace, or services to the Flavian cause.[2] The tribal *civitas Helvetiorum* continued to manifest a communal existence beside the new Colonia Flavia Helvetiorum. It makes dedications in the formula *Helvetii publice* until the third century, its townships retain their local organization, and the bulk of its citizens remain peregrines, formally designated as *cives Helvetii*.[3] Roman citizens in Helvetian territory were organized as a *conventus civium Romanorum Helveticus*, and distinguished in documents of Aventicum as *incolae* from the citizens of the colony. But no senior magistrates of the Helvetii are known, while those of the colony receive dedications in Helvetian townships, and occupy themselves with road-building outside the colonial territory. Whether the colony was of Roman,

---

[1] Tac. *Hist.* 4. 62, *Ann.* 14. 27, 33. *CIL* iii. 5215. Cf. above, 351 n. 7; but Tacitus may only have in mind the great provincial cities which were *coloniae c.R.*, such as Lugdunum, Tarraco, Carthago, Narbo. Note the suggestion of N. J. de Witt, 'Urbanisation . . . in Roman Gaul' (Diss. Lancaster, Pa., 1940) that *colonia* in the northern usage represents the translation of the Celtic term *dunum*, unofficially used: but this cannot apply to Tacitus.

[2] See F. Stähelin, *Die Schweiz in Römischer Zeit* (Basel, 1948), 139 ff., 221 ff., Howald–Meyer, op. cit. 140 ff., for discussion and evidence about Aventicum. For the Flavian connection cf. Suetonius, *Vesp.* 1. 3. Tac. *Hist.* 1. 67–9. For the *civitas* cf. Tac. mentioning Aventicum (69) and an unnamed township (67) in A.D. 69; *ILS* 7008, dated to Claudius' time by Stähelin, op. cit. 143 n. 2, though a date after the Flavian colonization is possible, since it may have been inscribed after the death of the dedicator, who survived the foundation (cf. *ILS* 2697, 7010, *CIL* xiii. 5094). For the foundation date *c.* A.D. 71 or 73–4 cf. Howald–Meyer, op. cit. 252 and n. 189. Of its titles (*ILS* 1020, 2697) *Emerita* suggests positive services, cf. Tac. *Germ.* 28. 5, 'Ubii colonia esse meruerint'; similarly Ann. 12. 21. 3; 62. 2, the *merita* of Cos and Byzantium. See also J. Reynolds, *Rev. Suisse Hist.* 14 (1964), 387 f.

[3] Howald–Meyer, op. cit. nn. 190–2, *ILS* 7009, distinguish between the *civitas* and the *colonia*; cf. Schönbauer, art. cit. 26–7. For the status of individuals, Howald–Meyer, op. cit. nn. 161, 171, 175–8, 474–6. For *vici*, ibid. nn. 156, 169, 179, 245.

or of Latin status, as some have surmised, the relationship of the Helvetian *vici* to it resembles some sort of 'attribution'.[1]

The closest parallel lies in the relationship between the tribal commune of the Germanic Ubii and the military colony, Colonia Claudia Agrippinensis, founded in their territory and at their central township on the lower Rhine in A.D. 51.[2] The two communities seem to be distinct in an incident of A.D. 58 recounted by Tacitus, who distinguishes the *civitas* and the *vici* of the tribal people from the newly founded colony.[3] But eleven years later some fusion has taken place according to the acount in the *Histories*. The Ubii themselves are now called Agrippinenses, their leading families are linked by marriage with those of the colony —which technically implies either Latin rights or Roman status —and the conduct of affairs seems to be in the hands of the council of the Ubian gentry rather than of the senate of the colony.[4] The language of Tacitus is ambiguous, and it is hard to be certain whether the governing bodies of the two communities have been formally united or not, though in the inscriptions of the later period only the officials of the Roman colony are known.[5] But together the evidence about the Helvetii and the Ubii confirms the impression that grants of special status in tribal areas did not always and immediately apply to the whole canton.

A different pattern is found among the peoples of the western Alps, north of Italy and Narbonensis, who were given Latin rights by Claudius and Nero.[6] In the Cottian and Maritime Alps

[1] For attribution see above, 356 f. Dedications, Howald–Meyer, op. cit. nn. 156, 168–9; *incolae*, nn. 179, 207–8, 211; road-building, n. 244.

[2] See the careful discussion of H. Schmitze (*RE* viiiA. 1 (1955), 532 ff.) who notes the parallel with Vienna.

[3] Tac. *Ann.* 12. 27. 1; 13. 57. 5. In *Hist.* 4. 55, 63–5, the Ubii share the colonial township with the *coloni*. Cf. *Germ.* 28. 5, cited 370 n. 2.

[4] *Hist.* 4. 28; 'gens Germanicae originis eiurata patria Agrippinenses vocarentur'; *conubium*, ibid. 65; *concilium, Agrippinensium*, ibid. 64; *Germ.* loc. cit. Throughout this narrative the *Agrippinenses* are Ubii, but Tacitus also uses Ubii separately. For ambiguity cf. 55: 'in colonia . . . in domum privatam conveniunt; nam publice civitas talibus inceptis abhorrebat; ac tamen interfuere quidam Ubiorum', and 63 'si . . . disiecta [sc. colonia] Ubios quoque dispersisset'.

[5] Cf. A. Riese, *Das rhein. Germ. in d. ant. Inschriften* (Leipzig, 1914), nos. 2294–2303. Schmitze (loc. cit.) notes that the term Ubius disappears as a personal designation after the Julio-Claudian period, cf. Riese, op. cit. nos. 2361–6. Possibly a part of the Ubii were included in the original *colonia*, that later swallowed up the *civitas* which had joined the rebel cause in 69.

[6] Tac. *Ann.* 15. 32. 1. (cited, 257 n. 6) with Pliny, *NH* 3. 135, and the Claudian

the title of *municipium* replaces that of *colonia*, though the earliest evidence for it at present comes from the later second century. At Vintium and Cenomelum, chief townships of the Maritime Alps, the term *municipium* appears rarely, though they use the normal municipal titles for their officers. At Cottian Brigantio and Segusio the title *municipium* is not authenticated until the later second and third centuries, and it has not yet appeared at Cottian Ebrodunum. At Dinia, capital town of the Bodontiaci, transferred in A.D. 68–9 from the Cottian province to Narbonensis, a new text reveals the title and the machinery of a *municipium Bodontiacorum* in A.D. 187.[1] Yet a lengthy inscription from the time of Diocletian shows that the identity of the tribal *civitates* of the Cottian peoples was still preserved in some form.[2]

In the Vallis Poenina and the Graian Alps of Switzerland there is a variant pattern. Four tribal *civitates* are documented in the Vallis Poenina from the time of Augustus to that of Gaius. Under Claudius Octodurum, central town of the Veragri, secures the title Forum Augusti.[3] After Claudius the names of the four tribes are replaced in inscriptions by the combined name of *Vallenses*, and Octodurum is restyled Forum Claudii. The common formula is *Foroclaudienses Vallenses* or *Forum Claudii Vallensium*, though the term Vallensis is also used by itself. There are few traces of regular municipal organization at Forum Claudii, and the term *municipium* does not appear even in late documents.[4] So too among the Ceutrones of the Graian Alps, the township Axima becomes Forum Claudii Ceutronum, though the people continue to use Ceutrones as an official designation after the Flavian period.[5]

titles, secure the fact—possibly all are Neronian, since the titles of Octodurum are ambiguous; below, n. 3.

[1] Cenomelum; officers, *ILS* 6759 (A.D. 181), 551, 6760; *municipium*, *AE* 1965, no. 193; *civitas*. ibid. no. 194. Vintium: *civitas*, *CIL* xii. 9 (A.D. 239), 11 (A.D. 250); officers, *CIL* xii. 17, 81–2, 84, *ILS* 553, 6758. Ebrodunum; Brigantio, *CIL* xii. 94, 95; possibly *civitatem per honorem consecuti*, ibid. 83. Segusio, *municipium*, *ILS* 3590. Dinia, *AE* 1961, n. 156; transferred to Narbonensis in A.D. 68–9, Pliny, *NH* 3. 37.

[2] *CIL* xii. n. 78; for the Capillates there named as *civitas* cf. Strabo 4. 6. 6, C. 204, Pliny, *NH* 3. 135, 137.

[3] Stähelin, op. cit. 164, Howald–Meyer, op. cit. 196–8 and nos. 37–42, *ILS* 169, 6754–5. For the tribal names, Nantuates, Seduni, Veragri, Uberi, cf. Howald–Meyer, op. cit. 37–8; Pliny, *NH* 3. 137 (text of 6 B.C.), Strabo 4. 6. 6, c. 204. For Forum Augusti *CIL* xii. 5528, in A.D. 47.

[4] Howald–Meyer, op. cit. nn. 289, 373–7. For Vallenses alone, ibid. nn. 147, 479; magistrates, ibid. nn. 48, 51, 62, 69, mostly not from Octodurum.

[5] Stähelin, op. cit. 159. *ILS* 289, *c.* A.D. 107, is the earliest documentation of Forum Claudii. Official texts concerning its boundaries use only 'Ceutrones', cf.

Here too the title *municipium* does not appear, and the Forum may be subordinate to the tribal commune. It has been assumed by Swiss historians that the grant of Latin rights was made to the whole population of these restricted territories, and that the tribal *civitates* were remodelled into municipalities of the Latin type. The same should hold for the development of the Maritime and Cottian districts. But there is room for doubt in the rather scanty evidence about the Fora. There is no sign of a rapid and total municipalization on the Spanish model, though the tribal names cease to be used to designate personal origin.

Eastwards in Austrian Noricum the development is more orthodox. Pliny lists five *oppida Claudia* and one *oppidum Flavium* in Noricum without further indication of status. Inscriptions, not certainly datable before the second century, confirm the title and mention normal municipal officers at five out of the six *oppida*, and the term *municipium* is applied to four of them, the documentation at Celeia being probably earlier than 100.[1] At Lauriacum, a military settlement, fragments of a Latin charter have been found, closely akin to the *lex Salpensana*, but dated to 212–17. Possibly there was an interval between the grant of Latin status, which is implied by the evidence, and the formal organization of the Claudian *oppida* as *municipia*, but this can hardly have been later than the Flavian promotion of Solva.[2]

In the Illyrian provinces there are some indications that tribal *civitates* were converted into *municipia* comprising the whole tribe in the later period. It seems that the extensive *civitas Iasorum* in central Pannonia became under Hadrian or Pius the *municipium Aelium Iasorum*, divided into *pagi* and *vici* which may represent former tribal sections.[3] The *municipium Latobicorum* may be a transformed tribal state, while in Dalmatia a *municipium Mal(vesatium)*

ILS 5957, 5868, of A.D. 74 and 163. The latter mentions Forum Claudii in another context.

[1] Pliny, *NH* 4. 146, with *CIL* iii, pp. 591, 597, 618, 631, 667. For *municipium* see *CIL* iii. 5227, 15205(3), Celeia; 11485, Aguntum; *AE* 1959, 151, Iuvavum; *CIL* iii. 5331, *AE* 1942–3, 69, Solva. Recent discoveries published in *AE* do not otherwise enlarge the picture. The two inscriptions from Celeia by their *nomina* and style (Julii, Claudii of the first generation) suggest an early date, cf. illustrations in Hoffiler-Saria, *Ant. Inschrift. Jug.* nos. 48, 82. My suggestion above, 242, that these were all *municipia c.R.* is not supported by Pliny's terms.

[2] *Lex Lauriacensis*, *FIRA*[2] i. 26, with *AE* 1953, n. 124. Solva, above, n. 1.

[3] See G. Alföldi, *Epigraphica* 1964, 95 ff.; *CIL* vi. 3197, *AE* 1964, 11, Pliny, *NH* 3. 147. Cf. the development of *municipium Batavorum* and *m. Canninefatium* in the study of J. E. Bogaers, cited *AE* 1962, 95.

and the *municipium Riditarum* are akin, though their names are local rather than tribal.[1] But the evidence from Illyricum is in general scanty and of uncertain interpretation.

In summary, the evidence from the Spanish provinces, and the great bulk of that from Africa, is against the thesis of Braunert, and favours a unitary explanation of Latin rights. So too what is known of Noricum and Illyricum. But in the Gallic and Alpine provinces the development is less orthodox. All the Gallic communes of Narbonensis about which there is any quantity of evidence, with the considerable exception of the Vocontii, demonstrate their Latin status by assuming the machinery of a *municipium* and using the archaic title of *colonia*. Among the Alpine peoples Braunert can find stronger support. The tribal folks of the central and eastern Alpine fringe, who were the objects of 'attribution' under Augustus or earlier, received Latin status, but were not expected to reorganize and manage their communities by themselves on the Latin municipal pattern.[2] The later extension of Latin rights under Claudius and Nero to the peoples of the western Alps, dispensed with 'attribution', and imposed or encouraged a varying degree of municipalization. This begins with the immediate establishment of the Fora Claudia at tribal centres, and tends towards the total reorganization of the tribal states as full municipalities. But it is not possible to date the stages of development or measure their duration within a hundred years.[3] The lack of formal organization of *municipia* in the Alpine zone in the first century A.D. may well be due to the remote and tribal condition of the peoples: it is not to be transported automatically to the context of the Mediterranean provinces.

The total separation of Latin rights from municipal status would hardly have been possible. 'Attribution' had provided an alternative to the municipalization of backward mountain peoples, but it had been found to have its drawbacks, as in the

[1] *CIL.* iii. 2774, 3925; Sasel, *Inscr. Lat. Jug.* 73, 86. For these Dalmatian *municipia* see Wilkes, op. cit. 240 f., 283 f.; their tribes were Delmatae and Dindari. It is remarkable that neither Alföldi nor Wilkes suspected the existence of Latin municipalities in Dalmatia except at Rider (above, 348 n. 3; as suggested by Mommsen *CIL* iii, p. 363), though Dr. Wilkes's description of certain Flavian and post-Flavian *municipia* of areas of inner Dalmatia (op. cit. 270 f., 280 f.), where the full citizenship seems to be restricted to a part of the population, strongly suggests Latin status, indicated by *CIL* iii. 14316, 14249 for Salvium and Magnum (peregrines *ex municipio*).

[2] Above, 356 nn. 5, 6.    [3] Above, 372 nn. 1, 5.

affair of Tridentum, where Claudius found the 'attributees' following illegal procedures through a misunderstanding of their status—the improper use of Roman names, illegal assumption of Roman offices, and enlistment in the wrong regiments.[1] This could be avoided only by the use of public regulations of the kind found in the municipal charters from Spain. Without the publication of rules dealing with the workings of the civil law, such as the sections of the *lex Salpensana* about the status of the children and freedmen of enfranchised Latins, the bare grant of Latin rights would have been a mystery to its holders.[2] It was never the Roman way to leave newly created or promoted communities in a political vacuum without any guidance for the management and understanding of their affairs.[3]

So it seems that 'charter Latinity' was the norm throughout the Mediterranean provinces, whether communes are styled *coloniae*—the original title—or *municipia*, later made universal by Augustus. In the Alpine zone a modified system appears under the careful Claudius, with newly organized *fora* as the focal points of former tribal *civitates*. During the second and third centuries these acquire charter Latinity, which alone makes its appearance in the Illyrian provinces. Nowhere except among the *gentes attributae* of the south-central Alps is there anything like the purely personal *Latinitas* of Braunert. But their condition dates back to the *lex Pompeia* of 89 B.C., and is an isolated archaism.

## CHARTER LATINITY

It is assumed even in the thesis of Braunert that Latin communes were eventually established as *municipia* by an act of Roman authority which included the issue of a set of rules, a *lex municipii*, similar to the lengthy laws that survive from Malaca and Salpensa in Spain, and are testified by the fragment from Lauriacum in Rhaetia. The alternative notion, promoted by some modern scholars but never adequately worked out, is that *municipia*, whether Latin or Roman, formed their own constitutions by combining a private selection from the corpus of Roman

---

[1] *FIRA*[2] i. 71, A.D. 46.

[2] *Lex Sal.* 22, 23, cf. ibid. 28, 29 (*manumissio, tutela*); cf. below, 378.

[3] Apart from the late Republican laws and charters, cf. the pretorian *praefecti iuridicundo* of the middle Republic, above, 43 f., 52 f.

municipal and civil legislation with elements of their previous native usages.[1] The only evidence for such a procedure lies in the statement of Gellius, enlarging upon a comment of Hadrian, that *municipia* were free to follow their own laws and usages, unrestricted by Roman legislation, and in the anomalous institutions of Mactar and Lepcis. But it was seen above that the latter are the exceptions which 'prove' the rule, and that Gellius and Hadrian were talking not about the *municipia* of the Empire but about *cives sine suffragio* and *municipia* of the middle and late Republic.[2] The solid evidence from the municipal laws of the late Republic indicates an increasing tendency towards central control and uniformity. The establishment of a new *municipium* or the reorganization of an old one by an official *conditor* or *constitutor municipii*, whose function includes the 'giving of laws', is well documented in the period of Caesar, and this usage continues in use through the Triumviral age into the Principate.[3] The term *lex data* appears equally in the charter of Tarentum (*c.* 88–49), the law of Urso (46), and in the section of the *Tabula Heracleensis* (46–4) concerning the laws of the ambiguous *municipium fundanum*.[4] In *c.* 63, Pompeius Magnus who closely followed Roman methods in his reorganization of the Greek cities of Bithynia and Pontus, imposed a uniform set of rules for the framework of local government, which frequently altered local usage.[5] The laws which reorganized the *municipia* of Cisalpine

[1] Cf. Picard, art. cit., above, 364 n. 1. Tentatively, M. Frederiksen, *JRS* 55 (1965), 191 f. The suggestion (ibid. 194 f.) that the miscellaneous collection of Roman regulations in the *Tab. Heracleensis* was a selection made for local purposes meets the objection that the rules would hardly have been published undigested and unadapted, on an expensive sheet of bronze, if they were to be combined with a local statute.

[2] Cf. above, 363. Gellius (*NA* 16. 13. 6–9 cited above, 257, 274) connects his view of municipal freedom with the Caerite franchise and regards such freedom as obsolescent; Hadrian's instances are all Republican.

[3] For republican *constitutio* cf. above, 160 n. 5, 167–8. For *conditores* of the Julian period cf. Grant, op. cit. 150, 160, 171, 181. For later examples cf. *ILS* 6773, 6779.

[4] *Lex mun. Tar.* (*FIRA*² i. 18), 2, 'post hanc legem datam'. *Lex Urs.* (ibid. 21), 67, 'quicumque . . . post hanc legem datam'. 72, 'uti hac lege data oportebit'. *Tab. Her.* (ibid. 13), 159 ff., 'quei lege . . . permissus fuit utei in municipio fundano . . . leges daret.' Under Trajan Hyginus refers generally to the *Leges datae* and *Leges* of all *coloniae* and *municipia* (B. 106–7).

[5] Cf. Pliny 10. 79, 112, 114, and my Commentary ad loc. A. H. M. Jones, *CERP* 159 f., 170 f. The *lex Pompeia*, which supplemented individual civic statutes enshrining much local custom (Pliny 10. 93, 109, 113), introduced the Roman

Gaul after its enfranchisement, and the regulations of the Caesarean *Tabula Heracleensis*, were similarly universal in application. That under the Empire a more liberal policy prevailed towards *municipia* seems improbable, when the general uniformity of institutions in the municipalities of the Romanized provinces is considered, despite the isolated anomalies.

The *lex Salpensana* itself can hardly be a statute of local provenance, since it is identified as the act which authorizes the grant of Roman citizenship to the annually elected magistrates, and is equated with an imperial edict to the same effect.[1] The whole *lex*, in the centre of which the sections about enfranchisement are imbedded, must rest on direct Roman authority. The surviving sections of the *lex Malacitana*, which happen not to overlap at all with those of the *lex Salpensana*, are concerned with the election of judicial magistrates, and with the definition of their jurisdiction over the local *municipes*, of whom the most influential were to become Roman citizens.[2] Like the rules of manumission and *tutela* in the *lex Salpensana*, which introduced universally valid forms of Roman manumission and guardianship, these sections can hardly have been formulated at the whim of the municipalities.[3]

When in the second century of the Empire a Latin *municipium* such as Gigthis refers to its imperial 'founder', it is probable that the process of foundation was similar to that found in the late Republic, when the *municipii constitutor* provided the more or less comprehensive *lex municipii*. The only discernible non-conformity in the imperial period lies in the very occasional variation of magisterial titles.[4] But the function of these officers

municipal census and censors, life tenure of decurions instead of democratic election and rotation, and a veto on plural citizenship, against normal Greek usage.

[1] *Lex. Sal.* 21, 22 : 'qui . . . ex hac lege exve edicto imp . . . Vespasiani . . . civitatem Romanam consecutus erit.' The clauses continue by laying down rules about the *ius civile* of the enfranchised-persons.    [2] *Lex Mal.* 54–60, 65–7, 69.

[3] *Lex Sal.* 28 : 'qui ita . . . manumissus . . . erit liber esto . . . uti qui optumo iure Latini libertini liberi sunt.' 29 : 'qui tutor h.l. datus erit is . . . tam iustus tutor esto quam si is c.R. . . . tutor esset.' These clauses might be regarded as examples of merely local adaptation of Roman usages for the Latin *municipes* alone, but they are worded so as to imply universal validity under Roman law, just like the rules cited above, n. 1, affecting Romans.

[4] Outside Italy such variation is rare. But one may cite the *sufetes duoviri* of Volubilis, the *sufetes* of Lepcis if not of Mactar, the *duoviri ad aerarium* of Narbonensis, and the *tresviri* of the Cirtan confederation. Above, 363–4 ; *ILA* 634, *ILS* 6858 f., 6996 f.

remained the same. The legislator of the *fragmentum Atestinum* meant just this when he enacted that 'whoever in that place has judicial power by virtue of a law, treaty, plebiscite, senatorial decree, or *established arrangement*, shall act as follows'. Whatever the title, the function was defined in detail by a Roman enactment such as the *lex Rubria*.[1] The procedure recalls the arrangements of Pompeius in Bithynia, who combined his general *lex provinciae* with individual city statutes which incorporated native usages that were not in conflict with the Roman rules. It is only so far that Latin or Roman municipalities might be said with Hadrian to be 'freer and less subject to Roman standards' than the cities with the uniform pattern of a Roman colony.[2]

Those who would separate the personal grant of *ius Latii* to a commune from its elevation to municipal status practically reduce Latin rights to the potential privilege of acquiring the Roman citizenship by holding local office (*per honorem*), and eliminate any positive content or advantage for the inhabitants outside the magisterial class. The charters show that this separation is unreal. They are concerned both with the public machinery of the *municipium* and with the personal status of the *municipes* as Latins. Enough survives to show that the *municipes* lived as Latins under a form of civil law which was essentially the Roman *ius civile*. The clause about the provision of guardians enacts that guardians appointed under the municipal law are to be 'as true guardians as if the minor concerned was a Roman citizen and the guardian were his nearest agnate relative'. Slaves manumitted by formal process are to be 'freedmen of the highest class of Latin freedmen', with analogous reference to the well-known classification of freedmen in Roman laws.[3] A rule that the previous relationship of *patria potestas* between fathers and children who become Roman citizens *per honorem* is not to be affected by this change of status proves that Latins as such had adopted a form of *patria potestas*, a custom otherwise confined to Roman citizens.[4] It is clear that the personal status of 'Latinity'

---

[1] *Fr. Atest.* 10–15, cf. above, 163 n. 4.

[2] Cf. 376 n. 5 above. For Hadrian, above, 376.    [3] Cf. 377 n. 3 above.

[4] *Lex Sal.* 22: 'ut qui c.R. consequantur maneant in eoru' . . . potestate . . . is . . . in eius qui c.R. h.l. factus erit potestate cuius esse deberet si civitate . . . mutatus . . . non esset . . . esto'; and 21 cited below, 379 n. 1; cf. Gaius 1. 95, where *Latini coloniarii* are the only category of enfranchised persons who automatically retain rights of *manus* and *potestas*. Despite Gaius' assertion (1. 55) that Romans

involved a reception or assimilation of Roman *ius civile*, a process that is already well documented in the Republican period. The fact is obscured by the total concentration of the textbooks of the classical lawyers on Roman law itself, though briefly indicated by the statement of Ulpian that Latins had the *ius commercii* and in some instances the *ius conubii*.[1] Since the charters were concerned with the judicial and administrative organization of this personal status, the two are interconnected and inseparable. The grant of Latin status necessitated the provision of a book of rules for its operation.

When Strabo as a Greek observer sought to explain the main features of Latin rights, he picked out the right of acquiring Roman citizenship *per honorem*, and the freedom of the communes from the intervention of Roman proconsuls.[2] The latter partly inaccurate statement is a reference to the provisions of the municipal charters. In them, as in the earlier rules for Cisalpine Gaul, the government of the communes, Latin and Roman alike, is established on a statutory basis which precludes the intervention of provincial governors except in spheres of action reserved for them.[3] The surviving sections of the Latin charters happen to deal only with jurisdiction over administrative offences. But the last of them indicates that the boundary between municipal and provincial jurisdiction was clearly defined.[4] Within that boundary the municipality is independent of the governor. Strabo in the time of Augustus thus anticipates and confirms the evidence of the Flavian charters that the grant of Latin Rights concerned the status both of individuals and of communes.

are practically the only persons to have the notion of *patria potestas*, the implication of these sections is clear. Gaius has very little to say positively about the rights of *Latini coloniarii* (cf. 1. 79, 131 against 1. 22, 29), as distinct from *Latini Juniani*, whose position was quite different. His omission cannot contradict the wording of *Lex Sal.* 21–2. Handbooks about Roman law for Italian use had no occasion to deal seriously with *Latini coloniarii*, who are, e.g., explicitly mentioned only once by *Tit. Ulp.* in 19. 4.

[1] Cf. above, 109 f. In effect the charters are spelling out in detail the meaning of *ius commercii. Lex Sal.* 21 may be thought to imply also the existence of *ius conubii* between at least the local Latins and Romans; '. . . liberis qui legitimis nuptiis quaesiti in potestatem parentium fuerint' etc. For *commercium* cf. *Tit. Ulp.* 19. 4. The statement of Gaius 1. 56–7 and *Tit. Ulp.* 5. 4 that Latini only had *conubium* by special grant may refer to *Latini Juniani*, who alone are considered in *Tit. Ulp.* 1 and 3.      [2] Strabo 4. 187 C.      [3] Above, 320–1.

[4] *Lex Mal.* 69: '. . . quodve cum eo agetur quod pluris HS CIↃ sit neque tanti sit ut (*de ea re proconsulem ius dicere . . . oporteat*).'

# XVI

## THE *CONSTITUTIO ANTONINIANA*: *DEDITICII* AND *RUSTICI*

ONTROVERSY about the edict of Caracalla continued unabated down to 1958, when C. Sasse published a masterly monograph which greatly clarified the 'state of the question', followed in 1962 by a critical catalogue of some ninety major discussions of the theme.[1] Since then the debate has declined in vigour, apart from a sustained effort by R. Boehm to undermine the commonly accepted bases of the restoration of the papyrus document.[2] This remarkable controversy, which has added singularly little to historical knowledge, has been concerned more with the formulation of Caracalla's pronouncement, his motives and intentions, than with the practical effects of it in the Roman world. Interest has been concentrated upon the clauses of the papyrus edict concerning the scope of the offer of Roman citizenship, the limitation affecting the *dediticii*, and the definition of this term. None who have written since 1939 have followed Bickermann and this book in regarding the text as a supplementary edict to a previous general announcement. Yet no one has established a meaning for the obscure definition of the beneficiaries in the introductory sentence that would fit the hard core of the *Constitutio Antoniniana* in the historical sources—the

[1] C. Sasse, *Die Constitutio Antoniniana* (Wiesbaden, 1958), cited below as Sasse, op. cit.; 'Literaturübersicht zur C.A.', *Journal Jur. Pap.* 14 (1962), 109–49, ibid. 16 (1963).
[2] E. Boehm, at immense length, in a series of polemical articles in *Aegyptus* 42–4 (1962–4), cited below by year numbers, following Bradford–Welles's inaccessible study of the papyrus in *Études Pap.* 9, 1 ff. (cited by B. from an off-print), claimed that the traces of the second delta of δεδειτικίων read by Meyer on the papyrus never existed, and hence that *dediticii* can be replaced by another term, as others had done earlier. He questioned the supplement τὴν before οἰκουμένην, and the initial υ of ὑπεισέλθωσιν, which he read as κ. He also claimed that ατων in line 9 may represent parts of two words such as κατὰ τῶν. But his own attempt to supply an alternative to δεδειτικίων involved the invention of the neologism ἀπολιτίκιοι; cf. below, 390 n. 4. Sasse cites an unpublished examination of the papyrus by E. Kalbfleisch (*JEA* 26 (1940), 16 n. 2) which reinstated traces of the delta; he also quotes evidence that war-time conditions of storage caused a deterioration of the papyrus, inhibiting further decipherment.

offer of the Roman citizenship to all the free inhabitants of
the empire. The words ὁσάκις ἂν ὑπεισέλθωσιν εἰς τοὺς ἐμοὺς
ἀνθρώπους implying entry into the Roman world from outside,
still baffle straightforward explanation, except for those who
ignore the precise meaning of words.[1] A few scholars have preferred to regard this document as a declaration of intent rather
than as a technical instruction for the enfranchisement of the
peregrine peoples.[2] This explanation, which was also tentatively
proposed above, is perhaps the best solution. For whatever the
meaning of the introductory section, the main statement agrees
with the literary evidence for the *Constitutio*: 'I give the citizenship [of the Romans] to all [those in the] world provided that
there remains . . . apart from the *dediticii*.'[3] As for the term
*dediticius*, there has been general agreement that this refers to
provincials who became subjects of Rome by formal surrender
in war, as in the Republican period, but it is disputed whether
the *dediticii* of the *Constitutio* were of remote or of recent origin,
and how far they were technically barred from receiving the
Roman citizenship. The term itself must however be used in a
well-established and familiar sense, since it appears in the Edict
without any explanation.

The central controversy concerns the limiting clause, which is
in the form of a genitive absolute introduced by the participle
μένοντος. Here a firm advance has been made. Sasse's detailed
analysis of the common use of the μένοντος formula in legal papyri

---

[1] Cf. above, 286. The iterative ὁσάκις, never used as a multiple, adds to the
difficulty of the meaning of ὑπεισέλθωσιν. Cf. Sasse, op. cit. 25 ff.; his linguistic
analysis decisively rejects the Stroux supplement τοσάκις μυρίους etc. He tries to
extract a reference to all present and future members of the Roman world—e.g.
'peregrinos quandocumque ad meos homines accedant', and perhaps rightly
insists that ξένους stood in the gap before ὁσάκις. Both terms are echoed in Dio's
account of the edict (77. 9. 5): Ῥωμαίους πάντας τοὺς ἐν τῇ ἀρχῇ αὐτοῦ . . . διὰ τὸ
τοὺς ξένους μὴ συντελεῖν ἀπέδειξεν. For the term 'my people' cf. Nerva's *cives mei* in
an edict cited by Pliny, *Epp.* 10. 58. 7, and Pliny's own use of *cives tui* addressing
Trajan, *Pan.* 21. 4, *Epp.* 10. 12. 2, though these nominally refer to Roman citizens,
and the later usage discussed below, 427, 434.

[2] Cf. E. Kiessling, *Z-S Savigny* 58 (1961), 421 ff. Boehm, art. cit. (1964), 236 ff.,
saw the advantage of regarding the text simply as an enabling act.

[3] Above, 280, I failed to stress that two contemporary administrators, the
lawyer Ulpian, who was probably on the imperial *consilium* at the time, and the
consular Dio, both describe the *C.A.* as a *universal* grant; *Dig.* 1. 5. 17, 'qui in orbe
Romano qui sunt'; for Dio, cf. above, n. 1. Sasse, op. cit. 9–11, lists all the
ancient descriptions of the *C.A.* Only Sidonius (below, 386 n. 1) mentions the
omission of slaves and barbarians.

sufficiently proves that this is the Greek equivalent of the Latin usage in such phrases as *salvis privilegiis . . .* or *salvo iure . . .*[1] The formula always prescribes that some positive condition is to remain unchanged. Hence it is now unlikely that the missing phrase in the papyrus refers to a class of persons who are to 'continue under' some *new* condition, as is assumed by one group of supplements.[2] Sasse also established that such formulae normally form the conclusion of the sentence in which they stand. Hence the exclusion of the *dediticii* should be connected not with the main verb but with the genitive absolute. Their exclusion is not from the grant of franchise but from the condition prescribed in the missing phrase.

That phrase had long been the subject of speculative restorations whent he discovery of a bronze tablet at Banasa in Mauretania provided fresh evidence. Oddly this still awaits full publication, but short extracts and a summary published by Seston and Euzennat in 1961 may suffice.[3] They show that the tablet contained three documents concerning the grant of the Roman status by Marcus Aurelius in A.D. 168–9 and 177 to a princely family belonging to a Mauretanian tribe. The grant was subject to two conditions. It was made *salvo iure gentis,* 'saving the privileges of the tribe', and also 'without detriment to the financial claims of the Treasury'. But while the first condition appeared in the two imperial rescripts contained in the tablet, the second is added only in an extract from the imperial registry of new citizens.[4] The first condition meant that the social and legal relationships between the enfranchised family and their native commune were to remain unchanged. It implies a developed form of that dual citizenship which is seen emerging in the Julian period in the instances of Seleucus of Rhosus and the enfranchised veterans of Octavian.[5]

This condition has been rightly connected with the limiting clause of the edict of Caracalla. Its discovery greatly enhances

---

[1] Sasse, op. cit. 48–58, summarized ibid. 58. In 47 instances of the genitive absolute in this sense, the participle always comes first. When a tense of μένειν is used instead, it comes first in 35 out of 37 instances.

[2] Sasse rightly observes that the sense of 'stay unchanged' is the sole meaning of μένειν only in this formula, against Schubart (*Aegyptus* 20 (1940), 36).

[3] W. Seston, M. Euzennat, *CRAI* 1961, 317 ff. But see above, 336, for final text.

[4] The tablet contains three documents.

[5] Above, 297 f. Cf. E. Schönbauer, *Jura* 14 (1963), 72 ff., the only scholar so far to exploit the new evidence since Seston.

the probability of the original supplement of Meyer in the sense that 'every kind of commune continues unchanged', or one of its numerous equivalents.[1] The second or fiscal condition of the Banasan tablet had also been anticipated by Bickermann's supplement, but apart from the verbal dissimilarity of the two, the fact that Bickermann requires the exclusion of the *dediticii* to be taken with the main verb, renders his version much less probable.[2] Meyer's supplement moreover makes good sense if the term *dediticii* is taken in its normal historical meaning; the whole phrase may well represent a Latin original of the type 'salvo iure [or *statu*] omnium ubique civitatium praeterquam dediticiarum'. The grant of the citizenship to the inhabitants of the empire was not to affect the present status of their communities except in the case of *dediticii*. This reflects the historical fact that existing *civitates* of every shape from *c. stipendiariae* to *c. liberae*, from *pagi* to *municipia* and *coloniae*, remained what they had been before. The *civitates* did not become *municipia*, and the colonial title remained the highest grade of communal status.[3] But since the grant of any permanent status automatically put an end to the condition of *dediticius*, any existing *civitates* or *gentes dediticiae* would become established provincial communities, if included in the grant.

This simple solution sets aside an accepted doctrine concerning the term *dediticius*. It is commonly assumed that *dediticii* had no communal organization until the restoration of their corporate status by the final decision of Rome, and hence that such a term as *populus dediticius* could not be used. This historically is not true, though many have persuaded themselves of it, largely through a misunderstanding of the treatment of the Campani in 211 B.C. and of a passage of Ulpian. The total destruction of the community of Capua and the narrowly defined *libertas* of the surviving Campani was not the automatic consequence of their *deditio*, but was due to specific decisions of the Roman authorities

---

[1] Seston, art. cit. 320. Schönbauer, art. cit. 106. Sasse, op. cit. 13–14, lists some twenty alternative supplements 'after' Meyer.

[2] E. Bickermann, who took χωρὶς τῶν δεδειτικίων with δίδωμι, proposed μένοντος [τῷ φισκῷ τοῦ λόγου ἀπαραβ]άτως.

[3] Yet scholars have persuaded themselves of the opposite against the plain facts of municipal documents in and after the third century (e.g. above, 350–1). Hence several supplements of the type μένοντος οὐδενὸς τῶν πολιτευμάτων figure in Sasse's list.

taken after the act of *deditio*. A tribunician bill was required to
enable the Senate to deal with the *dediticii* because they were
Roman citizens (albeit *sine suffragio*). They had not ceased to be
such either by their rebellion or by their *deditio*.[1]

Ulpian is talking of the category of inferior freedmen created
by the *lex Aelia Sentia* to whom the status of *dediticii* was assigned,
and who are regularly described by the Roman lawyers as 'qui
in dediticiorum numero sunt'—'in the category of surrendered
persons'. Of these freedmen *dediticii* Ulpian says that they lacked
testamentary rights under Roman law because they were *peregrini*, and otherwise lacked them altogether because they were
not citizens of any commune under the laws of which they
might act.[2] This does not mean that ordinary *dediticii* were
'citizens of no city'. The *lex Aelia* had deliberately refused any
specific status to its new category of freedmen except the bare
and precarious condition of being a *dediticius*. In this they were
unlike all other *dediticii*. In Livy the Campani are still Campani
after their *deditio*, even if their continued existence depends on
the grace of Rome. The Aelian *dediticii* are also unlike all other
*dediticii* in that they were positively barred from acquiring the
Roman citizenship. But this bar does not derive from their condition of *dediticius*, though many scholars have held this, because
*populi dediticii* both in the early and in the late Republican period
acquired Roman status on several occasions and in large numbers,
as after the last Latin war and after the Social War.[3] The bar
depends on the specific veto laid down by the *lex Aelia* and subsequent enactments,[4] and proves nothing about ordinary *dediticii*

---

[1] Livy 26. 16. 9–10; 33. 10; 34. 6–9. Cf. above, 60, 96. The final condition of the
Campanians as *corpus nullum civitatis* does not follow from their act of *deditio*. Note
also the identification in 90–89 B.C. of *dediticii* with *populi* in texts cited, 151 nn. 1–3.
The *deditio* of the Helvetii in Caesar *BG* 1. 27–8 is also corporate.

[2] *Tit. Ulp.* 20. 14: 'is . . . qui dediticiorum numero est quoniam nec quasi civis
Romanus testari potest cum sit peregrinus, nec quasi peregrinus quoniam nullius
certae civitatis civis est ut secundum leges civitatis suae testetur.' This is the only
legal text that associates any kind of *dediticii* with total lack of citizenship of any
sort. None of the texts in Gaius dealing with *qui in numero dediticiorum sunt* or with
*peregrini dediticii* do so; cf. *Inst.* 1. 12–13, 25–6, 67–8; 3. 74–6. For the distinction
between the two terms see below, 391 n. 1. Much ink has been spent arguing for
their identity or the inclusion of the latter in the former, by scholars who have not
read Gaius from the standpoint of his own purpose in these chapters, in which
those *in numero dediticiorum* are the category of freedmen below *Juniani*. For the
exclusion of Aelian freedmen from Roman status see below, 391 n. 1, and for the
specific case of Aegyptii, below, 392 nn. 1–2.

[3] Above, n. 1.                                              [4] Cf. below, 391 n. 1.

*peregrini*, to whom the Roman state could assign whatever final status it liked. Even the Campani, whose condition anticipates that of the Aelian freedmen, secured the partial restoration of their civic status within a generation of their degradation.[1] Hence there is no reason to regard the *dediticii* of the *Constitutio* as a class of persons to whom the Roman citizenship was permanently barred.

There have been doubts about the existence and condition of provincial *dediticii* in the Severan age. It was never very probable that the term in the *Constitutio* referred to blocks of old provincial subjects left casually in the status of *dediticii* for two centuries and more, because Augustus or his successors forgot to make a formal provincial settlement which by 'restoring their own things', in the antique formula, to the submissive peoples put an end to the temporary condition of *deditio*.[2] Sasse rightly observed that the definition in Gaius of *peregrini dediticii* proves that the meaning of the term did not change between the Republican writers and the age of the Antonines—'peoples who formerly after defeat in war have made a total surrender of themselves and their commune to the grace of Rome'.[3] The frontier wars of the Severan age would produce their quota of recently submitted *populi dediticii* along the Rhine and Danube, in Britain, and beyond the Euphrates. An inscription of A.D. 232 appropriately mentions a unit of *Brittones dediticii* serving in the Rhineland.[4] The status of such communes called for clarification under the terms of the Edict.

This seems the most probable explanation of the *dediticii* of

[1] Above, 211.

[2] *Deditio* and *dediticii* have been discussed at excessive length by Sasse, op. cit. 68–117, and Boehm, art. cit. 1964, 263, without improving on A. H. M. Jones, *JRS* 1936, 229 f. Cf. above, 60–1, 96, 284. For the paradigm of an act of *deditio* cf. Livy 1. 38. 2, 'deditis ... populum Collatinum urbem agros ...', which is supported by the early evidence of Plautus, *Am.* 1. 1. 74: 'urbem agrum aras focos seque uti dederent.'

[3] Sasse, op. cit. 117, citing passages from Caesar and Sallust down to Suetonius and later Ammianus. Gaius 1. 14: 'qui quondam adversus populum Romanum armis susceptis pugnaverunt deinde victi se dediderunt.' Too much has been made of *quondam*—it may imply the obsolescence of the old formula, but not of the condition itself.

[4] *ILS* 9184. For the elucidation of the text see H. T. Rowell, *Yale Cl. Stud.* 6 (1939), 74 ff. Boehm's counter-offensive does not convince (art. cit. 1963, 320 f.). The inscription certainly mentions a unit of *dediticii* and most probably of *Britonnes dediticii*. Dio 76 (77). 13. 4 mentions a relevant submission of Caledonians to Severus in *c.* A.D. 210.

*P. Giessen* 40: but it is still possible that when the rescripts from Banasa are known in full they may modify the view that the *salvo* formula must conclude the legal sentence. The order of words in the citation quoted by Seston is not quite that of the Greek documents cited by Sasse: 'non cunctamur [sc. his] civitatem Romanam salvo iure gentis dare.' If the Greek version of the edict of Caracalla represents precisely the word order of a Latin original, instead of following the formulary tradition of the Egyptian papyri, the possibility remains that after all the *dediticii* were excluded from the general grant of citizenship, as in the explanation of Bickerman. One might cite the observation of Sidonius Apollinaris in a much later age: 'in . . . unica totius orbis civitate soli barbari et servi peregrinantur.'[1] But this must now be the less probable explanation of *P. Giessen* 40. Meyer's restoration of the central section, or something similar, seems best because it is most in accord with all the external evidence, new and old.[2]

### THE CONSEQUENCES OF THE *CONSTITUTIO ANTONINIANA*

More important than the terms of the edict is its real effect. Evidence has continued to accumulate for the adoption of Aurelius as a formal 'gentile' name by ex-peregrines of all classes, urban and rural alike, as a token of their new citizenship. Recruitment lists of an auxiliary cohort at Dura on Euphrates, which cover the period A.D. 193 to 222, show a tremendous increase in the incidence of Aurelius as a second name among those recruited during the years 214–16, though 'peregrine' names do not disappear altogether.[3] Thus while *P. Dura* 98 can produce only eight Aurelii from A.D. 193 to 212, against twelve other Roman and thirty-three peregrine names, during A.D. 214–17 it produces fifty-five Aurelii against nineteen other combinations. But it is apparent from the Egyptian and the few Syrian papyri that the usage of the Aurelius name was far from universal, and that many peasants continued to use the old style of

---

[1] Sidonius, *Epp.* 1. 6. 2, dated *c.* A.D. 469. But see p. 393.

[2] For the myth that *dediticii peregrini* were incapable of acquiring Roman citizenship see further below, 391.

[3] J. F. Gilliam, 'Dura rosters and the *C.A.*', *Historia* 14 (1965), 81 ff. For the text C. B. Welles, 'Excavations at Dura', (v. i, 1959), nn. 95, 98, 100–2.

singleton peregrine nomenclature.[1] Yet elsewhere, in inscriptions from eastern and western provinces, and in some Egyptian papyri, persons who were already Roman citizens are found in the years following the *Constitutio* taking Aurelius as an extra gentile name.[2] There is also the odd fact that in one of the Dura rosters the clerk has—rightly or wrongly—added the name Aurelius to every entry.[3] The evidence suggests some uncertainty about official procedure, and the possibility of local directives. It is in an official and military milieu that the edict is given immediate effect, while persons in the backwoods may take no action.

Sidonius was certainly right when he asserted the continued existence of barbarian *peregrini* within the Roman world. Individuals and communities of peregrine status are documented in the two generations following A.D. 212, though some of the evidence is ambiguous. Some of the Thracian village inscriptions in the style *cives Romani et Bessi consistentes vico* are dated to A.D. 237–46.[4] But the title is a hundred years old, and its meaning could be adapted to the new circumstances. Similarly in the village township of Moguntiacum in the mid third century a closed organization of self-styled *cives Romani* continues an association—a *conventus civium Romanorum*—known from the second century.[5] It seems that these clubs maintained their closed existence after the Edict, recruiting members from the upper military personnel. Pride was taken in demonstrating the antiquity of one's status, personal or communal. Three legionary soldiers in A.D. 230 in a village dedication declare themselves 'Roman citizens and men of Taunus by paternal descent'.[6] Their

[1] E. M. Conduracchi, 'La C.A. e la sua applicazione', *Dacia* 1958, 304–5, exaggerates the absence of Aurelii from Egypt in the decade after A.D. 212; cf. Gilliam, art. cit. 87. The evidence for the exclusion of villagers is very thin: cf. R. Taubenschlag, *Law of Graeco-Roman Egypt*, ii. 2. 593 ff. For Aurelii at Cyrene, *S.E.G.* ix. 128, (224–5).

[2] Gilliam, art. cit. 86–7, cites sixteen instances from Egypt, Syria, Germania, Pannonia, and Rome between A.D. 213 and 221. Thus the well-documented Ti. Julius Balbillus, so known c. A.D. 199, becomes Aurelius Julius Balbillus in A.D. 215; cf. *CIL* vi. 708, 1027, 1603, 2130.

[3] *P. Dura* 100, a document of A.D. 219. Those who already had Roman names appear with two gentile names. Against this may be set the use of peregrine names by Mesopotamian villagers in a legal text of A.D. 227, *P. Dura* 26.

[4] Cf. above, 269.

[5] Cf. A. Riese, *Rhein, Germ. ant. Inschriften*, i. 2120, 2121, (A.D. 198), 2125 (A.D. 276), 2126 (A.D. 222–35).

[6] Riese 1176.

father was a former pretorian guardsman, though their mother was an Aurelian citizen. There is no reason to infer that the general mass of the Rhineland villagers (*vicani*) remained peregrines after 212.[1] There are in the later age lists of dedicants who mostly bear the double or triple names characteristic of Roman citizens, though in one dedication of A.D. 232 the villagers are styled *peregrini*, and a military list of A.D. 246 consists of singleton names.[2] The survival of pockets of peregrines in the northern frontier zones is not surprising. But some have sought to extend the range of this by invoking the evidence of the military *diplomata*, which continue to include throughout the third century the well-known clauses offering enfranchisement and *conubium* to time-expired auxiliary soldiers, generally drawn from tribal areas.[3] Here a combination of utility and legal archaism may be invoked. The documents served as certificates of honourable discharge, and in the military zones men could still find peregrine wives for whose issue the grant of *conubium* was required. The men themselves have names in the Roman style instead of the singleton barbarian names characteristic of the *diplomata* from the first and second centuries. The failure to delete an unnecessary clause in an otherwise necessary document is not surprising in the troubled times of the third century.

### STATUS OF THE RURAL POPULATIONS

Some scholars still argue from this sort of evidence that the populations of large tribal areas within the older provinces were excluded from the operation of the Edict, either as *dediticii*, or else because they lacked civic organization of the Italian, Hellenistic, or Phoenician style.[4] The contemporary description of the grant as universal in scope makes this improbable, but the

[1] As Sasse, art. cit. 127, following Conduracchi, art. cit. 290, who developed the ideas of E. M. Staermann, *Vestnik Driv. Istoria* 2 (16) (1946), 81 ff.

[2] For multiple gentile names cf. Riese 2135, 2136, 2218–19, 2227 (A.D. 236); *contra*, 1748 (A.D. 246) for singleton names. Riese 237: 'genio pagi Dervet peregrini qui pos. vico Soleciae'. The large body of nomenclature from the Germanies calls for a special study to determine the significance of these uses. Cf. also *CIL* xii. 94 for Roman citizens and *peregrini* at Brigantio apparently in the reign of Constantine (Saumagne, op. cit. 127 n. 161).

[3] Conduracchi, art. cit. 292–9. For doubts cf. Sasse, op. cit. 127.

[4] Notably Conduracchi, art. cit. 299–307. Boehm, art. cit. 1963, 54 ff., 307 ff., and especially Schoenbauer in a long series of articles, cited by Sasse, op. cit. 139, down to his restatement in *Iura* 14 (1963), 75 f.

theory also involves a widely held misunderstanding of the Roman empire. Social disregard for rural communities is a characteristic of Greek writers and politicians to which too much attention has been paid. The exaltation of the *polis* which characterizes the civic orations of Dio and Aristides has its counterpart in the cult of municipal forms in the Latin-speaking provinces. But the Roman government, though like Roman writers it approved of urban civilization, *urbium cultus*, as the highest form of social life, did not regard non-urban communities as incapable of self-government in the shape of a *res publica*. *Municipia* and *poleis* do not exhaust the list of recognized communes. Great tribal cantons, subdivided into parishes (*pagi*) and villages (*vici*), are characteristic of all the provinces of northern Europe. No one doubts that the sixty-four cantons of northern Gaul—the largest socially unified zone in the empire—administered their own affairs as tribal *civitates* organized in the Celtic style throughout the first century A.D. and later. Yet it is suggested that similar tribal cantons in the Alpine and Balkan provinces, and in North Africa, lacked genuine autonomy and were directly administered by Roman officials working through the villages and parishes in which the tribesmen lived.[1]

This notion is largely due to a misunderstanding of the role of the regional officers of the early Principate with such titles as *praefectus civitatium Moesiae et Treballiae*. These were indeed administrators in charge of troublesome tribal regions, some of whose commissions developed into independent governorships while others remained as the assistants of imperial legates.[2] But there is nothing to suggest that these prefects replaced elective or hereditary rulers in the internal administration of tribal affairs. It was seen above that in the Alpine and Illyrian zones the tribes either retained their identity or assimilated the municipal pattern of government in a form adapted to their needs.[3] There is a trend from the *gens Iasorum* to the *municipium Iasorum* despite the

---

[1] Conduracchi, art. cit. 306–7, Schoenbauer, art. cit. 73, 94.

[2] Cf. A. N. Sherwin-White, *BSR* 15 (1939), 1 ff. *Attributio* (above, 356) has its role here also. The nearest thing to a directly administered area outside Egypt may be the African *pagus Thuscae et Gunzuzi* with its sixty-four *civitates* and its ex-centurion *praefectus*, though nothing is known of his functions; cf. G. Picard, *CRAI* 1963, 115. *AE* 1963, no. 94. Cf. also Wilkes, *Dalmatia*, 288 f.: both district prefects and tribal *principes* appear there (*CIL* v. 3346, ix. 2564, iii. 8308, 14324).

[3] Above, 369–74.

predominance of rural life. There is no incompatibility between tribal culture and Roman status, and the notion that a *gens* cannot have a *res publica* of its own is alien to Roman thought and practice, as the new document from Banasa indicates. Hence there is no place for this notion in discussion of the *Constitutio Antoniniana*.

In the Hellenized provinces the pattern is different. There were rural peasantries in the territories of certain Greek cities which were excluded from political rights in the *polis* which governed them.[1] Strabo describes the Maryandani of Heraclea as serfs, but in documents from the villages of Nicomedia in the second century the peasantry appear as free men, partly Greek and partly 'barbarian' in their names, whose communes have officers similar to the *magistri pagi* of the western provinces.[2] A very few seem to be Roman citizens in the earlier period, but later a list of 'Aurelii' appears. So not even these subject populations were excluded from the possibility of Roman citizenship, which lay open to them at all times through military service as it did to the tribal peoples. A passage in the *Panegyric* of Aristides has been cited in support of the notion that the Roman government limited its favours to the urban populations. In this he states that 'the Romans have everywhere marked out the more civilized and powerful sort of men as citizens and even as members of their own race, while they have designated the rest as subordinates and subjects.'[3] This has been taken to mean that the Romans divided the world into three categories—city dwellers, Romans, and non-urban subjects. But throughout this section of the *Panegyric* the term 'citizen' or 'citizenship' refers to the Roman status, and the contrast is between the enfranchised upper classes and the peregrine proletariat of the towns, not between villagers and city-dwellers.[4] Aristides is particularly impressed by the fact

---

[1] Cf. the Maryandani, serfs of Heraclea in Pontus, Strabo 12. 3. 4 (p. 542), the subject 'farmers' of Cyrene, Jos. *Ant. Jud.* 14. 7. 2, and workers of Tarsus 'outside the polity', (Dio. *Or.* 34. 21 (11. 2) –23).

[2] F. K. Dörner, *Inschriften aus Bithynien*, n. 31 etc.

[3] Schoenbauer, Boehm, 388 n. 4 above. Aristides, *Pan.* 59: τὸ μὲν χαριέστερον . . . πανταχοῦ πολιτικὸν ἢ καὶ ὁμόφυλον πᾶν ἀπεδείξατε, τὸ δὲ λοιπὸν ὑπήκοόν τε καὶ ἀρχόμενον.

[4] For the context cf., e.g., s. 60: 'the barrier of the sea does not prevent anyone from becoming a citizen.' In s. 64 the same combination of πολῖται καὶ ὁμόφυλοι recurs, clarifying s. 59. By not considering the context Boehm (art. cit. 1963, 54 ff.) was misled into introducing the otherwise unknown term ἀπολιτίκιοι into *P. Giessen*

that the Roman franchise was given not as a merely honorary 'isopolity' but made its recipients 'one of themselves'. This passage is not evidence for incompatibility of status, or indeed for Roman official policy at all.

The sole evidence for the positive incompatibility of some provincial status with Roman citizenship is the letter of Pliny to Trajan about the promotion of Harpocras, the freedman of an Aegyptius. It is implied that the Aegyptii, the common folk registered in the rural districts and country townships of Egypt, could not receive the Roman citizenship unless they had previously acquired the local citizenship of Alexandria, or presumably that of one of the other two Greek cities of Egypt. This evidence has been combined with the common misinterpretation of Ulpian's definition of the status of Aelian freedmen *dediticii*, discussed above, to argue for the 'deditician' status of the Aegyptii.[1] By itself Pliny's letter does not prove so much, quite apart from the argument that if the Augustan settlement of Egypt restored their previous status to the Greek cities, it did as much for the Aegyptii. Peculiar though that status may be— neither tribal nor municipal—it is not that of *dediticii*, unless one invents a new meaning for that term, but that of free villagers living directly under the complicated legal and administrative system of the Ptolemies, as reorganized by Augustus. Sasse tried

40 in place of δεδειτίκιοι. By ὁμόφυλον Aristides may try to render *ius Quiritium* or *ius Italicum* into Greek, or may refer to Roman tribal registration, or to all of these. The term ἀπόλιδες is used by Ulpian and Marcian for 'stateless' men, *Dig.* 32. 1. 2; 48. 19. 17.

[1] Cf. above, 284 f. For Ulpian see 384 n. 2. Equally the statement of Gaius 1. 26 about the exclusion of Aelian freedmen *in numero dediticiorum* from avenues to the Roman citizenship does not apply to *peregrini dediticii*. Gaius proceeds in 28–35 to list numerous means for the full enfranchisement of *Latini Juniani* by imperial enactment which were closed to Aelian freedman. He makes it abundantly clear in his discussions of *qui in numero dediticiorum sunt* in 1. 12–15, 25–7 (and 3. 74–6) that this term was created by the *lex Aelia Sentia* for its new class of unprivileged freedmen. Subsequently in 1. 67–8 he uses the term consistently (*pace* A. H. M. Jones, art. cit. 230 f.) in the context of mixed marriages contracted in error. The person *in numero dediticiorum*—i.e. the Aelian freedman—is excluded from the favour which granted the Roman citizenship *per erroris probationem* to a Junian Latin or a peregrine lacking *conubium*, who married a Roman citizen in mistake as to their status. The Aelian freedman or freedwoman 'remains in his station'. The bar to promotion lay not in the condition of *deditio* (cf. above, 384 n. 2), but in the rule of the *lex Aelia*; cf. Suet. *Aug.* 40. 4. Like the *Campani dediticii* after 211 B.C. (above, 383 f.), they are limited in their *libertas* by a particular enactment. Boehm, art. cit. 1964, 285 ff., rightly remarks that Gaius does not absolutely exclude the possibility of a special grant of the franchise to Aelian freedmen by *beneficium principis*.

to eliminate the relevance of the Harpocras case by suggesting that the rule applied only to the freedmen of Aegyptii. But Pliny's words, stressing the term *Aegyptius*, support the normal interpretation.[1] The bar against the direct enfranchisement of Aegyptii may well be due to their lack of *any* form of self-government. In this respect the bureaucratized Egyptians differed from all other inhabitants of the Roman empire. In a Tacitean gibe they were 'ignorant of magistrates and laws', i.e. of municipal government, and Josephus remarked that they 'had no share in any polity'.[2] Only the *disciplina* of military service in the auxiliary army could compensate for this, and enable Aegyptii to gain the Roman citizenship directly.[3]

### THE *CONSTITUTIO* AND THE *IUS CIVILE*

The extent to which the *Constitutio Antoniniana* led to the *immediate* adoption of Roman civil law by former *peregrini*, *en masse*, cannot be adequately studied, though much discussed, because of the paucity of contemporary evidence. A. M. Honoré has drawn attention to the remarkable number of surviving imperial 'constitutions' issued in 212–13, as though in response to a new pressure of inquiries from private appellants about

[1] On the status of provincial Aegyptii cf. Schoenbauer, art. cit. 1963, 87 ff.: 'liberi ex lege provinciae'. Sasse, art. cit. 76 ff., notes that some Aegyptii succeeded in becoming *c.R.*, possibly through auxiliary military service (cf. below, n. 2). Pliny, *Epp.* 10. 6. 1: 'debuisse me ei Alexandrinam civitatem impetrare deinde Romanam quoniam esset *Aegyptius*'. On this see my *Letters of Pliny*, 10. 5. 2; 6. 1 nn. The Cappadocian villagers may have been analogous after the annexation of the kingdom in A.D. 19.

[2] Tac. *Hist.* 1. 11, cf. above, 284. Jos. *c. Ap.* 2. 4. Perhaps because of this Aegyptii were excluded from legionary service, though apparently not from all forms of auxiliary service; *Gnomon idiologi*, 142. Schoenbauer, art. cit. 1963, 81 f., cites Isidorus of Pelusium 1. 174, 175, 178, for the late continuance of prejudice against Aegyptii as men incapable of holding municipal office. (*Or.* I. 485, 489 in edn. 1606.)

[3] Cf. above, n. 1. The formal dating of the *Constitutio* to A.D. 212, due to its association with dated documents in the Giessen papyrus, has been challenged by F. Millar, *JEA* 48 (1962), 124 ff. But Gilliams, art. cit. 90 f., cites against a date within 214 proposed by Millar the evidence of two inscriptions in which a legionary soldier adopted Aurelius as a second gentile name before 13 Jan. 213, only to discard it in a dedication of 221 after Caracalla's death; *CIL* xiii. 7338, with *AE* 1962, 228. The date affects the immediate occasion of the *Constitutio*, and the identification of the 'victory' of Caracalla, but does not touch the historical interpretation of the grant. Cf. also A. M. Honoré, *Stud. et. Doc. Hist. Iur.* 28 (1962), 228, who argues for a date in 212 from the exceptional number of imperial *constitutiones* issued in 212 and 213.

problems of *ius civile*, who might be identified with the Aurelian citizens. An indication of the norm might be seen in the papyri from Egypt which reveal an Aurelian citizen using the Roman formula of manumission *inter amicos* in 221, and another using the testamentary forms of Roman law, though half a century later. But it remains in dispute whether the use of Roman legal notions and terms in provincial documents represents a total adoption of Roman law or its infiltration into and amalgamation with provincial usage.[1]

## A Conclusion

The full text of the *Tabula* of Banasa proved finally to contain nothing more that directly illuminated its enigmatic limitation, *salvo iure gentis*.[2] The anxiety of the two Juliani to secure Roman status for their peregrine wives and children implies that *salvo iure gentis* does not refer to the personal status of the Juliani in civil law. Their private standing is different from that of their *gens*, and they want to secure the same for their wives and children, just like the auxiliary veterans who secure this by similar grants of *conubium* and *civitas*.[3] Hence, as was suggested above, *salvo iure gentis* should refer to the complex of municipal claims and obligations, from which externs in the Republican period had been set free by automatic exemptions, and which were steadily reduced or abolished by Augustus and his successors, except for privileged groups of externs who received specific grants of *immunitas* and *muneris vacatio*.[4] The *salvo iure* condition of the *Tabula* summarily excludes the Juliani from such advantages. In the edicts of Octavian participation in the local life of the municipality depended upon the will of the extern. It is now mandatory. The internal life of the *gens* or *populus* is not to be dislocated by the exemption of leading men. So the limiting condition of the *Tabula* confirms the version of the limiting clause of the *Constitutio Antoniniana* that was preferred above: the grant of universal citizenship is not to affect the status of the communes.

---

[1] Cf. above, 312. Honoré, art. cit. *FIRA* iii nn. 11, 51, 61.

[2] Above, 336.

[3] Cf. also the grant of *conubium cum peregrinis uxoribus* to the enfranchised Volubilitani, above, 342.

[4] Above, 296 ff., 304 ff.

The full text of the *Tabula* also helps to clarify the exclusion of the *dediticii* in the *Constitutio*. The express caution of the joint emperors in granting citizenship to the *gentiles* of Mauretania Tingitana, and their comment that the ruling families were notably deficient in loyalty towards the Roman government, can be connected with a series of documents concerning the *gens Baquatium* of western Mauretania, a tribe much given to disturbing the peace of the province.[1] In these texts, which extend from A.D. 173 to 280 the leaders of the Baquates at irregular but frequent intervals hold conversations and conclude pacts with the Roman governors about the preservation of peace.[2] It has been noted that few of these *principes Baquatium* held the Roman citizenship, and some acquired it long after the *Constitutio Antoniniana*.[3] Such border peoples required periodical chastisement, which in Roman terms would reduce them to the status of *dediticii*. The exclusion of such *gentes* from the general enactment of Caracallus perpetuates the attitude of Marcus Aurelius to the *gentiles* of Mauretania.

---

[1] Discussed at length by E. Frézouls, 'Les Baquates et la province romaine de Tingitane', *Bull. Arch. Maroc.* 2, 1957, 65 ff. Cf. W. Seston, M. Euzennat, *CRAI* 1971, 475–6. For some texts see *AE* 1952, 42–3, 1953, 78–80. 1954, 110, 1957, 203–4, 1966, 602.

[2] Frézouls a.c. nos. 12, 14, 15, 'firmandae pacis . . . aram'; no. 10, 'foederatae pacis aram'; no. 11, 'ob diutinam pacem'. *CIL* 8. 9663 records a raid of Baquates against Cartenna in eastern Mauretania.

[3] Frézouls a.c. 87 ff., 94. In the *colloquia* inscriptions only the family of Julius Matif (ib. nos. 10–11; *ILA* 609–10), A.D. 276–80, have Roman *nomina*, derived from Philippus Arabicus, but Canartha (nos. 4, 5; *ILS* 855) acquires it later than the *colloquium*. In A.D. 226–9 'Urel' or 'Uret' is peregrine. For a fuller discussion of the *Tabula* see my article due to appear in *JRS* 1973.

# PART IV

# THE ATTITUDE OF THE PROVINCIALS TO THE EMPIRE

# THE PROBLEM

'SINCE Fate has given to the Romans the empire and mastery of the world, they should show mercy and generosity in the employment of their good fortune.'[1] The history of the later Republic seems to show an increasing failure to appreciate the value of this advice, tendered by the ambassadors of Antiochus in 191 B.C., and the result of this failure appears in the undoubted unpopularity of Rome throughout wide areas of the mediterranean world in the half century before the establishment of the Principate. This unpopularity sets the problem, although it is not a very profound problem, of accounting for the undoubted change of heart that is observable throughout the Empire by the time of the Antonines. It is not a very profound question since the answer so obviously lies, as has often been seen, in the vast change for the better in the spirit and method of imperial government introduced by the Principate. The true problem, infinitely more subtle, is to account for and interpret the complete change in the conception of the *Orbis Terrarum*, implied in the hackneyed phrases of the panegyrists of the late Empire, from the idea held about it by both the Romans and their subjects in the earlier period. Something more than the excellence of the imperial administration is needed to explain why the communities and peoples that took such pride in their partial independence and in their individuality, not only under the Republic, but also under the early Principate, should later reveal such a readiness to be absorbed into the Roman state, and to affect the garb and fashion of Romans. This difficulty is most urgent in the history of the Greek-speaking provinces. It is not hard to understand the attractions that a superior civilization had for the Iberian, Celtic, Germanic, or Numidian peoples. But in the eastern provinces Rome lacked this glamour. Here she had more to combat than her previous reputation—loyalties and traditions, whether Greek or oriental, set deeper in the hearts of the people than anything she had so far offered. Yet Rome ended by securing the allegiance of the East as firmly as that of the West. And the miracle of

[1] Polyb. 21. 16. 7–8, slightly paraphrased.

statecraft is that in accepting the mark of Rome the East remained always Greek. Even this does not exhaust the problem, for the divorce is not one-sided. The separation of Greek and Roman was undoubtedly willed also by the Roman government, not only of the second century B.C., but of the later Republic and of the early Principate. The problem is to discover not only why and in what sense the Greeks later began to want to become Romans, but why the emperors began to welcome them as such. The same acute problem appears in the western and northern provinces also, wherever, as especially in Gaul, there appears a growth of loyalty to Rome that is not accompanied by the transformation of the former political system into the Roman mode, since it is not always among the *coloniae* and *municipia* of the *provinciae togatae* that in the later centuries devotion to Rome is most manifest.

# XVII

## THE WINNING OF ALLEGIANCE

### DISLIKE OF THE ROMAN NAME UNDER THE REPUBLIC

WHEN Rome began her career as a world-power the auspices were fair enough. The Greeks welcomed her with as much respect as they showed towards her Hellenistic predecessors, and regarded her to a certain extent as one of themselves. This is shown by the early reference to Rome as a 'Greek City'[1] in the first historian to treat of her,[2] and in the early appearance of the cult of *Roma* as a goddess among the Greek city-states of Asia.[3]

The relations between Rome and the Greek states, towards which, in her career of conquest, she behaved as well as the Greek kings had done, remained at least officially cordial until the close of the second century. An inscription of about 129 B.C. describes, on the occasion of the publication of a treaty of alliance with Rome, at some place not far from Pergamum, public ceremonies and rejoicings of such a domestic and intimate nature that they cannot be dismissed as a mere attempt to please and flatter the Roman power, but must have been intended as a purely local expression of joy.[4] At least there is no attempt to inform the Senate of what is being done. Similar manifestations appear in the foundation of the Mucian festival by the province as a whole in honour of the governorship of Mucius Scaevola, and in the building of temples in honour of governors.[5] Neither the war with Aristonicus nor the formation of the Asiatic province

---

[1] πόλις Ἑλληνίς.    [2] Cf. Plut. *Cam.* 22. 3, and Strabo 5, 232 C.

[3] V. Chapot, *La Province romaine proconsulaire d'Asie*, 423, collects the instances, from 195 B.C. onwards.

[4] *SIG³* 694—not only a special prayer for the continuance of the alliance, with sacrifices to Demeter and *Dea Roma*, but a holiday for schoolboys and slaves, with public sports, is mentioned. This, however, being inspired by relief at deliverance from Aristonicus, represents not the normal but what might have been normal if the governors of the succeeding age had possessed the wisdom of Augustus.

[5] Chapot, op. cit. 462.

can be regarded either as a symptom or as a cause of the change for the worse in the relations of Rome and the Asiatic Greeks. The trouble with Aristonicus had other roots: it was both a slave war and a rising of the classes oppressed by the previous regime, more especially the rural classes,[1] whereas many of the Greek states stood firmly by Rome in these years[2]—and evidence for loyalty to Rome, such as the establishment of the Mucia, is not lacking after the foundation of the province.[3]

It was not so much the Roman administration of provinces as the financial activities of the 'Italici', both within and without the provinces, that led to an increasing dislike of the Roman name that protected them.[4] Doubtless bad government and the connection between the *negotiatores* and the *publicani* aggravated the crisis, but it is possible that the case against senatorial government has been somewhat exaggerated. Certainly the sources concentrate their attention on the horrors and the abnormalities. But when trouble came in Africa and Asia Minor, it extended far beyond the limits of the Roman provinces. The massacres inspired by Jugurtha and Mithridates are not local but continental in extent, and it is especially the Italici who suffer, whether at Cirta, Vaga, or in Asia Minor.[5] The unpopularity of Roman governors and Italian business men taken together finds a clear expression in the Sibylline verses that deal with the rise of Rome to the position of a world power.[6] These 'oracles' seem to reveal three special causes for the dislike of Rome: these are her 'disgraceful love of money',[7] the sack of Corinth,[8] and the brutality of the generals of the later Republic, such as Sulla.[9] It is worth noting that the general account of misery and oppression is connected much more with the name of Italia than of Roma, in such lines as 'A great Italian war shall burst forth, through which the world shall yield to the yoke and serve as the slave of Italy.'[10] This prominence of the name of Italia is due not merely

---

[1] Cf. Tarn, *Hellenistic Civilization*, 2nd ed., 115 f.

[2] Cf. *SIG*[1] 694 n. 3. *IGRR* iv. 134.                    [3] Cf. above, 399.

[4] Cf. Bloch, Carcopino, *Histoire Romaine*, ii. 123.

[5] Sall. *Bell. Jug.* 26. 3; 47. 1; 67. 3. App. *Mithr.* 22, ἐπιθέσθαι . . . Ῥωμαίοις καὶ Ἰταλοῖς . . . καὶ ἀπελευθέροις ὅσοι γένους Ἰταλικοῦ. The edict of Mithridates was sent σατράπαις ἅπασι καὶ πόλεων ἄρχουσι, e.g. to Rhodes, a *civitas foederata*, ibid.

[6] *Oracula Sibyllina* iii. 175–91, 470–3; iv. 102–6.

[7] αἰσχρόβιος φιλοχρημοσύνη. iii. 189.          [8] iv. 105.          [9] iii. 470.

[10] Ἰταλὸς ἀνθήσει πόλεμος μέγας ᾧ ὕπο κόσμος λατρεύσει δούλειον ἔχων ζυγὸν Ἰταλίδῃσι. Cf. viii. 95. Italy is μέγα βάρβαρον ἔθνος.

to metrical reasons but to the great part that the Italici played in
the period when the Hellenistic world was first becoming familiar
with the Roman power, a part amply demonstrated by the inscriptions of the Italian colony at Delos.[1]

The popular account thus seems to agree with the historical
tradition in connecting the decline of Roman popularity with the
events and tendencies that appear in the last quarter of the second
century B.C.—the period when the serious scandals of provincial
government begin to appear.[2] The full weight of governmental
oppression, as distinct from the exactions of the *negotiatores*,
could not after all be felt till the provincial system was more fully
extended by the conquests of Pompey. The colossal scandals
and the astounding exactions of magistrates seem to belong much
more to the very last years of the Republican period when
*tresviri* and *liberatores*, free from any fear of a day of reckoning
in the courts, pillaged the unfortunate Greeks at their pleasure.[3]
It is thus not surprising that few further manifestations against
Rome are recorded, after the rising inspired by Mithridates, till
this last period, in which the popular traditions of the Sibylline
verses preserve the curious 'oracle' elucidated by Dr. Tarn.[4] The
verses are very different in tone from the earlier passages, which
confined themselves to descriptions of the tribulation endured by
the subjects of Rome. These verses both condemn and accept.
Rome is to be 'cast down', but she is also to be 'raised up again',
a process connected with the inauguration of a new period of
'orderly life'. In other words the writer of these verses, which,
unlike most of the Sibyllines concerned with Rome, were not
composed after the event, had learned that in the world of his day
the power of Rome could not be eliminated. The lines combine
the two contrary traditions of respect for the Roman name and
hatred of Roman exactions, for the existence of both of which in
the worst period of the Republic there is evidence enough. Public
opinion about Rome would after all be divided, and show variations as numerous as the states that composed the Empire; but
the possibility of any unification or integration of the Empire
would depend upon whether or not the hostile opinion disappeared. Yet even this was but a *sine qua non*. As far as the

---

[1] Cf. T. Frank, *Economic Survey of Ancient Rome*, i. 275 ff.
[2] Cf. App. *B.C.* i. 92 (V.).  [3] Ibid. 4. 313; 5. 15 ff.
[4] *JRS* 22. 135 ff. *Or Syb.* iii. 350–61, 367–80.

Hellenistic world was concerned, Rome might remain the kindly mistress of the peoples, the *domina gentium* which Cicero and Sallust considered her, without ever becoming the state *in gremium victos quae sola recepit*,[1] unless her statesmen could devise forms of loyalty that would win over the enthusiasm of the Greek world, without coming into conflict with the essential peculiarities of the Hellenistic peoples.


CONVERSION

*Pax Augusta and the Imperial Cult.*

The emperors solved the problem of the world state, both in the West and in the East. In both parts the final solution lay in the influence which the imperial name came to exercise over the peoples of the Empire. But this influence was based in the last resort upon the *beneficia* which the establishment of the imperial power conferred upon the world, and these *beneficia* consist in the twofold blessing of the *Pax Augusta*, and the imperial administration. This double character is asserted again and again by the most diverse authorities, by the educated rhetorician Aristides and equally by the popular historian of the Sibylline oracles.[2] The methods by which a loyal spirit was built up in the two halves of the Empire were diverse. In the western and northern provinces the provincials literally became part of the Roman state.[3] In the Asiatic provinces the situation is different. The place largely filled in the West by zealous pursuit of the constitutional privileges and titles of the Roman state is taken in the East by an ever-expanding development of the imperial cult, a process that is followed only slowly and from afar by the spread of the citizenship. This spread of the actual *civitas* does not possess the vast importance that it has in the West; for the former municipal categories of the Greeks persist unchanged. The titles which the communities seek during the first two centuries of the Principate are not those of the Roman colonies, but of the imperial 'neokorate.[4] When rivalry for Latin titles appears, it is an individual and not a municipal matter. Men begin to search out the privileges of equestrian and senatorial status for themselves and for their

---

[1] Below, 464 ff. 'Which alone took the conquered to its bosom.'
[2] Below, 427, 429 f.
[3] Above, Part II in general.                              [4] Below, 403 f.

families. Such rivalries and jealousies are in fact confined to the highest circles of the provincial nobility.[1]

The cult of Rome and of Roman governors was nothing new in Asia.[2] What was new was the tremendous importance that the worship of 'Rome and Augustus' assumed when it was extended beyond the borders of the Asiatic province and grafted on to the system of provincial and sub-provincial Councils, and when it began to draw its strength from the enthusiastic spirit of municipal rivalry that animated the Greek states of Asia Minor.[3] Augustus in his wisdom saw how to turn to the profit of Rome and the ruling house the rivalries of the cities and the great families in a fashion that surpassed the inventiveness of the kings themselves, to whom the popularization of ruler-worship had been mostly due.[4] If the priesthood of the cult of the ruling emperor and his forbears was to be the prize for which men sought by all the means at their disposal, the final object of all this rivalry was likely to gain a continual increase of prestige.

The history of the adaptation of the Greek provinces to the *Orbis Romanus* thus becomes, for a time, the history of the imperial cult, provincial and municipal alike. The oft-told tale need not be repeated here, but some aspects of it and some questions that arise from it call for discussion. It is to be remembered that the imperial cult itself was only one way of expressing the enthusiasm with which the Hellenistic world greeted the establishment of the *Pax Augusta,* and which makes itself heard in numerous inscriptions to the emperors as champions and protectors of civilization.[5] Although the imperial cult was officially encouraged and stimulated from the beginning, yet the history of the origin of the particular cult-centres and their exuberant development suggests that it is wrong to regard their *inspiration* as official. Instead, the cult acted as a genuine focus for the expression of a pre-existent emotion. At the same time there were other objects with which the rivalries of the Asiatic cities were concerned, some of which had no direct connection with Rome or the emperors. Chapot remarks that the title of 'Neokoros' was not so popular as that of

---

[1] Below, 404 ff.                         [2] Cf. Chapot, op. cit. 423.
[3] Ibid. 436. Kornemann, *RE,* s.v. Κοινόν, col. 930, 938.
[4] Chapot, op. cit. 439, marks the distinction between the spontaneous municipal cult and the partly officially inspired cult of the province, cf. ibid. 466.
[5] Perhaps the best instance is the Oath of Assos, *SIG*[3] 797, too often dismissed as 'excessive' or 'mere' flattery.

'Metropolis' and 'First City', so bitterly disputed in the time of Dio Chrysostom, titles whose sole reference is to the dignity of the particular state within the province.[1] Yet the term 'Neokoros', which usually means that the city which held it possessed a temple of the imperial cult, seems to have been invented to supply the Greek states with fresh fields in which to exercise their municipal rivalries at each other's expense, at a time when the imperial cult had perhaps lost the first vigour of novelty.[2] It is at least certain that there was such rivalry; for example, the proud proclamation of Pergamum that she was the 'first city to become thrice neokoros', that is, to possess three temples of the imperial cult, was met by Ephesus with the riposte that she was the only city to become neokoros fourfold.[3] This institution, which represents the fullest development of the municipal *cultus*, reached its acme under Trajan and Hadrian in the first half of the second century, and enjoyed a second efflorescence under the Severan dynasty.[4] Chapot suggests that the somewhat curious check in the spread of the neokorate in the interval may be due to the fact that these were the emperors who gave most personal attention, actual visits, to these provinces.[5] This illustrates well the difference between the grounds of loyalty in East and West, where the extension of *Romanitas* was based more directly on a genuine assimilation of Roman institutions,[6] though it is true that the function of the imperial cult and the provincial Councils in the newer provinces of the West was much the same as that of the Councils in the East.[7]

Much more difficult to judge, and perhaps more informative, once a decision is made, about the relation between local and imperial loyalties, is the hard question of the provincial High Priests introduced by Rome, and the pre-existent officials known as Asiarchs, etc.—the most honourable posts that the various provincial Councils offered to the great families of the provincial nobility. Whether they represent two different offices or two names for one office, the same question seems to pose itself. Did the emperors try to submit to their service, or to supplant by

---

[1] Chapot, op. cit. 449.     [2] Ibid. 445.
[3] Ibid. 449 f.
[4] Ibid. 453.
[5] The obvious objection is that Lucius Verus also visited the eastern Empire.
[6] Above, 251 ff.; below, 413 ff.
[7] Cf. Kornemann, *RE*, s.v. 'Concilium', cols. 803, 810–11. Below, 412 n. 1.

a rival office, a post that savoured too much of provincial particularism and too little of loyalty to Rome? But further examination of the history of the provincial Councils disposes of this difficulty. The encouragement which the emperors gave to the existing Councils, and to the foundation of new ones where such had not existed before,[1] shows that they knew that Rome had nothing to fear from this type of local particularism. Certainly they turned to their service the old institutions, but the history of the municipal rivalries of Asia and Bithynia makes it clear that it was never the purpose of the imperial government to efface the old order, but to preserve it within the new. This appears very strongly from the study of Lycia. After the provincialization of the old federation of free cities, the organization of the Council remained as before, except for such offices, like the navarchy, as had been rendered unnecessary by the institution of the new province.[2]

If the Councils became an instrument of empire, that is not due to imperial action, except in so far as the emperors entrusted the provincial cult to them, but is what the Greeks themselves made of them. The evidence for this development in Lycia, where local traditions were very strong, and where the converse might well be expected, is unambiguous. The members of the Council seem to have made use of its position as the official organ of the province to thrust themselves upon every possible occasion on the attention of the provincial governor and of the emperor himself. The vast collection of edicts, letters, and decrees in honour of the Lycian millionaire Opramoas proves this.[3] It is the climax of his career when the Council writes to inform Pius that they have elected the man Lyciarch. In other matters the Council submits all sorts of honorary decrees to the approval of the governor, where not only was that unnecessary in law, but the procedure was likely to encourage interference by the governor with the liberties of the Council.[4] This conduct in Lycia, where the office of Lyciarch was never swallowed up by that of High

[1] Summed up by Kornemann, *RE*, s.v. Κοινόν, col. 931-4.
[2] Cf. Ruge, *RE*, s.v. 'Lycia', col. 2279. The best proof of the harmless nature of the old traditions lies in the frequent mention in the same inscription of a man's ancestors who were navarchs, etc., beside those who held the High Priesthood or properly Roman offices, cf. below, 410. [3] *IGRR* iii. 739.
[4] This does not apply to all votes of special honours, some of which were subject to veto, cf. *IGRR* iii. 739. 1; 14; 24; 28. For an example of unnecessary submission to the governor not drawn from the Opramoas inscription see ibid., no. 582. The governor remarks τὰ καλῶς γινόμενα ἐπαινεῖσθαι μᾶλλον προσήκει ἢ κυροῦσθαι.

Priest,[1] cannot be dismissed as due to 'flattery' or 'mere slavishness'. It is evidence of a general enthusiasm for the imperial power and the name of Rome, such as appears again in the inscriptions of men who proudly enumerate their ancestors and descendants who were of senatorial or consular rank.[2]

This enthusiasm manifests itself in one form at least that is common to the whole Roman world—this is in the assimilation of the divinized emperors to the gods of the Pantheon.[3] But, although Nero and Hadrian masquerade as Zeus Eleutherius and Panhellenius, the apparent lack of the reverse process, i.e. of the appearance of Zeus Augustus, is a reminder that Asia is not Africa or Spain.[4] Akin to this difference is the failure in the Greek provinces of the abstract deities of which the Latin world was so fond—including *Dea Roma* herself.[5] For the early history of the imperial cult shows that none of the attempts to mitigate the direct worship of the rulers by addition of the name of the Senate or of Rome was successful.[6] No second power could flourish beside the overwhelming majesty of the imperial kingship. For that is what the Greeks made of the emperors, and it is because they turned them into kings that the great acceptance of Roman dominion became something more than gratitude for the establishment of peace and order. If the worship of *Dea Roma* in Asia seems to fade silently away in the epigraphic records of the early Principate, this is due to the strength of the revival of the Hellenistic traditions.[7] This is a movement that concerns more than the upper stratum of society, and reveals, for once, something of the attitude of the small folk of the provinces

---

[1] Cf. its absence from the genealogical tree of Oenoanda, *IGRR* iii. 500, where always the Lyciarch, never the provincial priest, is mentioned. At the date of *OGIS* 556 they certainly appear to be separate offices.

[2] πατέρες, πάπποι, πρόπαπποι, υἱοί, κτλ., συγκλητικοί or ὑπατικοί. E.g. *IGRR* iii, 500, and below, 408 f.

[3] Chapot, op. cit. 428 ff.

[4] The nearest approach to this western practice is the apparently solitary instance of *Augusta Eubosia* at Acmonia, cited by Chapot, op. cit. 429 n. 8, who turns out to be Agrippina the Younger, for whom Augusta was an official title, Tac. *Ann.* 12. 26.

[5] Cf. Chapot, op. cit. 434 n. 3.

[6] Ibid. 436 f.

[7] In Lycia the cult flourished longer, cf. *IGRR* iii. 563, 692—Julio-Claudian, ibid. 595—late second century; it is still recorded in the third century, ibid. 474. This must be due to the late date of the provincialization, and to the great difference between the history of the Asiatic and that of the Lycian cities in the pre-Roman period.

towards the ruling power. St. Peter, one remembers, bade the people of Christ 'honour the king';[1] that was the object of the imperial cult also. These ceremonies, though performed by the provincial and municipal aristocracy, were conducted before a congregation composed of the masses, and the masses in the Asiatic provinces, though excluded from power, were well able to express their opinions and to influence custom.

There is no single formula that embraces the attitude of the subject peoples towards Rome in these early centuries. The empire was what men made of it, and it is not surprising to find that the Greeks made a 'kingdom' of it.[2] The general fact is familiar enough from the literary sources, but it is important to notice that behind the fact lies a great deal more than diplomatic convention and the polite formulae of international relations. For it was the acceptance of the emperors as legitimate 'Kings' in the full meaning of the term that brought the communities of the eastern provinces 'within the state' in a way which the old subject and provincial relationship to Rome was not able to achieve. The worship of the 'King-Emperor' did for the East what the extension of citizenship achieved in the non-Greek provinces, and perhaps a little more; for the new relationship was transcendent. It interfered not at all with the old bonds, loyalties, privileges, and freedoms. These were all forms of contact with the *senatus populusque Romanus*, and were not touched by, and did not touch, the new form of allegiance to the 'king-emperor'. It is almost as if the two orders existed side by side, both concerned with the same people, the same populations, but in a different manner.

The same end was served by this indirect means in the East as was achieved directly in the West; for from the concentration of attention on the 'kingship' the provincials were led on to the study and service of Rome, since the king was also the Princeps.

---

[1] 1 Peter 2: 17. That the idea of the king is ingrained in ordinary thought is shown by the triteness of the metaphor in Christian literature: e.g. Romans 6: 12, μὴ βασιλευέτω ἡ ἁμαρτία, where the metaphor seems to come from a more pagan source than in the idea of the βασιλεία τοῦ θεοῦ. Cf. the copious evidence in the orations of Dio Chrysostom, *De Regno*, and the crude expression of a popular pamphlet quoted by Nock, *Conversion*, 91, 'What is a god? That which is strong. What is a king? He who is equal to the Divine', from *Philologus*, 80, 339, second century.

[2] Cf. W. Schubart, *Klio* 30. 1, 'Das Gesetz und der Kaiser in griechischen Urkunden', 55 ff.

If the provincials wished to find any practical expression of their new enthusiasm, it could only be through the normal forms of the organization of the Roman state, i.e. as soldiers, centurions, prefects, tribunes, procurators, legates, magistrates, and proconsuls. Consequently, although the dual relationship towards the emperor and the Roman people exhausted the possibilities for the communities, individuals might go further, seek out the citizenship and progress through the social system of the Roman state. This is precisely the state of affairs that the epigraphic evidence reveals for the later Principate. The cities show their respect for the sovereign by the use of titles, drawn not from the organization of the Roman *civitas* but from the conception of their sovereign as a divine ruler, while the great families of the upper stratum of society have gone further and welcomed a metamorphosis that was possible for Greeks as individuals, to whom the practice of isopolity or exchange of citizenships was customary and familiar, but impossible for their city-states, to which the preservation of ancestral status and identity was all-important.

## ROMAN CITIZENSHIP AND CIVIC DIGNITIES IN LYCIA

The viritane extension of the Roman citizenship in the eastern provinces is not in general a remunerative study, because the process is desultory and for the most part unconnected with any principles of policy. The gift of the citizenship to Greeks is a favour, an honour, or even a bribe, but, except possibly in the mind of Claudius and in a passing thought of Nero,[1] it never formed part of a scheme. Nor is it easy to form from the inscriptions of the Greek *Corpus* any conception of the attitude of the eastern provincials in general to the citizenship by itself. But Lycia—a province in many ways peculiar—forms an exception to the rule. An examination of the Lycian inscriptions seems to lead to some conclusions that are more than merely statistical, and also provides a salutary warning against unduly wide generalizations about the citizenship, and against studying its spread without reference to local conditions. The attitude of men to the citizenship, to Rome, and to the emperors varied from province to province, and should be considered, to a certain extent, regionally,

[1] Above, 246.

where there is sufficient evidence to make this possible, as in Lycia.

Here it is clear that even in the second century the citizenship had not suffered that devaluation that appears in some parts of the Roman world. The greatest men of the province, not content with the *tria nomina*, add the description 'Romanus' to their titles. There is a series of such inscriptions of the type 'So-and-so was a Roman and a Xanthian', or 'a Roman and a Sidymean' etc.,[1] which reach to the middle of the century.[2] Their peculiarity is that the Roman citizenship is named as a type of isopolity—the same in kind as that of any other state. Sometimes a list of isopolities is given, in which the Roman is always named first but still as in the same category as the rest.[3] These men then, the greatest of the province—Lyciarchs and kin of Lyciarchs—regard the Roman citizenship as the most honourable of all the honorary civic 'freedoms' which it was possible to acquire, but they do not treat it as by itself bringing practical privileges. The situation recalls C. Jullian's remark that under the empire only the senators of Rome present the picture of the complete *civis Romanus*.[4] As long as this is not taken to imply the heresy of an actual *civitas sine suffragio* or *sine iure honorum*, started long ago by A. W. Zumpt, there is some value in this remark, and it can be illustrated by the development of the citizenship in Lycia. For when these Greeks wished to make any practical use of their citizenship they did so by securing advancement to the dignity of equestrian or senatorial status. Only as knights or senators can they take an active part in the service of the Roman state, such as fits their high place in provincial society.

Among those families from which the Lyciarchs were commonly drawn, equestrian and senatorial status do not appear as contemporary honours. Though the first 'consular' of Lycia belongs to the end of Trajan's reign, up to about A.D. 140 the equestrian career was the highest distinction commonly enjoyed by Lyciarchic families.[5] Then instances of 'the first consular' and

---

[1] ὁ δεῖνα Ῥωμαῖος καὶ Ξάνθιος, or Σιδυμεύς, etc.

[2] *IGRR* iii. 514, 526–7, 530–3, 603, 628, 634.

[3] e.g. ibid. 603, Ῥωμαῖον καὶ Παταρέα καὶ Ξάνθιον . . .

[4] *Histoire de la Gaule*, iv. 267. But cf. above, 265.

[5] Cf. C. S. Walton, *JRS* 19. 49. This date has been disputed—cf. ibid. n. 5—on insufficient grounds. Cf. in general the conclusions of Stein, *Römischer Ritterstand*, 412–15. The modifications of Walton's view made by Lambrechts, *Ant. Cl.* 1935, 111, do not touch Lycia.

'father of a son who was a senator', etc., become frequent. It is clear that the nobility of Lycia only worked their way up to the highest distinctions of the Roman state by a slow process. The study of the genealogical tree of Oenoanda demonstrates this.[1] In the first quarter of the second century the great men of the family —the Lyciarchs and municipal *flamines*—were military tribunes and imperial procurators.[2] In the period before this they had been plain *cives Romani*, but the authors of this document, which was drawn up about the date of the Constitutio Antoniniana, did not consider this worthy of special note. It is among the grand-children of this generation that the first 'consular' appears.[3] After this, honours come thick and fast, the father of this man being introduced with a great flourish as the founder of a senatorial and consular family, and the family ends up by producing, after the date of this inscription, a wife for the ephemeral emperor Regalian in the middle of the third century.[4]

The evidence of this 'tree' does not stand alone.[5] The history of the great families consists in a progress through the dignities of the Roman state, generation by generation. There is no sign of any opposition between the old Lycian and the new Roman traditions. It is true that the earlier Lyciarchs of the imperial period like to describe themselves as the 'descendants of navarchs and generals'—the old military offices of the free federation. But Opramoas' own wife has a similar claim made for her, while his father is advertised as 'progenitor of senators'.[6]

The place that the Roman citizenship held in this province can thus be fairly clearly defined. In the first half of the second century it was still the privilege of a narrow circle—a privilege that the great Opramoas himself did not possess. At a date only sixty years before the Constitutio Antoniniana this limitation would be somewhat surprising, if the rapidity with which the highest honours of the citizenship spread within this narrow circle, once

---

[1] *IGRR* iii. 500.

[2] Ibid. c. ii. 45–60. Gaius Julius Demosthenes, Lyciarch, ends up in A.D. 102 as *proc.* of Trajan in Sicily, cf. ibid. 487. His son follows an equestrian career, ibid. 500, c. ii. 31, c. iii. 24–42. Licinius Longus, Lyciarch, and his father-in-law, are simple *primipilares*, cf. Cagnat ad loc.

[3] Ibid. 500, c. ii. 65–70.

[4] Cf. Cagnat's note on ibid. c. iii. 5–10.

[5] Cf. *IGRR* iii. 524, 581, 618—another 'tree'—for the emergence of *senatorii* about A.D. 140–50. In general see Walton, art. cit. 54 ff.

[6] *IGRR* iii. 735, 736.

the principle had been admitted that Lycians could make useful senators, had not prepared the way for speedy development in this sphere. But it is firmly established that, if the masses of the Lycian population were won over to anything like the respect for the Roman power that the inscriptions of their betters betray, it was by courses that lie entirely outside the narrow categories of properly political relationship.

IMITATION OF ROME

*Municipal Rights and Titles.*

This peculiarity of Asiatic cities—this dualism in their development by which the ruling classes are taken up into the highest places of the Roman administration, while the communities themselves remain in their old status—contrasts strongly with the development of the western provinces. At a great city like Cirta in Africa the series of equestrian and senatorial families appear in their proper setting as the crown of a whole system—the *colonia* with its citizen population all ordered according to the forms of Roman political organization.[1] It is true that Lycia represents an extreme. In Asia and Bithynia, where citizenship seems to have been more widely extended, as is natural in view of the long establishment of the provinces, the formula of the type 'Roman and Xanthian', with its implications, does not seem to appear. But the other phenomenon, the growth of the equestrian and senatorial clique, although not so common, is by no means absent.[2]

The contrast of the eastern and western provinces is in this respect undoubtedly justified, but in another way there is no difference—that is, in the final effect that the attraction of the imperial power had upon the provincial communities. Augustus after all introduced the imperial cult into Gallia Comata and north-western Spain to serve the same purpose as it was to serve in the Asiatic provinces, and other emperors followed his example

---

[1] e.g. *CIL* viii. 7050–2, 7054–6, 7059.

[2] Mostly at Cibyra, *IGRR* iv. 906–12 (*saec.* II), where the same transition is observable as in Lycia. Cf. Juvenal 7. 14–17, for 'equites' from Asia, Bithynia, Cappadocia, and Galatia. Somewhat later also at Thyateira, *IGRR* iv. 1213, 1216, 1217, 1230–34, where the ἱππικοί are still prominent under the Severi. For Pergamum it is sufficient to mention the family of Quadratus Bassus, early *saec.* II. The last important use of this *instrumentum imperii* is in Palmyra in *saec.* III, where the family of Odenath are senatorial and consular, *IGRR* iii. 1034–5, while the municipal councillors are equestrian, ibid. 1036, 1040, 1045.

in the majority of the western and Balkan provinces. It is undoubtedly true that these provinces grew up, not only to be *provinciae togatae*, but to feel towards the emperor, or at least to express, something like the sentiments that animated the municipalities and provincial councils of the East.[1] There is, however, this important difference, that in the West the charm of the imperial name did not outbid but only rivalled, the attractions of Roma herself. Thus, while Greek cities seek out the titles of 'Neokoros' and so on, the western municipalities try to secure the position of *colonia splendidissima* or the privilege of *Latium maius*, according to their present status. But this does not exhaust the forms of expression which their admiration for *Romanitas* assumed. The increasing frequency of by-names or titles derived from the emperor's own *nomina* and *cognomina* is not peculiar to any one part of the empire. Among the great cities of Asia Minor and Syria it is somewhat sporadic but by no means absent. Tarsus bears the titles 'Alexandriana Severiana Antoniniana Hadriana',[2] Nicomedia is 'Hadriana Severiana',[3] Cyzicus calls herself Hadrian and Friend of the Emperor,[4] while at Prusias seven of the civic tribes are named after members of the imperial families,[5] not Julio-Claudian so much as Ulpian or Aelian, even as Paphos is called 'Augusta Claudia Flavia'.[6] This tendency is certainly weaker in the East,[7] where the title of 'Neokoros' to a large extent performed the same service, than in e.g. Africa, where in the second and third centuries the titles increase continually in length and number to an extent that would be amazing, were it not clear that in the western provinces the titles not only express a certain exuberant loyalty to the *Principes*, but mark the stages by which the municipalities have advanced in civic honours.

There is in the West a direct admiration of Rome and Roman institutions which did not need the mediation of the imperial cult, however much it may have been contemporaneously en-

---

[1] For the imperial cult in the West cf. Kornemann, *RE* s.v. 'Concilium', col. 803, 805–6. C. H. V. Sutherland, *JRS* 24. 39 ff.

[2] *IGRR* iii. 879, 880.    [3] Ibid. 6.    [4] Cf. ibid. iv. Index viii. 2.

[5] Ibid. iii. 67, 69.    [6] Ibid. 937, 947.

[7] The list can only be extended, apart from states that were renamed or refounded by emperors, like Selinus-Traianopolis, by a few early instances such as Laodicea Sebaste, Pergameni Sebasti, Sardiani Caesarei. Cf. op. cit. iii–iv, Index viii. 2.

couraged and strengthened by the latter. At the same time there is also the direct admiration of the imperial house expressed through the cult and through the innumerable honorific inscriptions. And it is both these tendencies that are expressed together in the complex form of the municipal and colonial titles of the second and third centuries.[1]

In this hunt after the title *colonia* it is clear that the provincials were not concerned for properly material advantages. Even without the statements of Gellius, the parallel history of the eastern cities would have suggested that provincial and municipal rivalry had something to do with the new passion. The inscriptions themselves occasionally refer to something of the sort, for example at Uchi Maius in Africa:[2] 'Concordiae . . . quod indulgentia Augusti nostri colonia Alexandriana Augusta Uchi . . . promota honorataque sit . . . ordo civitatis Bencennensis.' But there is more than the spirit of rivalry in this passion. In this very instance it is clear that the rivalry is not so much between Uchi and her neighbours as between Uchi and herself. Aulus Gellius clears up the situation.[3] The *municipia* sought after the status of *colonia* because this was the nearest approach in municipal form to the shape of 'the City' itself to which they could attain. They were eager to become *coloniae*—'in ius coloniarum mutari gestiverint'[4] because that condition, despite certain theoretical disadvantages—'cum sit magis obnoxia et minus libera'—carried tremendous prestige with it 'propter amplitudinem maiestatemque populi Romani, cuius istae coloniae quasi effigies parvae simulacraque esse quaedam videntur'.[5]

It is impossible to dispute the truth of this account, which is based upon, and in part consists of, quotations from a speech of Hadrian. Nor is there any obscurity in the reference to the greater freedom of the *municipia*. Gellius is speaking in the first

[1] The full development of this practice can be followed in detail in J. Assman's *De Coloniis Oppidisque Romanis quibus Imperatoria Nomina vel Cognomina imposita sunt* (Langensalzae, 1905). He points out that this first became a regular custom in the foundations of Caesar. Cf. briefly *ILS*, Index xi. 666–9.

[2] Above, 272 n. 2. 'The Council of the community of Bencenna to Concord, because by the grace of our emperor the colony . . . of Uchi has been dignified and advanced.'

[3] *NA* 16. 13. 4–5. Cf. Tertullian, *de Pallio* 4, 'si est Romanitas omnis salus'.

[4] *NA*, loc. cit. 'They were eager to exchange their charter for colonial status.'

[5] Ibid. 13. 9, 'because of the greatness and majesty of the Roman people, whose colonies have the appearance of miniatures and reproductions of Rome itself.'

place of the original Italian *municipia*, whose constitutions contained much that was handed down from earlier times. These privileges were now 'confused and obscure', and for the most part never belonged to the vast majority of the provincial *municipia*, which in their progress within the Roman state acquired a new constitution, on a stock model, at the stage of Latinity. But the rest of the account exactly explains the situation which the epigraphic evidence reveals. The great difference between the development of the *provinciae togatae* in the second century as contrasted with the first is that the provincials begin to take matters into their own hands. Instead of the Princeps giving *Latium* to a whole province, individual communities ask for it of their own accord. Hadrian's words are evidence enough that it was the provincials' desire and not the Princeps' policy that changed the nature of the *colonia* in the second century.[1]

Something similar is observable in the development of the *ius Latii* also, at least in the African provinces. The inscription of Gigthis shows that a tremendous effort was made to acquire what seems to be a not very considerable degree of promotion, elevation from plain Latin rights to the *Latium maius*. Twice they sent an embassy to the City *ad Latium maius petendum*, and at last the good news of success arrived—*tandemque feliciter renuntiavit.*[2] The same process is visible elsewhere in the same period, at Thisiduo under Hadrian,[3] and at Lambaesis, where the *Respublica Gemellensium* celebrates the gain of Latin rights, *Latium impetratum.*[4] These instances, together with the contemporary hunt of the *municipes* after Roman distinctions and honours, show the sheer absurdity of the old view that the invention of *Latium maius* was an attempt to palliate an alleged decline in municipal prosperity. Not long before Pius founds the Latin *municipium* of Gigthis, Hadrian awards to some of the more notable inhabitants the membership of the jury-panels at Rome, the *quinque decuriae*.[5] The clue to the understanding of these facts as a whole is not interest but sentiment—the sentiment of admiration for the Roman state, and the desire to win a high place within its fold. When the interest of the community is at stake, its expression finds other

[1] Cf. above, 413.

[2] *ILS* 6780. Cf. ibid. 6779. Pius is the *conditor municipii*. 'To get greater Latin rights.' 'At last he reported success.'

[3] Ibid. 6781, 'decuriones c.R. et municipes'.

[4] Ibid. 6848.　　　　　　　　　　　　　　　　　　　　[5] Cf. ibid. 9394.

forms. In A.D. 168 the *pagus* of Thugga celebrates the *caeleste beneficium iure capiendorum legatorum*, granted by the Princeps.[1]

This turning towards Rome takes many shapes. In this same Thugga it was expressed in bricks and mortar, or rather in stone and cement, in a fashion whose meaning is unmistakable. Between the later years of the principate of Marcus and that of Alexander the town-centre was converted, as far as public buildings were concerned, into the external likeness of a truly Roman city. It is notable, first, that this material metamorphosis somewhat outstrips the constitutional promotion of the *civitas*, which joined to the *pagus* became a *municipium* only under Severus, and *colonia* under Alexander,[2] and second, that the Numidian characteristics of the old town are retained under the garb of imperial architecture. The temples of Juno Caelestis and Saturn, magnificently rebuilt, remain what they were before, despite their porticos and colonnades; the Forum is fitted into the muddled plan of the old town as well as might be, and the little non-Roman shrine of African Mercury nestles beside the imposing temple of Capitoline Juppiter. As one passes from the narrow alleys of the oldest portion of the town to the fine buildings of the north-western quarter one seems to step from Berber town to Colonia Septimia. But that the change is external and formal there is no real doubt. The spirit of the place remain Numidian even when it is most Roman.[3]

## Contamination of Cults.

The metamorphosis of the town of Thugga exactly illustrates the transcendental quality of the attraction which Rome exercised over her subject peoples, and the way in which the old loyalties were not exchanged for, but were retained beneath and were largely untouched by the new ties. At most there is produced an amalgam. This is well illustrated by the influence which the imperial cult exerted in many departments of paganism. In the East the emperors became Zeus and so on,[4] and in the *provinciae togatae* a similar but less serious process is observable. Deities, especially minor deities, become associated with the emperor by

[1] *ILS* 9399. Cf. above, 333. 'The divine benefit of legally receiving inheritances.'
[2] Ibid. 6796, 541.
[3] For the building dates cf. *ILS* 9364; Cagnat, Merlin, *Inscr. Latines d'Afrique*, nos. 517, 521, 561. Juno and Saturn are Punic Astarte and Baal.
[4] Above, 406.

the addition of the title *Augustus*. As Nock suggests, this means little more than that they became 'the emperor's gods',[1] gods 'by royal warrant'. The precise meaning of the process is not here important, since any of the possible interpretations provide the same evidence for the continual problem of Roman history— the attitude of the ordinary man, the small folk or the masses, to the Empire. For the inscriptions of this type are by no means always the large official dedications of the municipalities and provinces, but far more commonly are the short records of individual men of humbler fortune than the *duoviri* and *decuriones*.[2]

The field of inquiry is large, and one in which it is difficult to secure dated evidence. It is a practice which seems to have begun in Italy, probably on the model of Juppiter Julius and the Lares Augusti,[3] and in Italy spread to a variety of deities. For the most part the title was given to the minor gods, but there are important exceptions;[4] one of the earliest instances is a dedication to Apollo Augustus at Rome in A.D. 46,[5] and one of the most frequent of the type in Italy is Minerva Augusta.[6] The practice appears commonly in northern Italy, and is found in the greater part of the northern and western provinces. The title is very seldom applied to Juno or Juppiter, or Venus, despite her association with the Gens Julia, in any part of the Roman world. The rest all seem to have their turn, although the lesser gods and heroes such as Hercules and Silvanus seem in general, outside Africa, more subject to the title, as though men sought to add to their dignity. The same custom early appears in the provinces as well as in Italy. At Lugdunum there was a dedication to Mercurius Augustus and Maia Augusta during the principate of Tiberius.[7] But the vast bulk of the in-

---

[1] A. D. Nock, Σύνναος θεός, *Harvard Studies in Cl. Phil.* 41. 59.

[2] Of those quoted below only a few, 10 out of 60 selected at random—those marked *—were set up by 'important' persons or official bodies; the rest are private, but include those of *seviri Aug.*, minor *collegia*, and *pagi*.

[3] The argument is purely chronological, the Lares Augusti are undoubtedly first in the field, being an institution of the Augustan Principate, cf. *ILS* 3611–14, while the 'dei Augusti' begin to appear under the Julio-Claudians. The idea, of course, goes back to that of Juppiter Julius, cf. Nock, art. cit. 57 n. 2. But surely after A.D. 14 Augustus was a *title*, not a name?

[4] *ILS* 3116, Junones (!); 3246, Diana; 3284, Neptunus; 3524, Silvanus, a great favourite; 5355*, Mercurius; 3876, Nymphae.

[5] Ibid. 3219.

[6] Ibid. 3128, 3129, 3136.

[7] Ibid. 3208.

scriptions naturally belong to the period of the fully developed empire—the later first, second, and early third centuries. Noricum and the whole range of Balkan provinces provide many examples, a scattering come from the Spains, and very few from the Gauls;[1] but Africa yields the richest harvest of all,[2] and some of the African dedications are truly significant of an attempt to harmonize or systematize the relationship of local and imperial loyalties. Here it is the gods whose Punic or Numidian character is most obvious who most frequently receive the title—Saturn, Hercules, Mercury and Neptune. Some of the inscriptions come from shrines whose non-Roman character is evident at a glance. The most telling are the numerous ex-votos to Saturnus Augustus Balcarenensis, whose shrine—no temple but a bare altar—was set among the clouds, between the twin peaks of Bou-Kornein which face Carthage across the gulf of Tunis.[3] But this is by no means an isolated instance.[4]

However cautious may be the interpretation of this evidence, its meaning is plain. Just as Augustine was in a later century able to use as a metaphor the idea of the empire as a whole, and to assume that the thought of an all-embracing *civitas* was familiar to the minds of his readers, so these innumerable dedicants, important imperial officials or slaves and freedmen or simple villagers alike,[5] had become familiar with the concept *Augustus* and transferred it as a whole from the imperial power to their local divinities. But this implies that they had accepted completely, or, at the very least, were ready to acquiesce in, the dominion of the emperors.

[1] *ILS* Noricum, 3231, 3745; Dalmatia, 3263, 3088–9, 3869, 9170, 3458; Pannoniae, 3655; Daciae, 3923*, 7139*; Moesia, 7172*; Baetica, 6910*, 6914; Tarraconensis, 3232, 5405; Lusitania, 3175; Gallia Comata, 3208, 3732–5, 7036, 3118, 3191*.

[2] e.g. ibid. Cirta, 3181*, Carthage, 4390, Cuicul, 5460; Giufi, 5073*, 5776*; Diana, 5355*; Mactar, 4908; Sua, 5572; Timgad, 6840*, 3368, 9396. Also nn. 3 and 4 below.

[3] Ibid. 4444 *a–d*. For the Punic cults cf. J. Toutain, *Les Cités romaines de la Tunisie*, 205 ff.

[4] Cf. the series ibid. 4443 *e–i*, from the Romano-Punic shrine at Thignica, a *civitas* whose history is similar to that of Thugga. Also ibid. 4447 'Saturno Palmensi Aquensio Augusto', 9291, from the sanctuary of Baal and Tanit at Siagu, cf. 9290 *a*. For Baalcaranensis cf. Toutain, op. cit. 221.

[5] Cf. ibid. 6805, 'Neptuno Aug. sacr. seniores et plebs Titulitana'. Cf. ibid. 9516 (from Gaul), 'Aug. sac. deae Souconnae oppidani Cabillonenses'.

PROVINCIAL OPPOSITION AND REVOLT UNDER
THE EARLY PRINCIPATE

In every part of the Roman world the provincial peoples of
every class and status were showing during the first two centuries
of the Principate an increasing interest in Rome, which expresses
itself in a variety of ways, and is by no means confined to the
imperial cult or to the extension of the citizenship either in the
East or in the West. 'The City' and 'The Emperor'—the two
cannot long be held apart, since the one leads to the other—
form a focal point for the attention of the provinces, however
completely these may differ in general characteristics from one
another. The great variety of these processes, formal and informal alike, by which the provincials began to venerate the
imperial state in all its manifestations, alone makes it possible
to understand the background of a measure like the Constitutio
Antoniniana, or the attitude of the panegyrists of the late Empire.

In this way the provincials prepared themselves, rather than
were prepared, for the formal unification of the *Orbis* within the
*Urbs*. Before considering the more self-conscious attitude of the
literary world toward the Empire, it is necessary to decide
whether this new spirit was universal, whether there were any
serious separatist movements during the early Empire to set over
against the philo-Roman tendency. The hostility felt towards
Rome under the late Republic in some regions had apparently
set its roots deep. Yet though there were occasional rebellions
within the Empire, and numerous instances of the strength of old
traditions, of pre-Roman and alien loyalties which maintain
themselves to a late date, neither the one nor the other disturbs
the main conclusion. The revolts are, with one significant
exception, rather outside the Empire, or in recently added
regions of it, and, when internal, are, with the same exception,
remarkable for their weakness. And the other phenomena are of
precisely that type which it was the genius of Rome to circumvent
or to transcend, where other imperial powers seek usually to oust
or to destroy.

Of revolt within the Empire all that need be taken seriously
are the Gallic movements and the Jewish troubles. The war
with Tacfarinas in Africa, the disturbances recorded in north-
west Spain under Nero, and the Cilician brigandage, are late

incidents of the conquest story rather than proof of dissidence within the established Empire. The Empire had its danger zones and uncivilized areas where resistance was prolonged, for the good reason that these areas had not been penetrated by the concomitants of the *pax Romana*, commercial or agricultural prosperity. But in Africa, when roads had opened up the interior, there was no second Tacfarinas. The occasional disturbances come from the nomads dwelling beyond the provincial boundaries. But the Gallic troubles are of another sort. Gallic peoples who had long accepted the Roman dominion certainly rose against Rome under Florus and Sacrovir, and again under the Batavian Civilis, and their leaders came from families that had possessed the citizenship apparently since the original conquest and had served as officers within the Roman auxiliary army. Yet, quite apart from the fact that these attempts were abortive and finally disowned by the Gallic peoples as a whole, they possess curious features, and are not to be interpreted as essentially anti-Roman. The rising against Tiberius seems to have been but a pale reflection of the troubles in Asia at the time of Mithridates. It was entirely due to debt,[1] and although there was some complaint about the 'continuous demands for tribute and the cruelty of the governor', sixty of the sixty-four states remained undisturbed, nor do the rebels seem to have expected that the provincial nobility as a whole would support the movement.[2]

Tiberius probably showed better sense than Tacitus in not treating very seriously an episode which demonstrated the growing reluctance of the Gallic nobility to challenge the accepted order, rather than the opposite.[3] Such was apparently Claudius' opinion of the affair, since, when addressing a somewhat hostile Senate, he was able to ignore entirely this interruption in the 'unbroken loyalty of a century' of the Gallic provinces.[4] It is difficult to believe that the risings in 68 and 70 were more serious as far as Gaul was concerned.[5] The real difference lies in

---

[1] Tac. *Ann.* 3. 40, 'ob magnitudinem aeris alieni'; 42, 'ut caesis negotiatoribus Romanis bellum inciperet'.

[2] Ibid. 43. 'Augustodunum . . . occupaverat ut nobilissimam Galliarum subolem . . . et *eo pignore* parentes . . . adiungeret.'

[3] Ibid. 41, 'consultus super eo Tiberius aspernatus est indicium'. 47, 'Tiberius ortum patratumque bellum senatu scripsit; . . . neque decorum principibus si una alterave civitas turbet', etc.

[4] *ILS* 212, 34.  [5] Cf. Tac. *Hist.* 4. 25; 31.

the circumstances, which were infinitely more favourable to a rebellion. The intentions of Vindex are perhaps inscrutable, but there can be no doubt that it was the vigour of the men from beyond the Rhine—Batavians and Germans—that made the movement appear serious. The neighbouring Gallic states merely joined what looked like the winning side, very probably to protect themselves from German violence,[1] and the movement entirely failed to stir the three provinces as a whole.[2]

There is no sign in the detailed Tacitean narrative of any general rebellion among the Gallic states as a whole. The movement was confined to a few of them, and among even those there are very obvious traces of dissensions and rivalries.[3] The Batavi take no part in the plans of their Gallic allies for a Gallic Empire, an *Imperium Galliarum*, and the presence of the Treviri and Lingones among the rebels means that the Sequani and others remain loyal.[4] The most curious feature of the revolt is the extent to which it is coloured by Roman concepts. Both Vindex and Civilis begin as supporters of a claimant to the Principate, while Vindex is represented by Dio as a patriotic citizen working in the interests of the Empire.[5] The new state of the Gallic rebels is to be an *imperium*.[6] Objection could be made that Tacitus is translating into Latin non-Latin notions, were it not that one of the leaders of the revolt—Julius Sabinus—proclaimed himself to be a descendant of Julius Caesar, and formally assumed his name.[7] Opposed to this are certain signs of Gallican feeling. The Druids raise their voice in prophecy, and Julius Classicus begins to recall ancient family traditions, more reputable than those of Sabinus—'ipse e maioribus suis hostis populis Romani quam socios iactabat'.[8] Possibly Mariccus the Boian was not the only fanatic prophet to become the 'champion of the Gauls' in these years.[9]

---

[1] Cf. Tac. *Hist.* 4. 65, reluctance of Colonia Agrippinensis to destroy her walls.
[2] Ibid. 69.                                        [3] Ibid. 61.
[4] Cf. ibid. 67 and 69.
[5] Dio, 63. 23. 1; 24. 4; Tacitus, of course, classes him with Florus and Sacrovir, *Hist.* 4. 57. Plutarch, *Galba* 4–6, inclines to Dio's view.
[6] Tac. *Hist.* 4. 58, 'Classicus . . . imperiumque et sacramentum Galliarum ostentat.' Ibid. 59, 'iuravere qui aderant pro imperio Galliarum.'
[7] Ibid. 55 and 67. 'Caesarem se salutari iubet.' Tacitus seems to think that this was a claim to the imperial title, as in his day it would have been.
[8] Ibid. 55. 'He boasted of ancestors that were enemies rather than allies of Rome.'
[9] Ibid. 2. 61, *adsertor Galliarum.*

The development of the Gallic provinces is at a halfway stage. Information is fullest about the attitude of the *primores*. They are already being attracted by the service and honours of the Roman state. In the time of Claudius the first move had come from them, when the so-called *ius honorum* was in question.[1] Their political ideas are becoming tinged with a strongly Roman dye. At the same time the old traditions are still alive, and no more can be said than that they accepted the Roman dominion indifferently.[2] The revolts were caused not so much by the existence of the regime as by its occasional harshness. Yet Tacitus alleges no motive for the spread of the revolt of Civilis among the Gauls except the hope of *libertas*.[3] He even names the concessions of Galba as a contributory cause.[4] There is not one word about the 'debts' or the tribute when he is discussing the motives of the Gauls alone. Only Cerialis in his speech of pacification mentions it, and then not as burdensome in itself, but as a sign of servitude which he is anxious to explain away.[5]

It is not likely that Tacitus' account is pure romance, though the theme *pax an libertas*, peace versus freedom, obviously offered temptation. The passing reference to the obscure Mariccus, *adsertor Galliarum*, adds considerable weight to these slightly rhetorical passages. There was in Gaul some anti-Roman feeling, which is perhaps best described by saying that the Gallic nobility was torn by two feelings, Gallican sentiment and self-interest. Peace won the day, party because the Gauls knew their own weakness, but also because the Romans had an insuperable argument to justify their dominion. Only the Roman power kept the Germans out of Gaul. The chapters where Tacitus elaborates this theme are of extreme importance; for this seems to be the earliest expression in a rudimentary form of the contrast between a single Roman world and the barbarians beyond the frontier.[6] The idea only came to full consciousness under the stress of the great invasions of the third century, and contributed much to the

---

[1] Above, 238 f.

[2] Cf. Tac. *Hist.* 4. 31, 'quis nec amor neque odium in partes'.

[3] Cf. ibid. 14-15. The levy, ibid., and the oppression of *negotiatores* concern only the Batavi. In 65 the *vectigal et onera commerciorum* touch only the free Germans. Note esp. ibid. 54-5 ad fin., 'coalita libertate disceptaturas Gallias quem virium suarum terminum velint'.

[4] Cf. Tac. *Hist.* 4. 57. 'Galbam et infracta tributa hostiles spiritus induisse.'

[5] Ibid. 74.

[6] Ibid. 73, 74. Cf. *Ann.* 4. 5; above, 283 n. 1.

ideal view of Rome elaborated by the later panegyrists. In Tacitus the doctrine is incomplete. The Gauls, who are regarded as enjoying the privileges of the Roman state, accept its dominion, and are protected against their enemies. The *primores Galliae*, to whom Cerialis addressed his oration, apparently acquiesce in this view.[1] Whatever the sources of Tacitus' narrative, he at least gives the philosophy of empire which was believed to represent provincial opinion in his own day; but the basic fact that the loyalty of Gaul was founded upon their fear of the free Germans must belong to the earlier rather than the later period, since Cerialis quotes not the German invaders of the Julio-Claudian period, but Ariovistus.

Thus in Gaul after a century and a quarter of Roman rule the blessings of the peace and the majesty of the Roman name seem to be securing their usual effect, while the sentiment of Gallic liberty is in rapid retreat. Two hundred years later, when it is next possible to assess the quality of Gallican feeling, the rout seems to be complete.[2]

The other instances of dissent under the early Empire are on a decidedly minor scale, excepting always the national risings of the Jews. The attitude of the Jewish communities, with a few exceptions, seems to have been one of utter intransigence. Roman statesmanship completely failed, despite its multiple ingenuity, to solve the problem, for the simple reason that the Jews were not prepared to co-operate. They could not come within the *civitas*, because they would not; for the essence of the *Orbis Romanus* in the fullest sense is that it was produced by the willing co-operation of both sides—subject peoples and Rome alike.[3]

In the hellenized provinces dissent was based upon the glories of Alexander and the traditions of the kings.[4] But except at Alexandria such dissent does not seem to have been dangerous. The all-embracing harmony of the *Orbis Romanus* could resolve

[1] Loc. cit., they alone can be described by the words *ipsi legionibus . . . praesidetis*, etc. Is this a rhetorical plural for Vindex? or is Tacitus elaborating a commonplace which in fact does not apply very well to Gallia Comata? Cf. above, 260.

[2] Cf. below, 446 ff.

[3] H. I. Bell, *Jews and Christians in Egypt*, 10, with the literature cited ibid. n. 1 Add Premerstein in *Hermes* 67. 174 f.

[4] Livy 9. 18. 6, 'levissimi ex Graecis qui Parthorum quoque contra nomen Romanum gloriae favent', etc. Ibid. 18. 13, 'quo sint mirabiliores quam Alexander aut quisquam rex'. Cf. 36. 17. 5; 37. 54. 18; 38. 17. 11.

these discords. All that was needed was sufficient time. The salute to Nero as 'The only emperor who was the friend of the Greeks'[1] suggests that even on this narrower issue goodwill was not lacking to overcome the friction of Hellene and Roman, noted by Livy in the Augustan age, and notably confirmed by the evidence of the Cyrenean edicts.[2] By the time of Trajan friction had been changed to an occasional bickering of an unimportant kind. Dio Chrysostom warns the Greek cities that the perpetual disorder of their municipal rivalries was regarded by the Roman government as 'Greek folly'.[3] A little later the sense of opposition vanished, the Greek traditions being preserved within the Roman framework.[4] The general fact is well documented by literary authorities, and some specific instances of what is meant have been preserved. In the third century the village of Baitokaike still preserved a letter from 'King Antiochus' granting them certain privileges.[5] Valerian confirmed their rights with the words 'Regum antiqua beneficia consuetudine etiam insecuti temporis adprobata is qui provinciam regit . . . incolumia vobis manere curabit'. Valerian here gives express recognition to the fact that the opposition between the Roman and the Hellenistic systems had been transcended.

The situation at Alexandria was more serious. The city—latest won of the Roman pearls—was very conscious of the grandeur of its past and very disinclined to yield pride of place to Rome. The squabbles lasted at least a century. Claudius' attempt at pacification was incomplete, for Vespasian by his exactions and by laying hands upon the royal palace seems to have provoked an anti-Roman outburst.[6] Admittedly the imperial cult was accepted, but the Alexandrines seem to have employed it

---

[1] εἰς αὐτοκράτωρ φιλέλλην γενόμενος SIG³ 814. Cf. Wilcken (Chrestomathie), no. 113.

[2] Above, 271 f. Cf. Tarn, The Greeks in Bactria and India, 35 n. 1, 37 n. 2.

[3] Ἑλληνικὰ ἁμαρτήματα. Or. 38. 37–8. Cf. Auctor de Bell. Alex. 15. 1, and later Tac. Hist. 3. 47: 'caesa ibi [at Trapezus] cohors regium auxilium olim; mox donati civitate Romana signa armaque in nostrum modum, desidiam licentiamque Graecorum retinebant'. But Tacitus perhaps echoes a literary commonplace, cf. Juvenal's Graecam urbem, etc., 3. 60 ff.

[4] Below, 425 ff., 430 ff.

[5] OGIS 262 = ILS 540. 'The benefits conferred by the kings of old and approved by the custom of the following period are to be secured to you by the governor of the province.'

[6] In general cf. Bell, op. cit. 8–9. Suet. Vespasian 19. 2. Dio Cassius 65 (66). 8, especially the sneer, οὐ γὰρ οἶδε καισαρεύειν.

largely as an effective weapon for Jew-baiting. That Alexandria was eventually reconciled to the Roman dominion, and accepted the second place in the rank of cities, seems to be proved by the description in the Sibylline oracles, but it is probable that the conversion came late.[1] Aristides the Sophist, although in one passage he explicitly recognizes Alexandria as the second city of the Empire and contrives to avoid almost any admission of imperfection in the Roman world,[2] makes an obscure reference to cities that cannot help disorderly behaviour because of their size and this looks like a recognition of Alexandrian discontent.[3] One suspects that the breach was not completely healed until Severus restored the city's council and its self-respect by one and the same edict.[4]

From all this it appears that the provincial opposition under the Caesars did not present an impossible problem to the Roman government. Its intensity varied considerably from province to province. The complaint might be sentimental or material; Rome had a remedy for both. The former was answered by the ready tolerance of almost any degree of local patriotism, which Rome could often twist to serve her own purposes. Disruptive patriotism was checked by Rome's trump card—the *pax*. It may be said, in the terminology of Tacitus, that men surrender their freedom to enjoy the peace and the prosperity—*aurum et opes*—which is its concomitant; these consolations lead them to 'love and cultivate'—*amate colite*—the City, until they finally come to 'possess' it—*victi victoresque eodem iure obtinemus*.[5]

---

[1] *Or. Sib.* 13. 48–9. τοσσούτους λυκάβαντας ἐκοῦσά σε [= Romam] σιτομετρήσει δῖα πόλις μεγάλη Μακηδονίοιο ἄνακτος. Here the proud claim of 11. 234–5, is renounced. But the trials of the Gymnasiarchs recorded in the 'Acts of the Pagan Martyrs' continue in the second century, cf. *P. Oxy.* 1, no. 33, under Marcus Aurelius (or Commodus?).

[2] Or. 26 (ed. Keil).      [3] Ibid. 67.      [4] Dio 51. 17. 3.

[5] Tac. *Hist.* 4. 74.

# XVIII

## THE ATTITUDE OF EDUCATED
## OPINION

### EXPLICIT EVIDENCE

THE previous discussion has concerned the way in which individuals, communities and provinces behaved towards Rome, the emperors and the Empire, and the conclusions were based mainly on the synthesis of what they did. Next comes the consideration of what they said. This study involves an advance in the actual history of events, since the evidence falls into two main groups. The writers of the Second Sophistic and the early Christian apologists, of whom Aristides and Tertullian are the most ample representatives, show how men talked of the Empire in the period preceding the Constitutio Antoniniana. The contemporary portions of the Sibylline books tell a similar story for a more popular audience, and lead on to the events of the third century, when the perpetual nightmare of the invasions caused the crystallization of men's attitude to Rome. The study of these events and of such phenomena as the so-called Gallic empire will prepare for the analysis of the second group of panegyrical writings about Rome—those of the Gallic rhetoricians of the age of Diocletian and Constantine. Closely connected with this is the evidence of the language and terminology of the historical writers who describe the period. The inquiry will then naturally conclude with the testimony of Augustine and the poets of the late fourth and early fifth centuries, which will be seen not to stand in any way alone but to form an epilogue to a long story, to which they have little to add except explicit statement and final canonization.

Aristides gives the classical exposition of the theory of the Empire at the highest period of its development. Whether or not his exposition is an exact description, universally true, of the facts of his own day does not very much matter. He provides an interpretation of the Roman world as seen with the eyes of a typical Greek of the upper classes. It is not exactly an official account; for some of his remarks, such as the disparagement of military service, must have drawn from an intelligent and responsible Roman an uneasy protest. A student such as Plutarch would not have applied to the Roman government the sentence, 'You reckon it unworthy of the empire that the citizens should serve in the army and endure labour'.[1] Nor would such an emperor as Marcus have accepted it, though he might have agreed that such service was 'unpleasant'. To Aristides the method by which the Roman army of his day was recruited was merely a clever dodge by which Rome circumvented the disadvantages of a mercenary army.[2] He recorded the fact, without fully appreciating its importance, that the loyalty of the new citizen-mercenaries was directed towards Rome.[3] His speech is an attempt to interpret what he saw from the point of view of a Greek. He lays some stress upon the peculiarities of the Empire, its special characteristics,[4] with which his wrestlings are not always a complete success.[5] His interpretation may thus be regarded as the common opinion of the class of men that includes, for example, the Lyciarchs discussed in the previous chapter.

Aristides gives formal explicit expression to the views whose emergence and earlier propagation have already been considered. Rome rules the *Orbis Terrarum*, and is the 'Common City' of the best elements within it. Starting from the principle that, for Rome, 'no one is a foreigner who is meritorious'[6] he sums up the characteristics of the citizenship as he knew it, thus: 'You have made Roman status the name not of a city but of a general species or race, not one of many races, but a race that balances all the rest'.[7] This is elaborated by the comparison of Rome to the sea which receives all the rivers of the world yet changes not in size, a phrase which carries a little further the process revealed

---

[1] Εἰς Ῥώμην 74, τὸ μὲν τοὺς ἀπὸ τῆς πόλεως στρατεύεσθαι καὶ ταλαιπωρεῖν οὐκ ἄξια τῆς ἀρχῆς . . . εἶναι ἐνομίσατε.                    [2] Ibid. 74–6.

[3] Ibid. 76, μηδὲ βλέπειν ἄλλοσε τοὺς ἐξελθόντας ἢ πρὸς ὑμᾶς.

[4] Ibid. 34 ff.

[5] Cf. 87–9, on the standing army, and 102, νόμους κοινοὺς ἅπασι τάξαντες . . . γάμους τε κοινοὺς ποιήσαντες καὶ συντάξαντες ὥσπερ ἕνα οἶκον ἅπασαν τὴν οἰκουμένην. This confuses the distinct idea of the extension of the *civitas* with the general picture of the world being under a single government.

[6] Ibid. 60, ξένος οὐδεὶς ὅστις . . . ἄξιος.

[7] Ibid. 63, τὸ Ῥωμαῖον εἶναι ἐποιήσατε οὐ πόλεως ἀλλὰ γένους ὄνομα κοινοῦ τινος καὶ τούτου οὐχ ἑνὸς τῶν πάντων ἀλλὰ ἀντιρρόπου πᾶσι τοῖς λοιποῖς.

in some detail by the inscriptions of Lycia. There Roman status was 'one of many races', though undoubtedly 'first among them all', and appeared in lists of honorary, or idle, isopolities because it was not regarded as entirely emptied of practical content. Here all the positive *iura* have been stripped away, and the citizenship is an active citizenship whose activity consists in mere possession, and whose function is simply to be a form of unity. Aristides, unlike Tacitus, says nothing of the senatorial and consular families drawn from the provinces, and when he speaks of the 'common laws'[1] and 'rights of intermarriage'[2] which Rome has introduced, he means little more, in so far as he thinks of the citizenship alone, than that the holders of this purely honorary status pass it down to their descendants.[3]

Aristides thus stands in the tradition both of Tacitus, with his phrase 'Romana civitas olim data cum id rarum nec nisi virtuti pretium esset',[4] and of Pliny the Younger, who insists on the 'tantus amor nominis nostri'.[5] But he comes close to a confusion of which a Roman official of the period would have been incapable. In describing the security of travel in the world of his day, he says that travellers pass 'from native-land to native-land'[6] and that to be safe 'it is enough to be a Roman',[7] and this he qualifies with the addition 'or rather to be one of your subjects';[8] this passage shows that, although Aristides is well aware of the proper distinction between citizens and *peregrini*, in popular thought the distinction was breaking down.[9] Half a century later Tertullian does commit the solecism.[10] Aristides does not, but it is clear that the distinction is only titular for him; all the subjects of Rome enjoy the advantages of the Empire alike,[11] whether Romans or non-Romans, and Aristides in notable passages describes the provinces as the *territorium* of Rome, and the boundary of the Empire as her city-walls.[12]

---

[1] νόμοι κοινοί.   [2] γάμος κοινός.   [3] Op. cit. 102.

[4] Tac. *Ann.* 3. 40. 'The Roman citizenship given of old when the gift was rare and made only as the reward of virtue.'

[5] Pliny, *Pan.* 37. 5. 'So great was their love of our name.'

[6] ἐκ πατρίδος εἰς πατρίδα.   [7] ἐξαρκεῖ 'Ρωμαῖον εἶναι.

[8] μᾶλλον δὲ ἕνα τῶν ὑφ' ὑμῖν.

[9] Aristides, op. cit. 100. Contrast 59.   [10] Below, 433 ff.

[11] Op. cit. 30, οἱ τῶν πεδίων . . . κληροῦχοι . . . ὑμέτεροι γεωργοί . . . ὥσπερ μία χώρα συνεχὴς καὶ ἐν φῦλον ἄπαντα ὑπακούει. Cf. 28, and 65–6, protection of πλήθη from δυνατοί.

[12] Ibid. 81–4.

The corollary of this view is expounded at length,—the old
rivalries within the Empire have disappeared.[1] The Hellenistic
world is flourishing anew under the material patronage of Rome,
and the former contrast of Hellene and Barbarian has given way
to the distinction of Romans and non-Romans—a fact which he
connects immediately with the persuasive majesty of the Roman
name.[2] This statement of Aristides can be checked not merely
by the negative proof that in this and the following period there
are no philhellenic manifestations of political dislike of Rome,
but by the curious way in which Herodian describes the educa-
tion of the young Severus Alexander. He was brought up as a
true 'Greek and Roman'.[3] The contrast is with the strange behaviour of Elagabalus who abominated all 'Roman or Hellenic'
forms of dress,[4] and worshipped a deity who possessed no 'statue
as is usual with Greeks or Romans',[5] but was a god 'of the natives'
and of 'the neighbouring princes and kings'.[6]

The association of the two ideas of Hellene and Roman, which
was given practical expression in the rise of the senatorial families
of the eastern provinces, was essential to the accomplishment of
the unity of the Roman world, and its importance was duly
recognized by contemporaries. Aristides after all is only one
representative of a whole school of thought; before him Dio of
Prusa had treated similar problems, and had contributed to the
final solution of the relation of the imperial power to the Greek
states with his tracts *De Regno*, whose doctrine Aristides accepts
and dismisses in a single paragraph of his panegyric. Since Dio
had cleared the ground, Aristides was able to develop the main
theme of Rome as the common native land, the *communis patria*
of the peoples of the world.[7] To this the only possible objection
was that in fact not all the peoples were included in the *patria*,

---

[1] Aristides, op. cit. 68. The loyalty of the cities, which cling to Rome like a string
of bats. Cf. 76, 94–9, Rome the city-builder, revival of prosperity, etc., 97, the only
ἔρις left is to make one's city ὅτι καλλίστη καὶ ἡδίστη.

[2] Ibid. 63, ἐπὶ τοσοῦτον ἐξηγάγετε τὸ τῆς πόλεως ὄνομα.

[3] Ἕλλην καὶ Ῥωμαῖος. Herodian, *Historia*, 5. 7. 5.

[4] Ibid. 5. 5. 4. But Lucian, *De Merc. Cond.*, shows strong social dislike of rich
Romans at some length.

[5] ἄγαλμα, ὥσπερ παρ' Ἕλλησιν ἢ Ῥωμαίοις, ibid. 5. 3. 5.

[6] οἱ γειτνιῶντες σατράπαι τε καὶ βασιλεῖς, ibid. 5. 3. 4.

[7] Aristides, op. cit. 60. Rome is a κοινή τῆς γῆς δημοκρατία under a Periclean
leadership, cf. 36, τοὺς ἄρχοντας καθίστατε . . . ἐπὶ προστασίᾳ τῶν ἀρχομένων οὐκ ἐπὶ
τῷ δεσπότας εἶναι.

and this thought does check Aristides from time to time. But he had another bolt to his bow. This is not merely the fact that all men enjoy the benefits of Roman rule,[1] citizens and subjects alike, but that the Roman government is a new thing in the world which men had not known before.[2] He criticizes the Achaemenid and Macedonian monarchies as never having understood the art of government, and calls the Hellenistic kings 'princes bereft of a king',[3] and then proceeds to deduce the Roman skill in government from the formal principle that 'ability emerges when the subject-matter is sufficient'.[4] Only when the Romans had united the world into one did the 'skill' emerge, thanks to the 'size' of the Empire.

This little piece of philosophy should not deceive many. For Aristides is simply enlarging upon the great Roman claim voiced by Virgil. 'Tu regere imperio populos, Romane, memento'. This becomes a regular panegyrical theme, of equal importance with the claim to have provided a *communis patria* for the world. In the Latin tradition of Rutilius the two themes are equally stressed,[5] and in the popular history of the Sibylline oracles the special virtue of Augustus is described by the line 'he shall establish laws for the peoples and subject all things to his command',[6] which appears in three passages.[7] The common inspiration of the panegyric tradition seems clear. Even the idea of the importance of the size and unity of the empire as an essential preliminary to the emergence of good government is not an original thought, nor of Greek extraction. The basic notion has been expressed by the Elder Pliny when he spoke of the 'orbis discors et in regna, hoc est in membra, divisus'.[8] He elaborated the theme in his description of the mission of Rome: 'quae ... sparsa

---

[1] Ibid. 59, τὸ μὲν χαριέστερον . . . πολιτικὸν . . . ἀπεδείξατε τὸ δὲ λοιπὸν ὑπήκοον.

[2] Ibid. 51, οὔπω πρὸ ὑμῶν ἦν τὸ ἄρχειν εἰδέναι.

[3] σατράπαι ἔρημοι βασίλεως, ibid. 27.

[4] Ibid. 58, ἐπὶ ταῖς ὕλαις ἀπαντῶσιν αἱ τέχναι. Ibid. 23; 27. Even Alexander is criticized in 24, because he did not 'rule' but only 'won' a kingdom.

[5] *De Reditu* 1. 77 f.—the *legiferi triumphi*; 91, 'quod regnas minus est quam quod regnare mereris'; 133, 'porrige victuras Romana in saecula leges'. Cf. Aristides, op. cit. 102, quoted above, 426 n. 5, and in the Christian tradition, Augustine, *de c. Dei*, 5. 17, quoted below, 462.

[6] καὶ θεσμοὺς θήσει λαοῖς καὶ πάνθ' ὑποτάξει.

[7] It is applied vaguely to the new ascendancy of Rome, ousting Macedon, in 8. 13 and to Augustus in 5. 19; 12. 23.

[8] *NH* 2. 117. 'The world lacking harmony and broken up into kingdoms, that is, parts'.

congregaret imperia ritusque molliret et tot populorum discordes ferasque linguas sermonis commercio contraheret ad conloquia et humanitatem homini daret',[1] a passage which concludes with the words 'breviterque una cunctarum gentium in toto orbe patria fieret.' This conjunction is significant of the debt that Aristides owes to his Latin precursors. He is, in his oration, elaborating the commonplaces of the dominant philo-Roman tradition in accordance with his own training and observation. His success was possible because the society of his day was in fact assimilating these Roman notions of *communis patria*, and of the special *artes* of Rome. What is in Pliny a bold thought, transcending both the Virgilian and the Ciceronian concept by combining them together, has become hackneyed simply because it has become accepted.

Aristides claims that Rome is popular both with the ruling classes of the cities and with the masses, whom she protects against the tyranny of the former, but he does not elaborate his statement. It can perhaps be elucidated with the help of the Sibylline history contained in the twelfth and thirteenth books of Sibyllines, which deals with the established Principate, and especially this period of it. The writers of these books have one test which they regularly apply to the emperors—the test of peace and war. Whatever their other merits, the emperors whose reign was a period of war within the empire receive a bad mark, while those who brought peace or fought successfully against barbarians outside the Empire gain a good mark, whatever may be held against them on other scores. In the early period dislike of Caligula[2] and Nero[3] is not allowed to obscure the fact that they were peace-bringers. Domitian[4] and Hadrian[5] win especial praise on this score, and Trajan, Marcus Aurelius, and even Severus are highly applauded for their foreign exploits.[6] The writers are chiefly offended by slaughter within the Empire. At

---

[1] *NH* 3. 39; cf. also Tac. *Ann.* 4. 5, 'regibus qui magnitudine nostra proteguntur adversum externa imperia'. 'To join together the scattered empires, to soften customs, to unite in common discourse the wild inharmonious tongues of so many peoples by use of her language, and to give humanity to man; briefly to become the single native land of all the peoples in the world.'

[2] 12. 51–3, ἀναιδῶς πλείονα συλήσας θήσει κατὰ γαῖαν ἅπαντα, εἰρήνη δ' ἔσται πολέμων δ' ἀναπαύσεται Ἄρης. Cf. ibid. 58, πολλὰ δὲ ποιήσει ἄνομα.

[3] Ibid. 78–94.

[4] Ibid. 127–8, καὶ τότε γ' ἄμπαυσις πολέμου κατὰ κόσμον ἅπαντα | ἔσται.

[5] Ibid. 172–3, εἰρήνη μακρὰ δὲ γενήσεται ὁππόταν ἔσται | οὗτος ἄναξ.

[6] Trajan, ibid. 147–63. Marcus, ibid. 180–4 (?), 196–203. Severus, ibid. 261–2.

the approach of the civil wars that succeeded the death of Commodus they give a great shout of despair,[1] and the account of the third century is one long complaint.[2] Only in the days of Philip the Arab is there any promise of relief from war 'for a little while, not for very long'.[3]

In addition to the test of peace and war, the emperors are judged by their activity as 'benefactors', as builders and as adorners of cities.[4] Both Domitian[5] and Hadrian[6] receive a tremendous ovation on this score, and Marcus or perhaps Verus is approved because of the splendour with which he invested the City itself.[7] These passages lead on to the magnificent appreciation of the external splendour of the 'Cities of Arabia' in the thirteenth book, coupled with a warning of the woe to come: 'Cities of Arabia, Bostra and Philippopolis, now do you adorn yourselves with temples, arenas and squares and streets, bright-shining wealth and statues, gold and silver and ivory.'[8]

The Sibylline writers clearly join hands with the rhetoricians of the Second Sophistic, though on a somewhat narrower issue. They have little to say about *Romanitas* and limit their appreciation of the Empire to the peace and prosperity which it brings, but they also show some trace of the idea that the provincials are members of a Roman world in their identification of the woes of the provinces with those of Rome and the reverse,[9] and in their dislike of the 'barbarizing' emperors. For example, they show disapproval of Elagabalus, with his 'barbarian' customs,[10] but strong sympathy for Alexander when, a Roman king, he is

[1] Ibid. 224–9, note κλαίει μοι κραδίη κλαίει δέ μοι ἔνδοθεν ἦτορ, and 239–44, the many forms of death.

[2] 13 throughout, especially 119–30, the wrecked cities, and 131–41, the ruined provinces.          [3] 13. 27.

[4] 12. 135–8, κτίσματα καὶ κόσμος granted to Σύροι.      [5] Ibid. 128–31.

[6] Ibid. 166–7, οὗτος καὶ ναοὺς πόλεσιν πάσαις ἀναθήσει, | κόσμον ἐποπτεύων ἰδίῳ ποδὶ δῶρα κομίζων. Cf. 5. 46–50. where he is πανάριστος; even in the highly unfavourable verses 8. 50–64, due to the Antinous scandal, he is δῶρα πορίζων, ibid. 53.                        [7] 12. 191–2.

[8]
νῦν κοσμεῖσθε πόλεις Ἀράβων ναοῖς σταδίοις τε
ἠδ' ἀγοραῖς πλατείαις τε καὶ ἀγλαοφεγγέι πλούτῳ,
καὶ ξοάνοις χρυσῷ τε καὶ ἀργύρῳ ἠδ' ἐλέφαντι,
. . . Βόστρα Φιλιππόπολίς τε.

13. 64–8, etc. Cf. 135–6, where the invaders ἄστεα γυμνώσαντες . . . ναοὺς ῥίψουσιν, a procedure which is deplored.

[9] e.g. 12. 224–8, for it was the provinces that suffered in the civil wars, cf. 250–5, where Thrace, Bithynia, Cilicia, and Syria are named, and above, n. 2.

[10] 12. 273–4.

deserted by the 'Roman Ares'.[1] Trajanus Decius is disliked as
a barbarian, 'sprung from Dacians',[2] but when contrasted with
the Persians he is a 'lord of Italy'.[3] Similarly the mysterious
'fugitive' who brings ruin to Rome from beyond the Euphrates is
described as 'no longer resembling the Romans but like to the
Persians'.[4] In these writers also the contrast of Rome with barbarians beyond the frontier has effect in consolidating opinion
of all sorts in favour of the Empire. The union of Palmyra and
Persia against the central government is strongly disapproved.
It was counter to the divine will, and only led to the exile of many
provincials in lands beyond the Empire.[5]

The consciousness of belonging to an *Orbis Romanus* is a
minor theme in the Sibyllines; it is implicit in the facts described
and in the judgements made by the writers, but it is never explicit. It does not receive any such expression as the representatives of the upper classes of the provinces, such as Aristides,
have given to it. The conception of the Sibylline writers is far
cruder, and owes little to Roman or Hellenistic thought. The
highest degree of attachment that they can imagine is expressed
by the forceful metaphor of 'willing slavery'. This is the formula
which Domitian's admirer considers most suitable to the description of complete imperial harmony: 'All shall be his willing
slaves and servants; cities shall willingly enslave and subject
themselves to him.'[6] The reciprocal relation on the emperor's
part is affection: 'These too the great king shall love and treat
kindly.'[7] This language represents the popular version of the
Hellenistic notion of 'philanthropy', and is the language of a
class rather than of a people. But the idea has this in common
with the more orthodox formulae, that the relationship is regarded
as reciprocal.[8] The Sibyllines leave the impression that in the

---

[1] *Or. Sib.* 12. 277–8.  [2] Δακῶν ἐξαναδύς.

[3] κοίρανος Ἰταλιητῶν, ibid. 100.

[4] οὐκέτι Ῥωμαίοις ἐναλίγκιος ἀλλὰ . . . Πέρσαις, ibid. 99–100.

[5] 13. 111–14. Ῥωμαίους δ' ὀλέσουσι Σύροι Πέρσῃσι μιγέντες,
ἀλλ' οὐ νικήσουσιν ὅμως Θεοκράντορι βουλῇ.
αἱ ὁπόσοι φεύξονται . . . ἐς ἀλλοθρόους ἀνθρώπους.

[6] 12. 129–31. πάντες δουλεύσουσιν ἑκούσιοι οὐδ' ὑπ' ἀνάγκης
καὶ πόλεις αὐτόματοι ὑποχείριοι ἠδ' ὑπόδουλοι
ἔσσονται.

[7] καὶ τούτους βασιλεὺς στέρξει μέγας ἠδ' ἀγαπήσει, ibid. 137, cf. above, 431 n. 4.

[8] Cf. Aristides, op. cit. 23, on the Achaemenid Empire, οὔτε ἐκεῖνοι ἄρχειν
ἠπίσταντο οὔτε οἱ ἀρχόμενοι τὸ ἀκόλουθον ἀπεπλήρουν.

lower strata of the Hellenistic provinces the new kingdom and the new kings were accepted and even welcomed. Up to this point the Sibyllines are on common ground with the Second Sophistic, but they are unable to accompany the latter in their appreciation of the less familiar virtues of the new power. The folk for whom these oracles were written were content to be the subjects of the new kings, recognizing the transcendent unity of the new order without probing the matter more deeply.[1]

Among the *provinciae togatae* of the West the recognition of the transformation of the old world is more complete, for the good reason that here a real material transformation had taken place. If the evidence of Tertullian can be extended beyond the coasts of Africa to the western world in general, it would seem that there was a complete recognition of the formal unity of the Roman world and of the approximation of the *imperium Romanum* to the Roman citizenship. Writing under the Severan dynasty, and, in his *Apology*, only a few years before the Constitutio Antoniniana itself, he uses language which means that in common speech the provincials as a whole thought of themselves as *Romani* or *cives*. The first hint of this comes in the opening page of the *Apology*, where the pagan enemies of the Christians complain that the Christians have taken over the State: 'obsessam vociferantur civitatem, in agris in castellis in insulis Christianos'. Here (as in other passages) the *civitas* is not just the city of Carthage, but the whole Roman territory.[2] In another tract he certainly regards *hic mundus*, the world of the living, as forming a single *civitas*; and this is an explicit extension of the normal language of Christian apologetics based upon St. Paul's phrase 'our citizenship is in Heaven', which Tertullian quotes.[3] The metaphor, as the Greek word πολίτευμα and Tertullian's rendering of it by *municipatus* clearly show, was intended originally to refer not to the imperial state but to the ordinary citizenship of the municipalities. Tertullian can alter the application slightly because he is drawing upon a conception that has grown up since the time of St. Paul, Roman citizen though he was; but the conception is

---

[1] Cf. the description of the emperors as σωτὴρ τῶν μετρίων in inscriptions and papyri, Schubart, art. cit., *Klio* 30. 62; 66.

[2] *Ap.* 1. 7, cf. 37. 4, cited below, 434 n. 6; for *civitas* 38. 2, 44. 1.

[3] *De Corona* 13, 'Sed tu peregrinus mundi huius civis civitatis supernae. Noster, inquit, municipatus in coelis.' Phil. 3. 20.

simply that of the world as forming a single state, and of the *imperium Romanum* as a single *civitas*.

In the *Apology* Tertullian speaks of *Romani* and of *cives*, apparently never of *cives Romani*. The term *Romani* is used in two senses. In historical or descriptive passages it has its ordinary meaning, as an adjective or as equivalent to *populus Romanus*.[1] But where Tertullian is arguing the special problem of his own day, where he is pleading the central theme of his *Apology*, *Romani* is contrasted with *Christiani*, and means 'the ordinary members of the Empire, the so-called loyal subjects'.[2] He is defending the case of the Christians, not merely of the African Christians who might have Roman or Latin status, but of all the Christians within the Empire. He deals at length with the prejudices against the Christians, which he sums up in the phrase 'laedimus Romanos nec Romani habemur qui non Romanorum deum colimus', where the double sense of the term is evident.[3] The ground for this abuse of the Christians is the belief that they are enemies of the Roman emperors, *hostes principum Romanorum*,[4] but since many instances can be found of *Romani* in the narrower sense who were traitors and *hostes*, Tertullian can make the excellent debating point 'non possumus et Romani non esse et hostes esse cum hostes reperiantur qui Romani habebantur', by playing upon the double meaning of the word.[5] In so far as Tertullian is defending the legal rights of the Christians in this tract, he is not concerned with Roman citizens alone, but with men of every degree and class—with the *gentes totius orbis*.[6] The fact that, in the part of the Empire which he knew by personal experience, the majority of men probably were citizens, made the transition from the narrow sense of *Romani* to the wider meaning easy both

[1] *Ap. passim*, e.g. 25, 'ergo non ante religiosi Romani quam magni'.

[2] e.g. ibid. 35, 'ne forte . . . deteriores Christianis deprehendantur qui nos nolunt Romanos haberi sed ut hostes principum Romanorum'. 36, 'cur nos qui hostes existimamur Romani negamus?' etc. Only 10. 5 contrasts *Romani, peregrini*.

[3] Ibid. 24. 'We hurt the Romans (they say), and are reckoned non-Romans in that we do not worship the god of the Romans.'

[4] Ibid. 35.

[5] Ibid. 36. 'We cannot both be non-Romans and enemies when those who were reckoned Romans are discovered to be enemies.'

[6] Ibid. 37, 'plures nimirum Mauri . . . vel quantaecunque unius tamen loci . . . gentes quam totius orbis . . . vestra omnia implevimus urbes insulas castella municipia conciliabula' etc.; ibid. 2 mentions the treatment of the Bithynian Christians; *ad Scapulam*—addressed to the African *Praeses*—quotes precedents from Cappadocia and Byzantium, ibid. 3, and Asia, ibid. 5.

for him and for his audience, but that he is not using the term in a legal sense is clear both from the actual passages and from the situation itself.[1] Nor is the word a technical term in ordinary practice. Tertullian's own usage makes this clear. Where he uses *Romani* in historical description it simply means the Roman people, as, in the example quoted, *Romanorum deum* means 'the god of the Roman people'.

His special use of *Romani* is allied to his use of the word *cives*. In one passage he makes the supposition that all Christians were to withdraw from the Roman Empire, and remarks that 'suffudisset utique dominationem vestram tot qualiumcumque civium amissio . . . plures hostes quam cives vobis remansissent'.[2] This is the same loose employment of a term capable of a more precise meaning as before. It appears again in his description of the Empire; 'hoc imperium cuius ministri estis civilis non tyrannica dominatio est'.[3] Here he uses a phrase, which is an appropriate description of the theory of the Principate, to sum up the whole Empire, to which it is inappropriate unless the population of the Empire can in some sense be called *cives*.

Tertullian has another word which he employs to describe the same people whom he calls *cives* and *Romani*. It is simply *vestri*. 'De vestris sumus,' he says, 'fiunt non nascuntur Christiani.'[4] But these *vestri* are simply the *Imperii Romani antistites* and their subjects as a whole, regarded as the opponents of the Christians. When disasters shake the Empire, 'et nos in aliquo loco casus invenimur,' he says, 'licet extranei a turbis aestimemur'.[5] With

---

[1] Cf. also *Ap.* 35, 'haec Christianus tam enuntiare non novit quam de novo Caesare optare. Sed vulgus, inquis. Ut vulgus, tamen Romani.' The reference is to *ipsos Quirites*. This shows that it was not the legal so much as the social or moral status that was in dispute. Tertullian scores because the *vulgus* is Roman in both senses.

[2] Ibid. 37. 'The loss of so many citizens of every kind would have overwhelmed your empire—more enemies than citizens would have been left to you.' The additional clause 'paene omnium civitatum paene omnes cives Christianos habendo', introducing the additional confusion of using *cives* as meaning *municipes*, is best left out of the discussion since the text is highly suspect. The usage is normal, especially epigraphically, but the meaning is irrelevant to Tertullian's point.

[3] Ibid. 2. 'This empire of which you are servants is a lordship over citizens, not a tyranny.'

[4] *Ap.* 18. 'We are from your people. Christians are not born but made.'

[5] *Ap.* 31. 'We are found in some corner of the tragedy, though we are reckoned strangers by the throngs.' Cf. 35, 'de Romanis, id est de non Christianis'. The contrast of *nos* and *vos* appears *passim*, e.g. 38 and 41. The terminology of Aristides and

the comparison of these terms the last temptation to give a rigid interpretation disappears. Tertullian, brought up in one of the most thoroughly municipalized of the provinces where *Romanitas* was the guarantee of civilization, *omnis salus*,[1] can and does speak of the inhabitants of the whole Empire as forming a single body, to which the name *cives* or *Romani* can be applied, without meaning that all were in fact in the legal status of Roman citizens. Not only could Tertullian use these phrases, but it is reasonable to assume that he was understood by his readers, and that his terminology corresponds to the popular usage of the class to which he belonged. He plays with the various connotations of the terms, but always there lie under the play of words certain political conceptions which are fundamental and which Tertullian did not invent but found ready for use.

This conclusion is fortified by consideration of the attitude of Tertullian to the Empire and the emperors. Beneath the Christian in him there lies the loyal subject. The emperors are necessary for the times, the existence of the Empire itself is in accordance with the will of God, and the Empire will last as long as the temporal order subsists.[2] Nor is this all; for Tertullian at times goes beyond this negative loyalty and recognizes the services which the Empire renders to humanity, not only in withstanding the disasters that loom in the future but in securing a positive prosperity for the peoples of the world.[3]

There are other, perhaps more numerous, passages in which Tertullian's attitude is less friendly, where he shows only a passive toleration and speaks of a unity of mankind transcending even the great unity of the Empire. But there is no need to set text against text. What is relevant to the present inquiry is the extraordinary degree of acceptance of the common enthusiasm

Tertullian is combined in Augustine's synthesis of history: 'Proponunt Graeci—adsumunt Romani—concludunt Christiani.' *De Civitate Dei* 2. 13.

[1] *De Pallio* 4.

[2] *Ap.* 21, cf. 33, 'Caesar a nostro deo constitutus.' *Ad Scap.* 2, 'Christianus . . . salvum (imperatorem) velit cum toto Romano imperio quousque saeculum stabit: tamdiu enim stabit'. *Ap.* 32, 'vim maximam universo orbi (!) imminentem ipsamque clausulam saeculi acerbitates horrendas comminantem Romani imperii commeatu scimus retardari'—hence 'Romanae diuturnitati favemus'.

[3] *De Pallio* 2. 'Quantum reformavit orbis saeculum illud, quantum urbium aut produxit aut auxit aut reddidit praesentis imperii triplex virtus . . . deo tot Augustis in unum favente . . . quot census transcripti, quot populi repugnati, quot ordines illustrati, quot barbari exclusi.'

which the austere and even cynical apologist of the Christians can permit himself, not only in the official *Apology*,[1] in which he offers an olive branch to the imperial government, but in tracts like the *De Pallio*, and even in the more theological works.[2] Apparently the people whom Tertullian represents found it impossible to maintain a complete alienation from the Empire. Where he admits so much of the panegyrical view of Rome, it is reasonable to suppose that the normal attitude of provincial society was a complete acceptance. For the evidence of Tertullian is superior to that of Aristides in this, that he is speaking for a set of persons not confined in class but drawn from all ranks of society. Possibly he reflects a certain degree of class prejudice; for, as Guignebert points out, there is almost contemporary evidence for the real alienation of the lowest classes among the Christian population.[3] But Tertullian with his divided opinions, accepting because he is a citizen what he would prefer to reject as a Christian,[4] provides excellent evidence for the sentiments of loyalty held by at least the upper classes of the Latin world at the very period of the Constitutio Antoniniana. His language shows that the panegyrical tendencies, and the real feeling underlying them, were not confined to the Greek-speaking world, and fully confirms the conclusions that can be drawn from the scattered testimony of the inscriptions.

## THE ROMAN WORLD AS *OMNES GENTES* OR Τὰ Ἔθνη

E. Kornemann briefly sponsored a view of the Empire which seems to be opposed to that set out in the preceding pages. In the place of a growing self-consciousness of the unity of the Empire he finds only regional or provincial self-consciousness in the second century.[5] But the general interpretation of the evidence

[1] Cf. C. Guignebert, *Tertullian, Étude sur ses sentiments à l'égard de l'empire*, 11, quoting *de Anima*, 49, 'nulla iam gens Dei extranea est', and *Ap*. 38, 'unam omnium rempublicam agnoscimus mundum'.
[2] e.g. *De Res. Carnis*. 24, where the existence of the Empire prevents the appearance of Anti-Christ.
[3] Guignebert, op. cit. 17–19, based upon the *Carmen Apologeticum* of Commodianus, a third-century African bishop who declares, ibid. 58, 'rudes edoceo', and proceeds to prophesy woe to Rome, and unlike the Sibylline writers, to exult over this, 805 (800) ff., cf. 923 (916), 'luget in aeternum quae se iactabat aeternam.'
[4] Cf. Guignebert, op. cit. 11; 23 f.
[5] J. Vogt and E. Kornemann, *Römische Geschichte* (Teubner, 1933), 80.

attempted above suggests that there is no real opposition between the two views. Provincial feeling was not only tolerated but encouraged, because the attachment of the peoples to Rome was mediated by the provincial system itself; for the organs by which provincial individualism was expressed were precisely those which secured the devotion of the provinces to Rome, while even in the Romanized provinces internal uniformity or conformity was not a basic secret of empire. The unifying element was external, consisting in the connection itself that bound the provincials to Rome, whether as allies, subjects, or members of the Roman state.

Even so, it is by no means certain that the evidence will bear the structure which Kornemann proposes to erect. The basic fact is that the Empire was commonly described by the Greek writers of the second and early third centuries as consisting of 'peoples' or ἔθνη instead of 'provinces'. The argument is apparently that this term was substituted for the more normal and official term ἐπαρχία, or province, because there was a growing feeling of nationalism in the provinces. But it is doubtful whether this is not merely a matter of literary history, and it is difficult to prove that the usage is really tendentious; for the term does not appear for the first time in the second century, and it continues as a stylistic peculiarity in later generations and even centuries.[1]

The usage has a Latin and not a Greek origin. It makes its appearance first in the speeches of Cicero and the *Histories* of Sallust, where Rome is called *gentium moderator*,[2] an idea that maintained itself as long as the Western Empire lasted. The contrast between this terminology and that of the late Hellenistic writers, who described Rome as the ruler of the οἰκουμένη, or inhabited world, shows that one is dealing with a truly Latin idea.[3] At first *gentes* was interpreted in the widest possible sense, as those peoples who fell within the sphere of influence of Roman military dominance; this is the usage of Cicero, in phrases like 'ille populus . . . dominus regum, victor atque imperator omnium gentium', or 'ut (Mars) urbem hanc gentibus vos huic urbi genuisse videatur'.[4] A more concrete meaning only appears as

---

[1] Below, 441.     [2] *Oratio Lepidi*, 11.
[3] e.g. Polybius 1. 2. 7; 5. 4. For the history of *gens*, cf. *Thesaurus Latinae Linguae*, s.v., esp. 1850 B 1.
[4] *De Domo* 90, cf. *pro Plancio* 11, *Phil.* 14. 32. 'That people which is master of the

the Empire itself takes a more concrete form with the provincialization of the *gentes*, and the growth of a more territorial conception of the *provinciae*.[1] Whereas Cicero calls the Roman people
*princeps gentium*, lord of peoples, Livy changes this to *princeps
terrarum*, lord of lands.[2] Though the two shades of meaning are
to be found in the later period, it is doubtful whether the Republican authors use the word in the more specific sense of certain
subject peoples who could, if necessary, be named, which is what
the writers of the Principate undoubtedly often do mean by it.
Livy with his phrase 'gentes humanae . . . aequo animo . . .
imperium patiuntur', and Horace's verses '(Juppiter) terruit
Urbem, | terruit gentes',[3] are well on the way to the precise and
limited usage of Martial, 'notus gentibus . . . Martialis, | et notus
populis',[4] and of the Elder Pliny, 'platanus . . . ad Morinos usque
pervecta ac tributarium etiam detinens solum ut gentes vectigal
et pro umbra pendant', a sufficiently explicit passage.[5] This process was never completed. The freedom of language in a creative
period, and the common usage of the term in other connections,
prevented the crystallization of the concept *gens = provincia*;[6]
always the more normal description of the Empire is not plain
*gentes* but *omnes* or *cunctae gentes*, a phrase whose persistence
illustrates the recognition of both the unity and the difference of
the component parts of the Empire.[7] But the dominant idea is

kings, conqueror and lord of all peoples.' 'Just as Mars begot this city for the
peoples, so he seems to have begotten you for this city.'

[1] Cf. Cic. *Flacc.* 2, 'omnium . . . salus . . . non civium solum verum etiam gentium'.
The same contrast comes in *Bellum Hisp.* 17. 3, 'qualem gentibus me praestiti similem
in civium deditione praestabo.' Cf. Cic. *Mil.* 19, 'non haec solum civitas sed gentes
omnes'.                                                          [2] Livy, *Preface*, 3.

[3] Ibid. 7. Horace, *C.* 1. 2. 5. 'The peoples of mankind endure our rule in calm-
ness.' 'Juppiter alarmed the city and the peoples.'

[4] Mart. 10. 9. 3. 'Martial, known to the nations and the peoples.'

[5] *NH* 12. 6. 'The plane tree was transplanted to the country of the Morini and
and occupied tributary soil, so that the peoples pay taxes even for shade.'

[6] Cf. *Thesaurus*, s.v., 1850 B 31 ff. e.g. Mart. 12. 8. 1, 'terrarum dea gentiumque
Roma'. Lucan, 7. 421, 'omne tibi bellum gentes dedit'. Pliny, *NH* 36. 111, 'illi qui
hoc imperium fecere tantum ad devincendas gentes . . . exeuntes'. Ibid. 120, 'nec
fuit rex Curio aut gentium imperator'. Suet. *Cal.* 35. 3, 'dominum gentium populum', Gaius' own words. Tertullian, *Ap.* 21, makes 'dominatores gentium' mean
'antistites imperii'. *Pan. Lat.* 11. 12. 1. Earlier, Pliny, *Pan.* 32. 1, *gentem* equals
*Aegyptum*; ibid. 70. 9, 'urbes populi gentes'.

[7] Most explicitly in Pliny, *NH* 3. 39, 'una cunctarum gentium in toto orbe
patria', cf. ibid. 3. 5. Mart. 8. 61. 5, 'spargor per omnes Roma quas tenet gentes'.
Pliny, *Pan.* 32. 2, 'omnes gentes discant . . . quanto . . . sit utilius unum esse cui
serviant'. At a later date, cf. Aug. *de Civ. Dei*, 1. 36; 5. 15; 17.

that the Empire is the *orbis terrarum*; *gentes* and *terrae* are alternative ways of describing its individual members, rather than synonyms for *provinciae*.[1]

No one would try to build on the Latin terminology any account of provincial development. All that can be extracted is what was known before—that the official view identified Empire and civilized world with one another as a whole composed of parts. It is curious that the idea of Rome as *domina (cunctarum) gentium* precedes that of the Empire as *orbis terrarum*.[2] If the latter is a translation of the Greek οἰκουμένη or 'world', and the former is purely Latin, this is intelligible. For just as the original expansion of Rome can be summed up by the formula *gentes universae in civitatem acceptae*, 'the reception of whole peoples into the citizenship', so the controller of a foreign empire is aptly described by the phrase 'lord of the peoples'.

The linguistic analysis seems to show that these terms have no special significance. Can anything more be made of their Greek equivalent, which came so much later into the field?[3] That the Greek writers of the second century used the phrase τὰ ἔθνη, the peoples, as a description of the Empire, and that sometimes this term is a literal equivalent of 'the provinces', is not disputed. Dio Chrysostom, Appian, Aristides, and Dio Cassius, who belongs to the late second and the early third century, all use the term thus at one time or another.[4] But they do not always employ it alone. The normal descriptive phrase is not simply 'the peoples', but 'the cities and the peoples'.[5] This does not exclude the former from the latter, but recognizes the smaller units

---

[1] Cf. *Pan. Lat.* 4. 35. 2, 'sensisti Roma tandem arcem te omnium gentium et terrarum esse reginam cum ex omnibus provinciis optimates viros . . . pignerareris ut senatus . . . ex totius orbis flore constaret'. This leaves nothing unsaid.

[2] At no period is the barbarian world forgotten. Pliny's use of *noster orbis* is almost always in passages where he is contrasting the Mediterranean world with the Far East: *NH* 8. 7; 18. 93; 19, 161; 28. 123; 37. 79. Only once does he apply *orbis terrarum* to the Empire, 2. 117. Contrast 5. 76: 'Gadibus extra orbem conditis.' *Orbis (terrarum)* remains for him a geographical concept, cf. 4. 96; cf. Vogt, *Orbis Romanus* (Tübingen, 1929), 25 f.

[3] The earliest instance is perhaps Jos. *Ant. Jud.* 18. 1. Quirinius is δικαιοδότης τοῦ ἔθνους. Perhaps the Greek version of the *Res Gestae* which uses ἔθνος as meaning *gens* had some influence, ibid. 26. 1; 33, etc.

[4] Dio Chrys., e.g. *Or.* 3. 104 R., 37 M.; 115. 45 M. Appian, *BC* 1. 173, ἡγεμόσι τῶν ἐθνῶν = *proconsulibus*. *Illyr.* 6. Dio Cassius 36. 41. 1; 37. 50. 4; cf. Boissevain, index s.v.

[5] Dio Chrys. 3. 104 R., 37 M. (βασιλεὺς) ὅτῳ παμπληθεῖς μὲν ὑπακούουσι πόλεις πάμπολλα δὲ ἔθνη. Cf. Aristides 26 (K.), 23; 28.

alongside of the larger, and as of equal importance. The use of 'the peoples' alone comes to full flower only in the *History* of Herodian.[1] In him 'people' is normally a substitute for 'province', and the older collocation of the type 'neither people nor city'[2] appears only occasionally.[3] Other uses of the term are rare except when he is speaking of the barbarian peoples.

The literary history of the word does not end with Herodian, but is passed on to the early Byzantine writers. In the reputable Zosimus, who normally employs the proper nouns to denote the parts of the Empire, a periphrastic use of the term sometimes appears,[4] and is regularly employed in place of provincial titles in one formula, 'the peoples beyond the Alps';[5] but the phraseology is entirely harmless and not tendentious, for he explains this term as meaning 'Gauls and Spaniards and the isle of Britain'.[6] The conception is simply geographic, and is the consequence of the fact that for many centuries the provinces had formed territorial units.

The same seems to be true of Herodian's language,[7] which is the result of a conflation of two ideas, the division of the Roman Empire into provinces and of the world into peoples. The two did not originally coincide, as a Sibylline verse shows: 'Neither Syrian nor Greek nor Barbarian nor any other People', a line which recalls the description of St. Paul as Apostle of the Peoples.[8] But within the Empire there were some recognized ethnic units which coincided with the area of the corresponding province—for example, Lycia. This mediated the identification of the two

---

[1] The list of passages is formidable. A few will suffice: for ἔθνος in the singular as *provincia*, 3. 8. 2 τὴν τοῦ ἔθνους ἐξουσίαν; 7. 9. 2 τοῦ ἔθνους ἐξελθεῖν; 8. 7. 8 τοῦ ἔθνους ἄρξας; 2. 7. 9 τὸ Σύρων ἔθνος. 3. 14. 9; 7. 5. 1; 7. 9. 1. In the plural, with further specification, 4. 8. 6 διὰ . . . Ἀσίας καὶ Βιθυνίας τῶν τε λοιπῶν ἐθνῶν; 3. 2. 7 ἐν πᾶσι τοῖς ἔθνεσιν ἐκείνοις. The sense of τὰ Ἰλλυρικὰ ἔθνη is not so explicit, cf. 8. 5. 6; 8. 2. 3; 6. 7. 2. Alone as *omnes provinciae*, 4. 6. 4 ἐς τὰ ἔθνη πέμπων. 8. 7. 6 τῶν ἄλλων ἐθνῶν οἱ ἀδικούμενοι ἀπέστησαν, cf. 6. 4. 5.

[2] οὔτε ἔθνος οὔτε πόλις.

[3] e.g. ibid. 1. 1. 4; 2. 10. 7; 7. 3. 6.

[4] e.g. Zosimus, 4. 12. 1, τῶν ἐν τοῖς ὑπὸ Ῥωμαίους ἔθνεσι γεωργῶν.

[5] τὰ ὑπὲρ τὰς Ἄλπεις ἔθνη. E.g. Zosimus 5. 2. 1; 27. 2; 2. 45. 2; 3. 2. 1.

[6] Γαλάται καὶ Ἴβηρες ἅμα τῇ Βρεττανικῇ νήσῳ. Zosimus 1. 64. 1. Cf. the usage in the late *Edictum de auro coronario*, Bruns, 96, 10–11, where the distinction of ἔθνος and πόλις is that of province and town, in official usage.

[7] Cf. the instances collected above, n. 1.

[8] οὐ Σύρος οὐχ Ἕλλην οὐ βάρβαρος οὐκ ἔθνος ἄλλο, *Or. Sib.* 8. 127. ἐθνῶν ἀπόστολος, Romans 11: 13.

ideas, but to argue from this literary usage to the existence of provincial nationalism is not legitimate. The proper method would be to establish the fact by independent evidence, province by province. Without this no generalization about the whole Empire is justifiable.

There is some good evidence for the existence of ethnic units within the eastern provinces, in the second and third centuries, to be drawn from the institution of the provincial assemblies or councils with their High Priests and Asiarchs, Bithyniarchs, etc. But even this evidence must be used with caution, since these offices are sometimes officially inspired creations of the Roman government, to which no strong feeling of local unity necessarily corresponds.[1] Only for Lycia is there ample evidence of such a feeling. Here the Council had a long and distinguished history in the pre-Roman period, which only ended in the time of Claudius.[2] In Lycia the confederation of cities is persistently described as a People,[3] and numerous inscriptions illustrate the identification of the terms People and Province.[4] But in the province of Asia the situation is very different. Although the Asiatic Council is of early date, the unity of the province remained a formality, divided between the great cities and the local ethnic groups, each with its own local assembly.[5] Like Achaia, Asia rather contained peoples than formed a People.[6] To argue from either the Lycian or the Asiatic precedent to the meaning of the assemblies of other provinces, such as Syria or Pontus, would be dangerous.

In general there is not sufficient evidence to establish anything beyond the formal recognition of what may sometimes be called ethnic areas, usually but not always coincident with the provincial boundaries, and often subdivided into smaller ethnic units.[7] Apart from Lycia and apart from the issue of a series of coins of

---

[1] For the distinction of pre-Roman and post-conquest assemblies, see Kornemann, *RE*, art. Κοινόν, col. 930.

[2] Cf. Ruge, *RE*, art. 'Lyciarch', cols. 2276–9. Kornemann, art. cit., col. 933.

[3] *IGRR* iii, Lycia, *passim*, cf. the use of ἐθνικός as opposed to πολιτικός. E.g. 739. 12. 64 ἀρχήν πολιτικήν τε καὶ ἐθνικήν; also 473 ἐθνικὸν ἄρχοντα; 527 ἔργα ἐθνικά.

[4] e.g. *IGRR* iii. 495 τῇ τε πόλει καὶ τῇ ἐπαρχείᾳ ... ἐν τῇ πόλει ... καὶ ἐν τῷ ἔθνει, cf. 513; and 739. 62. 35 πρωτεύων ἐν τῇ ἐπαρχείᾳ = ibid. 63. 50 πρωτεύων ἐν τῷ ἔθνει.

[5] Cf. Chapot, op. cit. 466 f.

[6] Cf. Kornemann, art. cit. 931.

[7] Ibid., col. 929. Brandes, *RE*, art. 'Bithynia', col. 540.

an Alexander-type by the Macedonian assembly in the middle of the third century,[1] there is no real evidence by which the importance of these Councils as focal points of local nationalism can be assessed. At the most they represent, outside the European provinces, only the Hellenic element, the city populations, and perhaps only the upper classes even of them.[2] But while little support can be found here for the existence of any national feeling in the high days of the Empire, it is true that the writers in whom the 'ethnic' terminology appears are drawn from that class for whom the existence of the Councils could mean most. If any reality lay behind the language of Aristides and Appian, it must almost certainly have found expression in the flaunting decrees and epistles of the provincial assemblies. At most the writers are following a habit that had been introduced by the very existence of these assemblies; but the problem is much more one of literary than of political history, and in any case cannot be confined in time to the later Principate, or in place to the eastern provinces, or even in expression to the Greek writers.

It is even possible that this terminology was not intended to stress the individuality of the parts so much as the unity of the Empire as a whole. When Aristides wrote 'No city, no people escapes you',[3] he was thinking only of the newly found harmony of the Empire in which the 'romantic but uncomfortable differences of former times and peoples' were obliterated.[4] The appearance of the term is not to be taken apart from the contemporaneous recognition of the Empire as 'the world'. The same men who exalt their office as Lyciarch set up inscriptions declaring that e.g. Pius 'provides many benefits for the world that is his'[5] or celebrate e.g. Severus Alexander as 'the lord of sea and land and every human people',[6] a variant of the familiar theme of 'Saviour of the whole world' which well illustrates the connection between the Empire considered as 'the Peoples' and as 'the World'. At the best the recognition of the ethnic element in this period is always secondary, outside Lycia, to the importance

---

[1] Kornemann, art. cit., col. 939. The ancient capital of the Macedonian kings at Pella was decaying and neglected in the second century, cf. Lucian, *Alexander* 6.

[2] Kornemann, art. cit., cols. 934–5. Cf. Chapot, op. cit. 462.

[3] ἐκφεύγει δὲ ὑμᾶς οὐδὲν οὐ πόλις οὐκ ἔθνος. Op. cit. 28.

[4] Ibid. 102.

[5] ἀγαθὰ πολλὰ παρέχει τῇ ἰδίᾳ οἰκουμένῃ. IGRR iii. 739. 68.

[6] τὸν γῆς καὶ θαλάσσης καὶ παντὸς ἀνθρώπων ἔθνους δεσπότην. IGRR iv. 1207.

assigned to the cities, but there is no reason to imagine any conflict between the two, still less between imperial and provincial loyalties. It was the function of the Roman state to include all these differences within its folds as a 'race that balances all the rest'.[1]

---

[1] γένος ἀντίρροπον πᾶσι τοῖς λοιποῖς. Aristides, op. cit. 63. Cf. 426 n. 7 above.

# XIX

# THE CONSOLIDATION OF LOYALTY IN THE LATE EMPIRE

## INTRODUCTION

IN various ways the world had prepared itself for the formal union within the Roman citizenship accomplished by Caracallus. There is no evidence to show what contemporaries thought of this act, except the statement of Dio Cassius that Caracallus' motive was entirely fiscal.[1] His failure to comment upon the act itself shows that in official opinion it was but the completion of a long process, and introduced no material alteration in the social conditions of the Roman world. But this formal unification came in the period immediately preceding a series of violent assaults upon the Empire from without, which, coming at a time when it was torn by civil strife, provided a crisis far more serious than the troubles that had faced Marcus Aurelius. The contrast of the present danger and past prosperity brought to rapid maturity the sense of membership in a Roman world; fear of the barbarians made what before had been only occasional and partly theoretical, universal and real. The normal description of the peoples of the Empire as *Romani* in the later third- and fourth-century writers[2] carries an intensified meaning when compared with the usage of the earlier period: for there is now a solid foundation in two elements that were lacking before, the complete formal unity of the *orbis* within the citizenship, and the recognition, forced from men by an ever-present fear, that the cause of Rome and of material civilization were bound up together. The attractive power of the majesty of Rome was reinforced by self-interest. Herodian puts the connection of sentiments very clearly when he says that the Aquileienses got from Rome 'in the place of wars, deep peace and the citizenship'.[3]

The conscious contrast between the peoples of the Empire and the barbarians must go back to the time when Hadrian accepted

---

[1] 78. 9. 5.    [2] Below, 451 ff.    [3] Herodian 8. 2. 4.

the necessity of delimitation and set the Empire upon the defensive. The feeling shows itself occasionally in such passages of Aristides as the description of Ares holding his dance 'on the banks of the frontier rivers'.[1] But in the writers of later times the contrast is universal and normal. The evidence is only good in and after the time of Diocletian. For the most serious period of the crisis, the only expression of provincial feeling which has left any large mark upon the tradition, and for which there is adequate testimony outside the meagre literary sources, is to be found in the establishment of the so-called provincial empires of Gaul, Palmyra, and perhaps Britain. These three, which, since they do not spring from a common root, must be treated separately, have been thought to exhibit a centrifugal tendency, and to be instances of the growth of nationalism within the Empire. This view, which may be true for Palmyra, is, however, very dubious in the other two cases, upon a close examination of the evidence.

### THE EMPIRE OF THE GAULS

The Gallic emperors differed from the other *tyranni* of the period only in the success with which they maintained themselves. This success was not due to any deep-seated national movement in the Gallic provinces, of which the literary sources, inferior though they are, know nothing,[2] but to the fact that these emperors had accomplished the primary task for which they were created, of keeping out the barbarians, and that their rivals in Italy had too much work on hand to deal with them. The Gallic emperors did not limit their claim to Gaul. There is evidence that their power was recognized for a time both in Spain and in Britain[3] and even north Italy.[4] Also they issued a series of coins bearing the titles of the Roman legions, of which the object was not so much to celebrate their own army as to claim the

---

[1] ἐπὶ ταῖς ὄχθαις τῶν ἔξω ποταμῶν, Aristides, op. cit. 105.

[2] The phrase *imperium Galliarum* is only used by Eutropius 9. 9. 3. The *Historia Augusta*, even, only calls them 'adsertores Romani nominis', v. Lolliani, cf. below, 448 f. Cf. A. v. Premerstein, *RE*, art. 'Esuvius', col. 700.

[3] Mattingly and Sydenham, *Roman Imperial Coinage*, 5. 2. 315–17. *CIL* ii. 4919, 4943; vii. 820, 823, 1150, 1160, 1161.

[4] Mattingly and Sydenham, op. cit. 327.

allegiance of the legions of other provinces which had not recognized their legitimacy.[1]

The final opinion about their intentions depends upon the
interpretation of a series of coins which they issued in honour of
Hercules. These have been held to prove that the spirit of nationalism inspired Postumus and his successors.[2] But of the sixteen
titles under which Hercules is celebrated six are drawn from
Greek legends,[3] five from the cult or service of Rome,[4] and
three from place-names or names of provinces outside Gaul.[5]
The title 'Gaditanus' is explained by the fact that the power of
the Gallic emperors extended to Spain. 'Libycus' may refer to the
same fact, since Gades was of Carthaginian origin,[6] or may with
'Thracius' be a part of the propaganda of the type illustrated by
the series of legionary coin-types.

Only two titles seem to refer to local cults within the Gallic
area, 'Deusoniensis' and 'Magusanus'; and of these two the
former is Germanic rather than Gallic, being the deity of a
village on the northern bank of the Rhine, the modern Köln-
Deutz.[7] Hercules Magusanus is a weak figure to bear the burden
of proof; from what is known of him his cult, in external form,
was Graceo-Roman.[8] Though this latter fact is by no means
conclusive against the argument for a nationalist revival, the
weight of the evidence, when set in relation to the history of the
times, favours another interpretation.[9] In the third century
Hercules was regarded as a symbol of the tremendous labours
which the emperors performed to save the Roman world from

[1] Ibid. 383 f. Carausius did the same, ibid. 440 f.

[2] This view was first combatted by Jullian, *CRAI*, 1896, 293 ff., repeated in
*Histoire de la Gaule romaine*, iv. ch. 15, 1–3. For the coins see Mattingly's lists, op. cit.;
also ibid. 331. For bibliography see P. Damerau, *Kaiser Claudius Gothicus*, 76 n. 1
(*Klio*, Beiheft 33). Most recent work, however, has been directed to the establishment of the chronology rather than to interpretation.

[3] Arcadius, Argivus, Cretensis, Nemaeus, Pisaeus, Erumantinus.

[4] Romanus Augustus, Comes Augusti, Pacifer, Immortalis, Invictus.

[5] Gaditanus, Lybicus, Thracius, cf. Mattingly and Sydenham, op. cit. 331 ff.

[6] Cf. its shrine of the Phoenician god Hercules-Melkart. Strabo 3. 5. 5 (170).

[7] Jullian, art. cit. 298 ff.

[8] Ibid. 298.

[9] The case for an earlier Gallic national revival under the Severi is also weak, cf.
Jullian, art. cit. 294. The basic evidence is the use of the *leuga* at that period, a
reappearance of Druidic influence according to the SHA, *Alexander*, 60, and of the
old tribal names, cf. *CIL* 5. 732. *Digest* 32. 11. 1 is irrelevant, 'fidei commissa . . .
relinqui possunt . . . etiam Punica vel Gallica vel alterius cuiuscunque gentis
(lingua)'. This proves too much.

destruction;[1] the cult found its final expression when Maximianus took the name 'Herculius'.

The imperial styles given to Hercules, such as *comes Augusti*, *invictus* etc., agree entirely with the testimony of the other coins and of the inscriptions, which show that the 'Gallic Empire' was in conception, execution and effect entirely Roman. Its official language and terminology owed nothing to Gallic feeling.[2] The coinage follows very closely the changes taking place within the legitimate Empire;[3] the few novelties that were introduced, such as *claritas Augusta* or *salus provinciarum*, only emphasized the thorough acceptance by the Gallic emperors of the imperial idea. That they were tolerated by and tolerated their rivals in Italy must be due to the situation itself.[4] They were securing what their coins proclaimed, the safety of the provinces. But they were also claimants, though sleeping claimants, to the whole imperial power.[5] The end of the story destroys any lingering belief in Gallic nationalism; for the abdication of Tetricus in favour of the 'legitimist' Aurelian, and the good understanding between them, prove that the movement was inspired only by the idea implied or explicit in many of their coin-titles, such as *defensor orbis*.[6]

If there was any Gallic feeling in the matter, it was of a very poor quality to peter out in a few years. The records show plainly that the Gallic provinces had completely assimilated the idea that they were integral parts of the Roman Empire, and had no wish to be separated from it. The choice of Tetricus as emperor reinforces this argument; for he was not the soldiers' man, but a civil administrator from the most peaceful quarter of Gaul.[7] Such a man should have been supported by the enthusiasm of whatever nationalist elements there were in Gaul; his abdication implies the formal recognition that the Gallic provinces, once they were 'safe', wanted nothing more than reunion with Rome. For once the *Historia Augusta* touches the

---

[1] Cf. Jullian, art. cit. 299 f.

[2] Cf. Mattingly, op. cit. 331 ff. Even *restitutor Galliarum* was no novelty, but Hadrianic, ibid., *Hadrian*, n. 326.

[3] Ibid. 322.

[4] Despite the possible attempt to seize north Italy, ibid. 327, the Gallic and the 'legitimate' coinage were interchangeable, according to the evidence of the finds, ibid. 318.

[5] Cf. ibid. 332 for the interpretation of the type *Roma aeterna* as a claim to legitimacy.

[6] Ibid. 385.　　　　　　　　　　[7] Victor, *de Caesaribus* 33. 14.

truth in calling these dynasts champions of the Roman name, *adsertores Romani nominis*.[1]

## CARAUSIUS

The adventures of Carausius in Britain form an appendix to the story of the Gallic emperors. There is the same claim to the imperial power as a whole,[2] the same modelling of the provincial dynasty upon the Roman pattern,[3] and the same temporary tolerance of the 'tyrant' by the central power,[4] all the more remarkable since that power is not the divided Principate of Gallienus but the strong *consortium* of Diocletian and Maximian. But there is a difference between the revolt of Carausius and that of the Gallic emperors, in that all the evidence tends to show that Carausius and his junior, Allectus, were thoroughly unpopular in their kingdom. Their military power was based not on the Roman forces but on an alliance with Picts and Scots;[5] to the middle classes, represented by the Panegyric writers and the source employed by Geoffrey of Monmouth, for what it is worth, they were pirates and brigands,[6] from whose desperate hands Constantius, after his victory near Southampton, delivered London when its sack was threatened.[7]

This literary tradition, in which the opinions of the *negotiatores* are echoed, is supported by some numismatic evidence. Britannia, when won back by Constantius, was feted not as a conquest, *provincia victa*, but as the sheep that was lost—*gaudens*,[8] and in the 'medallion of Arras' Constantius as *redditor lucis*

---

[1] Above, 446 n. 2. Cf. in general, concerning the dynasties of the third century, A. Alföldi, 'La Grande Crise du Monde Romain', *Ant. Class.* 1938, 13 f.

[2] Mattingly and Sydenham, op. cit. 440 f.; the legionary propaganda appears as in Gaul. [3] Ibid. 447.

[4] Ibid. 442; there are coins bearing the heads of the three Augusti, Diocletian being in the centre, with the inscription, 'Carausius et fratres sui' and 'pax Auggg'.

[5] Mattingly and Sydenham, op. cit. 427 f.

[6] e.g. *Pan.* 8. 12. 1, 'contractis ad dilectum mercatoribus Gallicis, sollicitatis per spolia . . . provinciarum . . . copia barbarorum', cf. ibid. 16. 2. In Geoffrey, *Historia* 75–6, Carausius and Allectus 'miserably afflict the Britons'.

[7] *Pan.* 8. 17. 1, 'cum direpta civitate fugam capessere cogitarent (barbari) . . . provincialibus vestris in caede hostium dederint salutem (Romani)', cf. 19, for the *gaudium* of the provincials. Carausius is never *named* but always *described*, e.g. ibid. 12. 1, 'isto latrocinio', 12. 2, 'impunitas desperatorum hominum', 15. 5, 'ipse signifer nefariae actioni', 16. 1, 'ille fugiens'; cf. *Pan.* 10. 12. 1, 'ille pirata'.

[8] *Num. Chron.* 1930, 225.

*aeternae* is depicted receiving the enthusiastic support of the provincial population.[1] When the behaviour of Carausis and Allectus is contrasted with that of Postumus, who refused to allow his victorious troops the plunder of his rival's city of Mogontiacum, and who dealt with the barbarians before he dealt with his rival,[2] the meaning of these events becomes clear: there was no secessionist movement in Britain, but an able and unscrupulous soldier took advantage for his own profit of the dismembered conditions of the Empire. The picture sketched by the Panegyrist of the loyalty of the British provinces, 'tandem liberi tandemque Romani tandem vera imperii luce *recreati*', seems to be justified.[3]

### THE PALMYRENE KINGDOM

The rebellion of Carausius is closer in spirit to the rise of the Palmyrene power than to the sad divorce, the *triste discidium*, of the Gallic provinces. The Palmyrene kingdom was regarded by contemporary and later writers as not merely non-Roman but anti-Roman, and its elevation as an invasion of the Empire from without, particularly contrasted with the civil wars that racked the Empire from within.[4] The titles that the Palmyrene kings took, to support their claim to rule over Roman provinces, were irregular. Gallienus and Aurelian had recognized them under the form of *rex imperator dux Romanorum*.[5] Vaballath finally called himself 'Augustus' to assert his independence,[6] but neither he nor Zenobia could seduce the affections of the city populations from Rome. When Aurelian appeared with an army, the cities rose in his

---

[1] Mattingly and Sydenham, op. cit. 429.

[2] Victor, *de Caesaribus* 33. 8, 'explosa Germanorum multitudine . . . (Laeliano) fuso . . . Mogontiacorum direptiones quia Laelianum iuverant abnuisset'.

[3] *Pan.* 8. 19. 2. 'At last free, at last Roman, at last restored by the true glory of the Empire.'

[4] Cf. P. Damerau, op. cit. 54 f. E.g. *Pan.* 8. 10. 2, 'tunc se nimium et Parthus extulerat et Palmyrensus aequaverat', contrasted with 'tota Aegyptus Syriaeque defecerant'; cf. *Or. Sib.* 13. 111, Ῥωμαίους ὀλέσουσι Σύροι Πέρσῃσι μιγέντες. Zosimus 1. 52. 3, who contrasts the Palmyrene forces composed ἔκ τε αὐτῶν Παλμυρηνῶν καὶ τῶν ἄλλων ὅσοι τῆς στρατείας αὐτοῖς εἵλοντο μετασχεῖν ( = Σύρων καὶ βαρβάρων, 44. 1) with the Roman armies, ibid. 52. 3 and 4, from Dalmatia, Moesia, Pannonia, Noricum, Syria, Phoenicia, etc.

[5] L. Homo, *Essai sur le règne de l'Empereur Aurélien*, 48 n. 4, 67.

[6] Ibid. 82.

favour.[1] The final destruction of Palmyra proves the complete distrust felt for the independent state which had ended by seeking Persian aid against Rome,[2] and contrasts strongly with the attitude of the emperors towards lost provinces whose recovery and 'restoration' were at this time the object of all effort.[3] This collapse of the Palmyrene power shows how strong a feeling of loyalty, in the East, was opposed to particularist sentiment of the narrow type shown by the Palmyrene kings. The element common to the three provincial dynasties under discussion is the claim to 'legitimacy' and the aping of Roman formulae. This was doubtless inevitable in the West, but the Palmyrene kingdom had extraneous roots. Here the assumption of the imperial titles must be due to the necessity of placating provincial feeling, and means that the Syrians and Asiatics would only accept a 'Roman' monarch. As *rex* Vaballath could claim authority only in Palmyra; to rule in Syria he must be 'Augustus', but even then he was only tolerated until a truly legitimate emperor appeared.[4]

## *STATUS ROMANUS* IN THE THIRD AND FOURTH CENTURIES

Where there is anti-Roman feeling in the third century, it takes the form of social disturbance, class movement rather than national rising. In Gaul there are the *Bagaudae*, men driven to brigandage by the hardness of the times.[5] But the main issue in the third century was not nationalism or imperialism or yet social revolution, but the struggle to save the Empire from the barbarians: this is set in the first place by every source, however meagre,[6] and must take precedence even over the very real

[1] Note Zosimus 1. 50, 1, εἰ μὴ βεβασιλευκέναι γνόντες Αὐρηλιανὸν τὴν Παλμυρηνῶν ἀπεσείσαντο προστασίαν (Βιθυνοί); cf. 51. 2, i.e. Antioch, 50. 2, Ancyra, Tyana, 52. 3, Apameia, Larissa, Arethusa; cf. 54. 1, καὶ τοὺς Ἐμισηνοὺς ἀλλοτρίως πρὸς αὐτὴν ἔχοντας.     [2] Zosimus 1. 55. 1, and 61. 1.

[3] Below, 456 nn. 1-4.     [4] Cf. above, n. 1.

[5] Cf. *Pan.* 5. 14. 3, 'quam multi ... quos inopia latitare per saltus aut etiam in exilium ire compulerat ... in patriam revertuntur ... desinunt odisse agrorum suorum sterilitatem', cf. 9. 4. 1 and 10. 4. 3, 'cum militaris habitus ignari agricolae appetiverunt ... cum hostem barbarum suorum cultorum rusticus vastator imitatus est', cf. Victor, op. cit. 39. 17.

[6] e.g. Victor, op. cit. 33. 3, 'rem Romanam quasi naufragio dedit (Gallienus) ... adeo uti Thraciam Gothi ... Mesopotamiam Parthi ... Alemannorum vis ... Italiam, Francorum gentes direpta Gallia Hispaniam possiderent ... amissa trans Istrum quae Traianus quaesiverat'; cf. Zosimus 1. 58. 4, ἐπειδὰν δὲ εἰς ἐκείνους

internal discord and oppression, from which the provincials sought relief not in nationalistic risings but in the imperial power itself, so that the crisis strengthened rather than weakened the hold of the Roman name on the Roman world.[1]

This new contrast of Roman and Barbarian, in which *Romanus* means both 'a provincial subject of Rome' and 'a foundation member of the Roman state', and, after the Constitutio Antoniniana, 'a Roman citizen', finds its complete expression in the works of the Gallic Panegyrists addressed to the *consortes*, Diocletian and Maximian, and their successors. These orations, being written for, and sometimes delivered to an imperial audience, give a highly one-sided account of *events*, but in their terminology they seem to reveal both the way in which men thought and spoke about the Roman world, and the leading hopes and fears of the Gallic nobility,[2] while on some topics, not directly concerned with the glory of the emperors, they supply valuable and trustworthy information about facts.[3] At times they even let slip something that tells against their picture of imperial harmony.[4]

The theme of all these panegyrists is simply that the Roman world has been saved from frightful disaster by the actions of the emperors concerned.[5] The language is largely drawn from a common stock, and is colourless and trite, but the feeling is none the less real, and the writers, though bound to celebrate only the glories of the hero of the hour, have a precise appreciation of what had been achieved. The author of *Pan.* vi was not led astray by the mere desire to praise Constantine's family, when he said that it was Claudius Gothicus 'qui Romani imperii

---

ἀφίκωμαι τοὺς χρόνους ἐν οἷς ἡ Ῥωμαίων ἀρχὴ κατὰ βραχὺ βαρβαρωθεῖσα εἰς ὀλίγον τι καὶ αὐτὸ διαφθαρὲν περιέστη of the period of Aurelian; cf. 4. 59. 3, βαρβάρων οἰκητήριον γέγονεν. These are formal recognitions of the new state of affairs in parenthesis to their regular account of the period; cf. the *Pan. passim*, especially 8. 10.

[1] This latter aspect tends to be rather neglected in Rostovtzeff's and others' treatment of the so-called social revolution; e.g. C. v. Sickle, 'Particularism in the Roman Empire', *Am. J. Phil.* 51. 343 ff. For bibliography of this subject cf. P. Damerau, *Kaiser Claudius Gothicus*, 48 n. 3.

[2] e.g. their landed interests, 5. 6; 8. 21; 9. 18.

[3] e.g. Eumenius' account of his school in 9, and the internal condition of the *civitas Aeduorum* in 5. 4; 5; 11; 14.

[4] e.g. the unrest among the *rusticani*, 10. 4. 3.

[5] e.g. 10. 5, 'cum omnes barbariae nationes excidium Galliae minitarentur ... Burgundiones et Alamanni ... Chaibones Erulique ... quis deus tam insperatam salutem nobis attulisset nisi tu adfuisses?'

solutam et perditam disciplinam primus reformavit'.[1] Similarly the author of *Pan.* 12 sums up Constantine's achievement truly, though the language is that of courtly panegyric, when he announces his intention to make a speech 'de recuperata urbe imperioque Romano tandem ex diuturna convulsione solidato'.[2]

The good sense here shown suggests that it will not be wasted labour to consider what these men say in detail about the world of their own day. The word *Romanus* is frequently used to mark the contrast between civilized peoples subject to Rome and barbarian invaders. The new sense of this word is far more explicit than in Tertullian, e.g. 'omnem illam rabiem extra terminos huius imperii in terras hostium distulistis . . . etenim . . . ruunt omnes in sanguinem suum populi quibus nunquam contigit esse Romanis'.[3] 'Nemo fere Romanus occiderit imperio vincente Romano. Omnes enim illos . . . campos . . . non nisi taeterrimorum hostium corpora fusa texerunt.'[4] The word is applied to lands as much as to men, e.g. 'quicquid ultra Rhenum prospicio Romanum est.'[5] Another passage, concerned with the quasi-university city of Augustodunum, shows that for these writers the word expressed a great deal more than a merely political bond: 'pater tuus civitatem Aeduorum voluit iacentem erigere . . . ut esset illa civitas provinciarum velut una mater quae reliquas urbes quodam modo Romanas prima fecisset.'[6]

The writers of these phrases are well aware that they are also Galli, and of their various peculiarities.[7] They make profuse

---

[1] 6. 2. 2. 'Who first restored the broken and perished discipline of the Roman empire.'

[2] 12. 1. 3. 'About the recovery of Rome and the final strengthening of the empire after lengthy upheaval.'

[3] 11. 16. 5, cf. 8. 19. 2, 'tandem liberi tandemque Romani'. 'You have expelled all that madness from the boundaries of the empire to the lands of the enemy. For all nations which have not the fortune to be Roman are rushing at each other's throats.'

[4] 8. 16. 3, 'No Roman perished in the victory of the Roman empire. Only the beastly enemy's dead bodies covered that battlefield.'

[5] 10. 7. 7, cf. 8. 10. 4, 'toto orbe terrarum non modo qua Romanus fuerat . . . sed etiam qua hostilis edomito', and ibid. 20. 2, 'tenet uno pacis amplexu Romana respublica quidquid variis temporum vicibus fuit aliquando Romanum'. 'Whatever I see beyond the Rhine is Roman.'

[6] 5. 4. 4. 'Your father wished to revive the prostrate city of the Aedui so that the city which first made the other peoples of the provinces Roman should be their metropolis.'

[7] e.g. 5. 3. 2, on the 'fraternitatis nomen', 8. 9. 2, 'insultare . . . communi Galliarum nomine libet'.

apologies for their rustic Latin—*incultum Transalpini sermonis horrorem*;[1] they speak of the use of the Latin language as a late arrival in Gaul, calling it, characteristically, *eloquentia Romana*.[2] It is impossible not to treat seriously these expressions of the feeling that the Gauls were integral parts of a Roman world at the same time that, and because, they were, in relation to the emperor, *his* provinces, *suae Galliae*.[3] These same writings make it clear that this sense of *Romanitas* had been sharpened by the conflict with the German peoples. Hatred and fear of *barbaria*, a noun which now makes its appearance in common use to correspond with a familiar fact, frequently find expression in phrases like the exultant cry, 'arat ergo nunc mihi Chamavus et Frisius et vagus ille praedator . . . frequentat nundinas meas pecore venali, et cultor barbarus laxat annonam'.[4] Or else the writers enumerate with joy the destruction of the hostile hosts.[5] Sometimes the two elements of the contrast are brought together in a single sentence —'(Britannia) ad conspectum Romanae lucis emersit aut haec ipsa quae modo desinit esse barbaria . . . feritate Francorum velut hausta'.[6]

This survey of the theory and practice of the third century shows that the effect of the invasions was to consolidate the heritage of the past, rendering explicit and universal what had been but dimly felt before when men were not forced to cast their reckoning. All the earlier features of panegyric expression are here, but the reality of the feeling is heightened by the reality of the dangers which threatened. Whereas the emperors of the second century exhibited a supererogatory generosity towards their subjects, Diocletian and his peers sought not to embellish but

[1] 'The rusticity of Gallic speech' 2. 1. 3, cf. 12. 1. 2, 'si quidem Latine et diserte loqui illis (Romanis) ingeneratum est nobis elaboratum'.

[2] 9. 19. 4.

[3] e.g. 8. 6. 1; 9. 6. 1; 10. 14. 3; 12. 21. 5, cf. the letter of the emperor, 9. 14. 1, 'merentur et Galli nostri' etc.

[4] 8. 9. 3. 'So the vagabond brigands of Chamavi and Frisi now plough my lands, and barbarian tenants bring flocks to sell at my market and lower the price of corn.'

[5] e.g. the long passage in 10. 5; cf. the sneers at the Franks, 12. 22. 3, 'gens levis et lubrica', ibid. 24. 2, the 'trux Francus' is contracted with the disciplined 'miles Romanus'.

[6] 9. 18. 3, cf. 7. 14. 1, 'te indefessum ire per limites qua Romanum barbaris gentibus instat imperium'. 'Britain has emerged to see the Roman light, or this land too which now ceases to be barbarian, though worn out by the savagery of the Franks.'

to save and restore the ruined *civitates*.[1] Rome and the emperors, because their cause is identified with a peaceful state of society which has become exceptional, receive a devotion beyond that of the second century when the *pax Augusta* represented a normal condition. That the centripetal tendency was accentuated rather than discouraged by the *triste discidium* of the third century is shown by the close examination of the so-called separatist movements,[2] and of other, minor, events. The schoolmaster who says of his map, 'nunc demum iuvat orbem spectare depictum cum in illo nihil videmus alienum',[3] is allied in spirit to that other pedagogue who collected an army to help Septimius Severus, and went into retirement without awaiting reward.[4] The curious attempt of the Civitas Aeduorum to give Constantine a right royal welcome reveals the same feeling; the panegyrist naïvely admits that 'omnia signa collegiorum omnium deorum nostrorum simulacra per compendia saepius tibi occursura protulimus'.[5] More serious in interest is the continued employment of imperial titles to honour the municipality: 'omnium sis licet dominus urbium . . . nos tamen etiam nomen accepimus tuum; iam non antiquum Bibracte, quod hucusque dicta est Julia, Polia, Florentia sed Flavia est Civitas Aeduorum'.[6]

The evidence is limited to the official utterances of an official class; sometimes this characteristic is made oddly conspicuous, e.g. 'sensisti Roma tandem arcem te omnium gentium . . . cum ex omnibus provinciis optimates viros curiae tuae pignerareris ut senatus dignitas . . . ex totius orbis flore constaret'.[7] Yet there is reason to believe that the sentiments which have been discussed were not limited to aristocratic circles. In these very speeches it

[1] Cf. 9. 4. 3; 5. 4. 4.

[2] Above, 446. Cf. 5. 4. 2, '(Aedui) Claudium . . . ad recuperandas Gallias primi sollicitaverunt'.

[3] 9. 21. 3. 'Now at last it is a pleasure to look at a map of the world, as we see nothing in it that is not Roman.'

[4] Dio Cassius, 76. 5.

[5] 5. 8. 4. 'We produced all the banners of our clubs, all the statues of all our Gods, and brought them round by the by-ways to meet you again and again.'

[6] 5. 14. 5. 'Though you are lord of all cities, we too have taken your name—old Bibracte no longer, once called Julia Polia Florentia, it is now called the Flavian city of the Aedui.'

[7] 4. 35. 2, cf. 9. 5. 4, 'hi quos ad spem omnium tribunalium . . . aut . . . ad ipsa palatii magisteria provehi oporteret'. 'Rome, you felt you were the citadel of the world, when you took the best of the provincials for your council that the dignity of the senate might consist of the flower of the whole world.'

is evident that both the terrors and the relief had been shared by all classes,[1] though often the writers speak from the standpoint of landed gentry alone.[2] In the epigraphic evidence from other parts of the Empire, the lower classes of the population, notably the *coloni*, regard the emperor as the man who not only can but will grant them aid,[3] in much the same way as the Civitas Aeduorum sought and gained assistance.[4]

To complete the picture of what *status Romanus* meant to the generality of the inhabitants of the declining Empire, it is necessary to pass beyond the limits of the badly documented third century. There are many incidents recorded in the history of the succeeding period which can only be understood as the final issue of a long process. It is reasonable to argue back from such evidence to the conditions of the previous age, and thus to establish on a firm basis the case that is at present built upon the somewhat suspect testimony of the *Panegyrici Scriptores*.

In Zosimus the contrast between Romani and Barbari has lost nothing of its vigour, but the bare outline is filled in with more detail.[5] When Jovian ceded Nisibis and other territories to the Persians, after the defeat of Julian, the inhabitants of the city showed the greatest reluctance to accept a new master, 'they urged that the Romans should not set them to experience barbarian manners after being educated for so many centuries in Roman civilization.'[6] In the end the city-dwellers of Nisibis

---

[1] e.g. the *c. Aeduorum* is assisted by a 20 per cent cut in its census assessment, and the remission of arrears, 5. 11; this would assist the 'rusticani vacillantes in aere alieno', ibid. 6. 2, as much as the 'latitantes per saltus', ibid. 14. 3. For the disasters which touched the smaller folk cf. 5. 6. 2, 'inopia rusticanorum', and 8. 21. 2, the disappearance of *artifices*, cf. 9. 4. 3.

[2] e.g. 5. 6. 1; 8. 9. 3 and 21. 1; 10. 4. 3.

[3] Relevant texts, conveniently collected in *A. and J.*, 139–44, cover the period 180 to *c.* 250, and link with earlier petitions to Hadrian and Commodus (ibid. 93, 111). Or *FIRA* i², 101, 103, 106–7.

[4] e.g. *Pan.* 5. 4. 3–4, cf. the 'Epistula de constitutione civitatis Tymandenorum', *ILS* 6090, and ibid. 6091, 'De iure civitatis Orcistanorum', in *circa* A.D. 330.

[5] The usual contrast is between the *barbari* and οἱ ὑπὸ τοῖς Ῥωμαίοις, e.g. 3. 6. 2, τὴν ὑπὸ Φράγγων . . . γῆν . . . τὴν ὑπήκοον Ῥωμαίοις. But in the later books he uses Ῥωμαῖος alone in the new sense, e.g. 4. 31. 1, ἦν οὐδὲ Ῥωμαίου διάκρισις ἢ βαρβάρου. Ibid. 34. 5, Σκύθας μηκέτι Ῥωμαίοις παρενοχλεῖν, ibid. 58. 5, προσήκει Ῥωμαίους ὄντας ( = certain rebels) ὡς τὸν βασιλέα . . . ἐπανελθεῖν, 5. 17. 2, συνέπιπτον . . . οἱ . . . βάρβαροι Ῥωμαίων παντί: ibid. 22. 2, πρὸς Ῥωμαίους ἐπανελθεῖν means to cross the Danube and return to Roman territory.

[6] ἐκλιπαρούντων . . . μὴ . . . εἰς πεῖραν καταστῆσαι βαρβάρων ἠθῶν τοσαύτη ἐτῶν ἑκατοντὰς τοῖς Ῥωμαίων νόμοις ἐντεθραμμένους. Zosimus 3. 33. 2.

emigrated to Amida, while 'the folk of the tribes and the strongholds', the country population, remained to endure Persian rule.[1]
Both elements in the story, the appreciation of Roman law and
the distinction between the attitude of city and country to Rome,
have appeared before. New is the translation of idea into action,
and the indication that, while loyalty might depend upon social
distinctions, the criterion was not one of class in the modern
sense, but of way of life or even of type of civilization. The
connection of laws and civilization with a certain type of life,
city-life, and the reason why the 'cities' so value the *status
Romanus* is perhaps self-evident; but there is another incident
in Zosimus which shows how conscious the subjects of Rome in
general were of what they had to lose. Certain Egyptian soldiers,
marching in company with some barbarian troops of Theodosius,[2]
tried to restrain the latter from robbing and maltreating the
provincial cities through which they passed, instead of buying
their provisions in an orderly fashion: 'This was not the behaviour', said the Egyptians, 'of men that were ready to live
according to the laws of the Romans.'[3] In all this there appears
a new conception of *Romanitas* which somewhat resembles the
development of Hellenism that resulted from the teaching of
Isocrates, and achieved practical expression in the spreading of
the Hellenistic civilization among the non-Greek peoples of the
nearer East.

The reason why the element of cultural unity is heavily
stressed in these anecdotes is not far to seek. The two orders,
barbarian and Roman, no longer faced one another on the
opposite sides of the imperial frontiers, but existed side by side
within the Empire as joint tenants. The Roman world was fast
becoming a 'dwelling place for Barbarians'.[4] They were first
admitted in the second century, saving a few experiments of the
early Principate, but it was the third century that first knew
wholesale invasion. Perhaps there was still some hope even then
that they could be kept within reasonable limits or driven out.
But in the fourth century men had grown accustomed to the fact

---

[1] οἱ τῶν ἐθνῶν καὶ τῶν φρουρίων οἰκήτορες. Zosimus 3. 34. 1.

[2] 4. 30.

[3] μὴ γὰρ εἶναι τοῦτο ἔργον ἀνθρώπων κατὰ Ῥωμαίων νόμους ζῆν ἐθελόντων. ibid. 30.
4. Cf. also 1. 71. 1, Πρόβος . . . Βαστέρνας . . . ὑποπεσόντας . . κατῴκισε Θρᾳκίοις
χωρίοις. καὶ διετέλεσαν τοῖς Ῥωμαίων βιοτεύοντες νόμοις.

[4] Zosimus 4. 59. 3.

that the barbarians could not be permanently dislodged, and that they were not good neighbours.[1] The *gens levis et lubrica Francorum*, with the treachery known to the panegyric writers,[2] was responsible for an incident of the fourth century when one Gaines, admittedly a rebel, massacred the Roman deserters who had joined him.[3]

'To be a Roman' or 'to be under the laws of the Romans' was thus a formula which comprehended all the subdivisions and categories of the Roman world; its implication is that such peoples formed a corporate body whose activity was regulated by more civilized standards than those recognized by the barbarians, within or without the Empire. That the distinction was cultural rather than ethnical is brought out clearly by the description of the general Fravittus, 'a man barbarian by race but otherwise a Greek, not only in external aspect but in mental outlook and in religious piety'.[4] The equation of Hellene and Roman goes back to the second century.[5] Zosimus' use of the term in this cultural context is due to his anti-Christian prejudices. Fravittus is singled out for praise because he was not only a civilized man but a pious pagan ;[6] but perhaps a more important point is the recognition that *barbari* is a relative term: the *Orbis Romanus* could assimilate even them, provided that they were willing. The first stage in such a process appears in the description of Baudon and Arbogast as 'Franks by race and very loyal to Rome',[7] and is summed up by a panegyrist as 'receptus in leges Francus'.[8] That the same conception of the unifying bond of civilization is contained in Aurelius Victor's phrase *status Romanus* is shown by a periphrasis which he once employs —'per omnes terras qua ius Romanum est (renovatae urbes)'.[9]

While these later writers agree in their appreciation of the

---

[1] e.g. Zosimus, 5. 13. 2, ἦρχε δὲ οὐ Ῥωμαικῶν ἰλῶν ἀλλὰ βαρβάρων ἐνιδρυμένων τῇ Φρυγίᾳ, a casual reference.

[2] Cf. *Pan.* 12. 22. 3.　　　　　　　　　　　　　　　　[3] Zosimus, 5. 21. 9.

[4] ἄνδρα βάρβαρος μὲν τὸ γένος, Ἕλληνα δὲ ἄλλως οὐ τρόπῳ μόνον ἀλλὰ καὶ προαιρέσει καὶ τῇ περὶ τὰ θεῖα θρησκείᾳ. Zosimus, 5. 20. 1.

[5] Above, 428 f.

[6] Cf. 4. 59. 3, where Zosimus ascribes the fall of Rome to the neglect of the *patrii ritus*.

[7] Φράγγοι τὸ γένος εὐνοί τε σφόδρα Ῥωμαίοις. Ibid. 4. 33. 2.

[8] *Pan.* 8. 21. 1. 'The Frankish folk were received into the Roman system.'

[9] Victor, *de Caesaribus* 9. 8; for *status Romanus*, see 24. 9; 39. 48. '(Cities were restored) throughout all lands where Roman authority held sway.'

Roman state or the Roman world as it was in their day, they are also familiar with the historical growth of the Roman power, and describe the Empire as the Empire of, belonging or subject to, the Romans. This dualism is made possible by the fact that, while strictly 'the provincial peoples', *populus Romanus, omnes gentes*, etc. were after the Constitutio Antoniniana interchangeable terms—always excepting the new categories of *foederati*, and *laeti*—at the same time all were the subjects of the emperor. This distinction is recognized in a remarkable passage of Zosimus, where he considers the Empire as the 'possession' of the Romans, and inquires whether they had ever lost any parts of it until the time of Jovian.[1] He surveys the history of the eastern provinces under the Republic, and decides that until the 'monarchy' nothing was lost despite many disasters, and that later none of the 'kings', not even Valerian, let slip any of the Roman possessions, until the death of Julian. But then 'the death of the emperor sufficed for the loss of these provinces, so that so far the kings of the Romans have been unable to recover any of them, and indeed have also lost the greater part of the other provinces gradually, some becoming free and some being surrendered to the barbarians'.[2] Gradually in this consciously historical passage Zosimus slips into the language of the later age. Instead of 'the kings' losing the provinces of the Roman people, it is the 'kings of the Romans' who lose 'their' provinces, which are either freed from the central power of the 'kings'—not of the Romans since the provincial peoples are the Romans—or as units of a Roman world are surrendered, like Nisibis, to the barbarians.

Among all these indications there is little that is new in the attitude of the post-Severan centuries towards Rome; even the quantitative completion of the unitary state by the Constitutio Antoniniana had been anticipated by her admirers themselves. The novelty consists in the strength and consistency with which the ideas are presented in the literature of a time when the material facts of daily life seemed to contradict in detail the grand claim which was made for Rome. This new fervour is due in part to the reassessment of values forced upon the world by the collapse

---

[1] 3. 32. 1–6.

[2] Ibid. 6. ἡ . . . τοῦ αὐτοκράτορος τελευτὴ πρὸς τὴν τούτων ἀπώλειαν ἤρκεσεν ὥστε ἄχρι τοῦδε μηδὲν δυνηθῆναι τούτων τοὺς Ῥωμαίων βασιλέας ἀναλαβεῖν, ἀλλὰ καὶ προσαπολέσαι κατὰ βραχὺ τὰ πλείονα τῶν ἐθνῶν, τὰ μὲν αὐτόνομα γεγονότα τὰ δὲ βαρβάροις ἐκδεδομένα.

of the *pax Romana*, but it also draws strength from the ancient familiarity of the ideas which were now made explicit, and of the beliefs which gained an added popularity at the very time when the material ground for them was beginning to melt away. All this will become clear after a study of the language of those writers who lived when the western half of the Empire was rapidly decomposing, notably St. Augustine, Rutilius Namatianus, and Claudian.

# XX

# THE RETROSPECTIVE PANEGYRISTS

WHAT St. Augustine, who is not a 'panegyrical writer', says explicitly about Rome is less remarkable than the implication of the metaphor which forms the basis of his book *De Civitate Dei.* Throughout this work he assumes that the idea of the unity of the Roman world in a single earthly state, the *civitas terrestris,* is familiar to his readers, and this implies that the equation of *Orbis Terrarum* with *civitas Romana,* in the sense of the Roman state, was an accepted belief in his day.[1]

Augustine can pass from a consideration of the Roman state and of the sack of the City itself to a defence of the kingdom of Christ, the 'peregrina civitas Christi regis', and then combine the two in the statement that 'perplexae sunt . . . istae duae civitates in hoc saeculo . . . donec ultimo iudicio dirimantur'.[2] The Roman Empire provides him with numerous parables of which the point is that there is only one *civitas terrestris,* of which all men are citizens.[3] There is doubtless an admixture of Christian terminology in the occasional contrast 'earthly' and 'heavenly', *terrestris* and *superna,* but the parentage of the metaphor is otherwise entirely Roman. This is shown by the frequent conjunction of the *civitas terrestris* with the *imperium Romanorum,* as well as by parallels which Augustine draws between the *cives* and the *munera* of the two states,[4] and by the common contrast between the earthly state doomed to perish at the last day—which was precisely the

---

[1] The evidence is to be found *passim* in the early books; in 2. 69 of the *Retractationes* he states that the following books contain 'exortum duarum civitatum . . . excursum earum . . . fines', and this resolves itself into a sketch of the history of the Roman Empire; cf. Lib. 1 *Preface,* where 'de terrena civitate quae cum dominari adpetit' refers to Virgil, *Aeneid* 6. 853. Cf., e.g., 5. 18, 'pro hac . . . terrena (civitate) filios Brutus potuit et occidere', 1. 36, 'Romanae reipublicae clades . . . et mala quae illa civitas pertulit vel ad eius imperium provinciae pertinentes'. For *civitas* as *orbis* see 5. 25, 'universum orbem Romanum unus Augustus tenuit et defendit'.

[2] 1. 35. 'The two states are bound together in this world until they are separated by the last judgement'.

[3] e.g. 5. 16, and *ad fin.* 'quanta dilectio debeatur supernae civitati . . . si tantum a suis civibus terrena dilecta est'.

[4] 5. 18; *ad fin.* p. 228 (Teubner) illustrates all these points.

Christian belief about the Empire[1]—and the 'eternal city' of the Christians.[2] The use of the epithet *peregrina* instead of *superna* or *caelestis* is likewise only intelligible if the contrast is not merely with 'this' world but with this world considered in a particular aspect.

The employment of this metaphor without explanation or apology shows not only that the Roman world had been unified in the course of time by the various processes that have been discussed, but that one of those processes ended by dominating the rest. It is the merging of the many peoples in the one *civitas* that is the leading idea both in Augustine[3] and in all of the last panegyrists.[4] Augustine describes almost in technical language how 'fieret ut omnes ad imperium Romanum pertinentes societatem acciperent civitatis et Romani cives essent', adding the comment 'ac sic esset omnium quod erat ante paucorum'.[5] But this is not all; for him as for the others Rome was also the great lawgiver: 'subiugatis imposuerunt leges suas . . . neque enim et Romani non vivebant sub legibus suis'.[6]

The subordinate theme of the majesty of Rome is familiar to Augustine, but is naturally treated from the Christian point of view.[7] In his attitude to the Empire he simply expands what had been established by Tertullian, that the Empire was due to the will of God,[8] that it was the reward of earthly virtue and was necessary to the earthly order.[9] He even justifies the existence of the pagans as being better instruments for the service of the divinely willed Empire: 'eos . . . utiliores esse terrenae civitati'.[10] There is also in Augustine the acceptance of the City itself as the symbol of the majesty of Rome, and the common confusion of the *Urbs* in the literal sense with the *Urbs* or *Civitas* in the

---

[1] Above, 436.

[2] Cf. the contrasted chapters 5. 15 and 16, 'de mercede temporali' and 'de mercede sanctorum civium civitatis aeternae'.

[3] e.g. 5. 15 and 17, quoted below, n. 6.          [4] Below, 464 f.

[5] 5. 17. 'It came about that all subjects of the Roman empire received the bond of citizenship and became Roman citizens, so that the privilege of the few was given to all.'

[6] 5. 17. Also cf. 5. 15, 'imperii sui leges imposuerunt multis gentibus'. 'They imposed their laws on the conquered, for the Romans too lived in accordance with laws of their own.'

[7] e.g. 5. 13, 'voluit Deus et Occidentale fieri . . . imperii latitudine et magnitudine illustrius (quam regna Orientis).'

[8] 5. 1.                                         [9] 5. 15, cf. 5. 18.

[10] 5. 19, p. 230, 'they are more useful for the earthly state'.

juristic sense.[1] Like others he makes the point that 'multi senatores sunt in aliis terris qui Romam ne facie quidem norunt'.[2]

From every test Augustine emerges as the typical intelligent
citizen who understands and accepts the Roman claim in its
entirety, saving only the concessions made necessary by the
Christian view that the eternity of Rome was relative to the
existence of the temporal order. His testimony is more impressive
because he is not an official panegyrist, and his admissions are
largely incidental or implicit. It is legitimate to assume that
what he accepted was accepted by his audience, the educated
Christians of his time, lay, clerical and monastic, perhaps even
by the ordinary congregation of the faithful.

The famous letter in which St. Jerome laments the capture of
Rome confirms the evidence of St. Augustine. He touches cur-
sorily upon the theme of the unity of the Roman world in the
words: 'capitur urbs quae totum cepit orbem',[3] but his letter is
more remarkable for the introduction of a new feeling which
grows ever more important with the crumbling of the Empire.
This is the sense of pity and regret for the failing power, and of
awe at the disasters befalling the Roman world. Jerome goes out
of his way to express his emotion with the help of quotations
from the Old Testament and from Virgil.[4] This sentiment is
different from the anger and fear felt by the writers of the third
century towards the barbarians.[5] It is inspired by the sense of
loss rather than of dread, and is close akin to the attitude of the
last books of the Sibylline Oracles.[6] It does not seem to touch
Augustine, although he records it of others; his words, 'exitium
vestrum . . . plangentibus orientalibus populis et maximis civitatibus in remotissimis terris publicum luctum maeroremque ducen-
tibus', are all the better evidence for the widespread existence of
a feeling which he himself did not share.[7]

[1] e.g. the transition in 5. 17, 'sic esset omnium quod erat ante paucorum; tantum quod plebs illa . . . de publico viveret'. In 2. 2, the symbolism is explicit, 'longe
ab eis Romanis degeneres . . . Romam foediorem stantem fecerant quam ruentem,
quando quidem in ruina eius lapides et ligna, in istorum autem vita omnia non
murorum sed morum munimenta . . . ceciderunt'.

[2] 5. 17. 'There are many senators in other lands who have not even seen Rome.'
[3] *Ep.* 127. 12. 1. 'The city is being taken that made the whole world its own.'
[4] Ibid. 2–3. The actual quotations, 'nocte Moab capta est . . . Deus, venerunt
gentes in hereditatem tuam', and Virgil, *Aen.* 2. 361–5 and 369, leave no doubt as
to Jerome's feelings.          [5] Above, 452 ff.          [6] Above, 430.
[7] *De c. Dei.* i. 33, 'Eastern peoples and great cities in the farthest parts of the
world are bewailing your destruction with public mourning and sorrow.'

This elegiac motive is present in all the panegyrical literature of the fifth century, and seems, as Augustine hints, to increase its strength in inverse proportion to the closeness of the city of Rome to the people concerned. Rutilius, who saw the city after the sack, is somewhat frigid in his treatment of the theme.[1] He compares Stilicho, because he was thought to have assisted the Goths, to the matricide Nero; but the lines[2]

> Hic immortalem, mortalem perculit ille,
> hic mundi matrem perculit, ille suam,

are very tame when set beside the words of his contemporary Jerome, 'terribilis de occidente rumor adfertur obsideri Romam'.[3] This comparison shows how much the Roman Empire and its outward symbol, the City, meant to the provincials, and how deeply rooted in their hearts this sentiment was. Certainly the less real the power of the Empire became, the more men wanted it, as long as the old traditions were remembered.

The past achievement of Rome is summed up by Rutilius in his famous poem; he incorporates all the familiar themes, presenting the age-long conception of the majesty of the Roman power as an introduction to the panegyrical passage.[4] In this, it is worth noting that the essential connection between the idea of the world-state and that of 'Rome the lawgiver' is very heavily stressed.[5] He returns several times to this latter Virgilian conception in such lines as 'Tu quoque legiferis mundum complexa triumphis', 'Porrige victuras Romana in saecula leges'.[6] While *Romanitas* is recognized as a quality which belongs to the whole Roman world, Rutilius makes the same easy transition from the glories of the Roman Empire to the glories of the imperial city

---

[1] *De reditu suo*, 2. 41–60.

[2] Ibid. 59–60. 'One slew an immortal, the other a mortal; one slew the world's mother, the other his own'.

[3] Loc. cit. 1. 'A frightful report came from the West that Rome was being besieged.'

[4] Op. cit. 1. 1–18, e.g. 3, 'quid longum toto Romam venerantibus aevo?'

[5] Ibid. 46–154; 56–66 are devoted to the theme of *communis patria* and *orbis Romanus*; 69–80 deal with the *pax Romana*; 87–92 with the peculiar genius of Rome, e.g. 'nec tibi nascenti plures animaeque manusque, sed plus consilii iudiciique fuit'; 93–114 deal with the material aspect of Rome; 115–32, her glorious past; 133–40, *aeternitas*; 141–54, prayer for the future.

[6] Ibid. 77; 133, cf. 80, *pacifico iugo*. 'You embraced the world in triumphs which spread your laws.' 'Bestow laws that will last through the centuries of Rome.'

as their symbol,[1] and the same identification of the two as in Augustine, so that he ends a long passage which hymns the Empire and city together by a prayer for the material prosperity of the urban population.[2] This would sound like a ludicrous anti-climax if the symbolism were not both obvious and familiar; but, since it is traditional and corresponds to a genuine belief of the contemporaries of Rutilius, it passes muster.

If Rutilius leaves anything unspoken, Claudian makes ample amends. In one tremendous passage[3] he elaborates the themes of *communis patria* and Rome the lawgiver in the manner of Rutilius, adding nothing that is new, but introducing an idea which, though it first appears in Aristides, is not stressed in any subsequent writer known to us. This is the appreciation of the material unification and organization of the Mediterranean world, from the practical point of view:[4]

> Huius pacificis debemus moribus omnes
> quod veluti patriis regionibus utitur hospes,
> quod sedem mutare licet; quod cernere Thylen
> lusus, et horrendos quondam penetrare recessus;
> quod bibimus passim Rhodanum, potamus Orontem.

This passage demonstrates the real connection between the sentiment of imperial loyalty and all sorts of seemingly separate matters, such as the building of roads and the improvement of communications. In fact Claudian slides directly into the main theme with the words, 'quod cuncti gens una sumus'.[5] In truth all this had been said before; Claudian only adds to the solidity of the tradition. It is the urgent note of pity and despair which is his speciality; whether direct or indirect, this is presented with equal force. When Claudian describes the 'restoration' of the Roman world effected by his heroes,[6] the hyperbole does not deceive;

[1] Ibid.93 ff.

[2] Ibid.151, 'ipse ... Tibris Romuleis famulas usibus aptet aquas' etc. This is the peroration, for in 155 he turns to his personal history.

[3] *De Consulatu Stilichonis* 3. 130–73, cf. *Pan. Probino et Olybrio* 126 ff.

[4] *De Cons. Stil.* 3. 154 ff., cf. Aristides, op. cit. 100–2. 'We all owe to Rome's peaceful ways that the stranger treats other provinces as his homeland; that one may change one's country of residence; that to visit Thule and to reach remote parts which once inspired terror is now a sport; that we drink at our pleasure the waters of the Rhone or quaff the Orontes.'

[5] Ibid. 159. 'That we are all one nation.'

[6] e.g. *de Cons. Stil.* 2. 184–207.

but such passages are not to be dismissed as flattery, since they represent his wishes, hopes, and fears, expressed in the guise of a statement of fact. In such lines as

> vidimus Hesperiam fessasque resurgere gentes,[1]

or

> restituit Stilicho cunctos tibi, Roma, triumphos,[2]

it is fair to see—without prejudice to our opinion of Stilicho—the complement of such passages as

> Quod tantis Romana manus contexuit annis
> proditor unus iners angusto tempore vertit,

or

>                          pulsata
> maiestas Latii deformataeque secures.[3]

Claudian is consoling himself, or making the best of a bad job.

The longing for the return of the lost glories and the feeling for the greatness of Rome are only accentuated by the frank recognition that such days are past,—

> si iuvat imperium penitus de stirpe revelli.[4]

There sentiments explain two peculiarities of Claudian's manner, his resurrection of themes drawn from Rome's Republican, especially early Republican, history, and his extensive invocation of the personified *Roma*. Claudian likes to dwell on the splendours of the imperial period also, the great days of *tranquillique Pii bellatoresque Severi*,[5] but the Republican period has an attraction for him that is not hard to explain.[6] The time of the *Decii pulchri fortesve Metelli* has become legendary, an exhibition of Roman strength in a world apart and untouched by corruption.[7] This interest in the earlier history of Rome, so neglected by the writers of the prosperity of the Empire, is perhaps a general tendency among literary men of the period. Augustine in his analysis

---

[1] *Pan. Probino* 168. 'We saw Hesperia and the weary peoples revive.'

[2] *De Cons. Stil.* 1. 385. 'Stilicho has restored you all your triumphs, Rome.'

[3] *In Rufinum* 2. 52 f.; *In Eutropium* 2. 129. 'The product of centuries of Roman strength a single lazy traitor wasted in a moment.' 'The majesty of Latium is overwhelmed, and the axes shamed.'

[4] In *Rufinum* 2. 207. 'If it is heavens' pleasure that the empire be plucked up by the root.'

[5] *De Sexto Cons. Honorii* 421.

[6] *Passim*, e.g. *de Cons. Stil.* 2. 379–90, *in Eutropium* 1. 441–65, *de Bello Gothico* 124–53, 385–99.         [7] *Pan. Probino* 147.

of the origins of Roman greatness reflects the same feeling, which forms part of the sentimental or elegiac attitude to Rome that emerged when the capture of 'the City' symbolized the final decay of the Western Empire.

The reappearance of the abstract personification of Roma, and the relegation of the dignity of the imperial throne—in the western world—to the second place is part of a similar process. The change is not surprising; the power of the western emperors was broken, while the value and importance of *Romanitas* remained. So in Claudian and Sidonius the expression of loyalty takes the form of panegyrical descriptions and idealized representations of Roma. Yet there is more than the repetition of what Rutilius summed up. It is natural in a formal panegyric to address Roma; but these writers tend to bring in the name of Rome whenever possible, even when the context does not demand it. Such apostrophes are frequent in the semi-historical poems of Claudian; whether his theme is some event or the praises of some man, he likes to connect his story with the praises of Rome as well.[1] But it is in a sort of mythology that this unofficial cult finds its fullest expression. Rome tends to be represented as a goddess in the company of other deities, receiving or giving consolation amid her 'children' —the wretched provinces —or dispatching new heroes to guard her world.[2] Despite the hackneyed conventions a real sentiment makes itself felt, the same mixture of pity and indignation that has already been noted as the characteristic of the period of decline, e.g.

> sum tota in principe, tota
> principis, et fio lacerum de Caesare regnum,
> quae quondam regina fui.[3]

The same idea appears continually. 'Bellatrix Roma' and her glorious past are contrasted with the gloomy present,[4] relieved only by the hope of help from some champion. The opening line

---

[1] e.g. *de Bello Gothico* 51, 77, 96, *de Cons. Stil.* 3. 27, 78.

[2] The whole of the panegyric to Probinus forms an elaborate illustration of this, also the long incident in *Pan. de Sexto Cons. Honorii* 360–493; cf. Sidonius 5. 13–369, 7 *passim*, esp. 17–120, also 2, 387 ff.

[3] Sidonius 7. 102 ff., cf. ibid. 51 ff. 'testor . . . quicquid Roma fui'. 'I exist entirely in the emperor, I am entirely his, and behold, I that was a queen of old am now the despoiled estate of Caesar.'  [4] Ibid. 5. 13 ff.

of the panegyric on Majorian sums up the attitude:

concipe praeteritos, Respublica, mente triumphos.[1]

The spirit of the panegyric writers must be comprehended as a whole. The themes of *communis patria* and *Roma domina gentium* complement one another, while the ardent appreciation of Roman unity is thrown into relief by the frank recognition of the badness of the times.

### CONCLUSION

It might be thought a far cry from the Constitutio Antoniniana to the writings of Sidonius, but the investigation has sought to show the solidarity both of the panegyrical and of the historical tradition throughout the limits of this long period. The importance of Caracallus' measure in completing the material basis for the idealistic theory of the *civitas* is clear; but that measure itself would have been meaningless and without effect, had it not been based in turn upon a rich medley of Romano-centric interests, some of which have been analysed above. The supervention of the barbarian invasions had the effect of stressing, in a way that no inhabitant of the Empire could miss, the advantages of the Roman order, and thus of increasing the force of the Romano-centric tendency, and of securing for it literary expression in terms that became ever more explicit as the triumph of barbarism advanced. Maybe this emotion was limited to the upper classes of society, and to the urban populations; but evidence has been adduced which suggests that at least during the first three centuries of the Empire this is largely untrue, and that the benefits of the Roman peace affected all alike. It is at least reasonably certain that the final attitude of those elements of the Roman world, which gave literary or epigraphic expression to their thoughts about Rome, can only be explained by postulating a high degree of loyalty permeating a considerable percentage of the provincial populations. This feeling of loyalty in turn manifests itself in various ways, which make it possible not only to work back from the panegyrical writers to a postulate, but to build up in historical sequence, from the earliest days of the Republic, the order of events or impulses by which the Orbis not only became but was recognized to be the Urbs.

[1] Sidonius 5. 1. 'Consider, commonwealth of Rome, the triumphs of your past.'

# BIBLIOGRAPHY

INDIVIDUAL articles upon particular points are cited in the footnotes to the text. The nature of the subject makes it impossible to provide a complete bibliography, but the following list contains the basic discussions of the major themes down to 1939 which are relevant to a study of the Roman citizenship.

## REPUBLICAN PERIOD

ASHBY, T. *The Roman Campagna in Classical Times.* London, 1927.
BELOCH, K. *Der Italische Bund (It.B.).*
—— *Römische Geschichte (RG).*
DE SANCTIS, G. *Storia dei Romani.*
FRANK, T. *Economic History of Rome.*
—— *Roman Imperialism.*
—— *Economic Survey of Ancient Rome,* vol. i.
GELZER, M. 'Latium' in *RE,* vol. xii, 1.
HENZE, E. W. *De Civitatibus Liberis.* Berlin, 1892.
HEUSS, A. 'Die völkerrechtlichen Grundlagen der römischen Außenpolitik in republikanischer Zeit', *Klio,* Beiheft xxxi, 1933.
—— 'Abschluß und Beurkundung des griechischen und römischen Staatsvertrages', *Klio,* 1934.
HORN, H. *Foederati.* Frankfurt am Main, 1930.
KONOPKA, Z. Z. 'Les Relations politiques entre Rome et la Campanie', *Eos,* vol. 32, 1929.
KORNEMANN, E. 'Colonia' and 'Municipium' in *RE,* vol. iv and vol. xvi. 1.
MADVIG, J. N. *De iure et condicione coloniarum populi Romani Quaestio Historica,* Opuscula Academica, 1834.
MOMMSEN, T. *Römisches Staatsrecht (St.R.),* 3rd ed.
—— *History of Rome.* London, 1901.
PAIS, E. *Storia critica di Roma.*
ROSENBERG, A. *Der Staat der alten Italiker.* Berlin, 1913.
RUDOLPH, H. *Stadt und Staat im römischen Italien.* Leipzig, 1935.
TÄUBLER, E. *Imperium Romanum.* Leipzig, 1913.
VOGT, J. *Ciceros Glaube an Rom.* Stuttgart, 1935.
WHATMOUGH, J. *The Foundations of Roman Italy.* London, 1937.
ZUMPT, A. J. 'De Propagatione Civitatis Romanae', *Studia Romana.* Berlin, 1854.

ZUMPT, A. J. 'De Coloniis Romanorum Militaribus Libri Quattuor', *Commentationum Epigraphicarum ad Antiquitates Romanas Pertinentium Volumen*. Berlin, 1850.

## PRINCIPATE

ABBOT, F., and JOHNSON, A. *Municipal Administration in the Roman Empire* (A. & J.). Princeton, N.J., 1926.

ASSMAN, J. *De Coloniis Oppidisque Romanis quibus Imperatoria Nomina . . . sunt*. Langensalza, 1905.

BICKERMANN, E. *Das Edikt des Kaiser Caracalla*. Berlin, 1926.

BRANDIS, C. 'Asiarches', 'Bithyniarches' in *RE*, vols. ii and iii.

BROUGHTON, T. R. S. *The Romanisation of Africa Proconsularis*. Baltimore, Md., 1929.

CHAPOT, V. *La Province romaine proconsulaire d'Asie*. Paris, 1904.

FABIA, P. *La Table claudienne de Lyon*. Lyons, 1929.

GUIGNEBERT, C. *Tertullien, Étude sur ses sentiments à l'égard de l'Empire*. Paris, 1901.

HIRSCHFELD, O. 'Zur Geschichte des lateinischen Rechts', *Kleine Schriften*.

JOUGUET, P. *La Vie municipale dans l'Égypte romaine*.

JULLIAN, C. *Histoire de la Gaule*, vols. iv–v.

KORNEMANN, E. 'Colonia' in *RE*, vol. iv; 'Concilium', ibid. iv; 'Conventus', ibid. iv; 'Koinon', ibid. Suppl. iv; 'Municipium', ibid. xvi. 1.

LAMBRECHTS, P. *La Composition du sénat romain*. Antwerp, 1936.

LIEBENAM, W. *Städteverwaltung im römischen Kaiserreiche*.

MATTINGLY, H., and SYDENHAM, E. A. *The Roman Imperial Coinage*.

MOMIGLIANO, A. *Claudius: The Emperor and his Achievement*. Oxford, 1934.

PREMERSTEIN, A. VON, 'Ius Italicum' in *RE*, vol. x. 1.

ROSTOVTZEFF, M. *The Social and Economic History of the Roman Empire*.

RUGE, W. 'Lycia' in *RE*, vol. xiii.

STECH, B. 'Senatores Romani', *Klio*, Beiheft x.

STEIN, A. *Der römische Ritterstand*.

TOUTAIN, J. *Les Cités romaines de la Tunisie*.

# SELECT BIBLIOGRAPHY SINCE 1939

THE following list is limited to monographs and treatises substantially concerned with problems of the Roman citizenship and to articles of primary importance. Subsidiary discussions are cited in the footnotes of the additional chapters and appendices.

### THE REPUBLICAN PERIOD: COMMUNAL GRANTS

AFZELIUS, A. *Die römische Eroberung Italiens* (Acta Jutlandica 14.3), Copenhagen, 1942.
—— *Römische Kriegsmacht* (ibid. 16.2) Copenhagen, 1944.
ALFÖLDI, A. *Early Rome and the Latins*, Michigan, 1964–5.
BADIAN, E. *Foreign Clientelae 264–70 B.C.* Oxford, 1958, chs. 8–9.
BERNARDI, A. 'Roma e Capua', *Athenaeum* 16 (1943), 21 ff., 86 ff.
BRUNT, P. A. *Italian Manpower 225 B.C.–A.D. 14.* Oxford, 1971, chs. 5–6.
EWINS, U. 'Enfranchisement of Cisalpine Gaul', *P.B.S.R.* 23 (1955) 74 ff.
GABBA, E. *Le origini della guerra sociale e la vita politica romana dopo l'89 a.C.*, Pavia, 1954.
GOEHLER, J. *Rom und Italien*, Breslau, 1939.
HEURGON, J. *Capoue préromaine*, Paris, 1942.
MEYER, H. D. 'Die Organisation der Italiker im Bundesgenossenkrieg', *Historia* 7 (1958), 74 ff.
OGILVIE, R. M. *Commentary on Livy I–V*, Oxford, 1965.
SALMON, E. T. *Samnium and the Samnites*, Cambridge, 1967, chs. 9–10.
SORDI, M. *I rapporti romano-ceriti e l'origin edella civitas sine suffragio*, Rome, 1960.
TAYLOR, L. R. *The Voting Districts of the Roman Republic*, Rome, 1960.
TOYNBEE, A. J. *Hannibal's Legacy*, Part I, Oxford, 1965.
WERNER, R. *Der Beginn der römischen Republik*, Munich, 1963.
WISEMAN, T. P. *New Men in the Roman Senate, 139 B.C.–A.D. 14*, Oxford, 1971, ch. 2.

### INDIVIDUAL GRANTS AND STATUS: REPUBLIC AND PRINCIPATE

BADIAN, E. *Foreign Clientelae 264–70 B.C.*, Oxford, 1958, ch. 11.
BRUNT, P. A. *Italian Manpower 225 B.C.–A.D. 14*, Oxford, 1971, ch. 14.

CARDASCIA, G. 'L'Apparition dans le droit des classes d'*honestiores* et d'*humiliores*', *Rev. hist. droit. fr. étr.*, 28 (1950) 305 ff., 461 ff.

GARNSEY, P. *Social Status and Legal Privilege in the Roman Empire*, Oxford, 1970, ch. 11.

NESSELHAUF, H. *Diplomata Militaria, CIL* 16, 147 ff., Berlin, 1936.

SCHULZ, F. 'Roman Registers and Birth Certificates', *JRS* 32 (1942) 78ff., 33 (1943), 55ff.

SESTON, W., and EUZENNAT, M. 'Citoyenneté romaine . . . d'après la table Banasitane', *CRAI* 1961, 317 ff., 1971, 468 ff.

SHERWIN-WHITE, A. N. *Roman Society and Roman Law in the New Testament*, Lecture 7, Oxford, 1963.

TREGGIARI, S. *Roman Freedmen in the Later Republic*, Oxford, 1969.

TRIANTAPHYLLOPOULOS, J. 'Ius Italicum personnel', *Iura* 14 (1963) 108 ff.

VISSCHER, F. DE, *Les Édits d'Auguste découverts à Cyrènes*, ch. v, Louvain, 1940.

WATSON, A. *Law of Persons in the Later Roman Republic*, Oxford, 1967.

WILSON, A. J. *Emigration from Italy in the Republican Age of Rome*, New York, 1966.

### THE CONSTITUTIO ANTONINIANA

CONDURACCHI, E. M. 'La *Constitutio Antoniniana* e la sua applicazione', *Dacia* 2 (1958) 281 ff.

GILLIAM, J. F. 'Dura Roster and the *Constitutio Antoniniana*', *Historia* 14 (1965) 81 ff.

SASSE, C. *Die Constitutio Antoniniana*, Wiesbaden, 1958.

—— 'Literaturübersicht zur *Constitutio Antoniniana*', *Journal of Juristic Papyri*, 14 (1962) 109 ff., 15 (1965) 329 ff.

SCHÖNBAUER, E. 'Eine wichtige Inschrift zum Problem der *Constitutio Antoniniana*', *Iura*, 14 (1963) 71 ff.

### MUNICIPAL STATUS IN THE PRINCIPATE

ALFÖLDI, G. *Bevölkerung und Gesellschaft der römischen Provinz Dalmatia*, Budapest, 1965.

BRAUNERT, H. VON, 'Ius Latii', *Corolla memoriae E. Swoboda dedicata*, Graz, 1966, 68 ff.

BRUNT, P. A. *Italian Manpower 225 B.C.–A.D. 14*, Oxford, 1971, ch. 15.

DEGRASSI, A. 'Quattuorviri nelle colonie romane', *Atti dei Lincei, mem. sci. mor.*, 1949.

GRANT, M. *From Imperium to Auctoritas*, Cambridge, 1946.

HENDERSON, M. I. 'Caesar and Latium in Spain', *JRS* 23 (1942) 1 ff.

HOWALD, E., and MEYER, E. *Die römische Schweiz*, Zürich, 1940.

LAFFI, U. *Adtributio e Contributio*, Pisa, 1966.

PICARD, G. CH. 'Civitas Mactaritana', *Karthago* 8 (1957) chs. 3–4.

—— 'Le *pagus* dans l'Afrique romaine', *Karthago* 15 (1969–70) 3 f.

QUONIAM, P. 'A propos des communes doubles . . . le cas de Thuburbo Maius', *Karthago* 10 (1959–60) 67 ff.

REYNOLDS, J. M., and WARD PERKINS, J. B. *Inscriptions of Roman Tripolitania*, B.S.R. Rome, 1952.

SAUMAGNE, C. *Le droit latin et les cités romaines sous l'empire*, Paris, 1965.

SCHÖNBAUER, E. '*Municipia* und *Coloniae*', *Anz. Österr. Ak. Wien*, 1954, 18 ff.

STAHELIN, F. *Die Schweiz in römischer Zeit*, Basle, 1948.

TEUTSCH, L. *Das römische Städtewesen in Nord-Afrika*, Berlin, 1962.

—— 'Gab es Doppelgemeinden im römischen Afrika?', *Revue internationale de droit antique*, 8 (1961) 286 ff.

VITTINGHOF, F. *Römische Kolonisation und Bürgerrechtspolitik unter Caesar und Augustus*, Wiesbaden, 1942.

WILKES, J. J. *Dalmatia*, London, 1969.

# INDEX OF CITATIONS

This index is limited to passages discussed critically in the main text.

# INDEX OF GREEK WORDS

# GENERAL INDEX

Personal names of statesmen and authors are given in their familiar style, e.g. Seneca, Gracchns, Vespasian. Others are indexed under *nomina*, where known.